Crimson Rain

东

WILLIAM T. ROWE

CRIMSON RAIN

Seven Centuries of Violence in a Chinese County

STANFORD UNIVERSITY PRESS 2007

Stanford, California

Stanford University Press
Stanford, California

Library of Congress Cataloging-in-Publication Data

Rowe, William T.
Crimson rain : seven centuries of violence in a Chinese county / William T. Rowe.
p. cm.
Includes bibliographical references and index.
ISBN-13: 978-0-8047-5496-5 (cloth : alk. paper)
1. Macheng Shi (China)—History. 2. Political violence (China)—Macheng Shi. I. Title.
DS797.48.M334R69 2006
951'.212—dc22

2006002605

Printed in the United States of America

Typeset at Stanford University Press in 10/12.5 Minion

Frontispiece: Drum Tower (Gulou), Macheng City. Photograph by the author.

In memory of DONALD CHRISTIAN ROWE

Contents

Map and Figures

Map

Figures

Preface

Approaching Macheng from the southwest, from the Hubei provincial capital, the visitor first encounters a blue arch over the highway, reading "Welcome to Macheng County." The quality of the road immediately improves, and the shops on either side begin to offer a larger range of amenities. The people seem better dressed than those in the areas passed along the way, and there are fewer farm animals blocking the road. Soon one sees another blue arch, announcing the Golden Needle Science and Technology Zone of Hubei Province. The county seat is large, sparklingly new, and squeaky-clean. It boasts a three-star hotel and offers a wide array of tourist-promotion literature, in English as well as Chinese. Its citizens look, for the most part, comfortably middle class. The surrounding countryside as well is dotted with newly constructed brick farmhouses, motorcycles parked alongside, and reveals a fertile and productive (though as yet largely unmechanized) agriculture. The impression one gets overall is of considerable prosperity, an activist and attentive county government, and a highly aggressive community boosterism. It is an evident success story of post-Mao China.

On June 10, 1999, the so-called 610 Office was set up in the town of Baiguo, in south central Macheng, and charged with eradicating the practice of Falun gong sectarianism. Subsequently this office was declared a model for the rest of the county. It was headed by the secretary of the Baiguo Township Politics and Law Committee. According to Falun gong sources, the persecution of their membership in Baiguo was especially "bestial" and "insane." Practitioners were ordered to renounce their teachers in violent epithets and were subjected to "brainwashing classes." In the unusually hot summer of 2000, they were locked in an unlit furnace of a room for over 100 days, for much of which time they were denied sleep. The following spring, four sect members were publicly tortured to death in the Baiguo town square. They were ordered to take off their shoes and were beaten on the face with these (some of the females wore high heels) until they were unrecognizable. Two of the victims were tied behind motorcycles and dragged around the square at high speed, until they were flayed alive. One sect member reportedly walked all the way to Beijing to report this incident but was arrested, sent home, and executed. Finally, in April 2001, a female sect member from Fengjia shan Village (most of the sect's members in Macheng County are rural, and many are unemployed) was beaten throughout the day in the Baiguo town square and then, just before sunset, was doused with gasoline and set afire. Township police detained all witnesses until they supported the police claim that this was a case of self-immolation (Clearwisdom.net, 2 July, 21 July, and 31 July 2001).

There is no necessary reason, I hasten to stress, why one should accept as factual these allegations from the Falun gong's sensationalist and highly developed propaganda machine. What is significant, though, is that the sect's proselytizers clearly expect the national and international audiences for their Web site to accept that this kind of behavior, which they themselves admit is extreme for the current Chinese regime, is potentially credible when set in the context of Macheng County. It is this stark contrast—between, on the one hand, a locale blessed with great natural beauty, economic prosperity (at least in better times, such as the present), and an extremely powerful sense of local pride and, on the other, a national reputation for dehumanizing violence that has, for much of the county's history, been well earned—that lies at the heart of this book.

When I began my academic career, in the early 1970s, it was clear to me that the great emphasis of Western historiography of China was on the countryside. It was assumed that China had enjoyed little in the way of a significant indigenous urban tradition before that tradition was introduced by the West. The overriding problems confronted by scholars were to explain the failure of China's "modernization" and to explain the victory of its Communist Party in the civil war, and both of these problems seemed to demand detailed and extensive analysis of rural conditions and agrarian history. In such an intellectual environment, it seemed to me, the most original and productive thing that an aspiring scholar might do would be to investigate, as closely as possible, the history of a large Chinese city, and that is what I did. Over the subsequent three decades, though, the situation appears to have been reversed. In the context of globalization, China's commercially fueled economic boom, and the triumph of "cultural studies" in academia (both in the West and, increasingly, in China as well), historians have come to focus their energies ever more heavily on Chinese urban history, particularly the cultural history of large metropolitan centers in the early twentieth century, a period for which, it is implicitly assumed, the models for post-Mao changes and cultural choices can best be explored. With the important exception of macroanalyses of comparative political economy, rural history seems, for the most part, to have fallen out of favor. Accordingly, as a dedicated contrarian, I feel the desire to turn my own efforts to the local history of a decidedly rural, even peripheral, area of China. This, then, is my personal *xiafang*.

Like the sent-down youths of a previous generation, I have depended on many people for my survival along the way. These include above all my colleague in the History Department at Johns Hopkins University, Tobie Meyer-Fong, who read the entire manuscript closely and corrected many errors. I thank also my other Hopkins friends Richard Kagan, David Nirenberg, Kellee Tsai, Eva González, and Yuanyuan Zeng. My present and former graduate students Di Wang, Grant Alger, Zhao Gang, Ma Zhao, Peng Juanjuan, Saeyoung Park, and Amy Feng have all provided very helpful advice and remained on the lookout for sources that otherwise might have escaped me. Others who have graciously commented on portions of my work include Timothy Brook, Lucien Bianco, Philip Kuhn, Mary B. Rankin, Keith Schoppa, Peter C. Perdue, Peter Bol, Robert Antony, Mary Elizabeth Berry, Joseph Esherick, Paul Pickowicz, Alfred Lin, Elizabeth Sin, Barend ter Haar, Wang Fan-sen, Ernest Young, Frank Dikötter, and my longtime friend and editor Muriel Bell. Odoric Wou, Jin Jiang, Barbara Volkmar, Ch'en Yung-fa, and Xiaorong Han have not only commented but also shared with me impressions gained in the process of their own studies of the Macheng area. An earlier version of portions of chapters 5 and 7 has been published as *From Ming to Ch'ing Along the Great Divide* (Taibei: Institute of Modern History, Academia Sinica, 2005); I am grateful for permission to reuse that material here.

I am deeply indebted to the faculty of the Institute of Modern Chinese History at Central China Normal University, Wuhan, most especially Professors Ma Min, Zhang Kaiyuan, Fu Haiyan, Liu Jiafeng, Zhu Ying, and Gao Zhuonan, and to several of their graduate students, including Tian Teng. Professor Feng Tianyu of Wuhan University has also been very helpful, as have the staffs of the Hubei Provincial Archives, the Hubei Provincial Library, and the Hubei Provincial Gazetteer Office. In Macheng I must deeply thank Deputy Mayor Fan Yizhong, Director Zhong Shiwu of the Macheng County Gazetteer Office, the staffs of the Macheng County Archives and the Macheng County Museum, and most especially the extraordinarily learned local historian Ms. Li Min. For indispensable assistance during my visits to rural areas of Macheng County I am grateful to the township administrators of Yanjiahe and Chengmagang, and above all to the wonderfully welcoming Zeng family of Zengjiawan Village.

As always, to my own family—Jill, Josh, and Sara—I owe most.

Crimson Rain

Introduction

IN MAY OF 1928, following the breakdown of the United Front between the Chinese Communist Party and its former revolutionary allies, the Chinese Nationalists, local people in Macheng County, in the Great Divide mountain range (Dabie Shan) separating the Yangzi Valley from the North China Plain, reported a remarkable natural event: a sudden drenching shower of crimson rain (*hongyu*).[1] Startled as they may have been, county residents were at no loss to comprehend what this meant. Their home district was at that moment the epicenter of a bloodbath (*xuexi*), an orgy of mass violence taking a terrible toll on local combatants and noncombatants alike. And this was by no means the first time this had happened. Deeply etched in the collective consciousness and local identity of Macheng people was the memory of recurrent bloodlettings of similar ferocity in times of disorder throughout the past, and of countless acts of routine brutality in times of peace. Their home, they understood, was simply a violent place.

As we shall see, Macheng's proclivity for violence was well appreciated by late-imperial and Republican officials and literati. Nor has it entirely escaped Western observers. For example, in an influential 1969 essay titled "The Ecology of Chinese Communist Success," the American political scientist Roy Hofheinz, Jr., sought to determine why certain areas of China had proved more fertile ground than others for Communist Revolution in the decades leading up to the Party's ultimate victory in 1949. His careful, computer-aided analysis concluded that, in *most* instances, there really was no observable correlation between social ecology and receptiveness to Communist appeals; rather, the revolution simply succeeded best in localities where the Party had happened most effectively to establish its own organizational presence. But Hofheinz did find a few exceptions—"hotbed counties," he called them—where the "rapid spread and prolonged success of the Communist movement" defied the overall pattern, and in which, he could only speculate, deeply ingrained "background social factors" must have yielded an unusual conduciveness to violent revolution. Hofheinz identified but eight of China's more than 2,000 counties as "hotbeds," two of which were Macheng and its neighboring county, Huang'an, which until 1563 had been part of Macheng itself.[2]

This book inquires: Why Macheng? Phrasing the question most narrowly, I ask: How different does the Chinese Revolution look when we place its most important crucibles—the so-called soviet base areas—in a very much longer historiographic perspective? More generally, however, I want to know why certain areas of China appear extraordinarily prone to violence, over time frames so long as to transcend the experience of very significant cultural, economic, social, and political change. Why, in such places, does the option of violent means of resolving problems appear such a habituated choice? Based on the experience of a single small place over a very long period of time—the seven centuries from the expulsion of the Mongols in the 1300s to the invasion of the Japanese in 1938—this book hopes to contribute to a broader exploration of the phenomenon of violence in Chinese rural society. I will suggest that collective memory, historical consciousness, and other routinized cultural practices played critical roles in this process.

Violence as a conceptual category has occupied writers in a number of Western intellectual traditions, including those of critical political thought,[3] functionalist social science,[4] and sociocultural history in the manner of *Annales*,[5] and collectively this body of reflection can help us think about violence in Macheng. It reminds us first of all that violent behavior may be normal or systemic rather than aberrant. While the notion of violence as irrational or immoral runs deep in contemporary Western culture, this is not the case in many others, and not in most societies of past times. The prevailing notion of just what constitutes violence, and of the legitimacy of such action, is in fact *relative* to the sociohistorical context. Moreover, even within each context there are usually *competing* conceptions of violence and its legitimacy, including a legal/political one defined by the state as crime (although states themselves, as well as private persons or groups, routinely engage in violent acts), as well as one or more different understandings operating in popular morality. Societies, states, and cultures set up conventions or norms to organize, routinize, or even ritualize the practice of violence within their bounds, in the hope of containing or channeling it. In the face of these conventions or norms, the commission of a violent act can constitute a deliberate contestation of legitimacy or a commentary on norms and discourses dominant within the society. Violence, in other words, has an *expressive* aspect; it is a vehicle of communication. Violence is also a *performance*, implying not merely the presence of an agent and a victim but also that of one or many witnesses. It may be undertaken for explicitly theatrical purposes—for instance, the display of severed heads as "symbols of transgression."[6] But even more pedestrian acts of violence often count on their visibility, and on "the probability that all involved are likely to draw, at the very least, some basic common understanding from the acts and images concerned."[7]

How, then, are we to interpret the meanings of violence within the specific, historical operation of Chinese culture? We must begin first of all with the recognition that in the practical day-to-day experience of its people throughout history, China has been *as* violent as most other human societies, and perhaps *more* violent than many. Not merely the evidence of this book but also most of what we know of China's history and society eloquently confirms this fact. At the same time, as in all societies, China devised cultural methods of domesticating or containing this practice of violence or, perhaps more appropriately, of providing people with means for coping with the everyday reality of violence in their lives. Indeed, it seems safe to say that in its literate (not merely literati) culture—most especially in that bundle of cultural items that we refer to in shorthand as "Confucianism"—China was considerably more energetic than many other cultural traditions in condemning violent behavior and establishing peaceful, harmonious coexistence among human beings as a moral norm. Prior to the twentieth century, at least, the textual tradition is so consistent in its bias toward harmony, peace, and decorum that it has led any number of historians—myself pointedly included—into depicting aspects of Chinese history as more tranquil than probably was warranted. We must continually be mindful of the fact that this entire textual tradition was in large part a coping mechanism, and that the normative vision was not a description of fact.

This deep cultural tradition has been emphasized by the anthropologist Steven Harrell, in a gallant effort to summarize the meanings of violence in Chinese history and society. Harrell argues that, by comparison to other cultures, Chinese culture condemns and abhors violence to an unusual degree: it "plays down the glory of military exploits, awards its highest prestige to literary rather than martial figures, and seeks harmony over all other values." In childhood socialization, Harrell notes, Chinese children are routinely punished for engaging in fights even when they are the victims rather than the aggressors, on the presumption that they have not been sufficiently resolute in avoiding conflict altogether.[8] My own rough-and-ready survey of the lexical items most often used in the Chinese language to refer to what we might call violence—words such as *bào, měng, hàn, héng, xiōng, lì, liè,* and, in some usages, *kuáng* (mad) and *luàn* (chaotic), as well as countless combinations of these with various shades of meaning—suggests some support for Harrell's view. These terms, in their most common usages, seem unambiguously condemnatory. "Violent" is used in reference to severe and irrational forces of nature (*baofeng, kuangxue*), wild and savage animals (*baohu, baoquan, hanma*), subhuman, barbaric cultures (*manheng*), and personal actions and temperaments decried as perverse, unruly, or malevolent. These adjectives are contemptuously applied to social types who defy consensus norms: to thieves and bandits (*hanni, baokou*), intractable lowlifes (*baotu*), undisciplined slaves or servants (*hanpu, hanbi*), women who resist their assigned gender roles (*kuangnü, hanfu, hanqi*), and that most despised of all social groups, government clerks and runners (*baoli, hanli*). At least as early as the third-century BCE classical text *Xunzi,* the language of violence was invoked to describe tyrannical rulers and their regimes (*baoguo, baojun, baozhu*).[9]

And yet there was also, from very early times, a way of reading this language against the grain, in usages that were far from unsympathetic. Valiant, fearless, and ardently righteous men might be referred to as *hanyong* or *mengyong,* as *mengshi* or *lieshi. Kuang,* which in conventional usage meant "mad" in the sense of a rabid dog (*kuangquan*), also came to refer to poets, painters, and philosophers of an admirably bold originality. And as early as the first century BCE, Sima Qian used *baokang* to refer to acts of political resistance that were both violent and righteous, a radical usage that would have many potent later echoes (*baoqi, baodong*). Such usages at least open the door for a view of Chinese literate culture as encompassing a receptivity to violence in at least some circumstances.

How, then, did Chinese culture reconcile itself to violence? There are probably many ways to answer this question, but recent scholarly literature suggests three. First, one might see Chinese elite culture as unequivocally antiviolent and thus read the sporadic practice and situational legitimation of violent behavior as deviant or (more charitably) countercultural. Harrell seems to incline to this view when he notes that "a real literatus" might fully accept the orthodox, unambiguous condemnation of violence, whereas the embrace of violence would suggest a less than fully "literatus" identity. Here I think he clearly goes too far, and the cases of such Macheng native sons as Mei Zhihuan in the seventeenth century (see chapter 5), Yu Yaxiang in the nineteenth (chapter 8), and even, in attenuated form, the twentieth-century warlord Xia Douyin (chapters 11 and 12) provide striking testimony to the seamless link, at least for some, of a self-conscious literati identity with an unmercifully violent behavioral orientation.

A second emerging method of reconciling violence and the dominant Confucian culture treats violence as a specific component in the construction of Chinese masculine gender. One of the pioneers of this line of inquiry, Susan Mann, sees, for example, a shared proclivity to violence as, in at least some instances, key to the "male bond," a central organizing device of late-imperial Chinese society.[10] Others, such as the literary historian Kam Louie, contrast the categories of *wen* (civil) and *wu* (martial) as alternative modes of idealized Chinese masculinity, noting, however, that in this pairing *wen* "subsumes" *wu*, just as *yang* subsumes its alternate, *yin*.[11] But, promising as such inquiries may be, it seems to me that they have not as yet produced a truly useful guide to understanding violence and its manifestations in Chinese history and culture.

The third method, which the substance of this book leads me to accept, begins with the frank recognition that there has been in fact quite ample space provided for "sanctioned" violence within Chinese culture, at the elite as well as the popular levels. Mark Lewis has beautifully demonstrated how such violence came to fit into the dominant culture of early China.[12] In a thoughtful recent article, moreover, Barend ter Haar has convincingly outlined the large range of violent behavior that *remained* fully sanctioned by and for literati themselves well into the late-imperial and modern eras. Ter Haar would concede that there was indeed "a long-term trend away from violence" in Chinese elite culture, but he insists that this was a highly "modified" and "differentiated" one. Elites moved away from using prowess at violence (in blood sports, for example) as a means of defining their status, and to an extent from approving it as a way of dealing with each other, but violence as "a means of controlling and subduing others"—servants, dependent family members, tenants—remained fully culturally approved, as were the most brutal of punishments against those construed as criminals, rebels, and other deviants.[13]

In the broader popular culture of late-imperial and modern China—against which elites were habitually at war even while they themselves participated in it—sanctioned violence assumed a yet much larger role: grassroots China was, as a number of scholars have recently pointed out, in many regards effectively a culture of violence. A child's socialization included everyday witnessing of the bloody butchering of chickens and fish, and, on exciting special occasions, the flogging or brutal public execution of criminals. Popular amusements included cockfights, violent contests of strength among local youths, and, in some localities, ritualized bloodletting through such means as community rock fights. The folktales and legends a child heard growing up, and the operas he or she might see from time to time, glorified violent behavior. Popular religion, featuring as it did blood sacrifice of animals and the extremely violent performances of shamans and exorcists, reinforced this habituation to violence as a natural element in human existence. Commoner males routinely sought to achieve local status through demonstrations of their prowess at violent activities, while the village community as a whole engaged in martial exercises to exclude outsiders—what one recent scholar terms "the violence entailed by the collectivity's production and reproduction of itself in persistently hostile circumstances."[14] And in Macheng those circumstances were nearly always hostile.

Focusing on the web of material interests that existed alongside (and helped sustain) this popular culture, David Robinson has described an "economy of violence" in late-imperial China that further helps us interpret Macheng's experience. "Illicit force," Robinson argues, "was as much a part of the social order as it was a threat to that order."[15] Violence was not merely chronic but in fact systemically embedded in the local society and economy, and in the state's administrative apparatus. Forces of order ("men of force" such as local strongmen and militia leaders) and disorder (often rather casually labeled "bandits") existed in a rough, negotiated equilibrium. In its effort to contain or domesticate violent activity, the regime relied rather uneasily on the former even while individual official and unofficial power holders routinely patronized the latter as well. Peacekeepers, of course, had a vested interest in keeping their antagonists in business, as a means of validating their own armed power, and indeed there was a great deal of fluidity across role boundaries. And these were the good times; in times of the collapse of central authority, the equilibrium in local society might break down catastrophically.

In the history of Macheng, two specific cultural models of violence, though hardly unique to this locality, seem to have had particular salience. One was the well-known ideal of the hero (*yingxiong*) or martial adventurer (*wuxia*), and its more widespread and attainable variant, the tough guy (*haohan*). Inasmuch as this alternative tradition to that of Confucian harmony had a special appeal to the underclass, it is tempting to call it a counterculture, but doing so masks the very great extent to which this set of attitudes intruded into the elite culture itself: one recent Chinese scholar, in fact, calls it none other than the literati's "millennia-old dream."[16] The trope is at least as old as Sima Qian's first-century BCE glorification of the *yuxia*—a term translated somewhat delicately by James Liu as "knight-errant" but more candidly by Burton Watson as "assassin"—and has enjoyed a continuous literary history down to the cinematic swordplay epics of today.[17] As W. J. F. Jenner has brilliantly shown, in its broadest form the cultural role of "tough guy" has captured the imagination of Chinese children and youth (mostly but not exclusively males) throughout the ages. Imperial criminal codes attempted at times to define this tradition out of popular acceptance, but never with great success.[18] As we shall see, this identification of true masculinity with an honorable, romantic, and even playful eagerness both to endure and to inflict violence had a special appeal in the rugged highlands of Macheng County. It ran through the fiction of one of the county's notable late-Ming visitors, Feng Menglong, and was central to the vision of moral heroism elaborated by its most notorious long-term sojourner, Li Zhi, above all in the novel *Shuihu zhuan* (*Water Margin*) that Li edited and substantially rewrote during his Macheng years (see chapter 4). The many entrepreneurs of violence whom we will encounter in Macheng's history were clearly, at least in part, acting out the heroic dictates of the *wuxia* and *haohan* roles.

The second cultural model was yet more basic and ubiquitous, and indeed made violence into a fundamental imperative of human existence. This model is what Barend ter Haar has termed the "demonological paradigm," a way of conceiving the world that ter Haar argues (convincingly in my view), belongs to "the oldest stratum of Chinese religious culture" and makes up the *normal* basis of Chinese popular religion.[19] Ter Haar builds upon the seminal study by Arthur Wolf, which divides supernatural beings in Chinese popular belief into the three categories of ancestors, gods, and ghosts. Each of these corresponds in human society to a set of persons with whom the subject stands in specific relation: ancestors equate with family, gods with officials or other social superiors, and ghosts (*gui*) with strangers or, more specifically, with dangerous human types such as drifters, beggars, bandits, and rebels.[20] Drawing out the malevolent implications of this third category, ter Haar argues that Chinese popular religion is built upon a basic presumption of "the persistent and fundamentally violent danger to human beings" posed by these *gui,* or, in his preferred translation, "demons." Some of these horrific, gory, nonhuman but human*like* entities "live on the outskirts of human civilization, but many live permanently among the people." They lurk especially at crossroads, under bridges, in doorways and window apertures, and in other liminal locations, but in fact they are everywhere. Demons are obsessed with eating human beings, most especially human blood and internal organs, and aim to "devour and crush" people in the most gruesome ways. Elaborate and consistent effort must be expended to ward them off; amulets, trigrams, the "life force" color red (*hong*), posting of statues or drawings of armed generals at doorways, and in fact the entire corpus of traditional Chinese medicine are part of the arsenal of defense. So too are exorcistic rituals, and so too is violence.

The gruesome violence threatened by these demons must be met with an equally determined response bent on bloody and complete extermination. The utter pervasiveness of the demonic threat and the unflagging need for a comparable response provides an underlying legitimation for violence in Chinese popular (and, to a modified extent, literati) culture.[21] It is what makes human violence, like the demonic violence that it confronts, both necessary and a fully "normal" facet of everyday life. The fact that demons are so adept at mutation, the fact that they routinely appear in human form (usually, of course, in the form of the corresponding social categories identified by Wolf), offers license for practicing extreme violence against other persons. In Chinese historical experience, the targets of intended violence—criminals awaiting punishment, rebels, hostile armies, and even (ter Haar rather more boldly suggests), in the modern period, "class enemies"—have routinely been *demonized* in order for the bloody acts visited upon them to be legitimated.

Though the demonic threat was omnipresent, there were moments in which it was especially dangerous. These moments demanded special responses. One such response was for leaders of the community to summon their own spirit armies (*shenbing*) to counter large-scale demonic forces marshaled against it; these spirit armies were of course themselves demonic and therefore perilous, but, if handled properly by a respectful and adept human intermediary, they might prove the people's salvation. Another type of response to a moment of demonic crisis—a response favored by those alienated from the settled community, such as bandits and rebels—was to invite, or to become oneself, a demon-smashing messiah. This "demonological messianic tradition," ter Haar argues, existed alongside the sectarian Buddhist millenarian tradition (for example, that of the White Lotus), which it somewhat resembled, but the two traditions grew out of differing cosmological systems, the latter somewhat alien to the indigenous Chinese popular religious system and the former directly spawned by it.[22] In both of these crisis responses, the license to enact cathartic violence in order to slaughter one's enemies (demonic hordes in human forms) was especially broad and permissive.

The Macheng County we will encounter in these pages was virtually a poster child for the "demonological paradigm." (Indeed, ter Haar himself cites one Macheng-centered eighteenth-century rebellion as a major illustration of his argument.[23]) Temples were built and offerings made to spirit generals who would purge the area of demons, and on at least one occasion a spirit army was seen to respond to these requests, saving the county from decimation (chapter 1). Local militias, rebels, bandits, and political parties alike draped themselves in red (Red Turbans, Red Armies, Red Spears, Red Guards) and invoked the language of demon smashing—demonizing their enemies, for example, as "Kings of Hell," or, like the prolifically murderous seventeenth-century rebel leader styled the Earth-Scouring King, personally assuming the mission of mass exorcist. Doing so made it perfectly palatable to demand the enemy's extermination, eradication, annihilation, or liquidation. The war against demons was a war without mercy.

The culture of violence in Macheng was inseparable from the operation of collective memory and the practice of local history; as one historian has nicely put it, "all memory is prelude."[24] Maurice Halbwachs pointed out that actual recollection is performed by individuals, but memories are necessarily formed at the level of, and in reference to, a social group, and such memories change over time, along with the group's constitution and concerns.[25] An individual can distance himself or herself from—can critique—the collective memories of the group, but this is extremely difficult; participation in new or multiple groups is one aid in doing so. Vehicles or sites of memory, such as written records, old objects and monuments, and commemorative ceremonies, participate in the construction (and continual reconstruction) of collective memory, but this process always takes place in reference to the present, to accord with current group understandings, attitudes, and needs. Collective memory is continually contested; since memory is an important factor in sustaining or challenging current relationships of power, it has a very active politics. One part of this politics is the invention of false memories, to be intermingled with accurate ones, and so too is "social amnesia," the collective forgetting of unpleasant, inconvenient, or seemingly anomalous past phenomena.

History, to Halbwachs and subsequent writers, has an awkward relationship to collective memory. Although there is a "lived" or "living" history that more closely accords with memory, written history is more usually antithetical to it. Its aims are different. History belongs to a few professional specialists, whereas memory is the property of the wider collectivity. History strives to be "objective" or "factual," whereas the memories of the group are unapologetically "subjective." History strives for univocality, whereas memory is infinitely multiple. History offers a "fixed" account of the past in linear time—it seeks to "keep the past in the past"—while memory situates past events in an ongoing dialogue with the present. One of Halbwachs's heirs, Pierre Nora, takes this dichotomization to romantic extremes. History is inherently suspicious of memory, is engaged in an ongoing effort to subdue or destroy it, and, in recent times, has appeared to succeed; Nora speaks of "the conquest and eradication of memory by history," a process he associates with the passing of "that quintessential repository of collective memory, . . . peasant culture."[26]

But the experience of Macheng, as I have come to understand it, belies or at least greatly complicates this polarity. In a culture with such a deep tradition of *local* historical production, written history, even at the county level and below, never displaced collective memory but has always engaged in a spirited dialogue with it, as it did with monuments, stele, popular legends, folk songs, theatrical and literary traditions, and countless other living (and continually produced) traces of the past. Regularly updated county gazetteers, lineage genealogies, and other written documents engaged in an ongoing negotiation with oral traditions, and with each other, over understandings of the shared local past. To a greater or lesser extent, these aimed to include a wide segment of the literate, and even illiterate, local population among their audience. There has been a great outpouring of this type of material in Macheng in recent decades—highly colloquial township-level histories, with romantic/martial story lines and stirring illustrations, celebrating the (violent) history of the revolution in our native place—but this is hardly original to the Communist era, as we shall see.[27]

All of this local historical production has sought to make use of the past for the purposes of the present, but it has never been free from contestation or resistance. Local histories have long been filled with heroes to cheer and villains to hiss, but the identification of these has always been subject to negotiation. Was Li Zhi, for example, a revolutionary martyr, a despicable threat to the social order, a champion of liberal individualism, or simply a famous man who conferred glory on Macheng County by his presence? Was a certain heroic action of the past—say, the resistance of the Forty-Eight Forts during the Ming-Qing transition—evidence of incipient "Chinese" nationalism, an expression of more localist strivings, or simply a means by which local strongmen sought to reassert control over their rebellious workforce? Social amnesia also plays a role in this reconstruction of the past, as in celebrating the "populism" of late-Ming native son Mei Guozhen while conveniently forgetting that he was the county's largest serfholder, or taking pride in the long local sojourn of Li Zhi while effacing how he was violently driven away by enraged residents, or commemorating the Northern Expedition by local Nationalist sympathizers while ignoring the brutal class warfare that this brought to Macheng, or finessing the embarrassing and suicidal *sufan* purge in local Communist Party histories.

Let me recount here but two modest examples of how this complicated interplay of memory and history has worked in Macheng. The late-Ming rebel Zhang Xianzhong, known to popular historiography as the butcher of Sichuan, on several occasions swept through the county, bringing great loss of life. Although he managed, at the time, to win considerable support among segments of the population, his wanton bloodthirstiness has ensured his not having received favorable notice from Macheng historians, not even from the most leftist among them. And yet a venerable local legend—associated with a physical monument and later transcribed into the 1993 county gazetteer—portrays Zhang not only in a more sympathetic light but also in one that reflects an element of local pride. As a young man, it is said, Zhang was working as a horse trader in Sichuan. He was arrested for theft and hauled before the deputy provincial judge, a Macheng native named Chen Chuchan. The judge observed that Zhang's physiognomy augured great things, and for this reason he ordered Zhang's release. Zhang promised to return the favor one day and asked Chen his native place. The judge, now turning cautious, cryptically replied, "In Huguang, where bundles of rushes hang from the house eaves and dried grasses from the trees, where no rivers run and yet there are two bridges—that is where I live." Years later, Zhang's rebel army occupied Macheng. Observing the rushes and grasses hanging as Chen had said, he was suddenly overcome by a sense of debt. He ordered a wall and an altar constructed, and there he sacrificed to the memory of the now deceased Judge Chen. The wall became known as the Sacrificial Wall (Baijiao cheng), and it remained a focus of popular sentiment until 1939, when the Japanese occupying army recognized its potential for galvanizing local resistance and had it destroyed.[28]

Our second example concerns a more obscure rebel, Macheng's own Bao Shirong. Bao was a local strongman and participant in the Dongshan rebellions of 1674 (chapter 7). His movement, centered at Zhangjiafan, in the southeastern Macheng hill country, reportedly festered for decades and eventually grew to 10,000 armed men. Finally, the famous Qing model official Yu Chenglong succeeded in putting together a force to defeat Bao, at terrible cost of life. Yu immediately ordered a stele erected at the site of Bao's defeat, to celebrate the permanent pacification of the area. This stele remained a memorial to the genuinely popular Yu Chenglong's effective tenure in the county. But another nearby local monument, a stone horse stable that had served intermittently as Bao's command headquarters, survives to the present day as a focus of popular memory of Bao's rebellion, seen as a fiercely localist act of resistance to imperial fiscal demands. In the last years of the Qing, the local historian Wang Baoxin built upon this legacy of popular sympathy for Bao Shirong in a semischolarly best-seller celebrating the rebels of this era as a model for the anti–Manchu Han nationalism of his own day. And in the People's Republic, Bao has been still differently enshrined in official historiography, as leader of a precocious peasant rebellion (*nongmin qiyi*).[29]

The method of this book is unabashedly that of narrative history. That is, the story I have to tell, as Lawrence Stone would have described it, is chronological, more literary than scientific, more descriptive than analytic in its presentation, focused on the particular and specific, and concerned with human experience in all its complexity.[30] It is a work of social history—a genre to which I remain deeply committed—but, in company with the more recent practice of cultural history (which this book likely is *not*), it reflects a degree of discomfort with the confident, structuralist schemes of social-*science* history. In common with the German historian Peter Jelavich, I confess that "the more clearly I see structures, the more clearly I also see the chaos in which they are embedded." To write a history informed by a central problem (in my case, violence), without shunning (admittedly structuralist) microanalyses, where these are appropriate, but relying on chronological narrative as the central organizing device, seems one way to stake out a methodological midrange zone between the extremes of structure and chaos.[31]

To call this book a microhistory might seem something of a stretch—throughout the period examined here, Macheng's population numbered in the hundreds of thousands—but the county was, in the eyes of local people and outsiders alike, most definitely a small place (*xiao difang*) within the wider Chinese world, and I share with microhistorians the goal of retrieving the perceptions and life experiences of ordinary people, to try to understand, as Peter Perdue has recently phrased it, how such people "interpreted the changes of their time."[32] At the same time, this book is local history of the *longue durée*, the once (and seemingly no longer) fashionable method of the *Annales* school. This book's long-term perspective allows us to explore continuity and change in production systems, microregional identities, urban-rural relations, local community solidarity and resistance to outside control, systems of hegemony and debasement, gender roles and relationships, institutions of coercion, modes of mobilization for collective action, and discourses in the local culture of violence.[33] But our story is hardly the "history with the events left out" for which *Annal*ists took much criticism. Indeed, it cannot be so, for Macheng County was deeply implicated in many of the most pivotal events in the grand narrative of Chinese history: the Red Turban rebellions at the end of the Yuan, the White Lotus rebellions at the end of the Ming, the Manchu conquest, the Three Feudatories rebellion of the early Qing, the Taiping and Nian rebellions of the mid-nineteenth century, the Nationalist Revolution of the 1920s, and the Nationalist-Communist civil war of the 1930s. It is my hope that the reader will come away from this book, as I have from the writing of it, with a renewed sense of the meanings *on the ground* of these great conflicts in Chinese history, and of how, for local people, they were linked with one another. This is, after all, one of the functions that microhistory and local history are especially well equipped to serve.

Let me offer here a single, fairly typical example of the way long-term continuity and change, the national and the local, were interlinked in Macheng. One accustomed response of Macheng people to the reality of violence in their county was a pattern of taking to the hills (*rushan*) in mountainside fortifications, under the protection of hereditary local elite strongmen. Typical of such strongmen were the Wanrenyai Huang. Confronted by the violent regional disorder of the late-Yuan era, Huang Wumeng, around 1350, led his family and neighbors into a fortress (*zhai*) that he had built on a precipice near his home in west central Macheng. Ultimately, very large numbers of persons were said to have sought refuge at Huang's fort, which he accordingly named the Lofty Cliff of Ten Thousand Men (Wanren yaigao). This name, or variations of it, became the toponym for Huang's lineage for centuries thereafter. For his heroic conduct during the dynastic change, Wumeng came to the attention of the founding Ming emperor, who offered him a post in his palace guard at Nanjing. Wumeng's offspring stayed in that office for several generations, moving to Beijing when the Yongle emperor relocated the principal capital there, in the early fifteenth century. One descendent—Huang Qi—however, returned to his native county and passed the Hubei provincial examination in 1456, taking up a career as a county magistrate. Over the remainder of the dynasty, three other Wanrenyai Huang passed the *juren* examination, and one, Huang Juan (chapter 4) took the *jinshi* in 1529 and rose to the post of Shaanxi provincial judge. But the lineage never lost its martial character. It rebuilt its cliffside fort to ward off the rebels of the late Ming, and, in the face of the Taiping and Nian disorders of the late Qing, the lineage added another satellite fort to accommodate still larger numbers of its neighbors. These forts were still in use, offering refuge, during the bloodbath of the 1930s. Thus, over some seven centuries, the Huang maintained their position as military protectors of a discrete segment of western Macheng County, aided by a single act of imperial patronage, modestly comfortable landholdings, and occasional enjoyment of examination success.[34]

The chapter arrangement of this book organizes Macheng County's history into two long cycles, culminating in two massive exterminations (*jiao*) in the second quarters of the seventeenth and twentieth centuries. This makes for a useful narrative device, but does it also suggest more? *Annales* historians looking at European regional societies over the long term have detected similar multicentury cycles, attaching to these a significant degree of repetitiveness and thus, presumably, predictability.[35] One *Annales*-influenced historian of China, Pierre-Etienne Will, has found ecologically determined cycles in China as well, which, because of patterned oscillations in the efficacy of the state's ecological management, largely coincided with the temporal contours of the Ming and Qing dynasties.[36] G. William Skinner, too, has famously argued for a cyclical pattern of development and decline in China, though he is keen to emphasize such cycles' regional specificity and lack of synchronicity.[37] In this regard, he challenges the more familiar model of the dynastic cycle generated by China's indigenous historiographic tradition and endorsed, at least implicitly, by Will. Of course, both may be substantially right.

The rhythm of violence in Macheng was that of recurrent episodes of large-scale carnage superimposed on the more routine practice of day-to-day killing, maiming, and coercion. Two of these episodes, those concluding the two halves of this book, were especially genocidal, inflicting unparalleled mortality on the county (see chapter 1). Both, though complicated by other factors such as alien conquest and imported ideology, were essentially the result of festering hatreds between essentially the same two categories of people: Macheng's clearly delineated haves and have-nots. With the understanding that the Qing cycle did not really end with the Revolution of 1911—the death toll from which, in Macheng, was precisely one (chapter 9)—but rather with the Nationalist-Communist civil war, it may not be unreasonable to suggest that the dynastic cycle had some reality in this remote mountain county. I invite readers to follow along with the saga of Macheng history and decide for themselves.

PART ONE

CHAPTER ONE

The Social Ecology of Violence

MACHENG LIES ON the southern slope of the Dabie Shan, the Great Divide mountain range separating the North China Plain from the Middle Yangzi Valley. The Five Passes (*wuguan*) cutting through this range, particularly the Pine Nut Pass (Songzi guan) and the Long Ridge Pass (Changling guan), in the county's northeast corner, played pivotal roles in imperial as well as local history.[1] Macheng is a place of great natural beauty, looking, in the words of one nineteenth-century magistrate, "like a painting of purple clouds over soaring peaks."[2] It is also a provincial frontier, sharing a long and porous northern border with Henan and a shorter but intensely trafficked one with Anhui, in the northeast. Along with adjacent areas of these provinces, and the prefectures of Huangzhou and Qizhou, in eastern Hubei, Macheng forms part of a natural highland subregion, whose "ten thousand mountains," wrote the local historian Wang Baoxin in 1908, "reach to the Milky Way."[3]

Population

This hoof-shaped chunk of central highland was one of the longest-settled areas of the Chinese empire. Despite periodic waves of immigration and emigration, it was home to a fairly stable and deeply rooted population—one capable of generating a rich local dialect sharply distinguished from that of even contiguous counties.[4] Except for the occasional sojourner merchant, it was quite ethnically homogeneous. Official reports of Macheng's population are compiled in this book's Appendix. With all the skepticism such official figures invite, the general trend is not surprising. That is, Macheng saw a steady tenfold growth of population, from about 100,000 in the early Ming to nearly 1 million in the 1980s. If one assumes a percentage of undercounting that would decrease over time, cumulative growth would be somewhat more modest but still very impressive.

It was not, of course, even over time. There was an unusual spurt of growth—a better than doubling—in the early and mid-Qing, which suggests how population in this moderately prosperous county might increase during a prolonged period of imperially imposed peace.[5] Conversely, two striking periods of population decline suggest the impact of massive violence, in death and flight of local people. The late-Ming decline (a drop of more than 25 percent between 1556 and the conquest year of 1644) likely reflects trends in the empire more generally,[6] but the sudden demographic collapse of the late 1920s and 1930s (a loss of nearly 20 percent over the period 1923–41) testifies more singularly to the horrific violence that this particular locality witnessed during those years.[7] These two catastrophic eras are those of the "exterminations" that conclude the two halves of this book.

According to government figures, Macheng County in 1923 had a male-to-female ratio of 129:100, which, I suspect, was roughly characteristic of the preceding centuries as well. Since Macheng was by no means a pioneer- or male sojourner–dominated society, this severely unbalanced sex ratio suggests a high incidence of female infanticide. (This supposition appears to be borne out by the more balanced ratio of 102:100 in 1964, following decades of both Guomindang and Communist anti-infanticide campaigns.)[8] It even more unambiguously reveals a high incidence of male bachelorhood. The controls on lower-class male nuptiality imposed by the agrarian bondservant system—which, as we shall see, marked Macheng society over the centuries—played a key role in perpetuating the bachelor population. This large reservoir of males without family ties participated in what has been termed late-imperial and Republican China's bachelor subculture, with its special proclivity for violent behavior.[9]

Macheng was and still is an agrarian society, part of what the American agronomist John Lossing Buck termed China's "Yangzi rice–wheat area." In the early twentieth century, an estimated 80 percent of its economic product still came from agriculture, very largely of grain. Much of Macheng's terrain is uncultivable. Local sources conventionally describe the county as "40 percent mountains, 30 percent foothills, 30 percent plain" or "70 percent hills, 10 percent water, and 20 percent arable land." Buck himself, in the 1930s, found only 790 of the county's total 4,531 square kilometers under cultivation, a 17 percent rate not out of line with Huangzhou prefecture as a whole but far lower than the 38 percent for the Yangzi area more generally.[10] Yet what arable there is has always been very good land, fertile and well watered both by sufficient rainfall and by runoff from mountain streams. For example, of the some 1 million *mou* of Macheng farmland the Qing administration listed as taxable in its seventeenth-century baseline survey, nearly three-quarters was first-quality rice paddy.[11] The local climate normally cooperates. It is temperate, with four distinct seasons and often very heavy snows, but a growing season long enough to allow double cropping on the county's best land. County gazetteers report no shortage of droughts, floods, blizzards, and so on, often with failed harvests, starvation, and epidemic disease in their wake, but their incidence or severity was not beyond the norm for central China; over its history, in fact, Macheng far more regularly *received* than *produced* refugees from agrarian dearth, usually from across the mountains in southern Henan.[12] Local writers—elite writers, to be sure—consistently represented their county as one of wealth and abundance, a normally happy land (*lerang* or *leguo*), if only violence and disorder could be kept at bay.[13]

A Prize of War

But of course war could often not be avoided, due to the county's strategic centrality in the geopolitics of empire. Huangzhou prefecture as a whole is a critical juncture in the east-west traffic of the Yangzi Valley, so dominant a factor in China's modern history. But millennia before the Yangzi assumed its modern significance as a transport artery, Macheng County, with its mountain passes, was a critical juncture between north and south. This was a strategic centrality it never relinquished, even as technological and demographic change allowed waterborne east-west trade to eclipse overland communication between north and south. In times of disorder (*luan*)—any breakdown at all in central control—Macheng instantly became a prize of war. In late-imperial parlance it was a *bingchong* (military keypoint) or a *yanyi* (strategic county), and in modern vernacular a *bingjia bizheng zhi di,* a site where militarists necessarily clash.[14] From antiquity, each era of dynastic decline brought with it invasion from outside and, as Wang Baoxin was quick to add, most often an internally generated rebellion to accompany it.[15] With ruins of battlements dating back to the Western Zhou ever before their eyes, their bloody local history could hardly escape the consciousness of Macheng people. Indeed, recitations of the county's martial past have opened nearly all of Macheng's local gazetteers, beginning with the very first, by Xiong Ji in 1535:

> With its lofty peaks and mighty rivers, its strategic passes and lairs for ambush, this Heaven-ordained boundary between north and south has been an inevitable battleground since the Three Kingdoms, the Six Dynasties, and the Tang and Song. It was here [in the Three Kingdoms era] that Man Chong made his crossing and Lu Sun erected his defense. It was here [in the Jin] that Mao Bao and Fan Jun battled to their death. Here [in the Tang] Wu Shaoyang plundered and Li Daogu seized the commanding ground. Ahai and Zhang Rou [in the Mongol conquest] sought it bitterly, while Li Zhi and Xia Gui defended it with valor. . . . In this war-wasted stretch of mountains and marsh, the greatest heroes of their times have always fought and died.[16]

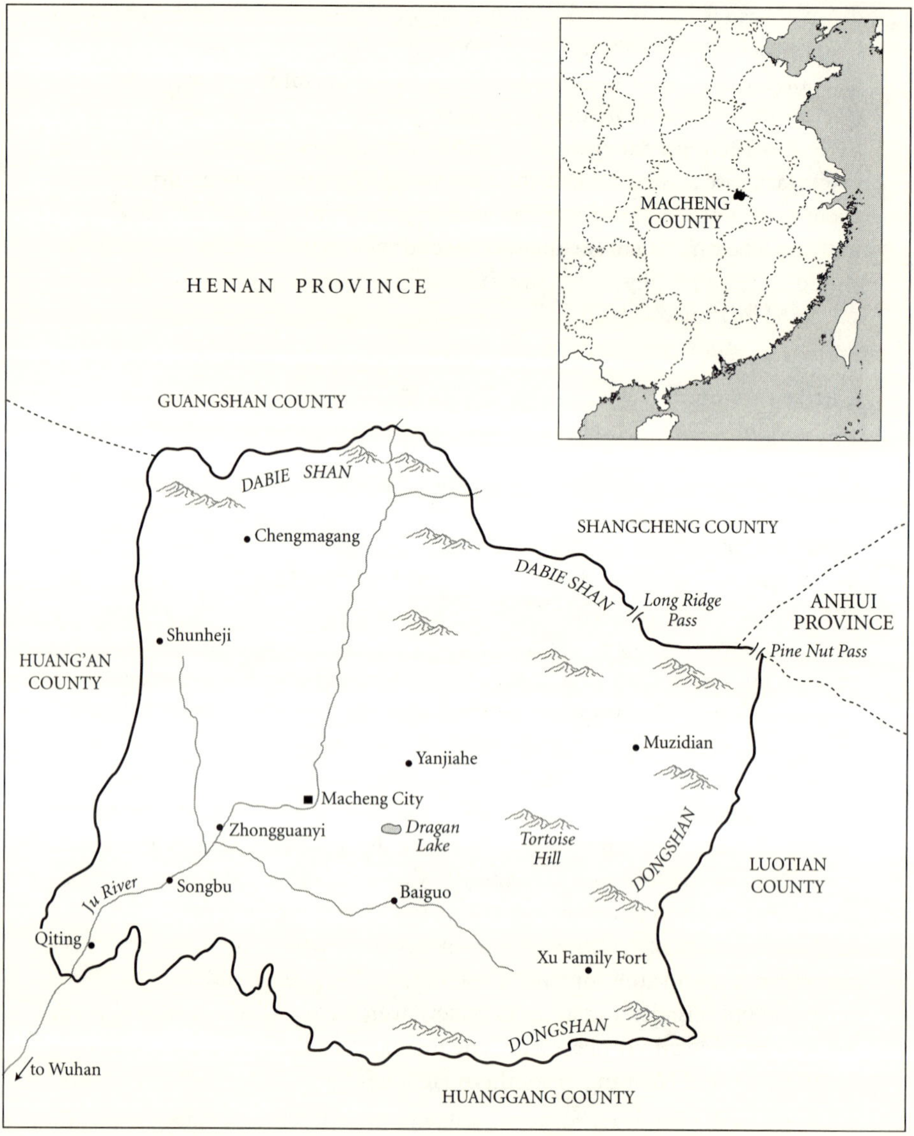

Macheng County

In local consciousness, none of these tales of martial valor had a greater imprint than that which gave the county its modern name, "Ma's Wall" (Macheng). During the Eastern Jin (317–419), an Inner Asian general named Ma Qiu served under the dynastic aspirant Shi Hu and occupied the site of present-day Macheng. To hold this favorable ground, he charged the local population with constructing a daunting set of battlements. Eager to complete this project as quickly as possible, he had the men work throughout the night, allowing them to go home to their families each morning only when the cock crowed and the chickens began to squawk. Legend tells that Ma Qiu's daughter, Ma Gu, felt sympathy for the people and learned the language of the birds. One night, well before dawn, she imitated the crowing cock, the roosters and chickens of the county all followed suit, and the workers went home early to sleep. When her father discovered the ruse he was furious, and Ma Gu was forced to flee to a mountain grotto, where she practiced Daoist alchemy and ultimately passed over into the realm of the immortals.[17] The site of her ascension, Ma Gu's Grotto (Ma Gu Xiandong), remains to this day a cherished Macheng landmark. Local poets who have visited the site over the centuries, and successive gazetteer compilers who recount its significance, each celebrate one or another of the various narratives of resistance that the Ma Gu legend may embody: the narrative of patriotic resistance to non-Han invasion, of pacifist resistance to militarist conscription, of localist resistance to central state commandism, or of popular resistance to elite expropriation.[18]

But Macheng was not merely a prize for militarists of dynastic scale, who most often swept in via the passes in the northeast or the rivers in the southwest; it also witnessed chronic combat of a more localized nature. Its long northern border, in the heart of the Dabie Shan, posed an obstacle to larger armies but was hardly impermeable to local traffic. We have already noted the county's receptivity to famine refugees from the southern portions of the North China Plain; reports of these, numbering into the tens of thousands, and plans for keeping them as tranquil as possible, form a recurring refrain in local sources through the centuries.[19] Far from shielding Macheng, the Dabie Shan served as an avenue to plunder and as an inviting haven for predators. As the 1920 *Hubei Provincial Gazetteer* observed, "The mentality of the prefectures of Runing, Guangzhou, and Nanyang in southern Henan is fierce and unruly (*kuanghan*). Local ruffians there habitually form themselves into bands for pillage and extortion."[20] As we shall see, these Henanese reivers were a routine irritant—often a devastating one—to the peace of Macheng. Though they came most often of their own accord in quest of spoils, their border crossing was also at times actively *solicited* by one or another party to the county's own indigenous violence. Nor was it necessarily a one-way affair. The early Communist organizer

Grotto of the Immortal Ma Gu (Ma Gu xiandong). Photograph by the author.

Wang Shusheng candidly admitted that his Macheng compatriots perhaps as often crossed the mountains into Guangshan and Shangcheng counties and despoiled the place: "The peasants of [Hubei] treated [Henan] as a foreign country and did what they liked as soon as they were [there]."[21] Mutual fear, hatred, and contempt characterized the populations on either side of the Dabie Shan.

Core and Peripheries

One can usefully imagine Macheng County as a leaf, lying at a 45-degree angle, with its stem in the southwest (pointing toward Wuhan) and its tip (the Pine Nut Pass) in the northeast. The center of the leaf is flatland, and its edges, mountains, with the Dabie Shan along the north and northwest, and the Dongshan (Eastern Hills) along the east and southeast. The veins of the leaf are waterways, tributaries feeding dendritically into the main artery, the Ju River (Jushui). The chief point of extraction, Songbu City, lies close to the stem, and the county seat lies near the confluence of many tributaries, at the leaf's center. Macheng thus broke down, in terms of both natural and human ecology, into three clearly defined zones—the stem and core of the "leaf," as it were, and its two flanking peripheries. At the start of the Ming, central authorities sought to divide the county into four townships (*xiang*) based on an artificial quadrant system—northeast, northwest, southeast, southwest—but by 1475 they had come to acknowledge the need to retailor this administrative structure to fit the ecology, folding one of the four *xiang* into the remaining three. These three were central and southwestern Macheng (Xianju Township), the mountainous north and northwest (Taiping Township), and the eastern and southeastern hills (Tingchuan Township).[22]

Central and southwestern Macheng, or Xianju Township, was by all measures the county's core. It hosted the county's greatest population density (some 44 percent of the total population in 1795, on much less than one-third of its land), and its greatest administrative density (not only the county magistrate, a subprefect, and a township-level submagistrate but also some 44 percent of Macheng's 124 Qing-era subtownships [*qu*]).[23] This area included by far the richest farmland, in the central plain popularly known as *guanxiang* (the house over the city gate) and in the fertile river valley draining the county to the southwest. This lush, intensely green terrain was largely double cropped, and planted overwhelmingly in wet-field rice until the cotton revolution of the mid-Ming pushed much of this paddy up to the hills that studded the plain. Silk, wheat, and vegetables were also produced in abundance. As we shall see, this lowland core was home to Macheng's wealthiest landlords, most successful

Prosperous mountain village, Yanjiahe Ward, central Macheng County. Photograph by the author.

scholar-officials, and most powerful lineages, but it was known as well for the comfortable life of its commoner population, including tenants.[24]

This core area also hosted the vast majority of the county's wholesale commerce, and all of its largest towns and cities.[25] Founded only in the Yuan dynasty, Macheng City had become, by the start of the period considered in this book, very much the political and cultural hub of Macheng, home to a substantial portion of the gentry elite, focal point of the county's elaborately interwoven lineage networks, and, as the point of linkage between the fertile central plain and the southwest river corridor, an important economic center as well. Its waterfront was ever active with river traffic, and by the close of our period it could boast nearly 600 shops and a population around 30,000. At the eastern perimeter of the central plain stood Yanjiahe, a substantial market town of well over 100 shops in the mid-nineteenth century, serving as intermediary in the exchange of lowland products for those of the mountains to the east. A similar role was played in southern Macheng by Baiguo, popularly known as the gateway to the Dongshan. More substantial still than Yanjiahe, Baiguo handled goods from all of eastern Hubei, hosted merchants from various Hubei counties as well as from Henan and Anhui, and, by the mid-Qing, had developed a significant handicraft sector in cotton textiles and metalworking.[26]

The greatest urban concentration in Macheng, though, lay along the banks of the Ju River, which linked the county seat easily and directly to the Wuhan cities—the great mid-Yangzi entrepot Hankou and the macroregion's administrative and cultural center, Wuchang. Tributaries of the Ju River integrated much of western and central Macheng County and carried the lion's share of interregional trade between the Middle Yangzi and the North China Plain. As the magistrate Guo Qinghua observed in 1882, the profits to be made along this waterway ranked "first in all Hubei."[27] The towns proudly known to locals as the three great markets (*sandaji*) were strung out in close proximity along the Ju River between the county seat and the river's exit from Macheng, in the county's southwest corner. All were sufficiently prosperous that by the nineteenth century they had been walled, at the local merchants' expense. Coming into the county from Wuhan, one first encountered Qiting. Both the political and commercial center of the county in the mid-imperial era, Qiting lost its administrative rank under the Yuan but recovered a bit in 1526, when it was designated the seat of a Huangzhou subprefect. Though the town remained a hub of intercounty trade through the nineteenth century, its long-term economic eclipse was accelerated when it was bypassed by the motor road built through the Ju River valley by the Nationalist regime in 1934. Farther upstream, en route to Macheng City, lay Zhongguanyi. As implied by its name, this town had started out as a postal station for imperial couriers, but its commercial importance grew rapidly, and by the close of the era examined here, it hosted over 300 shops.

Both Qiting and Zhongguanyi were dwarfed, however, by the market that lay between them: Macheng County's largest city, Songbu. Throughout the late-imperial and Republican eras, Songbu was easily the most cosmopolitan place in Macheng, hosting a variety of sojourner merchant guilds. Just as Macheng City was dominated by well-to-do county gentry, Songbu was controlled by sojourners and the county's own merchant diaspora. Popularly known as Little Hankou and as the gateway to Wuhan, Songbu in the Ming and Qing transshipped goods of forty-five major trades to destinations throughout central and northern China. In 1909 the British-owned Heji Egg Factory set up an office in Songbu for buying eggs to be shipped to Hankou, processed into powder, and exported to confectioners in Europe and America. German and Japanese firms followed shortly thereafter. By the late 1930s, Songbu claimed nearly 800 business enterprises, some of quite impressive scale.

The euphemistically named Taiping (Great Peace) Township, comprising roughly the northern half of Macheng County, could not have been more different—it was the periphery to Xianju's core. This was the true Dabie Shan, less densely populated than other parts of Macheng, and lair and chief victim of the bandits and border reivers to whom we have already referred. Though the larger-scale militarists who periodically swept through the county plagued all parts—more often than not heading to besiege the county seat—they, too, usually hit Taiping Township first and hardest. The area was roughly equally divided between high mountains and foothills, with nearly no level plain, and much of its territory was uncultivable. Livelihoods were overwhelmingly agricultural (as late as 1984 in Chengmagang subdistrict, only 1.5 percent of the population were nonfarmers), with some herding, fishing, and forestry, but with handicrafts very nearly nonexistent. Even to the present day, agriculture in this marginal scrubland has been basically subsistence-oriented. Adequate rainfall allowed some terraced cultivation of dry-field rice, along with millet, sesame, and—following the introduction of New World crops, in the sixteenth century—peanuts. There was little profit to be made from owning farmland, so landlordism, not surprisingly, was of much smaller scale than in the south; the ever-present specter of downward mobility, however, made the existing landlords unusually predatory.[28]

Given its persistently low level of commercialization, Macheng's northern township was not very urbanized. What towns there were remained small and devoted almost entirely to local retail marketing and a bit of short-distance petty trade across the provincial border; even today, in the wake of repeated "rural industrialization" campaigns, these towns hardly exceed 1,000 persons.

From west to east, the chief among them included Shunheji, Chengmagang (Horseback Ridge), Huangtugang, Futianhe, and Sanhekou. Communal identity was strong at the level of these local marketing systems but rarely transcended them. Futianhe, for instance, developed a distinctive genre of folk opera that, locals claimed, dated from the Tang dynasty; the performances, inspired by interprovincial porterage traffic through the area's Two Temple Pass (Shuangmiao guan), featured a female impersonator (*huadan*) carrying baskets of flowers on a shoulder pole along a mountain road and pausing to exchange suggestive verses with two clownish bumpkins (*chou*).[29] In the 1920s and 1930s, the districts around Chengmagang and Shunheji produced extraordinary numbers of Communist activists (Chengmagang alone spawned no fewer than twenty-six PLA generals); it is clear that local marketing ties played a critical role in recruitment into the movement.

Macheng's eastern and southeastern hills (Tingchuan Township) were significantly divided from the rest of the county by an intervening ridge of mountains known as the "roofbeam (*wuji*) of Macheng." The highest of these was Guifeng shan (Tortoise Peak), some sixty *li* east of the town of Baiguo. Site of a famous battle between the Qu and Wu kingdoms in the Warring States era, Guifeng was also where the Southern Song magistrate sought refuge when the Mongols first threatened in 1234. Well over 1,000 meters above sea level, the Guifeng range constituted a natural watershed, and the streams that drained this eastern township and linked its principal market towns—Muzidian, Zhangjiafan, and Yantianhe—fed not westward into the Ju River, like the rest of Macheng County, but instead southeasterly into Luotian and Huanggang.[30] This three-county borderland was the heart of the so-called Dongshan, the Eastern Hills.

The Dongshan was highland (only 15 to 20 percent plains), and it was wild.[31] Even today, panthers, wolves, badgers, and wild boar roam its hills, and hunting has always been a central feature of local life. Dongshan has also long been a favored wandering place for Buddhist and Daoist recluses. But, despite its wilderness atmosphere, the region is not especially impoverished. Pine, bamboo, and other forest products supply a comfortable source of livelihood, along with hides, tung oil, and a wide variety of medicinal herbs. Rice, millet, and chestnuts are the major staples, and both sericulture and tea cultivation add considerably to local prosperity. Timber and oil-pressing mills from early times offered local farmers supplementary employment. The town of Muzidian (Timber Market) was small—as late as the 1990s, it hosted no more than fifty businesses—but it was an important stage en route to Anhui and southeast Henan as well as to Luotian and eastern Hubei. More than once it was held for ransom by bandit gangs, rebel forces, or renegade soldiers sweeping in through the Pine Nut or Long Ridge Pass.[32] The town's principal Buddhist temple, the

Dinghui si, was something of a nerve center for local politics and society in the volatile northern Dongshan and, to a lesser extent, in the region as a whole.

Dongshan was a periphery of a very different sort from the Dabie Shan in the north. Though tied in administratively to Macheng County—and, as our story will relate, of growing importance over time in political and military control of the county as a whole—Dongshan was never really a dependency of the lowland core. It was instead—more, indeed, than any other part of the county—a locus of personal identity and communal solidarity unto itself. This autonomous urge was most typically expressed in violence: the Wuhan University historian Wang Baoxin, a Dongshan native, proudly noted in 1908 that, local customs in his homeland being brave and martial (*qiangyong*), men of the Dongshan took armed resistance as habitual local practice (*yi wukang wei xiangsu*).[33] Outsiders, including successive national political regimes, noticed this as well, and terms such as "Dongshan rebels" or "Dongshan bandits" (*Dongshan zei*) became, over the centuries, staple idioms in official discourse.[34]

By the late Ming, a popular quatrain gave poetic form to the stereotypes that Macheng people attached to inhabitants of the various sectors of their native county. Residents of the county seat and its surrounding plain were refined and educated (*xiu*) and accomplished (*da*) in attaining official service. Those of the commercial southwest were clever (*qiao*) and broadly traveled (*you*). By contrast, inhabitants of the Dongshan were rustic and unpretentious (*pu*) though capably self-sufficient (*zu*). The unfortunate denizens of the western Dabie Shan (Chengmagang and Shunheji) were impoverished (*pin*), surviving on a dog-eat-dog animal cunning (*jiao*).[35] A folk ballad of the early twentieth century was, if anything, more direct, reducing each sector to an emblematic image: in the central core it was the examination essay (*wenzhang*), in the commercial southwest the commission agent (*jingshang*), in the Dongshan the rustic farmhouse (*tianzhuang*), and in the Dabie Shan, alas, the distillery (*jiujiang*).[36]

There was a clear intersectoral rivalry, even mutual contempt, underlying such stereotypes. To cite but one example, the Ming-revivalist agitation of certain Dongshan strongmen in the 1670s was dismissed by more refined (and Qing collaborationist) civil literati of the central core as a typical hotheaded act of that region's impetuous small fry (*xiaochun*).[37] Attitudes such as this—heartily reciprocated, I might add—provided a lingering, tense undercurrent to Macheng's political life.

Town and Country

This dynamic overlay and interacted with another persistent tension in the county: that between rural and urban. Animosity between the countryside and the major urban centers of the county's core—most obviously Macheng City, but also to varying degrees Songbu, Zhongguanyi, Qiting, and Baiguo—was endemic. In this equation, the "countryside" might well include the rural elite (the township-level gentry, or *xiangshen*) equally with their poorer neighbors. There was much to intimidate and inspire rural resentment about even such modest cities as these. They were home to indisputably the county's wealthiest landlords and merchants, referred to locally as the county-seat gentry (*chengnei shishen*). The cities of the core were also storehouses of most of the county's food reserves and thus were regular targets in times of dearth. In times of economic distress, it was axiomatic that urbanites suffered less seriously and immediately than did the farmers.[38] And each of these towns, by the nineteenth century, had been walled and moated—Macheng and Qiting at the initiative of the state, and the others at that of the resident commercial elite. This highly visible distinction was probably, in practical terms, a mixed blessing for rural dwellers; labor and materials for construction of these battlements were often simply impressed from the countryside, as in the massive rebuilding of the Macheng City wall in 1573, but such labor could also be a means for the state to provide work relief for starving farmers in times of failed harvests.[39]

Equally significant, these cities (especially Macheng, but periodically, to a lesser extent, the others as well) were home to the local representatives of national political regimes. They housed government treasuries and courts of law. They were where the county's taxes were assessed and collected, with (as we shall see) the varieties of resentment that could invite. And they were the home of government troops, not merely the magistrate's, the subprefect's, and the submagistrates' modest detachments, charged with policing their rural neighbors in times of peace, but, more important, in times of unrest as bases for far larger military forces. Macheng's history gave ample testimony, as we shall see, to the principle that a governing regime defended its walled cities and ceded the countryside to its foes or, indeed, took the precaution of actively despoiling that countryside (*qingye*) before retreating to the town. This meant systematic favoring of urbanites' subsistence needs. For example, when the Macheng magistrate wrote to Hubei governor Hu Linyi in 1858, asking for advice on how to manage the county's food supply in the face of Taiping attacks, Hu was brutally candid in his reply: "In the defense of the walled cities, nothing is more critical than grain supply. The grain collected as rent by wealthy urban households must be allowed to come unimpeded to them in the city"[40] (rather than be retained or diverted for rural relief). Moreover, regimes from the Mongols to the Guomindang routinely used the cities of the core and the southwest as bases from which to "exterminate" uppity malcontents in the county's peripheries.

All of these factors also made the cities prime targets for rural assault, and this, too, was a constant refrain in Macheng history. When threat arose from within or without, elites from the central plain and the Ju River Valley flocked into the cities for refuge. There they fretted about the trustworthiness of the rural commoners. Would their tenants abscond and leave their lands lying fallow? Would they form into mobs (*chengqun*) and march on the towns? Or would they turn to the rebel side? Would the country folk prove, in fact, to be the elites' reliable compatriots in the face of outside forces, or would they instead be an "enemy within" (*neiying*)? Imperial officials charged with Macheng's defense repeatedly reported on the panicked mentality of these besieged urban and suburban elites.[41] No one, perhaps, voiced this mind-set better than Meng Guangpeng, a locally born, nationally renowned social scientist recruited by Guomindang County authorities to write a preface for the 1935 gazetteer. Reviewing the lessons of history as he saw them, Meng identified a recurring pattern of times of cataclysm (*shibian*), when mobs of uneducated kids (*shixue nianshao*) and propertyless traitors (*wuye jianmin*) streamed down from the county's mountainous fringes (*yanjie*) to inflict unspeakable calamities on the upright and productive citizens of the plain.[42]

But, as it happened, the rural-urban or core-periphery dynamic in Macheng County was considerably more complicated. One of the distinguishing features of Macheng's human ecology was the presence, growing rapidly over the late-imperial era, of alternative walled safe havens in times of unrest, replete with elite wealth and food supplies. These were the fortresses (*zhai* or *bao*) about which we will have much to say as our story progresses. The presence of these fortified *rural* settlements might even, at times, reverse the conventional practice of officials and literati elites hunkering down exclusively in *urban* centers in times of social unrest. This does not means that Macheng's major cities and towns were not subject to siege—they were indeed, and with great regularity. But when that occurred, the urban notables might, in extremis, actually abandon a city and hide out in a mountainside fort, as did the Southern Song magistrate when the county was overrun by the Mongols in 1234. It might mean that rural rebels could find themselves holding cities they had captured, and under siege by a combination of dynastic officials and fortress-based elites. It might also mean that rural strongmen from one of Macheng's peripheral areas (most typically the Dongshan highlands), rather than being excluded from the defense efforts of the administration centered on the county seat, could find themselves, by invitation or at their own initiative, actually in charge of such efforts. We will explore this complex dynamic in the chapters to follow.

Routine Violence

The historical narrative of this book inevitably tends to highlight episodic outbreaks of massive violence in Macheng County. And, indeed, the historian cannot help but be struck by the singular frenzy, ferocity, and scale with which, in moments of broader social disorder in empire or region, the population of this otherwise nondescript locality threw itself bloodily into the fray. For the moment, however, we need to look more to the commonplace, to stress how these larger "eruptions" were embedded in a human ecology in Macheng within which violence was endemic, chronic, and routine. As the late-Ming visitor Wang Shizhen wrote of the region, "Local customs there are fierce and bellicose, and there is little regard for law."[43]

Macheng County, as we have already seen, was at all times a dangerous place. The persistent plague was that most commonly referred to as *tufei,* or local bandits. Bandits were never really absent from Macheng's highlands, but the numerous reports in local sources suggest eras of greater and lesser scale and intensity of activity. These trends are hardly surprising in light of larger patterns of unrest in China's history as a whole.[44] We first hear Macheng *tufei* referred to with regularity in the mid-Ming (the 1470s), and they remain a growing theme through the Qing consolidation two centuries later, in the 1670s. Local sources routinely complain that government functionaries and rural gentry alike are complicit in the activities of *tufei*, confirming David Robinson's findings on the general importance of elite patronage, at least by the fifteenth century, in underpinning the empire's "economy of violence."[45]

The early-Qing "model official" Yu Chenglong, serving as Qiting subprefect in 1673, devised a typically resolute way of identifying and dismantling these patronage networks. He simply sent out his forces to seize nine individuals widely suspected of banditry, then convened a conference of local literati to ask if anyone would vouch, in Yu's presence, for any of the suspects. Only two were vouched for. Equally characteristically, Yu then freed the other seven on parole, deputing them as his personal agents in suppressing the activities of other *tufei* in the county.[46]

By comparison to the Ming, there is a remarkable silence on bandits in the era of the "high Qing"—eloquent testimony to the policing power of the dynasty in its heyday, and especially, as we shall see, to the implementation of that power locally. We begin to hear of *tufei* routinely again in the wake of the mid-nineteenth-century rebellions, and the problem escalates rapidly and disastrously through the Republican era. As late as the 1950s, the fledgling Communist government felt obliged to launch a determined and protracted "bandit extermination struggle" from a command post on the Macheng-Huang'an border.[47]

Tufei ravaged the county, at times causing calamitous damage to agriculture. They disrupted transport, depressing the county's commerce. They engaged in salt smuggling (though in this peripheral area there is surprisingly little evidence of their involvement in prostitution, opium, or other rackets). They kidnapped local elites for ransom. They torched local temples. Reivers routinely swept in from across the Dabie Shan, as we have seen, sometimes by the tens of thousands, and ransacked north-township markets like Chengmagang. But bandits also plundered and periodically occupied the more developed towns of the south—Songbu, Qiting, Baiguo. In 1512 they took the county seat itself, and in the spring of 1927, with Macheng and Huang'an occupied by United Front revolutionaries, they besieged both county seats again. In one of their boldest moves, in 1926 two local bandits accepted commissions as "militia division commanders" from the renegade militarist Yuan Ying, set up headquarters in the county orphanage (appropriating its endowment), and for months systematically extorted tribute from the county administration, local businessmen, and township "self-government" organizations; when Jiang Hualong, a gentry hero of the late-Qing reforms and of the 1911 Revolution, who headed the county's "self-government bureau," resisted, he and his son were abducted and killed.[48]

Just who were these *tufei*? As Mei Guozhen, the Ming general and eminent bandit-suppressor, observed around 1590, farmers of his native Macheng were well practiced at turning to banditry in extremis to survive times of dearth.[49] But the more serious *tufei* threat came from professionals. Full-time bandit gangs numbering in the hundreds and thousands have been endemic throughout the past millennium in the Dabie Shan, on both the Henan and the Hubei side, and, to a lesser extent, in the Dongshan. In troubled times their ranks swelled—as, for example, with the addition of defeated antidynastic rebel remnants in the 1370s, 1640s, and 1860s and, in the early Republic, the addition of splintered detachments of warlord armies (*huibing*). The relations of these forces with local militia and fraternal societies (*hui*)—such as the Red Spears—was a complex question, to which we shall return.[50]

The social analysis of banditry is much complicated by the readiness of aspirant and actual state regimes to refer to their armed political opponents as "bandits," in internal documents as well as public proclamations. Conquerors and consolidators in service of the Qing did this routinely in Macheng. Qing sources use the term *tufei*, or its variant *tuzei* (local bandits), most often to refer to professional outlaws but at times also to refer to Ming-loyalist holdouts or rebels. The word *tao* (thieves) was used in reference not only to robber bands but also to rebellious bondservants and, at times, even Ming remnants.[51]

The subsequent Guomindang regime learned from this, of course, becoming masters at defaming their ideological opponents as mere criminals: *gongfei*, or Communist bandits. (Macheng Communists may well have returned the favor by including Guomindang loyalists among the "bandits" to be "exterminated" in the 1950s campaigns.) There were indeed genuine bandits within Communist forces in the Dabie Shan, and others in loose alliance with them, but, as we shall see, the relationship was more often a tense than a comfortable one.[52] And Guomindang authorities in Macheng did spend a great deal of energy combating "bandits" who were not Communists at all. Government discourse sometimes reveals this distinction and sometimes elides it.[53] For example, local Guomindang sources in the 1930s, describing recent history, speak of a bandit calamity (*feihuan*) gradually giving way to a Red calamity (*chihuo*), and of a crisis of *tufei* (local bandits) eclipsed by one of *chifei* (Red bandits)—but never completely in either case.[54] In reading such documents and imagining oneself in the position of conservative local elites—struggling, as they always had, to preserve their society against forces of disorder—it becomes possible to see the origins of later Guomindang *gongfei* rhetoric as something more than cynical spin-doctoring. From the local perspective, at least, there was clear logic in viewing Communist guerrillas as simply one more gang in a long series of predatory bandits afflicting the county.

This persistent threat of banditry was the most basic factor in the progressive, long-term militarization of Macheng society that will be a major theme of this book. But local cultural responses went far beyond the institutional ones. Local heroes such as Mei Guozhen and his nephew Mei Zhihuan, and local officials such as Mu Wei and Yu Chenglong, were celebrated over the centuries for their bloody campaigns of bandit extermination. Such violence was legitimized by the popular view—reinforced by the posturing of many outlaws themselves—that saw bandits as incarnations of the ever-present demonic threat. For this reason as well, demon-extinguishing gods such as the Martial and Majestic King Yue (Wumu Yuewang), enshrined in the Yuewang Temple at the county seat, and the Lord of the Eastern Peak (Dongyue shen), in the Huiyun Shrine at the Mei ancestral home of Seven Mile Ridge, were continuously invoked to protect the county from demon-bandits.[55]

Bandits also, unsurprisingly, figured very largely in local folklore. One popular story concerned Li Zhongsu, scion of a very wealthy early-Qing gentry family. Kidnapped by bandits for ransom as a child, he instead joined the band himself, becoming an expert horseman and archer. He also wrote poetry about the joys of the brigand's life. Grand Secretary Gong Zhili was so impressed by this verse, and by the martial prowess it betrayed, that he commissioned Li an officer in the pacification army against the Zheng Chenggong regime in Taiwan.[56] Another local legend is more revealing of the black humor that Macheng people turned to in the face of the unremitting threat from bandits. The tale lampoons the mid-fifteenth-century literatus Liu Zhongpu, awakened one night by bandits who had broken into his family compound and demanded his valuables. He claimed that the only things he had of real worth were his wife's jewels, and he gave these to the intruders. They accepted the jewelry and left, warning Liu not to tell anyone (that is, the authorities) of their visit. Some days later, Liu's wife discovered the jewelry to be missing and asked Liu if he knew anything about the loss. "I'm sorry, dear," he replied, "but I've promised not to tell."[57]

Endemic violence in Macheng went well beyond the threat from bandits. Firearms appeared early, and in great numbers. By at least the seventeenth century, hunters of the Dongshan and Dabie Shan highlands were routinely armed with European-style muskets (*niaoqiang*), and vigilantes encouraged their use against human targets as well.[58] Heavier arms, including the cannon brought in by Mei Zhihuan from Gansu and southern Jiangxi in the late Ming, were imported by local defense forces each time the county faced an outside threat.[59] With the mid-nineteenth-century rebellions came a qualitative increase in the number of firearms in the county. In the reconstruction era, arsenals were established in the county seat and in more than half a dozen market towns, with the goal of trying to assert some control over leftover weapons, but the effort had little success. Bandits of the late Qing carried rifles by the hundreds. By the early Republic, in the proud words of the 1935 county gazetteer, the progress of civilization (*wenming jinbu*) had introduced new kinds of high-tech arms, and combatants of all persuasions now toted automatic weapons. The gazetteer recorded some 1,388 automatic weapons registered in the hands of government-friendly militia but conceded this to be a mere fraction of the actual total in the county.[60] Once imported, most of these vast numbers of arms remained in Macheng—on the street, as it were—to be used by any party into whose hands they fell.

But if guns were an accepted staple of local life, even more ingrained into the fabric of Macheng society were the martial arts (*wushu*), and most especially boxing (*quanshu*). As subprefect Yu Chenglong wrote in the 1670s, comparing Macheng to its neighboring Dongshan county, Luotian, "In the two counties the civil (*wen*) and the martial (*wu*) are not in equal balance. Whereas in Luotian the *wen* is the more highly developed, in Macheng it is indisputably the *wu*."[61] Schools and fraternal associations (*hui*) specializing in Shaolin, Wudang, and nearly a dozen other local varieties of boxing were ubiquitous in the county. Members of these associations (*huiyou*) themselves fanned out into surrounding counties of the Dabie Shan region and participated in the several wider diasporas of Macheng natives during the Yuan, Ming, and Qing eras, setting up schools of their own and giving their home county something of an empirewide reputation as a center of martial arts learning. So, too, did the county's prodigious contingent of military degree holders: nearly all of the sixty-one Ming-era and seventy-six Qing-era military *juren* that Macheng produced came originally out of one or another of the county's scores of boxing academies. In the troubled times of the late Qing and early Republic, even as firearms flooded the countryside, local devotion to the arts of hand-to-hand combat only deepened.[62]

In the Ming and Qing eras, Macheng developed a colorful empirewide renown for the contentiousness of its population. One vehicle for this contention—normally nonviolent, but nevertheless highly vindictive—was the civil litigation process. As one early sixteenth-century observer put it:

> The people of Hubei are customarily deceitful and conniving and addicted to litigation. At the slightest provocation they file false charges against each other, engage in mutual vendettas, and implicate their neighbors in imagined crimes. Such lawsuits can drag on for more than a century! And the very worst county of all in this regard is Macheng.[63]

One particular Macheng incident involving an accusation of murder became sufficiently celebrated, in the form of a virtuous-widow tale, to make it into the Ming dynastic history (*Ming shi*). A certain Ms. Li was married as the second wife to the Macheng-born prefect Wang Longlin. At Wang's death, his body was brought home, and his faithful wife refused to eat for forty days, weakening herself to the point of death. Local people thought she had indeed died, and they placed her in a coffin to await burial. A kinsman, a cashiered local official, coveted the household property, which rightly would be inherited by Wang's son by his first wife. To eliminate this son from the succession, the kinsman spread rumors that he had killed his stepmother. As Ms. Li's coffin was being lowered into the earth, a crowd assembled and, at the kinsman's direction, chanted "Matricide!" But Ms. Li called out from within her coffin: "I know of your evil plan. Go away from here!" The crowd dispersed in shame, the son got his rightful inheritance, and Ms. Li expired in peace.[64]

Another Macheng tale, this one involving an actual murder, gained notoriety in the genre of a Judge Dee–type detective story. Teng Zhao was a local official famous for his sleuthing technique. While serving as Huangzhou prefect in 1416, he was confronted with the suspected murder of a local soldier in Macheng. Teng thought he knew the identity of the murderer, but since no body had been found, he could not bring the culprit to justice. He decided to spend the night in the temple of the Macheng City God (Chenghuang miao) and ask that deity for inspiration. Awakened suddenly in the middle of the night, he saw a rat run into the temple, circle several times around his cot, then run out the door and dive into a nearby pond. In the morning, the prefect ordered the pond dredged at the point where the rat had jumped in, and, sure enough, the soldier's body was discovered.[65]

The Case of the Runaway Bride

In such a lineage-dominated local society as Macheng, conflicts among kin groups were a fact of life; the Mei, for instance, one of the county's preeminent families of civil/military officials in the late Ming, engaged in protracted conflicts with several of their neighbors, most famously, but not exclusively, with the Geng clan of philosophers and officials.[66] And in a population deeply acclimated to the use of force, recourse to violence among competing kin groups was hardly uncommon. In 1628, for instance, the neighboring township-level gentry (*xiangshen*) lineages of Hu and Tian became embroiled in a web of murder and litigation that ultimately attracted the attention of the Ming court.[67]

But the most celebrated of Macheng's local feuds, one between the Tu and Yang that lasted over a decade in the 1720s and 1730s, became the stuff of local folklore.[68] Moreover, through its recasting as a piece of "reality fiction" by the eighteenth-century poet Yuan Mei[69] (and again, in 1996, through its serialized retelling in a mass-market "law and order" magazine[70]), this affair came to reinforce prevailing images of Macheng's uncouth local lineages for an empire-wide audience, much as Faulkner's satirical portraits of rural Mississippians in his Snopes trilogy did for later audiences of urban literati.

Yuan Mei's version goes as follows: Tu Rusong, a substantial farmer from Macheng, took a girl from the neighboring Yang lineage as his wife. The two proved incompatible, and Ms. Yang ran back to her parents.[71] Persuaded to attempt reconciliation, the young woman returned to Tu, but he beat her constantly, and when his mother became ill she took the occasion to abscond. No one knew where she had gone, and suits and countersuits followed between the two families. The bride's brother, Yang Wurong, announced that Tu had killed her. He asked a local villain (*wulai*) named Zhao Dang'er to corroborate his case, and Zhao craftily lied: "I have heard that it is true." Yang thus dragged Zhao along to the county *yamen* as a witness, but Magistrate Tang Yingqiu found insufficient evidence to convict Tu of murder. When Zhao's father stepped forward to confess that his son was an inveterate troublemaker, the latter's testimony was thrown out, and so the case dragged on, unsolved.

Magistrate Tang's ongoing investigations revealed that Ms. Yang had previously been sent as a child bride (*yangxi*) to the household of Wang Zu'er, but when the prospective groom died before the wedding could be consummated, she had been reclaimed by her family. The magistrate further detected a broader pattern of "tigerlike" marital chicanery orchestrated by the head of the bride's lineage, lower-gentry member Yang Tongfan, and initiated proceedings with the Board of Rites to have Yang stripped of his rank. No longer believing that Ms. Yang was actually dead, he launched a police dragnet to find and arrest her.

In actuality, when she fled the Tu, the young woman had once again returned home. Her mother feared for her safety and, after hiding her from everyone for a month, decided to notify the officials. But the person she chose to perform this notification—her son, Yang Wurong—proved unwise: instead of going to the authorities, Wurong had gone directly to the lineage head, Yang Tongfan. Sniffing a chance for profit, Tongfan said, "Let's hide the girl away.

Since I am a degree-holding gentryman, who will dare come and snatch her away from me?" So together Tongfan and Wurong sealed up the unfortunate Ms. Yang, very much alive, in a secret double-partition wall in their compound. It was then that they filed the accusation of murder against Tu Rusong.

Before the year was out, a neighbor by the name of Huang buried his dead child in a shallow grave near the river. The river then flooded, partially exposing the child's corpse, which was dug up and partially eaten by dogs. The local constable asked Magistrate Tang to come and investigate, but because of stormy weather Tang was forced to turn back. Here was another opportunity for Yang Tongfan: with Yang Wurong, he plotted to falsely identify the corpse as that of Ms. Yang. He paid the local coroner, Li Rong, to verify that the corpse was that of an adolescent girl, but Li forthrightly acknowledged that he could not be sure. Two days later Magistrate Tang was finally able to come to the site, but by then the corpse was so decomposed that no identification at all was possible; all Tang could do was have the body dressed for burial and properly interred.

Foiled again, Yang at this point mobilized a force of several dozen armed kinsmen to lead a raid against the Tu, and a violent feud ensued. News of this affray reached as far as the Huguang viceroy Maizhu, at Wuchang, who ordered the magistrate of nearby Guangji County, Gao Renjie, to reinvestigate the entire case. Gao, who secretly coveted the post of Macheng magistrate for himself, sought to use this opportunity to discredit Magistrate Tang. He enlisted some corrupt *yamen* underlings to find the corpse of a young woman, conspired with Yang Tongfan to falsely identify the corpse as that of Ms. Yang, and reported to Maizhu that Magistrate Tang had been taking bribes from the Tu to hush up the murder. Maizhu accepted this account, cashiered the honest Magistrate Tang, and the duplicitous Magistrate Gao took Tang's post. Not surprisingly, Gao proved a tyrant. He extorted money ruthlessly from the falsely accused murderer Tu Rusong, driving him and his family to attempt suicide; and, to hush up the honest coroner, secretly had Li Rong murdered.

An elaborate series of efforts followed, on the part of both the Tu and the Yang, to prove that the corpse in question was or was not that of Ms. Yang (these efforts are described with macabre delight by Yuan Mei). Gao, declaring the body to be that of the murdered Ms. Yang, submitted his case report to his superior, Huangzhou prefect Jiang Jianian, but the prefect was not convinced. Jiang ordered a coroner from a neighboring county to disinter the corpse for reinvestigation, and on this basis he determined that it was, after all, that of a male. Gao was not yet finished, however. He claimed that there had been a switch of corpses, and he submitted this report directly to Viceroy Maizhu, who forwarded it approvingly to the throne.

The people of Macheng all knew very well, of course, that justice had not been served in this case, but they could not prove it without a living Ms. Yang to produce as evidence. Their chance came when, early one morning, an old neighbor woman discovered traces of blood spattered about the Yang compound. (It was the blood of the coroner, Li Rong, who had been beaten to death there.) The neighbor respectfully asked Yang Tongfan about it, and he dismissed her, saying, "None of your business, old woman!" Now very suspicious, the neighbor poked around the compound one day when Tongfan was away, and she heard moaning from within the wall. It was Ms. Yang, of course, and the imprisoned bride responded to the old woman's questions by describing her sorry fate. Yang Tongfan suddenly returned and leaped at the woman in rage, but she managed to escape. She told her son what she had found and sent him to report the news to the county magistrate.

At that time the new Macheng magistrate was one Chen Ding, an extremely upright man from Haining, Zhejiang.[72] Having heard about this case upon his arrival, Chen immediately suspected fraud, but he had needed evidence of the sort that the neighbors now provided before he could bring the true culprits to justice. Chen reported the new development to Hubei Governor Wu Yingfen, who in turn reported it to the Huguang viceroy, still the same Maizhu. The enraged Maizhu, finally realizing that he had been duped, demanded that Ms. Yang be immediately brought before him. Magistrate Chen feared that if he did so too openly, there was the risk that Ms. Yang would actually be murdered or would commit suicide, and that the key to resolving the case once and for all would thus be removed. So he instead trumped up a charge of his own: that the Yang were operating a whorehouse. On the strength of this charge he personally led a raid on the Yang compound, tore down the wall's secret interior partition, and seized Ms. Yang. He then proceeded to the county law court, with Ms. Yang and the other parties in tow along with "several tens of thousands" of the good people of Macheng, whom he invited to witness the proceedings. In front of this audience, Magistrate Chen had Tu Rusong confront Ms. Yang, publicly acknowledge her as his wife, and profusely apologize for all the grief he had caused her. The assembled crowd, we are told, wept loud and long. Yang Tongfan and Yang Wurong knelt quietly and accepted their guilt.

In the late summer of 1735, Governor Wu memorialized the throne on the final resolution of the case. There was one final act to be played, however, and it was a dilly. In the time between the submission of Wu's memorial and receipt of an imperial rescript signaling closure of the case, Viceroy Maizhu had second thoughts about how bad this whole affair had made him look. He therefore concocted an alternative narrative, one more favorable to himself, by proclaiming as truth the false whorehouse charge devised by Magistrate Chen. In Maizhu's revised account, the young woman who had been discovered in the wall was not, in fact, Ms. Yang but rather a prostitute in Yang Tongfan's employ. The viceroy coerced Ms. Yang, by now exhausted, into going along, and he convinced Yang Tongfu to spare himself the death penalty by falsely confessing to keeping a brothel. Maizhu then memorialized his own version of the case's resolution.

Presented thus with two conflicting memorials, the emperor—probably the neophyte twenty-five-year-old Qianlong, who had acceded to the throne in October 1735—dispatched Shi Yizhi, president of the Board of Revenue, to Wuhan, to confront Viceroy Maizhu and Governor Wu directly and get to the bottom of things. Eventually the account of Magistrate Chen Ding (and Governor Wu) was determined to be the truth. Tang Yingqiu, the cashiered Macheng magistrate, was exonerated and restored to his rank. Yang Tongfan and Yang Wurong were convicted and executed. Justice is not always speedy, Yuan Mei concludes; but, with patience and perseverance, the truth will always be revealed.

While Yuan Mei's fascinating tale emphasizes deceit, civil litigation, careerist bureaucratic scheming, and imperial justice, the slightly varying version of this story that survives in local Macheng legend significantly places more emphasis on the militaristic elements of the feud. In this account, the raid that rescued Ms. Yang from the secret partition of the compound wall was not undertaken by the crusading Magistrate Chen and his trusty retainers but rather by a gang of local thugs in service of the Tu lineage. When the desired legal result was not achieved by the reappearance of the supposedly deceased, the Tu responded by mobilizing a still larger force of "several hundred men" that leveled the entire Yang compound to the ground. Still not satisfied, the men excavated a hole three feet deep where the buildings had stood; today it remains a marshy pit: the Yang-compound pond (Yangji tang). In local folk reckoning, it is not clever official detective work that brings resolution to this sort of nagging conflict; rather, it is armed might. *Wu*, in Macheng, prevails over *wen*.

Protest

Lucien Bianco has shown, on the basis of quantitative analysis of thousands of incidents, that the "big" entrepreneurially organized rebellions in modern Chinese history were embedded in a context of, and numerically overwhelmed by, much more routinized and smaller-scale mobilizations of popular collective force: food riots, tax resistance, and rent resistance. The experience of Macheng, so regularly the site of these "big" eruptions over the centuries, nevertheless bears out Bianco's point.[73] This was a county, as we shall see, where class-based tensions at all times ran perilously high. Wang Shizhen, the famous literary critic who served as Hubei provincial judge in 1573–74, wrote of Macheng: "There is no place in the empire of which it is more often said that its population is irreconcilably divided by class [*geyi buyijun*]."[74]

I have found documentation of food riots in the county in 1472, 1590, 1831, 1855, 1898, and 1929; but, quite clearly, there were many more submerged below the written record.[75] When harvests failed and grain prices escalated, hungry villagers were well schooled in orchestrating demands that the government prohibit further price hikes, compel private sales at "fair" or "stable" prices (*pingjia*), and open the granaries. When these demands were not met, state and private granaries were forcibly looted, often by armed popular associations (*hui*) formed for just such purposes. So familiar were these actions, and so understandable were they to local authorities, that they were almost officially tolerated. Macheng magistrates like Li Zhaoyuan, in 1831, would dutifully arrest and convict the major rioters, then sentence them merely to remain at home and reform their conduct; or, like Liu Qi in 1855, they would bow to popular pressure to release the ringleaders from jail.[76]

Tax resistance movements were an even more familiar form of collective protest in Macheng, stemming in part from the persistent patterns of center-locality and state-society tensions that we will observe repeatedly throughout this study. Unsurprisingly, such incidents became epidemic during the era of state breakdown under the Republic, but protests of significant scale against the imposition of taxes—in cash, in kind, and in corvée labor—were regular occurrences throughout Ming and Qing times as well. A Macheng native named Li Tianbao, for example, led a local tax rebellion, and when it failed he fled to the hills of western Hunan; there he allied with local "Miao" peoples, claiming to be a descendant of the Tang ruling house, and led a short-lived uprising of several thousand men.[77]

Tax protests might unite elites and commoners against the administration, divide the two (especially when local magnates were engaged in *baolan*, proxy remittance rackets), or even fragment a social class based on geographic or other factors. Two examples will offer some of the flavor of these protests.

The first involves the county's grain-tribute assessment. After the fifteenth century, Macheng, falling as it did under the "southern" portion of the tribute, owed a total of 4,200 catties of tribute rice per year, with the assessment divided among local property holders. Because of Macheng's mountainous terrain, however, this assessment constituted an unusually burdensome imposition on the county's taxpayers, who were, like others elsewhere, responsible for bearing, in surtax form, the transport costs of tribute rice to the government's collection stations. This was an especially onerous burden when scheduled payments happened to coincide with periods of low water on the county's tributary arteries, a situation necessitating a tremendously costly shift to overland collection. *Yamen* clerks as well as transport laborers used this situation to exploit taxpayers even further. Commutation of grain-tribute payments to payment in cash seemed to be the answer. In the later sixteenth century, local officials and elites sat down repeatedly to seek out ways of effectively implementing this solution, but intrataxpayer squabbles were the usual result. Commutation to cash at a blanket rate, with average transport costs built in, actually disadvantaged those wealthy lowland rice planters who were within relatively easy shipping distance to the collection stations, and these planters, who preferred that payment in kind be continued, more than once resisted payment. Only in the 1590s, after several decades of bickering and a personal inspection tour on the part of the Hubei governor, was some reconciliation achieved.[78]

The second example of tax protest involves the assessment of seasonal payments of firewood on highland populations. These assessments, made by Qing county officials and clerks, were for those officials' own use of firewood—a clear irritant to the ever-latent tensions in Macheng between state and society, and between urban and rural areas. Over the early eighteenth century, property holders of the Dongshan, in growing numbers, had forcibly resisted this imposition. Finally, in 1753, the newly arrived magistrate Dan Yanyang, a crusader against bureaucratic high-handedness in general, abolished the firewood assessment altogether. Dan engraved in stone the proclamation "Hereafter all wild vegetation in uncultivated areas belongs entirely to the people, who may harvest it for their own fuel needs." The Macheng literati lauded Dan's action as a major factor in maintaining subsistence on the county's agrarian margins.[79]

Class-based rent resistance in Macheng was less persistent than were crowd-based actions over food or taxes, but it was hardly absent. In the turbulent late 1920s and early 1930s, violent antirent movements were an everyday occurrence in the county, and, as an investigator sent down from Party Central in Shanghai reported in 1929, the majority of these actions seemed to spring from entirely local roots, with little or no direct Communist orchestration.[80] But if the frequency and ferocity of these movements was greatest in the early twentieth century, they were nevertheless far from new to that period. In the early eighteenth century, for example, in the Tiantang zhai area of Dongshan, on the Macheng-Luotian border, several men of the wealthy Jiang lineage purchased large tracts of hillside land and brought in members of the Ma surname to clear and till it as their tenants. The arrangement worked well until the yields of the land began to decline, after several years of continuous farming. In 1750, when Ma demands for corresponding rent reductions were rebuffed by the Jiang, Ma Chaozhu and two kinsmen known as "the three young Ma" (Ma san shaonian) rose in rebellion. Only the combined forces of Huguang viceroy Yongchang and Liang-Jiang viceroy Yinjishan were eventually able to subdue them.[81]

Much of this popular collective violence over the centuries was essentially of a reactive character, in defense of accustomed livelihoods and ways of doing things in the face of perceived threat. In the late nineteenth century, this logic extended to the cultural innovations introduced by the West, notably Christian missions. Macheng was relatively late to experience a missionary presence. It came in the form of the nonconformist Swedish Missionary Society (Svenska Missionsforbundet), or SMS, which set up operation in Wuhan in 1890 and determined to fan out into portions of the Hubei hinterland not yet touched by personnel of other denominations. Two years later, two SMS members, O. S. Wikholm and A. D. Johansson, arrived in Songbu and rented a merchant's shop to serve as their mission. They were not made welcome. Members of the town's martial arts academies, led by the sixteen-year-old boxing prodigy Li Peixiang, mobilized popular hostility against the foreigners, and, under the heady nativist enthusiasm of the Duanwu festival and the Dragon Boat races that fall, the boxers accused the missionaries of molesting a young girl of the Huo family and beat them to death in the open street at midday.[82] Over subsequent decades, repeated attempts to proselytize in Songbu (by far the most cosmopolitan place in Macheng) and elsewhere in the county were met with more muted but nonetheless determined resistance.

On occasion, these sorts of popular disturbance could promote themselves into *luan* (disorders) or *bian* (rebellions) of greater than local, even regime-changing, pretension. Such, of course, were those major violent upheavals of the 1350s–60s, 1620s–40s, 1670s, 1850s–60s, and 1920s–30s, which form the basis of this study. But there were also many other, more routine *bian* that never got so far and yet were sufficiently threatening to panic local society. For instance, Dong Guanpan, in the 1490s, and Hu Tingfeng, in the 1520s, were both Macheng bandits who proclaimed themselves *wang* (kings) and for a time waged antidynastic campaigns; in 1524, a Macheng purveyor of sorcerous literature (*woshu*) named Wan Minfu managed to stir up such alarm that Ming troops were brought in from the Han River Valley to quash him; and in 1905, a self-styled White Lotus movement, under the local activists Li Shiying, Deng Dapeng, and Hu Qucheng, systematically gathered rebel supporters to uphold the Qing and snuff out the foreigners (*fu Qing mie Yang*).[83] By no means was deep-seated apprehension of disorder (*pa luan*) a monopoly of the authorities and the upper classes. In 1513, for example, great fear of the approach of an army of spectral demon-rebels (*guibing*) gripped the rural population, prompting demands that the county officials and elites move to a heightened stage of defensive alert.[84] But fears of *bian* and *luan* were especially deep-seated elements of consciousness among the property-holding Macheng elite.

State Violence

At times, the prospect of popular *luan* could influence the authorities to take a more timid path in policy implementation: in the Macheng City wall-building project of 1573, for instance, this prospect prompted the authorities to shift in part from conscripted to hired labor. More routinely, such fears underlay elite campaigns over the centuries to propagandize "civilized"—properly docile and deferential—behavior (*jiaohua*) among the lower classes, and to inculcate the four social bonds and the eight virtues (*siwei bade*) among the population at large.[85] More customary still in Macheng, however, were efforts of the state and the elite to confront popular disorder, incipient or actual, with a patterned terrorist violence of their own—a practice epitomized in the single ominous word *jiao* (extermination).

Much of the narrative in the remaining chapters focuses on just such sanctioned inhumanity. Aggressive, even preemptive violence against demonized enemies of the state was chillingly defended in the 1630s by Mei Zhihuan as the repression of evil apparitions (*tanya yaofen*), and its grisly arts were perfected three centuries later by the Guomindang ward leader Lin Renfu, the self-styled King of Hell.[86] It was no less than a divine mission: a blood-drenched defense of the cosmic moral order versus the perceived forces of chaos. In this particular local setting, such battles were joined with great frequency and ferocity.

CHAPTER TWO

Kings of Light

DURING THE WINTER of 1346, recalled the late Yuan–early Ming literatus Ye Ziqi, the sun in central China suddenly turned blood-red.[1] This augured an era of ferocious rebellion and massive carnage throughout the region, lasting nearly a quarter of a century—the death throes of the Yuan dynasty. In this cathartic process, as Ye himself would chronicle, Macheng and its neighboring counties would play a pivotal and very violent role.

Macheng under Mongol Rule

What did Macheng society look like in the early fourteenth century? Insofar as this history can be recovered, it seems to have appeared considerably different from the picture that will become familiar to us for the sixteenth century and after. Macheng by the Yuan period was already an anciently settled place, the site of famous past battles between dynastic contestants. But it lacked the dense population of retired government officials and eminent literati that would emerge in the mid-Ming. The great lineages of the Ming and Qing had for the most part not yet established themselves. Rough it must have been, but we do not, in the Yuan, see much of the organized militarization of local society that would characterize later eras. The county was a significant avenue of trade, hosted a substantial number of transport workers, and was canvassed by itinerant peddlers, but there is no clear evidence that it had as yet developed a wealthy indigenous merchant class or an export-oriented commercial agriculture. It produced grain, largely for subsistence, and local agriculture was seemingly in the hands of a class of free tenants and owner-cultivators. Bond-servants, who would play such a large role in the county's later history, seem not yet to have been a social force: agrarian slaves (*nuli*), common in much of the former Jin domains of northern China and active in the mid-fourteenth-century rebellions in Jiangxi and Jiangnan,[2] are essentially absent from the historical record for Macheng and its neighboring jurisdictions in this era.

Local society had not been stagnant, however. Under the Tang (618–907), not a single one of the several hundred nationally powerful, choronym-bearing, aristocratic clans mentioned in court records identified Macheng as their home, nor indeed did they so identify anywhere else in the wider Dabie Shan or eastern Hubei (Huangzhou and Qizhou) region.[3] As far as the hereditary nobility was concerned, Macheng was simply not on the map. Throughout the three centuries of Tang rule, local sources claim only a single native son who held government office: Yan Boyu, who served as prefect of nearby Hongzhou, in northwest Jiangxi.[4] (Though the Yan are commemorated in local Macheng geography in the name of the market town of Yanjiahe, they had by Ming times effectively disappeared from the roster of the local elite.) But with the great demographic and sociopolitical changes of the later middle period of Chinese history, Macheng's position improved. In Robert Hartwell's analysis, Huangzhou and Qizhou Prefectures were among those central and southern regions that benefited most from the introduction of early-ripening rice, and from the greater demographic density this allowed; Hartwell places them, by Song times, firmly in the core area of the Middle Yangzi Valley. Macheng also became a major producer of tea for the Song government tea monopoly; by the late eleventh century, its plantations (*chachang*) yielded around 300,000 catties per year.[5] The ascendancy of the civil service examination as the chief instrument for bureaucratic recruitment, the displacement of the older aristocracy by the degree-holding "gentry," the rise of neo-Confucian (*lixue*) moral scholarship, and the "localist turn" in elite communal identity described by Robert Hymes—all seemed, similarly, to open greater opportunities for Macheng County.[6]

That Macheng was poised to really "make it" nationally was signaled by perhaps the one event in county history most celebrated in the subsequent consciousness of the local literati: the visit there of the great Northern Song poet-official Su Dongpo (Su Shi, 1037–1101). Su spent several of his mature years in Huangzhou Prefecture, wandering the hills, visiting Buddhist temples, and discussing the area's martial past with such friends as the recluse Chen Zao. On several occasions during this sojourn, Su was invited by a wealthy Qiting native, Wang Yi, to stay with him in his hometown, then the Macheng County seat. Su obligingly composed hagiographies of several past Macheng luminaries and occasional poems about various local sites—poems that were proudly reprinted in successive county gazetteers for centuries thereafter. (Macheng has even engaged in a persistent struggle with neighboring Huanggang about whether the "Dinghui si" in the title of one of Su Dongpo's Huangzhou poems refers to the temple of that name outside the Huanggang County seat or to the temple in Muzidian Town, in Macheng's Dongshan highlands.)[7]

There was clearly an evangelical element in Song neo-Confucianism in Macheng, as there was elsewhere, the beginnings of a new style of literati attack on popular culture that would become known as *jiaohua*—instructing and civilizing. For example, another prominent visitor of the day was the wealthy Sichuanese scholar Zhang Xingqi, who had come initially to explore Macheng's hills and compose verse about its natural beauties. But, appalled by the proliferation of hair-raising heterodox cults that he discovered among the natives, he moved his residence to the county, allied himself with reformist local officials, and dedicated himself to a protracted crusade for these cults' eradication. He tore down as many *yinsi* (lewd altars) as he discovered, and established in their place the Ziwei hou Temple on Mount Wunao, just outside the west gate of the county seat, for more proper worship of the orthodox Fuzhu shen (Lord of Good Fortune).[8]

The centerpiece of Macheng's new *lixue* literati culture—and the physical embodiment of the "localist turn"—was a pavilion constructed in the mid-eleventh century on the Wansong ling (Ten Thousand Pines Ridge), in the highlands west of the Ju River, by magistrate Zhang Renfu. Here local scholars and prominent visitors met to expound and debate the heady new moral and ontological issues of the day, and here Su Dongpo wrote a famous poem, playing on the homily "In planning for a decade plant trees, but in planning for a century plant virtue."[9] Gradually the Ten Thousand Pines pavilion (*ting*) evolved into an academy (*shuyuan*), developed an impressive library, acquired a growing endowment of rental lands, and at some later time was relocated into the new county seat of Macheng City. The Wansong Academy also developed a national reputation (until the eighteenth century, its successive headmasters were all nonlocal scholars of wide renown), and it remained the vital center of the county's scholarly scene through the close of the imperial era.[10]

With all this wave of high intellectualism, however, Macheng scholars were, surprisingly, unable to turn it to examination success and official prominence. Granted, there may be some gaps in the surviving historical record, but the usually attentive local gazetteers report only a single Macheng native who achieved the *jinshi* degree during the Song: he was Tian Hui of the subsequently prominent Tian lineage of Tianjiazhai. Only one other man besides Hui, his brother Tian Gui (who lacked a higher degree), is claimed to have held a significant official post under the Song. The succeeding Yuan did not hold civil service examinations until 1315, but in the half-century from that time until the fall of the dynasty only two other Macheng natives—Zhao Yufeng, a *jinshi*, and Mao Wenmu, a *juren*—attained higher than local degrees, and only a few others, kinsmen of Zhao and Mao, attained office by recommendation. Macheng's remarkable burst of examination and office-holding success as yet lay centuries in the future.[11]

The imprint of the Mongol occupation itself may have been rather light. Macheng *xian*, under the newly created Huangzhou *lu* (route), was overseen by a Mongol *daruyaci* (in Chinese, *daluhuachi*) but administered on a day-to-day basis by a county magistrate (*xianyin*) and a number of subordinate officials, all of whom were northern Chinese.[12] Although, as we have seen in chapter 1, the county was threatened by Jin armies on several occasions, it never fell under Jin imperial administration, passing instead directly from Song to Yuan rule. And although Dongshan elites mounted sporadic resistance throughout the 1270s to Mongol advances,[13] the Yuan takeover of Macheng, in 1279, was relatively peaceful. As was the case with most of China south of the Huai River, Macheng was peopled, in Yuan racial taxonomy, not by Chinese (Hanren) per se but rather by Southerners (Nanren), former subjects of the Southern Song. Accordingly, Yuan policy in general was to leave the local social structure, and the land tenure system on which it was based, relatively undisturbed, in contrast to the experience of much of the north, where the Yuan, building upon Jin innovations, expropriated much of the holdings of large Chinese landowners to create large princely and official estates farmed primarily by unfree labor.

As Paul Smith has argued, in former Southern Song territories such as Macheng, the Yuan state was in fact a relatively weak one. It relied for governance largely on subofficial *yamen* clerks, a social group always viewed as predatory and parasitic by Macheng elites and commoners alike, and for social control on large private landholders (including Buddhist and Daoist temples, which in Macheng, as throughout the rest of the empire, emerged ever more obviously as large corporate owners of tenant-farmed lands).[14] As we shall see in a moment, Yuan Macheng had some very large landholders indeed, but the likelihood is that the rural population was comprised primarily of small landholding households. After the reign of Qubilai (Emperor Shizu, 1280–94), an intensified Yuan effort to extract taxes from the agricultural surplus of the south led to the statutory appointment of certain local landholders as village heads (*lizheng*) and as fifty-household-unit community heads (*shezhang*), but there is some doubt about how widely these mandated posts were ever actually filled in most localities, and there is no evidence that they were filled in Macheng.[15] As Meng Siming argued in a classic 1938 study, despite the Yuan dynasty's stated policy of favoring Mongols and other Inner Asians over Hanren and Nanren, in practice it was property ownership, for the most part, rather than administratively determined ethnicity, that remained the principal determinant of social status.[16]

A few Macheng natives, as we have seen, attained degrees and accepted political office under the alien regime. And in at least one case a non-local man, the Jiangxi native Zou Qianba, was brought into the county as an official by the Yuan, acquired a favorable piece of land in the county, and spawned one of the area's most enduring, wealthy, and illustrious lineages over the course of the Ming and Qing.[17] But while Zou's case was a notable one, it was likely not representative (as we shall see, the majority of Macheng's late-imperial elite established themselves *after* the Ming founding). A more typical case of large local landlords under the Yuan is probably the Qin lineage, about which near-unique documentation survives in the text of a stone stele written around 1350 by their neighbor, the Confucian scholar Liu Shen, and transcribed in the 1935 county gazetteer.[18]

"The Qin," begins Liu, "are the foremost lineage [*jiazu*] of Macheng," and there is little reason to doubt him. The current lineage head, Qin Chaoqing, is the sixth-generation descendant of a set of brothers who migrated to the county in the 1160s and 1170s, under the Southern Song. It is not specified from where they came, but we are told that they have several relations throughout Jiangxi; very likely they were part of the southern migration accompanying the Jin conquest of the north, moving first into Jiangxi in the mid-twelfth century, and the Macheng Qin relocating again from there. Once in Macheng, they acquired land at various sites in the vicinity of Songbu, and branches of the lineage developed around each site. Their landholdings grew rapidly (from where did their capital come? were they involved in mercantile activities at Songbu?), but they always feared loss of their property due to Macheng's precarious position in the military contests between south and north—Song versus Jin, then Song versus Yuan. The eventual Yuan victory and consolidation, though, proved very beneficial. In 1337, the newly installed lineage head, Qin Chaoqing, conferred with several members of the senior generation about the possibility of endowing a lineage *yitian* (charitable estate). They did so, and then, in the late 1340s, launched a drive to reclaim additional land (*kaiken*) to augment their holdings. Altogether, the estate reached the astounding size of 700,000 *mou* (more than 100,000 acres). It was run by a professional estate manager (*da sinong*), and its proceeds were used (ostensibly) to fund a granary for the support of indigent relatives, to underwrite weddings and funerals, and to operate a lineage school. With all of this, the Qin seem not to have carried their status very effectively over into the Ming and Qing: only a very few Macheng *juren* and no *jinshi* of the Qin surname are recorded for those eras.[19] But in the Yuan itself they did very well. The stele records negotiation between lineage leaders and Yuan local officials over a favorable tax rate on estate lands, and a pledge by the latter to safeguard Qin property rights. Thus it is hardly surprising, as we shall see, that indigenous landed elites such as these would rally to the defense of the "alien" dynasty when it was threatened by a revolution of the dispossessed.[20]

Red Turbans

In the early fourteenth century, Mongol rule began to show serious signs of strain. A cadastral survey of southern landowners, announced in 1314, sparked rebellion in Jiangxi under the self-declared king, Cai Wujiu; essentially a tax revolt of the elite, Cai's uprising nonetheless attracted support from tenants and other commoners. Beginning in the 1320s, the Yellow River repeatedly flooded, causing failed harvests and massive movements of refugees, whom the Yuan court insisted on labeling as bandits (*taozei*). In 1325, one Zhao Chousi led a sectarian uprising in Henan's Xizhou, and a decade later, in 1337–38, Hu Run'er, or Hu the Venerated (Peng Hu), rebelled in the same province's Runing Prefecture, just across the Dabie Shan from Macheng. At the same time, Zhou Ziwang and his wife, the Buddha-mother (*fomu*), led a 5,000-strong rising to the south, in Yuanzhou Prefecture, on the Jiangxi-Hunan border; Zhou proclaimed himself king of Zhou and promulgated his own dynastic calendar.[21]

The man who emerged as the most promising force for reform within the court was Toghto, a Mongol of the Merkid tribe, a Confucian scholar, and chancellor of the right. Having won the affection of the Chinese literati for his principled retirement in 1344 in the midst of factional struggles, he was recalled to office in 1349 and immediately began to devote his attention to hydraulic affairs. Nevertheless, his ambitious plan to reroute the Yellow River to the north of the Shandong Peninsula, announced in 1351, proved politically costly. The imposition of new salt taxes and monetary debasement (issuance of unbacked paper currency) to finance the project earned Toghto the disaffection of the elite, and his conscription of more than 150,000 Han commoners to build the new dikes touched off widespread rebellion in the North China Plain.[22]

In Hubei, antipathy to the Yuan regime had intensified with the enfeoffment at Wuchang of Saichepuhua, a particularly venal and despised Mongol prince.[23] Then, just as the troubles were worsening in the north, the central Chinese highlands were struck with a series of failed harvests. Macheng itself suffered devastating drought in three successive years (1352, 1353, and 1354), with epidemic disease in its wake. Famine was so severe that local sources tell of widespread cannibalism (*da xiangshi*), one of the rare instances of this in the area's long history of periodic food shortage.[24] By this time, though, the county was already awash in bloodshed of a different nature.

Macheng's own contribution to the Yuan demise came in the form of a blacksmith named Zou Pusheng. Not a great deal is known of this man.[25] His given name, Pusheng (Universal Victory), was a nom de guerre, shared (as were variants of it) by several other late-Yuan rebels. On the basis of his surname, it would be tempting to see Zou as a disaffected offspring of the elite lineage founded by the former Yuan official Zou Qianba, whom we have already met, but this seems unlikely, since Zou Pusheng did not hail from the area of northwest Macheng in which Qianba had carved out his estate. Instead, he came from Huaqiao (Flower Bridge), a small settlement some 15 *li* east-southeast of the county seat, where the central plain just begins to rise into the Dongshan; Huaqiao seems to have become reasonably prosperous after the construction of the eponymous bridge on that site in the late thirteenth century.[26] Zou Pusheng appears to have been a man of genuine military talent. He was a religious leader as well. In 1338—the coincidence of this date with that of the Yuanzhou rebellion is probably not accidental—he founded in Macheng a sect known as the Shengren tang, the Lodge of the Holy One. A decade later, he encountered Peng Yingyu, the spiritual leader of that earlier rising, who was then passing through Macheng, in part on the run from Yuan authorities and in part in an effort to broaden his already widespread network of potential millenarian rebels.[27]

Peng Yingyu was a native of Yuanzhou (present-day Yichun), in Jiangxi, and he operated out of a highland base on the Jiangxi-Hunan border—the same highlands, not coincidentally, that spawned the Ping-Liu-Li Uprising of 1906 and formed the heartland of the Jiangxi Soviet in the 1930s. (The historic links and parallels between these Jiangxi-Hunan highlands and the Dongshan and Dabie Shan highlands to the north—the latter the heartland, in the 1930s, of the Eyuwan Soviet—date at least to this late-Yuan era.) Peng, born around the turn of the fourteenth century to a family of indigent farmers, had been sent at the age of nine to become a monk in the Cihua Temple of Yuanzhou's Mount Nanchuan (his family members were very likely tenants on the temple's endowment land). By young adulthood he had become adept at occult medical arts and began to wander the borderlands, making his living at religious healing or, in the eyes of more orthodox elites, *woshu* (sorcery). He began as well to proselytize rebellion. Zhou Ziwang and his Buddha-mother wife were among his most ardent converts, but when their 1338 rebellion collapsed and the Zhous were captured and executed, Peng escaped. He spent the next decade wandering throughout the broader Middle Yangzi highlands, distributing sutras, cultivating a network of disciples, and overseeing the establishment of sectarian lodges. One of his converts was another Jiangxi itinerant monk and the eventual founder of the Ming dynasty, Zhu Yuanzhang; for a time, Peng's Cihua Temple, in Yuanzhou, was considered the headquarters of the movement's western branch, and Zhu's Huangjue Temple, in Haozhou, was considered the headquarters of its eastern branch. A second disciple, as we have seen, was Zou Pusheng, likely converted in person during Peng Yingyu's sweep through Macheng in 1348. Yet a third was a native of Liuyang (just across the Hunan border from Yuanzhou), the later "Tianwan emperor" Xu Shouhui.[28]

This Xu Shouhui was a tall man, possessed of a magnificent physical appearance and, by most accounts, only very modest intellectual gifts. By midcentury he had left his native Hunan for Hubei, relocated to Luotian County on the eastern slope of the Dongshan range, and found work as an itinerant cloth peddler on the Huangzhou-Qizhou circuit. Sometime in the year 1351, in a scene highly befitting the Chinese operatic tradition, Xu came on commission from Peng Yingyu to visit Zou at his Macheng smithy. Recognizing some secret sectarian signal, Zou understood that what Xu really wanted was armaments, which Zou was skilled at producing. Their serious mobilization for rebellion began to take shape.[29]

At the same time, Han Shantong (d. 1355) and his son Han Liner (d. 1367), scions of a hereditary line of sectarian leaders claiming descent from the Song ruling house, were recruiting followers in the western Huai River Valley of Anhui and Henan. The elder Han styled himself the Greater King of Light (Da Mingwang) and his son the Lesser King of Light (Xiao Mingwang). The Han had apparently worked a loose confederation with Peng Yingyu and his disciple Zhu Yuanzhang, to the effect that the Han's sect was declared the northern branch and Peng's the southern. Taking advantage of popular anger at conscription levies for Toghto's dike-repair projects, Han Shantong launched a rebellion in Yingzhou, Anhui, in the fifth month of 1351 and had remarkable early success. His initial 3,000 followers, the Red Turban Army (*hongjin jun*), soon grew to nearly 10,000, and his uprising spilled over into southern Zhili and western Shandong. This success also gave the signal for Zou Pusheng and Xu Shouhui to rise on their own in the eighth month of that year.[30] The Zou-Xu rebellion, in turn, provided what Edward Dreyer has called "the proximate cause of the collapse of Yuan power in the Yangtze area."[31]

Zou and Xu called their force the Southern Red Turban Army, in direct imitation of Han Shantong's forces in the north, though they are routinely referred to in fourteenth-century sources by the abbreviated and (to modern ears) jarringly anachronistic name Red Army (*hongjun*). They gathered recruits in Macheng and throughout the wider region, offering promises of invulnerability through the spells of Peng Yingyu. They gradually seized control of the major transport routes of the region, drove off the Yuan administrators, and in the ninth month converged on the Qizhou prefectural seat, which an unusually determined Yuan official, Prefect Li Xiaoxian, defended to his death. The Red Turbans, now masters of all northeast Hubei, set up their seat of administration in the Lotus Pavilion Palace (*liantai sheng*) at the Qishui county seat. The stout and handsome Xu Shouhui, with his impressively shaggy eyebrows, took a bath in a salt pond and emerged giving off a regal glow; he was immediately pronounced *huangdi* (emperor), with the more effective Zou Pusheng settling for the title of *taishuai* (grand marshal). A government was established which mimicked that of the Yuan: a central administration featuring a secretariat (*zhongshu sheng*), six boards, a censorate, and a Hanlin academy, and a field administration comprising four provinces (*xingsheng*) and subordinate circuits (*lu*). Xu took the reign title Zhiping (govern in peace) and named his dynasty Tianwan (fulfillment of Heaven). In case Zou's and Xu's intentions were not as yet sufficiently manifest, the *wan* of Tianwan was the character for the Yuan dynasty—with a cap over it.[32]

The scope of the Tianwan domains grew rapidly throughout 1352 and early 1353. Attracting to its side large numbers of boatmen and fishermen from this central China "interior delta," it used naval power to expand its control of the region's intricate maze of waterways. The Red Army was claimed by one contemporary, Wang Feng, to have exhibited extraordinary military discipline, strictly observing an announced policy of *busha buyin* (no killing and no sexual molestation) with respect to conquered civilian populations.[33] Zou Pusheng's forces incorporated or allied with other, disparate rebel groups and rolled over central and western Hubei. In the early spring of 1352, Zou captured Hanyang, just across the Yangzi from the provincial capital at Wuchang, and shortly afterward he took Wuchang itself; the despised governor, Prince Saichepuhua, fled by boat, an action for which he was subsequently cashiered by the Yuan court. Zou then led his troops downriver to take Jiujiang, the most important Yangzi port in Jiangxi, while his subordinate commanders took the Jiangxi provincial capital of Nanchang and the Hunan capital of Changsha. In subsequent years, Tianwan armies also occupied much of Sichuan and parts of Shaanxi.[34]

The key figure in the thrust into Sichuan was one Ming Yuzhen (1331–66). Born Min Rui in the Han River County of Suixian, Ming was a county constable at the time his native area came under siege by the expanding Tianwan regime. After leading local defense for a year, he saw his opportunity in 1352 and went over to the Tianwan side. Xu Shouhui put Ming in charge of consolidating his hold on Macheng and other nearby counties until, in 1357, he dispatched him to lead a western expedition through the Yangzi gorges into Sichuan. Commanding a force of a reported 10,000 men, very largely recruited in Macheng, Ming captured both Chongqing and Chengdu. He survived the demise of Tianwan itself, styling himself the Master of Light (Mingzhu) and declaring his own Sichuan-based Xia dynasty in 1360. Ming Yuzhen's son, the Lesser Master of Light (Xiao Mingzhu), succeeded him in 1366, only to be deposed by Zhu Yuanzhang's own Ming regime five years later.[35]

Already by 1353, however, the Tianwan regime had begun to suffer reversals. The year began promisingly enough: the culmination of the three-year drought and famine led in the spring to a number of independent, sympathetic uprisings in the Yangzi Valley, including that of Zhang Jiusi in Jiangsu. But Mongol forces rallied under Toghto, and by summer an army of some 400,000 loyalist troops (*yibing*) had converged on the center of Tianwan power in eastern

Hubei. In early autumn a Yuan force captured the capital at Qishui; although Emperor Xu Shouhui escaped, some 400 top Tianwan leaders—including the chief military commander, Macheng's Zou Pusheng—were killed. Xu and his court took refuge in one after another of the Dongshan region's mountain forts (*zhai*) and, as each of these in turn was besieged by Toghto's army, took to running the hills of Huangmei County. Imperial politics came to their rescue, however; Toghto's enemies at the Yuan court took advantage of his relative slowness to extinguish the Tianwan regime altogether, and argued that this stemmed from the chancellor's massive unpopularity among the people. He was relieved toward the end of the year, and the rebellion's prospects immediately improved. By the winter of 1355–56, Xu Shouhui had reestablished his Tianwan court at Hanyang, at the confluence of the Yangzi and Han Rivers, in the very heart of Hubei.[36]

Very quickly, however, the internal discord and murderous intrigues that would ultimately bring down Tianwan began to emerge, in the persons of the Xu's lieutenants Ni Wenjun and Chen Youliang. Ni came from a hereditary fishing family of Huangpi County, a family that, like many others of the violent central Hubei waterworld, was traditionally armed and bellicose. He was clearly ambitious, circulating the legend that a white tiger had miraculously appeared at the door of his mother's bedchamber at the moment of his birth. An early adherent of the Tianwan cause, Ni had been granted the post of *chengxiang* (prime minister) in the Qishui court and placed in charge of its naval forces. After the loss of Qishui and the death of Zou Pusheng, he became even more central to the Tianwan regime; his navy engineered the capture first of Mianyang, in early 1355, and then the subsequent recapture of Hanyang. Most sources concede that from this point on it was Ni rather than the "lax and lenient" (*kuanzong*)[37] Xu Shouhui who was the regime's de facto head. He enfeoffed his son as king of Changsha to control the southern portions of the Tianwan realm. But Ni apparently overreached. In 1357 he attempted to seize the emperorship in his own name, by trying to have Xu Shouhui assassinated; when the plot failed, Xu had him assassinated in turn.[38]

The assassin was none other than Ni's trusted subordinate Chen Youliang, a man of no less ambition than his master. Born in 1320 to another armed fishing family, and having served intermittently as a county clerk (*tieshu*), Chen had taken service under Ni Wenjun during the latter's campaigns of 1354–55 in Chen's native Mianyang. In these battles and the subsequent capture of Hanyang, he fought so effectively that Ni appointed him *yuanshuai* (marshal) in the Tianwan military; after murdering Ni, Chen promoted himself to *pingzhang* (minister of state). Chen left Xu Shouhui to occupy the throne in Hanyang and gradually shifted his own base of operations downriver to northern Jiangxi Province. In early 1360, he proclaimed himself Hanwang (king of Han), with his capital at the major Yangzi port of Jiujiang, and the following month he dispensed with the niceties of allegiance to Xu Shouhui by having him and most of his court butchered at Hanyang. Chen's succeeding Great Han dynasty inherited most of the eastern portions of the former Tianwan domains (as Ming Yuzhen's Great Xia regime did the western portions) and engaged in ongoing warfare against the forces of Zhu Yuanzhang's Great Ming. Local legend has it that a turning point in the campaigns came at Macheng's own Great Victory Mountain (Dasheng shan), just east of Songbu, where Zhu and his contingent held out heroically for seven days against a siege by Chen.[39] Ultimately, in one of the great naval battles in Chinese history, at Boyang Lake in the autumn of 1363, Chen was defeated and killed by Zhu. Tianwan was no more.[40]

Religion, Class, and Nation

Surviving sources allow us only to speak in speculative terms about the mix of motivations behind the Red Turban rebellion and the social bases of the Tianwan state. Was this a Han-nationalist revolution against alien rule? It was certainly anti-regime, and very viciously so. The Red Army brutally killed every Yuan official it could lay its hands on: in one instance, the *Yuan shi* reports, the army flayed an official alive and cut out his stomach.[41] The Red Army was equally merciless toward captured Yuan soldiers: according to the contemporary observer Liu Renben, Tianwan troops dealt with these demonized enemies by "placing them in shackles, poking them with knives, binding them with cloth, putting sacks over their heads, and parading them around accompanied by drumbeating and derisive chants."[42] But there is scant evidence that this anti-regime violence was racially or ethnically inspired. None of several reported slogans of the Red Army (see below) betray specifically anti-Mongol (or antiforeign) sentiments. Indeed, apart from the hated—and apparently rather inept—Prince Saichepuhua at Wuhan, there seem to have been precious few Mongols among the Yuan officials and landed elites in the Middle Yangzi to invite popular wrath. The proliferation of predatory clerical types in the Yuan local administration is sometimes presumed to have inspired anti-dynastic resentment on the part of conquered populations, but it is worth recalling that two of Tianwan's key leaders, Ming Yuzhen and Chen Youliang, had themselves been county subbureaucrats. It seems perhaps safest to conclude that the evident anti-Yuan orientation of the rebellion represented less a nationalist movement than the proactive response of martially adept and highly ambitious aspirants to imperial power—in effect, entrepreneurs of violence—to the perceived opportunities created by a weakened dynastic regime.

A more compelling question is the extent to which the Red Turban rebellions were an outgrowth of class-based economic grievances, or perhaps even of an agrarian revolution. In his classic 1938 study of Yuan social structure, Meng Siming argued that inasmuch as the supposed race-based status hierarchy of the Mongols was never effectively instituted, especially in central and southern China, the "revolutions" (*geming*) that toppled the dynasty were necessarily economic in character—essentially a class war among Han Chinese themselves.[43] Unsurprisingly, historians in the People's Republic have even more unequivocally identified the Red Turban movement as a "peasant uprising" (*nongmin qiyi*) and the Tianwan regime as a "peasant government" (*nongmin zhengfu*).[44] Western scholars, however, have frequently been more skeptical; for example, Frederick Mote, in his standard *Cambridge History of China* article on the subject, concludes that this "strained search for abortive class warfare in the late Yuan period" is "far-fetched" as social history.[45]

Yet contemporary witnesses were fairly unanimous in using economically defined terms to describe the parties to the violence they observed. Tang Guifang, son of a high Yuan official, and tireless writer of epitaphs for victims of the central China bloodbaths, described the Huangzhou rebels as *xiaoren* (lower class) and their targets as *haoyou zhi jia* (households of the rich and powerful); Ye Ziqi blandly identified the constituency of the Red Armies as *pinzhe* (the poor).[46] Though I have found no independent confirmation in fourteenth-century documents, there seems little reason to disbelieve the unanimous testimony of Chinese historians that a central rallying cry of the Zou Pusheng/Xu Shouhui rebellion was "Take from the rich to relieve the poor" (*cuifu yipin*).[47] Tang Guifang likewise reported a confiscatory, redistributionist mentality among the insurgents: "The gold and pearls are all properly ours [*woyoude*]. The oxen and sheep are all ours. The grain is all ours."[48]

There is no record of Tianwan rebels explicitly invoking slogans like "Servants, kill your masters" (*cangtou shizhu*), as did contemporary rebel movements downriver—the absence of such slogans in reports from eastern Hubei may reflect that area's as yet less rigidified social structure—yet there is plenty of behavioral evidence that class tensions were at work here as well. Large numbers of Macheng landowners were sufficiently alarmed that they took to the hills and fortified themselves until the rebellions passed over.[49] And Tang Guifang's obituaries chillingly convey the ferocity with which the Middle Yangxi elite were indeed attacked, and the terror and contempt with which this elite confronted the poor. A certain Ms. Lu, widow of a Chinese Yuan official, was repeatedly set upon by "local villains who didn't know their place" (*xiangli xiaoren bu anming*); having given them in turn her jewelry, grain, and livestock, they further threatened to violate her sexually. "I am the wife of a Confucian [*ru*] family," she protested. "It is improper that I be defiled. I beg you to kill me instead." They obliged. Petrified elites took flight but were hunted down like fish and game (*yulie*) and, when caught, minced, and pickled (*zuhai*).[50] It is tempting to dismiss such talk as conventionalized hyperbole, but, given reports that starving victims of Macheng's repeated failed harvests resorted to cannibalism, it is indeed possible that we see here a literal episode of eating the rich.

This ravenousness, indeed, may be more than incidental. It seems likely that the vicious attacks on landed interests in Macheng and its wider region were based less on any impulse toward fundamental economic reform than on a classic food-riot mentality: surplus hoarded in elite and government granaries properly belonged to the wider community of the hungry. Beyond this, of course, the landed elite was identified (rightly) as complicit in Yuan dynastic rule, and it was this elite that in fact led local efforts at military counter-mobilization against Tianwan. It is striking that even the most vehemently Marxist chroniclers of Tianwan's rise and fall concede that, once the Red Turbans were in power, the redistributionist and class-warfare components of their platform quickly evaporated. Qu Shusen notes that Tianwan local administrators unhesitatingly copied Yuan fiscal extraction systems; even the periodically announced programs to lighten the corvée and land-tax burden (*qingyao bofu*) seem designed to appeal to landholders as much as to any other group. After 1353, under Ni Wenjun and Chen Youliang, landed elites were actively courted to participate in the governance of Tianwan and its successor state, Han. Above all, there is general agreement among specialists that no evidence whatsoever exists of programs to alter existing regimes of property ownership on the part of the fourteenth-century Red Army.[51]

Nor does a single peasant or practicing farmer of any kind appear among the rebellion's leaders; they were itinerant monks and diviners, traveling peddlers, ironmongers, fishermen, boatmen, constables, and *yamen* clerks—a motley group of men whom the *Yuan shi* at one point convincingly lumps together as "the rootless ones" (*wulai*).[52] Indeed, it may not be too far amiss to see in Tianwan a rebellion of dispossessed, familyless, marginalized males against a landed (or at least settled) agrarian establishment. As we have seen, Xu Shouhui's initial power base was a floating one, cruising the maze of the Middle Yangzi Valley's rivers and lakes and "terrorizing all those dwelling along the shore."[53] Under such circumstances, it is very hard to depict the Red Turban movement, at least in Macheng and its environs, as an agrarian revolution. In this, as we shall see, it would differ markedly from subsequent waves of mass violence intended to sweep the area in the late-Ming period and after.

What held this group of desperadoes together, apart from hunger and the elusive prospect of dynastic power, was an apparently gripping religious faith. Ever since the work of Wu Han in the 1950s, even the most materialist scholars of the late-Yuan rebellions have acknowledged the genuine religiosity of these movements and observed that, for Tianwan at least, millenarian ideals proved more central and lasting than economic or class-based ones among the movement's mixture of rationales. Tianwan leaders throughout the regime's existence continually burned incense, chanted sutras, and shouted religious slogans. Alas, Marxist historians lament, the failure of the fourteenth-century "peasantry" to constitute a self-aware class (*zijue de jieji*) led to its tendency to sublimate economic class-interest into religious superstition (*zongjiao mixin*)—the "opiate of the masses."[54] I would opt instead for a view of Tianwan millenarianism more empathetic to systems of popular imagination and belief. As E. P. Thompson expressed it, responding to similar materialist caricatures of millenarian movements in the West, we sell such movements short by dismissing as "fanaticism" or delusion "the *imagery* . . . with which minority groups have expressed their aspirations for hundreds of years. . . . When we speak of 'imagery' we mean much more than figures of speech in which ulterior motives were 'clothed.' The imagery is itself evidence of powerful subjective motivations, fully as 'real' as the objective, fully as effective . . . in their historical agency."[55] And in fourteenth-century China there is indeed every reason to see religion as being at the very forefront of class identity. Much as earlier neo-Confucian crusaders had waged war on popular belief by smashing all the *yinsi* they encountered in Macheng, the late-Yuan Red Army countered by razing such emblems of elite religious hegemony as the Confucian school-temple (*xuegong*) at the county seat.[56]

What was the precise nature of Tianwan religion? Let us start with the relatively little that we know with some certainty. The religious slogans of Peng Yingyu's Huangzhou and Qizhou followers were variously reported as proclamations that a deity named Mi-tuo, Mi-le, Mi-le-fo, or Mingwang (the King of Light) will appear in the world (*chushi*), descend into the world (*xiashi*), or become incarnate (*xiasheng*); in some variants, it is further specified that this deity will assume his rightful place as lord of all the world (*dang wei shizhu*).[57] The *Ming shi* reports in these prefectures a number of smaller late-fourteenth-century uprisings organized around the anticipated appearance of Mi-le, and others identified as White Lotus (Bailian jiao).[58] And the contemporary observer Ye Ziqi enumerates a range of popular sects providing the mix out of which Tianwan and its competitors and successors arose, including among them not only Bailian jiao and Touto jiao (presumably the worship of Mi-tuo/Mi-le) but also Manmo jiao—a rather unambiguous reference to Manichaeism.[59]

Evidently the Red Turbans were a millenarian movement, dedicated to ushering in the earthly reign of a divine savior who would cleanse the world of its accumulated demons and defilements—and, in the process, overthrow the Yuan. It was a classic example of what Barend ter Haar has called the "demonological messianic tradition" of Chinese popular religion, clothed in this instance with Buddhist and, most likely, Manichaean overlays.[60] Movement leaders claimed to be prophets of this savior's arrival or, in certain instances, claimed to be the savior himself. In other contexts, the name Mi-tuo is usually interpreted as a Chinese rendering of Amida Buddha, devotion to whom will lead the faithful to personal rebirth in the Pure Land (*jingtu*), and the name Mi-le is understood to be a reference to the future Buddha Maitreya; in Peng Yingyu's case, however, it seems clear that the two deities had been merged into one, and that it was Maitreya's function as world avenger and world deliverer that figured most centrally in mobilizing the rebellion. As for the White Lotus characterization of the movement, it is clear that this is not the Bailian jiao of later eras, associated with worship of the Eternal Mother (Wusheng laomu), but rather an older variant dedicated more closely to Amida/Maitreya; Yang Na suggests as evidence of the Red Turbans' link to White Lotus the fact that the "*pu*" adopted in the noms de guerre of Macheng's Zou Pusheng and various of his followers was one of four characters designated as appropriate for sect leaders' names (*dingming zhi zong*) by the Song-dynasty White Lotus patriarch Mao Ziyuan.[61]

But it is the possible Manichaean link for Tianwan that has aroused the greatest scholarly interest. The slogan "The King of Light will appear" (*Mingwang chushi*), the adoption of "Ming" as surname by the Red Turban leader Min Rui and of "Ming" as dynastic name by Zhu Yuanzhang, and the self-designations as Greater King of Light and Lesser King of Light by Han Shantong and Han Liner and as Greater Lord of Light and Lesser Lord of Light by Ming Yuzhen and his son would all seem to point to a central influence of the so-called Ming jiao—the Doctrine of Light, or Manichaeism—on Red Turban ideology. So, too, would Ye Ziqi's testimony to Manichaeism (Manmo jiao) as being prominently on the local cultural scene in this era. The most emphatic proponent of the Manichaean roots of the late-Yuan rebellions has been the biographer of Zhu Yuanzhang, Wu Han.[62] Wu argued that one of the principal scriptures firing Red Turban beliefs was the Song-dynasty *Da xiao Mingwang chushi jing* (Sutra on the Coming to the World of the Greater and Lesser Kings of Light), and that this was indisputably a Manichaean text.

According to Wu Han's reconstruction, the religion of the Persian prophet Mani (216–277 CE), focusing on the primordial struggle between dark and light, good and evil, and worshiping the savior Mingwang as its cardinal deity, had first come to China under the rule of the Tang Empress Wu, in 694. It became the predominant religion of the Huigu state, a border principality absorbed by the Tang in the early ninth century; in the 840s, Manichaeism was proscribed and its temples were seized as part of the more general attack on the Buddhist church by Emperor Wuzong. Thereafter, with no established church and no foreign missionary support, Ming jiao became a more fully sinicized and locally diverse underground sect, its light-conquering-darkness eschatology appealing to various plebeian rebel movements during the Five Dynasties and the Song. It was very strong along the southeast coast, but by Southern Song and Yuan times it had taken hold as well in Jiangxi, Anhui, and the southern portion of the North China Plain. Ming jiao followers were strict vegetarians and organized themselves around vegetarian halls; they advocated abstemious poverty and mutual aid, were strongly communal and solidary, and frequently feuded with their wider host populations. There was also a gradual intermixing of some Ming jiao congregations with Maitreyan and White Lotus adherents, based in large part on their common identification of the existing world as corrupt and in need of violent purgation. It was this tradition that was embodied in the teachings of Peng Yingyu and his various armed supporters.

Wu Han's arguments have received a mixed reception from later scholars. Most Western historians dealing with the Red Turban rebellions, including Edward L. Dreyer, Frederick W. Mote, and Ming Yuzhen's biographer John Dardess, have followed Wu's lead in seeing Manichaean influences but are rather more cautious and tentative in this identification. But Samuel N. C. Lieu, a prominent scholar of Manichaeism in the West (and coincidentally of Chinese descent), denies that the connection is anything more than the accidental presence of the word *ming* ("light" or "bright") in both traditions. Lieu concedes the importance of the *Da xiao Mingwang chushi jing* to the anti-Yuan rebels, but he sees this text as a fairly standard Maitreyan Buddhist sutra, with no evident Manichaean overlay.[63] Working separately from Lieu, the Chinese scholar Yang Na has found Maitreya himself identified in Buddhist texts as the "Bright and Glorious King of the Boddhisattvas" (*zhu fo guangming zhi wang*), and on this basis he argues that the appellation "King of Light" (Mingwang) may not necessarily derive from Manichaean influences.[64] Most recently, though, Richard Shek has emphatically reaffirmed the central role of Manichaean teachings in the Red Turban movement.[65]

In my own view, the scant surviving evidence is more supportive of Wu Han than of Lieu, but I also feel that the question of just how attenuated the influence of a once-prominent foreign creed was on late-Yuan rebels in Macheng—interesting as that question may be—is not really the most compelling one. In the periodic outbursts of massive carnage that punctuated Macheng's history from the fourteenth to the mid-twentieth centuries, chiliastic religion rarely if ever played as central a role as it did in the late-Yuan rebellions. But there *were* lingering, and highly disturbing, continuities. The American journalist Edgar Snow, visiting the Dabie Shan area in the 1930s and at once sympathetic to the Communist Revolution and horrified by its savagery, described local attitudes as distinctively "Manichaean."[66] By this he intended no reference to the millenarian beliefs of the area's late-Yuan rebels, of which he was doubtless unaware, but rather to an absolute and uncompromising hatred of one's enemies that would sanction, across the spectrum of political ideology, the most hair-raisingly savage actions bent on their total extermination—the kind of totalistic light-versus-dark mentality that might give rise in the twentieth century, as it had in the fourteenth, to flaying alive, disemboweling, and "mincing and pickling" one's adversaries.

Flight

The Yuan-Ming transition occasioned significant social change in Macheng, not in the structure of the social hierarchy but in the composition of the local population. Throughout central China, many elite families who had achieved prominence and even official service under the Yuan fought bitterly against the Red Turbans and other mid-fourteenth-century insurgent groups, yet with remarkable ease they made their peace and maintained their status under Zhu Yuanzhang's Ming regime once it had established itself successfully in their locality. This was the case with all of the literati who have bequeathed to us accounts of Tianwan atrocities—the Anhui (Huizhou) native Tang Guifang, the Jiangxi native Quan Heng, the Zhejiangese Ye Ziqi, and the Hunanese Song Lian.[67] It was also true of the Yuan official Zou Qianba, in Macheng, whose descendants, as we have noted, achieved great and continued official prominence under the Ming. Other Macheng elites seized the opportunity to elevate their standing even higher under the new regime. For example, Zhu Boming, a wealthy landowner from the county's northern township, made a timely contribution of several thousand piculs of grain to provision Ming armies engaged in subduing Chen Youliang; his descendants received special imperial favor ever after.[68] When, in 1365, an enterprising Luotian rebel named Lan Niu'er claimed to be the (by now disappeared and presumably dead) "sorcerer" Peng Yingyu, proclaimed himself emperor, and deployed his own local officials, a local Macheng notable named Yuan Bao managed to capture Lan and present the trophy to Zhu Yuanzhang's representatives "as tribute."[69]

But the turnover in Macheng's population, at both the elite and the commoner level, was probably more striking than the continuity. Beginning around 1360, large numbers of Zhu Yuanzhang's Jiangxi compatriots began to move into the county, as fighters in his conquering forces or in their immediate wake.[70] The new Ming-era Macheng elite, to be discussed in the next chapter, was largely drawn from their ranks. An even more impressive number of persons migrated *out* of the county during the dynastic transition. Most of them went to Sichuan. The mid-Qing *Sichuan Provincial Gazetteer*, for example, reproduces twenty-one tomb inscriptions of persons who had relocated to the province during the Yuan-Ming transition: six of the twenty-one came from the single county of Macheng.[71] Of the ninety-three lineages whose genealogies (*zupu*) are held in the Sichuan Provincial Library and the Sichuan University

Library, thirty-seven claimed to have relocated from Macheng in the late fourteenth century.[72] Macheng immigrants established themselves in various counties of Sichuan; in Hechuan, for instance, eight of fifteen immigrant households recorded for imperial times came from Macheng in the early Ming.[73] But nowhere were they as dominant as they were in Jianyang County and its surrounding Jianzhou prefecture. The Republican-era Jianyang gazetteer notes that, out of 329 total families recorded as having immigrated to the county, no fewer than fifty-nine came from Macheng in the fourteenth century alone; combined with later waves of migration, Macheng natives made up some 83 percent of all immigrant families the county had ever received![74]

Macheng migration to Sichuan was a continuous pattern, beginning as early as the 1320s and continuing into the latter decades of the century as part of an apparently deliberate policy of resettlement undertaken by the victorious Ming emperor Zhu Yuanzhang.[75] Yet the bulk of the fourteenth-century migrants claimed to have left in order to flee the disorder of the Red Turban rebellions in their native place. In this, most, at least, were disingenuous. The truth was that these men had come as rebels themselves, in the service of the "Greater Lord of Light," Ming Yuzhen. Dispatched ostensibly to colonize Sichuan by the Tianwan court (but really, in large measure, to remove his forces and alleviate the severe food pressures in the central Tianwan domains in Hubei), Ming Yuzhen eventually declared his own Great Xia state in 1367, only to have it absorbed after his death by Zhu Yuanzhang's triumphant Ming dynasty, in 1371. The great bulk of the troops that Ming Yuzhen brought west through the Yangzi gorges came from Macheng, with smaller portions from adjacent northeast Hubei counties, and the heart of the Great Xia empire that they carved out lay precisely in Jianzhou Prefecture.[76]

Jianyang, Hechuan, and the other counties conquered by Ming Yuzhen and peopled by Macheng migrants were not, for the most part, peripheral, but lay in the most productive plains and river valleys of the Sichuan basin. And though generations of Sichuan local officials thereafter complained about these querulous and bellicose immigrants, a substantial number of them prospered quite well in their new surroundings. Indeed, several scions of late-Yuan émigrés from Macheng to Sichuan became high officials under the Ming—one, Yang Tinghe, became grand secretary in the early sixteenth century.[77] As these Sichuan lineage records suggest, such men did not forget their Macheng roots. They were the first wave of a Macheng diaspora that would be in place for, and of great service to, the surge of prosperity that would greatly transform their native locality in the mid- and late-Ming era. That is the story to which we now turn.

CHAPTER THREE

Boom Time

Over the course of the Ming dynasty, and most notably in the early sixteenth century, the economy, society, and culture of Macheng were fundamentally transformed. In his preface to the 1535 county gazetteer, a local literatus, Mao Fengshao, described the county's recent experience this way:

> Confucius long ago observed that when a population grows numerous it will become rich, and when it is rich it will turn to scholarship. This principle has been understood by officials for countless generations. In Macheng, the land has now widely been reclaimed for cultivation and the population has greatly increased. Thus it has for some time been the case that, with our large and ever more wealthy population, neighbors compete with one another to improve their status through education.[1]

Mao was correct about the population increase: according to Ming official figures, Macheng's population had grown by about 40 percent in the century before he wrote, and it continued to grow steadily over the subsequent half century.[2] This growth was due in part to the relative peace of the era and in part to a protracted period of favorable weather and good harvests.[3] It was facilitated by the hillside land reclamation that Mao observed; a very considerable number of Macheng settlements dating from this era include in their names the character *fan* (rice terrace), and, revealingly, several of those produced some of the most prosperous lineages in the county under the Ming, among them the Zou, Deng, and Wang of Balifan, the Xiong and Liu of Baitianfan, and Mao Fengshao's own lineage from Guchengfan.[4] The growing prosperity of mid-Ming Macheng did not reflect merely extensive growth, however; even more important, it also reflected intensive growth, a notable rise in per capita productivity and wealth.

Agricultural Commercialization

The key factor was the commercialization of the county's agriculture, to feed external markets of both intra- and interregional scale. As noted by Iwami Hiroshi, the conventional expression "When Huguang has a good harvest, all the world has enough to eat" ("Huguang shu tianxia zu") can be dated to a text of 1528, an indication that the large-scale commercial export of Middle Yangzi rice to feed an increasingly cash-cropped, industrialized, and grain-deficient Jiangnan was already well under way in the early sixteenth century.[5] Satō Fumitoshi traces the origins of export-oriented rice cultivation in Macheng itself—notably in the double-cropped areas of the county's central plain and the southeast river valley—to the same era, the Ming Zhengde and Jiajing reigns.[6] Nor was rice the county's only export. The 1670 gazetteer catalogues nearly 300 specialty items produced in the county—textiles, vegetables, oils, animal products (notably deerhide), teas, medicinal herbs, minerals, and a wide variety of luxury timbers and forest products—nearly all of which were marketed locally, and a significant number of which found buyers farther afield. Several of these commodities, such as hawthorn fruit, *jiepian* (a root used in making cough medicine), and *bai'ai* (a root used in making red ink), developed empirewide reputations as distinctive Macheng products.[7]

First among the items listed in the 1670 gazetteer was cotton. Though Ma Duanlin's thirteenth-century encyclopedia *Wenxian tongkao* had reported that Macheng people at that time were clothed primarily in hempcloth, by the late Ming this fabric had given way to the more comfortable cotton. The county now produced in abundance not only raw cotton (*mianhua*) but also cotton thread (*mianxian*) and cotton cloth both plain (*mianbu*) and patterned (*wenbu*), products initially of cottage industry, then also of the spinning and weaving workshops that began to appear in the county in the later sixteenth century.[8] A substantial portion of each of these was produced for export. In other words, Macheng's mid-Ming boom came about primarily as a result of a newfound export of rice, of raw and processed cotton, and of a wide range of subsidiary commodities.

It was in this era that the hierarchy of markets discussed in chapter 1 began to take its modern shape, and the county's major commercial towns began to spawn rich and prominent families: the Li of Songbu, the Lin of Zhongguanyi, and the Zhong, Ruan, and Lu of Baiguo.[9] Initially, the transport and marketing of Macheng's newfound export commodities was controlled by nonlocal merchant groups, most likely building upon the activities of their forebears involved in the long-standing north-south trade *traversing* the county. The key group was that from Jiangxi—indeed, Macheng's central extractive market, Songbu, took its name from a Jiangxi merchant surnamed Song who had pio-

Rice terraces, central Macheng County. Photograph by the author.

neered the town's commercial development in the late fourteenth century. But groups from Fujian and other areas quickly followed, and at some point in the Ming each of these merchant diasporas established a permanent guildhall in the town.[10]

Gradually, however, the exclusive hold over local exports exercised by extra-provincials was broken by the organized efforts of merchants from Macheng itself and from its neighboring counties, an enterprise that would become known as the Huangbang, or Huangzhou guild. Although, as we shall see, the true glory days of the Huangbang's economic power came under the Qing, the beginnings of this effort are to be found in the sixteenth century. Already by that time, local convention identified natives of Macheng's Ju River Valley as not merely mercantile but also unusually mobile.[11] It appears that a geographic and commodity-specific division of labor eventually came to pertain: Jiangxi and other outsider merchants continued to control (as indeed they always would) the county's *rice* exports *downstream* to the east and southeast, but Macheng natives by the mid-Ming were already personally carrying *cotton* and other local products *up* the Han River into northeast Hubei and southern Shaanxi, and, taking advantage of the presence of compatriot émigrés in Sichuan, developing new markets *upstream* along the Yangzi for their native place's goods. There are also already indications of "gentry merchants" from Macheng allying in commercial ventures with those from Huanggang and other neighboring counties, laying the groundwork for the emerging regional-level Huangzhou guild.[12]

One impact of this growing agricultural and commercial prosperity was a marked concentration of landownership. Over the course of the 1950s and 1960s, Chinese and Japanese Marxist historians of the Ming era collectively demonstrated the existence of such a process throughout the rapidly commercializing central China. In a series of detailed and closely documented articles, for example, Li Wenzhi explored the various means by which, in the words of a late-Ming Board of War memorial, "land owned by the rich has become ever greater, and that owned by the poor ever less."[13] More locally, in central Hubei, Yasuno Shōzō in 1962 chronicled the case of a single sixteenth-century landlord who gradually acquired from his failed owner-cultivator neighbors some 500 *mu* of choice "interior delta" land; he planted this with rice for interregional export, utilizing a mix of tenant and bondservant labor.[14] Despite some contention over aspects of the argument during the past several decades, most historians today continue to accept the general validity of this Ming "land concentration thesis."[15] There is no question that it is applicable to the experience of Macheng.

Some of the new large concentrations of landholding locally were accumulated through reclamation of formerly uncultivated acreage; we have seen in the last chapter that at least one powerful Macheng lineage, the Qin, had already begun, in the 1340s, systematically bringing under cultivation thousands of *mu* of new land, and the testimony of Mao Fengshao and others indicates that this process only accelerated after the restoration of social order under the Ming. Then, to an appreciable extent, the wealth of merchants coming into Macheng to exploit its new commercial possibilities was turned to the purchase of large agrarian estates in the county.[16] If, however, land reclamation on the part of established families and land purchases on the part of arriviste merchants accounted for much of the land concentration of the early and mid-Ming, by the later fifteenth century the chief means of property aggrandizement had become commendation of title (*touxian*) by cultivators unable to meet their land-tax obligations, and the major leverage had become the tax privileges enjoyed by Macheng's mushrooming civil and military degree–holding elite.[17]

A significant amount of the new land concentration was in corporate hands. Some such corporations were schools, like the increasingly powerful Wansong Academy.[18] Others were temples. In the 1920s, for example, the Longtan Temple held over 5,000 *mu* of land, farmed by more than 100 long-term laborers (*changgong*) boarded and fed by the temple itself, a practice almost certainly dating to the Ming era.[19] Still other corporate landholders were lineage trusts (*sichan* or *yitian*), dedicated ostensibly to financing the performance of ancestral sacrifices and other collective and philanthropic purposes.[20] These charitable estates controlled a substantial fraction of Macheng's arable land continuously through the early twentieth century, perennially serving as targets of complaints from poorer-lineage members that their proceeds were subject to expropriation by elites.[21] In the twentieth century, moreover, a further percentage of Macheng farmland was tied up in private estates known as manors (*zhuangyuan* or *zhuangtian*), which were identified with no particular "charitable" purpose other than profit. Each *zhuangyuan* was centrally managed in terms of crop selection (usually a commercial crop) and labor budgeting, and often up to a dozen were owned by a single individual or lineage.[22] Concrete evidence is lacking, but it seems most probable that these institutions, too, were legacies of the agricultural commercialization and land concentration of the Ming era.

Lineage Building

The centrality of lineages in the fabric of late-imperial and Republican-era Macheng society cannot be overestimated. A social survey undertaken by the Nationalist Hubei Provincial Government in 1934 paints a dismal picture of social anomie and cultural despair in contemporary Macheng, blaming these most directly on the fact that the great gentry lineages (*haoshen dazu*) on which the county had for centuries relied for its sustenance, order, and, indeed, morale had had their backs broken by decades of warfare and predatory taxation.[23] The regime's Communist opponents reached similar views. In 1925 the first Communist organizer to operate in the county, Dong Biwu, determined on the basis of his own social survey that the ancestral cult and the lineage system—the effective embodiments of feudal superstition—were the most central institutions in Macheng and demanded concerted attack. Over the course of the next decade, however, local peasant association and Red Army leaders came to understand that genuine attachment to kinship-based organization ran so fundamentally through the very plebeian constituency they sought to mobilize that they decided to keep their hands off lineage temples and gravesites, seeking instead to link the threat posed to the ancestral cult with their radically modernist Guomindang opponents.[24]

Both parties were right. Lineage consciousness was probably the most fundamental element in Macheng people's personal identity; as the sixteenth-century philosopher Geng Dingxiang put it, seeking out and remaining mindful of one's pedigree (*congshi*) was a basic moral obligation.[25] The lineage was also a unit of spatial and social organization. One has only to glance at the names of most Macheng villages (for example, Wang Family Village) or at those of the streets in its major urban centers (such as Cao Family Lane) to see the ubiquitous pattern of identifying place with collective residence by kinship. Though many of these initial names became vestigial over time, as one kinship group declined and another moved in, there was also much continuity: the Zeng of Zeng Family Cove, for example, are still today the exclusive residents of the village they founded in the early Ming.[26] While such smaller settlements remained the turf of a single surname group, larger settlements might be jointly controlled by two or more lineages, as in the shared dominance of Xindian (New Town) in the Ming by the Zhou, Xie, and Peng.[27] As late as the 1920s, the Guomindang efforts to regiment local populations into a revived residential surveillance system (*baojia*) most often took lineage-specific neighborhoods as the components of such a system, and the corresponding ancestral temples as its local headquarters.[28]

Through their proprietorship of granaries, lineages aided in local subsistence, and through management of militia, they oversaw collective defense. They were also central to local cultural practice. The seventeenth-century gazetteer of Henan's Runing Prefecture, Macheng's neighbor in the highlands of the Dabie Shan, is eloquent on how sponsorship of annual festivals by the area's official elite lineages (*shihuan wangjia*) both cemented a lineage's internal solidarity and helped the lineage exert hegemony over the wider neighborhood.[29] In Macheng itself, neighborhood-based lineages sponsored celebrations of the new year's "dragon lantern" displays and provided the units of competition for the massively popular Dragon Boat races at Songbu during the fifth lunar month; the loss of lineage-based wealth as a result of civil war in the late 1920s and early 1930s put a halt to this centuries-old festival, reportedly at great loss to popular morale.[30]

Although certain of Macheng's most exalted lineages—the Zou, the Tian, and the Mei, for example—were already powerful under the Yuan, it is clear that the institutionalized dominance by several dozen prominent kinship groups which has characterized Macheng County over the past seven centuries was effectively a product of the early Ming. Indeed, recent scholarship has shown that much of the lineage elite that dominated the entire Middle and Lower Yangzi regions over the late-imperial and Republican eras was a systematic creation of the Hongwu reign. Detailed studies of the "hegemonic" local lineages of the Xiang River Valley (Hunan), of the Yangzi-Han confluence area (Hubei), and of Lower Yangzi jurisdictions such as Huizhou (Anhui), Wuxi (Jiangsu), and Ningbo (Zhejiang) have all revealed a disproportionate number of such lineages to have arrived and established their local dominance in the late fourteenth century. Many or perhaps even most of their founding ancestors arrived—either as military officers, civil officials, commercial support staff, or grantees of agrarian estates—in train with the movement into the area of the forces of the Ming founder, Zhu Yuanzhang, and the majority came from Zhu's own native Jiangxi.[31] The four lineages of Macheng County for whom the most detailed genealogical records survive all conform to this pattern.

The Li of Luotan, in the Songbu suburbs, came to Macheng from the Lushan area of Jiangxi (just south of Jiujiang), initially in the late Yuan. The man subsequently honored as progenitor of the line, Li Shengqi, was a Macheng sojourner—possibly but not certainly a merchant at Songbu—who returned to his native place when the Red Turban forces devastated the area. Shengqi's son, Jufu, took service in Zhu Yuanzhang's rebel army and eventually rose to the rank of brigade general (*zongbing*), dying in battle in 1377. After his son's death, Li Shengqi returned to Macheng, now a decorated client of the victorious Ming. Shengqi's grandson, Li Zhao, inherited the military rank of his father, Jufu, and began the systematic acquisition of prime paddy land in the Luotan neighborhood. Li Zhao's military duties, however, frequently brought him back to his native Jiangxi County of Luling, and he established lines of descent there as well as in Macheng.[32] Eventually, in the 1470s, the Li lineage organized itself into three branches (*fen*)—allegedly when representatives of all three descent lines chanced to meet in Beijing while sitting for the metropolitan examination—with the Macheng branch identified as the most junior of these.[33]

According to a preface to the surviving 1947 genealogy written by the principal of the local elementary school, "The Li of Luotan is one of the oldest established lineages of western Macheng County. . . . Their offspring have continued to proliferate, so that they have come to inhabit several dozen walled villages [*cunbao*] on both sides of the Luotan River. Over 600 years and more than thirty generations, they have accumulated much property and many examination degrees."[34] The evidence of the genealogy itself suggests a pattern of settlement expansion, property accumulation, and local "philanthropic works"—dedications and regulations transcribed from local stele suggest that the Li had founded and subsequently controlled bridges, ferries, and indeed the entire communications infrastructure of the Luotan area—but there is little corroborating evidence in other Macheng sources to suggest an unusually glorious pattern of examination success. (The Macheng Li lineage, which did establish just that sort of pattern, was from another sector of the county and was almost certainly unrelated.) Again, Luotan's proximity to Songbu suggests some connection with commercial activity, but the genealogy does not advertise this. It seems safest to conjecture that the Luotan Li's longevity and prosperity derived essentially from the profits of commercialized agriculture on this prime portion of county real estate that they had seized or otherwise occupied in the late fourteenth century, combined with some pattern of economic, coercive, and cultural domination of their less favored neighbors.

Another dominant lineage of the Songbu area, the Shijiafan Shi, was not so coy about the mercantile basis of its wealth. The Shi, after tracing their origins from the Zhou dynasty Duke Hui of Lu and several eminent officials of the Tang and Song, more convincingly identified their true founding ancestor (*shizu*) as one Shi Xianfu, who came during the Yuan-Ming transition from Jiangxi's Yugan County, on the eastern shore of Poyang Lake. Over time they settled into various places of southwest Macheng and adjacent northern Huanggang.[35] Although they owned considerable farmland, when they got around in the eighteenth century to constructing a grand ancestral temple, they did so in Songbu City itself. By this time the kinship/commercial diaspora of the Shi had fanned out to many parts of western and northwestern China. The Shi genealogy proudly records the existence of one sixth-generation descendant who achieved his *jinshi* and served as a county magistrate in Guangdong in the 1570s, and another of the ninth generation who was a *juren* of 1612, but it is clear from other local sources that the Shi were never among Macheng's major degree-winning lineages, civil or military. Nevertheless, the genealogy's lavish illustrations of Shi villages, temples, mansions, and tombs announce that they *were* among the county's wealthiest.[36]

Our third lineage, the Cheng of Xicun (West Town), we have already met in connection with their substantial collective "sacrificial" landholdings (*sichan*). Like the Shi, the Cheng claim a Zhou-dynasty pedigree, placing their origins in the ancient feudal state bearing the same name as their surname. Somewhat more persuasively, they argue for descent from one of the great merchant-official lineages of Huizhou, established there in the tenth century and meticulously documented in the *Xin'an Chengshi tongzong shipu* (Collective genealogy [of all branches] of the Cheng lineage of Xin'an). Be that as it may, like the Li and the Shi, the Cheng of Macheng actually came to the county from northern Jiangxi. The founding ancestor of the local lineage was one Cheng Chao'er, alleged offspring of a branch of the Huizhou Cheng that had established itself in Jiangxi's lakeshore Poyang County in the Song, and who relocated again from there to Macheng under Ming Taizu in 1374. They established themselves at various locations along the Ju River, in the southwestern core triangle between Songbu, Qiting, and Baiguo, where they seem to have been especially dominant. At some point in the mid-Ming, they constructed their first ancestral temple at suburban West Town.[37]

The Cheng genealogy states baldly, "The hereditary occupation [*shiye*] of our family is that of merchant."[38] They were very clearly a leading force in the Huangbang commercial diaspora, and their fortunes continued to rise along with those of that group more generally; for the eighteenth and nineteenth centuries, the Cheng genealogy provides nice detail on Huangbang commercial

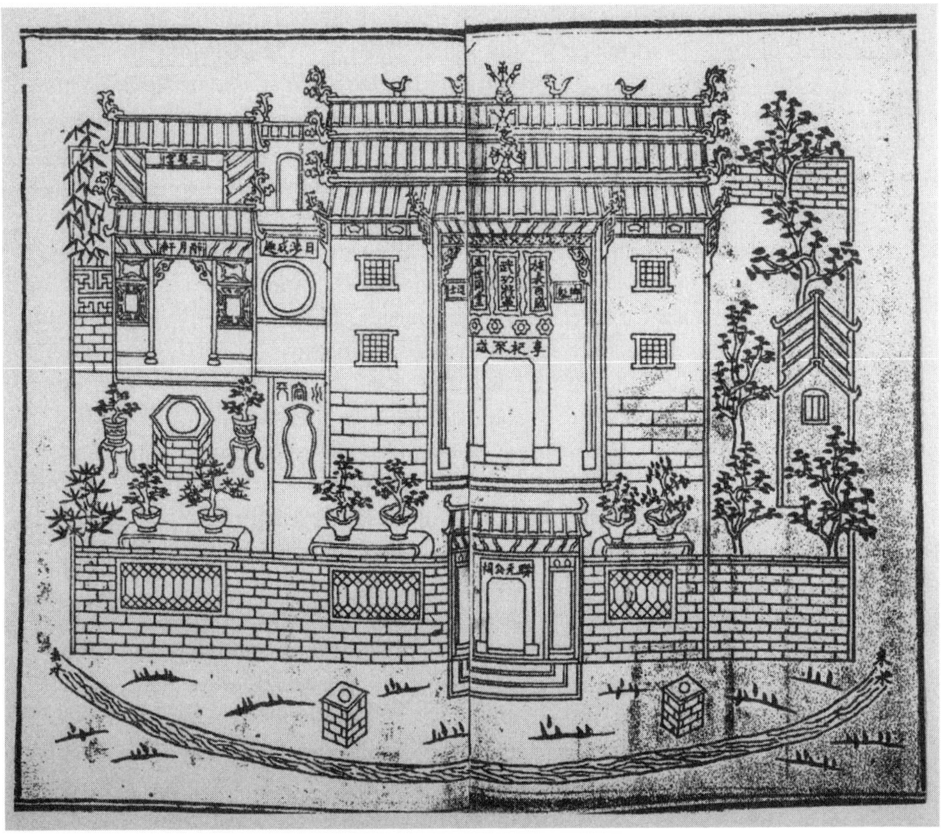

Cheng Lineage Temple, West Town, Songbu. From *Xicun Chengshi zongpu*, juan 1.

activities, to which we shall return. Besides the collective endowment property, the profits of this trade were plowed back into education so that, whereas under the Ming the Cheng were virtually absent from Macheng's large and growing list of upper-level degree holders, increasingly after the Qing conquest lineage members accumulated an impressive number of degrees and official posts.[39] This only increased in the Republican era. Cheng Yinnan, for instance, the compiler of the 1919 Cheng genealogy, was a remarkable figure, successively a Western-trained mathematician, a member of the Hubei Provincial Assembly active in the 1911 Revolution, a magistrate in various counties of his old native province of Jiangxi, and an intimate of Yu Jinfang—a Guomindang establishment intellectual, editor of the 1935 Macheng gazetteer, and one of the most important figures in Nationalist-era county politics.[40]

The Lin, finally, came not from Jiangxi but from Futian County, in Fujian.[41]

Though very likely of mercantile origins, they had enjoyed some literati success under the Yuan. The founder of the Macheng lineage, Lin Gusong, was, for example a *juren* of 1348 and a brevet rank holder in his native province. But the Lin, notwithstanding their acceptance of degrees and ranks under the Yuan, converted very adroitly to the Ming cause. Gusong's brother, Lin Mian, took a *jinshi* under Zhu Yuanzhang and in 1376 was appointed provincial treasurer of Hubei. Gusong accompanied him, and when Mian was reappointed metropolitan censor at Nanjing, Gusong stayed on to carve out an estate in the section of Macheng's Ju River Valley around the town of Zhongguanyi. The family remained a dominant force in the town ever after. By their fourth and fifth generations in Macheng, they had constructed an ancestral temple,[42] laid down lineage rules (*zugui*), and accomplished most of the other tasks involved in lineage formalization. Their first published genealogy appeared in 1803. There is no question that for the Zhongguanyi Lin interregional commerce came first and land development second, but they were highly successful at both. They were less interested—but not totally uninterested—in examination success, and they produced a modest total of two upper-level degree holders in the Ming, and a somewhat larger number in the Qing. Under the late Qing and the Republic, with the still greater success of their commercial ventures and the arrival of the railroad at Zhongguanyi, they emerged as one of the preeminent economic and political families in Macheng, scioning among other figures the notoriously brutal anti-Communist ward leader Lin Renfu.

These four lineages—the Li, the Shi, the Cheng, and the Lin—can, I think, tell us something about Macheng County's lineage elite as a whole. All four families arrived in the lifetime of the Ming founder and came, in some measure, because of him. In this, the four families were hardly atypical: five other Macheng lineages whose genealogies I have seen at least in part—the Cai, the Chen, the Xiong, the Zeng, and the Zhou—arrived from Jiangxi or (in two cases) from contiguous eastern Hunan in the early Ming.[43] All nine of these lineages engaged in long-term processes of land acquisition and reclamation (on the basis of an initial early-Ming grubstake), in expansion of lineage turf and partition into federated branches, in pursuit (sometimes with great success) of upward status mobility through scholarship and official service, and in a dedicated effort at local philanthropy, infrastructural development, and community leadership. Many—notably the Shi, the Cheng, and the Lin, but likely to a lesser extent the others as well—combined these pursuits with mercantile activity. All made the transition into modern-sector careers and political leadership in the late nineteenth and early twentieth centuries. And, far from coincidentally, they all engaged in a process of lineage formalization for purposes of both internal discipline and solidarity regarding the outside world: the plebeian mass around

Genealogy of the Wucheng Zeng lineage. Photograph by the author.

them, neighboring lineages, and the central state. Formalization of their lineage organization was a major key to their longevity.

A look at the relatively rich surviving record of formal and informal family rules gives us a fuller picture of lineage strategizing and of elite mentality in Macheng. Four of our genealogies, those of the Shi, the Cheng, the Lin, and the Chen, include full sets of lineage regulations (*jiagui*) or compacts (*guiyue*).[44] A principal concern in all of these was the maintenance of internal order and group integrity. Harmony among kinsmen was repeatedly stressed, especially among those of greater and lesser degrees of wealth (*fupin xiang'an*). Emphasis was put on the need to maintain and, in the wake of social crises, reconstruct accurate genealogical records. Generationally specific naming patterns for offspring were laid down along with rules for adoption of children among households within the group. As the lineages grew, they were divided into branches, based on descent and residence. Heads of branches (*fangzhang*) and individual households (*huzhang*) were nominated by the overall lineage leaders, then ratified by the membership of the component unit. The regulations offered detailed provisions governing the duties of these headmen: they were responsible for instruction in ritual propriety (*lijiao*), encouraging scholarship and other desirable endeavors, arbitrating disputes, and, as necessary, imposing disciplinary sanctions (*yueshu*) upon their constituents.

The lineage rules also treated matters of corporate finance. An annual business meeting for the group was held on the occasion of the sacrifice to the founding ancestor at the lineage temple. At the same time, audits were conducted for budgets of the lineage as a whole and of each component branch. These budgets were used to underwrite the maintenance of the temple itself and of the lineage graves, to procure utensils and implements for the celebration of the ancestral rites, to support promising scholars within the group, and, in at least one instance (involving the Lin), to operate a lineage orphanage. Revenues came from annual dues paid by lineage members (those seventy years of age or older were exempt) and from rents on endowment land, collected in the eighth month. In the selection of tenants for these lands, preference was given to lineage members, but it was acknowledged that it was not practicable to restrict it to them altogether; in years of dearth, of course, tenants had to be granted rent remissions, but if they fell too severely in arrears, they were to be evicted by the estate managers.

The rules paid close attention to the decorous behavior of lineage members, who were admonished to avoid luxury, extravagance, and waste. Gambling was forbidden. The early-fifteenth-century Shi lineage rules commented that neither wealth nor poverty was a permanent condition ("fu buchang fu, pin buchang pin"), and so it was well to preserve one's own wealth but at the same time to be nice to poorer kinsmen or neighbors who might someday be more financially secure than oneself.[45] Maintenance of good relations with these neighbors—the fostering of an explicitly extragovernmental local solidarity (*liren*) at the level of the village or even the township—was a special and recurring theme in Macheng lineage genealogies.[46] Correspondingly, lineage members were enjoined to shun, as much as possible, the mechanisms of the formal state, and above all the villainous county clerks and runners (*xuli*). They were to avoid any heterodox or subversive doctrines (*xieshuo*). Above all, they were not to engage in any conduct resembling that of the economically and culturally deprived servile underclass (*nupu xiaren*) of the local society.[47]

Of great concern in most of these regulatory codes was the topic of gender relations within the lineage. Present from the earliest Ming versions, restrictive rules governing gender segregation (*bie nannü*) and decorum (*zhengsu*) became even more intensive in later eras; lineage discipline was explicitly presented as a bulwark of resistance against twentieth-century liberationist movements. Females were to remain in the interior (*nei*) and males outside (*wai*). When womenfolk did leave the inner quarters (*guimen*), they had to wear the veil (*yongmian*). In poorer-lineage households, women were permitted to leave the house only to bring food to their husbands tilling the fields (*nangeng nüye*). In wealthier households, male servants were not to enter the house (an exception was made for cooks), and female servants were never to leave it. Detailed rules were provided for proper treatment of concubines as opposed to principal wives. Above all, it was most unseemly for neighbors to hear women of the household wailing or scolding their husbands.

The lineage rules presented the accumulation of wealth (*jicai*) and its stable maintenance (*hengcai*) as moral imperatives, a duty owed both to one's forebears and to one's heirs. The regulations were quite frank about the fact that scholarship and agriculture were esteemed vocations, but so were "the 100 artisanal trades" and commerce; after all, the 1919 Cheng genealogy acknowledged, in recent generations the Cheng had "mostly been merchants."[48] The important thing was to pursue one's chosen occupation honorably and industriously (*qin shiye*). Male offspring were to be assigned careers in accordance with the patriarch's perception of their capabilities so that the lineage would avoid squandering its human capital (*wu qicai*). Those lineage sons who became resident or traveling merchants (*zuogu xingshang*) would be apprenticed to uncles or cousins and instructed in keeping their accounts in order, selecting business partners of good character, avoiding get-rich-quick schemes, and being circumspect and morally upright in their professional dealings.[49]

Zou Laixue's Advice to His Son

These rules participated in a broader discourse on family continuity and preservation of the patrimony shared among the Macheng lineage elite over many centuries. A relatively late example of this discourse occurs in the tomb inscription for Cheng Xuehan (1825–85) composed by his son-in-law, Dai Alu. Dai begins by noting that Xuehan was able to pass down considerable and growing wealth to his heirs and that this was "not accidental"—it was a natural outgrowth of Xuehan's lack of extravagance and sound financial management. Dai then proceeds:

> It is evident that the happiness or misery that human beings enjoy in this world is based on whether they are rich or poor. The rich eat their fill of the finest meats while the poor subsist on coarse grains. The rich adorn themselves with opulent silks while the poor wear only the roughest of clothing. The one group lives in warm, comfortable mansions while the other shelters itself in hovels and reed shacks. As much as people may depre-

cate money, their happiness or misery hinges directly upon it. One's wealth, in large part, is based on the vicissitudes of fate [*yunshu*]. Heaven is impartial in this regard. But there is yet a role for virtue in this process, and the wealthy must reflect on this.

Keep in mind that the food in my bowl, the clothes in my wardrobe, the tiled roof and doors and windows of my house, and the utensils on my table are each and every one the product of the blood and sweat of farmers, the weaving of women, and the 100 trades. They are mine to enjoy in comfort. But if they are not enjoyed appropriately, Heaven will ensure that they are used up and not replenished, still more so if they are arrogantly and recklessly flouted. Reflect on this fact, keep your pride in check, and be moved to treat others less fortunate than you with proper consideration. Mr. Cheng Xuehan's approach to life was based on this recognition, and so he was able to preserve his wealth [*baofu*] and create a legacy for his posterity.[50]

This tomb inscription came, as I have said, from the late Qing, and its unabashed celebration of riches certainly betrays some elements unique to that era. But the single text that the Macheng elites themselves accorded pride of place in this discourse on preservation of wealth came in fact from the fifteenth century. This was the *Jie zi shu* (Letter admonishing my son) of Zou Laixue, a *jinshi* of 1445 and a long-serving metropolitan official. Though the Zou, unlike the Cheng, were not primarily a mercantile family, the thematic overlap here with Cheng Xuehan's late Qing epitaph is undeniable. This letter of a Ming-dynasty Lord Chesterfield is worth citing at some length:

To Zou Han, son of my principal wife, Madame Yang:

There is so much to say to you! I have been away from home now for nearly two years. The affairs of the town and countryside [at home]; our relatives, neighbors, and friends; the comings and goings of people; our houses, irrigation works, trees, and crops; the prosperity of your elder brother's family; the health of the younger children—about all of these things I have no detailed knowledge. Although you have written me once or twice, you only give me the general picture of things. Think of your father so far away, who constantly cherishes you! Your conduct has always been so slovenly and lackadaisical, and your treatment of others so cavalier and rude. A young man who treats his own parents this way will certainly not know how to behave toward relatives and neighbors.

You read almost nothing, and your experience of life is terribly shallow. Your reading level is that of a small child. You do not know how to live harmoniously with your neighbors, nor how to treat the aged with veneration, nor to show consideration to those in distress, nor to show compassion to those stricken with grief. You don't know how to reject those who would be bad examples for you, nor how to emulate those who are good. Neither do you know how to reciprocate those who are gracious to you, nor how to shun those who would do you harm.

When you drink wine you don't know your limit. Your words on such occasions are wild and reckless, without either courtesy or forethought. When drunk, you act without regard for who is watching, and spend money heedless of what is reasonable and proper. . . . You eat without proper etiquette, making yourself a laughingstock among polite society. . . .

You fail to grasp the essentials of what is necessary to raise our family fortunes and status. Don't you understand that success in agriculture requires hard work—that raising farm animals requires feed and water, and raising crops requires planting and sowing? In the same way, raising children requires education and moral instruction. Your home must be kept clean and in good repair, the inner and outer must be kept segregated, and entering and leaving properly regulated. At nighttime, avoid gambling. In bountiful years, avoid extravagance. Avoid wasting your time. Ensure that your hired workers are warm and well fed, and that your household retainers are treated with compassion and respect. I am greatly vexed that your inability to act as a mature man [*buneng weiren*] has persisted for so long!

Your letter is very short on details. You say that the oxen are dying, but don't indicate whether this is also true of those of other families in the locality. There are proper methods for caring for oxen. For example, they must be fed according to a proper schedule. If you force an ox to haul a load that is too heavy for it, naturally it will be injured!

Your letter also claims that the household has no liquid capital [*wu benqian*]. You must watch what other households do, and pay your taxes accordingly. Pay hired laborers according to the dictates of compassion [*renqing*]. In every single matter you must match expenditures to income [*liang ru wei chu*]. You cannot give too much thought to this! You must always keep the improvement of family fortunes foremost in your mind, lay aside what will be needed to meet our tax obligations, and anticipate the possibility of harvest shortfalls. Always calculate for the long term, not simply on the basis of present conditions.

In my official career, I too must always be prepared for the possibility of disaster, for my obligations to your mother and to all of my children. From morning to night I am constantly mindful of the responsibility I bear, and acutely conscious of the limits of my own virtue and abilities. Several times I have submitted memorials, and several times received approval for these, but each time I receive a commission from the court I am fearful lest I possibly do something that will besmirch my name and thus bring disastrous consequences upon my descendants.

Zou concludes by counseling his son to make peace with the neighbors with whom he has been feuding, to properly observe mourning rituals for the ancestors, and, in general, to reform his conduct in the direction of thrift, prudence, and social responsibility.[51]

The goal of elevating one's family, repeatedly identified in Zou Laixue's letter, was one that his lineage richly achieved. The Zou, indeed, may have been the single longest-lasting dominant kinship group either in Macheng or in neighboring Huang'an (after that county was severed, in 1535—an event that effectively divided the Zou's home turf between the two counties).[52] As we saw in the preceding chapter, the Zou were the one late-imperial great family of Macheng whose local pedigree could reliably be traced to pre-Ming times, heirs as they were to a Yuan official who had been posted to the county in the early fourteenth century. Over the course of the Ming, after the great success of Laixue himself, the Zou produced a total of twelve recipients of higher-level civil examination degrees. As we shall see, they then moved again, with equal adroitness, to shift their dynastic loyalties in the seventeenth century. Following the notable career of Grand Secretary Zou Shicong (*jinshi* of 1688), they became the Macheng lineage that produced the largest number of upper-level degree holders under the Qing—a total of five *jinshi* and fifteen *juren*. Laixue's advice apparently worked.

Zou's letter, moreover, was faithfully reprinted in successive county gazetteers (those, at least, that were produced by politically conservative regimes) down to the twentieth century, with a growing number of endorsements from enthusiastic readers. The early-Qing magistrate Qu Zhenqi was one of these, noting that the letter had by his time become required reading among sons of the Macheng literati. Qu credited this fact with no small part in the prodigious examination and official success that the county as a whole had enjoyed in the years since its writing.[53] He may have been right. But what is missing from the letter, and from virtually all the rest of the lineage-centered discourse on family and wealth, is that none of this success would have been possible without the systematic exploitation of others' labor, the systematic debasement of their status, and the systematic subjection of these debased others to coercive and often violent restraints on their freedom of action. It was these phenomena that would fire the massive (Manichaean) violence which the county would repeatedly suffer in the centuries after Zou Laixue wrote his letter.

Scholarship and Official Service

In an essay celebrating the reconstruction of the local Confucian school-temple, Liu Bian—a *jinshi* of 1529, intermittent president of four of the six boards, and junior guardian of the heir apparent—wrote: "Macheng has been a famous county since antiquity, but under the present dynasty our native sons' mastery of the classics and of [examination] essay writing has been remarkably flourishing."[54] Our old friend Mao Fengshao boasted, in 1535, "It is said throughout the empire that, in terms of literary production, no province can match Hubei, no prefecture in Hubei can match Huangzhou, and no county in Huangzhou is the equal of Macheng."[55] Liu and Mao were Macheng natives and local boosters; but the magistrate Guo Qinghua, an outsider compiling the Macheng gazetteer in 1882, likewise marveled at what that county—in Guo's day, no more than a mediocrity in terms of empirewide educational prominence—had achieved in the past: "Local culture here emphasizes literacy and poetry, and local people compete fiercely for examination success. This has always been true, but under the Ming the county achieved truly spectacular results."[56] Given Macheng's obscurity among the national elite in earlier centuries, the success that its native sons enjoyed in passing higher-level civil service examinations and attaining bureaucratic office (high and low) in the mid- and late-Ming was nothing short of astonishing. This success was the result both of the county's rapidly growing economic capacity to produce leisured and highly educated elites, and of an energetic process of network formation and local boosterism, which Liu Bian and Mao Fengshao themselves epitomized.[57]

The profits of early-Ming commerce and of commercialized agriculture were systematically plowed into the development of an educational infrastructure. The most formal of these institutions was the Confucian school-temple (*xuegong*), inside the Shengmen Gate of the county seat. Constructed originally in the Song, and destroyed in Zou Pusheng's late-Yuan rebellion, the temple was rebuilt in the late fourteenth century, renovated in the 1470s, and entirely reconstructed once again in the 1530s. By this time, the tablets to the Sage and to members of the Song-era *lixue* pantheon could be joined by an altar to local worthies (*xiangxian si*)—in effect, a Macheng hall of fame of those local boys who had gone on to gain empirewide reputations as scholar-officials. Eventually, no fewer than fifty-three men from the Ming era would achieve such recognition. During the annual performance of the Confucian rites at the temple, aspiring local scholars would convene and reflect on how they themselves could perpetuate this glorious tradition.[58]

Of more practical significance in preparing for the examinations was Macheng's mushrooming number of lineage- or village-sponsored elementary schools (*jiashu, zushu, cunshu*) and the higher-level private academies (*shuyuan*) into which these fed. Most prestigious among the latter was the already venerable, nationally famous, and increasingly richly endowed Wansong Academy; even more striking, however, was the new wave of founding other and, in some cases, nearly as eminent schools at sites scattered throughout the county. The Longji, Baiquan, and Dongji Academies were established in the fifteenth century; the Daofeng, Furen, and Mingde, in the sixteenth; and the Huiche, Baiyun, and Jingzheng, in the early seventeenth. To take one example of the latter group, the Huiche [Returning Cart] Academy, in the southern portion of the county, near the border with Huanggang, educated the offspring of the gentry and merchants from both counties. It was first established in the 1620s by two brothers, Zhou Ming and Zhou Chang, who purchased a statue of Confucius from the Sage's native place in Shandong, installed it in the Xiangqishan Temple, and turned the temple into a school.[59]

In the educational fever of the Ming, other local temples—while they did not, like the Huiche, formally morph into Confucian academies—did take on the roles of local centers of learning. Several, such as the Daxiong Grotto Temple, served as local libraries. The Daxiong, bequeathed a handsome collection of texts by the eminent Macheng philosopher-official Zhou Sijing, was credited after that with affording several neighborhood boys the opportunity to study for and attain higher-level civil service degrees. Another example of such transformation was the Yushi Temple, on Mingshan Mountain, dedicated to the martial deity Tietou shi (the Iron-headed General). Taken over in the late sixteenth century by a local scholar, Liang Xueting, the Yushi Temple was rededicated as a center for study of the life and works of Wang Yangming. (While others of his era chided Wang for his Chan Buddhist leanings, Liang and his followers venerated him for his doctrine of *liangzhi*, or innate moral wisdom, and most especially—apropos of the Yushi Temple's own martial orientation—for his seamless linkage of military and scholarly virtues.)[60]

Here are the remarkable numbers: Over the course of the Ming, Macheng produced 110 metropolitan (*jinshi*) and 421 provincial (*juren*) civil degree holders. At least ten of these *jinshi* passed in the very top rank and were appointed to the Hanlin Academy. Given the county's rough-and-tumble character and its historic strategic centrality, it is less surprising that Macheng also produced twenty-two military *jinshi* and sixty-one military *juren*. It also produced hundreds of purchased degree holders (*gongsheng*), a fact reflective of its growing agrarian and commercial prosperity.[61] These totals did not place Macheng quite on a par with the very most wealthy and exalted counties of the Yangzi Delta—Yin County (Ningbo), for instance, produced 293 *jinshi* and more than 1,000 *gongsheng* in the Ming[62]—but they far outstripped most other localities of central China. Macheng's total of 110 civil *jinshi* was considerably higher than that of any other county in Hubei Province; the second highest was neighboring Huanggang, with eighty-seven, followed by Jiangling, with seventy. Jiangxia, the county incorporating the provincial capital of Wuchang, itself only produced sixty-four.[63]

These examination successes were not evenly spaced over time; rather, they accelerated over the course of the dynasty. In the first 120 years of the Ming, Macheng produced seventeen *jinshi*, a very impressive number by contrast to the county's almost totally negligible pre-Ming numbers, but not particularly striking in comparison with the totals in other contemporary localities; the metropolitan Jiangxia County, for example, did better during this same period, with twenty *jinshi*. It was in the second half of the fifteenth century that Macheng County's startling elevation to empirewide prominence occurred. A signal of what was to come can be seen in a commemorative essay from the early 1470s by Shanxi Provincial Treasurer Li Zhengfang on the occasion of the renovation of the Macheng Confucian school-temple. Li notes with pride, but also with no little amazement, that his home county has managed to produce seven *juren* in the year 1467 alone.[64] From the start of the Hongzhi reign, in 1488, through the end of the dynasty, Macheng's productivity in *jinshi* really soared: a total of eighty-three, not counting another seven produced in that part of the county that was severed to form Huang'an in the late sixteenth century. It is revealing, I think, that the productivity of Macheng's neighbor to the south, Huanggang, showed a similar jump, from ten *jinshi* in 1368–1487 to seventy-seven in 1488–1644. The success of both counties clearly came, in some measure, as a result of the practice of investing in education the commercial profits of the emerging Huangzhou guild.[65]

Nor was the higher-level-examination success of Ming Macheng evenly distributed by lineage. Some lineages that we know to have been quite wealthy and powerful during this era—for example, the mercantile Cheng of the southwest, and the strongman-type Xia of the Dongshan—virtually failed to participate at all in this literary boom, while others did incredibly well. Indeed, the county elite maintained a record of just which lineages, of which local settlement, did best; the remarkable document that resulted looks, on the one hand, like a local peerage register and, on the other, like a scorecard for a vitally intense interfamilial competition.[66] The criterion for inclusion in this list was production of more than one provincial degree holder, and a total of sixty-two lineages made the cut. The single most successful lineage, the Zhou of Xindian, produced no fewer that twenty-seven *juren* and seven *jinshi* under the Ming. Next came the Suokouhe Liu, with seventeen *juren,* eleven of whom went on, remarkably, to win the *jinshi.* The Bashang Li boasted sixteen *juren* and seven *jinshi.* And so on. In some cases there were several Macheng lineages of the same surname that did very well, a fact that makes it difficult to disaggregate individuals by lineage and local settlement; besides the Xindian Zhou, for instance, two other Zhou lineages made the register (one, the Juedanshan Zhou, itself produced an impressive thirteen *juren* and six *jinshi*), and three other Liu lineages are listed besides the one from Suokouhe. It is hard to know to what extent, if at all, these common-surname lineages shared a distant common descent. In other cases, though, all successful bearers of a given surname claimed to be from a single lineage, as with the Baiguo Dong (thirteen *juren*, five *jinshi*), the Qiligang Mei (eleven *juren*, four *jinshi*), the Naowushan Mao (nine *juren,* three *jinshi*), and the Xiangshan Zhao (eight *juren*, two *jinshi*). Moreover, certain local settlements served as formal homes to more than one scholarly family; Xindian, for instance hosted not only the Zhou but also the very successful Xie and Peng, while Baiguo hosted the Ruan and the Lu in addition to the Dong.

Examination success in mid- to late-Ming Macheng was regularly followed by official service. According to the late-Qing magistrate Guo Qinghua, over 500 Macheng natives served in one or another kind of official post during the Ming. This total included those who served in relatively humble posts, such as those of submagistrate or county director of studies, as well as a prodigious number of county magistrates and prefects (even more modest elite lineages of this era, such as the Baiguo Dong, might boast several successive generations of local officials).[67] But the total of 500 also included very high-ranking ministers of state. According to one modern source, Macheng produced no fewer than

143 metropolitan officials in the late-imperial era, the vast majority of them during the Ming. Of the men honored in Macheng's Temple to Local Worthies (*xiangxian si*), fifty-three were from the Ming and only eight from the Qing; of those enumerated in the Famous Native Sons (*mingxian*) chapter of the Republican-era gazetteer, fifty-eight were from the Ming and only nine from the Qing. These Ming honorees included one senior guardian of the heir apparent (*taizi taibao*), one junior guardian of the heir apparent (*taizi xiaobao*), seven board presidents (two of whom served as presidents of four different boards during their careers), four board vice-presidents, two board department heads (*zhushi*), fourteen provincial governors or other provincial-level officials, and a large number of military officials of very high rank. A substantial number of these higher-ranking officials merited biographies in the *Ming shi* (Ming dynastic history), and seven of them were accorded the *yin* privilege of designating one of their heirs to inherit their rank. No fewer than ninety Ming-era Macheng natives were accorded posthumous official rank (*fengzeng*) because of the meritorious service of their sons and grandsons. The county, then, succeeded under the Ming in promoting its native sons into the highest echelons of political power, to an extent that no one could have anticipated and that was far out of line with Macheng's economic and cultural centrality.[68]

Certainly a major role in these accomplishments was played by an aggressive process of patronage whereby aspiring local scholar-officials were helped along by their compatriots who had already made it. In the mid-Ming, for example, the establishment at Beijing of a Macheng local-origin club (*huiguan*) attests not only to the critical mass of central government officials that the county had accumulated by that time but also to a process by which those men solicitously cared for their junior colleagues of common local origin (*tongxiang*) who were visiting the capital to sit for the metropolitan examination or to lobby for official employment.[69] Apart from exercise of the *yin* privilege, most of the personal machinations involved in this local boosterism remain discreetly out of the historical record. However, one episode in the career of Mei Zhihuan (about whom much more later) offers us a rare glimpse of Ming-era pork-barrel politics. Returning home from his tenure as Gansu governor in the late 1620s, Mei was approached by a delegation of forty-five Macheng candidates for the prefectural examination at Huangzhou. Given the strict quota of passes for that exam, and the fact that the number of candidates was estimated to be more than 3,000, it was clear that only a very few of these Macheng men could hope to succeed. But Mei sent the delegation back to Huangzhou, accompanied by a personal letter to the chief examining official; out of deference to Mei, that official individually examined each of the forty-five Macheng students and awarded passing marks to the disproportionate total of seventeen of them.[70]

Like their examination success, the breakthrough of Macheng native sons into the higher levels of officialdom was a cumulative phenomenon of the middle to late years of the Ming. The first to really make a mark was Zou Laixue, scion of the venerable Zou lineage that had already tasted official success under the Yuan. A *jinshi* of 1433, Zou was appointed a department head in the board of war, in special charge of logistical matters in the northwest. He distinguished himself during the Tumu incident of the 1440s, and for this he was promoted to Jiangnan governor. In this post, he did what model officials do—relieved taxes, curtailed clerical corruption, extended hydraulic works, built up granary stocks, promoted sericulture—but he did it so well that he ended his career as a metropolitan censor (*du yushi*).[71] In the latter half of the century, three generations of men from the Bashang Li lineage—Li Zhengfang (*jinshi* 1442), Li Qing (*jinshi* 1469), and Li Wenxiang (*jinshi* 1487)—served in turn in provincial posts in the northwest, where each gained national fame in the intense frontier warfare of that era; and Wenxiang, having returned home after a bitter defeat in battle, drowned himself at the age of twenty-nine, thus winning both a martyr's biography in the *Ming shi* and a cult readership for his collected works (published with a preface by the eminent late-Ming scholar Wang Shizhen).[72] In the mid-sixteenth century, Macheng men did even better, spearheaded in the 1540s by Liu Tianhe and in the 1560s by Zhou Hongzu, scions of the two most prominent local lineages of the Ming.

The Liu lineage of Suokouhe was descended from one Liu Mingmeng, an officer in the conquering army of Zhu Yuanzhang who had later served as a subprefect and received an imperial grant of land in the county for the subsequent maintenance of his family. Mingmeng's descendants included Liu Congzheng, who in 1394 became Macheng's very first Ming-era *jinshi* winner; Liu Xun (*jinshi* 1439), who rose to the post of governor of Shanxi; and Liu Xun's sons, Zhongqi and Zhongquan, both *juren* of 1453 and local officials.[73] It was Mingmeng's great-grandson Liu Tianhe (1479–1546), however, who took the patriline's fortunes to a yet higher level. According to his eulogy in the *Ming Veritable Records,* Tianhe served with great distinction as governor-general of Shaanxi and Gansu, as president of the board of war and the board of works, and as senior guardian of the heir apparent. He was renowned for his expertise both in frontier defense (a Macheng local specialty) and in water conservancy; his book *Wenshui ji*, based on his experience as Yellow River commissioner, was regularly reprinted throughout the Ming and Qing.[74] Liu Tianhe merited a eulogy by Wang Shizhen, the imperially conferred posthumous name Zhuangxiang gong, and a biography in the Ming dynastic history. His progeny included many lower officials as well as Liu Shouyou, assistant grand tutor of the heir apparent; the renowned bibliophile Liu Chengxi; and the famous late-Ming poet Liu Tong.[75]

The Zhou lineage of Xindian presents a similar story of gradual elevation, by the latter part of the dynasty, to the highest echelons of Ming official service. As we have seen, the Zhou were the single most successful Macheng lineage in the higher-degree sweepstakes—they went so far as to publish a book of biographies of family members who had achieved civil and military office.[76] The first important official to rise out of this lineage was Zhou Jian (*jinshi* 1445), who enjoyed a highly checkered bureaucratic career, featuring appointments as provincial treasurer of both Shandong and Yunnan (where he reportedly accumulated a large fortune, only to lose it in a shipwreck on his journey home) as well as many factionally inspired impeachments. Jian's grandson Zhou Tingzheng (*juren* 1489) was a field commander with a distinguished record of military service in the northwest in the 1510s. Both of Tingzheng's sons, Zhou Zai and Zhou Yi, enjoyed only minor local official careers; but in the next generation, the lineage hit pay dirt.[77]

Of the many bearers of the "Hong" generational character, three were spectacularly successful. Zhou Hongmo, a military *juren* of 1576, achieved such decisive success at rebel suppression throughout the empire that he was awarded the *yin* privilege of hereditary rank. The two sons of Zhou Yi, Hongzu and Hongyue, became national heroes of a more political kind. The elder, Zhou Hongzu (*jinshi* 1559), served as metropolitan censor at Nanjing and won praise for his dogged crusade to combat corruption in the disbursement of military pay. The younger, Zhou Hongyue (*jinshi* 1574), served in various metropolitan and provincial posts, from which, on two famous occasions, he remonstrated the Wanli emperor, first to protest the court's extravagance in the face of a troubled economy and then to decry the emperor's withdrawal from direct management of his realm. Both times Hongyue was dismissed and then recalled to service, but in progressively lesser posts; at the beginning of the succeeding Tianqi reign, however, he was posthumously awarded the rank of assistant grand tutor for his courage and sagacity.[78]

Eventually the brothers Zhou Hongzu and Zhou Hongyue both returned home to Macheng in retirement, serving as proud local exemplars of political integrity in an uncertain age. Both left distinguished publication records. And both played important roles in developing the rich cultural infrastructure that would grace Macheng County during the troubled final half century of Ming rule.

CHAPTER FOUR

The Heretic

THE ERA OF progressive and painful decline of the once mighty Ming empire was, ironically, that of greatest glory in all of Macheng's history. With its long martial tradition, the county was well positioned to offer the dynasty the military heroes it so badly needed. Moreover, its patient process of cultivating local educational opportunity and intergenerational official patronage gradually built up to its grandest era of examination and bureaucratic success. Not least, the celebrity of a pantheon of native sons as officials, scholars, and writers—for one shining moment before the holocaust—transformed this obscure locality into a nationally renowned center of intellectual activity and political debate.

Macheng Takes Center Stage

Nearly all of the major local scholar-officials of the era left collections of their political writings, but also classical commentaries, philosophical and historical treatises, encyclopedias, gazetteers, and travel guides, not a few of them worthy enough to be collected in the imperial library (*Siku quanshu*). Subsequent gazetteers are packed with the poetry of local men of the late Ming, not merely those (such as Liu Tong and Cao Yinchang) with enduring extralocal reputations but also dozens of verses by other men, such as Mei Guozhen, whose real distinction lay in the realms of civil and military service. Local literati, such as Liu Chengxi, became book collectors of such note that scholars came even from Jiangnan to consult their rare editions.[1] Indeed, the county in the late sixteenth and early seventeenth centuries became something of a mecca, attracting the empire's most glamorous literati. In the 1590s, the Hunanese Yuan Hongdao (1568–1610), described by Jonathan Chaves as "the single greatest poet of the Ming dynasty," visited on several occasions, along with his brothers Zongdao and Zhongdao, and wrote numerous poems in praise of the local scenery; these and others were later edited and published by Macheng's own eminent scholar-official Li Changgeng.[2] The historian Jiao Hong (1541–1620) resided here during the same period.[3] The great classicist and fiction writer Feng Menglong, as we shall see, sojourned in the county two decades later. Most famously of all, it was in Macheng that the iconoclastic Taizhou-school thinker Li Zhi wrote his most notorious works and fought his most bitter intellectual wars.

Men such as these, and others who aspired to emulate their grand refinement, congregated at one or another of the county's summer houses (*lengting*) for scenic viewing, tea and wine drinking, and exchanging verse in the cool of the mountains. Established centers of elite sociability, such as the Wansong Academy, the Grotto of Ma Gu, and Dongshan's Dinghui Temple, received new luster and were joined by newly constructed ones, such as the Xingfu Temple of Baiguo, the Azure Cloud Temple (Biyun si) built by Mei Guozhen, and the Hall of the Three Elders (Sanlao tang) in the county seat. Gradually there emerged a recognized itinerary of approved sites for such gatherings of local notables and tourists, Macheng's Three Pavilions and Eight Vistas (*santai bajing*). Some of these had been especially sanctified by the great cultural heroes of the past. One, Henghua cun (Apricot Blossom Village) outside Songbu, could boast visits from Du Fu in the Tang and Su Dongpo in the Song; the Qianlong emperor dutifully followed suit in the Qing.[4] Most favored of all in the late Ming was the complex of new and existing temples around Dragon Lake (Longhu), in the central plain some 25 *li* east of the county seat. Domain of the powerful Zhou lineage, this deep, clear lake formed by the runoff from mountain streams was a magnet for all visitors of prominence, who paid tribute in verse or essay to the charms of the lakeside Angler's Terrace (Diaoyutai).[5] At such sites, Macheng's notables self-consciously displayed to all their cultural elegance and their consequent worthiness to dominate local society as thoroughly as they did.

Buddhism flourished in late-Ming Macheng, epitomized by scholarly monks such as Daoyi (birth name Zhou Mingming), the scion of a very eminent local lineage. In a near-perfect metaphor for the broader contemporary literati retreat from the deteriorating public life, Zhou, while en route to Wuchang to sit for the provincial examination, became so disgusted with the indecorous behavior of other candidates, who were fighting for seats on a river ferry, that he abruptly turned back to take the tonsure and wander the hills of his native county in quest of personal enlightenment.[6] Many other prominent members of the local elite, though not taking up monastic life, also maintained a deep engagement with Buddhist metaphysical and ethical inquiries.

At the same time, these men were far from withdrawn politically. Indeed, Macheng natives, at least from the generation of Zhou Hongzu and Zhou Hongyue, in the third quarter of the sixteenth century, not only enjoyed a persistent presence in the higher echelons of imperial officialdom but also played an active and complex role in the bitter factional politics of the late Ming. They were persistent vocal critics of the throne, of eunuchs, and of the imperial clan. They were deeply involved with the "left wing" Taizhou school of neo-Confucianism in the late sixteenth century, but in the early seventeenth they became equally engaged in that school's intellectually conservative but politically radical opponents, first in the Donglin and later in the Fushe movements.

One emblematic case is that of Peng Zungu. In 1586, the celebrated whistle-blower Hai Rui, already famous for his dismissal from office a decade earlier, was recalled to serve as metropolitan censor at Nanjing. Hai's first act, unsurprisingly, was to call for torturous punishment for any official engaging in even the slightest corruption. This invited a call by the superintendent of education, Fang Huan, that Hai be dismissed yet again, on grounds of hypocrisy and arrogance, and the Wanli court concurred. Macheng's Peng Zungu, however, in Nanjing for the metropolitan examinations, organized several of his fellow successful *jinshi* to submit a collective petition calling for Hai's reinstatement. They attacked Fang Huan's own deviousness, and praised Hai Rui as the great man of his age (*dangdai weiren*). The court defended Fang from these charges, ordering that the presumptuous Peng and his classmates return home and remain aloof from political action thereafter. Peng did indeed spend the balance of his life as a productive private scholar but was posthumously honored by the Tianqi court in the 1620s for his heroic remonstrance.[7]

Mei Guozhen and the Tax Reform of 1570

Macheng's incendiary political scene of the late sixteenth century—a local politics with major national implications—was most visibly embodied by three groups of kinsmen: the Mei, the Geng, and the Zhou. Probably the county's most nationally eminent native son in the century's last decades, and clearly its most energetic local booster, was Mei Guozhen (1542–1605). Guozhen belonged to what was likely the single wealthiest planter lineage in Macheng. The Mei had first arrived in the county very early and expropriated for themselves huge chunks of the county's very best farmland, in the area of the central plain just southeast of the county seat, at Seven Mile Ridge (Qiligang). The man subsequently identified as their founding ancestor (*shizu*), Mei Heng, was not new to the area when, in the early Yuan, he was selected by his neighbors for (or appropriated to himself) the post of militia commander (*baiyi*) in the face of banditry and social breakdown. His son and grandson expanded on this achievement to build ever-larger militia networks of their own (under the titles *qianyi* and *wanyi*, respectively). The lineage started, that is, as a group of local strongmen.[8]

As with others of Macheng's great literati-landlord families, examination success came slowly, but when it came it was glorious. The first of the lineage's four metropolitan and eleven provincial degree holders in the Ming was Guozhen's great-grandfather, Mei Ji (*jinshi* 1499), who served a contentious term as prefect of Huizhou (Guangdong).[9] The next was Guozhen himself (*jinshi* 1583), the eldest of six brothers. The second of these, Guolou, was a *jinshi* of the same year, a long-serving official in Guangdong, Sichuan, and Jiangxi, a decorated warrior in the border-defense campaigns of the era, and, in retirement, a great patron of local Macheng education and culture; the third, Guosen, was a *juren* and father of the county's late-Ming local hero Mei Zhihuan (see chapter 5). Guozhen married one of his daughters to Li Changgeng, offspring of the only Macheng lineage more powerful than his own, who rose to the empire's most exalted rank, that of grand secretary.[10] Guozhen's only son, Zhiyuan, was a noted classicist and bibliophile, a famous philanthropist who gave away thousands of taels of his patrimony to relieve the dearth of the Ming's final decades, and a member of the Donglin and Fushe movements who refused service under the conquering Manchus and lived the balance of his life as an ascetic Buddhist monk in the hills of his native county.[11] Despite Zhiyuan's example, however, the examination success and official prominence of the Seven Mile Ridge Mei continued apace, throughout the Qing era and beyond.[12]

Mei Guozhen himself was seen by contemporaries as a brilliant polymath, an accomplished poet who also excelled at riding and archery, and a man of no-nonsense candor, easy affability, and "chivalrous demeanor," fond of participating in drinking and poetry parties with friends.[13] Like many of his contemporaries, he was also attracted to Buddhism and eagerly engaged in theological discussions with acquaintances both secular and monastic.[14] He began official service as a county magistrate, was promoted to salt censor, and then moved on to a long and distinguished military career on the northwest frontier and throughout North China. He was especially known for his expertise in constructing defense fortifications and for his planning of siege campaigns, notably that which crushed the Pubei rebellion of 1592.[15] Though he was repeatedly involved in factional disputes, his growing reputation as a dynastic military hero shielded him from repercussions, and he ended his career as vice-president of the board of war and assistant grand tutor to the heir apparent. Returning to his native place in 1605 to mourn his father, Guozhen himself soon thereafter died of illness; his death was immediately reported to the throne, and he was posthumously granted the *yin* privilege of hereditary official rank.[16]

Throughout his career, Mei Guozhen still found time to patronize the construction of schools, temples to demon-exterminating deities, and so on, in his home county. In times of dearth, he interceded with higher levels of administration to allocate government grain for relief of Macheng.[17] More interestingly,

Guozhen and his brothers actively involved themselves in a number of contentious tax reform campaigns in their native place, in which they frequently appeared as point men for local popular interests as a whole. For example, Guozhen, in 1600–61, worked closely from his post in northwestern China with the incumbent Macheng magistrate Liu Wenqi to root out clerical tax engrossment at home.[18] The Hanlin laureate Mei Guolou was chief lobbyist in the campaign (discussed in chapter 1) to effect commutation of Macheng's grain tribute assessment to silver, in order to save local taxpayers at least a portion of the heavy transport costs entailed in shipment of actual grain to government collection depots. Here, in spite of the fact that the Mei family holdings were concentrated within relatively easy shipping distance from the Ju River and downstream, Guolou seems to have patiently worked to achieve a compromise on the issue, potentially dividing landowners like himself—whose locations allowed them to bear transport costs fairly easily, and who therefore opposed commutation at a standard rate (with *average* transport costs factored in)—from others, more remotely situated, who were quite happy to have assessments commuted at such a rate.[19]

On other matters of fiscal policy, however, while still claiming the mantle of spokesman for the people (*min*), Mei Guozhen seems rather to have pressed the interests of a more narrow planter class or, even more exclusively, his own lineage. This appears most strikingly in the case of a cadastral survey of all Macheng lands, carried out in 1570 by the magistrate Mu Wei, which quite clearly served as a flash point for local intraelite animosities and conflicting interests. Mu was a Jiangxi native and an energetic crusader against wrongdoing. Very quickly upon his arrival at Macheng, he gained universal elite praise for his campaigns against banditry. Then, however, he turned his attention to the problem of inequitable tax assessments, and this issue proved more divisive.

The magistrate convened an assembly of (carefully selected, it would appear) gentry and elders (*dafushi fulao*) and asked their views of the problem. All complained about the excessive fiscal burden faced by the county as a whole. The throne misinterpreted the strategic centrality of Macheng as a function of its prosperity, they claimed, whereas it was in fact really a frontier fortress (*watuo*), militarily critical but only marginally productive. On top of this, the tax burden was unfairly distributed within the county itself. Powerful households (*qiangzhe*) had much land that went untaxed (*bushui zhi tian*), whereas the weak (*ruozhe*) paid taxes on land that wasn't theirs to farm (*wutian zhi shui*). One result was an explosion of vicious litigation; another was the immiseration of the poor, who had either to flee or to die (*budu ce si*).[20]

Mu Wei determined that the root of the problem in Macheng lay in the dual classification system of riceland as either official land (*guantian*, that is, land held in the name of one or another of the county's numerous high officials) or commoner land (*mintian*). Both types of land were freely marketed and frequently divided. Since the lands, once sold, usually retained their former designation, the question of actual ownership by officials or commoners quickly became an artificial issue. The dynamic in this market lay in the fact that the two types of land were differently taxed, with *guantian* exempt from labor-service assessments but carrying a correspondingly higher land-tax assessment per se than commoner land. Consequently, a landowner wishing to lower his land-tax burden, but willing to accept labor-service obligations, would be anxious to trade *guantian* for *mintian* (*gaiguan weimin*), whereas one wishing to escape labor-service obligations altogether would seek the reverse exchange (*gaimin weiguan*). This in itself would not have constituted a problem of inequity but for the deceptiveness with which parties to land transactions disguised or manipulated the tax classifications of their lands. Theoretically, the market value of a piece of land moved in tandem with its tax assessment, which was presumed to be an index of its productivity. But great families (*dajia*), eager to gain a high return for land they sold, often claimed for their land a higher tax assessment than it actually had; the buyers of such property were often doomed to pay high taxes on land that was, in reality, of quite marginal yield, and they not infrequently defaulted on their titles rather quickly. Conversely, there was incentive for others to portray the tax burden on a piece of land as lower than it was, either to seek a buyer or to buy the land themselves at an attractively low price. Yet another corrupt practice was to sell a portion of one's land, typically to an overeager and undercapitalized buyer, and stick the buyer with a disproportionate share of the tax assessment formerly borne by the undivided property.

The result, confronted by Magistrate Mu in 1570, was a fiscal system in total disarray, with county tax registers totally unreflective of reality, and with tax burdens distributed grossly unequally among the population. He determined that the only effective way to deal with this was to conduct a full cadastral survey (*zhangtian*). He brought in a team of experts of unimpeachable integrity and ability to conduct this survey, and managed to totally recompile Macheng's tax registers and reassess all property holders within two years. Reclassifying most of the county's official land as commoner land, so as, he hoped, to lighten the tax burden of the county as a whole, he simultaneously sought to equalize the tax burden (*junliang*) between rich and poor.[21]

Quite clearly, a newly arrived magistrate, no matter how energetic and competent, could not have achieved this outcome had there not been significantly broad preexisting support for such a project among the local elite. The figure who seems to have embodied this consensus opinion was Huang Juan (1504–79), by now a quite aged local elder, who enjoyed wide veneration among the Macheng gentry; at his death, Huang's many friends secured for him a tomb inscription by the most glittering literatus of the day, Wang Shizhen.[22] Huang had achieved his *jinshi* more than four decades earlier, in 1529, and after serving in several midlevel official posts had returned home to pursue a career of local public service. In the late 1530s, he had led the subscription drive and compilation project that produced the county's first gazetteer, receiving widespread accolades from compatriots who saw this volume as a signifier of the new prominence to which their county had by this time risen. Huang also had a reputation as a man of the people. Wang Shizhen notes that he nearly never went into Macheng City to hobnob with the county elite. Rather, as Huang's biography in the Kangxi-era gazetteer stresses, he personally managed the work in his fields (*gongdu tianshi*), shared prosperity and adversity with his bondservants (*yu nupu tong ganku*), and was always ready to lend his farm implements to needy neighbors. Even more, he was an outspoken critic of overly rigid readings of the ritualized social-status system (*mingli*).[23]

This populist, reformist member of the county elite—and, evidently, not a few of his colleagues—saw the arrival of the activist magistrate Mu Wei as a blessing from Heaven. Upon Mu's departure, Huang prepared a commemorative essay identifying the magistrate with the great model officials of antiquity. Like these lofty exemplars, he had demonstrated in every way his love of the people (*aimin*)—by planting trees, extending cultivation (*kentian*), constructing hydraulic and other infrastructures, and, most important of all, equalizing the tax burden (*junping fuyi*). Huang argued passionately for the crucial necessity of the cadastral survey that Mu had effected, noting that in recent decades growing tax inequities had given rise to an alarming trend of land concentration in Macheng. A situation had arisen in which the rich had a great deal of land and little tax burden (*fuzhe tianduo shuishao*), while the poor had lost their property and yet retained tax obligations (*pinzhe chanqu liangcun*). Huang had no doubt whatsoever that the imminent result, failing Mu's drastic reform, would have been class war: the county was on the brink of devastation (*zhan yu weiwang*), the agents of which would be its masses of bondservants (*pushu*). As it turned out—and perhaps Mu Wei's tax reforms had some genuine palliative effect—the devastation that Huang envisioned was visited on Macheng only some half a century later.[24]

But Huang Juan hailed from a family of only modest wealth and academic achievement, by local late-Ming standards; the Wanrenyai Huang, though of venerable pedigree, had produced a paltry four *juren* in the entire dynasty, and Juan himself was their only *jinshi*.[25] It may be that the constituency which provided backing for Mu Wei's fiscal crusade was a broad stratum of just such modestly affluent elites. When it came to lineages of more fabulous opulence and national prominence—arguably the chief perpetrators of the tax exploitation and land grabbing that Huang decried—support for reform was evidently not so universal. It was this stratum to which the Qiligang Mei, and their then up-and-coming star Mei Guozhen, clearly belonged.

Probably on the basis of Huang Juan's nomination, Magistrate Mu Wei drew consideration for an imperial commendation (*yingjiang*), and Hubei Governor Luo Qiyu was placed in charge of investigating whether in fact Mu merited such honor. Advocates of Mu's tax reforms mounted an aggressive campaign in his behalf. Several local gentry, including the nationally known philosopher Geng Dingxiang (see below), visited Provincial Judge Wang Shizhen in 1573 and tearfully persuaded that luminary to write a brief praising Mu as a model official (*shunli*) who had succeeded where countless others before him had failed, and praising his reforms as of benefit to the rich as well as the poor (*xia yu shang jiaoyi*).[26]

When Governor Luo turned to these same wealthy interests, however, selecting Mei Guozhen as their spokesman, he received a somewhat different assessment. In response to Luo's inquiries, Mei effectively damned Mu with faint praise. His bandit-suppression activities were certainly commendable, Mei noted, and he conceded that the more controversial cadastral survey itself was unquestionably a well-intentioned exercise and had been conducted with due fairness. But was it really such a good thing? Speaking as a local landowner of the first magnitude, Mei suggested that the true test of any fiscal reform was its impact on *aggregate agricultural productivity*, and that, on these grounds, it was as yet too soon to tell whether Mu's project was a success or a disaster. His own family clearly having been economically inconvenienced by the reform, Mei discreetly declined to offer his own view of the outcome. In passing, though, he did hint that Mu Wei's fiscal reforms had not been conducted with prudent preparation: while they undoubtedly looked impressive to Mu's bureaucratic superiors, they had in fact been undertaken without proper regard for local public opinion (*minqing*).[27]

Geng Dingxiang and the Founding of Huang'an

The philosopher-statesman Geng Dingxiang (1524–96) was born in the northwest corner of Macheng. According to legend, a nobleman (*gongqing*) happened to pass by his residence and identified the two-year-old Dingxiang as a future sage. With this stimulus, the child applied himself vigorously to *lixue* studies and was rewarded with receipt of the *jinshi* degree in 1556. Appointed censor for the Yunnan circuit in 1559, he immediately gained notoriety by impeaching Wu Peng, president of the board of civil office. A frenetic chain of other impeachments and counterimpeachments followed, with Geng emerging relatively unscathed. He gradually climbed the administrative ladder, reaching the post of president of the board of revenue in the late 1580s. Upon his death, he was posthumously named junior guardian of the heir apparent, awarded the *yin* privilege of hereditary official appointment, and eventually merited a biography in the *Ming shi* (Ming dynastic history).[28]

Geng was notably prominent during his lifetime in his home locality as well; in 1575, for instance, he was one of the very few Huangzhou natives invited to contribute a preface to the newly compiled prefectural gazetteer. But this influence was something essentially won in Dingxiang's own lifetime. The Geng of Tri-Corner Mountain (Sanjue shan), in Macheng's Dabie Shan periphery, were not, like the Qiligang Mei of the central plain, a family of very great wealth and pedigree. Throughout the Ming they produced only three upper-level degree holders. Their first provincial examination success was won by one of Dingxiang's forebears, Geng Guang, a *juren* of 1501 and minor educational official. The first *jinshi* was Dingxiang himself. His immediate ancestors, in the words of Dingxiang's biographer Julia Ching, were small-time "gentlemen farmers" holding no academic or official rank. There is also no record of any Geng involvement in Macheng's prestigious local elite collective projects of the fifteenth or early sixteenth centuries, such as the reconstruction of the Confucian school-temple at the county seat or the compilation of the 1535 county gazetteer. But in Dingxiang's own generation, the family hit the big time. His younger brother Dingli also won the *jinshi*, in 1570, and rose to become vice-president of the board of war. The eldest brother, Dinglii, purposefully eschewed the examination sweepstakes after winning only a prefectural degree but was widely renowned for his expertise in neo-Confucian philosophy and Buddhist theology.[29]

Throughout his life, Geng Dingxiang wrestled very publicly with the heavy philosophical issues of his day, and with their implications for politics at both the imperial and the local level. He was attracted to Chan Buddhism and knew its precepts well. He held faith in the existence of the innate human moral wisdom (*liangzhi*) central to the teachings of Wang Yangming and was frequently associated by contemporaries with the "left wing" of Wang's disciples, known as the Taizhou school, which included Geng's sometime close associates He Xinyin and Li Zhi. But, as we shall see, the growing bureaucratic corruption and demoralization and the corresponding social anomie that he perceived in his times gradually led Geng to emphasize the values of moral choice and social hierarchy as well as the concrete prescriptions for achievement of sociopolitical order (*zhi* versus *luan*) that he found in Song-era neo-Confucianism. He was one of the first scholars outside northwestern China to appreciate the contributions of the Guanxue (Shaanxi) school—a firmly Zhu Xi–centered prescription for ritual and moral reinvigoration combined with devoted study of practical statecraft (*jingshi*) and useful technologies of all types—that would become central to the substantive learning (*shixue*) movement of the early and mid-

Qing.[30] Geng himself did not live to see the founding, in 1604, of the Donglin Academy by Gu Xiancheng (1550–1612), but his gradual turn away from Buddhism and moral intuitionism, and toward a "Song learning" commitment to public service nationally and social discipline locally, clearly anticipates this later scholarly movement.

Geng Dingxiang's emerging passion for institutionalizing social discipline in the face of an increasingly restive underclass is nicely epitomized in his proposal, sometime around 1575, to revive the community compact (*xiangyue*) system, famously championed by Zhu Xi in the Song and revived to great effect by Wang Yangming in the Ming itself.[31] Geng argued that the *state*-mandated decimal-group household registration system (*baojia*) was a crucial weapon in the fight to clamp down on traitors and curtail disorder (*jinjian zhiluan*), but that its necessary complement was a local *elite*-imposed institution for improving social mores and directing social practices (*daosu weifeng*): the community compact. This was especially true, he said, since the alternative system of local control implemented by the Ming founder—the *lijia*, or canton system—had clearly lost its effectiveness. Geng observed that a collective, communal, almost congregational commitment to moral reinvigoration was demanded by his unsteady times, and he echoed a common theme of late-Ming reformers in calling for a newly formalized means for elites to reach or get to the people (*tongmin*), from whom, it was clear, they had begun perilously to divorce themselves. Most intriguingly, Dingxiang noted that the peculiarly unruly, frontier character of his native area had generated a trio of especially vexatious problems—rampant banditry, proliferating litigation, and debt and tax arrears—that a functioning *xiangyue* system could help redress.

Although Geng did not go into details about just how this change could be accomplished, he was explicit that a community compact system, controlled by the local landed elite, would allow the more equitable assessment and collection of land-tax and labor-service dues (*yaofu ke ping*). He made a similar point in a testimonial essay, composed around the same time, honoring the Macheng magistrate Wang Sanzhai for having cleaned up local subbureaucratic tax racketeering and, in the process, firing several dozen county clerks.[32] Here, then, as throughout the rest of the area's long history, the festering issue of taxes appears as an area of friction between locality and state, providing an opening for demands for greater elite-led local autonomy.

Geng Dingxiang sounded these themes even more adamantly in the protracted and ultimately successful campaign he waged to have his native area of northwest Macheng severed from that district and established as a county in its own right.[33] In this episode, moreover, we get a further glimpse of the normally disguised contention *within* the local landed elite. The creation of Huang'an County was clearly a controversial and highly politicized process. Landholders of the area consistently argued that their need for administrative separation hinged most directly on the issue of public safety, and that the Macheng magistrate had neither the capacity nor the inclination to dispatch his modest security forces to defend the slopes of the Dabie Shan northwest of the county seat, thus leaving them perpetual prey to bandits and border reivers crossing over from Henan. A new and closer county seat with a substantial armed contingent would help alleviate this problem. There is no reason to suspect the validity of this concern. Nevertheless, it is clear that a more general factor underlying the movement was a desire for a higher level of local autonomy vis-à-vis the far more powerful elite lineages of Macheng City and the county's central plain—lineages like the Xindian Zhou, the Bashang Li, the Guchengfan Zeng, and, not least, the Qiligang Mei. Administrative autonomy would certainly bring with it greater home rule over the collection and allocation of fiscal resources, and a better chance to compete for the scarce resource of quotaed examination passes that these venerable, well-connected lineages of the old county core had managed to claim so disproportionately in the past. These were advantages that the core-area elites would evidently not willingly give up.

The idea of a new, detached county was first formally broached in a petition submitted in 1542 by two northwestern *jiansheng*, Qin Yue and Li Daxia. Despite preliminary endorsement by the censor for the Huguang circuit, Lu Jie, the petition was ultimately rejected on the basis that it gave rise to too many complications—presumably, opposition from the kind of literati-based public opinion (*minqing*) that Mei Guozhen later chided magistrate Mu Wei for ignoring in the cadastral survey case. Five years later, in 1547, Huangzhou prefect Guo Fengyi himself asked provincial authorities to reconsider the matter, but the result was the same. Then, in 1552, newly minted *juren* Geng Dingxiang joined the fray. He lobbied censor Feng Yue to reopen the case but was roundly rebuffed by the provincial authorities. Consequently, the *Huang'an Gazetteer* reports, the area continued to suffer the repeated pains of social disorder.

A year after his promotion to *jinshi*, in 1559, Geng found himself posted to the Ming southern capital at Nanjing, and he immediately seized the occasion to press again for the autonomy of his native township. He asked Hubei governor Liu Lunxin to reconsider the issue and seemingly was on the point of securing Liu's approval when the governor was suddenly transferred and replaced by another man, Zhang Yu, who was less persuaded of the move's necessity. Almost certainly, this new arrival was gotten to early by the Macheng opponents of severing the northwest. Geng Dingxiang himself was at the time too far away in Nanjing to rebut them effectively, but when, the following year, he was reposted to Gansu, he passed through his native place and the Hubei provincial capital, using all his energies to lobby local and provincial officials in favor of creating the new county. Toward the end of 1562, Geng's persistence paid off, and Governor Zhang submitted a lengthy memorial to the throne endorsing his case. Over the winter and the spring, all sides made their voices heard, with much contentious bickering, especially over the details of fiscal reapportionment. In April 1563, the board of revenue finally granted formal permission to create Huang'an (Peaceable Huangzhou), taking most of the new district from Macheng but small segments from two other adjacent counties as well.

Geng Dingxiang had emerged triumphant over the more entrenched Macheng County elites. Indeed, the extent of his victory is overwhelmingly conveyed by the Kangxi-era Huang'an County gazetteer. There were clearly other northwest Macheng lineages who benefited from the new county's severance, but the gazetteer—in its biographical notices, its selection of local literary works, its attribution of patronage for local infrastructural development, and so on—strikingly reveals just how exclusive a Geng-lineage turf the new county had become over the century and a half since its creation. And whereas in Macheng the Geng had enjoyed only modest success in the examination sweepstakes, once on their own ground in Huang'an the lineage produced literally dozens of credentialed literati, not only through the remainder of the Ming but also well into the succeeding Qing dynasty.[34] Geng Dingxiang had effectively been enfeoffed.

The Zhou Brothers and Dragon Lake

Intimately associated with Geng Dingxiang and his brothers was another set of siblings from the Zhou lineage. At least eight Zhou men bearing in their given names the generational character "Si"—Sijiu, Sijing, Siji, Sizhao, Sizhi, Sidan, Sida, and Sishan—achieved the *juren* or *jinshi* and served as county magistrates or in higher offices in the second half of the sixteenth century. These men belonged to the Juedanshan Zhou, one of the oldest elite lineages of the Dabie Shan region. They claimed a local presence as early as the Southern Song (the 1190s), when their founding ancestor, Zhou Ailiu, is said to have migrated from Jiangxi. Their lineage headquarters, Juedanshan, was located in the western portion of Macheng, which was detached in 1562 to form Huang'an (Zhou Sijing's biography appears in the Huang'an County gazetteer, where he is claimed as a native son[35]), but the Zhou estates in fact sprawled over both counties, with a heavy presence in the Macheng central plain, north of the market town of Yanjiahe.[36]

Politically most influential among this generational cohort were the brothers Zhou Sijiu (Zhou Liutang, *jinshi* 1553) and Zhou Sijing (Zhou Youshan, *jinshi* 1568). Sijiu never served in a post higher than prefect, but he was extremely well connected nationally. No less a figure than the celebrated *qingguan* (incorrupt official) Hai Rui wrote glowingly of Zhou's achievements in the difficult post of prefect of Hainan Island, as a result of which Sijiu was summoned for consultation by the Jiajing emperor.[37] Zhou Sijing, like Geng Dingxiang, was a protégé of Zhang Juzheng (1525–82), the consummately powerful chief grand secretary. In his lifetime he rose to the post of vice-president of the board of works and was posthumously awarded the rank of grand secretary.[38]

Both locally and beyond, however, the cultural influence of Macheng's renowned "two Zhou" surpassed their considerable political clout. They were intellectual celebrities. Sijiu and Sijing built grand Confucian halls and libraries and Daoist temples in Macheng City and throughout the county. Most famously, they constructed a complex of pavilions and temples around the shores of the beautiful Dragon Lake (Long hu or Longtan hu), in the northern suburbs of Yanjiahe. In addition to the Angler's Pavilion (Diaoyutai), these included the Cold Jade Pavilion (Hanbitai), the Dragon Lake Temple (Longhu si), and the Cloister of the Iris Buddha (Zhifoyuan), all of which became destinations of choice for touring literati. From these sites, Sijiu and Sijing launched boating parties on the lake, with much drinking, and with elegant but frequently impassioned conversation. These temples also reflected the deep fascination that Buddhism held for the Zhou brothers. Macheng's famous ascetic Daoyi was, after all, the son of their cousin Sishan, and Sijiu and Sijing were intimate as well with another nationally known monk, Wunian, an offsping of the Xiong lineage of the Dongshan, whom they installed as abbot of the Cloister of the Iris Buddha.[39] Zhou Sijiu conducted a correspondence over many years with Geng Dingxiang on various issues of Buddhist belief, most centrally on how it could be reconciled with the Confucian imperatives of personal ethics, ritual propriety, and public service they both equally held dear.[40] This Buddhist element in their ideological mix would be central to the scandal that, in the final decades of the sixteenth century, would surround the Zhou brothers, along with the Geng, and also the Mei: the activities at Dragon Lake of their notorious houseguest Li Zhi.

Li Zhi Comes to Macheng

The iconoclastic philosopher Li Zhi (1527–1602) was born into a mercantile family of Muslim ancestry in Quanzhou, Fujian.[41] After service as a local official during the 1550s, including a term as prefect of Yao'an, Yunnan, he retired to the life of a private scholar in Nanjing. There he became involved in heady philosophical debates with fellow disciples of Wang Yangming, including He Xinyin (1517–79), Macheng's own Geng Dinglii and Dingxiang, and Dingxiang's student Jiao Hong. From He Xinyin the group adopted the practice of discussing learning (*jiangxue*), the deliberate exercise of defending one's views in open debate, with emphasis on the physical act of public speaking, on communicating with the general populace, and on a relativist receptivity to others' points of view. It was indeed a highly syncretist circle: Dingxiang championed Wang Yangming's doctrine of innate moral wisdom (*liangzhi*) as interpreted by the idiosyncratic Taizhou scholar Wang Gen (1483–1541), Dinglii worked at perfecting the regimens of Chan Buddhism, and Li and Jiao began the intense collective reading of Daoist texts that would occupy them for several years.[42]

In 1581, the Geng brothers returned to their newly carved-out home county of Huang'an in mourning for their father, and Dinglii invited the fifty-four-year-old Li Zhi to join them as their guest. Jiao Hong followed as well at the end of the year.[43] For a while Li and Geng Dingxiang continued to get on well; the Huang'an County gazetteer reprints a selection of linked verses that they composed and exchanged during this period.[44] But philosophical and political differences began to divide them, with increasing acrimony. Geng Dinglii and their mutual friend Zhou Sijiu sought to reconcile the two, but with diminishing success. He Xinyin had been arrested for sedition and executed at Wuchang in 1579, under circumstances that remain to this day somewhat obscure. Although Geng Dingxiang had served as He's protector for some five years before that, Li Zhi gradually came to blame Geng's moral cowardice for the death of the man Li considered a heroic martyr (*yingxiong*) for his beliefs.[45] Then, when Dingxiang chose to accept a new appointment as vice-censor under the regime that had killed He, Li vehemently condemned Dingxiang's self-serving hypocrisy. In the summer of 1584, Geng Dinglii died of illness, whereupon Li, increasingly pressured by Geng Dingxiang, sought to vacate Huang'an. Initially he thought to return to Nanjing, but when Jiao Hong protested that their finances were inadequate, the two instead accepted the Zhou brothers' invitation to move to neighboring Macheng.

Li Zhi arrived in Macheng in 1585 and would spend most of the next fifteen years in that county. He lived in the massive Cloister of the Iris Buddha, on a serene wooded cliff overlooking Dragon Lake. Though housing upward of forty monks, the cloister was not formally registered as a place of Buddhist congregational worship; in the words of Li himself, it was, strictly speaking, "neither a temple [*si*] nor a monastery [*an*]" but rather a place for personal, nonsectarian prayer and meditation, which had been built by Zhou Sijiu in a patriotic effort "to invoke good fortune upon the country/dynasty" ("weiguo qifu").[46] Jiao Hong lived here as well until his departure for the metropolitan examination and his subsequent appointment to the Hanlin in 1589. Frequent visitors included the Zhou brothers and their nephew Daoyi, Yuan Hongdao and his brother Zhongdao (on one of his visits, Hongdao stayed for more three months), Mei Guozhen, and other luminaries from both the locality and beyond. This so-called Dragon Lake Group coalesced into a quasi-permanent feature of Macheng society in the last decades of the sixteenth century, a center of nonconformist thought with a growing national notoriety.[47]

The abbot of the cloister was the charismatic Dongshan native Wunian, friend and spiritual mentor to men as diverse as the general Mei Zhihuan (Guozhen's nephew, and soon to be military overlord of Macheng) and the poet Yuan Hongdao. In one poem addressed to Wunian, Yuan teased him about the abstruseness of his message:

A hundred times I heard you lecture
but my mind remained a tangled knot.
I was like a man born blind
who has never seen red or purple—
try explaining the difference to him
and the more you speak
the more confused he'll get.[48]

Li Zhi felt Wunian's influence as well. In 1588, he sent his family home to Fujian and took the tonsure. In keeping with his syncretist leanings, Li insisted that this was not incompatible with his status as a public-minded literatus: he protested to Zhou Sijing, "My devotion to the Buddha and reciting sutras is but an effort to secure prosperity for the country and security for our people" ("guotai min'an"). Nonetheless, it was cause for scandal. Geng Dingxiang was particularly incensed, and neither Zhou Sijiu nor the sympathetic Macheng magistrate Deng Shiyang could mollify him.[49]

At Dragon Lake, Li Zhi read broadly and intensively; his reading included not only the great Tang poets but also, according to Yuan Zhongdao, "eccentric writings of Song and Yuan masters" and "short stories of the marvelous and strange." For days at a time he holed up in his study with a bottle of wine and his books and spoke to no one. He was obsessed with personal cleanliness, and his simple clothes were meticulously neat.[50] But he also drank and exchanged poetry with his friends, and he was a prolific correspondent.[51] The works for which Li is best known—his critical historical studies, and his essays and letters that have been collected as the two-volume *Burn This Book!* (*Fenshu* and *Xu fenshu*) and *Hide This Book!* (*Cangshu*)—were all products of his Macheng sojourn. And he continued his practice of public discourse (*jiangxue*): his open lectures at Dragon Lake attracted not only literati but also petty merchants and other curious townspeople, further inviting the animosity of conservative local elites.[52]

Fuel for their attack was provided by Li's perceived sexual transgressions. By Li's own admission, whereas in Huang'an he had lived a secluded and strait-laced existence, he took advantage of his move to Macheng—and away from the prudish eye of Geng Dingxiang—to "frequent the pleasure quarters and mingle with fellow sensualists."[53] After taking the tonsure, the sixty-year-old Li by no means abjured the company of women. Under Wunian, the Cloister of the Iris Buddha indeed had something of a reputation for attracting female disciples, inviting even the jests of the abbot's friend Yuan Hongdao for the sexual license this may have allowed:

> The Master's mind is like quiet water
>   reflecting this moon.
> His body is a cold forest
>   putting forth this blossom.
> How many times can she remember
>   the hand of ordination
>   on her brow?[54]

Under these circumstances, when Li Zhi himself accepted as a disciple no less notable a woman than Mei Guozhen's twenty-year-old widowed daughter, Danran, tongues were set to wagging, and Li's enemies had all the ammunition they needed.[55]

And he had no shortage of enemies. Li routinely condemned, in the most ad hominem manner, even his closest friends and protectors when they failed to live up to his standards. He publicly criticized Zhou Sijing, for example, for not resigning from office to protest the posthumous degradation of Zhou's patron Zhang Juzheng; a true scholar, he thought, should never in this way defer to holders of political power: "If that were the case, then Confucius and Mencius would never have opened their mouths!"[56] The worst of his wrath, however, even long after he had left Huang'an for Macheng in 1585, was reserved for Geng Dingxiang. In Li's *Fenshu* (1590) and *Cangshu* (1598), Geng emerged as the very epitome of *wei daoxue* (phony neo-Confucianism), counterposed to the *zhen daoxue* (genuine strain) that Li himself, despite his apparent apostasies, claimed to represent. His own conduct of interpersonal relations, Li protested, was based on authentic human responsiveness (*zhenji*). The phonies, by contrast, demanded adherence to arbitrary norms of right and wrong (*shifei*), and they insisted on enforcing ritually based principles of social hierarchy (*mingjiao*) but really did so only out of self-interest. Their so-called scholarship was directed toward passing the examinations and groveling for political office, which in turn was simply a hypocritical pursuit of wealth. Merchants, who sought their wealth honestly and productively in the marketplace, were in fact more ethical than these scholar-officials who belittled them.[57]

Li Zhi's scathing attacks on Geng Dingxiang took the form primarily of letters—to Zhou Sijing, Jiao Hong, and Geng himself—which Li had the effrontery to collect and publish in his own lifetime (and many in Geng's as well). Geng Dingxiang's written responses likewise came in epistolary form, specifically in three letters written to Zhou Sijiu in the early 1590s. These were discreetly withheld from publication until after Geng's death, appearing in his posthumous collected works, although they look very much as if they were intended for private circulation at the time of writing. None of these letters, at least overtly, deals with the two men's deteriorating personal relationship: Geng takes the high road of sticking to his growing discomfort with Li's ethical and social ideas.

In the first letter, Geng defends his adherence to the *mingjiao* and critiques Li's stated preference for rooting social relations instead in *zhenji* (authenticity). Geng notes that he takes his own mission as that of carrying down workable social models from antiquity and transmitting them to future generations (*jiwang kailai*), whereas Li's insistence on living solely in the moment dangerously disregards the lessons of the past. Geng insists that his own valuation of textual learning and tradition-sanctioned family rituals is far better suited to imposing order on chaos (*luan*), never more necessary than in his own time. He concedes that there is indeed a discourse of authenticity within the Confucian-Mencian tradition but notes that it is necessarily bound up with moral categories, the authentic pursuit of benevolence (*ren*) and propriety (*yi*). Li's own version of authenticity seems clearly derived from Buddhist rather than Confucian sources. There is nothing inherently wrong with this, Geng concedes, noting that he himself has spent many years in study of the Buddhist canon. It is necessary, however, to keep Buddhist teachings in critical perspective, especially in regard to their social utility.[58]

Geng's second letter focuses on the practice of *fenbie*, drawing proper distinctions. Li Zhi, Geng states, does not believe in this imperative. For example, whereas Geng himself avoids prostitutes out of concern for *fenbie*, Li openly consorts with them, even in a time when he should be in mourning for his deceased wife. Li, of course, justifies his conduct as fidelity to his principle of spontaneous authenticity (*ziran zhi zhenji*), to which Geng counterposes his own preference for decorum and morality (*mingyi daoli*). Characteristically, Geng again concedes that there is a Confucian discourse of "nondistinction" upon which Li Zhi might base his case. Cheng Yi, for example, said that "inasmuch as the ten thousand things are of one essence, there is really no distinction between myself and other human beings" (*wanwu wai yiti, shi renwo wu fenbie*). But this is a very different sort of nondistinction from that championed by Li: it is an argument for the moral responsibility to care for others, not a justification for self-indulgence.[59]

The final letter organizes itself as a point-by-point rebuttal of each of Li Zhi's professed beliefs. Most interesting among these points is Geng's refutation of Li's incendiary dismissal of the moral dictates concerning ruler and subject, and father and son. Li had famously inverted the Confucian *wulun* (five relationships), arguing that the egalitarian relationship between friend and friend, and that between husband and wife (which he redefined in a manner much more egalitarian than had been done by any previous Confucian thinker), were of much more consequence than the transparently hierarchical relationships of ruler and subject, father and son, and elder and younger siblings.[60] Geng emphatically disagrees with Li's argument that the ruler-subject and father-son dyads are "false" or "arbitrary" pairings (*jiahe*), presenting them instead as dichotomies that are "wondrously" or primordially ordained (*miaohe*). For Geng, the affection that binds father and son, and the obligation that bonds ruler and subject, are inherent and may never be abrogated. Here and throughout his critique, Geng Dingxiang routinely deploys such words as *zi* (spontaneous) and *yuan* (original) in order to wrest from Li Zhi any claim to naturalized or a priori truth for his own philosophy of (in Geng's view) moral license. According to Geng, Li Zhi is doing nothing less than undermining the natural, cosmic, moral, and social orders.[61]

Although Geng, in his written criticisms of Li, kept the debate an intellectual one, he clearly felt personally betrayed, and there is evidence that he used his substantial clientage networks to push the attack on a more visceral level. Already by the late 1580s there was swelling literati opinion in Macheng against Li's presence. He was decried for his heretical views (*yiduan*), his corrupt (*bichun*) and debauched (*yinzong*) personal life, for spreading immorality (*xuanyin*) and leading the world astray (*huoshi*), and even for his rumored engagement with the occult (*yihuan yuwen*).[62] With the publication, in 1590, of Li's strident attacks on Geng in his *Fenshu*, even Li's Macheng host Zhou Sijiu broke off personal relations with him (the younger Zhou brother Sijing apparently did not). In 1591, Cai Yizhong (*jinshi* 1600), an ambitious former student of Geng Dingxiang from Guangshan County, across the Dabie Shan divide, published his *Fenshu bian* (Critique of the Fenshu), which was far more scatological than anything the master himself would put in print; there was general understanding that Geng had put him up to it. When at the end of that year Li and Yuan Hongdao visited Wuchang, Geng allegedly sent his family retainers to fan public criticism of Li's perversion of the Way (*zuodao*), with the result that Li faced physical attack by a mob while touring the provincial capital's famous Yellow Crane Tower (Huanghe lou).[63]

Things only went downhill from there. In 1594, another professed disciple of Geng Dingxiang, the Hubei provincial judge Jing Xian, came to Macheng to lodge a charge against Li of great degradation of public morals (*dahuai fengsu*). Li adamantly refused to leave the county, reportedly saying "You can kill me, but I will not leave. You can cut off my head, but my person will not be disgraced."[64] Two years later, however, when Li went to visit a friend in Shanxi, he was driven out of the county by the local officials; attributing his expulsion to the agents of Geng Dingxiang, he returned to Macheng and drew up his will, confiding to Zhou Sijing that he believed his murder was imminent. The following year, he fled the county, again going to Shanxi and taking refuge in Mei Guozhen's governor's office. Jiao Hong, now back in Macheng, wrote to Li to ask him to return to their old haunts at Dragon Lake, but Li demurred, claiming that too many people in Macheng wanted to see him dead. He went instead to Nanjing, seeking the protection of friends, and taking the occasion to publish his parting shot at the now deceased Geng Dingxiang, his *Cangshu.* The book carried prefaces by Mei Guozhen and, remarkably, by the surviving Geng brother Dingli. Mei wrote in part:

> Of old, the thought of heroic [*haojie*] scholars was often out of harmony with those of their contemporaries. Only in times of crisis could they be appreciated; in normal times, they could not be seen for what they were. . . . My friend Li Zhi is just such a hero. The writings of scholars today are all so bound up by convention and formality that they discuss merely the dross of human existence. Li Zhi stands alone. No one dares consider the true implications of his thought. . . . He holds emphatically to his own ideas, regardless of whether they conform to the standards of morality imposed by tradition. Aware of just how out of step he is with his times, he writes down his views and hides them away. Whether they will indeed be handed down and better appreciated by later generations, who can say?[65]

Mei's discussion of heroism in this passage is quite significant, and revelatory of both Li Zhi's evolving thought and its special relationship to the Macheng setting. One of the "stories of the marvelous and strange" to which Li especially devoted himself while at Dragon Lake was the swashbuckling novel *Shuihu zhuan* (*Water Margin*). While there, with the help of the young local scholar Yang Dingjian and other assistants, Li produced a 120-chapter critical edition of this work, now held to be the novel's "most definitive form."[66] His manuscript was safeguarded by Yang, and ultimately, with the assistance of others among Li's admirers, it was published posthumously in Suzhou around 1614.[67] Li's interest in the *Shuihu zhuan* was born of his quest for paradigms of virtuous behavior beyond those of the conventional Confucian *wenren*, or bureaucrat, as well as his interest in styles of prose outside the placid norms of literati discourse. It was in this light that he revered the martyred hero (*yingxiong*) He Xinyin. Most specifically, Li's attraction was to the ideal of a courageous, highly physical manliness—a masculinity that did not shun violence and in some instances even gloried in it. He was especially attached to the notion of the *haohan*, the tough guy. In his *Shigang pingyao* (Critical commentaries on historical figures), he invoked the term repeatedly to describe men who took bold and unconventional political action in times of crisis—men such as the classical proto-Legalist officials Shang Yang and Shen Buhai, and the Tang founder Li Shimin. The *haohan* ideal suffuses the *Shuihu zhuan*; in Li's edition, by one count, the term appears 369 times.[68] It also, as self-consciously exemplified by men like Mei Guozhen, ran very deep in the local culture of Macheng and the Dabie Shan.

In the spring of 1600—self-consciously exhibiting his own heroism—Li Zhi returned to Macheng for what would be the final time. His mood was sardonic and defiant. They accuse me of being a sectarian leader, he writes to Jiao Hong, yet I have never done anything but shut myself up in my study and read books. I am what county gazetteers usually include in their category of visiting dignitary (*liuyu*). Most counties are delighted to record persons such as this, and yet here all they can think of is how best to chase me away! Think of it! If these local literati, who think of themselves as so many Confucian gentlemen (*junzi*), really believe me to be a sectarian leader, is it truly gentlemanly for them to inflict my evils on some other locality? Already a movement was afoot in local elite circles to tear down the Cloister of the Iris Buddha in which Li lived. In protesting this movement, Li Zhi again plays what may be seen as the "class card." My enemies, he observes, are themselves persons commanding great wealth (*caizhu renjia*). How petty is it that they would tear down the humble abode where for years I have been living in poverty?[69]

In the winter of that year, these elites won over to their cause the new Macheng magistrate Feng Yingjing. Feng hired a band of retainers—referred to in sources friendly to Li as hoodlums (*liumang*)—and marched on Dragon Lake, intending to evict Li once and for all. Li's disciple Yang Dingjian refused to surrender the seventy-four-year-old master and instead helped him escape over the Dabie Shan to Shangcheng, and from there another ally, Ma Jinglun, spirited him off to Beijing. The furious magistrate ordered that Yang be arrested for trial and that the Cloister of the Iris Buddha be razed to the ground.[70]

At Beijing in 1601, the nature of Macheng's elite society, and Li Zhi's ambiguous role within it, became grist for scandal and debate among the entire metropolitan literati. The censor Zhang Wenda memorialized to decry the many corruptions that Li had visited over the years on Macheng, and to warn that similar horrors would take place in the imperial capital itself if Li were not immediately thrown in jail. Ma Jinglun, Li's new host and a censor himself, responded with three publicly leaked letters defending Li's conduct in Macheng and condemning the actions of the "pack of wolves" in driving this harmless old man ("laoweng") out into the cold. Li Zhi is not different from the great Confucian sojourner-exiles of the past, argues Ma, men such as Li Bo and Sima Guang, who in drinking and fishing took refuge from the difficulties of their age. Whereas the Ming Code clearly demands that people respect retired officials living in their midst, and that they venerate elders who have lived to over seventy years, both stipulations have been grossly violated by Li Zhi's Macheng persecuters. Moreover, the allegations against Li in that county are merely rumors stirred up by a narrow faction of his enemies there; they by no means reflect the general public opinion (*yulun zhi gong*) that they represent themselves to be.[71] But Zhang Wenda and the accusers won the day. In a Beijing prison, in 1602, Li Zhi took his own life.

Li Zhi and Lineage Feuding in Macheng

One of the most interesting of Ma Jinglun's arguments defending Li Zhi concerns the way his case served as a flash point for intraelite feuds internal to Macheng County itself. In his first letter, Ma vaguely hints that the false accusations against Li of propagating lewdness (*xuanyin*) are in truth nothing but a means of vilifying the most illustrious and noble lineage of the locality (*yixiang xiangui zhi zu*); as such, it is the accusers rather than the accused who are guilty of propagating lewdness. He discreetly leaves unnamed just which lineage this might be.[72] Apparently pushed to greater specificity, however, Ma identifies the target of this slander as none other than Mei Guozhen, "a man of strict rectitude and a highly skilled military commander, who has served the dynasty well in combating rebels." His enemies at home, Ma says, have sought to discredit him through insinuations about his daughter Danran, who, although she has studied with Li Zhi at the Cloister of the Iris Buddha, is actually a chaste widow who became a Buddhist nun. Ma argues that the false allegations of sexual dalliance on the part of Danran "owe entirely to petty enmities within the Macheng elite [*shifu*]" and are intended less to get at Li himself than to defame the Mei lineage and destroy Guozhen's official career. He notes that there are many Macheng literati who are or have been in relatively high official service, and he suggests that the specious attack on Mei Guozhen may involve not only local lineage feuding but also, to some extent, a local reflection of bureaucratic factionalism on the broader imperial level. Ma never identifies Mei's enemies by name.[73]

If indeed Mei Guozhen was the target, Li Zhi was a natural way to get at him, since by the last years of the century Mei had emerged as Li's major surviving champion among the regional elite. He had, as we have seen, visited Li at the Cloister of the Iris Buddha on his visits home, had offered Li sanctuary in his Shanxi governor's mansion, and had contributed a laudatory preface to Li's incendiary *Cangshu*. Mei and Li maintained a running correspondence on matters of Confucian and Buddhist thought, and it is clear that, at least in some sense, Mei saw Li as his spiritual and philosophical guide.[74] It is especially noteworthy that Mei Zhihuan, Guozhen's nephew and effective political heir, both nationally and socially, remained loyal to Li Zhi's memory even after Li's imprisonment and suicide, writing a eulogy in which he refers to Li as "the master" (*zhangzhe*).[75]

Was Li Zhi in fact merely a sacrificial pawn in a conflict between the Mei and Geng lineages? In a recent article, Jin Jiang hints at as much, identifying the Mei as a long-established Macheng lineage and the Geng as an "upstart" challenger to their local hegemony.[76] And, indeed, the key issues in Macheng's local politics of the 1570s and 1580s found the Geng and the Mei on different sides. Geng Dingxiang was one of the most ardent supporters of Magistrate Mu Wei's tax reforms, an enthusiastic advocate of Mu's imperial commendation, and an intimate friend of Mu's local confidante, Huang Juan; Mei Guozhen was, as we have seen, highly skeptical of Mu's initiatives. It seems likely as well that the conflict of interest over the separation of Huang'an County formed a further wedge between the Geng and the Mei.

Without naming names, Ray Huang also notes the fact that Li Zhi's local defenders were comfortably established local magnates (like the Mei), whose economic and political security seemingly could allow them to tolerate Li's freethinking ways, while his attackers were smaller-scale and less established local scholars (like the Geng), who were forced to fall back on a puritanical guardianship of public morals as one basis of their power in local society.[77] It is difficult to accept this position with confidence, however, since nothing that I have found in the surviving late-Ming writings of the Geng or the Mei mentions the other directly (in later generations, the two lineages intermarried[78]). This hypothesis is also complicated by the fact that Geng Dingli joined Mei Guozhen in writing a preface to Li Zhi's *Cangshu,* with its ongoing attack on Dingli's (by now deceased) brother Dingxiang. The Zhou brothers, Sijiu and Sijing—whom it seems reasonable to see as mutual friends of the Geng and Mei and as intermediaries between the two, literally having one foot in the Gengs' new Huang'an County and the other in the Mei turf of the Macheng central plain—were by the 1590s themselves divided in their loyalties, Sijiu cutting off relations with Li Zhi and Sijing remaining his confidante.[79] At minimum, it seems necessary to recognize that interpersonal and interlineage politics in late-Ming Macheng were in fact far more complicated—one might say Byzantine—than a simple Mei-versus-Geng hypothesis would allow.

What we can say with certainty is that Mei Guozhen, long absent from his native county in official service, had nevertheless gotten himself and his lineage, by the turn of the century, deeply embroiled in a maze of disputes within the local elite. Feng Yingjing, the Macheng magistrate who led the expulsion of Li Zhi in early 1601, was presumably acting in league with Mei Guozhen's local enemies, but within a few months Feng was succeeded by the Sichuanese Liu Wenqi, a man who, as we have already seen, was effectively in Mei's pocket. The tenor of local politics changed immediately. Mei wrote to Liu from his post in the northwest, shortly after the latter's arrival in Macheng, to ask his intervention in a personal dispute, and Liu obliged. A number of lower-gentry members, he writes, led by one Wu Ketong (there are no Gengs on the list), have begun slandering Mei's family and stirring up the local commoner population (*lixiang pingmin*)—tenants on Mei estates?—turning them against him. Wu is involved in a tax-proxy racket, Mei charges, but to deflect guilt has accused the Mei family of the same offense. Will the new magistrate please look into this? Mei writes that during his absence he has tried to remain aloof from local Macheng politics, but it seems that the situation has reached a point where he must come home and intervene personally.[80]

Before the end of the year, he did just that. In a later writing, he notes that this is his first extended visit home since 1588, and that the deterioration in the morale and esprit of the local elite since that time is deeply alarming. Surface pleasantries are observed among the county's leading lineages, but these just serve to mask a pattern of mutual backstabbing. Defamation, libel, and slander have become the order of the day, and he notes—in an oblique reference to Geng Dingxiang's pattern of attack on Li Zhi?—that established scholars even enlist their young students in these campaigns. Among other material factors, he says, the persistent problem of distributing tax assessments underlies this fractiousness, and it needs to be addressed; but, Mei says, what really distresses him is that scandalmongering and nuisance litigation have in themselves become such entrenched elements of the local elite culture.[81] Thus, if Mei Guozhen can be believed, the elite solidarity that had so facilitated Macheng's rise to national prominence over the course of the sixteenth century was in the process of unraveling, and just at the moment when those elites would be most sorely tested, by revolution from below and armed invasion from beyond. When those challenges came, they would make the literati squabbling that Mei decried seem like the petty bickering of spoiled children.

Li Zhi and the Fall of the Ming

Historians of Chinese thought nearly all agree in assigning a pivotal significance in that history to Li Zhi, and see him as in some way progressive, but they tend to divide into two camps regarding the nature of Li's contribution. Those arguing from a socialist perspective stress the revolutionary antifeudal character of his thought and depict him as a bitter opponent of the landlord class. Highlighting his attacks on literati hypocrisy and his intermittent championing of the profit motive, Marxists most frequently associate him with an emerging commercial-capitalist bourgeois thought (*shimin sixiang*), but they also emphasize the resonance of his egalitarian views with the interests of both urban laborers and the peasantry, allied against the forces of the feudal "great landlords."[82] By contrast, historians in what might be called the liberal camp—beginning with the pioneering work of Shimada Kenji in 1949, and followed by that of Wm. Theodore de Bary, Ray Huang, Willard Peterson, and many in the post-Mao People's Republic, all working in their own distinctive ways—stress instead Li's modernist individualism, seeing his quest for a personal voice as an implicit or explicit championing of the intellectual freedom of the individual (*geren*), or, in Li's own usage, the self (*wu*), liberated from the crushing pressures of society (*shehui*).[83] These non-Marxist and post-Marxist scholars tend to downplay the class character of Li's thought, a tendency most notable in Huang, who emphasizes Li's rather obstinate "elitism," his insistence on being carried even very short distances in a sedan chair and being read to by a servant rather than reading for himself, and his coziness at Macheng and elsewhere with the wealthiest landed interests of his day.[84]

In Macheng local memory, Li has been variously assessed. The first truly historical notice was the tomb inscription written by the Macheng poet and Ming loyalist Liu Tong. Liu's essay is scrupulously neutral, reporting on Li's travails in the county in a matter-of-fact manner, neither endorsing nor condemning his or his antagonists' positions: the important thing, it seems, is simply that this dignitary of empirewide stature was in *our* Macheng, and for so many years. This is essentially the position taken in the standard local gazetteer biography as well, first included in the "important visitors" section of the gazetteer of 1670 and reprinted in that work's successors all the way down to 1935. Li may be controversial, perhaps even blameworthy, but his presence here is evidence of our county's historical greatness.[85]

By 1935, however, this studied neutrality could not stand alone. The Republican-era gazetteer was produced, as we shall see, at the moment of greatest triumph of social conservative power in Macheng. Thus the work bears a preface by the establishment social scientist Meng Guangpeng in which Li Zhi is explicitly identified with the kind of breakdown of social discipline that underlay both the late-Ming rebellions and the Communist insurgency of Meng's own day. The lesson of history is that such wild and perverse teachings as those purveyed by Li must be suppressed. Fortunately, Meng continues, the population of the county is deeply loyal and righteous (*zhongyi*), and consequently rose up and threw Li Zhi out, just as they have united to crush the leftist elements of today.[86] The direct counterpart of this Guomindang demonization of Li's social impact is of course the gushing praise of that impact in official and semipopular Macheng historiography during the Communist era. The fact that Li once pointed out the hypocrisy of his host Zhou Sijing—who professed public-mindedness while hoarding grain during a food shortage—is cited as an indication of Li's concern for the plight of the masses and of his social-leveling instincts. His public lectures are claimed to have opened the eyes (*xingmu*) of his socially diverse audiences, liberating them from cultural inhibitions to rebellion.[87] Li Zhi emerges in twentieth-century Macheng—as in the wider historiography—as a touchstone for each author's own political attitudes, and as an emblem, for better or worse, of social revolution.

The charge that Li Zhi fomented social breakdown was not new to the twentieth century, of course; it was already being leveled against him in the seventeenth. No less influential a conservative voice than Gu Yanwu, for example, directly linked Li's mad (*kuang*) ideas with the cataclysm that followed. "What was most despicable," Gu wrote, "was Li's outrageous conduct at Macheng, hanging out in a Buddhist temple with a crowd of worthless drifters, and enticing daughters of the gentry into his chambers to hear lectures on the *dharma*, playfully dressing them up as Guanyin, and luring them into his bed. His young followers imitated their master in this dissolute behavior, thumbing their noses at Confucian familial norms [*Kongzi jiafa*]. Thank goodness some upright local people threw him out of the county and burned down his temple!"[88]

Li's attackers notably included partisans of the Donglin movement. As Jin Jiang has pointed out, two of the most stringent critics of Li's Macheng performance, the author of the *Cangshu* rebuttal Cai Yizhong and the censor Zhang Wenda, would both become fervent Donglin partisans in the years to come.[89] But factional alliances in the late Ming were never very simple. Also among the Donglin party, as we shall see, would be Mei Guozhen's nephew Mei Zhihuan, who as a youth idolized Li Zhi and throughout his life remained devoted to his memory. And among the staunchest partisans of the Donglin's successor movement in the Ming's last decades, the Fushe, would be Macheng literati like Liu Tong, who were deeply proud of Li's presence in their county. What united Li Zhi, Mei Guozhen and his nephew Zhihuan, and Liu Tong, at least in part, was an ideal of personal heroism that each in his own way sought to act out.[90]

The role of the Mei lineage, indeed, seems to becloud any presumed direct link between Li Zhi and the social revolution that would begin to appear some two decades after his death. The Mei, as it happened, were among the largest serf-holders in all of the empire. Mei Guozhen was very far from a social liberal, and his nephew Zhihuan would emerge as the single fiercest enforcer of social discipline in the county in the final decades of the Ming; yet they both treasured their association with Li Zhi, and he happily accepted their hospitality and protection. Though criticisms of literati-landlord hypocrisy and self-interest certainly abound in Li's works, there seems very little in his Macheng writings suggesting any awareness at all of the enormous agrarian underclass of the county, still less any attempt to incite them to rebellion.

Yet Li Zhi did spend all those years in this relatively remote county, and very active and vocal years they were. And the massive carnage that erupted in the last years of the Ming dynasty did break out earlier in Macheng than any other locality in the empire—indeed, on the very estates of the Mei lineage. What Li indisputably did contribute to in the Dabie Shan was the deepening fissures *within* local elite society, breakdowns of solidarity visible to those below who wished to bring about that society's destruction.

In the Tiger's Mouth

> In Macheng, the people's lives [*minsheng*] show extremes neither of gentility [*gui*] nor servility [*jian*].
>
> Mei Guozhen, 1602[1]

> Hubei has more bondservants [*puli*] than any other region of the empire, and Macheng has more than any other place in Hubei. The great families of Mei, Liu, Tian, and Li have no fewer than three to four thousand apiece.
>
> Wu Weiye, 1652[2]

THE GLORIOUS literati culture and society of late Ming Macheng was, in a sense, built upon a lie. In the representation offered to the throne by Mei Guozhen, cited above, all local people (*min*) had equal access to education, and it was the sorting process, based on academic talent, that determined whether the individual became a scholar-official, a functionally literate clerk, or a largely illiterate agricultural worker. In this mythic world, those who fell behind in the scholarly sweepstakes were treated with "compassion and respect" and kept "warm and well fed" by their more successful neighbors; they "shared prosperity as well as adversity" with those whose literary achievement allowed them to accumulate landed property.[3] But, as the chronicler Wu Weiye pointed out, in a post-holocaust critique of this lost world of genteel privilege, truly enormous numbers of Macheng's late-Ming population actually experienced no such chance for advancement nor fraternity with the grand literati whom they served and fed, and who were effectively their owners. Instead, they were subject to institutionalized physical restraint on their pursuit of opportunity and to routinized status debasement and personal humiliation.[4] They had, in practice, been defined out of the category of "the people." The growing resentment and savagely violent response of this servile underclass would ultimately not only bring down the Ming ruling house but also forever strip Macheng of the national prominence it momentarily enjoyed in the antebellum era.

Bondage

The vocabulary of agrarian servitude employed in Macheng admittedly allows some ambiguity regarding the exact status of many individual farm workers. The ubiquitous term *pu* (servant or slave), though always disparaging, almost certainly refers in some usages to persons who enjoyed relative legal freedom as well as to those who did not. The term *dianpu* is yet more vexing, combining as it does the elements of (free) "tenant" and "servant."[5] *Tongpu*, combining elements of "child" and "servant," when used of adults, would seem clearly to emphasize the aspect of personal dependency on the master. The terms *nupu* (slave) and *shipu* (hereditary servant) seem still more unambiguous about the unfree status of the person whom they describe; moreover, they appear with such frequency in local sources as to suggest that the simple unqualified *pu* is, in the majority of cases, used as a shorthand version of one of these.

The single most revealing statement on servility in Macheng—a statement regularly cited both by later local sources and by modern social historians—comes in the 1670 county gazetteer. It reads:

> Agricultural work here is all done by tenants [*dianmin*]. The great households [*dahu*] employ mostly servants purchased for cash [*jiamai pu*] to till their lands. As these servants grow up and have sons and grandsons, the latter come to be considered "hereditary servants" [*shipu*].[6]

The key elements of marketable chattel status and inherited servitude are here clearly stated, and there is nothing in other local sources to suggest that this description is invalid or exaggerated. As the statement also suggests, free tenancy existed alongside servitude. Servitude, it seems, was most concentrated on the lands of the elite lineages and in the county's core areas, where, as Wu Weiye reported, families like the Mei and the Liu each owned bondservants numbering in the thousands. In these areas, rural villages were often entirely composed of such persons.[7] While there is clear evidence that servitude existed as well in the Dongshan and other peripheries, it was somewhat less pervasive there.[8]

As many scholars have shown, agrarian bondservants were a phenomenon of the late-imperial era, common to many areas of China.[9] They were most concentrated in a number of discrete local systems: Huizhou, Ningguo, and Chizhou Prefectures in Anhui, Nanyang, and Runing Prefectures in southern Henan, Hanchuan County in Hubei, Leiyang County in Hunan, Taihe County in Jiangxi, Taicang County in Jiangnan, Nanhai County in Guangdong, and various localities of Fujian. The details of the particular servile arrangements varied, and Ye Xian'en has argued convincingly that, as a formalized and contractualized institution, it was in Wan'nan, southern Anhui, that the *nupu* system was "most developed."[10] But there is likewise no reason to disbelieve Wu Weiye's testimony that, in terms of percentage of the overall population affected and of total bondservant holdings of individual masters, no locality of the empire could match Macheng County itself.

Servile status and dependency had of course been a familiar phenomenon throughout earlier Chinese history and, as we have seen, was a special social irritant in some parts of China (though not Macheng) under the Yuan. However, most scholars agree that the widespread employment of unfree labor in agriculture of the *nupu* or *dianpu* variety was a specific phenomenon of the mid- to late-Ming period, an element of what Fu Yiling called the "refeudalization of the countryside" during that era.[11] Large landholders of Macheng's central plain, such as Huang Juan, acknowledged farming their lands by means of *nupu* labor at least as early as the first half of the sixteenth century.[12]

What brought this about, and why was it so much more evident in some localities than in others? Fu, along with such Japanese scholars as Oyama Masaaki, Yasuno Shōzō, and Satō Fumitoshi, suggests that the rise in agrarian bondservice was a means of invoking extraeconomic compulsions to keep labor "down on the farm" in an economy that was rapidly opening up new avenues of employment outside of agriculture. As such, it was especially turned to by planters who viewed that labor as most profitable to themselves—those who simultaneously were engaged in the accumulation of large rural landholdings, were involved in commercialized agriculture (particularly of rice), and actually lived in the countryside and played at least some role in the management of their own estates. There also seems to be a clear connection between those areas of greatest bondservant presence and those of remarkable examination success and high official service. Possession of *nupu* was formally prohibited after 1397 to anyone below the third rank of the bureaucracy;[13] and, though this particular prohibition proved largely unenforceable in the fifteenth through seventeenth centuries, many or most of the sub rosa arrangements that consigned agrarian workers to unfree status were sufficiently illegitimate that enjoyment of high official status was a great help in getting away with them. Bondservice also seems to have been most prevalent in areas of highly formalized lineage organization. Indeed, Ye Xian'en, on the basis of his study of Huizhou, posits a rather direct line of causality linking (1) profits from commercialized agriculture and participation in trade, (2) attainment of examination degrees and official rank, (3) a literati culture of self-conscious Cheng-Zhu *lixue* orthodoxy, (4) fetishistic attachment to the hoary notion of *zongfa* (core-line principle) and construction of powerful and ritually heavy lineage organizations, and, finally, (5) large concentrations of bondservants.[14] By all of these indices—commerce, office holding, and lineage development, as well as the accessibility of alternative off-farm employment in the booming entrepôt of Wuhan—the exceptional prevalence of agrarian servitude in mid- to late-Ming Macheng begins to make sense.

Fortunately, Jin Changzhen, prefect of Runing (Henan) in the 1650s, left us a detailed analysis of the actual mechanisms of descent into servitude as they operated in Guangshan County, directly adjacent to Macheng.[15] Jin identified four distinct paths. One of these was coercion (*qiangzhan*). In the highland peripheries of Guangshan, Prefect Jin noted, there were numerous petty strongmen (*tuhao*) who intimidated their neighbors by means of the armies of familyless goons they had impressed into their service. Similar strongmen and similar goons existed throughout Macheng's own peripheries, in the Dabie Shan highlands it shared with Guangshan, and even more evidently in the Dongshan. Though these hooligans did occupy a fairly abject servile and dependent status with respect to their *tuhao* master, in many cases they had been voluntarily attracted to this service, and they not infrequently broke away as they pleased. In such cases, they were even more of a menace to public order. Jin Changzhen observed that this variety of rural servitude was patently illegal, and he vowed to put an end to it. He could not have been very successful. Such martial clientage was, in fact, not a phenomenon of the late Ming per se; rather, it was always endemic to these areas. The region's various militia mobilizations throughout the Qing, and the Red Spear organizations of the early twentieth century, clearly traced their roots, in part, to this phenomenon.

The second path to servility identified by Jin—commendation (*touxian* or *toukao*)—was both more specifically a product of the times and more a phenomenon of the prosperous county cores. Among the great office-holding lineages (*shihuan zhi jia*) of the area, the number of agrarian bondservants had shot up over the past decades "like a forest." Most of these small cultivators had voluntarily sold themselves into servitude (*zimai* or *maishen*) or had married a bondservant and accepted the same unfree condition in the process. This status was then passed down to their posterity. We noted in chapter 4 the alarming trend of commendation of land title by persons unable to meet their tax or corvée obligations in Macheng, a trend that already in the 1570s had precipitated the controversial cadastral survey of magistrate Mu Wei; frequently (though not always) such a transaction involved commendation of the cultivator's person as well.[16] In other cases, personal commendation was independent of any transfer of land. For example, because gravesites were an increasingly scarce resource, an immiserated cultivator household might voluntarily opt for servitude in exchange for the right of burial in the master's lineage cemetery; sometimes (but, again, not always) acceptance of the master's surname occurred along with this agreement.[17] Though I have not seen specific evidence of it in Macheng, Wei Qingyuan finds that by the seventeenth century personal commendation had become such a pervasive phenomenon that professional brokers and markets (*renshi*) sprang into existence to facilitate the process.[18] Prefect Jin interestingly notes that "commended" bondservants, like the "coerced" bondservants of the periphery, are not in every case passive victims. Some have adopted this tactic in order to escape a different and less liberal master to whom they were already indentured, and others have used this ploy to gain the additional leverage of their master's name for use in litigation or other conflicts with their peers. Yet Jin concludes that this form of bondservice is in most cases spawned out of economic necessity and, while a regrettable product in some cases of inept government policies, cannot be considered illegal.[19]

In this, commendation is distinguished from the third and fourth paths to servitude, the legality of which are debatable, and the clarification (*qingyan*) of which are Prefect Jin's major goal. The two categories were that of hired farm laborers and that of tenants. Neither group had contracted itself into a status of personal dependency, but their masters, over time and in practice, had nevertheless reduced both to an unfree and servile status. In the first category, that of the farm laborers (*gugong*), Jin singled out especially the locally prevalent institution of temporary son-in-law (*nianxian nüxu*) under which a free hired worker takes up employ in the household of a master, then marries and has a child by a maidservant of that household. Jin stresses that such a man should *not* be considered equivalent to a true bondservant (*yu nupu butong*); in practice, however, when his contracted term of employment expires and he wishes to leave, he is frequently restrained from doing so, with the master claiming that the offspring of the marriage is his property. When, as often happens, the laborer leaves anyway, taking his wife and child, he is declared a runaway bondservant (*taopu*), and the mechanisms of government or vigilante justice are used to hunt him down. The employer may choose to settle for a cash ransom to allow the laborer and his family their freedom, or he may forcibly recover the laborer's wife and child and sell them to another. In the second category, that of tenants, Jin reserves his greatest indignation for the institution of *dianpu*, or "tenant-serf," which, he insists, is a patent contradiction in terms. Such individuals are locally made to perform extracontractual and uncompensated menial duties, and their female dependents are commanded to come to the master's house to provide various (sexual?) services. Sometimes when the head of a *dianpu* household dies, his household assets are expropriated, and his dependents are sold off rather than, as is proper, allowed to return to the wife's natal family. Jin is especially offended by cases in which the master and the tenant are members of the same lineage. Locally, in defiance of the statutory provisions that kindred tenants should be treated with still greater empathy than unrelated ones, kinship is used as an excuse to debase the tenant and his household into the status of slaves (*nuli*).

Finally, in a statement that sounds remarkably like an expression of natural-rights theory, Prefect Jin concludes his analysis by arguing that all individuals who have not voluntarily and expressly contracted themselves *in writing* into personal servitude should be deemed individuals of full competence (*liyi zhi ren*) and should not be reduced to the status of chattel slavery (*zanghuo*). To reduce their status in this way is a violation of dynastic law (*lüli*), of Confucian precepts of interpersonal relations (*lunchang*), and, moreover, of basic human decency (*renqing*).

Jin Changzhen's fulminations notwithstanding, bondervice remained a basic fact of life in Macheng, as it also did in Jin's own jurisdiction, on the opposite slope of the Dabie Shan. There is evidence, as we shall see, that it continued in disguised form well into the twentieth century, despite the well-known efforts of the Yongzheng emperor in the 1720s and 1730s to impose on it just such narrow restrictions as Jin himself sought to do in the 1650s.[20] The persistent efforts of Macheng elites to maintain the social order by a never-ending campaign of instructing and civilizing (*jiaiohua*), a project as active in the 1930s as in the Ming, seldom spoke frankly about bondservants, but such persons were the campaigns' chief intended targets. Persons of servile status were expected above all to be content with their fate (*anfen*), and those who were not were violently disciplined.

Mei Zhihuan and the Donglin Movement in Macheng

Mei Zhihuan (1575–1641) was by all accounts an extraordinary person, a figure much larger than life, and possibly the single most influential man in Macheng history.[21] Nephew of the eminent Mei Guozhen and scion of the county's grandest serfholding lineage, Zhihuan was born near the ancestral home of Seven Mile Ridge, in the suburbs of the county seat. As a young boy, he startled his friends by jumping off a high cliff into Li Zhi's Dragon Lake. But when he was nine his father, Guosen, died, and he moved with his mother to her nearby natal village of Shenzhuang. There the boy became known as a reckless and gifted horseman and archer, repeatedly alarming his elders by galloping though the streets and showing off his prowess with the bow. At the age of thirteen he rode presumptuously into the midst of the county military examination, and when the irate examiner asked him what *he* could do with a bow, he reportedly put nine successive arrows in the bull's-eye and spurred his horse away. But Zhihuan was also given to intense and hermetic classical study, an inclination that allowed him to pass, precociously, the *shengyuan* exam that same year. He received his *jinshi* in 1604 and was appointed to the Hanlin Academy, where he remained for seven years.

In the words of the local historian Wang Baoxin, Zhihuan exemplified the cultural type of heroic, martial masculinity associated empirewide with the men of Hubei (*Jing-Qu yinghao*). He was uncompromisingly loyal and sincere to the extreme (*zhicheng*), but this sincerity was also manifested in a free and easy (*titang*) spirit—relaxed, unpretentious, openhanded, and, in a sense, populist. He was famous for inviting visitors and even passers-by into his home, killing a chicken for dinner, and entreating them, with deliberate disdain for hierarchical seating arrangements, to join him wherever they chose at his table. Mei loved to laugh, and his own writings, even in crisis situations, often display a genuine ironic humor.[22] He gave liberally to the poor. In his youth, Mei had been close to Li Zhi (he remained loyal to the latter's memory long after Li's death in disgrace) and was a lifelong intimate of Li's Buddhist drinking companion Wunian.[23] He regularly engaged in meditative "quiet sitting," in the fashion of Wang Yangming. And Mei was a prolific poet, of a romantic, soul-searching bent. His biographer Wan Yanqi extolled his poetry as "the most beautiful of any in the empire" for avoiding the surface elegance favored by contemporary poseurs and for cutting directly to the practical (*shijian*) essence of what he had to say.

At the same time, Mei Zhihuan was a man of steely resolve in defense of the causes he embraced: the social and moral order, the well-being of his friends, the security of his home locality, and the survival of the Ming dynasty. In a revealing poem, he reflected very candidly on the problem of violence, arguing that, contrary to what many seem to think, "administering beatings is part of the expression of imperial grace, and so too is killing. If one is unwilling to kill or even to beat other people, how can one ever consider oneself up to the charge of protecting the realm?"[24] He backed up this defense of state violence in his conduct of office, at one point shocking his superiors by summarily beheading some 840 surrendered rebels.[25]

Zhihuan's official career included stints as lieutenant governor of Guangdong, educational commissioner of Shandong, governor of Nan-Gan (southern Jiangxi), and governor of Gansu, with an eventual promotion to the vice-presidency of the board of war. Like his uncle Mei Guozhen, he became something of a specialist in the frontier defense of the beleaguered Ming empire and won many notable victories, including several over the growing power of the Qing regime. Both during his lifetime and after his death, he received handsome honors from the grateful Ming house. But in the increasingly factionalized world of the late-Ming bureaucracy, Mei also came under repeated attacks, which were by no means blunted by his outspokenness and his fierce defense of his own factional allies. From the moment he received his first substantive post, as supervising censor of the board of civil office in 1611, Mei proved an unrelenting critic of official corruption and court extravagance, and as early as his first provincial appointment in Guangdong he attacked the eunuch superintendent of maritime trade, Li Ling, for his extortionate persecution of merchants.

Some time in the 1610s, Mei Zhihuan became affiliated with the strident political reform movement that grew out of the Donglin Academy (founded in 1604 in Jiangsu's Wuxi County) and with the network of largely Jiangnan literati who comprised the movement's core.[26] In particular, it seems, there was a textual basis for this bond in their mutual attachment to the classic *Chunqiu* (*Spring and Autumn Annals*). Macheng native Li Changgeng observed that study of the *Chunqiu* had "always been a specialty" of his home county,[27] and Mei himself wrote as follows:

> Our humble county of Macheng is nestled like the palm of a hand amidst ten thousand mountains. And yet, since the rise of the Ming, it has become a center of leisurely retreat for specialists in the *Unicorn Classic*.[28] Over the past decade, men from such families as the Zhou, the Geng, the Tian, the Li, and my own Mei have achieved higher-level degrees and set out on careers far and wide. Experts on the *Spring and Autumn Annals*, whom they have encountered along the way, have in turn converged on our humble county.[29]

There was a great vogue of attachment to the *Spring and Autumn Annals* in the 1610s and 1620s, and, as Mei suggests Macheng was at its center. More specifically yet, there was an affection for the controversial interpretation of the classic proffered in the commentary by the Southern Song neo-Confucian Hu Anguo (1073–1138). The relevance of Hu's text to the late Ming is obvious, stressing as it did the urgent need for political reform in face of the northern "barbarian" threat and for moral regeneration along the lines of "the values encoded in the *Annals*."[30] It was a particular favorite of hardliner specialists on issues of frontier defense, a group that included Mei Zhihuan, Li Changgeng, and many other officials of Macheng birth.

Foremost among the *Spring and Autumn* "experts" of whom Mei spoke was the brilliant Suzhou short-story writer Feng Menglong (1574–1646), who spent several months in Macheng in 1620. The direct invitation was issued to Feng by Chen Wuyi, a Macheng native then serving as Suzhou prefect, and Feng's living expenses while in the county were largely borne by the fabulously wealthy Tian lineage, for whose sons Feng served as tutor. But the driving force was clearly Mei Zhihuan. At Macheng, Feng came under the residual influence of the county's infamous sojourner of several decades past, Li Zhi, and met with Li's friends Yuan Zhongdao and Yang Dingjian (Feng had already assisted the latter in securing a Suzhou publisher for Li's edition of *Water Margin*) as well as with Mei Zhihuan himself; in the words of one of Feng's biographers, his Macheng sojourn was a watershed moment in the forty-six-year-old writer's career.[31]

Under Mei Zhihuan's patronage, Feng Menglong convened at Macheng a literary society (*wenshe*) dedicated to explicating the *Spring and Autumn Annals*, a group that at its height attracted some 88 men. When Feng was set to depart for home and the group to disband, they collectively published their proceedings under Feng's editorship, with a lead preface by Mei Zhihuan. The work, titled *Linjing zhiyue* (A monthly guide to the *Unicorn Classic*) is enormous, running, in a modern edition, to over 1,300 pages. One of its features is a list of contributing readers (*canyue*), who, one supposes, comprise members of the study society and selected others invited to help promote the work or subvene its publication.[32] There are precisely 100 such "readers," plus two of Feng's brothers and a cousin listed after them. It is a very interesting roster. No fewer than forty-one of the 100 list Macheng as their native place, and another ten list Huang'an. This was not really a regional product, however, for very few of the remaining forty-nine readers were from Hubei, most instead hailing from Jiangnan or elsewhere in the southeast. (One of the most identifiable of these is Hanlin senior compiler Wen Zhenmeng, a Donglin partisan who was cashiered two years later for a scathing remonstrance of Tianqi.[33]) The Macheng natives included Mei Zhihuan, his cousin Zhiyuan, his uncle Guolou, and seven other kinsmen, plus several members each of the Tian, Liu, Zhou, and Li lineages—the county's superelite. (Li Changgeng, for some reason, is not among them, but the family is represented by his brother Changnian.) As evidence that old wounds stemming from the Li Zhi case had healed over in the face of worsening dynastic crisis, seven of the Huang'an representatives were from the lineage of Geng Dingxiang.[34] The list is a remarkable testament to how a "study society" dedicated to reading a hoary classic in a contemporary light might serve to establish a county-level elite solidarity, transcending lineage particularisms, and at the same time link this remote locality's most powerful and politically engaged men with those of more cosmopolitan regions. As Mei Zhihuan boasted in his preface, "We have assembled here most of the leading *Spring and Autumn* scholars from throughout the empire."

Mei goes on to betray a particular political motive for the book's publication. Mastery (*zhi*) of the *Spring and Autumn* is a painfully laborious task, he notes, by comparison to the study of its gloss, the *Zuo zhuan* (Zuo chronicle), which many men can claim. Those who have achieved this mastery, he says—members of our group, and above all Feng Menglong himself—deserve consideration for the highest official posts. (Despite his renown as a leading classical scholar, Feng had never passed a higher-level examination and hence, to the chagrin of many reformers, had never been granted bureaucratic office.) Fortunately, Mei continues, the throne is now occupied by a new Son of Heaven (*xin tianzi*), who, we are confident, will recognize his duty to appoint new officials of true merit (*gongling*) and, by this means, bring about a restoration (*zhongxing*) of the flagging Ming dynastic fortunes. The book, then, is a manifesto by 100 Donglin sympathizers, in Jiangnan and Macheng, intended for the newly enthroned Taichang emperor, who, it is hoped, will reverse the decline of the long, painful reign of his father, Wanli, and throw the bastards out of the palace. Mei dates his preface "ninth month of the first year of Taichang."[35]

There is a poignant irony here, however, in that there never was such a date. The thirty-eight-year-old eldest son of the Wanli emperor, Zhu Changluo, whose reign title was Taichang, and whose succession had been vociferously championed by the Donglin party, had indeed, on assuming the throne, moved quickly to appoint "new officials of true merit." But Taichang had died—presumably he was murdered by his doctors, under orders from the eunuch faction—on September 26, 1620, less than a month after his inauguration. Very probably he was already dead when Mei Zhihuan wrote his hopeful preface. Mei in fact wrote in what was still formally the forty-eighth year of the Wanli reign, and the following new year would be the first in the reign of the emperor Tianqi (1620–27), who would prove a gruesomely violent foe of the Donglin faction.[36]

One of the earliest and most celebrated victims of Tianqi's Donglin purges was another Hubei native, from Yingshan County, Yang Lian (1571–1625). In the relatively lowly palace post of supervising secretary, Yang had been present at Taichang's deathbed and had submitted a bold memorial that was critical of the way the succession crisis had been handled. He then retired to his native county, dedicating himself to the memory of Taichang and to the task of ridding his successor, Tianqi, of the nefarious influence of Wei Zhongxian and his eunuch cronies. Recalled to duty in 1622 and promoted to vice-censor-in-chief two years later, Yang almost immediately submitted his famous "Twenty-Four Crimes" memorial, demanding the ouster and punishment of Wei. Yang was courting martyrdom, and he knew it. Retiring again to Yingshan, at the end of 1624, he was arrested by palace guards on a trumped-up bribery charge at his home the following May, an act that provoked a popular uprising in that county and other uprisings in Henan along Yang's route to Beijing. Once at the capital, Yang was brutally tortured for several weeks and was secretly murdered in his jail cell on August 26.[37]

Mei Zhihuan counted Yang Lian, whom he referred to affectionately as "the tiger," among his most intimate "friends"—a heroic construct of masculine bonding that had special emotional power in the politically troubled late-Ming era.[38] The two men had been *tongnian*—fellow successful candidates—in the Hubei provincial examination of 1603. Mei had returned home to Macheng in mourning for his mother in 1623, and he was still at home two years later, when Yang was arrested and sympathetic disturbances broke out throughout the central highlands region. Imperial suspicions were raised by Mei's close ties to Yang and, despite Mei's proud military record in dynastic service, he was summoned to Wuchang for questioning about his complicity in the rebellions. Mei was cleared on this count and shortly returned to duty on the frontier, but he knew that the days of his official service were numbered.[39]

Among Mei's special friends was the aesthete and intellectual Qian Qianyi

(1582–1664); Mei playfully referred to Qian as the "dragon" (and to Yang Lian as the "tiger"). Frederic Wakeman describes Qian as "the most brilliant literary critic and one of the greatest poets of his generation." In his native Jiangnan, Qian became patron of a group of talented young poets, female and male alike, and he married one of the era's most famous courtesans, Liu Rushi. Politically, he was something of a chameleon, and he eventually earned widespread contempt for negotiating the surrender of Nanjing to Qing forces in 1646. In the 1620s, however, Qian was an ally (though not formally a member) of the Donglin reformist faction. He was one of the Jiangnan "readers" who affixed their names to the Feng Menglong/Mei Zhihuan *Spring and Autumn* commentary of 1620, and he was a vocal critic of the Donglin nemesis, Wei Zhongxian. In 1628, this criticism landed Qian in prison, impeached by Wen Tiren, president of the board of rites; Mei Zhihuan took the lead in the campaign to have Qian released, an act that earned Mei the enmity of Wen and led in part to his own dismissal from office five years later. Eventually, the grateful Qian turned his gifts to an affectionate posthumous biography of Mei, penned on the very eve of the fall of Beijing, in 1644.[40]

The politically volatile links among Macheng, Feng Menglong, the Donglin faction, and the *Spring and Autumn Annals* were kept alive by Mei's affinal cousin (Mei Guozhen's son-in-law), Li Changgeng (*jinshi* 1595).[41] A Hanlin academician and noted expert on the *Annals* himself, Li had served as Shandong governor and in other provincial posts throughout the later Wanli and Tianqi reigns, gaining wide respect for his skills in such practical statecraft matters as tax collection, currency management, famine relief, and military logistics on the northern frontiers. But he also made himself a pest by his repeated impeachments of corrupt behavior on the part of court favorites and by his noisy advocacy of the interests of taxpaying households, both of which activities led to his periodic removal from office. He took advantage of one such forced retirement to work closely with Feng on the manuscript of the latter's definitive commentary on the classic *Chunqiu hengku* (An expansive treasury on the *Spring and Autumn Annals*), published in 1625 with Li Changgeng's preface.

The death of the Tianqi emperor and the installation of his reform-minded successor, Chongzhen, in 1628, brought Li back to metropolitan office; he held, in quick succession, presidencies of the boards of punishments, revenue, works, and civil office and ultimately was appointed a grand secretary. In these posts he worked tirelessly to rehabilitate and restore to office many degraded officials (*shidong xueji*), victims of the factional strife of the preceding two reigns. He did so in a way that one local historian charitably describes as "favoring men whom he deeply trusted because they were from his own native area." Li would also seem to have played a role in the final triumph of Feng Menglong, who, despite his lack of a higher-level examination degree, received his first official appointment by special imperial decree in 1631. Around 1635, however, Li Changgeng's perceived "faction building" cost him his support at court, and he retired to his native county, where he assisted Mei Zhihuan in defense of home, dynasty, and civilization. It was an awesome task.[42]

Bondservant Rebellion

The second quarter of the seventeenth century—the very time when Macheng, like all of the empire, was undergoing the traumatic passage from Ming to Qing—saw the contradictions inherent in the bondservant system erupt in the most cataclysmic way. It would be wrong to view bondservants and their masters in Macheng as in a constant state of battle; for example, persons of servile status were routinely and successfully drawn upon by local elites to fight in the various and bloody local defense efforts that punctuate local history, including those of the late Ming and early Qing. But it is also clear that there was a persistent undercurrent of conscious bondservant solidarity and resentment, and that it reached a boiling point in the era of dynastic transition.

In the context both of the erosion of the social controls of the Ming *lijia* system and of the intensifying marketization and monetization of the economy, a growing movement spread throughout the Middle and Lower Yangzi regions for bondservants to resist service obligations imposed on them and to destroy their contracts of servitude. Those servile tenants who had managed to do well in commercialized agriculture, in Macheng and elsewhere, demanded in specific the opportunity to redeem their freedom by cash payments to their master (*shupu*).[43] The perennial problem of bondservant flight was worsening day by day. Taking light of this situation, some Macheng landlords sought to free themselves of the problem altogether by manumitting their *nupu*: on the occasion of his sixtieth birthday, for instance, the *shengyuan* Bao Shifa gathered together all his bondservants, ceremoniously set fire to their contracts of indenture, and presented each of them with a plot of land.[44] But *nupu* resentment continued to grow, and with it the threat of violence. Already in the very first years of the century, the magistrate Liu Wenqi had been called upon to put down a small yet deeply troubling movement of rebellious servants (*panpu*), and a decade later his successor Song Yilin did the same.[45] As the chronicler Wu Weiye described the situation in Macheng of the 1620s, "the bondservants swaggered about the villages, stealing and plundering what they pleased. They spouted an ideology of equality [with their masters] [*siqi*] and organized into tight little bands [*chiwu*] to pursue their own interests."[46] The crisis was nearly at hand.

Harvest failure and the utter collapse of both state and private famine-relief mechanisms provided the context: Macheng experienced unusually great flooding in 1628, followed by drought and severe famine the following year. During the winter of 1630, a rumor swept through the county that a dynastic or world-era change had occurred, and that the new ruler had issued an edict that all bondservants be allowed to redeem their freedom. One night toward the close of the year, a large number of the *nupu* of various prominent landholders assembled at a sectarian temple-cum-training camp, hoisted a red banner emblazoned with the slogan "Ten thousand men of a single will" (*wanren yixin*), and, armed with swords and knives, set off to enforce their demands on their masters. Apparently, they had no connection to any extralocal rebel movement, and were thus left to rely upon their own strength, which quickly proved inadequate. The Macheng magistrate, a newly arrived, no-nonsense military *jinshi* named Jiang Yu, immediately proclaimed that the rumored edict could only have come from a pretender to the throne, that service to the true emperor demanded abject obedience, and that any disloyalty to one's master was a capital offense. On these grounds, he arrested and summarily executed every participant in the uprising he could lay his hands on.[47] The 1630 rising thus quickly fizzled out. But the sentiments that had spawned it, and the organization that lay behind it, not only persisted but progressively spread to the surrounding region.[48] Indeed, in the view of the well-informed Chinese historian Fu Yiling, the events of 1630 in Macheng constituted the very first salvo of the empire-wide bondservant rebellions (*nubian*) that precipitated the fall of the Ming.[49]

Mei Zhihuan Comes Home

In 1633, Gansu governor Mei Zhihuan, caught in a flurry of charges and countercharges over blame for a military defeat in the northwest, was cashiered and returned for the final time to his native place. The eight years of Mei's retirement were perilous ones for his Macheng. As Mei himself described it, the county had "its head in the tiger's mouth."[50] It was under continual siege, for the most part by regional bandit-cum-rebel forces, led by men with such colorful noms de guerre as the Earth-Scouring King (Soudi Wang)—announcing its bearer's assumed mission as demon-exterminating savior—and the Old Muslim (Lao Huihui).[51] Although these rebel forces were mostly not indigenous to Macheng, Mei repeatedly complained that the local population was of divided loyalty (*erxin*); that the rebels, flush with cash from plunder, easily bought the allegiance of the local riffraff; and that with the approach of these daunting armies, even many good commoners (*liangmin*) ran out to greet them, shouting, "Wansui!"[52]

In 1634, a significant rebel army crossed the Yangzi from the south, spreading into Macheng. The county seat was not threatened, but there were many spirited engagements with rural militia, and a number of ambitious local strongmen in the county's various peripheries set up sympathetic regimes, calling themselves the Eight Great Kings (Badawang). The following year, 1635, was one of the bloodiest in the area's entire history—as the Huang'an County gazetteer described it, a "slaughter of tragic proportions." Just after the new year, forces under the major rebel leader Zhang Xianzhong passed through Macheng for the first time, were successfully rebuffed by Mei and Magistrate Liu Xingyao in their siege of the county seat, and proceeded to butcher the urban-commercial southwest corridor and other rural areas. In the latter part of the year, protracted combat between Ming troops and a motley array of rebel armies devastated the county's east and southeast. After a period of more modest skirmishes, massive bloodshed erupted again in 1637, when Ming general Qin Yimin conducted an extermination campaign against Lao Huihui and the Eight Great Kings, succeeding only in splintering the rebels into smaller groups that holed up in Qiting and other area strongholds. Sporadic fighting characterized the remainder of the decade, with the local civilian population the recipient of most of the violence. Finally, in 1641, Hubei governor Song Yihao organized a massive, coordinated counterinsurgency campaign, with Macheng as its epicenter. It culminated in a grand battle late that summer at the county's Dongyi Island, a glorious victory for Governor Song, and a festive beheading of some 1,200 rebels.[53]

When Mei Zhihuan returned home, he was nearly sixty; he was seen by local people as an old man and was treated initially with patronizing skepticism.[54] But in the event, he proved incredibly vigorous. The first task he undertook was to reconstruct the walls and defenses of the county seat, a task for which his long official service on the frontiers had amply prepared him. He then turned to walling and moating his own childhood village, Shenzhuang, which he dubbed the Lifesaving Fort (Husheng bao), building catapults along its ramparts to heave stones down on would-be besiegers. Mei's plan was to make Shenzhuang and Macheng City, respectively, the eastern and western poles of a countywide defense axis, which would be swept clean of rebels and used as a base for operations on the perimeters. He built a formidable personal fighting force, which he called the Shenzhuang Army, and which came to serve as the prototype for many other mountain armies (*shanbing*) throughout the central China highlands. Mei began by impressing his tenants and neighbors into a *tuanlian* militia of over 10,000 men, training them, and then adding an awesome array of mercenaries and armaments: a mobile guerrilla unit composed of vagabond delinquent youths (*wuji eshao*), a unit of crossbow archers specialized in the use of poison arrows (*yaonushou*), and a brigade of fearless Dongshan tiger hunters (*shahushou*). From the site of one of his old campaigns, Guangdong, he brought in European-made cannon (*hongyipao*) and, from another, southern Jiangxi, several hundred trained artillerymen (*congpaoshou*).

Foraying out from Shenzhuang, he captured and decapitated any suspected rebels he encountered, parading their heads around the area on pikes.[55] It rapidly became clear that Mei meant business.

Mei emerged as lord protector of the entire county. His army was credited with having saved the county seat during an attack by Lao Huihui, in early 1635. Mei himself describes the situation:

> On the second day of the second month, I rode out [from Macheng City] toward Shenzhuang. When I had got as far as Yujiagang, I turned around and saw, along the ramparts, guns and cannon densely crammed together as far as the eye could see. I was satisfied and returned to the city. The next day, several tens of thousands of rebels passed by the county seat but were afraid to approach it. Along the roads, the Shenzhaung Army could be seen everywhere. I stopped my horse and dismounted at Yulinghe, called the local womenfolk to gather around, and paused under the trees for a drink. "We have had a very close call, old friends," I said. "The rebels, for the moment, have come and gone."
>
> In the area of Baitianfan, there were several places where the passing rebels had plundered and kidnapped local people. I heard much murmuring in that area: "Let us take our dependents and withdraw to the safety of Mr. Mei's fortress at Shenzhuang." I was also told that Lao Huihui himself had jokingly complained of me, "Why must that man lure me into eating his big guns?"[56]

Reportedly *hundreds of thousands* of local people did flock to Mei's mountain stronghold for protection, and he did not refuse them. Others found their own refuges in the hills, and Mei used his forces to safeguard them as well. In one instance, colorfully recounted by Mei's biographer Wan Yanqi, the threat came not from proclaimed rebels but from renegade Ming troops. A contingent of these had seized the Jade Mist Mountain Fort belonging to the Zhou lineage, comported themselves riotously, and threatened mutiny. The rightful proprietor—a younger brother of Li Zhi's former patrons Zhou Sijing and Zhou Sijiu—locked himself up in the fortress's keep and sent word to Mei Zhihuan for help. Mei allegedly rode alone to the fort, galloped into the midst of the troops, and shouted at them derisively "as one would address a dog": "You slaves dare contemplate disobedience? I will tie you up like trussed hares!" The soldiers all cowered in awe. Mei administered beatings to the ringleaders, and the troops all went meekly back to their barracks.[57]

Mei Zhihuan's personal power was reaching truly extraordinary proportions. He continued to enjoy the declared support of most local officials, and he periodically received honors from the throne itself—promotions in grade in 1636 and 1638, and the *yin* privilege of hereditary office in 1640—for his contributions to the Ming cause. But the fact was that he was increasingly autonomous. He was popularly lauded as a Macheng local hero, and "there was no one [even in the wider region] who did not acknowledge him as their leader."[58]

His Shenzhuang fortress became, in effect, the judiciary center of the county as local people increasingly came to him rather than the magistrate's court to press their grievances. Even Mei's devoted hagiographer Qian Qianyi candidly admits that the local authorities and other elements within the local elite began to look askance (*zemu*) at his unbridled exercise of power, but none dared challenge it.[59] Besides, the alternatives were much worse.

What did Mei Zhihuan himself think of his position? Mei had long been acutely critical of the Ming regime's decadence; in a poem, written while he was on campaign on the northwest frontier, he explicitly ponders the difficulty of loyalism to an ungrateful and perhaps undeserving dynasty.[60] His *tongnian* and close friend Yang Lian had chosen the path of rebellion. Mei chose local defense of his native place. Writing upon Yang's death to his executioner, Grand Secretary Feng Quan, Mei articulated his view of the relationship of localism and loyalism: the old saying goes, he wrote, "Destroy your home in order to resolve the larger crisis" (*huijia shunan*), but I do not accept this. Relieving the local crisis contributes directly to relieving the national one. Indeed, in the saying, we should substitute "protect your home" (*baojia*) for "destroy your home." Keep the eggs intact even though the nest has been destroyed, and the nest will eventually regenerate. In the present context, when the localities remain strong while the center is weak and indecisive, the only recourse is for private individuals personally to take up arms, and for households to look to their own defense.[61]

Yet, as Mei's correspondence from the 1630s poignantly reveals, he grew increasingly frustrated at the incompetent and counterproductive assistance offered by the tottering Ming regime to his own local defense efforts.[62] Precisely because the forces of the central government have no effective overall warplan, he complains, all we can do is repeatedly drive the rebels out of our county, only to see them return from another direction. It is ever more clear, he points out, that imperial strategy, such as it is, is simply to avoid the (indefensible) Macheng like the plague (*bi Ma ru jin*). Imperial commanders haven't the slightest clue (*wufen shengfa*) about how to conduct a campaign, he charges, and increasingly, as at the Jade Mist Mountain Fort, it is their own unruly troops who have become the enemy. Officials at the southern capital of Nanjing, who should be actively coordinating the defense efforts in central China, are for the most part a bunch of effete literati, whose talents lie in the area of belles-lettres and nothing more. There *are* occasional strong and decisive Ming officials, he points out, like the Huang'an magistrate Zhao, who, with the assistance of Geng Dingxiang's descendant Geng Jiuyi, has almost singlehandedly kept that county from falling into rebel hands. Yet, as Mei himself knows, both from his official career and from his experiences here in retirement, the world is full of ineffectual bystanders who will carp about men like Zhao and Geng for the same decisive actions that have saved their own hides.[63] Mei has his personal candidate for the vacant Macheng magistracy (a current acting submagistrate), whom he lobbies to get installed by Nanjing.

In crises such as this one, Mei observes, "relying on government troops is not as good as relying on the people themselves" (*yongbing buru yongmin*), and at the moment it is increasingly "my army" (*wobing*), and that alone, on which survival depends. Zhihuan's messianic sense of personal mission to save Macheng, and hence the world, grows along with his despair regarding the Ming. "The fate of Macheng is in my hands," he declares, "and I will see it through no matter how long it takes."[64] Only my own arms, he says, remain to "prop open the tiger's jaws," keeping it from devouring the millions of souls in this county. Mei repeats with pride a statement he has heard attributed to a rebel leader: that there is only "this one Mei guy" ("Mei mou yiren") standing between themselves and victory.[65]

All the time he was fighting rebels, Mei Zhihuan was waging another campaign: to win the hearts and minds of Macheng's own people. One aspect of this effort was keeping them fed during the successive years of bad harvests in the late 1630s. The inhabitants of Mei's rapidly growing fortress at Shenzhuang were housed in temporary shelters that he had constructed, and they were sustained by grain fields, vegetable gardens, and fish hatcheries that he oversaw. Tens of thousands more county residents subsisted via a network of gruel kitchens that Mei had established at various sites.[66] He also, as already noted, took an active role as community mediator; his offices were available to all—"petty laborers, male and female peddlers, beggars," and so on—to hear and help redress their grievances against those they felt to be exploiting them.[67] There is little reason to doubt these reports of Mei's generosity and populist sense of justice, since they seem to accord with all we know of his personality. But they were only one facet of an overall program of local control that he instituted, other aspects of which could be stern and even brutal.

An element of this program was his attention to civilizing (*jiaohua*), that is, the persistent crusade of the Confucian elite for mass indoctrination in correct and deferential thought and conduct. One of Mei's biographers notes, admiringly, that the chief characteristic of all Mei's writing was a shift away from the *jiangxue* (open debates on moral and ontological issues) that had characterized the previous generation and toward a more univocal and inflexible *jiaoren* (instruction of others in how to behave). We have already observed Mei's patronage of a number of important local temples—both in his ancestral village of Seven Mile Ridge, in the central plain, and as far afield as the Dongshan highlands—all of which he dedicated to past dynastic loyalists and to martial, insurgency-suppressing deities; in one such temple, Mei installed a stele that read, "The minds of the people and the fate of the realm are inextricably linked" ("renxin guoshi you daguan").[68]

An even more basic aspect of his campaign to mobilize the populace, however, was the violent suppression of all suspected enemies within. Very quickly upon his return to his native county, in the early 1630s, Mei succeeded in putting Macheng under his own martial law. Associated with his conviction that the "minds of the people" were in fact untrustworthy was his deep-seated, at times near-paranoid, fear of spies (*jianxi*) and traitors (*neiying*). In his letters, Mei delights in recounting how he has exposed some of these. The following is typical:

> One of these traitors had formerly been an obedient bondservant on my own estate. Four years ago, he had been exposed to some rebel propaganda, on the basis of which he began to turn against me and ran away. During the third watch on an early-spring evening [in 1635], the sound of a boat was heard outside the Chaosheng Gate of the county seat. The gunners on the walls fired into the water, and the sound could be heard of the boat pulling away.
>
> The next morning, this former bondservant of mine jumped up onto the ramparts, took off his hat and plain overcoat, revealed himself to be clothed entirely in resplendent silks, and shouted to the defenders: "The rebels are coming and will take this city! Flee back to your homes!" Many in the defense force believed him. Then I spoke up myself: "What do these fine silks on this man signify? He can be no other than a high official in the rebel army! Formerly, he fled Macheng to evade punishment for his crimes, and now he returns finely decorated by the rebels. In the past he turned his back on his master's grace, and now he has returned as his master's enemy. Can you imagine greater villainy than this?"
>
> I seized him and examined his silk garments, discovering that their lower portions were all wet. Clearly, he was the man who had sneaked in aboard the boat that had approached during the night. We subjected him to torture and interrogation three or four times, and finally he confessed that he was planning to light a signal beacon for the rebels atop the rear Daozhong Gate. I then immediately decapitated him. Thus came to an end one rebel plot![69]

Instances like this one invited criticism from softhearted souls, who condemned Mei's penchant for summary execution. He in turn belittled his critics and sturdily defended those few comrades who resorted with equal readiness to capital punishment in the public interest (*binggong zhengfa*).[70]

Beyond stamping out traitors when they appeared, Mei Zhihuan had a more proactive agenda to push during his exercise of martial law.[71] It was an agenda that no doubt had been shared by many Macheng elites over many centuries, but Mei, because of the extraordinary nature of the times and of his power, was in a rare position to pursue it. Shortly after his return home, Mei announced his intention to rectify the three great evils (*sandahai*) that were besetting not only Macheng but the empire as a whole, and that underlay the large-scale rebel movements then "devastating all the world." The three were marauding bandits (*taozei*), verminous government clerks (*yadu*), and uppity bondservants (*shipu*).

Mei described the first of these groups as "mean people" who inhabited the Macheng high country and who banded together for raids of the lowland. Officials and local elites had for decades allowed them to run rampant. The way to root them out, Mei said, was to go after their usual safe havens—in a modern-sounding rhetorical flourish, cleansing (*xidi*) the countryside. Any individual found guilty of brigandage, and anyone who had sheltered or failed to report him, would have to be made to fear the law (*weifa*). Mei launched his own dragnet operation, sending his handpicked troops into the hills to apprehend a few well-known bandits, and interrogated them under torture about any prominent family that might be serving as their protector. He then went after these families. He released the bandits themselves on their promise that they would mend their ways; those who failed to do so were recaptured, and their feet cut off.

While it is not surprising to find a member of the elite, one with strong localist leanings, fulminating against intrusive government clerks, it is nevertheless curious to find Mei including them as one of the three targets of his cleanup campaign in a time of dynastic upheaval; it seems clear that they are a target of opportunity. Mei insisted that the Macheng population was most adept at managing its own affairs, via lineages and other types of social organizations, and yet in Macheng City there were no fewer than 4,000 underlings in the service of the magistrate alone, not to speak of the hundreds of others employed by the county director of studies and other local functionaries. Nearly every one of them, according to Mei, was corrupt. This overblown workforce, he said, had to be immediately purged (*tai*) or cleansed (*xi*), and he beseeched the incumbent magistrate to do so at once. But, Mei said, one of the most nefarious ways in which these villains worked was in directly infiltrating and manipulating the service staffs of the county's great families. Mei thus resolved to conduct a purge of his own lineage's households and to root out and dismiss any bondservant who was moonlighting as, married to, or in collusion with a *yamen* underling. Other lineage leaders had to do the same, he stated; any villager who felt exploited by a government clerk was to come to him personally for redress.

Finally, the bondservants themselves. Over the years, Mei said, too many Macheng masters (*zhuren*) had become complacent or inattentive to what their bondservants were doing, and the latter had become arrogant and presumptuous. Such servants were now not only more pervasive and vexatious than the brigands or *yamen* vermin, they were also, in many cases, actually the *source* of the other groups. Mei provided a detailed catalogue of the kinds of ways in which "uppity bondservants" operated, among them manipulation of hydraulic repair projects and of the criminal justice system for their own profit. Worst of all, Mei charged, they had effectively isolated the masters from the bulk of their servile workforce and had become, in practice, the masters themselves. When Mei Zhihuan spoke of this evil, his "whiskers bristled" in anger and resolve. I take it as my own personal mission (*yisheng renzhi*), he said, to put these cruel and crafty slaves (*jiexia nu*) in their place. As we shall see in the following chapter, his success was far from complete. But one can only imagine the gloves-off way in which Mei went about his task.

Mei's rhetoric throughout his stand at Macheng emphasizes the totality of the life-or-death struggle that he saw himself engaged in. The rebels, in his view, were not only engaged in destroying civilization and desecrating the Heaven-imposed order (*fanzheng tiandao shenming*) but were also bent on "annihilating us to the last man" (*gege shajin*). If we allow the county to fall, he said, "its streets will overflow with blood" (*mancheng liuxue*). The forces of evil had already committed unspeakable atrocities (*pocan burenyan*) in nearby places, and, Mei warned, they intended similar genocidal slaughter (*tujin*) right in Macheng.[72] Under such conditions, the most pitiless "cleansing" of the population was not only justified, it was demanded. The resonance of this Manichaean rhetoric with that of the fourteenth century, as well as with that of the nineteenth and twentieth, is striking, and the predictability of its recurrence in this one troubled locality no less than chilling.

Fortification

It is a truism of Chinese history that administrative cities were walled and defensible, whereas the surrounding villages and towns were unfortified and thus indefensible. In times of crisis, people and valuables were to be withdrawn to the county seat and a stand made there, with the countryside left to the predators.[73] We have seen how, in Macheng, Mei Zhihuan's first initiative, in 1633–35, was to fortify the county seat and vigorously defend it from the ramparts. But his parallel efforts at walling, moating, and arming the hillside village of Shenzhuang—his creation of the Lifesaving Fort—were more indicative of how local defense actually was conducted in the history of the Dabie Shan. Throughout this highland region, in times of crisis rural landholders, and often even urban elites, characteristically took to the hills (*rushan*), built mountain fortresses (*zhai* or *bao*), and established themselves there as mountain lords (*shanzhu*), hunkering down until the time was ripe for them once again to descend. As we shall see, it was not at all unusual to concede a walled city to the attackers and then besiege the rebels there from a mountain fortress base.

Fortified villages were also to be found in other parts of the empire; Elizabeth Perry, for example, has vividly described the existence of over 600 so-called polder forts (*yuzhai*) in the Huaibei floodplain at least as early as the middle of the nineteenth century.[74] But though these other rural forts, and perhaps especially those of Huaibei, might be at times functionally similar to those of Macheng and the wider Dabie Shan, the latter were distinctively mountain fortresses (*shanzhai*) and as such had a special history and mystique all their own.

In Macheng today there are ruins of two forts, the Hongmiao zhai and the Tucheng zhai, said to date as far back as the Western Zhou dynasty (ca. 1000 BCE). Historical evidence of fort-related activity, however, begins in the middle of the imperial era. The Huangchao zhai, southeast of Yanjiahe, was built by local residents to defend themselves against the Huang Chao rebellion in the late ninth century CE. The Shizi shanzhai, in the Dongshan, which survives to this day, was originally constructed to house the local administration after rebels had captured the county seat in 1234–36. Other mountain fortresses were built by Song loyalist elites to resist the Mongol conquest in the late 1270s and were then in turn occupied by the Yuan itself to suppress local rebellion.[75] At the end of the Yuan, as we have already seen, still other fortresses were constructed to shelter refugee elites during the rebellion of Zou Pusheng's Red Turban army. Mei Guozhen, who established himself as a fort-building expert during his tenure on the northwest frontier in the late sixteenth century, was certainly applying, in his official service, techniques he had absorbed in his native Macheng.[76]

With all this local history behind it, the late-Ming fort-building movement in Macheng was nevertheless of a wholly new scale and style. The immediate model of *shanzhai* construction almost certainly came from the Han River highlands, to the north and west of Macheng. Like the Dabie Shan/Dongshan highlands, this was a transprovincial region, encompassing Hubei's Xiangyang Prefecture and portions of adjacent Henan and Shaanxi. It had been undergoing a protracted phase of decline and peripheralization ever since the removal of the imperial capital from Chang'an, under the Song, and had been especially devastated by the late-Yuan rebellion of Meng Haima. The conquering Ming had responded by prohibiting permanent resettlement of this now depopulated area, only to find it increasingly overrun by roving bands of vagabonds (*liumin*), sometimes numbering in the hundreds of thousands, who engaged in salt smuggling and other illicit activities. In the 1460s, the area erupted once again into massive rebellion, an event that prompted the Ming to carve out a new prefecture, Shiyang, and to station there a permanent imperial inspector (*du yushi*) in charge of pacification. The occupant of this post in 1634 was the young Jiangnan native and Donglin partisan Lu Xiangsheng (1600–49), who established a network of *shanzhai* to combat Li Zicheng's rebels.[77] Lu was promoted the next year to the governorship of Hubei, where he turned his rebel-suppression efforts to Macheng and its neighboring counties along the Henan border.[78] Although Lu did not feature the *shanzhai* strategy as centrally in the Dabie Shan theater of operations as he had in Shiyang, his presence and his reputation as a fort builder inevitably would have influenced the efforts of indigenous fortress lords in the making, most notably Lu's old colleague from the northwest front, Mei Zhihuan.

Lu Xiangsheng's Han Valley initiative did differ from the one in Macheng in that it was mandated by the government rather than undertaken autonomously by local elites (there were few such established elites in Shiyang), and especially in that it was paired with a scorched-earth program for the surrounding countryside. As we shall see, this kind of effort would appear in Macheng in later centuries, but during the Ming-Qing transition it was unheard of; the large estate holders who retreated to *shanzhai* during this era had no intention of effecting unnecessary damage to their lands. But Lu's well-publicized efforts did have other influences, or at least parallels, in the Dabie Shan. In the seven-item regulatory code he proclaimed, Lu specified that *shanzhai* should be built in relatively flat pockets within the mountains, that each one should encompass between four and eight natural villages and a population of at least several hundred, that each should have its own water supply and large stores of provisions and livestock, that each should be *named* (as Mei had named his mountain fortress at Shenzhuang the "Lifesaving Fort") and led by a publicly selected local elder, and that the inhabitants of each fort should be drilled as militia and should intimately coordinate their activities with those of other forts.[79]

Macheng's local elites began to take to the hills and build forts as early as the late 1620s, as confidence in the peacekeeping power of the Ming regime began to falter. The process accelerated after the crisis of early 1635, when, as we have seen, Macheng City barely escaped falling to the rebels; but neighboring Luotian, on the eastern slope of the Dongshan, was not so fortunate, and Magistrate Liang Shiren lost his life in its defense. Altogether, more than a dozen major fortresses (*mingzhai*) were constructed in Macheng during this era, and several preexisting ones were rebuilt in addition to perhaps scores of smaller forts that were simply fortified hamlets. The larger ones bore names derived from their founders (Yang Family Fort), from their appearance (Tricornered Fort, Stonewall Fort), from hoped-for Buddhist protectors (Guanyin Fort), or from Confucian-loyalist mottoes (Benevolence and Propriety Fort). Perhaps most common were names—such as Mei Zhihuan's Lifesaving Fort or the Peace-Preserving Fort or the All-Pacified Fort—that simply reflecting the function their builders hoped they would serve. The Benevolence and Propriety Fort (Renyi bao) was perhaps typical of the larger *shanzhai*, surrounded by a brick wall some 15 feet high and 4,000 feet in circumference, with three gates. The men who built such battlements were powerful local magnates, acting ei-

Stonewall Fort (Shicheng zhai) with beacon torch, Yanjiahe Ward, central Macheng County. Photograph by the author.

ther individually (as Mei had done) or collectively; the collective projects were often built by members of a single lineage, but this was not necessarily so. In most cases, local commoner neighbors (bondservants included) were not kept out but instead actively invited to enter and seek shelter, adding their strength to the fort's defense. *Shanzhai* sprang up most prominently in the Dongshan, where the tradition had its deepest roots, but also in Chengmagang and other northern townships, and in hilly areas in the suburbs of southern market towns such as Songbu, Zhongguanyi, and Baiguo, built as places of ready refuge by urban-commercial elites. As Zhang Xianzhong's major rebel force approached

Macheng, in 1642–43, resident gentry of the county seat collectively undertook to renovate and evacuate to the venerable Shizi shanzhai, in the Dongshan some seventy *li* to the east.[80]

Macheng's mountain fortresses quickly acquired a rich corpus of heroic legend. Forts of great antiquity, such as the Tiantai zhai and the Shizi shanzhai, had great stocks of lore surrounding them, including tales of each of their many historic uses; populations in the immediate neighborhoods deeply associated themselves with these local landmarks, and their behavior was said by others to reflect this tradition of martial valor. Stories were passed down about the heroic labors involved in the forts' construction. A literary retelling by Zou Hexin of the forced march of urban gentry, along with beasts of burden and laborers, through mountain mist and snow, to the Shizi shanzhai in 1643 was regularly reprinted in subsequent county gazetteers. Another sort of foundation myth added a religious dimension. Bifan (Precious Jade), a wealthy Buddhist abbot from Macheng, had financed the construction of a fort for the defense of his neighbors. Some time afterward, one of the abbot's disciples was pestering him about ordination. Bifan refused, and the novice went off to another monastery. When the young man returned, ordained, Bifan was furious. He tore the monk's habit to shreds and smashed his begging bowl. That night in his sleep, he had a vision of the deity Weituo, who terrifyingly threatened him: "What right do *you* have to destroy the sacred emblems of my priesthood?" Bifan tremblingly asked forgiveness. "You have accumulated good karma for having built that *zhai*," Weituo responded, "so I will forgive you this time."[81]

Many "trickster" legends dealt with the perennial problem of provisioning the *shanzhai*. The Baimi zhai, for example, was under siege by rebels, and its grain supply was perilously low. The defenders took their last remaining rice and threw it over the ramparts to the rebels, graciously offering them something to eat. The rebels passed on, assuming this gesture to mean that the fort could not be starved out. Ever since, the *zhai* had been known by its new name, White Rice Fort. In similar circumstances, the defenders of the Fuhe zhai stuffed their last remaining rice into a pig and sent the animal out the gates toward the besieging army. When the rebels, predictably, slaughtered and ate the pig, they saw all the rice it had consumed; remarking that the defenders were so comfortably provisioned that they even fed good rice to their pigs, they gave up the siege.[82]

Other legends, however, emphasize the more ominous, tragic nobility of fortress defense. For example, the *shengyuan* Lu Yuansun hailed from a prominent lineage of Baiguo Township that had produced several upper-level degree holders during the Ming. In the 1630s, Yuansun organized the construction of the Yunwu shanzhai, but when Zhang Xianzhong's forces approached the fort, in 1643, the Lu defenders were greatly outnumbered. Zhang's officers called for Yuansun to surrender and go over to the rebel side. He replied, "My family has been loyal to the Ming for generation after generation. How could I possibly forsake it for your cause?" The incensed rebels then overran the fort and butchered the entire Lu lineage—scores of individual families—and the lineage disappeared forever from the roster of the county's local elite.[83] In Macheng's experience of the Ming–Qing transition, such tales were by no means uncommon.

The Forty-Eight Fort League of Qi-Huang

Macheng was not alone in witnessing a proliferation of *shanzhai* during the final Ming decade. The county's forts were but part of a broad pattern extending throughout the wider Dabie Shan highlands, encompassing most of Huangzhou and Qizhou Prefectures in eastern Hubei along with Henan's Guangshan, Shangcheng, and Gushi Counties to the north, Anhui's Huoshan, Qianshan, and Taihu Counties to the east and northeast, and parts of northwestern Jiangxi. In all, many hundreds of mountain fortresses of varying scales—some with tens of thousands of inhabitants—came to dot this landscape. Systematic network formation gradually took place among these, the most formalized network being the so-called League of Forty-Eight Forts of Huangzhou and Qizhou (Qi-Huang sishiba zhai).

The exact process of the league's formation is not completely clear, but all sources agree that its founder and first commander was none other than Macheng's own Mei Zhihuan. It was a practical implementation of the political and military vision he had articulated in a letter to Grand Secretary Feng Quan: each individual village must fortify itself and link up with its neighbors, Mei argues, so that the enemy will be dissuaded from attacking it; as this model is reproduced in thousands upon thousands of contiguous small localities, the crisis of the empire as a whole (*tianxia*) will ultimately be resolved.[84] Mei's grassroots network building found sympathetic official patrons in Shi Kefa, Anqing Governor and president of the board of war, and in Shi's military subordinate, Song Yihe.[85] Shi had been ordered by the court to establish a four-province defense zone to guard the western approaches to Nanjing, and he and Song selected Mei to head, first, its eastern Hubei sector and, later, the wider fortress network as a whole. Eventually, as the situation in the north deteriorated desperately, Shi, Song, and Mei were ordered by the ruling house to attach their loyalty to the imperial prince enfeoffed in central China, Zhu Yunyan. Mei's network eventually incorporated nearly 400 *zhai*. Essentially, he was told, leave it to the Ming armies to battle for the cities while you safeguard the countryside and its refugee populations as best you can.[86]

To govern this population, Mei and his allies in the Forty-Eight Fort League drew up a regulatory code, in effect a constitution of sorts. The regulations included the following:

1. Individual *zhai* would be commanded by individual lineage heads or by an agreed-upon cohort of lineage heads from a single residential area.

2. *Zhai* would be systematically linked to one another through a chain of command and communication. Those in western Anhui were considered the most central to the network as a whole—nearest to Shi Kefa's Anqing headquarters—and those in the Dongshan were considered to be the most central of those in Hubei.

3. Precautions would be taken against epidemic disease and would include expulsion of those infected. (In one instance, the mother of the fortmaster of the Chaoyang zhai, in Hubei's Yingshan County, was expelled on these grounds.)

4. Strict orders of precedence and social distinction would be maintained within each fort. For example, inappropriate mingling among male and female residents was forbidden.

5. Charitable provisions for relief would be made, both within and among *zhai*, concerning food and medical treatment of the (noninfectious) ill.

6. The education of youths would be vigorously carried on, even in times of warfare.

7. Proper fealty and service to the members of the Ming imperial family would be required when these persons took shelter in any fort under the command of the League of Forty-Eight. (This requirement was in effect both before and after the loss of Beijing.) Specific *zhai* would be assigned responsibility for the security and maintenance of individual Ming princes and their retinues. The forts were also charged with offering protection to any Ming official who sought refuge within them.

The Forty-Eight Fort League rapidly became known and imitated throughout the empire, as far away as Sichuan, and became the stuff of a very potent cultural memory that persists to this day. Its history was written first, cautiously, by the obscure Huizhou scholar Wu Dezhi in the Yongzheng reign[87] but then more defiantly by Wang Baoxin (1867–1944), a Luotian native who was a professor at Wuhan University and Beijing University, an activist of the 1911 Revolution, and a friend of the early Communist organizer Dong Biwu. Wang's erudite yet highly romanticized book on the Forty-Eight Fort League has a clear anti-Manchu undertone; it was written for private circulation in 1908 but published only six years later, when the Qing regime had safely passed from the scene. The work, and especially its discussion of the league's self-regulatory code, resonates with the intellectual currents of the New Policies (*xinzheng*) era, influenced by Western political thought but at the same time seeking to locate in the (local) Chinese past an indigenous model of self-governance. Mei Zhihuan's own writings—and especially his letter to Feng Quan, cited above—postulate a model of nested loyalisms that resonates strongly with the discourse of lineage- and native place–based corporatist nationalism of early-twentieth-century China.[88] But Wang Baoxin takes his subject one degree further, depicting in the history of the Forty-Eight Forts something akin to an indigenous social contract theory.[89] "Before the *shanzhai* were constructed," he writes, "the primitive masses [*wanmin*] were governed by the struggle for survival." In this Social Darwinist universe they lived in fear of each other, and only by developing a spirit of group cohesion (*jieji* or *jiezhong*) could this fear be overcome. To implement the sense of community in practice, they spontaneously created their own set of rules (*zisheng guilü*). In the process, they generated the principles of community formation (*hequn zhi gui*), but also the institutional foundation of their political independence (*duli zhi zhi*).[90]

The historical memory of the Forty-Eight Forts is indeed an extremely dangerous and multivalent one, laden with implications of class warfare, Han nationalism, and, perhaps most strongly, armed local autonomy of the Dabie Shan region itself. As Wang Baoxin observed, this is a warlike place, and each time in Chinese history when the center has appeared weak, elites such as Mei Zhihuan—or, centuries earlier, commoners such as Zou Pusheng—have seized the opportunity to assert the region's effective secession from the surrounding polity.[91] The pattern would repeat itself yet once more in Wang's own lifetime—in the form of the Eyuwan Soviet.

CHAPTER SIX

Extermination

In early fall of 1641 (Chongzhen 14/8/12), Mei Zhihuan died of illness at the age of sixty-seven. A sense of loss and panic swept through Macheng County. Public weeping was reported everywhere as the news spread. On the first anniversary of his death, a great ceremony of mourning was held at his grave, with several thousand persons in attendance. Half of those present, Mei's biographer tells us, were those he had disciplined in one way or another during his lifetime.[1] The public funeral was not only a sign of the continuing symbolic power of Mei's persona but also an orchestrated effort to rally local community solidarity versus the forces arrayed against it, not least those of the collapsing Ming state. For nearly ten years, Mei Zhihuan had effectively propped open the tiger's jaws, but in 1643, two years after his death, the jaws slammed shut. The story of the succeeding decade in Macheng is that of a continuing wave of bloody bondservant uprisings, punctuated by alien conquest and a to-the-death resistance movement combining, in some complex mix, loyalism to a refugee Ming regime and a fierce regional localism. There was much intrigue and shifting of allegiances, but there were few survivors.[2]

Tang Zhi and the Village Benevolent Association

The early 1640s were critically difficult times for Macheng. Both 1640 and 1641 were years of severe drought, locusts, harvest failure, and unchecked inflation of grain prices. Wang Baoxin notes, with perhaps some hyperbole, that half the population of the wider Huangzhou-Qizhou region starved to death. As in the last years of the Yuan, the Macheng County gazetteers record widespread instances of cannibalism. They also report a wave of devastating epidemics. On top of this, the county became a battleground for combatants of empirewide scale. Zhang Xianzhong's troops repeatedly passed through, and in mid-1641 Hubei governor Song Yihe decided to make Macheng the epicenter of a massive rebel-annihilation campaign. Large armies under the Ming generals Wang Yuncheng, Liu Liangzuo, and Zuo Liangyu moved in to occupy sectors of the county while local residents increasingly took to the hills. After months of bloody fighting, a decisive Ming victory was achieved at Dongyi Island at year's end, climaxed by General Zuo Liangyu's mass beheading of some 1,200 captured rebels. Governor Song could declare to the throne his operation's "complete triumph." Throughout 1642 and early 1643, nevertheless, rebel forces under Li Zicheng repeatedly came and went, pursued doggedly but futilely by Ming troops.[3]

Ironically, the relative and short-lived pacification of Macheng by Ming armies had added still further to local immiseration when General Zuo decided to institute a misguided program for amnesty and resettlement of rebel forces. Zuo declared that anyone who accepted his amnesty would be declared a new citizen (*xinmin*) and be granted a grubstake of farmland in the highlands. To finance this scheme, he levied a new tax on the existing populations, who were at the moment most ill equipped to bear this added burden. Widespread local elite protests, and accelerating disaffection from the Ming cause, were the predictable results.[4] In early 1643, the Board of War reported to the throne that, in contrast to the local elites of Hunan and other areas, those of the Huangzhou region could not be reliably counted upon for loyalism to the Ming cause.[5]

One of the most interesting instances of this disaffection came in the rebellion of Macheng's Bao Shirong. Born into a prosperous lineage on the western fringe of the Dongshan, the young Shirong had taken orders in the Guanyin monastery, which was patronized by his family. Bao, however, angered by oppressive Ming taxation and sympathetic to the cause of Li Zicheng, gathered a group of monastic and secular allies in 1642 or 1643 and launched a rebellion in the townships of Tortoise Peak and Yanjiahe, killing tax collectors and government clerks. His army reportedly grew to nearly 10,000 and established a base in the Dongshan near the Shizi shanzhai fort. Dislodged by Ming troops in late 1643, Bao linked up with Li Zicheng's larger forces in Shaanxi, survived Li's defeat and death in 1645, and returned to his native county. For nearly two decades thereafter, Bao remained in constant rebellion in the Dongshan hills.[6]

Of greater immediate consequence, though, was the rebellion of Tang Zhi.[7] The rebellion began among the tenants and bondservants of Macheng's most illustrious families, those who owned vast estates in the county's central plain. During the chronic military unrest of the last Ming decade, self-defense associations (*hui*) had begun to spring up among villagers on these estates. Formation of such *hui* was a long-standing historical practice in Macheng and elsewhere, a manifestation of the basic organizational genius of Chinese rural society. They were a later version of the more overtly sectarian *tang* set up by the same villagers in the late Yuan, including the famous Shengren tang of Zou Pusheng. They had analogues in Macheng's numerous village associations, recorded in the Qing and Republican eras: the Eight Directions Association (Bafang hui), the Brotherly Society (Xiongdi hui), the Drumbeat Association (Lougu hui), and so on. They were the precursors of both the rightist Red Spears associations (Hongqiang hui) and the leftist Peasant Associations (*nongmin xiehui*) that would engage in such fratricidal combat during the 1920s and 1930s. Some, like the Double Ninth Festival Association (Chongyang hui), were ostensibly organized to manage village cultural activities, but most, like the county's numerous boxing associations (*quanshu hui*), were oriented to the practice of the martial arts and to village self-defense.[8]

Among the *hui* of the late Ming were two set up on the estates of the hyper-elite Bashang Li lineage, the lineage of incumbent board president Li Changgeng.[9] These were the Village Benevolent Association (Liren hui) founded by the free tenant Ming Chengzu and the True Way Association (Zhidao hui)—also called the Clean Ear Association or the Reverence Association (Xi'er hui)—set up by the bondservant Hong Louxian. As their names imply, the ideology of these groups was fully orthodox, steeped in the knight errantry, sworn brotherhood, and muscular Confucianism of swordplay romances. The *liren* (benevolent treatment of neighbors) of the Liren hui had been a recurring injunction in the moral codes that the Macheng elites had drummed into their dependents over the centuries; it was seen as the indispensable solvent of village community.[10] Members of the Liren hui and the Zhidao hui collectively drank the blood of slaughtered chickens to affirm their fraternity, donned military garb, and drilled in the village streets. Initially these activities were performed with at least the tacit blessing of the landholders, who were busy at the same time organizing their own collective defense against marauding rebel armies. But things seemed to get out of hand; there were complaints in various elite quarters that the *hui* were dressing in unwonted finery, that they were growing intoxicated by their collective power, and that they were beginning to intimidate their masters. They were becoming a threat in their own right.

The threat became a crisis when, in 1642, leadership of the Liren hui fell into the hands of Tang Zhi, a bondservant with apparently some education and an agenda fired by the same demand for redemption of servitude that had underlain the Macheng *nupu* uprising of 1631. Large numbers of disaffected young men gravitated to Tang's organization, which reportedly grew to over 10,000 members. In the spring of 1643, under cover of an enormous blizzard, Tang declared war. He killed more than sixty local literati (*zhusheng*)—an act that the social critic and chronicler Wu Weiye described as divine vengeance (*paoluo*) for generations of decadent extravagance on the part of the Macheng local elite.[11] As Satō Fumitoshi observes, the leaders of the rebellion were for the most part high-ranking bondservants, often holding managerial positions on the great estates surrounding Macheng city. In normal times, they all conducted routine business for their masters in the city and so found ample opportunity for networking.[12] In March, therefore, when Tang's Liren hui marched on the county seat, Tang was able to mobilize other groups of disaffected bondservants from nearby estates to converge on the city along with him. Most of the urban elite had already abandoned the county seat for the mountains, to such an extent that Li Zicheng, passing through Macheng the month before, had deemed the city not worth the taking. Tang's bondservant army, finding it defended by a mere token force under Magistrate Lu Jinxi, occupied it without difficulty. Magistrate Lu, effectively under house arrest, issued a call for help to the militia of the various surrounding mountain fortresses, and the latter mounted a collective siege to retake the city. At least one member of the local elite, however, did not join them: Zhou Wenjiang, a lower-gentry member (*xiucai*) from the western township of Shunheji, had opted, perhaps by prearrangement, to accept a leadership role in Tang Zhi's rebel army.[13] But as the fortress-based siege of the county seat tightened and urban food supplies grew short, Tang personally slipped out and made his way to Zhang Xianzhong's camp at Qizhou. Zhang's army had been sweeping back and forth through eastern Hubei for several years, though Zhang had never succeeded in taking Macheng City. Tang Zhi now offered to present the city to him, in exchange for his relieving the siege.

Legends about the charismatic Zhang Xianzhong circulated in Macheng like scenes from a folk opera. Many stressed his roughhewn Confucian rectitude, as in the tale, recounted in the introduction to this volume, of Zhang's construction of the Sacrificial Wall (Baijiao cheng) in Macheng in honor of a locally born judge who had dismissed a robbery charge against him in his youth.[14] It was also said that when Zhang, on a sweep through the county in 1642, had encountered the grave of Mei Zhihuan himself, he reverently sacrificed to the spirit of this upright antagonist and ordered that no harm be done to any resident of Mei's native village.[15]

But other stories of Zhang's conduct were more unnerving to the Macheng elite. At the beginning of 1643, for example, Zhang had taken the prefectural seat of neighboring Qizhou. Word was that he had demanded huge sums of blood money from the urban gentry, and then, after they paid, ordered them all to march into the city's east gate and out the west, where he butchered them to the last man; the women of the city committed mass suicide.[16] When, the following month, he took the Huangzhou prefectural seat as well, a local Buddhist monk who had been leading a separate, bloody sectarian uprising declared him an avenging boddhisatva, Amitaba Zhang. Zhang crushed the resistance efforts of one Huangzhou militia leader and then vengefully exterminated fifty-one of his relatives.[17]

In fact, however, Zhang Xianzhong was at the moment at a relative ebb in his fortunes. His army had begun to engage in divisive combat with that of Li Zicheng and had not fared well. At the time of Tang Zhi's overture, his forces were much reduced, and the offer of easy pickings in Macheng and of some strong new allies was one he could not refuse. In late April (Chongzhen 16/4/6), Zhang broke the siege and occupied Macheng. He killed the deputy magistrate, Li Timing, and the county director of studies, Xiao Gongsheng, although Magistrate Lu managed to escape to the mountains. Zhang rechristened Macheng seat of the Ever-Compliant Department (Changshun zhou), named the maverick literatus Zhou Wenjiang its magistrate, and set up a local administration staffed by former Macheng bondservants. The few urban gentry who had been left behind in the general flight to the hills, anxious to avoid the fate of their Qizhou brethren, paid Zhang ready obeisance. One was the aged Liu Qiao—great-great-grandson of Liu Tianhe, *jinshi* of 1592, a former military guardian of the heir apparent (*dudu gongbao*) who had been cashiered after running afoul of the eunuch Wei Zhongxian, and head of one of Macheng's grandest serfholding lineages.[18] Via the offices of Zhou Wenjiang, Liu offered Zhang concubines and tens of thousands of gold coins in exchange for his life, accepting an honorary commission in Zhang's army.[19]

With the incorporation of the Macheng rebels, Zhang Xianzhong's forces swelled greatly in strength, from 7,000 to some 57,000, a force he appropriately dubbed the New Battalion (Xinying). Tang Zhi was appointed a major and given some 4,000 men to consolidate control of Macheng itself.[20] He proceeded to counterattack the militia of the fortress lords and succeeded in bloodily reducing many of the county's *shanzhai*. The principal holdout was the Crimson Mountain Fort (Zhushan zhai), where Magistrate Lu Jinxi had installed his county government in exile. The bulk of Zhang's New Battalion—overwhelmingly composed of Macheng natives—then marched on the provincial capital of Wuchang. After protracted fighting, during which Zhang's men slaughtered the merchant population of Hankou, they vanquished the Ming Prince of Chu in July and occupied the capital. The rejuvenated Zhang Xianzhong now declared himself the Western King (Xiwang), proclaiming his reign from the same Yellow Crane Tower where Li Zhi had been attacked by a mob some fifty years earlier. The Western King held civil service examinations, passing seventy-eight men, and formed an expanded bureaucracy of imperial pretensions. Unsurprisingly, Macheng men received most of the plum jobs: Li Shirong was named governor of Hubei, Zhang Yize became military governor of the Huangzhou-Qizhou circuit, Huang Yuankai was appointed prefect of Huangzhou, and Shen Huilin was named prefect of Hanyang. The renegade literatus Zhou Wenjiang was promoted to minister of war.[21]

But, just as suddenly, the tides of combat shifted once again. In late summer, Zuo Liangyu, probably the most capable Ming general operating in central China, returned to eastern Hubei from downriver and succeeded in resuscitating the Forty-Eight Fort League. Zuo (1598–1645) was a native of Linqing, Shandong, who had risen to his position through a string of military successes over Li Zicheng and Zhang Xianzhong; though nearly illiterate and defiant of higher authority, he had reformist leanings and was associated with both the Donglin and Fu She movements.[22] Zuo's force of combined Ming regulars and *shanzhai* militia retook the prefectural seat of Qizhou, and under his wing Yi Daosan, lord of the White Cloud Fort (Baiyun zhai, on the Huanggang slopes of the Dongshan) retook Huangzhou City. Huang Yuankai, Macheng-born and recently appointed Huangzhou prefect by Zhang Xianzhong, took flight. At the news of Zuo's approach, Shen Huilin, the Macheng literatus whom Zhang had made prefect of Hanyang, ran back to the hills of his native county.

At this point, Fengyang governor-general Ma Shiying entered the fray. Ma, a Guizhou native and *jinshi* of 1619, was one of the most notoriously corrupt officials of the era. A eunuch protégé who warred constantly with the reformist Shi Kefa and with Zuo Liangyu, he was a virtual warlord who consistently intimidated the Ming court with his impressive Huai River naval force.[23] Sweeping into Macheng through the pass from his Anhui base, Ma and his forces retook the county seat in midsummer (Chongzhen 16/6), a mere two months after it had fallen to Zhang Xianzhong. A furious round of betrayals and recriminations followed. Liu Qiao, who had offered financial support and taken a titular post in the Western King's regime, shaved his head and ran off to the mountains as a monk; as Wang Baoxin observes, "literati opinion reviled him." Apprehended by the Ming governor of Hubei, Huang Shu, Liu bribed the ever-receptive Ma Shiying to restore him to his former imperial rank (Huang Shu instead was cashiered), then denounced his compatriot Zhou Wenjiang as the real traitor. The resilient Wenjiang extended his own bribe to Ma Shiying, in return for which he was pardoned and installed as commander of the Macheng militia. Zhou also produced his own scapegoat, Tang Zhi, and the former bond-servant had less to offer Ma in exchange for his life. He was pursued out of the county, and his head was brought back on a pike to Ma's headquarters.[24]

Massive bloodletting ensued. In late summer, Zhang Xianzhong was forced out of Hubei altogether. He took most of his forces into Sichuan, where he engaged in one of the most hair-raising genocides in imperial history.[25] Participating in this butchery as Zhang's key lieutenants were a number of former Macheng gentry, including brigade commanders Hong Zhenglong and Shang Yuan. Literally scores of Sichuan lineages today trace their origins to Macheng migrants of this era, most of whom, it seems, arrived as fighters in Zhang Xianzhong's genocidal armies.[26] Back home in Macheng, however, the forces of Ma Shiying rounded up and exterminated (*jinzhan*) all the remaining kinfolk—male and female, adult and child—of every man he believed to be in Zhang's service. Some splinter elements of Zhang's Hubei regime fled into Hunan, where 350 of them were hunted down and treated to a mass beheading at the hands of Zuo Liangyu.[27] Ironically, though, some of the most prominent of Zhang Xianzhong's remnants (*yudang*) in Macheng had a much different fate. Well-connected literati collaborators, such as Liu Qiao, Shen Huilin, and, most notably, Zhou Wenjiang, retreated to the Dongshan forts, where they eventually fought—and died—as heroic "loyalists" to the Ming cause.[28]

A Change of Dynasty

On April 25, 1644, Li Zicheng captured Beijing, and the Chongzhen emperor hanged himself on the hill behind the Forbidden City. Six weeks later, on June 6, Qing conquering armies, led by the erstwhile Ming general Wu Sangui, in turn took the city from Li and established the six-year-old Shunzhi emperor on the Dragon Throne. One type of response to this news in Macheng was that of the erudite book collector Mei Zhiyuan, son of Guozhen and cousin of the county's recently deceased protector, Mei Zhihuan. Like his cousin, Zhiyuan had been for several years an active partisan of the reformist Fu She (Revival Society)—perhaps even more active since having shunned the exams and official service, whereupon he spent much of his adult life socializing with the Fu She leadership in Jiangnan. When informed of the Qing succession in the northern capital, Mei Zhiyuan proclaimed that the fall of the Ming was an accomplished fact (*qian Ming yi shi*) and led a delegation of other Fu She members to Beijing, where they acknowledged the authority of the new rulers and petitioned them to grant the former emperor an appropriate burial. Mei Zhiyuan then returned to Macheng, took the tonsure (thus diplomatically sidestepping the issue of whether to retain the Ming hairstyle or wear the Qing-mandated queue), divested himself of his considerable patrimony, and moved to Tortoise Hill, where he lived out his life in hermetic classical scholarship.[29] (One is led to wonder whether growing frustration with Ming rule might have led Mei Zhihuan himself, for all his vigorous life of dynastic and local defense, to make a similar choice had he still been alive.) As it turned out, however, despite Mei Zhiyuan's plea to his compatriots that they remain stoically aloof (*kanggan*) in the face of dynastic change, most of the Macheng literati-turned-fortress lords would choose to take another tack.

The prevailing response of the literati elite, one that Frederic Wakeman has aptly termed "romantic,"[30] was epitomized by two brash disciples of Macheng's greatest native-born poet, Liu Tong (1595–1637). Liu himself was a member of the hyperelite Liu lineage and a younger kinsman of the disreputable Liu Qiao. Along with Tan Yuanchun, Liu had founded the "Jingling school" (from the name of Tan's native county) that, along with the "Gong'an school" of Yuan Hongdao to which it was consciously opposed, has been called the most important poetic movement of the late Ming.[31] An aggressive and controversial promoter of his own unorthodox poetics, Liu also received criticism for the book for which he is best remembered, the 1635 *Dijing jingwu lue* (Guide to the sites of the capital).[32] Liu spent more than five years as a student at Beijing's Imperial University (Guoxue), and his guidebook offers a rich and colorful potpourri of poems, essays, and legends associated with each landmark that a culturally minded tourist might wish to visit. It is not without elements of social criticism and factional politics, however, and includes, among other things, a sympathetic description of the tomb of Li Zhi (and one of Matteo Ricci's as well). Liu Tong was also, like his senior compatriots Mei Zhihuan and Mei Zhiyuan, an active partisan of the Fu She and critic of the political decadence of the late Ming. One of his poems, for example, passionately attacks the inequitable and corrupt way in which agrarian taxes are levied to provision the faltering defense of the Manchurian frontier, leaving villagers to eat nothing but thin gruel even after a bountiful harvest. "Why should we care," he has his local-minded villagers ask, "whether or not Liaoyang is secure?"[33]

Having finally passed the metropolitan examination in 1637, Liu was dispatched to his first official posting, that of Suzhou magistrate. He never took up the post, however, having died en route of illness at the age of forty-three, and thus was spared the difficult decision of how to greet the Qing conquest. The same was not the case for his two younger acolytes, Cao Yinchang and Zhou Sun. Cao and Zhou were inseparable, having studied with Liu Tong for more than a decade, first in Macheng and then in Beijing, where they worked as research assistants on the *Dijing jingwu lue.*[34] After Liu's death they returned to Macheng, where they both passed the Hubei provincial examination of 1639 (Cao won the primus) and, again together, sat successfully for the *jinshi* exam in 1643. Both men came from impeccable local elite families, and both were famous bibliophiles as well as accomplished poets. Cao in particular became something of an empirewide cult figure among the youth of his day, who loved to chant his poetry to musical accompaniment.

In keeping with the culture of their native county, both young men assumed personae of martial bravado. Cao had spent a portion of his adolescence in frontier Yunnan, where his father had served as a county magistrate, and after the old man's death he had endured heroic hardships in bringing his father's corpse back to Macheng for burial. Upon receiving his *jinshi*, Yinchang was himself posted as magistrate of Jiading, in the Yangzi delta, where his devotion to drinking parties and his disdain for fiscal administration brought a speedy end to his career in field administration; his superior, Hong Chengchou, described him as *wuyi yu shi* (caring nothing about worldly affairs). He returned to Macheng to build his famous Wave Garden (Liangyuan), where he drank, wrote poetry, and practiced the martial arts.

Zhou Sun's career had a bit more substance. Even while at Beijing, in the entourage of Liu Tong, he had sped back to Macheng in 1633 to join with his brothers in chasing away rebels from his native village. A decade later, as magistrate of Raozhou, Jiangxi, he had the temerity to stand up to Ma Shiying, whose troops had plundered several local villages, and negotiate a solution that saved face for all parties. While Sun was away, his kinsmen had constructed the Crimson Mountain Fort in western Macheng, where, as we have seen, the county government relocated during Tang Zhi's occupation of the county seat. With the fall of Beijing, in 1644, Zhou Sun returned home to take command of the fort and to join with Cao in organizing Macheng's local defense.

The League Revived

As it turned out, the dynastic transition year of 1644 was one of remarkable tranquility in Macheng, the lull before the storm. Qing armies were busying themselves with consolidating their hold on northern China. As Wakeman notes, the news of the death of the Chongzhen emperor "seemed to signal the end of civil order," touching off bondservant and other plebeian uprisings in many localities.[35] Macheng saw little of this, however, the bondservant discontent there having played itself out, for the moment, with the Zhang Xianzhong interregnum. In the latter part of the year, the Southern Ming court at Nanjing deputed Zuo Liangyu to Wuchang as imperial commissioner in charge of the defense of Hubei, and for the remainder of the year he, too, quietly went about his business.

In the spring of 1645, the clouds of war again began to gather. Qing forces pushed south, and the strategic city of Yangzhou fell in March, in a suicidal defense orchestrated by Shi Kefa. Li Zicheng, having been dislodged from Beijing, likewise fled south, and early in the year he attempted to establish a regime at Jiujiang, in northwestern Jiangxi. He linked up with indigenous rebel groups, extended his control to nearby Huangzhou, and, some reports claimed, sought to forge a makeshift anti-Qing alliance with his old enemies, the leaders of the Forty-Eight Forts. By summer, however, his position was increasingly untenable, and while on the run through southeastern Hubei he met his end at the hands of local militia units. Meanwhile, at Wuchang, Zuo Liangyu had become increasingly fed up with the machinations of Ma Shiying at Nanjing, and in April he proclaimed an "eastern expedition" to rescue the Southern Ming court from its ostensible protector. He made it as far as Jiujiang, where he died of illness later that month. Zuo's lieutenant, Jin Shenghuan, thereupon offered his services to the advancing Qing commander, who gladly put him in charge of stamping out Ming-loyalist resistance throughout Jiangxi. The southern capital of Nanjing fell to the Qing in June, and the Ming Prince Fu, who since the suicide of Chongzhen the year before had assumed the title of Hongwu emperor, was captured and subsequently executed. The rump Ming court was fractured and on the run.[36]

The eastern Hubei prefectures of Qizhou and Huangzhou were increasingly isolated and, for a time, effectively autonomous. But, as Wakeman observes, the decision of a given county—or, indeed, a portion of a county—to engage in active resistance was the result of a highly complex calculus based on "specific local conditions," including the local property regime, class relations, and the cohesiveness of the indigenous elite.[37] In eastern Hubei, most of Qizhou's Qishui, Guangji, and Huangmei Counties and Huangzhou's Huanggang County were progressively brought onto the Qing map (*ru bantu*) with little resistance over the latter part of 1645, but Macheng and its two adjacent counties, Huangzhou's Huang'an and Qizhou's Luotian, were not effectively incorporated until much later—perhaps, as we shall see, as much as *two decades* later. As the Luotian native Wang Baoxin noted with pride, this outcome was owing primarily to the martial bravado (*wuyong*) that formed the central element in these counties' cultural style (*fengqi*).[38]

Perhaps; but what turned passive Ming loyalism into active resistance to Qing rule was a specific act of July 8, 1645 (Shunzhi 2/6): the edict ordering every Han male to shave the front of his head (*ditou*) and adopt the Manchu queue, and all Qing magistrates to enforce this edict on their populations. Throughout the Yangzi Valley, this act led to violent uprisings. In Jiangning, Jiangsu, the newly installed Qing magistrate was attacked and killed; in Macheng, where no Qing magistrate had as yet been installed, a crowd of urban gentry and commoners (*chengnei shimin*) contented itself with burning down the magistrate's *yamen*. But in Macheng, as elsewhere, the city was not the major problem. When the first Qing magistrate, Li Heng, arrived the following year, he rebuilt the *yamen* and, with seemingly little difficulty, pacified the urban populace.[39] The *shanzhai* were a different story. According to Jiang Yuxu, the new Qing governor of Hubei, the haircutting edict suddenly turned the hills throughout Huangzhou into a battleground.[40] The Forty-Eight Fort League, formed initially to quell domestic rebellion, not to resist conquest, had deputed Zhang Jinchan, former board of war president in the Nanjing regime of Prince Fu, to negotiate a peaceful accommodation with the new regime, and several of the most influential Dongshan fortress lords, including Yi Daosan of the White Cloud Fort and Wang Guangshu of the Great Cliff Fort, had already informally capitulated to local Qing commanders. The mandate to adopt the queue changed all that.[41]

The Forty-Eight Fort League was speedily revived. Sources vary on how many *zhai* it now incorporated—anywhere between 300 and 800—and it now spanned three provinces and dozens of counties. As the league's hagiographer Wang Baoxin observed, the passage from antirebel defense to anti-Qing resistance was a logical one, given that at all times it was local boundaries (*tujing*) which were being protected.[42] But the "locality" at issue was not an administrative one; the league was, in effect, a state within a state, within which imperially imposed jurisdictions had little relevance. And by now most of the administrative seats were comfortably in Qing hands. In effect, it was the highlands that had seceded from the river valleys and the plains.

The position of master of the league (*zhumeng*) now fell to one Wang Ding. A *juren* of 1627, Wang had spent most of the 1630s at home in Luotian County, constructing his Walled and Orderly Fort (Guozhi zhai) and, like Mei Zhihuan in adjacent Macheng, "advising" the magistrate on how to keep the rebels at bay. He had also aided Mei in extending the original fort alliance beyond its Macheng origins. Wang left to accept local office in Henan in 1643, but when Kaifeng fell, in early 1645, he returned home and began vigorously to mobilize the resistance.[43] His second in command was Macheng's Zhou Sun. To tie the league's operations to the broader loyalist cause, Zhou paid a visit to the court of the Longwu emperor at Fuzhou (the former Prince Tang, who had assumed the imperial title following the death of Prince Fu in 1645) and came home rewarded with a presidency of the board of war.[44] The Qi-Huang forts thereafter were plugged in to a wider resistance network, its members loosely linked by common retention of the Ming hairstyle, allegiance to one or another of the Ming pretenders, and use of the Ming calendar. According to one contemporary, this network incorporated a variety of regionally specific "local strongman" types: the old gentry (*gushen*) of Sichuan, the cave lords (*dongzhu*) of Zhejiang, the island lords (*daozhu*) of the southeastern coast, and the mountain lords (*shanzhu*) of Qi-Huang and central China. A few of these scattered localist/loyalist regimes managed to retain their autonomy from Qing rule for decades—even, like the regime of southern Fujian's Zhang Jinlong, for more than a century.[45]

To suppress the organized Forty-Eight Fort resistance, the Huguang viceroy, He Mingluan, and the Hubei governor, Jiang Yuxu, called upon the dour General Xu Yong, a Liaodong native who had formerly served the Ming in the army of Zuo Liangyu. With Zuo's death, in April 1645, Xu, along with his comrade Jin Shenghuan, had gone over to the Qing side. He spent the summer and fall mopping up remnants of Li Zicheng's and Ming-loyalist forces in northwest Jiangxi, then turned his sights westward to the Dongshan forts.[46] Viceroy He's orders were for Xu Yong to pacify by extermination (*jiaofu*) the Forty-Eight Fort League. In standard military practice, there were two alternative means of pacification: on the one hand was the well-developed repertoire of techniques aiming toward a negotiated surrender with amnesty (*zhaofu*), and on the other was a straightforward military solution directed toward total annihilation (*jiao*) of the opponent.[47] In the campaigns against the late-Ming rebels in eastern Hubei, Ming officials such as Lu Xiangsheng, and their local allies like Mei Zhihuan, had themselves adopted the extermination strategy, as, indeed, had Macheng local authorities in suppressing bondservant uprisings as early as 1631.[48] By the time the Qing forces organized themselves for the campaign against the Qi-Huang forts, in the winter of 1645, they, too, had determined that amnesty was no longer an option and that extermination was the only satisfactory solution. They proceeded accordingly.

Moving westward up the Yangzi from Jiujiang, Xu Yong first encountered the forts of Huanggang County, on the southeastern slopes of the Dongshan. According to Xu's report, the resistance here comprised several tens of thousands of men, all experienced in upland fighting techniques. The Qing forces first laid siege to Yi Daosan's White Cloud Fort in late December, and initially they were driven back. Over the next few days, however, they reinforced their position and took the fort in extremely bloody fighting; Xu's troops hacked to death (*kansha*) several thousand rebels, and burned all structures in the White Cloud Fort to the ground. Within the next few days, they advanced to the Great Cliff Fort manned by Wang Guangshu, with similar results. Just after the new year, they took down the Doufang Fort in Qishui County, defended by Zhou Congkuang. As each fort fell, the surviving defenders fell back to other *shanzhai* behind the front line. By the beginning of February 1646, the Qing forces had obliterated nearly 100 of the dependent forts on the eastern slopes of the Dongshan, mopping up most of the residual resistance. The fort masters Yi Daosan, Wang Guangshu, and Zhou Congkuang, along with several Ming-appointed county officials who had sought their protection, were captured alive and hauled off to Wuchang. There they were decapitated, and their severed heads displayed as a warning to all those who dared stand in the way of the Qing juggernaut.[49]

Macheng, though, remained a center of defiance. In the words of Governor General He Mingluan, this area was strewn with forts and overrun with fortress rebels (*zhaini*). A year earlier, before the inflammatory haircutting edict had turned these forts to active rebellion, He had concocted a precautionary plan to raze them all, but it was not carried out in time. One critical leader of the Ming-loyalist resistance in Macheng and Huang'an in early 1646 was none other than Zhou Wenjiang, former collaborator of Tang Zhi and president of the board of war in Zhang Xianzhong's fleeting Hubei regime. Among Zhou's unlikely allies were men bearing some of the most illustrious surnames in the region, including Mei Zhihuan's kinsman Mei Zeng and Geng Dingxiang's kinsman Geng Yingqu, both of whom had been granted high military rank by the Southern Ming court.

In April and May, emboldened by his perception of an overstretched Qing army fighting a multifront war against various Ming pretenders, Zhou Wenjiang descended from his Yellow Cedar Fort (Huangbo zhai) to besiege the county seats, first that of Huang'an and then, two weeks later, that of Macheng. With few Qing troops as yet in Macheng, the city was defended chiefly by another, countervailing force of local militia. Their leader was one Zou Xing, a scion of the county's single most venerable lineage, the Balifan Zou, and a man who (as we shall see) had made his choice for the Qing very early and would become Macheng's most important power broker for decades to come. Zhou Wenjiang did not manage to take either city, but he did invite the concerted attention of Xu Yong, whose forces hunted him down and killed him at the Great Buddha Temple of Zoudunzhai. Thus came to an end one of the most colorful and multivalent careers in Macheng local history: of all the county's national dignitaries of the late-imperial era, Zhou Wenjiang nearly alone merits biographical notice in the Communist-era gazetteer.[50]

Over the course of the summer, Zhou's allies were captured one by one and executed by Xu's troops. The most elusive of these allies proved to be Geng Yingqu, who escaped the Qing siege of his Newly Arisen Fort (Xinxing zhai) and thereafter hopped back and forth across the Hubei-Henan border, hiding out in one fort after another. Xu Yong's troops were said to have destroyed thirty-two *shanzhai* in the process of pursuing Geng alone. Finally, in midsummer, he was trapped in the Yao Family Fort (Yaogong zhai) by an assembled force of some 7,000 men. After a three-day siege, a huge blaze broke out in the fort, killing a large number of defenders, many of them women. Geng again escaped, but shortly afterward was captured and executed.[51]

Zhou Wenjiang's old haunt, the Yellow Cedar Fort, remained one of the most impregnable in all of Macheng. Several of his former lieutenants managed to hold out there for months after Zhou's own adventures in the plains had brought his own demise. Late in 1646, they were joined there by Liu Fengzhi, a Ming-loyalist leader from Henan's Guangshan. In December, a massive Qing force converged on Yellow Oak but for over a week could not compel its occupants to surrender. Xu Yong brought in excavation machinery to try to tunnel under the fort's walls, but the defenders used cannon and explosives to thwart him. Eventually the Qing commanders succeeded in setting the fort afire, killing the majority of those inside. Yu Chenglong reports that 397 persons, many of them women, managed to escape the blaze but were caught and executed by Xu Yong's troops.[52]

Even so, the Macheng area could not be fully incorporated into the Qing domain. After the Qing capture and execution of Prince Tang, in October 1646, the focus of loyalist sentiment turned to the former Prince Gui, now declared the Yongli emperor. Yongli initially established his court at Zhaoqing, in Guangdong, but he was very quickly forced to evacuate, on a route that led him, in the late 1640s, through Guangxi, Hunan, and Yunnan and eventually to Burma, where he quietly died in 1662. The leader of the Qi-Huang Forty-Eight

Fort League, Wang Ding, was granted a presidency of the board of war by the Yongli court, but this peripatetic and by all accounts largely ineffectual pretender really offered little coherence to the resistance, other than his thin (and contested) claim of legitimacy. In practice, the league's fortress lords pledged fealty to two minor Ming princes who remained visibly in their midst. One of these was Zhu Yunyan, the Frontier Prince (Fanwang), whose seat was originally at Wuchang but who by the late 1640s had taken refuge in the Tricornered Fort (Sanjian zhai), in Qizhou's Yingshan County; the other was Zhu Tongqi, the Stonewall Prince (Shichengwang), in hiding in the hills of Qianshan, Anhui. Both of these men occasionally passed through Macheng, seeking the protection and hospitality of one or another fortress lord.[53]

By the late 1640s, Qing partisans had effectively established civil authority in the Macheng County seat and were engaged in restoring property rights for the surviving landholders who gathered there.[54] The highlands were a different story altogether. Even after much of Qizhou Prefecture had been subdued in a bloody campaign of 1648, the Macheng rebels remained a constant annoyance. In the summer of that year, a failed Qing assault on Macheng's Drumbeat Fort (Dagu zhai), reportedly inhabited by 30,000 Ming loyalists, resulted in great loss of life to the attackers.[55] When, that same year, the erstwhile Qing convert Jin Shenghuan recanted and led his army upriver from Jiangxi toward Wuchang, a short-lived but bloody sympathetic offensive was launched by the Macheng fortress lord Zhou Chengmo.[56] With the lowland cores of the Hubei counties now lost to them, the loyalist militia of the Dabie Shan took to reprovisioning themselves via raids across the border into Henan. A massive campaign led by Xu Yong in the winter of 1649 to establish Qing control over the Pine Nut and Long Ridge Passes reduced this practice but could not end it altogether.[57]

As midcentury approached, there were ever fewer of the original several hundred forts in the Forty-Eight Fort League still in active rebellion. League master Wang Ding made the circuit of these, to keep up morale and solidarity. Something of a quixotic last-gasp offensive was undertaken in the spring of 1649, when the Stonewall Prince fell back from Yingshan to the White Cloud Fort, Yi Daosan's old stronghold on the Huanggang-Macheng border, and proclaimed there a shadow imperial government. His supporters drew lots (!) for ministerial portfolios: the poet Cao Yinchang drew that of imperial commissioner (*du yushi*), Wang Ding and Zhou Sun were made board presidents, and even Shen Huilin—the turncoat Macheng gentryman who had served as Hanyang prefect in Zhang Xianzhong's 1643 Wuchang regime—took the presidency of the board of war. The prince determined to launch an eastern expedition to liberate Luzhou, in Anhui, and selected Wang and Cao as its commanders. The campaign was a spectacular failure, and the two veteran loyalists quickly retreated to their mountain forts.[58]

Again, boldness only invited more active Qing efforts at extermination. The year 1650 saw Huguang viceroy Chi Riyi conducting an intensive counterinsurgency operation in Macheng with a force of nearly 5,000. The Stonewall Prince was captured and sent to Beijing for execution; Wang Ding was killed in battle that same year. Macheng's Zhou Sun was defeated in Anhui by the twice-serving official Hong Chengchou, and, according to which account can be believed, was killed, escaped to wander the hills as a Buddhist monk, or (as described below) accepted Qing amnesty.[59] With the loss of both its symbolic and actual leaders, the league alliance gradually fell apart.

The poet-loyalist Cao Yinchang had a more colorful fate. With no wish for martyrdom, Cao responded to the collapse of the Forty-Eight Fort resistance by moving discreetly back into his native village and acting as if he were insane. But his old nemesis Hong Chengchou—who as a Ming official had been Cao's frustrated superior in Jiangsu, and who now, by 1651, had risen as a Qing official to the position of grand secretary—wrote to local military officials in Hubei that Cao was merely feigning madness. Using this cover, Cao was writing scandalous verses and issuing drunken insults against both the Qing regime and Hong personally.[60] Under pressure, Cao fled to Yunnan, where he had spent his adolescence in his father's county *yamen*, and where the fugitive Yongli emperor relocated in 1652. He died there sometime in the 1650s.[61]

But Cao Yinchang proved as contentious in death as in life. At least according to local legend, a sordid melodrama played itself out about the transport of his corpse back to Macheng. At the center of this melodrama was a Huanggang native named He Lingluo. Lingluo and Yinchang had a great deal in common. Both had been protégés of the famous Macheng poet Liu Tong, and both were sons of Ming officials who had served in Yunnan in the early seventeenth century. Lingluo's father, He Hongzhong, had been provincial education commissioner and, as it happened, had died in Yongchang County, where Yinchang's father was the magistrate. The younger He had managed, presumably with the aid of Cao *père* and *fils*, to transport his father's corpse back to Huanggang for burial, just as Yinchang shortly thereafter would bring his own father's remains back to Macheng. With this history (Cao Yinchang's biography in the Macheng County gazetteer implies), one would expect He Lingluo to have done everything in his power to assist Yinchang's younger brother Yinming in bringing the corpse home to rest in the 1650s. But over their later years, Cao Yingchang and He Lingluo had become estranged: the gazetteer notes circumspectly that the two "were certainly not friends." What is perhaps most especially important here, Cao had been a prominent leader of the Huangzhou resistance movement, whereas He had quickly taken service under the conquering Qing. We are led to believe that Lingluo, in a position to help, had pointedly not done so. Cao Yingchang's corpse never made it back to his native place.[62]

One final, rather anticlimactic act remained to be played in the drama of Qing conquest in Macheng. Over the years 1652 and 1653, virtually no rain fell in much of eastern Hubei, resulting in failed harvests and disastrous dearth (Macheng was hardest hit of all) as well as frenetic efforts at relief on the part of the fledgling Qing administration. Splinter groups of loyalists in Hunan attempted to use this distress to prompt their Hubei neighbors once more to join their cause.[63] One who did so was Li Youshi, the new occupant of the White Cloud Fort on the Huanggang-Macheng border, in the heart of the Dongshan. In one sense, Li's last-gasp 1653 rebellion was a transitional event: local sources tend to identify it as a specifically *Dongshan* movement and hence as more closely related to the troubles that would be endemic to this area in later decades and centuries than to the more broadly based regional resistance that had gone before. Li, dislodged from his safe haven by the end of that year, continued for years thereafter to fight a guerrilla-style resistance campaign, relying on the intermittent protection of various fortress lords. For their part, the Qing authorities now moved away from their energetic but largely futile efforts to raze the *shanzhai* once they were taken, and hence prevent their future use by local rebels; they adopted instead a policy of at least partially incorporating the forts into the state's own defense structure. In late 1653, for example, a Qing military detachment was permanently assigned to Dongshan's Stoneman Fort (Shiren zhai), to keep watch over that vexing area.[64]

Shortly after the new year of 1656—some thirteen years after the Qing conquest—Grand Secretary and Five-Province Pacification Commissioner Hong Chengchou memorialized on the progress of his ongoing mop-up operations in Macheng. The way to achieve lasting pacification of the highlands, he argued—and, in the process, to deny sanctuary to the still at-large Li Youshi—was to offer amnesty to each *shanzhai* commander once he was defeated, in exchange for "leading his dependents in acknowledging Qing rule (*shanghua*)." Granting imperial benevolence (*huangren*) would secure the lasting peace of the area better than imposing the ultimate sanction; the era of pacification by extermination (*jiao*), he implied, might now finally come to an end. Hong counseled that the fortress lords of Macheng should be "individually dispersed and resettled, in order to alleviate lingering grievances."[65] Hong did not specify where this resettlement might take place. Might it have included Sichuan, the target of energetic Qing resettlement and homesteading drives during these years, and already home to a large and growing Macheng diaspora community? If so, Hong's project may have constituted less the ultimate pacification he advertised it as being than simply a shifting of the problem upriver. Throughout the early-Qing decades, Upper Yangzi officials routinely complained about the predations inflicted on their jurisdictions by purportedly Ming-loyalist marauders from Macheng County, that damnable exporter of violent souls.[66]

Loyalism and Localism

The loyalists of the Qi-Huang Forty-Eight Fort League have been presented in a wide variety of ways—the movement was one of many overlying meanings. In contemporary Qing documents, the loyalists were most often referred to as *ni* (rebels), with an emphasis on their disobedience to properly constituted orders, or as *zei* (another customary term for antidynastic rebels, but with connotations of "thief" or "despoiler"), emphasizing their plunder and disruption of local society. In one intriguing case, a 1645 *Qing Veritable Records* reference to Yi Daosan and Wang Shuguang, they are derided as *changjue* (wild beasts), a characterization that emphasizes the irrational, subhuman violence of their behavior.[67] From all accounts, however, including those of Qing functionaries themselves, it was *state* or *regime* violence that in this time and place was far the more savage. The Qing had its ideology-generating machinery busily at work from its very first approach to Macheng society.

By contrast, every single reference to the Qi-Huang loyalists that I have encountered in modern scholarship is unambiguously sympathetic, though sympathetic in widely differing ways. This begins as early as Wang Baoxin's 1908 paean to the Forty-Eight Fort League. As a credentialed academic historian, Wang Baoxin offers a convincingly complex breakdown of the parties to the eastern Hubei resistance, including Ming princes, former Ming high officials, local gentry and commoners "of righteous intentions," more scurrilous turncoats who had run afoul of the Qing conquerors and had fallen back into the opposition, and not a few simple opportunists.[68] As a committed revolutionary in the last days of the Qing order, however, Wang is less enthusiastic about the loyalist component in the Qi-Huang cause than about its Han nationalism. At the same time, as an ardent local booster writing in the heady era of the local self-government (*difang zizhi*) movement, he is even more rhapsodic in his praise of the Qi-Huang patriotism elements in their motivational mix: in the Dongshan and Dabie Shan, he notes, aspirations to local autonomy fester at all times and invariably rise to the surface at moments of dynastic breakdown (including, presumably, his own times). A populist, Wang is not unsympathetic to the grievances of local bondservant rebels, but it is clearly high-minded elites such as Mei Zhihuan, Zhou Sun, and Cao Yinchang who are his romantic heroes.

By contrast, scholarship in the People's Republic values the Qi-Huang resistance because it is seen as, precisely, a manifestation of class struggle. Documents and narratives related to the Forty-Eight Forts are triumphantly (and rather myopically) lumped into the category of peasant uprisings (*nongmin qiyi*) or that of peasant wars (*nongmin zhanzheng*). Even the great historian Xie Guozhen, while acknowledging that such leaders of the League as Wang Ding must be recognized as local gentry (*xiangshen*), quickly adds that the majority of its personnel were drawn from the peasant masses (*nongmin qunzhong*) and that it was this group that gave the movement its essential class character.[69] Japanese historians, even those with Marxist sympathies, are more cautious. They note that whereas the bulk of the manpower engaged in the anti-Qing resistance in Macheng and its neighbors was clearly of tenant or even bond-servant origin, these persons were capable of being co-opted for a variety of causes, including that of the Qing. It is a mistake, they note, too readily to assume enthusiasm or even general sympathy on their part for the literati-loyalist cause (or for that matter, in the absence of personal testimony, to deny the same). As Taniguchi Kikuo rightly points out, many leaders of the Forty-Eight Fort League, and above all Mei Zhihuan, were not simple country squires but enormously wealthy individuals and extremely high-ranking Ming officials with empirewide contacts. They were *very* powerful men, and it would have been extraordinarily difficult for their tenants and servile dependents to resist their localist/loyalist agenda once it had been determined upon.[70] Even so, as we shall see in a moment, such resistance did occur.

An alternative or companion interpretation, offered in many instances by the same scholars who invoke the "peasant uprising" trope, sees the Forty-Eight Fort resistance as a protonationalist effort—in effect, a class-bridging United Front against a foreign invader. Xie Guozhen, who began his study of the Ming-Qing transition well before "Liberation," in the heyday of the anti-Japanese resistance, refers to the Qi-Huang militia as a people's army (*minjun*) combating Qing aggression. Taniguchi, who also seems to have the wartime United Front in mind, refers to it as nationalist resistance (*minzokuteki hankō*). Even apart from the anachronism inherent in such a characterization, however, there seems scant evidence on which to advance this claim.[71] The old warhorse Mei Zhihuan, to be sure, repeatedly invoked the "*guo*" as the object he sought to defend, but this probably more directly meant the Ming dynasty than it did the Han patria. In any case, it is by no means clear that Zhihuan, had he lived, would not, like his cousin Zhiyuan, have capitulated to the Qing in the interests of preserving the social order and the Confucian way of life. By all accounts, the edict mandating the queue was the spark that decided the Qi-Huang fort masters in favor of to-the-death resistance, but this, too, may be read in ways suggesting something other than protonationalism.

What seems relatively clear is that, whatever its larger object—Confucian civilization, the Han patria, the Ming ruling house—the most compelling way in which loyalism could be expressed in seventeenth-century Huangzhou and Qizhou was through *localist* appeals, through what Wakeman has called "the mystique of the locale."[72] For some, perhaps, such as Mei Zhihuan, the local community was the building block in assembling national spirit, but for most others it was sufficient in itself to prompt resistance to conquest, be that conquest by uncivilized, low-class interlopers like Zhang Xianxzhong or by heathen border tribes like the Aisin Gioro. Both of these forces threatened the locality with genocidal violence, and a defensive alliance forged to combat one could logically, perhaps even necessarily, be turned to resist the other. Yet the presence within the *shanzhai* resistance of men of such convenient allegiances as Zhou Wenjiang, Liu Qiao, and Shen Huilin should caution us against crediting even the local community with too encompassing an appeal. Every party in the loyalist alliance would seem to have had his or her own distinctive motivation. What they had in common was a habituated acceptance of violence as a mode of social action.

Dynastic Change as Personal Liberation

Any comforting illusion of a class-transcendent localist resistance to alien conquest in Macheng was dispelled in 1651, with the outbreak of a war within the war—the last wave, for the time being at least, of bondservant rebellion. Indeed, there was every reason for many in Macheng society—perhaps even the majority—to actively welcome imperial regime change as being of positive benefit to their life condition. Some well-informed scholars have argued that this optimism toward Qing rule was in fact not misplaced, since the new rulers were no necessary friends of the kind of literati privilege that had served as the governing principle of local society under the Ming.[73]

More concretely, in their first decade of rule in North China a number of difficult issues had confronted the Qing conquerors regarding systems of personal servility inherited from the Ming. One of the most vexing involved the rising incidence of violence and litigation between landowners and tenant-serfs over which of the two was responsible for the tax and corvée impositions attached to the land over which they shared proprietorship. Local officials complained that they were caught in the middle, and they asked for clear resolution of the problem from above. Finally, after the new year of 1651, an exasperated Shunzhi court issued an edict attempting to clarify the limits and conditions of bondservice, specifying, for example, that an individual who had commended himself to another nevertheless retained full personhood under the law and was responsible, like any free commoner, for crimes he might commit. This edict was received in most localities with confusion, which only further complicated local social relations.[74]

In Macheng, by 1651, Qing officials had achieved fairly secure control of the fertile lowland core, where the largest numbers of bondservants were found, and were well on their way to mopping up the residual *shanzhai*-based loyalist resistance. But the new county administration faced contentious fiscal issues of its own. For reasons of both politics and finance, Hubei governor Luo Xiujin had issued an order canceling corvée and tax exemptions on property held by retired Ming officials (a category, of course, that included many of the largest landholders in Macheng). Macheng local magistrate Xu Ding determined that one of the most effective ways to implement this directive in his district would be to "clarify" the status of bondservants, who composed the bulk of the labor on former Ming officials' estates. The details of his nine-item proclamation do not survive, but one item was a declaration that servile tenants on retired officials' lands were personally responsible for the corvée and tax assessments on their leaseholds, regardless of their landlords' privileged status.[75] For the masters, this was unequivocally a hostile move, and local and provincial authorities were deluged by petitions from eminent Macheng landholders on the improper (*buzheng*) nature of Xu's new policy. For the servile tenants there was more ambiguity: on the one hand, they might logically interpret this as the Qing government's recognition of their status as free subjects of the throne, but, on the other, they were faced with a new fiscal burden, at the very time when the local agrarian economy was in crisis. On either score, direct action seemed called for.

Rebellion broke out in late spring of that year, on the estates of the Qiligang Mei lineage's Mei Tian, in the suburbs of the county seat.[76] The leader of the movement was a literate bondservant and estate manager named Fang Jihua. Fang bombarded local officials with petitions decrying what he saw as a tax-engrossment racket (*baozhan dingliang*) conducted by retired officials resident in the county seat (*yizhong guhuan*)—his own master Mei Tian among them—in collusion with *yamen* clerks. Magistrate Xu Ding's proclamation came, it seems, at least in part in response to Fang's agitation. At the same time, Fang began to reassemble the survivors of Tang Zhi's Liren hui of 1631, utilizing funds expropriated from the Mei estate accounts. Runaway servants (*zanghuo*) and rootless villains (*wulai*) flocked to his banner by the hundreds. Probably inspired by the Shunzhi edict of early spring "clarifying" the status of bondservants, Fang told his followers that their long-sought quest for redemption of servile status (*shupu*) had now received imperial endorsement. They mobilized to realize this by force, if necessary. Magistrate Xu was informed of Fang's activities by alarmed estate holders but, flustered by the variety of conflicting orders and information with which he was presented, equivocated for several days.

Frustrated by the magistrate's inaction, a group of influential urban literati undertook personally to inform Governor Luo of the crisis looming in their county. One of these literati, naturally, was Mei Tian; another was the same Zhou Sun who had so recently been a leader of the anti-Qing Forty-Eight Fort resistance, but who was also a member of one of Macheng's largest serfholding lineages. The most influential of these men, however, was Zou Xing, a very early Qing convert and leader (as we have seen) of the 1646 defense of the county seat when it was besieged by Ming-loyalist fortress lords.[77] It was Zou Xing who was now deputed by his colleagues to go in person to Wuchang and invite Governor Luo's intercession.

Zou protested to the governor that there had never been any tax-engrossment racket such as the one Fang Jihua alleged. At least with regard to the corvée (*ding*), he explained, this was not possible, since in Macheng County the *ding* assessment had already been converted from a head tax to a supplementary imposition on agricultural land (*congtian tanding*)—in effect, a local precursor to the empirewide *tanding rudi* reform of the 1720s and 1730s.[78] Thus it was being paid by landowners like himself, not by their bondservant-tenants such as Fang Jihua. The governor, convinced, authorized Zou to return to Macheng and take whatever action he felt necessary, even without the approval of the ineffectual Magistrate Xu Ding. Zou Xing returned home and, with his estate-holder allies, arrested and summarily executed Fang Jihua and seven of his key lieutenants. The removal of Fang did not, however, destroy the *hui*, incensed members of which violently attacked their masters. In one instance, they massacred the entire household of the estate holder Wang Shijie. The literati elite, many of whom only recently had been persuaded to come back down to their estates from their hillside havens, once again fled to their mountain fortresses. The rebels then laid siege, in time-honored fashion, to the Macheng County seat.

Governor Luo Xiujin personally led a contingent of Qing troops to relieve the siege, which proved a relatively easy matter. He then took three actions, clearly designed to mollify the various parties to the dispute while establishing the solonical authority of the new Qing regime. First, he cashiered Magistrate Xu Ding, effectively scapegoating him for the entire mess and exonerating the county gentry from any allegations of wrongdoing. Second, he rounded up and executed all known residual members of Fang Jihua's organization. Third, however, he issued a new set of guidelines specifying the only appropriate conditions for bondservant status. These were (1) persons whose service had been bestowed on another by direct imperial order (*laizi*), (2) captives of war (*zhenhuo*), (3) persons born within the master's household (*jiasheng*), and (4) those who had expressly, in writing, sold themselves in service to another (*jiamai*). This set of guidelines basically accorded with the categories of legitimate servitude then being worked out by the Shunzhi court in Beijing, but it by no means exhausted the categories of persons who were actually living in servitude in Macheng.

The events of 1651 in Macheng were part of a broader regional pattern in the Shunzhi reign. A separate bondservant rebellion, led by one Zhang Zhengzhong, took place the same year in Huang'an and was put down by armed literati-landlords.[79] A more serious rebellion erupted in Macheng's neighbor to the north, Guangshan, in the winter of 1658–59. With prompting, again, from a rumor that the new Qing court had issued an edict of emancipation (*fangpu*), bondservants under Wang Mingyu organized a society (*tang*), acquired weapons, and intimidated their masters into giving them documents of manumission. The movement spread to the adjacent Dabie Shan counties, Shangcheng and Gushi, and was eventually quashed by troops under the command of Prefect Jin Changzhen. Jin then issued a set of regulations similar to those previously issued in Macheng, tightening the criteria for legal bondservice. He especially condemned the common practice of impressing free tenants and farm laborers into servitude, insisting that the only legal basis for servile status was a written document of indenture, freely signed by the individual and held on file at the county *yamen*. Even with this requirement met, however, a similarly unfree status could not be imputed by extension to the contracted bondservant's wife and descendants. In an argument sounding remarkably like one for natural rights, Jin insisted that all tenants and laborers who had not voluntarily abrogated their freedom were "fundamentally persons of full competence and capacity" (*liyi zhi ren*), and that to treat them as chattel (*zanghuo*) was contrary not only to Qing law, but also to the basic principles of human nature and society (*renqing*).[80]

As has been pointed out by Satō Fumitoshi, the most thorough scholar of bondservant rebellions in the Dabie Shan region, it was the Qing response to the troubles of 1651 that decisively convinced the estate-holding elite of Macheng that they could and should work as partners with the alien dynasty. The Qing response was the key indicator that in this interior highland region the throne-gentry alliance had, in the end, survived the conquest.[81] Throughout Huangzhou Prefecture, in the wake of 1651, newly installed Qing officials made overtures intended to legitimate and co-opt for the imperial cause the elite-led paramilitary forces that had been formed over prior decades in order to combat, variously, local bondservant insurgencies, broader antidynastic rebellions, and the Qing invasion itself.

The chief sticking point was, of course, the institution of bondservice. Had such regulations as those of Luo Xiujin, in Hubei, and Jin Changzhen, in Henan, been rigorously enforced, their effect would have been broadly emancipatory. At least in Macheng, however, they clearly were not. To the contrary, in the Shunzhi reign and the early part of the Kangxi, Qing official efforts in this area seem to have concentrated less on addressing the bondservants' lingering demand for purchased redemption (*shupu*), than on the *masters'* chief complaint, which was the problem of runaways (*taopu*).[82] Even here, however, the events of the 1670s (our concern in the next chapter) suggest that before that decade, Qing active intervention in the Macheng social-economic regime was rather minimal.

The early-Qing initiatives of Luo, Jin, and others to strictly clarify (*qingyan*) the status of unfree tenants and farm laborers anticipated the more strenuous empirewide emancipation edicts of the Yongzheng emperor some seventy years later. Their message was essentially the same: agrarian bondservice was not illegal in and of itself (the Qing, of course, used it extensively on their own imperial and banner estates in the north and the northeast), but many and, very likely, *most* instances of it in practice, especially in central and southern China, were counter to law and propriety. In general, the state would countenance only those cases in which a signed written contract of indenture was on file with local officials, pertaining only to the single individual who had signed it.[83] But even Yongzheng's efforts had only partial success. Agrarian bondservice continued to be widespread in many areas, and in some, such as Anhui's Huizhou Prefecture, it continued to be *the* predominant labor regime for a century or more thereafter.[84]

In post–seventeenth-century Macheng, the major instances of collective violence no longer revolved around the issue of personal servitude. But although it is difficult to ascertain how widespread such servitude remained, there is ample evidence of its persistence. A famous mid–nineteenth-century monk named Yaozhan, for example, had been a personal slave (*rennu*) until, at the age of eighteen, he was consigned by his owner to Dongshan's New Temple (Xinsi).[85] Liang Gongchen's *Beidong yuan bilu* (Jottings from the Northeast Garden, ca. 1845), contains the following passage:

> Hubei's Chen Fusheng is a great and powerful lineage head from Huangzhou Prefecture [county unspecified]. He has six sons, all of whom have become eminent officials. In his household there are countless servile dependents. When one of these and his wife have a daughter, if she is beautiful she is made into a serving maid. When they have a son, that son becomes a *nupu*.[86]

Ultimately, bondservice in Macheng outlasted even the Qing's own demise. The All-Hubei Peasants Conference, held at Wuchang in March 1927 with considerable Macheng representation, explicitly condemned the continued existence of "serfdom" and "landslaves" throughout the province.[87] And as late as 1946, the regulations of Macheng's Shi lineage placed formal restrictions on the behavior of male and female servants who, by their terms of reference (*nanpu* and *nünu*, respectively), appear to have been unfree.[88] Despite repeated and savage waves of violence, old institutions died hard.

PART TWO

CHAPTER SEVEN

Dongshan Rebellion

IN THE THIRTEENTH YEAR of the reign of the Qing emperor Kangxi (1674), Macheng experienced a linked series of incidents that have remained to this day a vivid part of the county's stock of lore and legend. The timing was exactly thirty years after the murderous trauma of the Ming-Qing transition, and the events of 1674 reprised each of the major themes of that earlier holocaust—localism, loyalism, and class warfare—intermixed, as before, in a heady and often confusing blend. But they did so now in a more neatly encapsulated form. The year Kangxi 13 brought to the fore as never in the past the distinctive identity of the Dongshan highlands that Macheng shared with Luotian and Huanggang Counties to the east, and the endemic tensions between this area and the county's lowland core. The drama of this year, moreover, featured a starring role by one of the most colorful personalities in all of Macheng history, the model local official Yu Chenglong. And the process of resolving the conflicts set in place a unique infrastructure of systematic power sharing between center and locality that would pertain in the county through the remainder of the Qing, and beyond.

Macheng Lineages Survive the Conquest

The great era of high official service that so many Macheng lineages had enjoyed under the late Ming was never again repeated. However, although the transition from Ming to Qing did eventually bring a significant decline in the county's level of educational and cultural prominence, this was neither complete nor immediate. Macheng men welcomed and took adept advantage of opportunities for examination degrees and official posts as soon as the new regime offered them. Some of the grandest of the Ming-era lineages, to be sure, did not fare as well thereafter. The Zhou, the Liu, and the Mei, producers of scores of Ming higher-degree holders, could claim a paltry thirteen *juren* among them over the entire course of the Qing. Yet others, like the Wan, the Wu, and the Dai, did far better under the new dynasty.[1] Quite a few Macheng men from theretofore undistinguished families—men with surnames such as Hu, Xiang, and Wang—won provincial or metropolitan degrees in the Shunzhi reign and moved into local official posts in service of the conquerors. Some who had enjoyed preferment under the Ming unblinkingly accepted the same under the Qing. Dong Chang, for instance, was a Ming *juren* but served the Qing as a county magistrate; his son Shisheng (named by his father, aptly, "rise when the opportunity occurs") was a *jinshi* of 1659 and a magistrate in Shandong. Cheng Hao, scion of a wealthy Baiguo mercantile lineage and son of a Ming local official, purchased a lower degree in 1651 and served as Taizhou subprefect (where he won glory in the campaigns against Zheng Chenggong), as Guangzhou prefect, and as Henan provincial judge. Unsurprisingly, the Cheng were among those Macheng families who enjoyed far greater examination success under the Qing than they ever had in the past.[2]

The biggest winner of all in the Ming-Qing transition were the Balifan Zou. The Zou, as we have seen, were the one enduring Macheng lineage who had been powerful local magnates as far back as the Yuan. In the Ming, they produced two *jinshi* and twelve *juren*—respectable totals, but far from competitive with the county's greatest official lineages. But in the Qing, while most of these others were experiencing dramatic decline in their examination success, the Zou did notably better than before—five *jinshi* and fifteen *juren*, far the most of any local family. Almost all of this success, significantly, came in the dynasty's early reigns; the last Zou *jinshi* was won in 1708.

This spurt of good fortune was largely due to one individual, our old friend Zou Xing. The offspring of a modest household within the Zou lineage, Xing never himself attained a higher examination degree or served in an official post, but he was very clearly the single most influential man in Macheng County in the third quarter of the seventeenth century. He lost his mother at the age of five and was sent to live as the adopted son of a neighbor, Zhao Zhiying, then serving as a Ming military official in Beijing. In Zou Xing's adolescence, Zhao was posted to Liaodong, where he died in battle against the advancing Qing forces. Xing took charge of transporting Zhao's remains the thousand *li* back to their native place for burial. During the chaos of the Qing conquest, Xing sent his aged natural father off to the relative safety of their ancestral fort in the Dabie Shan while he himself stayed on to supervise affairs in the Macheng County seat. As Qing forces moved up the Yangzi in 1645, Zou Xing saw the handwriting on the wall and declared his fealty to his old enemies from the northeast. As we have seen, when loyalist fortress lords under Zhou Wenjiang besieged the city in 1646, Zou Xing aided the Qing by supervising its defense. He was also the local notable most responsible for crushing Fang Jihua's bondservant rebellion of 1651. We will see that he was a key local figure in countering the uprisings of 1674 as well. During the early-Qing decades, moreover, Zou was also able to parlay the gratitude that the dynasty owed him for this allegiance into deals favorable to local landed interests; he led, for example, a campaign to remove land-tax surtaxes levied by county clerks to finance the postal service. According to the county gazetteer, it was the strong guiding influence of this man that was most responsible for the official success of his descendants, most notably his own son, Zou Shicong, grand secretary in the 1710s and the highest-ranking official produced by Macheng throughout the Qing.[3]

In other words, residual Ming loyalism beyond the 1640s did not prevent many among the Macheng elite from taking service under the conquering Qing. But it was not altogether absent. As Wang Baoxin pointed out, discrete pockets of Ming loyalism—for the most part passive, effectively autonomous, and living in tacit coexistence with Qing state authorities—persisted for many decades after the conquest. In the Macheng highlands in the 1670s there remained many adult males who had not yet adopted the queue. The actual rebels of 1674, moreover, were in many instances the direct genealogical descendants of the loyalist heroes of the 1640s. The physical survival of many of the mountain fortresses, and the memory of the Forty-Eight Fort League, provided ready institutional models for rebellious mobilization.[4]

The chief pocket of residual loyalism in Macheng County, and the site of the 1674 uprisings, was the Dongshan. Though the Ming-loyalist resistance of the conquest era had in large part played itself out in this highland region, that movement's chief architects had been lowland elites, such as Mei Zhihuan, Zhou Sun, and Cao Yinchang, who had deliberately gone into the mountains (*rushan*) to conduct local defense. As we saw in the preceding chapter, it was only in its very last phase, with the final rebellious holdout Li Youshi in the 1650s, that resistance to the Qing conquest had begun to take on a distinctly Dongshan coloring. The leaders of the 1674 rebellions, however, would be highly self-conscious Dongshan natives. And though the rebellions themselves were quashed, certain of these leaders would emerge to wield influence that went far beyond what any Dongshan men had ever previously enjoyed.

Thus began a long-term shift of power—peaking only in the Nationalist era of the 1930s—in which extraordinarily wealthy, ultracivilized (though in many cases militarily adept), cosmopolitan, and nationally connected literati from the plains and river valleys were supplanted as the most important actors in the county's history by smaller-scale, marginally educated, and deeply parochial strongmen of the eastern highlands. Whereas the former group could certainly be militarized in defense of family, locality, and dynasty, it was made up essentially of classical scholars, nationally famous poets, and disciples of avant-garde thinkers like Li Zhi; members of the latter group, by contrast, were imbued with a fierce backwoods sociocultural conservatism. Relations between the two groups were always testy at best.

Macheng in the San-fan Rebellion

In the general history of the Qing dynasty, the Dongshan rebellions of 1674 were but a sideshow to the larger San-fan (Three Feudatories) rebellion. Wu Sangui—the Ming general who, upon the fall of Beijing to Li Zicheng, had joined the Qing and led their forces into North China and then played a major role in mopping up rebels in the southwest—had been granted a fiefdom in Yunnan. By the early 1670s, the Kangxi emperor had grown impatient with Wu's autonomy and was increasingly putting pressure on him to resign and allow full integration of the southwest into the Qing bureaucratic administration. Wu responded on December 28, 1673, by declaring a rebellion under the slogans "Overthrow the Qing and restore the Ming" ("fan Qing fu Ming") and—more convincingly, since Wu also proclaimed his own new "Zhou" dynasty—"Oppose the Manchus and support the native Chinese" ("fan Man xing Han"). He ordered his subjects to cut their queues and his troops to wear white garments and caps in mourning for the Ming. Wu quickly advanced into western Hunan, and then, in early 1674, he took the Hunanese capital, Changsha, as well as Jingzhou, in western Hubei. By March he had established a forward headquarters at Yuezhou, not far from the confluence of the Xiang and Yangzi Rivers. To counter this advance, the Kangxi emperor led his own troops south into Jiangxi, and from there he experimented with various routes into Hunan to recapture Yuezhou, a feat he was not able to achieve until early 1679.[5]

Macheng and the Dongshan make no appearance at all in most general histories of the San-fan rebellion, but it is clear that their strategic importance in the campaigns was considerable. Had Wu Sangui been able to consolidate his hold on them, he not only would have attained a significant further expansion of his territory to the north and east but also would have commanded one of the time-honored points of linkage between his central China stronghold and the Lower Yangzi, where his allies from the southeast coast had made their own advances early in the war. He would also have nearly surrounded and cut off the Kangxi emperor's troops in western Jiangxi. And the Dongshan area did seem ripe for the picking. Huangzhou Prefecture had been unsettled by a fairly severe drought during the first half of 1674, while the majority of Qing troops stationed in the area had been redeployed to the fronts in northern Hunan and western Hubei. Wu seems to have enticed a certain Tan Yicong into rebellion in Huang'an County in the spring of that year.[6] His parallel efforts to convert various residually Ming-loyalist Macheng strongmen to his cause likewise enjoyed success, as we shall see. From the Qing point of view, rebellion in the Dongshan was a very serious prospect indeed.

An obscure yet pivotal series of events, the Dongshan rebellion—or, more properly, rebellions—bears a complex array of meanings, and this complexity is reflected in the way the history of these events has been transmitted. There are three near-contemporary accounts, which have served as the basis for most subsequent historical treatments, both in successive county and prefectural gazetteers and in the work of more recent historians.[7] First are the reports to superiors and the proclamations to the local population of Yu Chenglong (1617–84), the official most directly charged with the rebellions' suppression. These are first-person documentary sources, produced simultaneously with the events they describe and published by Yu's literary executors, with a preface of 1683, less than a decade after the events they describe.[8] They are decidedly subjective. Yu quite naturally paints his own actions in a favorable light, but he does not necessarily disparage the character and motivations of all his opponents; indeed, we shall see that Yu, even at the time, quite clearly altered the truth in order to portray the rebellion in the light he wished it to be understood. The second account is by Yu's younger contemporary, the eminent Kangxi court official Chen Tingjing (1639–1712), appearing in a biography of Yu written very likely in the late 1680s, shortly after Yu's death, but published in Chen's collected works of 1708.[9] This version is far more effusive in its praises of Yu Chenglong than even Yu's own accounts—indeed, it reads like a stirring heroic romance—but at the same time it is more candid about the motives of his opponents, especially of their Ming loyalism, which Yu, for a variety of reasons, actively sought to efface. The third source is an essay by a contemporary Macheng scholar, Zhou Weiju (*jinshi* 1672), clearly written in the wake of the events themselves and appearing in the county gazetteer of 1795. (The preceding edition of the gazetteer, that of 1670, just shortly antedated the rebellions.) Zhou, clearly no friend of any of the various rebel groups, and angered at the threat their hotheaded action has posed to the county, likewise tilts his story to the praise of Yu Chenglong, less for the romantic heroism celebrated by Chen Tingjing than for Yu's statesmanlike avoidance of recriminations against the local population.[10]

But one additional source—the late-Qing quasi-academic, quasi-popular account of the Forty-Eight Forts by a Dongshan native, Wang Baoxin—draws on new evidence from family records and popular folklore and turns these earlier narratives on their heads. Wang is still respectful of the motives and actions of the model official Yu Chenglong. But at the same time, far from obscuring the anti-Manchuism of the Dongshan rebels, as Yu himself had done, Wang is anxious to rescue this from the cultural amnesia into which it had fallen under centuries of Qing rule. And, far from the embarrassment that the earlier Macheng scholar Zhou Weiju (a product of the county core, *not* of the Dongshan) had felt about the small-fry (*xiaochun*) rebels of 1674, Wang is keen to redeem them as part of his own proud highland heritage.[11]

Liu Junfu Meets Yu Chenglong

The story begins with the arrival in Macheng of a sorcerer (*yaoren*) named Huang Jinlong, or Golden Dragon Huang. A native of Hubei's Daye County, Huang had spent years wandering various mountain regions plying his wares and trying in one way or another to organize a rebellion. Most recently he had been doing his work in Guangdong, from which he had managed to escape just one step ahead of the law. In a passage of rare ethnographic insight, the editor of Macheng's 1882 county gazetteer links Huang Jinlong to a broader pattern of Chinese who had traveled to the south and southwest under the Three Feudatories regime and there picked up a variety of techniques from the Miao-Man indigenes, techniques that, for example, allowed the adept to mutate into many bizarre forms (*bianhua huanxing*). So equipped, these shamans then returned to central China—perhaps loosely as Wu Sangui's advance propagandists—and fanned out to cut queues and otherwise preach against the Qing occupation.[12]

Golden Dragon showed up in Macheng just after the new year of 1674, brandishing a *baojian* (precious sword) and bearing a *tianshu* (letter from Heaven) that proclaimed his mission to exterminate Qing demons.[13] He took refuge at the fortress estate of Liu Junfu, in the village of Caojiahe, near the Luotian-Huanggang border. Liu was in many ways a typical strongman of the Dongshan but was somewhat more swashbuckling than most. He commanded a band of desperadoes (*wangming*) and was prone to give shelter to just such fugitives as Huang Jinlong. Nevertheless, he was notoriously shrewd (*zhixia*) and knew how to win the favor of the local officials by using his vigilantes to capture and turn in any unsuspecting bandits who stumbled onto his turf. As Chen Tingjing notes, he was one of those men whom the regime sought to make use of because it could not otherwise control them.

Liu Junfu's nephew and adopted son, Liu Qingli, was as truculent as he, and far more hotheaded. He was more given than his uncle to banditry of his own. And it was said that he had actually visited Wu Sangui in Yunnan. Either through the medium of Qingli or through another emissary, Liu Junfu came into possession of a communiqué (*zha*) enlisting him in Wu's imperial enterprise and authorizing him to lead a sympathetic rebellion in the Dongshan. Qingli then began systematically to mobilize support from neighboring strongmen throughout highland Huangzhou Prefecture and beyond into the neighboring provinces of Henan, Anhui, and Jiangxi, drawing in part on the collective memory of the Forty-Eight Fort resistance and in part on the network of disciples accrued over the years by Golden Dragon Huang. He also communicated with men already actively in rebellion, such as the Henanese Iron Claw Zhou (Zhou Tiezhao). Qingli argued that the officials' own misdeeds would rouse the people to rebel (*guanji minbian*). Somewhat hesitatingly. it would seem, Liu Junfu was drawn into his nephew's campaign, adding his considerable aura of power to the movement. He was said to have at his command, directly or indirectly, several hundred thousand armed men. To allow time for adequate preparation, Junfu set a date for his rebellion that was several months off, in the seventh lunar month of 1674.

Rumors of Liu Junfu's impending rising brought to the fore a complicated and very bitter set of schisms within Macheng society: between the propertied elite and the subbureaucratic county functionaries, between those elites who had early converted to the Qing cause (*yuanguizhe*) and those who remained stubbornly loyal to the Ming (*yimin*), between the refined literati of the county seat (*chengshen*) and the roughhewn strongmen of the highlands, and, not least, among the perennially feuding latter group themselves. The longest-standing rival (*chouren*) of Liu Junfu was Xia Ding'an, head of the sprawling and feisty Xia lineage of Cassiawood River (Muxihe)—a venerable Dongshan presence about whom we will have much to say in later chapters. Ding'an dispatched a kinsman to the county seat to inform Magistrate Qu Zhenqi of the pending rebellion of the Liu and of their commission from Wu Sangui. When news of this petition in turn filtered back to Liu's own theater of operations—the sector of Macheng County southeast of Baiguo, most especially the townships of Xu Family Fort (Xujia bao), Wang Family Fort (Wangjia bao), and Riverbank Fort (Shuiyuan bao)—it sparked panic at the prospect of massive Qing retaliation. Elites of the area took to the hills yet once more and manned their fortresses.[14]

Qing functionaries in the affected sector saw things differently, however. On the fifteenth day of the fifth lunar month, one of these, a local constable (*xiangyue*) from Xu Family Fort named Zhou Meigong, ran to Magistrate Qu's *yamen* to report that the ongoing fortress mobilization was *not* a means of self-defense but rather was itself a manifestation of antidynastic rebellion. Provocatively, but convincingly to many urban literati, Zhou expressed his view that the fort masters there were untrustworthy evil gentry (*lieshen*) and that there was no one outside the county seat who was not of the rebel party. The magistrate hesitated. Faced with official inaction, a number of Macheng City gentry and clerks from the county *yamen*—a coalition of parties who had actively gone along with, if not profited from, the Qing conquest—began systematically arming themselves for their own defense.[15] Just as in the 1640s and 1650s, the chief stabilizing force in the Macheng City of 1674 was none other than Zou Xing. Zou decried the rural gentry for their inconstancy in the face of legitimately established Qing authority, and he invoked his considerable con-

Ancestral portrait of Yu Chenglong. Reproduced by permission of Freer Gallery of Art and Arthur M. Sackler Gallery, Smithsonian Institution, Washington D.C.: Purchase, S1997.39.

nections in an effort to fragment the rebel coalition and defuse the threat. Over the long trauma of the Ming-Qing transition in Macheng, in other words, it was Zou Xing who most consistently kept the lid on social turmoil, and who effectively succeeded Mei Zhihuan as the county's "godfather"—its single most authoritative and powerful figure. He was probably the last member of the county's core elite who would have the chance to do so.[16]

As for Liu Junfu, he now saw the impossibility of continuing any longer to husband his time, and around the twentieth of the month he hoisted the banner of rebellion, joined by Chen Huihui and several other neighboring strongmen. Magistrate Qu declared the county seat under martial law and called for reinforcements. A small Qing battalion from the Huangzhou prefectural seat advanced to Macheng's Xingfu Temple while Qu himself led a force of local militia (*xiangyong*) as far as Baiguo. Together the two forces engaged Liu Junfu's rebels but were rebuffed. Magistrate Qu, still accompanied by the Qing battalion, fell back to the relative safety of the county seat.[17]

Enter Yu Chenglong. Yu hailed from Yongning County, Shanxi, and held merely a purchased lower degree. (This Yu Chenglong should not be confused with another prominent early-Qing official bearing the same name, a Han bannerman whose dates are 1638–1700.) At the time of his arrival in Macheng, Yu was a seasoned fifty-seven-year-old local official, having served long and distinguished terms as a county magistrate in Guangxi and Sichuan. His ancestral portrait shows him with a bright red nose—a candid admission that he "was fond of his cups"—but he was otherwise severely abstemious and gradually gained popular acclaim as the most incorrupt official of his generation. Moreover, in the words of one biographer, "despite his bookish appearance he commanded troops like a god." At the time of his death, Yu had risen to governor general of the Lower Yangzi region and was posthumously canonized in the Temple of Eminent Statesmen by the Qing court.[18]

The post that Yu held in Macheng was that of Huangzhou subprefect, an office first established in the mid-Ming and stationed at Qiting, the town farthest downstream on the Ju River and the county's closest point of contact to the provincial capital of Wuchang. Formally, the incumbent of this post was the highest-ranking official in the county, senior to the county magistrate at Macheng City, but there is little evidence that at any time prior to Yu Chenglong's tenure the Qiting subprefect took any kind of active role in local administration. Yu himself had held the post since 1673 but seems to have barely set foot in the county, having merely rounded up a few local bandits before he was offered a collateral "acting" appointment as Wuchang prefect and assigned the task of securing the Hubei-Hunan border from falling into the hands of the northward-advancing Wu Sangui. When rebellion began brewing in Yu's own jurisdiction of Macheng in midsummer 1674, however, Hubei governor Zhang

Chaozhen recalled him from the south and dispatched him back to pacify that new trouble spot. The governor's meeting with Yu is described by Yu himself, and even more dramatically by Chen Tingjing, very much in the manner of a scene from a Chinese opera: Yu notes that the population of Macheng is notoriously violent (*piaohan*) and belligerent (*shandou*), and, besides, there are all those forts! I know that, replies the governor, but I also believe that, if not led astray by hotheads, they can be taught to become loyal subjects. In any case, despite your notorious drinking, you are my man, and I have great faith in your ability to win their hearts and minds. Yu, his confidence bolstered, resolutely sets forth.[19]

Upon his arrival in Qiting, Yu opted to bypass the county seat and Magistrate Qu altogether. On the twenty-fourth of the fifth month, he proceeded instead to Baiguo Town, the gateway to the Dongshan, where he set up his field headquarters. He immediately issued a series of proclamations to the fort masters of Xu Family Fort and the neighboring townships, in which he adopted a paternalistic approach, familiar enough from imperial Confucian discourse in general but, under the circumstances, nevertheless striking. When I was first posted here, Yu says, I found the literati and commoners of the Dongshan to be remarkably sincere. There were a few bandits, to be sure, but we apprehended them, and the area was peaceful. This was my own good fortune, and also that of the hardworking cultivators of the area. Then I was called away to the south, and imagine my surprise when I was told that Dongshan was in rebellion and I must return to put it down! I could not believe this would happen in such an upright locality. Have parents here been neglectful in raising their children to be obedient? Can the productive labor of several years be overturned in a single day? I call upon the good people (*liangmin*) of this area to come down from the mountains and return to your farms (*guinong*). If you do not, I will be forced to bring in troops from Wuchang, and the devastation to your families and lands will be terrible.[20]

The response was nearly all Yu could have hoped for. If the various fort masters of Xu Family Fort had in fact harbored any thoughts of joining Liu Junfu's cause, they quickly thought better of them. A series of remorseful collective petitions streamed in, fronted by the lower-degree holder Zhu Jue. Zhu stated, "The gentry and commoners of this township are customarily hardworking farmer-scholars (*gengdu*) and are never involved in any kind of illegal activity. Between the tenth and fourteenth of the month, a handful of troublemakers (*feilei*) from elsewhere in Dongshan came into our township, spreading rumors [of rebellion]. We sent several local elders to investigate these rumors, and they determined there was no truth to them. Then, on the fifteenth, Constable Zhou Meigong falsely denounced us to the magistrate, claiming that the entire township are all rebels. In fact, we were all loyal subjects (*shanliang*), and our agitated reaction was based simply on our fears of impending military disaster." Other leaders of the wider region petitioned to vouch for Zhu, calling him a good Confucian scholar (*liangru*) but adding coyly that if he *had* committed any crime, he was anxious to confess and beg for pardon. Zhu himself then petitioned again, allowing that there might still be a few troublemakers around in his township but that they, too, would be eager to seek Yu's amnesty. Yu Chenglong assured them all that he would forward their petitions to the provincial governor, along with his favorable endorsement. Appealing again to the timely necessity of tending their crops and to their interests as property holders, he assured them that no major military action would be forthcoming.[21]

Even more striking than all of this was the way Yu Chenglong reported to Governor Zhang the success of his mission thus far. Whether out of temperament, his reading of the local scene, or deliberate political purpose, Yu Chenglong opted emphatically to side with the highland elite against the urban establishment, both bureaucratic and literati. True to his word, he depicted Zhu Jue and his party as innocent (*wugu*) of any serious wrongdoing. But Yu then went on to argue that, *even if* the Xu Family Fort strongmen had momentarily flirted with rebellion, this was a case of being pushed into rebellion by official misconduct (*guanji minbian*).[22] He singled out for blame the "stupid" county magistrate, Qu Zhenqi, and—remarkably—the dean of the urban gentry and the Qing's staunchest Macheng literati ally Zou Xing, whom he intemperately described as unfilial and unfeeling, lacking all sense of benevolence and propriety (*buxiao buci, wuren wuyi*). Most culpable of all in Yu's estimation—and this is less surprising coming from such a man of statecraft (*jingshi*) leanings—were the county clerks, who sought to scavenge profit from any disorder. It was these "rats and crows" who had convinced the urban population that the entire countryside was awash with rebels and thrown them into panic. The clerks, in Yu's view—in league with Zou Xing (who may have been using the disorder to settle some old scores[23]), and behind the back of the obtuse Magistrate Qu—sought, on the one hand, to loot the property of the urban elite should they flee and, on the other, to blackmail any individual who came under suspicion of rebel sympathies. The petitions of the honest Zhu Jue and his Xu Family Fort neighbors, Yu told the governor, clearly revealed the rights and wrongs of the matter. He asked for, and received on their behalf, the governor's pardon.[24]

This left the matter of the declared rebel Liu Junfu. Yu Chenglong, having stripped Liu of several potential allies in the region, then determined to confront Liu directly and present him—boldly—with the same terms of amnesty that had succeeded in flushing out Zhu Jue. After an exchange of written communications, the extraordinary climactic act of the drama played itself out. On the twenty-seventh, Yu Chenglong rode out from Baiguo, virtually alone, the ten or so *li* to Liu's mountain fort. There he personally confronted Liu, who was accompanied by a bodyguard of some 300 heavily armed men. Yu's official account does not shirk from implications of his own romantic heroism but offers few details of the encounter itself.[25] Other reports stress its theatrical emotionality and moral implications.[26] But Yu's eminent biographer, Grand Secretary Chen Tingjing, gives it the unrestrained literary treatment. It is at once a comic portrayal of personal intimidation and a classic Confucian knight-errant recognition scene: two powerful personalities, initially on opposite sides of a conflict, size each other up, perceive each other's intrinsic moral rectitude, and then form a bond to pursue the good of all humankind.[27]

Yu Chenglong rode to Liu Junfu's fort, Chen tells us, on a black mule. As he approached, he sent a retainer ahead to beat a gong, declaring his intention to approach. When he had reached a point no more than two *li* from the fort, he again sent the servant ahead, continually beating his gong and calling out, "The subprefect has come to meet with you, men of the mountains." Liu, unsettled by Yu's boldness, withdrew into the inner recesses of his stonghold. He ordered several hundred of his men, armed with muskets and bows and arrows, to line the path of approach and lie in waiting. When these men saw Yu ride up, they lit torches and drew their bows, aiming at Yu and awaiting Liu's order to shoot. Yu Chenglong, unfazed, pretended not to see them and continued to spur his mule forward. Liu's men were confused and dared not fire, allowing Yu calmly to run the gauntlet.

As he approached the front gate of the fort, it was opened for him and he rode in. He dismounted in front of the rebel sleeping quarters. Hearing scuffling about inside, he called to Liu Junfu in a calculatedly haughty tone: "Come out now, you old slave [*laonu*]!" He waited there for over an hour. One by one, Liu's subordinates came out of hiding to examine this strange man, and Yu addressed them: "This year, hasn't the rainfall been adequate in these mountains? Haven't the crops been growing well? If so, why have you good people [*ru liangmin*] turned to rebellion? Why have you invited so much butchery and slaughter upon yourselves? The weather now, in midsummer, is extremely hot. At this time of year you should be attending to your aged parents, and your wives and children, in the cool comfort of your homes, rather than acting in this rash and suicidal way." Gradually, the rebels began to weep.

Yu then declared, "It really is extremely hot. I must rest here awhile." He ordered one of the rebels to help him take off his riding boots and another to bring him some water. He drank his fill. Several of the rebels brought out a reclining sofa for him, and others fanned him. The remainder stood around him on all sides, in a reverent and attentive posture. Yu went soundly to sleep. His snoring was as loud as thunder. The rebels were increasingly nervous and terrified. When Yu awoke, he again called to Liu Junfu, through half-closed eyes:

"Old slave, why have you not come out from your hiding place for so long? You have a guest, and yet you don't set up a table of wine and food for him!" Liu had thought at first that Yu's bold approach to his fort could only mean that he had brought a large armed force along behind him, but slowly he realized that Yu had indeed come alone. Overwhelmed by the official's sincerity and lack of duplicity, he came out, kowtowed, and begged forgiveness for his rebellion.

Whatever the actual details of what transpired that day, this event proved to be one of the most pivotal in the entire history of Macheng County. For the moment—and only for the moment, as we shall see—it spared the county yet another round of extermination (*jiao*) as Yu permitted Liu and his followers to accept the strategic alternative, peaceful surrender (*zhaofu*). Far more important in the long term, the personal encounter between Yu Chenglong and Liu Junfu on that summer day would ultimately set in place the conditions for state–local elite power sharing, on the one hand, and dominance of Macheng politics by roughhewn strongmen of the Dongshan, on the other, which would obtain down to the time of the Japanese invasion, in 1938.

Subprefect Yu returned on the evening of the twenty-seventh to his makeshift headquarters at Baiguo, where he remained for the following weeks. He ordered the major exit road from the county closed down, to prevent panicked flight. He notified the terror-stricken urban population of Macheng City that the crisis had been defused and that they should go again about their normal routines. And he began the process of formally reeling in the mountain lords who had declared themselves in rebellion—a process he variously termed *jiaoyang* (instructing and nurturing), emphasizing its Confucian normative aspects, and *suqing* (mopping up), a more chilling term that would reappear in Macheng political discourse in reference to the far less polite purges or liquidations of the Eyuwan Soviet. In proclamations to the rebels to lay down their arms, he maintains his paternalistic tone. Take the interests of your wives and families to heart, and turn back to productive farm labor. Do not become embroiled in—or, for that matter, fear the war between north and south (*nanbei zhi bing*);[28] trust me to keep you secure from its impact. He addresses the rebels patronizingly as children who have been playing at being soldiers (*chizi nongbing*); to his superiors at Wuchang, he refers to them as ignorant mountain people (*shanyu*). He explicitly contrasts them to the genuine San-fan rebels, madmen who have thrown the world into chaos (*kuangfu changluan*). Whereas the proper response to the former is simple pacification (*fu*), the response to the latter must be extermination (*jiao*).[29] This distinction would have ominous implications for Macheng itself in the months to come.

On the third day of the sixth month, Liu Junfu and his nephew led Liu's entire army to prostrate themselves at Yu's Baiguo headquarters, formally accepting his amnesty and proclaiming their allegiance to the Qing dynasty (*xiang-*

hua). Yu responded by actively appointing Liu his agent in proclaiming the amnesty to his fellow rebel fort masters and assisting in the full pacification of the Dongshan region. Between the seventh and the seventeenth, Chen Huihui and the other parties to Liu's rebellion one by one followed his lead, paying court to Yu Chenglong at Baiguo and accepting the Qing pardon. Reading Yu's own correspondence on the matter, it all seems natural and automatic. But the account of Wang Baoxin, the hagiographer of the Dongshan fortress lords, stresses the tensions that lay beneath the surface of this uneasy truce. For one thing, the intraelite armed feuding that characterized Dongshan society (and that had contributed to the rebellion's having been so quickly aborted) was by no means diminished by the strongmen's common submission to the imperial regime. Moreover, Wang suggests that the commitment to the Qing of Liu Junfu and his allies was more tactical than heartfelt. Tellingly, they deliberated whether or not to turn over to Qing authorities the ideologue of their rebellion, Golden Dragon Huang, and opted instead to hide him for some months and then spirit him out of harm's way, where he might ignite further loyalist rebellion.[30]

None of this appears in Yu Chenglong's formal report, *Dongshan guangji minbian zhi an* ("The case of Dongshan people forced into rebellion by official misdeeds"). Yu clearly read the facts of the case in a highly individual way, in line with his own preconceived "statecraft" agenda. Xia Ding'an, in Yu's account, had effectively precipitated the affair by lodging a false charge of treason against Liu Junfu and Liu Qingli, out of personal enmity. According to Yu, Magistrate Qu Zhenqi ought at that point to have issued a declaration of Liu's innocence and thus avoided the entire mess, but he failed to pay proper heed to popular opinion (*renyan*) regarding the true facts of the case and so did nothing. This, Yu continues, opened things up for the clerical "Mafia" of the Macheng County seat, who were routinely in the business of blackmailing rural elites through false accusations of one kind or another, and who had long nursed a grievance against the Liu in particular because they had refused to pay bribes demanded by the clerks in connection with an old lawsuit. Liu Junfu had eventually been left with no alternative to rebellion, Yu reports. To make matters worse, he adds, the clerks then coerced Zhou Meigong and other rural constables into extending the false charges of sedition to other fort masters of the Dongshan, thus drawing the entire region into panic and militarization.

Yu then devotes the bulk of his report to a detailed rebuttal of the testimony of several parties regarding the alleged commission that Liu had received from Wu Sangui. He claims that the supposed emissary from Wu to Liu has never existed, and that although a document of some kind has been found in Liu's possession, its contents are entirely unclear, and in any case the document never makes mention of Liu or his nephew by name. Indeed, Yu insists, there have been no Ming loyalists (*yimin*) whatsoever in this area for many years. Case closed.[31]

He could not possibly have been right. Not merely Wang Baoxin, with his barely disguised late-Qing anti-Manchuism, but also Yu's own biographer Chen Tingjing, not to mention successive editions of the county and prefectural gazetteers, treat the genuine Ming loyalism of Liu Junfu and his allies as an unquestioned fact. Was Yu, then, simply naive? Was he misled? This, too, seems impossible. For example, he could not but have known of the activities in the area of the anti-Qing agitator Golden Dragon Huang, and of Liu Junfu's harboring of this highly wanted man. And yet, with clear and deliberate intent, Yu never allows Huang's name to appear in any of his reports on the affair.

The possibility that Liu Junfu had been an antidynastic rebel simply did not suit Yu Chenglong's agenda. As a loyal Qing official fresh from the front in the Wu Sangui campaign, Yu must have felt that conducting a witch-hunt for Ming loyalists so far behind the front lines, when such matters might easily be dealt with by other means, would constitute a distraction that the embattled Kangxi emperor simply did not need. Nor could Yu very well mention this to his superior and confidante Governor Zhang Chaozhen (who probably, in any case, knew the truth himself) without forcing Zhang to pass the information on to the court. Equally important, a confession that Liu Junfu et al. had been at one time confederates of Wu Sangui would render them useless for the tasks that Yu still had in mind for them.

In recognition of his spectacular success in pacifying (for the moment) the vexing Dongshan, the court promoted Subprefect Yu to Huangzhou prefect. Rather than having Yu proceed directly to that jurisdiction, however, Governor Zhang asked him to stay in Macheng for a time to undertake the process of reconstruction (*shanhou*).[32] Yu set up a reconstruction bureau (*shanhou ju*) and began to conduct a cadastral survey.[33] More important, he required that all individuals who had "gone into the mountains" apply at his bureau for a clearance ticket (*piao*) prior to their reintegration into normal rural society (*guinong*). Possession of the ticket signified that they were covered under the blanket amnesty issued by Governor Zhang, and that they willingly accepted its terms. Yu justified this requirement as necessary to prevent his favorite whipping boys, the county clerks, from blackmailing the returnees as former rebels.[34] Given his more general political stance, there is little question that he was sincere in this argument. Yet the ticket system was useful for Yu in another way as well: it provided the initial registration of one segment of the population, an especially elusive one, for what would become the prefect's most enduring contribution to Macheng society: implementation of an extremely compelling system of grassroots social control known as *baojia*.

Baojia, Militia, Forts

The *baojia* system of regimenting local populations into ten-, hundred-, and thousand-household mutual responsibility groups had its locus classicus in such hoary texts as the *Rites of Zhou* and the *Guanzi* but was given its first historically verifiable implementation under the regime of the great eleventh-century statist official Wang Anshi. In the sixteenth century, the philosopher-statesman Wang Yangming had famously imposed his own version of it in the southern Jiangxi highlands, demonstrating its utility to the state in pacification of frontier peoples and, at the same time, by infusing it with the moral value of local community solidarity, rehabilitating it from the taint of state commandism it had acquired in the hands of Wang Anshi.[35] It was in this guise that the system became an inviting policy option, though always a highly ambivalent one, for a long succession of Qing "statecraft" thinkers,[36] a tradition into which Yu Chenglong very clearly fit.

Yu Chenglong's experiment with *baojia* in Macheng was in fact a pivotal step in the evolution of the system empirewide under the Qing. The new regime began issuing proclamations ordering decimal-group regimentation as early as 1644, but most scholars agree that it was only in the 1720s, under the energetic local administration initiatives of the Yongzheng emperor, that the system became a reality in most localities.[37] Between the halfhearted efforts of the Shunzhi reign and the more strenuous efforts of Yongzheng, it was above all Yu Chenglong, first in Macheng and then more visibly and on a grander scale in his subsequent governorship of Zhili Province, who provided the model of *baojia* workability that the court needed to see.[38]

And yet Yu Chenglong's Macheng system was a very different creature from the *baojia* system as it existed empirewide after the eighteenth century, and perhaps farther still from the image of that system prevalent in Western historiography. In his massively researched study of the system, written at the height of the Cold War, Kung-chuan Hsiao characterized it as an ambitious (though not very successful) instrument of state terror. In Hsiao's view, "A nineteenth-century Western writer correctly said of the [Qing] dynasty that 'what is ostensibly a paternal government ruling its subjects through filial affection is in reality a tyrannical administration that maintains its power through *fear and distrust.*' The [*baojia*] was one of the instruments employed by the emperors for this very purpose."[39] But this is not the way that Macheng people viewed the system over its long history in the county, at least not at all times. *Baojia* local headmen seem for much of the time to have enjoyed a favorable local reputation. A local folktale, for example, tells of one headman (*jiazhang*) who encountered a farmer about to cut down a roadside tree. "Why do you wish to cut down this tree," the headman asked, "when it provides needed shade to passers-by?" When the farmer replied that the tree was his property and that he needed to sell its timber to pay off a debt, the headman, though not hailing from the immediate area, offered to buy the tree himself in order to leave it standing.[40]

For Yu Chenglong, even engaged as he was in a campaign of conquest in the Dongshan, the totalitarian model of *baojia* portrayed by Hsiao Kung-chuan was very far from his mind. Quite the contrary, Yu genuinely imagined his system as a means of protecting the people (*min*) from the predations of the state apparatus, in order to "govern the people by means of the people themselves" (*yimin zhimin*).[41] In line with the sentiments of late-imperial statecraft reformists, and especially those of the *fengjian* (elite-led local autonomy) wing epitomized by his eminent contemporary Gu Yanwu (1613–82), Yu vilified beyond all others the petty functionaries of the local administration.[42] Coincidental with his *baojia* initiatives—and echoing Mei Zhihuan four decades earlier—he issued a proclamation ordering Macheng elites to prohibit any of their lineage members from serving in such capacities.[43] Moreover, Yu considered the personnel of preexisting *baojia* systems in Macheng, men such as Zhou Meigong of the Xu Family Fort, to be no more than lackeys of this clerical "Mafia"; it was intimidation by these men, as well as by the clerks themselves, that he sought to short-circuit by means of his system of amnesty tickets for repentant rebels. As agents to enforce standards of disciplined conduct among the "people," Yu found far superior to these villains the ritually sanctioned institution of the lineage, and he sought as much as possible to incorporate the authority of the lineage head and the sentiment of lineage solidarity—what he termed *huxiang shenjia zhi xin* (the mind-set of individual and familial mutual self-interest)—into his reformed (*qingli*) household regimentation system in Macheng.[44]

Yu began in late summer to make personal rounds of the Dongshan forts that had been drawn into the Liu Junfu affair, and he began implementing his *baojia* system there. Over the remainder of the year, he expanded its scope to include the Dabie Shan and other border areas of Macheng County, then the county as a whole, and finally, in his new capacity as Huangzhou prefect, all of that prefecture. Yu employs a sometimes confusing range of nomenclature to discuss the leadership of his system, but in general three tiers of authority seem to have been his goal. The lowest level he usually termed the *huzhang* or *hushou* (household or lineage head), a post he charged with instructing and training dependents (*jiaoxun zidi*).[45] The next largest unit was the *jia*, headed by a *jiazhang*. The highest and, by all evidence, the most significant level of leadership was the *quzhang* (ward headman) or *baozhang* (*bao*-unit headman).[46]

Just who were these ward headmen? Here again, Yu Chenglong's Macheng system differed markedly from later, empirewide models of *baojia*. Kung-chuan

Hsiao argues—correctly, I believe—that *baojia*, in its ultimate manifestation under Yongzheng, was designed to include local literati among the population to be regulated while deliberately *excluding* them from any role in the system's leadership hierarchy; it was a way of establishing a type of local authority independent of indigenous economic and cultural elites, and thus it undercut potential local elite autonomy from the throne.[47] Yu's system in Macheng was very nearly the opposite: it was a joint state/local elite endeavor designed to undercut the power of subofficial bureaucratic functionaries. By making these elites (many of them, though not the majority, holders of civil service degrees) full partners in his social-control apparatus, Yu confidently hoped to align their interests with those of the Qing state. Not only were the local elite the highest-tier leaders of Yu's *baojia* system, the jurisdictions they governed were coterminous with existing, *militarized*, local communities—the catchment areas of the *shanzhai*. Thus Yu grafted his public security structure not only onto the existing hierarchy of wealth and bloodline but also onto the existing structure of local defense, an arrangement that was made transparently clear by his routine substitution in his proclamations of the term *baozhang* (fort master) for the homonymous term "*bao*-unit headman."[48]

This does not mean that Yu Chenglong was overly casual in bestowing quasi-governmental authority on those who already enjoyed the lion's share of private economic and coercive power. On the contrary, his reports to Governor Zhang make clear his careful calculations regarding precisely whom among the county's many existing fort masters he selected for the posts of *qu*- or *bao*-unit headman.[49] He describes all of these individuals as wealthy, substantial, and well behaved (*yinshi liangshan*) and, moreover, as heads of great lineages and rich manors (*juzu fushi*). But there were other considerations at work as well. In Erlihe Ward, for instance, he appointed as ward head a lower-level degree holder named Tian Chuyang, bypassing a more likely degree holder, Li Gongmao. He explains in his report that in recent years the Tian and Li lineages had been in involved in a blood feud, stemming from a perceived offense committed by Li Gongmao against the Tian, and that the Tian had gradually begun to get the upper hand. Their mutual hostility had just begun to abate somewhat when Liu Junfu announced his rebellion, and Li threw Liu his support, while Tian did not. Although Li Gongmao later accepted Yu Chenglong's amnesty, Yu (rightly, as we shall see) considered him still unreliable. He chose Tian Chuyang as *baozhang* not merely in order to recognize Tian's own wealth and power but also, and specifically, to take advantage of Tian's enmity in order to offset the more problematic power of Li.

Similarly, in Cassiawood River, Yu appointed as *baozhang* several kinsmen of the whistleblower Xia Ding'an. He notes in his report to Governor Zhang, "The Xia lineage has over 200 adult males. In the past social unrest, they were unanimously and unwaveringly against the rebellion. Moreover, they are bitter enemies [*chouren*] of those on the rebel side [above all, enemies of Liu Junfu and of his supporters: the Bao, the Li, and the Cheng]. Relying on them, we have no need to worry about the future security of this area."

It might appear, then, that Liu Junfu was odd man out, but this was far from the case. Yu's correspondence does not reveal whether or not Liu had been formally installed as a ward headman, but it is very clear that he was taken into the prefect's confidence and assigned critically important paramilitary tasks as an agent of the Qing local administration. He was involved, for example, in the systematic suppression (and summary execution) of bandits, who had utilized the disorder of Liu's own rebellion to intensify their predations against the rural clite. Liu's armed power became so imposing that his enemies sent assassins into the county to do away with him; he asked Yu Chenglong to post guards at major roadways to intercept them.[50] The early-twentieth-century scholar Wang Baoxin infers from this that the real winner in the dramatic staredown between the vanquishing Yu Chenglong and the repentant Liu Junfu was none other than Liu himself.[51] More precisely, they both won. The brilliance of Yu's success in quelling the Liu Junfu rising, and in establishing his *baojia* in the Dongshan and beyond, was that he was able to capitalize on existing local antagonisms for governmental purposes while simultaneously utilizing all, or very nearly all, of the mutually hostile parties for his own ends.

What were those ends? Yu was rather specific about just who were the targets of his *baojia* surveillance scheme. Even before the system was in place, he ordered Liu Junfu and his fellow fortress lords to turn in to him the *xiongni wangming zhi tu* (violence-prone desperadoes) and *yushou haodou zhi lei* (itinerant mercenaries), suggesting that both the area's recent brush with rebellion and its preceding history of endemic feuding had attracted a class of rootless and geographically mobile professional fighting men.[52] In a follow-up directive, Yu added to this list *zeian weixiao, rochu linsou* (fugitive criminals who hide out in the forests and marshes everywhere), that is, the classic *Water Margin*–type of Chinese outlaw. But two final target groups identified by Yu make strikingly clear the economic-class basis of his campaign: *juji shanzhong, yishi buzu* (the underfed and underclothed who congregate in the mountains) and *wujia kegui, wuye kewu* (the familyless and propertyless unemployed).[53] A very profound shared fear of the poor underlay Yu Chenglong's makeshift alliance with the Dongshan elite, and this would shortly have gruesome consequences, as we shall see.

With his *baojia* apparatus effectively in place by early autumn, Yu Chenglong sought to expand its activities in a number of directions. He draped upon it a routinized program of moral indoctrination (*jiaohua*) in norms of social deference, so that "the aged [would] receive due respect" and "rich households [*yinshi fujia*] [would] no longer need to live in fear."[54] When the 1674 harvest proved inadequate, he urged his *baojia* leaders to undertake a modicum of food relief but, more important, to regulate the good conduct of (or keep out altogether) refugees from across the Dabie Shan, where the famine was, as always, worse.[55] Far more lasting and significant than either of these applications, however, was Yu's attachment to his public security system of a more proactive network of local militia.

Proceeding from the assumption that the Dongshan area was rife with paramilitary groups anyway, and that it would be easier to co-opt than disarm them, Yu called upon all men of martial temperament (*you yongli*) and all who possessed hunting muskets or other weapons (*you wuqiang wujie zhe*) to enlist in his militia.[56] The commanders of these units were to be those fort masters whom Yu had already enfeoffed as his ward leaders, and these men were now granted the authority to administer military justice. Though this recruitment was obviously linked to his concurrent *baojia* registration drive, Yu chose to refer to his militia not by the term most usually associated with a *baojia*-based militarization—*tuanlian*—but rather by terms like *xiangyong* or *xiangbing* (local braves or local army), emphasizing its more mobile and semi-professional nature. Part of the reason for Yu's choice of terminology was his insistence that enlistment (*chongwu*) be a voluntary act, unlike *baojia* registration, which carried severe penalties for noncompliance. Yu evidently felt that any attempt on his part to coercively conscript the local population would meet with serious resistance, and he reiterated several times that this was not his intent. Anticipating that his despised county clerks would attempt to solicit bribes from would-be draft-evaders, he issued stern warnings against such a practice. Moreover, his local braves were to be handsomely paid: Yu announced a pay scale that would vary according to weapon and prowess, with musketeers receiving the highest salary (one and a half *taels* per month). It seems likely that one of Yu Chenglong's major motives for this militarization was simply to get local armed men to come forward and voluntarily identify themselves, and in this he was quite successful. But the paramilitary units he created—or, more likely, merely legitimated—very quickly were turned to actual campaigns in the field.

In his landmark 1970 study of government-sanctioned, elite-led paramilitary organization in central China, and its implicit impact on tipping the balance between state and local elite power, Philip Kuhn proposed that the deciding moment in that shift came in the *tuanlian* and *xiangyong* mobilizations led by such luminaries as Hu Linyi and Zeng Guofan in the anti-Taiping campaigns of the 1850s.[57] In a subsequent rethinking of this thesis, Kuhn himself suggested that this shift may in fact have come earlier than he had previously supposed, in the first few decades of the nineteenth century.[58] What the evidence of Macheng County in the 1670s reveals is that, in at least some parts of central China, sanctioned local militarization and the resultant redefinition of state-elite power sharing came far earlier still than Kuhn imagined. In fact, it may have reflected little in the way of "shift" at all—more properly, a de jure recognition by agents of the imperial state, such as Yu Chenglong, of the existing de facto power realities to which the Qing regime would be wise to accommodate itself in order to rule effectively. In Macheng, Yu did very astutely come to this recognition, and with it he achieved a lasting measure of local legitimacy for the imperial regime he served.

More Troubles in the Dongshan

In the winter of 1674–75, armies of the Three Feudatories under General Sun Tingling began to push west from Jiangxi into Qizhou Prefecture in eastern Hubei. Several strongmen of Huangzhou Prefecture sympathetic to their cause responded with a series of linked local uprisings.[59] The man who emerged as chief of this rebel alliance (*mengzhu*) was one He Shirong. Shirong commanded the He Family Fort, on the outskirts of Huanggang County's Yangluo Town, at the southern tip of the Dongshan. Along with his elder brother, Shirong had earlier in the year ventured to Changsha and taken a military commission under Wu Sangui, but with his brother's death in battle he returned to his native place and began to plan for rebellion. On Kangxi 13/10/28 He Shirong rose up, fought his way across the Huangtu Ridge into Macheng, and rallied a network of supporters from throughout the Dongshan. He began to issue proclamations to the local populace in the name of the Wu Sangui regime.

Many of He's supporters were the usual suspects. Among them was Macheng's Li Senpu, son of the Ming-loyalist guerrilla Li Youshi. At the beginning of the eleventh month, a second rebellion broke out in Macheng's Baishuifan Ward, centered in the Tortoise Hill range just to the west of Dongshan. This second rebellion was led by Bao Shirong, the former ally of Li Zicheng and leader of various insurgent movements since the early 1640s, and by Li Gongmao, the lower degree holder who had earlier joined Liu Junfu's rebellion and then strategically accepted amnesty from Yu Chenglong. A few days later, the veteran Henanese rebel Iron Claw Zhou crossed the Dabie Shan to join up with the Tortoise Hill group.

By the end of 1674, He Shirong had loose command of a force popularly estimated at 100,000 men, with ties to much larger San-fan forces in Hunan and Jiangxi and throughout the Yangzi Valley. Huangzhou prefect Yu Chenglong presumed their goal to be, first, consolidating control of southeastern Macheng and the Dongshan border area; second, converging on and capturing Huangzhou City itself; and, third, uniting with Sun Tingling's army from

Jiangxi in order to move up the Yangzi from Huangzhou and take the provincial capital of Wuchang. The result might have proved devastating to the Qing cause and could have tipped the balance of power in the larger war decisively to the Three Feudatories. Thus, although most of the Qing regulars assigned to defend Huangzhou had been redeployed to other campaigns, Yu deemed it imperative to defend the city "to the death," which to him meant stamping out the rebellion at its source. He moved his own field headquarters to a cliffside temple in the Dongshan.

On Kangxi 13/11/8, Yu issued a direct appeal for aid against He Shirong to the fortress lords and their forces of "local braves," and they, we are told by Wang Baoxin, "tearfully and enthusiastically" responded.[60] He promised official decorations and monetary rewards to the leaders, and cash stipends (*daigong qian*) of twenty to thirty cash per day to the braves themselves.[61] Altogether, more than a thousand men answered his call, a hundred or so from each major fort. Yu assigned each unit a different-colored regimental banner, assuming personal command of the coalition force. His subordinate commanders made unlikely bedfellows. The senior officer was none other than Liu Junfu, who so recently had himself been, like He Shirong, a sworn confederate of Wu Sangui. Junfu's hotheaded nephew Liu Qingli was also among them. But so were Xia Zhongkun and Xia Jing, members of the Lius' most bitter Dongshan rival, the Cassiawod River Xia. And so too was Mei Tian, the same offspring of Mei Guozhen who had been chief target of the 1651 bondservant revolt, and, as the wealthiest and most refined of Macheng's lowland estate holders, a man who would in other circumstances have opposed the power of all these upstart Dongshan elites.[62]

Prefect Yu also requested that a small number of Qing regulars be sent in from Wuchang, but when they arrived he deployed them solely to occupy the major passes into and out of Macheng County, and to divide Bao Shirong and Iron Claw Zhou in Tortoise Hill from He Shirong in the Dongshan. Presumably to avoid any cause for mass localist solidarity against outside conquerors, he chose to assign to his indigenous militia the task of direct engagement with (and annihilation of) the rebels. This was a prudent thing to do, for, as it turned out, the denouement of the He Shirong rebellion was far different from the anticlimactic, comic-opera resolution of Liu Junfu's uprising of six months before. It was serious carnage.

Throughout the last weeks of the year, "the beacon fires could be seen from mountain top to mountain top, all the towns sealed their gates both day and night, and many of the villages were abandoned." On the eighth day of the eleventh month, just ten days after he had declared his rebellion, He Shirong was engaged in a fierce battle in a thick bamboo forest at Huangtu Gorge. According to Yu Chenglong, the dead numbered in the thousands: "The corpses piled up like mountains and the blood ran like rivers." The units of braves routinely beheaded their captured adversaries, and, in a local equivalent of Native American scalping, cut off the left ear (*zhanguo*) to save as a trophy. He Shirong himself was taken alive and sent to Wuchang, where Governor Zhang had him decapitated; his head was carried on a pole through the city streets. Back home in Huanggang, every known member of the He lineage was rounded up and beheaded.[63] The next day, Yu turned his forces toward Tortoise Hill. After another bloody engagement, the rebel leaders Bao Shirong and Iron Claw Zhou managed to escape. Yu put a bounty on their heads of twenty taels apiece. Within three days, Liu Qingli had cornered them at Dongshan's famous Dinghui Temple, killed Bao and Zhou, and claimed the bounty. Some sixty-eight of Bao's kin, male and female, septuagenarians and infants, were summarily exterminated by Liu's militia.[64] One by one, the remaining rebels were tracked down and executed, the last being Li Gongmao at month's end.

All the while, Yu Chenglong was also busily engaged in a propaganda campaign to limit the scale of the insurgency. In order to prevent tenants and bondservants from running off into the mountains to join the rebels, he ordered even stricter implementation of his *baojia* registration; with all this terrible bloodshed, he observed, none of it took place in those areas where registration had effectively been accomplished. He appealed with much success for the continued good conduct of those fortress lords—probably the majority—who had neither declared for the rebel side nor taken up arms in his own Qing-loyalist militia. Those local elites who, like He Shirong and Bao Shirong, "vainly seek for riches and power," only bring about their own deaths (*shenwang*) and the destruction of their families (*pojia*).[65] Yu also appealed to the relatives of the active rebel leaders to disassociate themselves from the uprising and pledge fealty to the Qing, promising if they did to spare them the stipulated incrimination to nine degrees of kinship (*zhulian jiuzu*).[66] In this, as we have seen, he was less successful.

Beyond the question of ensuring dynastic loyalism, the He Shirong rebellion presented Yu Chenglong with a more general crisis of popular disorder. He was repeatedly confronted with reports of plundering on the part of *xiangyong* militia units, and of looting on the part of the population at large.[67] To a considerable extent, the events of 1674 in Macheng constituted a civil war within the local elite, and Yu feared a widening breakdown of social discipline. This danger was further aggravated by the tendency of the elite to use the rebellions as a means to pursue unrelated, ongoing mortal vendettas (*shengsi qiechi*). We have seen that in setting up a system of mutual surveillance in the summer and fall, Yu had been able to turn this social dynamic to his own use; but in the aftermath of the winter troubles, elites routinely denounced their enemies as rebel sympathizers, using this as leverage to extort women, livestock, cash, and other property.

In waging his ideological campaign of pacification, Yu made extensive use of popular religion. He condemned the rebels, of course, for their unfilial "offenses against the rites." But he also invoked the specter of recrimination against wrongdoers on the part of *guishen* (ghosts and spirits): those who plundered their neighbors' property would surely face the wrath of the gods. He hinted to members of the local elite engaged in the opportunistic settling of scores that the agents of these avenging spirits might turn out to be none other than their own tenants. Your unseemly conduct, he warned, can only invite "the collective anger of spirits and men" (*shenren zhi gongfen*). Most offensive of all were vigilante massacres of entire lineages. To counter this, at the end of the year Yu proclaimed:

> The New Year festival is fast approaching. This is the time when the gods descend to reward and punish the good and bad deeds of the people. I myself each night weep and pray [in anticipation of their judgment on me]. If the unlettered rural folk cold-heartedly murder those who are guiltless but implicated in the rebellion by kinship or association, they will only bring upon themselves and their own descendants the immediate punishment of the gods![68]

The challenge to Qing legitimacy in the Dongshan was now over—the final significant challenge for centuries, it would turn out. Yu Chenglong had achieved a victory that would secure the area for the dynasty and preserve its elite-dominated social order for many generations. As we have seen, he did so in part by circumscribing as much as possible the number of those implicated as rebels, preventing lingering intimations of complicity against other parties, whatever their actual initial sympathies had been. In this bloody affair, just as in the bloodless Liu Junfu rebellion of the preceding spring, Yu also sought to put a spin on the events so as to minimize the culpability of the local elites. Both in his report to his provincial superiors and in his local public pronouncement of the rebellion's end, Yu produced a highly idiosyncratic narrative, locating the rebellion's cause in an invasion by outside (*waisheng*) agitators from Henan, Hunan, and Jiangxi. While he could not efface the record of local rebellion altogether, he explained it away as a more or less natural response to such an invasion on the part of a strategically central local society. In so doing, Yu characteristically strove to create a climate in which the various survivors could live in accommodation with other agents of the imperial state, and with one another.[69]

Class War

But if Yu displayed the velvet glove in the Liu Junfu affair, and the iron fist when it came to He Shirong, it was in an intervening disturbance that the truly savage face of state/elite violence was revealed. In this instance, the endemic viciousness that lay beneath the propriety and gentility of Macheng society pushed to the surface. In the process, it starkly exposed the limits of Confucian paternalism, even as it was so effectively championed by a model official like Yu Chenglong.

After a month's service in Wuchang, Yu had returned to Huangzhou in late summer to oversee the state's response to the expected bad harvest of that year. Here we find him acting the role of the model official to its fullest: repairing and extending water-conservancy works, importing grain to meet anticipated dearth, reducing tax and corvée demands on the strained local economy, sagely resolving litigation, and utilizing his new *baojia* apparatus to apprehend bandits.[70] Then, in the seventh lunar month, a new round of troubles erupted. The persistent Golden Dragon Huang left the shelter of Liu Junfu's estate and joined up with a longtime villain (*laozei*) in the neighborhood of Paper Mill River (Zhipeng he) named Zou Junsheng. They were quickly joined by another local troublemaker, Fang Gongxiao, and together they went on a rampage throughout southeastern Macheng. Yu Chenglong immediately returned to Qiting and mobilized a force of some 2,000 to 3,000 braves from the gentry-led units he had so recently established, with Liu Junfu appointed extermination master (*jiaozhu*). Yu personally led this force into the Dongshan, setting up a field headquarters at Floral Vista Mountain (Wanghua shan).[71] There, he and his local gentry allies "drank wine together every night, and shared warm mutual affection."[72]

The arrival of Sorcerer Huang with his millenarian message no doubt gave Zou's local predations a new antidynastic tone, but Han-nationalist politics does not appear to have played any real role in his uprising. Instead, from the state's and the elite's point of view, what set Zou's movement apart from those of Liu Junfu and He Shirong was a hint of class warfare, which had not really been seen locally for more than two decades. In his public declaration of the end of the Liu Junfu affair, Yu Chenglong very candidly announced his own perception of Macheng society as neatly divided into two social classes. On the one side was the landed and settled population, organized into patrilineal groupings with ancestors to honor, children to care for, and, not least, property (*chanye*) to protect. On the other side were the dispossessed, the drifters, the troublemakers and rumormongers, none of whom had familial compulsions or property interests to keep their behavior in line. Yu made it clear that he saw not only Liu Junfu and his would-be rebel party but also Liu's elite rivals as sharing membership in the first class. Don't let these other villains drag you into anything you will regret, he warned; use the reliable test of public opinion (*gonglun*) to sort out for yourself the good from the bad, and in this way protect your real interests.[73]

He was even more specific with regard to bondservants. To them he declared, "Be contented in your servitude!" He ordered his newly constituted *baozhang* headmen, "Do not by any means tolerate runaway bondservants!" As he worked out the details of his new *baojia* system over the course of the summer, Yu took ever greater care to ensure that bondservants did not escape its registration mechanisms, and that their masters fully understood their responsibility for their servants' conduct.[74] From Yu Chenglong's perspective, disobedience on the part of members of the lower social orders was a matter far different from the misguided naughtiness of a bastion of society such as Liu Junfu, and it would call for a very different sort of response.

And it was precisely the lower orders of society that formed the backbone of the Zou Junsheng uprising of early fall. Zou very quickly attracted renegade soldiers and bandit types, but the considerable bulk of his armed force was made up of runaway or rebellious bondservants (*taopu, panpu*).[75] Why did Zou's cause attract so many of them, whereas the causes of Liu Junfu and He Shirong did not? Part of the answer may rest with the nature of the leader. Zou Junsheng was clearly a man of some substance, but, unlike most of the fortress lords whom Yu Chenglong had converted to his cause, Zou was not a degree holder. Most likely he was simply an independent local strongman who periodically ventured into banditry, but Yu Chenglong suggests in passing that Zou may himself have been of bondservant origin.[76] More important, the militant resistance of Macheng bondservants seems in its timing, after more than two decades of quiescence, to have occurred in direct response to Yu Chenglong's *baojia* registration drive itself, and especially in response to the fears of mass lower-class conscription, fears that, as we have seen, Yu was anxious to dispel. The prefect himself noted that although he considered his *baojia* implementation to have been an overall success, there were in fact large numbers of persons who had deliberately evaded (*lou*) its compulsions. These persons, and especially bondservants, flocked to take refuge under Zou Junsheng's banner.[77] When the rebellion erupted, Yu Chenglong directly ordered all its bondservant participants to return to their masters and beg their forgiveness,[78] but their masters, as it turned out, had different plans for them.

The campaign against Zou Junsheng was short, decisive, and pitiless. On the twenty-fourth day of the seventh lunar month, one of Zou's subordinates, Yang Keli, was captured and beheaded, and his head was sent to Macheng City to be displayed atop the city gate. The following day, Fang Gongxiao was taken and decapitated, and his head in turn was placed on a pike in the main street of his native town, Li Family Market. The main rebel force was quickly driven back into a mountain fort, which Yu's militia besieged and took with rapid success. The prefect's confrontation with Golden Dragon Huang on the twenty-ninth provided one final operatic touch to the affair, at least as recounted by Yu's biographer Chen Tingjing:

> Sorcerer Huang, cornered, attempted to use his occult arts to make himself invisible. But Yu wielded his sword and scoffed at him, "Your magic does not work on me!" He immediately lopped off Huang's head and sent it to Wuchang to declare his victory. Governor Zhang Chaozhen took out the head and displayed it to his provincial colleagues, saying, "People all say that I should never have appointed a drunkard to this job. What, then, do you say to *this*?" They all laughed. Indeed, Yu Chenglong was truly a drunken sot [*jiukuang*], but just look at what he achieved in the Dongshan![79]

Finally, on the first day of the eighth month, the militia leader Xia Zhongkun captured Zou Junsheng along with some forty of his followers who were hiding out in a local temple. The entire group was summarily decapitated.[80]

Thus, although Liu Junfu's and Zou Junsheng's rebellions were both inspired by the same provocateur, Golden Dragon Huang, the treatment accorded the rebels was very different. Over the next several days, elite-led militia units formally created by Prefect Yu precipitated an orgy of vigilante violence in which any and all suspected rebels they encountered were beheaded. The gentry commanders took it upon themselves, where possible, to "exterminate the families [of rebels], with no surviving progeny." The total number of dead was described by Yu himself as very great (*shenzhong*) and by local historian Wang Baoxin as countless (*wusuan*). Renegade braves (*youyong*) operating independently of their units ran further amok, killing the males and kidnapping females from villages allegedly sympathetic to the rebels. Initially, Yu Chenglong sanctioned these mop-up operations, putting a bounty on the heads of surviving rebel leaders. Very quickly, however, he realized that he had let out of the bottle a very unpleasant genie. He had vastly underestimated the savage hatred felt by the Macheng elite toward the county's servile underclass—as great, perhaps, as the hatred that this underclass had displayed toward the elite during the Ming-Qing transition. Apparently genuinely aghast, Yu urgently and repeatedly proclaimed "Stop the killing! . . . I cannot bear this wanton slaughter!"[81]

Only gradually, over the course of the autumn, did Yu Chenglong manage to restore order to the area. In statesmanlike fashion, he petitioned for rewards for the victorious militia leaders (the Lius, Xias, Meis, and others) while working to reintegrate, as much as possible, the surviving rebels into local society and to restore women and property to those from whom they had been appropriated. According to his reports, midway through the ninth month Hubei governor Zhang announced to the throne that the troubles in Dongshan were finally over (they would erupt again, as we have seen, but two months later).[82] The problem of bondservant rebellion in Macheng had been quelled once again. For generations thereafter, however, it would continue to plague the area, if on a more circumscribed scale.[83]

The Dongshan Rebellion as Memory and History

On the thirteenth day of the eleventh lunar month of 1674, Yu Chenglong ordered an assembly of the local population at Huangshi, a market town located at the intersection of roads leading up to the year's highland battlegrounds. He stood on a bridge at the town's center and declared the Dongshan rebellions to be at an end, reciting a quatrain to commemorate the occasion:

> Tortoise Hill is now at peace.
> Dragon Lake now runs clear [of blood].
> The people have returned to sowing and reaping.
> And peace will endure for ten thousand generations.[84]

Several years later, the now very eminent Yu returned to this spot to oversee the installation on the bridge of a stone stele bearing this quatrain, a stele that could still be seen and read well into the twentieth century.

In so doing, Yu contributed directly to the launching of a cult devoted to his honor in the collective memory of the Macheng people, or at least in the memory of the county's people of property. His heroics have been celebrated in county gazetteers from the Qianlong era on, each author stressing not only that Yu defeated numerically superior forces and did so in a matter of weeks but also, and strikingly, that his reliance on the local militia saved the locality and the state a potentially great expense of tax dollars.[85] (The subtext of this classic "statecraft" argument is, of course, that the county was also spared the expected predations of outside troops.) An altar to Yu, commemorating especially his compassionate handling of the provisioning crisis that accompanied the rebellions, was set up at Red Cliff (*chibi*), the site outside the Huangzhou County seat indelibly identified in local consciousness with the sojourn of Su Dongpo. Thus Yu was forever linked with one of the empire's greatest cultural icons.[86] Beyond these semiofficial markers, "the people" of Macheng (*Mamin*) wrote numerous poems in his honor, and his legendary exploits were popularly enshrined in a rich body of local folklore. In these tales, he walks in disguise among the "people," hearing their concerns and drawing upon this grassroots intelligence to see through the phony claims of elite petitioners. In times of dearth, he invokes magical powers to multiply the county's stores of grain. When a local brigand masquerades as a constable, Yu invites him to a banquet and exposes him through clever questioning. An admiring local "man of the wilds" (*yeren*) presents Yu with an enormous fresh-killed deer; the prefect has the antlers polished "to gleam like jasper" and wears them around his waist as a girdle.[87] As the right-Guomindang gazetteer of 1935 concludes, Yu was "much loved by the people."[88]

Indeed, the popular cult of Yu Chenglong became a national one, and it continues down to the present day. The collections of tales of official sleuthing known as *Yu gong'an* (The court cases of Mr. Yu), a staple of storytellers throughout the Qing and Republican eras, conflate and embellish historical accounts of both this Yu Chenglong and his identically named Han-bannerman colleague.[89] A staple play of the Beijing opera tradition, *Lianli Yu Chenglong* (The incorruptible official Yu Chenglong), celebrates our own Yu's integrity and personal frugality. A television series based on the latter—timely, in light of recent concerns about rampant cadre corruption—aired on Central Chinese Television in 2000–2001 and included a dramatization of Yu's experiences in Macheng.[90]

And yet, while there seems little reason to doubt the genuineness or social breadth of Yu Chenglong's cult in Macheng, sources from the People's Republic also record traces of a countermemory in which the hero of 1674 turns out to be, not Yu, but rather the persistent and ultimately failed rebel Bao Shirong. Despite effective suppression in successive elite-produced gazetteers, we are told, tales of Bao's heroic defiance were passed down and extolled (*zhuansong*) by later generations of Macheng "people," to be collected and published by local historians of the late twentieth century. A stone horse stable said to have been used as a headquarters for Bao's rebels was popularly revered as a kind of shrine, just as the Red Cliff altar and the Huangshi Bridge stele were revered in the cult of Yu Chenglong.[91]

In this version, Bao Shirong reemerges as leader of a *nongmin qiyi*, a peasant rebellion. In truth, it is difficult to see how a man born to one of the county's more prominent lineages and raised as a monk in the temple patronized by his family can be seen as a *nongmin* (peasant), but surely he at least belonged to the *min*, the people. As so often in the rhetoric of late-imperial sources and historiography, the contest is precisely over the appropriation of this latter category. In the typical establishment account of the Dongshan rebellions, only those who supported the victorious Qing regime merit description as *min*, while those who rebelled or deviated are dismissed by terms such as *qun* (the crowd) or *zhong* (the mob).[92] Of course, in the historiography of the People's Republic, the labels are nearly reversed. The contest over the legitimating category of "the people" was yet one more way in which the violent hostilities inherent in Macheng society played themselves out.

The local historian Wang Baoxin, writing in 1908, identified the principal lasting result of the 1674 Dongshan troubles to be that, from that time on, Qing officials proved too timid to regulate the area directly, and the native population "took armed resistance [to the state] as a local customary practice." He cited Yu Chenglong's superior, Hubei governor Zhang Chaozhen, as saying that, in the Dongshan, "disorder was the norm, and political order very hard to achieve."[93] Wang, of course, knew the area well, both as a native and as a well-informed scholar.

From our perspective, however, we can see a kind of stable accommodation having taken hold in Macheng County in the wake of 1674, and remaining very largely in place until the catastrophic violence of the mid-nineteenth century. This accommodation included several basic elements. First was an as yet incomplete but now definitely visible transfer of the weight of local power from core-area estate-holding elites, such as the many eminent officials the county produced in the last century of the Ming, to less wealthy and accomplished but equally venerable elites of the highlands, whose chief asset was simple control of armed force. Second, we see (as Wang Baoxin emphasized) a greater degree of elite-led local autonomy, or at least a more systematic sanctioning of this autonomy by agents of the Qing state, an accord arrived at out of recognition by both parties of a general congruence of their interests in social hierarchy and control. And third, on the basis of this accommodation, we see a systematic use of the disciplinary mechanisms of *baojia* regimentation, local militia, and the fortress system to effectively suppress any collective expression of plebeian discontent—until the arrival in the area of the Taiping in the 1850s. For nearly two centuries, repression worked.

CHAPTER EIGHT

Heavenly Kingdom

THE EIGHTEENTH and nineteenth centuries witnessed a slow but steady decline of Macheng into the same peripherality that had characterized the county prior to its meteoric late-Ming ascendance, a decline that would only be hastened in the twentieth century. And yet this was not, for the most part, an unhappy time. At least it was not so until the county's catastrophic experience of the Taiping and Nian rebellions of the 1850s and 1860s.

For one thing, the mid- to late-Qing period was the absolute heyday of the area's enterprising commercial diaspora: the Huangbang, or Huangzhou guild. Based in the thriving commercial towns of Macheng and its surrounding counties—preeminently Songbu—Huangbang merchants came to dominate the booming trade in Middle Yangzi cotton cloth and other commodities up the Yangzi to Sichuan, up the Han to the northwest, and throughout a broad local region encompassing southern Henan and northern Hunan. Members of the guild established branch families in Chongqing and other Sichuan cities, in Shashi and Yichang in western Hubei, in Hunan's Yuezhou, and in Laohekou and other Han River ports.[1] In Hankou, the Huangbang set up the Hall of the Imperial Lord (Dizhu gong)—dedicated to the guild's patron, a Song-era Macheng merchant named Zhang—and from this base came to dominate the entire textile trade of central China's commercial metropolis.[2] Long-established Macheng commercial lineages—such as the Shi of Songbu, the Lin of Zhongguanyi, and the sprawling Cheng of Songbu, Qiting, and Baiguo—made extraordinary fortunes and reached the pinnacle of corporate power.[3] As the Cheng triumphantly recorded in their 1919 genealogy:

> The hereditary occupation [*shiye*] of our family is that of merchant. Following the Ju River [out of Macheng], we arrive at the confluence of the Yangzi and Han. Following the Yangzi, we get to the Xiang River [Hunan], the Li River [Hunan and Jiangxi], the Zu River [Shaanxi], the Zhang River [Henan and Hebei], and through the gorges into Si-

chuan. Following the Han River, we pass through Xiangyang and numerous other ports, en route to northern Sichuan and the northwest. This is our own commercial district (*shangqu*), in which we have done business since the time of our ancestors.[4]

Other Macheng merchants of less exalted family origin—Xiaos, Chens, Zhangs, and Luos—likewise parlayed the wealth accrued from this riverrine trade into philanthropic notability at home and, on occasion, into official careers.[5]

Moreover, the success of Macheng's commercial diaspora abroad had a pronounced backward linkage effect on the county's own internal economy. The number of registered market towns grew rapidly, to a total of forty-one by the end of the eighteenth century.[6] Songbu merchants, flush with wealth, continually renovated and embellished their town's major landmark, the Jade Frost Tower (Ningrui lou) and, in the wake of the midcentury rebellions, constructed their own city wall.[7] The nineteenth century also brought a considerable spurt of local protoindustry. Baiguo and its environs, a major center of cotton weaving and dyeing since the Ming, became a center of metalworking as well. In the 1840s, the Li family opened a wok foundry, growing rapidly over several decades to a workforce of more than seventy, and in 1851 the Liu family set up a plow-blade and shovel factory, quickly spinning off branches at other Macheng market towns. Caijiashan's centuries-old pottery kilns greatly expanded both their scale and their reach, finding new markets as far away as Southeast Asia. Yanjiahe spawned a paper mill in 1876.[8]

But the continued economic well-being of Macheng was not reflected in a corresponding maintenance of the striking educational and political prominence the county had claimed for itself over the course of the Ming. By any standard, in fact, it witnessed a retreat into the mediocrity that its geographic isolation from the empire's major cultural centers would suggest. In the Qing, there were no more Li Zhis, Jiao Hongs, Yuan Hongdaos, or Feng Menglongs making scholarly pilgrimages to the county. In the Ming, Macheng produced 110 civil *jinshi* (ranking first among all Hubei counties), but under the Qing this total declined to forty-six (with Macheng ranking a more plausible eighth in the province). Macheng's 421 provincial degree winners in the Ming similarly dropped to 206 under the Qing. Even the production of military *jinshi*, an area in which Macheng, with its self-conscious martial tradition, might have been expected to excel, fell from twenty-two under the Ming to a mere four under the Qing. The yield of nationally prominent officials—those meriting recognition as *xiangxian* (local worthies) in the county's Confucian temple—dropped even more dramatically, from fifty-three in the Ming to eight under the Ming's comparably long-lived successor.[9] Timothy Brook, noting an analogous decline in examination and official success in Zhejiang's Yin County (Ningbo) from Ming to Qing, attributes it less to a weakening of local elite means than to a shift (or broadening) of elite priorities to the "pursuit of other goals, such as accumulating landed or mercantile wealth."[10] Given the steady development of Macheng's economic base over these centuries, it is likely that Brook's observations would apply there as well.

Certainly, elite wealth was not turned to the support of higher education, at least not to anything like the extent it had been previously. Of the ten private academies that the county could boast at the time of the Ming-Qing transition, only three were still in operation by the 1880s, among them the Wansong shuyuan, that venerable centerpiece of Macheng intellectual life, and the Huiche shuyuan, dedicated to educating the sons of the Huangbang merchants. The different direction that education would take under the Qing, in Macheng as elsewhere, was epitomized by two "public schools" (*yixue*) set up in the 1720s and the 1820s, respectively. They were founded and maintained by local officials rather than private elites, and they were oriented toward elementary literacy and moral training (*yangmeng*) rather than successful passing of higher-level examinations.[11]

Scholarly Revival

Macheng did, however, experience something of a scholarly revival in the nineteenth century. The content of this was far different from the freethinking and broad-ranging intellectual inquiry of the late sixteenth and early seventeenth centuries, but once again, in its own way, it was symptomatic of vanguard intellectual trends in the empire more generally. The initial figure in this revival was one Bao Peng, a provincial degree holder of 1788. Men of the Bao surname had enjoyed a modest degree of examination success in the late Ming and early Qing, as we have seen, but it is impossible to determine how, if at all, Peng was related to them. Bao Peng, we are told, was a brilliant and defiantly principled scholar, not infected by the intellectual fashions of his time—an apparent reference to the ultrarefined demonstrations of philological skill flaunted by Han-learning (Hanxue) scholars, so much in ascendance during the later Qianlong reign. Bao Peng failed repeatedly to pass the metropolitan examination in this hostile intellectual milieu, but he did succeed, late in life, in attaining one lower official post, serving as director of studies in western Hubei's Yicheng County in 1809. He spent most of his career, however, as a teacher in his native township, where he trained a generation of students in his new reformist ideology.[12]

Bao Peng adhered to a strict Song-learning (Songxue) or *lixue* (school of principle) mind-set, which his admirers considered remarkable for its sincerity and purity. Song learning, in the context of the day, meant a number of things, some of them highly conservative and others potentially radical. Most literally, it meant defense of the canonical status of the so-called Four Books (compiled in the Southern Song by Zhu Xi) from attack on the part of Han-learning philologists, who argued for the priority of the much older Five Classics. This valuation of the Four Books meant, by extension, an intense (often angst-ridden) dedication to personal moral improvement, coupled with a belief in the social efficacy of family and community ritual in preserving the established order. In this regard, Song-learning partisans (Bao Peng included) can be seen as working more feverishly than many of their opponents to maintain genealogical, gender, and even class hierarchies.

Other aspects of the Song-learning agenda, however, place its proponents in a less traditionalist light. The Han-learning attack on Zhu Xi's Four Books was based in large part on the claim that they were merely historical artifacts of the Song era rather than timeless founts of revealed truth like the Five Classics. For many Song-learning partisans, however, this historicity—a sensitivity to shifting contextual realities—was something actively to be prized. It was a mandate to administrative and social reform, in a radically empirical and often strikingly pragmatic fashion. Taken to its extreme, it was a validation of technological prowess in such areas as cartography, hydrology, agronomy, and—especially applicable in its manifestation in Macheng—military science. It thus provided an intellectual underpinning for the mid- to late-Qing literati movement frequently dubbed *jingshi*, or practical statecraft. For scholars of this persuasion, the pursuit either of literary stylistic refinement or of esoteric philological technique was a frivolous and, indeed, immoral squandering of intellectual energy. Song learning was a way of thinking that proved especially attractive to literati from areas away from such entrenched centers of cultural production as Jiangnan and Beijing—most famously, Hunan Province. The existence of Bao Peng and his school suggests that it found adherents in other semiperipheral areas as well, including northeastern Hubei.[13]

Among Bao's students was a neighboring lad named Yuan Xian.[14] Though hailing from a family of no previous academic distinction, Yuan enjoyed a meteoric rise to prominence. He received his *jinshi* in 1811 and was appointed first to the Hanlin Academy and then, in 1814, to the volatile post of censor for the Jiangnan circuit. There he conducted a vigorous and highly visible campaign to clean up corruption in the grain-tribute and granary systems. In 1820, Yuan was made coexaminer for the Shuntian (Beijing-area) *juren* examination, and in that capacity he wrote a scathing and widely circulated memorial condemning a number of irregularities, including the sale of degrees. He formed partisan connections with some of the most prominent reform-minded intellectuals of his day, including the elder statesman and reformist hero Hong Liangji (1746–1809) and his own contemporary Lin Zexu (1785–1850); the latter contributed a preface to Yuan's fervently Song learning–oriented primer *Sishu tijie*

(Introduction to the Four Books). Yuan, in other words, found himself at the heart of the "statecraft revival" of the Daoguang era.

Around 1825, Yuan Xian returned to Hubei, where he accepted the headmastership of the Jiang-Han Academy at Hanyang.[15] While there, he penned a series of impassioned broadsides denouncing regional literati for, among other things, condoning female infanticide in their households[16] and failing to contribute adequately to relieve the famine refugees who routinely thronged the Wuhan area. Within the academy, he instituted a rigidly Song learning-cum-statecraft curriculum that he dubbed, with deliberately provocative irony, "*Chuzhong puxue*" (the rustic learning of central Hubei). Though the precise linkages remain unclear, it is virtually certain that Yuan's activities in Wuhan were closely tied to the programmatic pursuit of statecraft studies at Changsha's Yuelu shuyuan and other Hunanese academies, which in the next generation produced Hu Linyi, Zeng Guofan, and other Xiang army commanders and reformist officials of the third quarter of the nineteenth century.[17] At Jiang-Han, Yuan Xian personally trained a generation of similarly committed activist students, the majority hailing from his own native Macheng. Many of these young men, such as Yu Poquan, Shen Sichang, Zhang Wenzao, and Yuan's own son Xuejun, would soon, like their more famous Hunanese counterparts, emerge as anti-Taiping militia leaders, Confucian statecraft theorists, and Restoration-era officials.

It is not recorded from which precise portion of Macheng County Yuan Xian and Bao Peng were drawn, but it was very likely from the self-consciously rustic Dongshan. This, in any event, was true for the majority of their students. Ultimately, the most influential of these would be Yu Poquan. Yu was a native of Dongshan's Cassiawood River (Muxihe), a neighbor and ally of the Xia lineage, whose activities as local strongmen we observed during the San-fan era, and whose star as powers in the county and beyond would soon be on the rise. In the immediate term, however, it was the Yu themselves who would take center stage. Yu Poquan became a locally renowned scholar, historian, and writer on famine relief and other practical matters. He never proceeded beyond the *shengyuan* degree, but after studying at the Jiang-Han Academy he returned home and set up a lineage school, passing on his strict moral message to his descendants. Poquan's nephew and ward Yu Linxie (1814–95) studied first in this lineage school and later with Yuan Xian at the Jiang-Han, then taught at the latter institution for some years. Eventually he came home to manage his lineage organization in accordance with the Song-learning statecraft agenda he had absorbed. Poquan's and Linxie's kinsman Yu Yaxiang—imbued with the same intellectual orientation, and now tied in more directly (via the Xiang army) with his Hunanese counterparts—would, as we shall see, emerge as lord and protector of all of Macheng during the midcentury rebellions.

Macheng in the "Prosperous Age"

But for the moment we run ahead of ourselves. In Macheng as elsewhere, the story of the "long eighteenth century"—the era that Susan Mann has usefully identified as running from the 1680s to the 1820s—was one of relative political and military stability accompanied by dynamic social development.[18] Throughout most of this period, dubbed by many Chinese scholars the "prosperous age" (*shengshi*), the Qing central administration attended to keeping the peace on an empirewide scale while working in a generally supportive yet not especially interventionist way with local elites on matters of infrastructural development. In Macheng, local magnates contributed to the renovation and expansion of the irrigation network (much battered by the constant warfare of the preceding century) and extended the county's system of local transport—bridges and ferries. To ameliorate periodic dearth and stabilize grain prices, the local administration set up a *changping cang* (ever-normal granary) at the county seat, which, prior to the retrenchment of 1748, held upwards of 16,000 piculs (*shi*) of rice; another 12,000 piculs were housed in community granaries (*shecang*) set up in the county's various market towns by joint official-private initiative over the 1710s and 1720s. A thirty-two-chamber poorhouse (*pujitang*) was established in the 1720s, attached to the Eastern Chan Temple outside the county seat. Over the course of the period, scores of government-approved memorial arches (*pailou*) were constructed throughout the county, to honor famous native sons and virtuous widows. To further signify this condominium of government and private interest, continually reaffirm the sociocultural hegemony of the local elite, and (it was hoped) forge a sense of county-level community transcending lineage and township, Qing authorities and Macheng notables participated in a cycle of elaborately orchestrated annual rituals—*xiangyin yizhu* (the "community libationer" ceremony), *yingchun yizhu* (the "welcoming spring" ceremony), *jiuhu yizhu* (the "local salvation" ceremony), and many others—at such sites of state-society interface as the City God Temple, the Guandi Temple, the Confucian School temple, and the Temple to the God of Literature.[19]

The long eighteenth century was not a time of dramatic change in agrarian relations in Macheng. New mercantile wealth was continually invested in land, and large estates remained common, both in individual and corporate (lineage) hands,[20] but there is no evidence that the mid-Qing period was, as the mid- to late-Ming period had been, an era of frenzied land concentration. Landlord-tenant relations maintained the familiar balance between animosity and paternalist good feeling; the occasional large landholder who was lionized for remitting his tenants' rent in years of dearth may suggest that this was not normal practice.[21] In an increasingly monetized rural economy, usury became an ever more attractive instrument of expropriation. On two occasions, in 1737 and again a century later, reformist local elites established pawn shops whose interest rates (2 percent per month) were explicitly designed to undercut market rates that they considered threatening to social stability—the latter reform drew the praise of no less a local hero than Yuan Xian—but any success they enjoyed was likely short-lived.[22] The energetic reforms of the Yongzheng era no doubt did bring some decline in the incidence of servile labor in agriculture in the Macheng region, but they far from eliminated it altogether. On the very eve of the Taiping rebellion, one observer wrote:

> Hubei's Chen Fusheng is a great and powerful clan leader from Huangzhou Prefecture. . . . In his household are countless servile dependents. When one of these and his wife have a daughter, she is made into a serving maid. When they have a son, he becomes a bondservant [*nupu*].[23]

The coercive presence of the Qing regime remained rather light: under normal circumstances, the combined force of government regulars throughout the county numbered well under 100 bodies.[24] As we have already seen, the truly effective agents of social stabilization or repression (as one chooses to view it) were the local militia, organized via the *baojia* system and headquartered alternately at market towns and mountain forts, all of which in Macheng, though sanctioned and loosely coordinated by the local administration, exercised an unusual degree of autonomy. The success enjoyed by these militia units was strikingly demonstrated by three events, one each at the outset, the middle, and the end of the long eighteenth century.

The first of these events was a troop mutiny, which broke out in the provincial capital of Wuchang in midsummer of 1688, and which provincial authorities failed to contain. The mutineers spread their rebellion into much of northeastern Hubei, gathering various underclass elements to their side, adopting some popular religious eschatology, and proposing to overthrow the Qing. According to a stele composed about the affair by the Hubei native and board vice-president Wang Fengrong, local officials and government troops simply fled in fear of the advancing rebels, who eventually, under the command of one Zhang Hanyi, laid siege to Macheng's walled market town of Qiting. "The rebel forces," we are told, "stretched as far as the eye could see." Nevertheless, Qiting subprefect Wang Minhao—a worthy successor in that post to Yu Chenglong—heroically rallied the gentry militia of southern Macheng County to withstand the siege. Once the rebels had passed on, the subprefect mobilized the entire militia structure of the county, explicitly inviting the aid of the mountain fortress lords, to sweep his jurisdiction clean of remnant troublemakers. This, Wang Fengrong tells us, was the moment that broke the back of the rebellion. In his account, he repeatedly emphasizes that this was not a locally generated uprising—it was, in effect, visited on the county from above, originating as it did in the provincial capital. But when all the supposedly formidable government defenders failed, the rebellion was thwarted by the hardy elite-led militia of Macheng, rallied by a single courageous minor official.[25]

The second event was the mid-eighteenth century rebellion of Ma Chaozhu. Ma hailed from eastern Hubei's Qizhou Prefecture, along the perennially troubled Anhui border. His uprising reprised various themes that we have already encountered, including Ming loyalism, Manichaean millenarianism, and demonic messianism. Like Macheng's rebels of the Three Feudatories era, Ma claimed to hold a commission from a separatist regime in the southwest, heir to that of Wu Sangui. The rebellion generated there, however, would be not only Ming-restorationist but also apocalyptic; it would be led by a world-saving King of Light (Ming wang) akin to those prophesied in the fourteenth century by Peng Yingyu and Zou Pusheng. Like Golden Dragon Huang in the 1670s, Ma brandished a letter from Heaven (*tianshu*) and a precious sword (*baojian*) as symbols of his legitimacy. But he also claimed to have discovered in the mountain grottoes of his native region various exorcist items—mirrors, amulets, tablets—that would enable him to exterminate the demon hordes (that is, the Qing) currently plaguing the world. To this end as well, he summoned spirit armies (*shenbing*) from the four cardinal directions, armies composed of soldiers who had suffered violent deaths in battle. Mounting his rebellion initially along the Anhui border, he fought his way westward until, in 1749, he occupied a network of mountain forts in the Dongshan, along Macheng's eastern border with Luotian. But that is where he stalled. Prevented by local militia from making effective headway into Macheng itself and beyond, Ma's rebellion dissipated in 1752, and he himself disappeared without a trace.[26]

Our final event is the far more celebrated White Lotus rebellion of the late eighteenth–early nineteenth century. This decade-long civil war, ravaging much of northern and northwestern China and plausibly seen as the turning point of the entire Qing dynasty,[27] was in fact the only major upheaval of the past eight centuries that largely passed Macheng by, primarily as a result of the powerful elite-led local security apparatus that governed the county in the late-imperial era. There was clearly no absence in the county of the set of popular religious beliefs that underlay the rebellion. Indeed, from the time of Peng Yingyu and Zou Pusheng in the late Yuan, down to the early twentieth century, men and women had orchestrated risings in Macheng that either loosely shared this millenarian eschatology or explicitly invoked the term "white lotus" (*bailian*) in reference to their beliefs. In early 1795, in fact, a Macheng expatriate named Zhou Qiwen was arrested and executed in northwestern Hubei for proselytizing the same heterodox teachings (*xiejiao*) that would very shortly spawn the great rebellion.[28] And later that year, in the home county itself, an omen was reported that the local authorities interpreted as an attempt by White Lotus provocateurs to spark a local movement in sympathy with the one just then coalescing in the northwest: a chicken belonging to the Tian family was said to have laid an egg bearing, in crimson characters, the hexagramic legend "Qiankun huoshui taiyi yinyang" (male and female—fire and water—the undivided void—*yin* and *yang*).[29] But if the potential for millenarian mobilization was amply present in Macheng, the efficacy of the local repression apparatus never allowed it to take hold.[30]

When the sectarian threat eventually did come, not from within but from outside, Macheng's local elite protectors found magic of their own—sanctioned, orthodox magic—to invoke in defense of their county. The one and only moment during the protracted White Lotus campaigns when the Huangzhou region might have been engulfed in the war came in the spring of 1797, when a large force of rebels under the female commander Widow Qi (Qi Ergua) swept in from the northwest. The rebels entered Huang'an County, where they were bloodily engaged by gentry-led militia. Under pressure, they sought to cross the stream that formed Huang'an's border with Macheng. Macheng's own militia forces stood at high alert, but on the eve of battle the commanders held a prayer vigil at the Ziweihou Temple, on Wunao Mountain outside the county seat's west gate. They invoked the aid of the temple's chief deity, the Lord of Fortune (Fuzhu shen), a preserver of law and order and a special patron of Hubei Province. Fuzhu did not disappoint: when the White Lotus troops attempted to forge the stream into Macheng, a tall godlike horseman was observed riding back and forth along the banks, whipping up the waters. In spite of the fact that it had not rained for weeks, the stream flooded violently, and the rebels were deflected elsewhere, never to return.[31] Macheng's long eighteenth century of peace and stability was not yet at an end.

Yu Yaxiang, Hu Linyi, and the Hubei Army

That peace would be shattered, catastrophically, in the early 1850s. During the winter of 1852–53, the northward-advancing armies of the Taiping Heavenly Kingdom captured and torched the Wuhan cities. In January, turning east down the Yangzi River toward Nanjing and Shanghai, they occupied the prefectural seat of Huangzhou, and in the process swept ominously through the southern portions of Macheng County. Magistrate Yao Guozhen, acting under the central government's directive, called upon the leading gentry of the county seat (*chengshen*)—most notably the brothers Li Keshen and Li Keming—to mobilize people's militia (*mintuan*) for local defense. He also took one other intriguing step, a step that uncannily anticipates the intervention of the socially conservative Red Spears during the Nationalist Revolution of the 1920s: to preserve the peace of Macheng, he called in some 200 well-armed loyalist mercenaries from across the county's northern border with Henan.[32]

In March 1853, the Taiping captured Nanjing and established their capital there. But in midsummer, Qing troops had themselves succeeded in recapturing Wuhan, and rebel forces from both downriver and the north (Henan) were prompted to turn back and liberate for a second time the great riverrine metropolis of central China. This would become a routinized pattern over the course of the next decade: the Taiping army would march up and down the Yangzi between Nanjing (which they held fairly securely through 1864) and the Wuhan cities (which they took and lost, repeatedly and devastatingly, several times over this period). On nearly every occasion, their route took them through Macheng, and on each occasion, Macheng's increasingly militarized local population resisted their incursion, at ever more gruesome cost.

The first two instances were deceptively benign. In the late summer of 1853, a force of several thousand rebels, who had become detached in Henan from the main army, besieged Songbu, but Magistrate Yao and his local militia allies repulsed them.[33] Two months later, another Taiping force retook Huangzhou and moved into southwestern Macheng, but again Yao led the militia to deflect them elsewhere. On the basis of this demonstrated success, when Yao, later that year, was relieved as Macheng magistrate by Han Baochang, his provincial superiors ordered him to remain in the county to coordinate yet further *tuanlian* mobilization.[34]

The first massive bloodletting in Macheng during the Taiping wars came the next year, in 1854: the county gazetteer records by name some 500 local militiamen killed in battle in that year, and many more dependents and other noncombatants must also have perished.[35] In early spring, a major Taiping force determined to occupy the county on a permanent basis. It took Qiting and Songbu, and then it proceeded to march up the Ju River toward Macheng City. Yao Guozhen chose to make a stand midway, at the market town of Zhongguanyi, but his Henanese mercenaries deserted him, and he and Li Keshen were killed. Magistrate Han and Li Keming then mounted a second defense at Longkun Bridge, the gateway to the county seat, and in a bloody battle Han was also killed. With the county's official defenders now dead, the rebels captured Macheng City with ease, razed much of the town, and set up an occupation government demanding "tribute" payments (*jingong*) from the county's property holders. For the most part, the latter complied, but a sporadic resistance campaign continued.

Li Keming's *mintuan* remained active in the lowland core, as did other village- and township-level militia forces throughout the county, but by far the most effective resistance to Taiping rule was mounted—unsurprisingly—in the Dongshan highlands. There, over the course of the summer, a network of secret communication and fundraising for township self-defense was established among a number of gentry fort masters-cum-militia leaders, a group that included, among others, Zhan Zhaozhu, Hu Dingsan, Zheng Jiaju, the Xia lineage's Xia Wu and Xia Yuan, and, most prominent of all, Yu Yaxiang. This was a cohort of old friends, all of them reared in the hardheaded Song-learning, statecraft pedagogy that was coming to dominate the intellectual life of Hubei and Hunan, in the peculiarly martial form that it assumed in the Dongshan. Yu Yaxiang and Xia Wu, in particular, were famous countywide for their youthful earnestness, routinely holing up in Cassiawood River's Yuntai Temple to debate neo-Confucian texts and engage in moral self-criticism; a Macheng magistrate playfully referred to them as *Dongshan erjun* (the two luminaries of the eastern hills).[36] Zhan Zhaozhu—the senior member of the group, and a former county director of studies—assumed formal leadership of the alliance, plotting a strategy to divide and exterminate (*fenjiao*) the Taiping overlords. The alliance mounted encirclement campaigns of Taiping detachments in the two principal Dongshan towns of Muzidian and Cassiawood River, annihilating the rebels to the last man. Zhan then invited the ranking Qing officials still alive in the county—a police warden and a brigade commander—to take asylum in his fort. In early autumn, this snowballing militia alliance rolled down from the eastern hills toward the county seat, besieged the town, and routed its Taiping defenders; the alliance then reinstalled the agents of Qing administration.[37] As in 1674, the rustic heroes of the Dongshan had delivered the lowland elite and placed the county under their protection. This time, at the outset, there was no model official such as Yu Chenglong to co-opt and direct them; that official would shortly appear, however, in the person of Hu Linyi.

Over the remainder of 1854 and early 1855, the Qing regime, under Hubei governor Yang Pei, succeeded in reconstituting itself and mounting an effective offensive in the eastern part of the province. The governor appointed He Qi the new magistrate of Macheng, and He immediately ordered the leading local elites of each ward (*qu*) to establish for each ward its own bureau (*ju*) for the financing and training of militia; the response was enthusiastic. Two supervisory agencies, the Benevolent and Righteous Bureau (Enyi ju) and the Loyal and Righteous Bureau (Zhongyi ju), were set up in the county seat to coordinate *tuanlian* leadership and financing at the countywide level. Yang also appointed Huang'an magistrate Xu Guangcao to the post of acting Huangzhou prefect, charging him with the recapture of the prefectural seat and points east; Xu marched through Macheng en route and recruited many of that county's Dongshan militia commanders to his cause. (Governor Yang had explicitly urged these militia leaders to expand their theater of operations beyond their home turf.) Zhan Zhaozhu, Yu Yaxiang, and their allies thus pushed the campaign as far east as Qishui County, where one of their colleagues, Xia Yuan, was killed.

By the late spring of 1855, however, the situation began to deteriorate. Governor Yang had overextended his forces in the eastern Hubei campaign, allowing the provincial capital to fall once again to the Taiping. Macheng's various militia units thus fell back from their eastern expedition to see to the defense of their native county; Hu Dingsan and others dug in at Dinghui Temple in the Dongshan, while Yu Yaxiang took charge in the lowland core, forming at Songbu an elite corps of some 500 braves, dubbed the Wuhuang ying (Huangzhou Army). Yu brought in a professional drillmaster, a former member of the imperial bodyguard from Luoyang, to train his crack unit.[38]

Over the next few years, the larger regional command structure of central China began to consolidate control over the Macheng area. The Hunanese liberator Zeng Guofan marched north in late 1855 to once again retake Wuhan, and he placed the county's now battle-hardened militia under the command of his own Xiang army. Huguang governor-general Guanwen brought a force of banner troops all the way from Heilongjiang to dislodge the rebel occupiers from Huangzhou City, and in 1857 Governor Hu Linyi himself moved his headquarters to Huangzhou in order to more directly oversee campaigns in eastern Hubei and farther down the Yangxi.

Hu Linyi (1812–61) was one of the most fascinating and pivotal figures in the final century of imperial Chinese history. A Hunanese, and a product of the fervently Song-learning tradition of the Hunan academy scene of the 1820s and 1830s, he was, like his father, a brilliant scholar, having achieved his *jinshi* and appointment to the Hanlin Academy at the age of twenty-four. Between his posting as acting Hubei governor, in April 1855, and his premature death from illness, six years later, he labored energetically to carry out a wide range of statecraft-tinged reforms in that province, most of them emphasizing reliance on wealthy and presumably public-spirited local elites, in place of hired subbureaucrats, to manage fiscal administration and other governmental tasks. All of these reforms were designed to win the hearts and minds of "the people" for the Qing-loyalist cause. But this was wartime, and Hu was even more notable for his achievements on the battlefield. Among the pleiad of Hunanese soldier-statesmen that emerged in this era, it was arguably Hu, above all, who worked out the particular arrangements for mobilizing the local *tuanlian* militia and implementing their extrabudgetary means of financing: the provincially imposed *lijin* commercial-transit tax, and a gentry-staffed local subscription and land-surtax bureau (*ju*). As we shall see, nowhere was he more intensely involved in these activities than in Macheng itself. Indeed, when forming what would become his Hubei army (Chujun), shortly after his appointment to the governorship, Hu explicitly identified Macheng, because of the area's long-established martial tradition, as one of the most fertile recruiting grounds for his army's "braves."[39]

Liquidation

On several occasions from late 1855 to early 1858, Qing regulars and Hubei and Hunan army braves fought side by side with Macheng's own militiamen to inflict major defeats on Taiping units in the region. But battlefield success was accompanied by yet more suffering for the beleaguered local population. In late summer of 1856, torrential rains flooded the county and all but wiped out the harvest; over the remainder of that year and into the following spring, grain prices rocketed upward, and famine refugees streamed in from Henan; with county granaries already plundered by the rebels, local philanthropists fought a losing battle to keep the population fed, and therefore securely loyal. As one report observed, "Corpses of the starved littered the fields."[40]

This was only the prelude to a greater cycle of carnage to come. As the new year of 1858 began, Hu Linyi reported from his makeshift provincial *yamen* at Huangzhou that his newly formed Hubei army was stretched dangerously thin. While his troops had been trying to clear the eastern part of the province and foray downriver toward Jiujiang (Jiangxi), a large Taiping force had circled around to the north. The rebels had moved westward from Anqing (Anhui) toward the Anhui-Henan-Hubei border, forming a battlefield alliance with Nian rebels in southern Henan and massing at the prefectural seat of Gushi. A local source says of their number, "It was popularly claimed to be over 100,000 men but in reality was between 60,000 and 70,000."[41] Macheng County lay directly in the path of their anticipated march toward Wuhan. Hu accordingly dispatched a Qing force under the Manchu general Shubao to defend the county, but soon thereafter he opted to advance this force further across the provincial border to attack Gushi itself. He notified Macheng magistrate Wang Dunren (the first of several Hunan-born local officials whom Hu had posted to the county) and Macheng's own local militia that they must at all costs defend the strategic Pine Nut Pass, the main gateway to the Middle Yangzi region.[42]

In mid-April, an 8,000-man rebel force brushed by Shubao and entered the pass. Its commander was a brilliant and bespectacled eighteen-year-old named Chen Yucheng, known to all as Four Eyes. Magistrate Wang made a gallant attempt to defend the pass but was forced to retreat. He chose to rally his troops in the foothills of the Dabie Shan so as to defend the northern and most direct route to the county seat. Four Eyes took the southern route instead, which led through Cassiawood River and the heart of the Dongshan. Here the battle-hardened Dongshan militia, under Xia Wu, contested the advance of Four Eyes but were badly outmanned and forced to retreat one step at a time. The decisive battle was fought at Huangtu Gorge, near the geographic center of the county, where the eastern hills gave way to the lowland core. The militiamen were defeated, and many of their commanders, among them several of the Xia lineage, were killed. Four Eyes was thus able to rampage his way on to Macheng City, where he butchered the local inhabitants and torched most of the city—not merely the expected government offices but also hundreds of private homes.[43]

Hu Linyi then personally directed a three-pronged campaign to besiege and exterminate (*weijiao*) the rebels occupying the county seat. Qing general Shubao returned from Henan to attack from the north, the Dongshan militia of Zhan Zhaozhu, Yu Yaxiang, and Xia Wu attacked from the east, and merchant-financed *tuanlian* units from Songbu and the other Ju River ports attacked from the south and the west. The campaign stretched on bloodily for two months, until, in mid-June, Four Eyes broke out and escaped to Henan. His followers were not so fortunate: several thousand Taiping partisans were killed in the Qing recapture of the city—as Hu Linyi boasted, "annihilated at one stroke" ("yigu er jian")[44]—and hundreds of others were caught and summarily executed as they fled.[45] Governor Hu then enlisted the victorious Macheng militia leaders to join his liquidation (*suqing*) campaign, pursuing the rebels throughout the wider four-province region, which they continued to do throughout the rest of the year. They received handsome honors and promotions as tokens of imperial gratitude.[46]

But for the people of Macheng as a whole, the events of these three months in 1858 were catastrophic. The immediate task in the wake of the Taiping occupation was to identify and bury the dead. A vast mass cemetery was constructed outside the west gate of the county seat for burial of unidentified corpses—joining similar suburban graveyards built centuries earlier for casualties of the Ming-Qing transition. On this site, the incoming magistrate, Yi Guanghui, erected the White Bone Pagoda (Baigu ta) and composed a stele to memorialize the "fathers and sons massacred side by side."[47] The names of the victims, when available, were diligently recorded for inclusion in the martyrologies to be printed in successive county gazetteers. For this year alone, several dozen gentry martyrs are listed along with nearly 500 commoner militiamen and—for the first time during the rebellion era—hundreds of nonlocal loyalist fighters who had died on Macheng soil.[48] The death toll among noncombatants can only be imagined.

Scorched Earth

A great many Macheng people, in time-honored fashion, took to the hills (*rushan*) to escape the bloodbaths of 1854 and 1858, and it would seem that much of the population spent most of the late 1850s and early 1860s actually residing in mountainside forts. The 1882 county gazetteer records a total of ninety-five such forts in existence at that time. Many of these, like the venerable Hall of Heaven Fort (Tiantang zhai), dated from the Ming or even earlier, but others had been newly built in response to the midcentury crisis, and the older ones were all substantially expanded and strengthened.[49] Certain fortresses were lineage-specific, like Yu Yaxiang's Cloud Dragon Fort (Yunlong zhai), on the Luotian border, and Xia Wu's Stonewall Fort (Shicheng zhai), outside of Cassiawood River. Others were joint-lineage enterprises, like the Heavenly Well Fort (Tianjing zhai) of the Dong, Xia, Yu, Wang, and Xiao families. Still others were communally financed through impositions on local commercial transactions and per-acre assessments on the harvest.[50] As noted earlier, the merchants of both Songbu and Baigu, with local official permission, walled their towns during this era; Songbu's wall was over 6 meters high and boasted eighteen gun towers. Many hillside stockades were large enough to enclose farm and pasture land, and even tracts of forest. Some, like the famous Lion Fort (Shizi zhai), perched on a cat-shaped cluster of peaks in the Dabie Shan, had their own patron deities whose divine power (*ling*) further shielded their inhabitants.

Over the course of 1859, however, the old *shanzhai* were joined on the Macheng landscape by an entirely new sort of mountain fortification. This was the *diaobao* or *diaolou* (blockhouse). Its purpose was specifically to guard the passes that provided entry into the county and the province across the Dabie Shan from the north and (especially) the northeast. In all, nine blockhouses were erected: two at the Pine Nut Pass, one each at the other Five Passes, and two atop adjacent mountain ridges. Also built were several *kamen* (supporting "guardposts"). Typically, a blockhouse was four stories tall, with internal ladders to the upper stories, and was topped by a parapet and artillery emplacement. The blockhouses were quite formidable. Their construction, like that of the guardposts, was financed by a special assessment levied on all Macheng property holders by the county's General Militia Bureau (see below), and it was managed by a special committee of "neighboring gentry" from the adjacent wards in the Dongshan and Dabie Shan hills. The chair of the committee was Xia Wu.[51]

Local historical accounts invariably credit the innovation of the Macheng blockhouses to Hu Linyi, and this attribution is not totally unwarranted, but examination of Hu's own correspondence on the matter reveals that the actual initiative came from literati-cum-militia leaders at the county level—undoubt-

Stonewall Fort (Shicheng zhai), front gate. Photograph by the author.

edly, above all, Xia Wu himself and his comrades Yu Yaxiang and Zhan Zhaozhu—who were anxious to prevent recurrence of the kind of invasion through the Pine Nut Pass that had so wasted their native place just the year before. Hu, in fact, was somewhat reluctant at the outset to sanction the new construction when the indigenous elite's grandiose blueprints were presented to him by Macheng magistrate Yi Guanghui. While Hu clearly acknowledged the need to defend these passes, his initial reaction—running somewhat counter to his more general encouragement of local elite activism—was wariness about the additional power that these new battlements might grant to the notoriously contentious and independent-minded Macheng elite. Why here and not elsewhere, he asked?[52] It was only after the governor had worked out the means to exert his own systematic control that he sanctioned and effectively co-opted the blockhouse project.

In a set of regulations that he drafted to oversee blockhouse construction throughout Huangzhou Prefecture, Hu Linyi laid heavy emphasis on the identity of interest between local elites and the Qing state. He noted that the population of Macheng had suffered massacres (*can*) on a nearly annual basis as a result of rebels entering through the passes, and he commended the local elite for taking the initiative in blockhouse building, comparing them favorably to the blockhouses of other areas, such as Qizhou, where even the *shanzhai* left over from the warfare of the Ming-Qing transition now lay in ruins. But at the same time he instructed his magistrates to take personal charge of the blockhouses and guardposts, and to standardize and bureaucratize their operation. Magistrates were to (1) assign the forces to man the blockhouses, (2) assume control over the blockhouses' financial management, (3) keep detailed accounts of the lands assessed for blockhouse construction and maintenance, and (4) deliberate with the local elite over standard procedures for blockhouse defense—all at the county level. Failure to do so, Hu stated, would amount to neglecting the essential responsibility of officials to defend their jurisdiction and its people, while fulfilling these duties would also (as Hu did not say but transparently meant) keep those people from appropriating an unseemly autonomy.[53]

Finally, in a strongly worded directive to Macheng magistrate Yi Guanghui (Hu's Hunanese fellow provincial and protégé), the governor began by chastising him in time-honored "statecraft" style for allowing *yamen* underlings, thugs, and pettifoggers to run rampant over popular livelihoods (*minsheng*) and private property (*mincai*). (The specific complaints to which Hu referred are unclear—were they specifically related to fortifications?) "The enrichment of the people [*minfei*]," Hu pointed out, "is directly proportional to the burden of labor assumed by the local official." It was especially critical, of course, to gain popular goodwill in times like these, he said. He then moved on to the crux of his message, the blockhouses:

> Blockhouses and guardposts are a particular form of the overall military strategy of fortification [*jianbi*]. We already have the general plans for building these, but implementing them with genuine results requires perseverance on your part. To effectively harness the capacity of the people [*minli*] for this project, you must first gain popular support [*minxin*], and to do this requires the support of the local elite [*shixin*]. You must work day and night to seek out and consult with upright local literati, to learn about and help influence the way things are actually done in this area [*difang shili*]. The common people are in awe of the literati and will follow their lead. This is true in regard to *baojia* registration, to *tuanlian* mobilization, and to blockhouse construction as well.

Once again, Hu urged his magistrate to keep *yamen* underlings out of the loop altogether. And he concluded by assigning the defense of the new blockhouses squarely to the local population: "Defending the city walls and moats is the job of government troops; manning the blockhouses and guardposts is that of the local militia."[54]

This conceived division of labor—state agents defending urban administrative centers while leaving the rural population largely to defend itself—also underlay what was Hu Linyi's other major contribution to the long history of fortification in Macheng: the draconian scorched-earth policy known as *jianbi qingye* (build forts and waste the surrounding areas) or simply *qingye*. As had been the case in the late Ming, the innovations in official-directed fortification policy in nineteenth-century Macheng followed the lead of policies introduced in the Han River highlands of northwestern Hubei. This area, long characterized by a transient and internally fractured population, had been the spawning ground of the massive White Lotus rebellion of the late eighteenth century and consequently had also witnessed frenetic official experiments in counterinsurgency methods specifically tailored to upland settings.[55]

A number of policy papers generated by Han Valley officials during this era became widely circulated during the subsequent decades and had a particular influence on the cohort of self-consciously statecraft-oriented scholars emerging out of the Hunan academy scene in the 1820s–1830s, not least among them Hu Linyi. In his 1842 *Shengwu ji* (Record of the conquest of the northwest), the Hunanese Wei Yuan reprinted a memorial of the Manchu general Mingliang (1735–1822) applauding the spontaneous efforts of Han highland elites to build forts and, specifically, to gather in as much as possible of the foodstuffs from the surrounding areas in defense against White Lotus attack. Mingliang's successor, Lebao (1740–1819), and especially Lebao's Fujianese subordinate and advisor Gong Jinghan (1747–1802), went a bit further, arguing in 1804 that the reason why White Lotus suppression had not gone well up to that point was that local officials had not had the resolve to promote fortification or to couple it with an aggressive policy of torching all surrounding farmland so as to starve out the rebels. The prescriptions of Gong Jinghan's 1799 *Jianbi qingye yi* (Essay on fortification and scorched earth)—calling for a coordinated policy of fort building, crop destruction, fortress-head nomination, militia organization, and financing via countywide supplementary tax assessments—provided the model drawn upon by Hu Linyi and his subordinates during the Taiping wars in the Dabie Shan and Dongshan areas.[56] Perhaps even more influential was the series of policy papers—on fort building, militia organization, and establishment of a defense perimeter via linked, armed, and fortified villages (the so-called *liancun fa*)—issued during the White Lotus campaigns by the Hunanese frontier-defense specialist Yan Ruyi (1759–1826). Yan's essays were reprinted by Wei Yuan in his quasi-canonical 1826 *Huangchao jingshi wenbian* (Statecraft compendium) and were internalized by students in the Changsha academies where Yan himself was a venerated presence during Hu Linyi's student years. In Yan's view, a scorched-earth strategy (*qingye zhi ce*) was "absolutely essential" to the task of sweeping any area clear of rebels.[57]

Local sources in Macheng are remarkably discreet about the actual details of *qingye* implementation in the county, and its possible implications. Most accounts credit it with the decisive role in defeating rebel incursions of the 1860s, and one writer suggests that it was the final phase in a defense-policy cycle, carried out only when the policies of *zhaomu fangjiao* (summoning troops for defense and rebel extermination) and *liantuan helian* (coordinating and training local militia) had exhausted their efficacy.[58] But what was the cost? We know that the early 1860s were years of increasingly severe dearth in Macheng—many individuals are honored for their self-sacrificing efforts to keep the local population from starving[59]—and deliberate destruction of crops, on top of the ordinary decimations of constant warfare, must have considerably aggravated the crisis. An undated directive of Hu Linyi to the Macheng magistrate insists that rents in kind due to residents of the county seat not be forcibly diverted to relieve rural food shortages, for to do so would jeopardize the security of the city itself as well as risk alienating the elite, already heavily burdened by demands for military contributions.[60] Under such strained conditions, one can only wonder what might have been the impact of *qingye* compulsions, however necessary and effective they seemed, on relations between the Qing state and local society, between urbanites and rural dwellers, and between the local wealthy and the poor.

Total Militarization

Just after the new year of 1859, Hu Linyi ordered a systematic restructuring of militia organization in all Hubei counties. A *zongju* (general bureau) was to be established in each county seat, with branch bureaus in each ward, and both financing and military strategy were to be more centrally coordinated. In Macheng, Magistrate Chen Rufan complied, staffing the system with gentry members largely drawn from the county seat, and headed by one Feng Tingxiang. For some reason, Chen's reorganization proved unsatisfactory, and a second reorganization was undertaken the following year, once Chen himself had been replaced by Hu Linyi's handpicked Macheng magistrate, Wu Lin. A native of Jiangnan's Jiading County, Wu proudly described himself as a man of rustic simplicity (*zhipu*), with no literary refinement, and had been personally recruited by Hu Linyi for his Hubei task force during Hu's stint as chief examiner for the Jiangsu provincial examinations the preceding year. In Macheng, Wu immediately overhauled the county *tuanlian* management corps. The general bureau was renamed the Yushou ju (Defense Participation Bureau), and its management was assigned to Li Keming—an urban gentryman, to be sure, but one who by now had long militia-command experience in the field. Li immediately undertook a major reconstruction of defense works surrounding Macheng City. The critical east ward bureau was headed by the old Dongshan warhorses Zhan Zhaozhu, Yu Yaxiang, and Xia Wu. Xia simultaneously was charged with organizing a 500-man mobile strike force known as the Liyou ying (Safeguard the Rites battalion).[61]

Macheng's newly centralized *tuanlian* apparatus would be put to severe test during the early 1860s. In the spring of 1861, the redoubtable Four Eyes Chen once again massed his forces on the northern slopes of the Dabie Shan, this time in league with a local rebel leader going by the name of Gong Xiazi (Blind Gong, or Gong the Reckless). Popularly known as the Scourge of Henan for his fierce and merciless conduct of war, Gong was further identified as a leader of the Nian, a somewhat ambiguous category referring to predatory rebel groups then operating in central and northern China. Among the many scholars who have wrestled with the nature of the Nian, Philip Kuhn and Elizabeth Perry both see them as mutated versions of local militia units that had achieved some degree of autonomy from the Qing state and had moved into various criminal rackets and had then, with the political breakdown occasioned by the Taiping rebellion, taken the further step into open revolt. (The two disagree on the White Lotus sectarian content of their ideology, Kuhn seeing it as relatively important and Perry as far less so.)[62] The Republican-era Hubei provincial gazetteer, for its part, was content to disparage these units simply as those perennially intractable outsiders from over the Dabie Shan:

> The local cultures of Runing, Guangzhou, and Nanyang, in southern Henan, are fierce and savage [*kuanghan*]. Local ruffians there form into bands [*tudang*] for the primary purpose of plunder and extortion. They call such bands Nianzi. Beginning in the early Xianfeng reign, under cover of the Taiping rebellion, they began opportunistic raids into our province.[63]

The first such raid of importance into Huangzhou came in 1855 but bypassed Macheng. The second was the joint project of Blind Gong and Four Eyes Chen, in 1861.

In the second lunar month, Gong and Chen led an army estimated at 100,000 in an effort to storm the Pine Nut Pass and fight their way to Wuhan. Zeng Guofan saw the coming confrontation as, in many ways, the most pivotal of the entire rebellion. He wrote to Hu Linyi: "If Huangzhou Prefecture cannot be held, then Wuhan will also be lost, and our entire position . . . south of the Yangzi may collapse. Nanchang will fall as well, and our forces will panic. It is up to you and me, commanding these Hubei troops, to rally our side. If we fail, I dare not consider the consequences."[64] Zeng therefore sent five Hubei battalions, led by the provincial commander-in-chief (and Hunan native) Cheng Daji, plus a united force of several thousand Macheng militia, led by Xia Wu, to intercept the rebels just inside the pass. It was an epic battle. After rebuffing the invaders, Cheng and Xia pursued the rebels through the pass itself, with great slaughter on both sides: "since no one in either army would retreat," it was reported, "the corpses piled up like mountains." Cheng beheaded over 3,000 captives, including Blind Gong himself. But after this great loyalist victory over the main rebel force, other Taiping and Nian units crossed over into Macheng through other passes in the Dabie Shan and Dongshan. At Goose Rock Mountain, Magistrate Wu Lin managed to rebuff their march on the county seat, but loss of life throughout the county over the next several months was reported to be "extremely tragic" (*shencan*).[65]

Through all of this, provincial esteem for and reliance upon the seasoned *tuanlian* forces of Macheng, and especially of the Dongshan, steadily grew. Following the glorious victory over Blind Gong in late 1861, no less influential a man than Zeng Guofan had personally recommended Xia Wu for a county magistracy; he was granted such a post in Zhili's Wuqiang County, currently overrun by racketeering gangs of salt smugglers (*yanfei*). Xia died (in combat?) en route to taking up this post, bringing to an end the career of one of the most powerful figures in Macheng's long history.[66] Xia's demise left effective power in the county in the hands of his fellow "luminary of the eastern hills," Yu Yaxiang.

In late 1861, an incident occurred that, though relatively minor in relation to the major regional warfare going on all around it, seems highly emblematic of both the rising power and the attitude of Macheng's Dongshan local protectors. A force of *jiaofei* (sectarian rebels) from Henan's Shangcheng County—a group apparently not directly linked to either the Taiping or the Nian, and very likely an antecedent of the Red Spears who would routinely foray into Macheng from Shangcheng in the Republican era—crossed into the Dongshan highlands and attracted some local support on the basis of their demonstrated *yaoshu* (occult arts). The highlands were in chaos, and the Luotian magistrate requested higher-level military aid. At this very time, the prefectural examinations were being given in the Huangzhou prefectural seat, and Yu Yaxiang, enjoying a momentary respite after the defeat of Blind Gong, was a candidate. Huangzhou prefect Huang Yijie, overseeing the exams, rallied the candidates to go to the magistrate's aid, but as he did so he pulled Yu Yaxiang aside to ask his views on the magistrate's request to call in Qing regular troops. Yu advised against it. Among the *xiangyu wuzhi* (untutored bumpkins) of this, my native place, he suggested, the vast majority are upright subjects and only a very few are sectarians. In such a place, Yu cautioned, sending in a large force of Qing occupying troops would more likely spark wider rebellion than preserve the peace. Far better to leave the matter to my own indigenous militia forces, who will make short work of it. Prefect Huang concurred. The Dongshan tradition of home rule by armed local elites, sanctioned in the seventeenth century by Yu Chenglong, was decisively reaffirmed.[67]

The following years—the first of the new Tongzhi reign—saw nearly continuous fighting in Macheng. In the spring of 1863, a Nian force crossed the border from Henan, captured the northern market town of Futianhe, defeated a county-defense force at Huangtu Gorge, and laid siege to the county seat. The next month, a very formidable joint Taiping-Nian force crossed the Dongshan from Luotian and Huanggang (the rebels held much of Luotian County throughout the early 1860s) and occupied Baiguo, which they progressively fortified into a major regional stronghold, foraying out occasionally to raid the surrounding plain for food. To counter this occupation, Yan Shusen, Hu Linyi's successor as Hubei governor, visited the area and ordered the establishment of a Macheng-Huang'an-Luotian tricounty militia command, which was put under the direction of Yu Yaxiang. In the fall, yet another rebel army moved up the Ju River from the southwest, occupied Songbu and Zhongguanyi, and again besieged the county seat. There were heavy losses of life on both sides; over the course of the year, nearly 4,000 captured rebels were decapitated in Macheng by government forces.[68]

For much of the Great Qing empire, the year 1864—witnessing, as it did, the formal collapse of the Heavenly Kingdom regime at Nanjing—was a milestone in the return to normalcy, the effective start of the optimistic era of Tongzhi "restoration." In certain localities, however, especially those in the path of the fleeing rebels, it was a very bad year. Macheng was one such place. The local food crisis, progressively worsening over the previous decade and aggravated by government scorched-earth policies, reached its most intense, and in the summer a series of severe epidemics ravaged the county. Local philanthropists and Qing military officers scrambled to keep the population alive.[69] No sooner had Zeng Guofan gathered up the Hubei army and pushed downriver to pursue the siege of Nanjing than rebel groups filled in the areas he left behind. The rebels, repelled in their effort to capture the county seat, congregated in the central foothills of the Dongshan, torching and pillaging every place they passed. The now heavily fortified rebel stronghold of Baiguo became the base for all joint Taiping-Nian activity throughout central China. When Nanjing itself fell to Qing forces in July, many of its defenders fought their way into Macheng, and Baiguo became in effect the Heavenly Kingdom's rump capital. Meanwhile, Nian forces based in southeastern Henan held most of Luotian County and much of Huanggang County, thrusting regularly across the Dongshan into Macheng. Governor Yan Shusen ordered a yet more rigorous scorched-earth campaign throughout the county.[70]

Dislodging the rebels from Baiguo became the major Qing objective in central China. Hubei-Hunan viceroy Guanwen moved his office to Huangzhou, provincial commander-in-chief Cheng Daji set up his field headquarters in Yu Chenglong's old office at Qiting, and the great and fearsome Mongol general

Senggelinqin was ordered in across the Dabie Shan, accompanied by units of the newly formed Henan army (Yujun). Together, heavily supported by Macheng's own militia units, they launched a three-pronged attack. Finally, in the autumn of 1864, after a protracted siege and incredibly high casualties on both sides, some 30,000 rebels abandoned their stronghold and fled, into the Dongshan to the east and the Dabie Shan to the north. Qing forces reported their liberation of the local population, which had been trapped in the town for over a year, but in the process they leveled Baiguo to the ground. The scattering rebels were gradually mopped up (*suqing*) by Qing regulars and Macheng militia, but as they fled, groups of them besieged and briefly occupied many of the county's mountain fortresses along the way; Qing authorities, as they had done during the conquest era two centuries earlier, sought to level (*pingmie*) many of these forts as a precaution. General Cheng Daji surrounded a group of fleeing Taiping in Luotian and, as was his wont, beheaded more than 2,000 of them in a single day. At the Dongshan market town of Muzidian, Qing armies and township militia ambushed and massacred a group of Nian retreating out of Huanggang toward their native Henan. The rebels held out longest, unsurprisingly, in the same rugged Jinjiazhai Plateau just outside the Pine Nut Pass that, some seven decades later, would provide the secure base for the Eyuwan Soviet.[71]

For all intents and purposes, 1864 was the final year of terrible bloodshed in Macheng during the midcentury rebellions. There were repeated Nian incursions up through 1867, when Zeng Guofan moved a large military force to the county to use as a staging ground for campaigns in the north. On each occasion, local people retreated to their mountain fortresses and dutifully destroyed the crops in their fields, and the rebels moved on to plunder another locality. Imperial troops, the Hubei army in its final years under the new governor (Zeng Guochuan, Guofan's younger brother), and the county's own and ever more powerful militia apparatus under Yu Yaxiang routinely conducted *suqing* sweep operations against any heterodox elements. Peace was restored.[72]

Rebellion within the Rebellion

Unlike the mass violence of the late Yuan, the late Ming, and the 1670s, the bloody mid-Qing rebellions had been a plague largely visited on Macheng from outside, the result simply of its strategic location in the geopolitics of empire. The county was not itself the spawning ground of appreciable rebel movements. The Macheng of the 1850s and 1860s produced no sectarian kingmaker like Zou Pusheng, no bondservant avenger like Tang Zhi, nor even any maverick gentry warlords like Zhou Wenjiang or Liu Junfu. Yet there are subtle hints in the sources, thoroughly laundered as they were by subsequent Qing partisans, of at least some breakdown in local solidarity, growing out of deeper social tensions during the chaotic rebellion years.

For one thing, we know precious little (for the empire in general) about how the massive Taiping armies, originally composed of a motley assortment of true believers and opportunists from the deep south, regenerated themselves during their sojourn of more than a decade in the Yangzi Valley. In a place like Macheng, how much willing collaboration or even enthusiastic reception was there for an army of rebels promising national liberation from the Manchus, economic equality, and personal salvation? The evidence suggests that the power of the local social-control apparatus, perhaps combined with genuine popular attachment to the lineage system and to the pantheon of popular religion (both explicitly targeted by the Taiping), ensured that receptiveness to the long-haired southerners was fairly minimal. The compiler of the postrebellion-era county gazetteer notes frankly that Macheng people were generally loyal to the Qing "state" (*guojia*), out of gratitude for the enlightenment and nourishment (*jiaoyang*) they had received at its hands, but that a more compelling motive for antirebel mobilization was the venerable and deeply entrenched *bangfeng* (localist spirit) of this place. As in the late Ming, loyalism grew primarily out of localism.[73]

Even so, complicity in the rebel cause could not have been altogether absent. The county gazetteer produced under the People's Republic—under which regime the taboo against mentioning Taiping collaboration had been lifted—relates, in the biography of a local hero of the Republican Revolution, that his grandfather had joined the Taiping army (*canjia Taiping jun*), gone off to Sichuan, and never been heard from again. What makes this passing comment all the more intriguing is the fact that the Taiping conscript in question seems to have been an uncle of the preeminent Dongshan militia leader Yu Yaxiang![74] Yaxiang himself repeatedly conceded that the *xiangyu* (ignorant bumpkins) of his native township were dangerously susceptible to rebel appeals, and he may well have been speaking from personal, even familial, experience.[75] Throughout the later years of the rebellion, moreover, there is routine mention in the sources of more localized groups of *jiaofei* in the area, groups with no apparent direct link to either Taiping or Nian but with a time-honored attraction to marginalized local residents. In early 1866, an uprising of the Society of Elder Brothers (Gelaohui), allied with but distinct from local Nian rebels—perhaps mutinous troops of the Xiang or Chu Armies?—evicted General Cheng Daji from Songbu and burned his troop barracks there.[76]

There are also periodic hints that economic grievances in the area could spark local conflict, given intense pressure due both to the cost of militarization and fortification (recall Hu Linyi's chastising the Macheng magistrate for insufficient sensitivity to the distribution of this burden) and to the growing subsistence crisis that accompanied the rebellions. As early as 1855, for example, *tuanlian* units that were mobilized in the county's southeastern Ju River Valley mutinied, refusing to fight the Taiping until they were paid for doing so.[77] In the same year, Zhan Zhonglian—holder of a purchased degree, militia leader from Dongshan's Muzidian, and kinsman of the more eminent *tuanlian* commander Zhan Zhaozhu—organized a 300-man association called the Pinnong ju (Poor Farmers Bureau) at the Dinghui Temple, seized grain from government granaries, and sold it off at a "fair price." For doing so, he was denounced to the county authorities, but his past and continuing valor in the anti-Taiping campaigns secured his exoneration (as well as a eulogy from the magistrate when he died in battle the following year).[78] As the rebellion progressed, another Dongshan militia leader, Zheng Jiaju of Cassiawood River, became so alarmed by the growing intimidation and oppression carried out by powerful families (*youzu*) against their poorer neighbors that he felt compelled to institute a community compact (*xiangyue*) in his native township to inculcate moral restraint in the elites and thereby prevent local class warfare.[79] The prospect of rebellion within the rebellion was a constant elite fear.

Reconstruction and Commemoration

The postrebellion decades in Macheng were a time of physical rebuilding and healing of wounds. In the county seat, it was said that the only important structure to have survived the Taiping forces intact was—miraculously—that symbol of local identity, the shrine to the Macheng's patron deity Ma Gu. Up through the mid-1870s, officials and private philanthropists—notably, of course, merchants of the Huangbang[80]—continually drew upon their surviving resources to reconstruct the examination hall, the drum and bell towers, the Confucian temple, and the magistrate's and submagistrate's office compounds. Temples throughout the county also needed rebuilding. The county's agricultural base required solicitous mending. Its granary system—once a mark of local pride, but plundered by the rebels and unavailable to serve the desperate needs of the population during the crises of the rebellion years—began to be reconstituted as early as 1861 by magistrate Wu Lin. By the time of the great northwestern China famine of the late 1870s, Macheng was proudly able to send some of its accumulated surplus as outside relief. After years of chaos, the structure of local administration, including a workably equitable system of tax assessment and collection, had to be reconstituted as if ex nihilo.[81]

Heroic service in the loyalist cause had brought imperial recognition and honors to many of Macheng's sons, but the elite, with peace restored, turned once again to the pursuit of social advancement through nonmilitary means. The urban literatus Feng Tingxiang, who had been granted official rank in recognition of his brief leadership of the county's General Militia Bureau, petitioned for Macheng County to be allowed a greater quota of passes on the local and provincial examinations, as a token of gratitude for the sacrifices of its residents. In two stages during the 1860s, Governor-general Guanwen did arrange such increases, the first by twenty per annum (ten civil and ten military) and the second by an additional seven, in addition to a one-time bonus, in 1870, of fifteen more.[82]

Even the county's greatest surviving militia hero and de facto "godfather" of the postwar years, Yu Yaxiang, returned to the scholarly vocation of his youth. He sat successfully for the provincial examination in 1864 but declined an official post, opting instead to assume the directorship of the Wansong Academy, a position that he passed on to his son Yu Yingyun (*jinshi* 1886) some twenty years later. An 1882 inventory of the library holdings of this academy, the most venerable and prestigious of the county's educational institutions, clearly reveals the direction that scholarship had taken there under its new headmaster. Central to the collection were the *Rizhi lu* (Record of knowledge accumulated day by day) and *Tianxia junguo libi lu* (Assets and liabilities of the empire's local jurisdictions) of Gu Yanwu, the *Wuzhong yigui* (Five sourcebooks on moral conduct) and *Zaiguan fajie lu* (Rules for disciplining government clerks) of Chen Hongmou, and the collected correspondence of the savior of Hubei (and Yu's own militia superior), Hu Linyi—virtually a genealogy of the "statecraft school" as constructed by Middle Yangzi intellectuals as of that date.[83] In other words, whereas once, in the late Ming, the Wansong Academy had been a hotbed of freewheeling intellectual speculation, this cultural centerpiece of Macheng had now been fully converted to the kind of socially conservative, morally fundamentalist, yet pragmatically activist scholarship that was reflective of Yu Yaxiang's roughhewn Dongshan origins but that now had become mainstream, in Macheng as in much of the rest of the late-Qing empire.

The dead had not only to be buried but also properly remembered. Mass eulogies were composed, and memorial monuments were erected. The county gazetteer of 1882 records the names of thousands of local militiamen, as well as those of heroic civilians, who gave their lives in the conflict. For example, it devotes five full chapters to listing the names of local virtuous women; more than half of the thousands included had died in the mayhem of the midcentury rebellions. The publication of this gazetteer was clearly seen as giving closure to the trauma of the rebellions and marking the triumph of the reconstruction project; that it took until 1882 for it to be published (a prefectural gazetteer followed close upon it, in 1884) suggests how long this closure took to achieve. The victories and defeats of the rebellion years in Macheng were meticulously recorded in its pages, to provide the orthodox script for social memory of the mid-Qing holocaust.[84]

The man who largely oversaw the work both of reconstruction and of commemoration, and who edited with evident personal devotion the 1882 gazetteer, was Guo Qinghua. A Guilin native who served six separate terms as Macheng magistrate between the late 1860s and the early 1880s, Guo accompanied this chronicle with an eloquent requiem of his own, which seems to capture very deeply local readings of what the county had experienced.[85] Guo begins by recalling the loss of North China to the Jurchen in the 1120s, providing an explicitly feudal/familial grounding for the link between localism and loyalism: "The feudal lords set up ancestral temples and tutelary shrines within their fiefs and sacrificed there [in rites of local identity]. When the Son of Heaven faced a great military challenge, the lords necessarily took up arms to defend their ancestral domains." In recent years it has been the same: "The counties conduct local spring and autumn sacrifices, as coordinated [empirewide] by the Board of Rites. When rebels arise, local people must inevitably take up arms to defend their native place." When the Taiping arose in the south, and the Nian in the north, it was only through mobilization and digging in at the local level that the empire as a whole could be saved. The situation was the same, Guo says, as in flood control, where dikes must be patched up locally to avert inundation of the entire system.

Guo then shifts his rhetoric from the more general rationale for local defense, emphasizing now the nearly unique quality of Macheng's self-reliance. Given its strategic position in the defense of central China, he says, the county has always served as a battleground (*zhancheng*) in contests for the empire as a whole. And yet in this instance, Guo states, it was never really singled out by the Qing administration as a key point to be defended (*shidi*). Instead, repeatedly over the midcentury years, it became an orphaned locality (*gucheng*), besieged by all and protected by no one but itself. With a zealous local solidarity that transcended lineage, gender, and class, Macheng people united to confront the common enemy (*tongchou*). And, Guo says, it is precisely this sense of abandonment that explains the unusual ferocity and viciousness of the campaigns fought on Macheng soil: the local people, dying in great numbers themselves, responded with a vindictive rage (*fenji*) that Guo himself finds a bit unsettling—a compulsion to massacre the rebels totally and without mercy (*shazei zhiguo zhi si*). As we shall see, observers in the twentieth century would express similar wonder and unease about the propensity for total war built into Macheng's local culture.

For others, however, there was no such queasiness. On the basis of Guo Qinghua's carefully reconstructed local record, the gazetteer of Hubei Province as a whole, when it was first compiled in the early Republic, gave pride of place, in a special essay, to the heroic contribution of Macheng's militiamen to the entire province's salvation. And the county's own gazetteer of 1935, produced by a

Guomindang local administration in celebration of its own seemingly successful "Communist extermination campaign," retold once again the story of how, in the nineteenth century, an upright local population, guided by honest officials like Hu Linyi, had annihilated a deviant and wildly uncivilized insurgent group.[86] It was the very model for present policy.

CHAPTER NINE

An Interlude of Modernity

In early 1924, Qu Peilan, native of Songbu, hero of the 1911 Revolution, and president of the Hubei Provincial Assembly, convinced a group of his fellow Macheng sojourners at Wuhan to invest in a Cotton Cloth Factory in their native county, the first steam-powered manufacturing plant the county had seen. He used his connections to get special assistance from the Provincial Enterprise Office and hired a Macheng-born graduate of the Hubei Institute of Technology, Wang Hongfan, to serve as the factory's manager. Wang persuaded the Macheng magistrate to convene a meeting of the county's leading merchants, among whom he circulated a stock subscription. He bought thirty power looms to make large and small bolts of cloth, headbands, and handkerchiefs and began formal operations in September. Within two years, however, the factory and its funds were held for ransom by the renegade general Yuan Ying during his occupation of the county. The following spring, Communist activists denounced the factory as an organ of the local "bourgeoisie," forced it to turn its operations to the manufacture of "peasant army" uniforms, and organized the factory workers into an armed brigade. When, at the end of 1927, the factory was again occupied by the militarist-bandit Ren Yingqi, its operations ceased once and for all.[1]

As the Cotton Cloth Factory's brief history epitomizes, "modernity" came to Macheng late and did not stay very long. Significantly, in his lengthy and careful survey of economic "modernization" (that is, the introduction of Western-style industrial, communications, and agricultural organization and technology) throughout the province in the era through the First World War, Hubei historian Su Yunfeng does not mention the county even once.[2] Rather, Macheng's history in the final quarter of the nineteenth century and the first quarter of the twentieth was essentially one of growing marginalization, of relegation to a neglected but highly volatile periphery.

Macheng as Periphery

For much of the period, this history was not necessarily one of impoverishment. Agriculture—in familiar crops such as grain, beans, vegetables, and peanuts, and utilizing long-familiar techniques—continued through the early 1920s to be reasonably productive. There was continued marketing of timber, bamboo, tung oil, and medicinal herbs and some specialized production of tea and silk. The county proudly exhibited several of these "native products" at the Nanyang Entrepreneurial Trade Fair at Nanjing in 1909.[3] Biographies of local Huangbang guild merchants likewise indicate that they continued, well into the Republican era, to ply very successfully their routes along the Upper Yangzi and Han Rivers and to repatriate a significant amount of profit to the home county.[4] But the modest prosperity that Macheng continued to enjoy increasingly fell into the "backward" sector of China's widening dual economy in the late Qing and Republican eras. As Chinese society and culture likewise increasingly divided into a peripheral, conservative sector and a more cosmopolitan, self-consciously "progressive" one, tensions between the two would come to play themselves out with exceptional violence in Macheng.

With the opening of Hankou to foreign residence in 1861, and the rapid development in the decades thereafter of steamship traffic along the Yangzi, the economy of much of central China had been gradually reoriented toward global networks of trade. Then, with the substantial industrialization of the Wuhan cities themselves beginning in the 1890s, much of the surrounding region quickly switched over to production of industrial crops to feed the factories both of the provincial capital and areas beyond. Most important in Hubei's sprawling "interior delta" was the transition to cotton and other textile crops. But, despite the riverborne proximity to Wuhan that had spurred so much of its economic development in the past, and its own long history of cotton cultivation, Macheng County remained remarkably insulated from these developments. As Albert Feuerwerker long ago demonstrated, cotton textiles was one sector of China's economy that became separated most visibly into two equally thriving sectors. Thus while Macheng's distribution of its own handspun cloth via the Huangbang continued to hold on to its centuries-old interregional markets, the county's economy never participated in the wholesale shift to industrial cotton cultivation that marked many nearby areas. Hence its *relative* position among Hubei counties as a cotton producer significantly declined.[5]

The Ju River, Macheng's commercial lifeblood, was not readily accommodating to steamer traffic, and it was not until 1934 that the first motor road linking the county to Wuhan was constructed.[6] The Beijing-Hankou Railroad, completed in 1905, was laid out through Xiaogan and Yingshan Counties, to the west of Macheng, rather than traversing any of the county's own Five Passes through the Dabie Shan. This layout guaranteed the end, once and for all, of Macheng's venerable role in the empire's north-south trade (long in decline in any case). More important, the county was deprived of the dramatic stimulus effect on its economy, via newly cost-effective access to the Wuhan and Beijing markets and those beyond, that quickly accrued to rural areas straddling the railroad's route.[7] Similarly, Hubei's comprehensive telegraph system, in place by 1906, linked and integrated all parts of the province *except* its increasingly peripheralized northeast—Macheng and its neighboring Huangzhou counties.[8] Despite the area's proud commercial heritage, Macheng's chamber of commerce was established only in 1908, one of the last founded in any Hubei county.[9]

Nor was the highly nativist and militarized local culture at all receptive to direct foreign penetration, commercial or otherwise. We have already seen (chapter 1) the beating to death in 1892 of the first two Swedish missionaries to venture into the county, an act committed by outraged local martial arts adepts on the occasion of the Dragon Boat festival. The Swedes returned; but six years later, in sympathy with Yu Dongchen's anti-Christian agitation in Chongqing (news of this had no doubt been sent home by the large Macheng diaspora in Sichuan), the Swedish church at Songbu was once again razed and its staff driven back to Wuhan.[10] The first lasting missionary presence in Macheng came only in the early twentieth century, and in the hypernativist Dongshan only two decades later.[11] In 1905, several local youths, clearly inspired by the Boxers but styling themselves "White Lotus," unsuccessfully plotted an uprising to uphold the Qing and destroy the foreigners (*fu Qing mie yang*).[12] Even as late as 1915, elites of the county seat filed a successful legal plaint, which went as high as the foreign ministry at Beijing, to have Western missionaries expelled from a vacant Daoist temple that they had transformed into a church.[13]

As for foreign merchants, none established themselves locally until 1909, when the British Heji Powdered Egg Factory at Hankou set up a purchasing station at Songbu.[14] In the decades to follow, German and Japanese buyers of rural produce came to Songbu as well, but up until the Japanese occupation of 1938 the foreign presence in Macheng County never numbered more than a handful of persons overall. There was no significant experimentation with Western industrial technologies until the Cotton Cloth Factory of 1924, whose dismal history we have already recounted.

Reform

Macheng, then, entered the twentieth century with a social and economic structure not greatly altered from that which had emerged over the mid- to late-Ming period. Yet there *were* frenetic elite reformist currents taking hold in the empire as a whole that could not but affect the county from above and outside and find at least some local response. Several Macheng literati became close associates of the progressive Huguang viceroy Zhang Zhidong, most notably in his vigorous educational reforms. Wu Zhaotai (1851–1909), for example, passed the *jinshi* examination and was appointed a censor; he lost that post in 1890 after submitting a bold memorial (like many of his Macheng forebears of the late Ming) lambasting the court for spending critically short funds on reconstruction of the Summer Palace. Wu then joined Zhang Zhidong's staff. Assuming leadership of the viceroy's pet project, the Jingxin Academy at Wuhan, Wu in the late 1890s renamed the academy (*shuyuan*) a modern school (*xuetang*) and restructured its curriculum to feature Western sciences alongside classical study. In the last years of his life, Wu directed Zhang's new provincial Educational Affairs Commission (Xuewu gongsuo).[15] Yu Yingyun (*jinshi* 1886)—the son of anti-Taiping hero Yu Yaxiang, and his father's successor as headmaster of Macheng's Wansong Academy—also studied at Jingxin and lectured at various of Zhang Zhidong's reformist academies in Wuhan. While so employed, he served as the viceroy's troubleshooter in several delicate matters, including the 1892 murder of the Swedish missionaries in his own home county. (Yu's efforts to spare the murderers from execution created an international furor, and the viceroy quickly arranged his transfer to a magistracy in Guizhou.) Eventually Yu returned home to represent Macheng in the late-Qing Provincial Assembly and worked to compile the gazetteers both of his native county and of Hubei Province.[16]

Educational change came more slowly within the borders of the county itself. An Italian priest in 1901 opened a Catholic elementary school at the county seat. Following the abolition of the civil service examination in 1905, several hybrid *xuetang* sprang up throughout the county, most of them founded by Huangbang merchants and, as elsewhere in the empire, often appropriating the precincts of Buddhist or Daoist temples for their campuses. In the last years of the Qing and the first of the Republic, Western-style elementary schools (including some specifically for girls) were set up in Songbu, Baiguo, and other market towns. Graduates of these early Western-style schools went on to take higher degrees elsewhere: in Wuhan, in Beijing, and, as early as 1902, in Tokyo.[17] But the school that was destined to have the most profound impact appeared first in 1897, in the wake of the shocking defeat of the Sino-Japanese War, when Qu Kaiyan, a radicalized gentryman from a long-established scholarly family, convinced the magistrate to cede the premises of Macheng's civil service examination hall (*kaopeng*) to form the Higher-Level Elementary School (Gaodeng xiaoxue), drawing students selectively from throughout the county. As we shall see, this school would become the spawning ground for several generations of radical activists and would deeply transform the county's political life.[18]

One can well imagine that educational innovation was an area fraught with tension in this locality that so prided itself on the "rustic simplicity" of its people. Beginning in the 1910s, Western-style schools in the region became routine targets of terrorist attacks on the part of self-conscious upholders of public morality like the Red Spears.[19] No less "modernized" a man than Zheng Zhong—the locally born Guomindang Macheng magistrate, New Life Movement leader, and overseer of the 1935 county gazetteer compilation—recalled the New Policies era as a time when radical and perverse (*beiyin*) new ideas began to circulate in the county, as in the days of Li Zhi some three centuries earlier, and greatly threaten the social order.[20] The new educational trends could not be ignored, but they had to be brought under control. The instruments of such control, countywide, were the Office to Encourage Education (Quanxue suo) and the Macheng Educational Association (Macheng xuehui), established around 1905 in, significantly, the Baojia Bureau at the county seat. The Macheng Educational Association, later renamed the Bureau of Instruction (Jiaoyu ju), gradually accrued a substantial amount of endowment land, the proceeds of which it disbursed to schools of which it approved. The association was led for the first decade of its existence by the reformist gentryman Wu Dongjia. Beginning in 1918, however, it was directed by a succession of highly conservative intellectuals and local magnates: Zheng Kangshi, Yu Jinfang, and Cheng Yinnan; beginning in the early 1930s, Magistrate Zheng Zhong himself assumed personal control. Bureau of Instruction funds were lavished during this period on the most anti-modernist of projects: the centerpiece of Zheng Kangshi's tenure was his restoration of the venerable Temple of Literature (Wenmiao), of Yu Jinfang's the reconstruction of the Confucian Temple (Kongmiao), and of Zheng Zhong's the refurbishing of the Shrine to Local Sages and Worthies (Xiangxian minghuan si) at the substantial cost of 2,369 Mexican dollars.[21]

For much of the Macheng landed elite, and perhaps most of all for those from the Dongshan, such as the Yus and the Zhengs, "modernity" was at best a mixed blessing. Well into the Republican era, for example, local philanthropists preferred to act in the same way their colleagues in more cosmopolitan localities had done a century or more earlier. Yu Jinfang—a Western-educated social scientist—endowed a Confucian wastepaper-collection bureau (*xizi hui*) at the county seat in 1923, to prevent dishonoring of the sacred written word. Benevolent halls (*shantang*)—Confucian institutions for dispensing rice gruel and medical care to the local urban indigent—which had begun to proliferate in many Yangzi Valley cities and towns as early as the 1820s, first appeared in Songbu only in 1919, and in Macheng City not until 1932.[22] The one area in which innovation was actively welcomed was, unsurprisingly, public security. In 1908, the county's *baojia* apparatus was dismantled (temporarily, it would turn out) and replaced by a "modern" police force (*jingcha*), headquartered at the county seat but with branch offices in each of the townships. The following year, Songbu City, in the spirit of local self-government, set up a police force of its own, superseding that of the county administration, and other major market towns soon followed suit. Arsenals were also established at each major urban center, in an attempt to assert control over the growing amount of modern weaponry on the county's streets.[23]

A(nother) Change of Regime

In the midst of this, in the third year of the reign of the young Xuantong emperor, came a "revolution." As described by Joseph Esherick, the spread of the 1911 uprising throughout central China, after an army mutiny of October 10 in the Wuchang barracks, was an affair wholly of the reformist elite, entirely urban, and almost completely bloodless.[24] So far as Macheng was concerned, Esherick is absolutely right. The late Yuan and early Ming, the late Ming and early Qing, and the Taiping and Nian wars in this county had been bloodbaths, and even more wanton bloodshed lay just around the corner, in the late 1920s and early 1930s. But the Republican Revolution in Macheng was different—it was romantic, even genteel. Locally, the story of the overthrow of the imperial system that had governed China for more than two millennia was essentially a tale of the heroic exploits of a few young men, culminating in a single and colorful case of murder.

No doubt there were social and political tensions building up within the locality that contributed to the revolution's eventual acceptance, but these all seem to have been more symptomatic than causative. As we have seen, tension between local taxpayers and tax collectors had been a regular feature of politics in Macheng over the entire late-imperial era (as undoubtedly it was everywhere else); and in the final two decades of Qing rule accusations of grain-tax engrossment (*zhongbao*) by *yamen* underlings had grown ever more strident, prompting a complete overhaul of the county's fiscal system by the magistrate in 1897.[25] The following year, neighboring Huang'an County witnessed a full-fledged grain riot. Despite several seasons of lean harvest, county granaries remained full and locked while grain prices tripled. Magistrate Wu Guoyu, a man himself of plebeian origin who had been promoted to his post after years of clerical service in the provincial treasury, imposed price controls and ordered the elite to sell off their surplus, but he was ignored. Crowds of hungry people assembled at Wu's *yamen* door and, with his implicit sanction, looted the county granaries. Local elites went to Wuhan to seek Wu's ouster, but Viceroy Zhang Zhidong opted to demote Wu in grade while keeping him in his post. The elite were cowed into acceptance of Wu's populist policies, but antigovernment sentiment ran ever higher.[26]

Granaries were an incendiary issue in Macheng as well. Over the course of the late nineteenth century, a series of lawsuits by local literati had prompted magistrates to assert greater county-level centralization over the area's many grain stocks. Finally, in 1904, Magistrate Teng Song ordered all governmental and communal granary holdings and management concentrated in the Baojia Bureau at the county seat. A succession of good harvests alleviated food pressure and allowed Teng's bold move to pass without widespread opposition. But at the outset of the Xuantong reign, in 1908, the central government announced local self-government (*difang zizhi*) as a key goal of its ongoing New Policies reforms, and in compliance Macheng's central grain stocks were again dispersed to the new township-level self-government organs. The result was chaos, and was immediately perceived as such by all. For decades thereafter, a series of reformist measures all failed to safeguard local grain reserves from continual expropriation by local self-government leaders and from looting by various military forces.[27]

In other ways as well, the local self-government movement helped pave the way for the elimination of Qing rule in Macheng. In 1909, Magistrate Zhang Xiyun convened a conference of leading literati from throughout the county to deliberate how best to implement the self-government dictates sent down from above. The literati divided the county into twelve self-government districts (*zizhi qu*), each with its own district office, district manager, and assistant manager, and a district assembly composed of perhaps a score of local elite representatives. Supplementary tax assessments were imposed to pay for this. In May 1911, a District Assembly (*yishi hui*) was set up, with its headquarters at what was by now the all-purpose Baojia Bureau. As was the case in so many other areas of China, it would be this Assembly that eventually declared for revolution in Macheng.[28]

What kind of individuals were Macheng's first generation of self-government leaders? Although very quickly in the early Republic these figures became targets of attack for their extortionate behavior, at the outset their local repute seems to have been somewhat higher. The leader of the convention that implemented the system in the county, and the man who succeeded to the presidency of the district assembly once the revolution had won the day, was Jiang Hualong. Jiang hailed from the far north of Macheng County, in the Dabie Shan foothills, and was a lower civil service degree holder of 1894. He commanded great local esteem for his fairness and financial acumen, having directed various grain-relief projects over the years. Eventually, in 1926, he and his son were kidnapped for ransom by marauding bandits and were executed when they steadfastly refused to pay. We are told that the entire county observed a rally of mourning for them.[29]

On a more humble level, we know a bit about two men who served as early self-government leaders in the southern portion of the Dongshan, near the Huanggang border. Ding Zhengbo and Ding Zhengsong were brothers, neither holding a gentry degree (both failed early attempts), but they hailed from the leading family of their home village, Ding Family Mountain, and held favorable but contrasting local reputations. Zhengbo embodied the virtues of *wen* (civil leadership), in a very traditional way. He was renowned as a local conflict mediator who strove to work out solutions in the interest of all parties, shielding them from the machinations of the corrupt legal process, and he was a leader of relief efforts, in his lineage and beyond, spearheading a drive in the early twentieth century to resuscitate the now dilapidated Huiche Academy, the center of local elite culture in his township. Zhengsong, by contrast, embodied the martial virtues of *wu*, once again in a highly traditional mold: a famously skilled archer and horseman and a very tough *hombre* who had won much honor on the battlefield, he assumed in his home locality the aura of a knight-errant (*xiaqi*) and champion of the downtrodden. The 1935 county gazetteer tells us that whenever he saw local villagers (*xiangyu*) being oppressed by the rich and powerful, he stepped in to enforce his own rough-and-ready interpretation of the public good (*gongdao*).[30]

Throughout the county's history, as we have seen, Macheng's extremely strong localist sentiment had intersected in complicated ways with imperial or dynastic political causes. In this era, when it was actually encouraged to an unprecedented degree by the central state, localism could become an incendiary political weapon. So, too, could local history. The circulation in 1908 by Wang Baoxin of his stirring history of the Huangzhou Forty-Eight Fort League, lionizing Macheng's Mei Zhihuan and his successor holdouts to the Manchu conquest, could not but galvanize regional pride in a way highly unfriendly to the interests of the tottering Qing court. In his preface, Wang coyly points out that his job of historical reconstruction has been made much harder by the court's paranoid destruction of unfriendly sources during the Qianlong literary inquisition. He seeks to protect himself from charges of treason by arguing that his evident enthusiasm for the Ming cause has echoes in the Qing's own magnanimous celebration of heroic Ming figures in the *Erchen chuan* (Biographies of twice-serving officials) and other anthologies. But he concludes his defense by claiming a compatibility of his intensely localist work with the current compelling need for patriotism (*aiguo*), with the object of that patriotism—the precise identity of the *guo*—left conveniently undefined.[31]

None of these factors—not the growing tension over tax and grain policies, nor the development of a local self-government infrastructure, nor the Han nationalism apparent in Wang Baoxin's work—gives one the sense of widespread antidynastic sentiment in Macheng on the eve of the 1911 Revolution or even the sense of a popular mood in favor of political change of any sort. (Just as most Macheng residents in the late Yuan had probably never seen a Mongol, those in the late Qing had little contact with "Manchus"; all the county's magistrates and subprefects in the late nineteenth and early twentieth centuries, for example, seem to have been Han Chinese.) The revolution was largely imported. To the extent that there were active *local* agents of revolution, they were a few local lads from the upper ranks of the elite who for the most part had developed their political ideas well outside the county's borders.

One of these was Yu Cheng (1884–1910).[32] A native of a Yu-lineage village on the outskirts of Cassiawood River, Dongshan, Yu Cheng came from a politically conflicted family. His grandfather, Yu Mouduan, had run off with the Taiping armies, while his uncle, Yu Yaxiang, was the county's most celebrated anti-Taiping fighter. Cheng's cousin Yu Yingyun was one of the county's most eminent late-Qing educators and a confidante of the reformist viceroy Zhang Zhidong. But whereas Yingyun, as a member of the Provincial Assembly, vehemently opposed the revolution (and, for his pains, had his Wuchang mansion razed and his prized library destroyed by New Army mutineers), Cheng was a pioneering revolutionary activist.

With Cheng's grandfather's disappearance, in shameful circumstances, Cheng's father, Yu Yashi, had been forced to give up his modest official career and had moved discreetly to Shangcheng, across the Henan border. There he worked as a Huangbang merchant, and there Yu Cheng had been born. The boy returned to his native county in 1895 to continue his studies, becoming enthralled by the works of such Ming-loyalist scholars as Gu Yanwu, Huang Zongxi, and especially the rabidly anti-Manchu Wang Fuzhi. He persevered at classical studies long enough to pass the prefectural examination in 1902 and was among the very last to pass the Hubei provincial examination in 1904, on the eve of its abolition. But all the while, Cheng had been drifting into radical politics. When a cousin returned from Beijing and told him of the tragic collapse of the 1898 reforms, Cheng determined to devote the remainder of his life to revolution.

Upon passing the provincial examination, Cheng formed his own Scientific Study Society and was recruited into Huang Xing's larger Society to Revive China (Xingzhong hui). When the Hubei provincial authorities began investigating his activities, he fled to Japan, where he enrolled briefly at Waseda University—studying bombmaking, among other things—and was a founding member of Sun Yat-sen's Revolutionary Alliance (Tongmeng hui). He helped edit the Alliance's journal, *Minbao*, and was appointed head of its Hubei branch. This brought him back to Wuhan in 1905, where he set up the Association for Daily Acquisition of Wisdom (Rizhi hui), named in honor of Gu Yanwu, but in practice a front organ for Revolutionary Alliance recruitment. He published his diary for that year, which argued that moral decline was the reason for the national crisis, and urged revolution as the only means to love and save the country (*aiguo jiuguo*). Cheng returned to his native Dongshan for the New Year festival of 1906, lecturing at Macheng's increasingly radicalized Higher-Level Elementary School against footbinding and in favor of queue cutting.

Back in the provincial capital in the spring, he got word of the Ping-Liu-Li Uprising in the highlands of the Hunan-Jiangxi border, led by his fellow radical students, and he planned a sympathetic rebellion in Wuhan. The rising aborted and Cheng once again fled, first to Shanghai, where he worked again for the *Minbao* and gave stump speeches in opposition to Kang Youwei's moderate reformist Society to Preserve the Emperor (Baohuang hui), and then again to Tokyo. In 1908 he returned home for the final time, continually outrunning the Qing authorities while doing organizational and propaganda work for what remained of the collapsing Tongmeng hui. He retained a highly flamboyant style—a photograph from these years shows Yu in a jaunty hat with a hunting dog, looking for all the world like a Van Dyke cavalier. But in fact Yu's health was deteriorating, and in February 1910 he died of illness at the age of twenty-six. He had not lived long enough to witness, and perhaps be martyred in, the revolution for which he had worked so long.

Another of Macheng's revolutionary students was Zhou Weizhen (1880–1911), who hailed from a wealthy mercantile family of Qiting and Songbu. At the age of fifteen, Zhou went off to Wuhan to study at Zhang Zhidong's Jingxin Academy and was one of Hubei Province's first scholarship students in Japan. He returned to Wuhan in 1900 to participate in Tang Caichang's failed Independence Army (Zili jun) rebellion but escaped the Qing dragnet and returned to Japan. There he was recruited by Huang Xing into the Revolutionary Alliance, wrote broadsides attacking Kang Youwei's loyalist program, and, under Yu Cheng, helped organize the alliance's Hubei branch. Around 1906, these activities got him expelled from Japan. Zhou continued revolutionary organizing in Hubei, Hunan, and (drawing upon Huangbang diaspora ties) Sichuan. After briefly returning to Macheng to set up a military academy in his native township, he set off on Tongmeng hui propaganda work in Shaanxi, Gansu, and Manchuria, where he led protests against Japanese encroachment. At the moment of the October Revolution, Zhou was in Shijiazhuang, working for the revolution's spread into Henan. He was arrested and executed by agents of Yuan Shikai on November 6, 1911.[33]

The third of Macheng's revolutionary martyrs, and ultimately the one with the greatest impact on the locality itself, was Qu Kaiyan (1851–1911), whom we have already met as founder of the county's Higher-Level Elementary School.[34] A generation older than Zhou Weizhen, Qu was like him in his wealthy urban-commercial roots, and their families routinely intermarried. The formal home of the Qu lineage was a street bearing its name (Qujia xiang) in

Yu Cheng, ca. 1906. Photograph courtesy of the Museum of the 1911 Revolution, Wuhan.

Songbu. During the Taiping occupation of that town, however, Qu's father had taken his family to seek shelter with relatives and business partners in Sichuan. There the young Kaiyan attended an academy set up specifically for Macheng émigrés. When his father died, in 1873, Qu's mother (nee Zhou) brought the family back to Songbu, where Kaiyan took first place in the prefectural examination of 1879 and passed the provincial exam three years later. In 1891, he headed off to Wuhan for advanced study at Zhang Zhidong's new-style Lianghu Academy, where he concentrated on economics.

Qu Kaiyan looked as if he was set for a career as an elite reformer of the late Qing, and indeed his family took an important lead in these activities, both locally and regionally: two of his cousins, Qu Kaichi and Qu Kaifang, were among the progressive gentry summoned to court by the new Xuantong regents in 1908 to advise on the future path of the New Policies.[35] But Kaiyan had long chosen a different route—a romantic, conspiratorial one that would end in his murder and subsequent glorification as a revolutionary martyr. In a stirring 1958 *waishi* (sensationalized unofficial history) known as *The Bloody History of Hubei*, for example, Qu is encountered on the opening page, huddled in the prow of a moonlit boat in Hankou harbor and plotting the overthrow of the Qing; he is the swashbuckling hero of that operatic saga's first act.[36]

An early acquaintance recalled that Qu Kaiyan had as a youth read the Qing-conquest massacre account, *Yangzhou shiri ji* (A record of ten days at Yangzhou), and conceived a lifelong hatred of the Manchus.[37] While at the Lianghu Academy in the early 1890s, he had already formed a study group among students from his home region, the Society for Study of Direct Action (Zhixue hui), dedicated to Han-nationalist revolution; among the society's members were the soon-to-be historian of the Forty-Eight Fort League, Luotian's Wang Baoxin, and the subsequent guiding spirit of the Communist movement in Hubei, Huang'an's Dong Biwu. Also at the academy was Tang Caichang, who recruited Qu into his own revolutionary Independence Society (Zili hui).

When news arrived of the outbreak of the Sino-Japanese War in 1894, Qu organized a paramilitary force in Songbu called the National Salvation Militia (Jiuguo tuan), ostensibly for defense of the native district from foreign invaders but in fact in preparation for armed antidynastic rebellion. He remained in correspondence with Tang Caichang, then in Japan, placing his Songbu militia at the service of Tang's larger Independence Army in the coming revolution. The scheduled moment for Tang's uprising, August 1900, found the fifty-year-old Qu Kaiyan in Huangzhou doing propaganda and organizing work among the students sitting for the prefectural examination. He was helped considerably in this effort by a cheating scandal. The widely detested Hubei education commissioner, Jiang Shifen, overseeing the exams, accused a particular student from Guangji County of secreting a crib sheet into the hall, and that county's director of studies, serving as assistant examiner, rallied to his student's defense. Escalating ad hominem attacks and counterattacks ensued, followed by violent clashes that led to at least one death. Qu Kaiyan opportunistically rallied all 30,000 exam candidates to surround the local *yamen*, with Commissioner Jiang, the prefect, and the magistrate inside, and held them there for two full days. But the besieged officials managed to telegraph Zhang Zhidong at Wuhan, who sent a cavalry detachment to disperse the students to their respective homes. Qu was fingered as an Independence Army operative and a warrant was issued for his arrest. However, a nephew, then a student at Wuhan's Jingxin Academy, got word of this and managed to spirit his uncle into hiding in Henan. The Qu lineage at Songbu sent out a notice of Kaiyan's death, to deflect official interest in his capture.[38]

After a few years, the heat died down, and Kaiyan was able to return to Macheng. There he dedicated himself to setting up Western-style schools. In 1908, however, he sought to revive his National Salvation Militia, and—clearly inspired by his friend Wang Baoxin's research on the Ming-loyalist Forty-Eight Fort league—tried to link his militia up with similar units in other Huangzhou and Qizhou counties. His efforts were frustrated by the alert response of provincial authorities, however, and Qu was once more on the lam. He taught briefly in Henan at the provincial normal college, then in Beijing at the middle school established by the Wuhan sojourners' club, and ultimately in the relative safe haven of Japanese-dominated Heilongjiang. In the spring of 1911, Qu felt secure enough to return to Macheng. Appointed head of the county's education bureau, he installed his old classmate Dong Biwu—a man already with clear socialist sympathies—as headmaster of the Higher-Level Elementary School that Qu himself had founded more than a decade earlier. He cemented his ties to revolutionary cells in Wuhan. And he got himself elected president of the newly convened Macheng District Assembly.

Murder in the Assembly

Eight days after the outbreak of the Wuchang rebellion, the Huangzhou Prefectural Assembly on 18 October 1911 declared for the Republic and sent emissaries to the prefecture's various counties, urging them to do the same.[39] In Macheng, Qu Kaiyan very quickly produced a banner proclaiming Han independence, won over his fellow assemblymen, and proceeded to the Qing magistrate with a demand that he join their cause. The irate Magistrate Zhang Xiyun refused, labeling Qu a "bandit" (*fei*). Qu mobilized his old militia force and rallied popular opinion to put pressure on Zhang, who responded by calling in the loyalist county brigade commander, a man by the name of Liu Jintang. Accounts vary on the motivation of Commander Liu, but none of them are very flattering. One source, reflecting deeply ingrained elite prejudice against the clerical subbureaucracy, claims that both Liu and Magistrate Zhang were simply obtuse puppets manipulated by the county's evil chief clerk. Another source argues that Commander Liu opportunistically used the news of the revolution to demand of the magistrate a long-desired pay raise for his troops; Magistrate Zhang cagily responded that he had not the funds to support this demand because they were being held up by Qu Kaiyan and his fellow assemblymen. In any case, Liu was persuaded that Qu, whose support was rapidly growing, needed to be eliminated. On the evening of October 20, while Qu and his colleagues were enjoying a celebratory banquet in the assembly precincts, Liu and his troops burst in and cut him down.[40]

There was a massive popular outcry demanding justice for Qu Kaiyan's murder, a mood only heightened by the protest suicide of Qu's daughter the following day. Kaiyan's nephew, Qu Peilan—who a decade earlier had rescued his uncle in the Independence Army affair—sought the intercession of the new revolutionary government at Wuhan.[41] Through the agency of another Songbu man (and likely affinal kinsman), Zhou Longxiang,[42] who was highly placed in the revolutionary government, Peilan got President Li Yuanhong to send a substantial armed force under New Army general Luo Hongsheng to punish the culprits and claim Macheng once and for all for the Republican cause. Luo arrested and executed Commander Liu (and, for good measure, the county's chief clerk) and relieved Magistrate Zhang of his office.

General Luo remained in Macheng throughout the winter of 1911–12, putting down dispersed pockets of *luan* (chaos) and consolidating the revolution's control. In the Jiuxie Mountain area, a captain of the border patrol, claiming to be "carrying out the revolution," extorted large sums of money from local residents. Constabularies in neighboring villages joined in his racket, setting up their own toll stations to demand gifts from travelers. Other soldiers in the Long Ridge Pass acted similarly, and various *youmin* (disloyal inhabitants) joined the mutineers' cause. Anticipating the Eyuwan Soviet of the 1930s, the entire Dabie Shan region, on both sides of the provincial border, became effectively autonomous until Luo moved in and, piece by piece, took it over.[43] By February 1912, the Republican Revolution in Macheng was an accomplished fact. Like Mei Zhihuan some three centuries earlier, Qu Kaiyan was given a grand funeral by the adoring local populace, and a monument to his heroism—and to that of the county's other "revolutionary martyrs," Yu Cheng and Zhou Weizhen—was erected at the ancient walled town of Qiting. Kaiyan's nephew Qu Peilan was voted Macheng's representative to the newly reconstituted Hubei Provincial Assembly at Wuchang.

But whatever promise the revolution seemed to offer to those who gave their lives in its achievement, this promise was never remotely fulfilled in Macheng

County. The legacy of 1911 in Macheng, in both the short and the long term, was little other than calamitous and escalating violence. Yu Yingyun—son and heir of the county's savior from the Taiping and the Nian, *jinshi* of 1886, and pioneer reformist educator both locally and throughout Hubei—observed this outcome with a growing sense of despair. As the New Army's revolution gradually deteriorated into chaos, and as the voices of the new politicians a generation younger became a confused and confusing babble, Yu abandoned both his native place and the provincial capital and embarked on melancholy wanderings throughout the struggling new nation, in self-imposed exile.[44]

The Rise of Xia Douyin

If China ever truly experienced a moment of liberalism, of the sort we usually associate with the May Fourth Movement of 1919 or the New Culture Movement of the late teens and early twenties, this moment never visited Macheng. There were isolated symbolic gestures in honor of May Fourth—the Temple to the God of War at the county seat, for example, was transformed into the Macheng Elementary Girls' School—but already by that time many of the Western-style schools that the county had established had been expropriated to serve as troop barracks.[45] A trickle of Macheng's native sons went overseas to study subjects such as business and law; by 1935, four young men had received overseas degrees, two from the University of London and one each from Meiji University and the Sorbonne. But these young men were greatly outnumbered by those who, sensing the direction of the times, opted to study war. In the teens and twenties, three local men attended Japanese military academies, and no fewer than thirty-one studied at the Central Army Officers' School in Beijing. In 1912, the Dongshan native Zhang Sen enrolled in the first class of the Baoding Military Academy, and more than a score of his neighbors quickly followed, including subsequent long-serving Macheng magistrate Zheng Zhong.[46] It was this most illiberal, hardboiled, and merciless cadre of individuals who were destined to comprise the dominant power structure of Macheng County in the decades to follow.[47]

There were subtle changes in the composition and orientation of the local elite as a whole. Guy Alitto, studying a portion of southern Henan on the opposite slope of the Dabie Shan from Macheng, observes the emergence in the 1910s and early 1920s of "a new rural 'establishment': a symbiotic coalition of bandits, militant, officials, functionaries, and various types of 'local bullies and evil gentry.'" The sudden elimination of the Son of Heaven, distant as that institution had been and hollow as it may have become over the Qing's final decades, yielded a terrifying anomie. In Alitto's analysis, "Disintegration of the political and moral communities and the absence of any single, objective, universally accepted standard of legitimacy produced a new rural elite whose power, although acquired through complex and diverse channels, *rested ultimately upon direct or indirect control over forms of organized violence*."[48] There was perhaps no better local example of this phenomenon than Macheng County.

China's experiment with representative government quickly proved a failure. By 1914, the monarchical ambitions of Yuan Shikai, president of the Republic, became sufficiently clear that the Hubei Provincial Assembly sent a delegation, led by Macheng's Qu Peilan, to Beijing to protest. Yuan dissolved the Assembly. When Yuan himself was removed from the scene the following year, the Assembly reconvened, with Qu as vice-president, and in 1918 he was elected the body's president.[49] But it was amply clear by that time that the Assembly had little power. By then that power lay in the hands of Beiyang army militarists, notably Hubei military governor Wang Zhanyuan and the Henanese general Wu Peifu. Among the natives of Macheng, and most especially those of the Dongshan—where localist resistance to outside rule had become an established cultural value over at least four centuries—this Beiyang occupation was deeply resented. That resistance would crystallize in the figure of the man who would become the single most powerful (and brutal) individual in both county and region for much of the Republican era: Xia Douyin.

Xia Douyin (1884–1951) was at once the heir to a centuries-old line of Dongshan martial heroes and a relatively "modern" man. He hailed from a sprawling and venerable kinship group that dominated the environs of Dongshan's chief market town, Muzidian. The 1935 county gazetteer (the compilation of which Douyin largely financed) described the Xia as an "exalted lineage" (*wangzu*) but also as one of "secret merit" (*yinde*).[50] The "secret" part seems to have been a diplomatic way of conceding that, over their many centuries as one of the largest landholding families in the area, the Xia had enjoyed remarkably little examination success. Indeed, the proud record of several hundred provincial and metropolitan winners of civil degrees that was included in this and earlier gazetteers includes no mention of a Xia in the Ming and only one (a *juren* of 1848) in the Qing; there are only one or two Xia winners of military degrees, and there is a single *gongsheng* by purchase.[51] But this paltry record of examination success clearly reflects lack of interest in the process more than lack of means or even of public engagement. As early as the 1440s, Xia notables are repeatedly recognized as contributors to local relief and other charitable activities in their native township.[52] More important, however, their "merit" lay in their role as armed and aggressive protectors of the local peace.

The Muzidian Xia were in fact the very model of what Johanna Meskill has portrayed, in areas of low penetration by the central government (such as Meskill's Taiwan Plain and Macheng's Dongshan), as the "strongman" type of Chinese local elite: reasonably prosperous in a not very highly developed local economy, locally influential, armed to the teeth, but not especially engaged in the high literati culture (unlike the scions of most of Macheng's other venerable elite lineages, no Xia man ever left a poem to be included in a compilation of local literary prowess) or in its ideal of bureaucratic public service.[53] Just like Meskill's early-Qing Taiwanese strongmen, however, the Xia *were* prepared to place their ever-present paramilitary force at the service of the ruling dynasty when they perceived a harmony of interests among family, locality, and state. We have seen, for example, that the Xia were among the first and most reliable armed Dongshan lineages recruited by Yu Chenglong to combat anti-Qing (and bondservant) rebellion in the Three Feudatories era of the 1670s. In the mid-nineteenth-century rebellions, they were even more stalwart in defense of dynasty and locality, with Xia Wu (the lineage's lone *juren* of the late-imperial era) emerging as one of the county's preeminent militia leaders and as a trusted subordinate of Hu Linyi, and with Xia Shipeng (Xia Douyin's own great-grandfather) recognized as one of the county's most prominent martyrs to the loyalist cause.[54] While Luo Ergang long ago argued for the *institutional* origins of Republican-era Chinese "warlordism" in the militias and personal armies of the anti-Taiping mobilization, the Xia of Muzidian offer at least one case of a *genealogical* linkage as well between militarists of the two eras.[55]

As had been the case for Mei Zhihuan three centuries earlier, Xia Douyin's father died in the lad's early childhood. His mother—intriguingly surnamed Mei—raised him in poverty, but very strictly. To support her son, a childhood friend recalled, she gathered charcoal during the day and spun yarn in the evening. Douyin spent a few years in a local elementary school, but when the financial burden proved too great, he dropped out. Despite several years of subsequent education, he is said to have remained only marginally literate (*shi zi buduo*) all his life. At the age of fifteen, Xia enlisted in the new public security force (*weifang ying*) at the county seat and then drifted to Wuhan, enrolled in a "modern-style" military school, and received a junior officer's commission in the Hubei New Army. He also joined the Revolutionary Alliance in 1906 and, as an assistant company commander, took part in the Wuchang Rebellion of 1911. Upon returning home to Muzidian, he tried his hand as a teahouse proprietor but quickly failed. He married and fathered the first of his three sons. Then, in the fall of 1912, he drew upon the patronage of his Dongshan neighbor Zhang Sen to gain admission to the Baoding Military Academy.[56]

After graduating from Baoding, in 1915, Xia took service in Shanxi under a series of his fellow provincials, rising rapidly in rank to the post of battalion commander under General Shi Xingchuan. In late 1917, General Shi was converted to the Constitution Protection Movement declared by Sun Yat-sen's military government at Canton. He mutinied from Beijing's command, renamed his force the Hubei Army for National Pacification (Hubei jingguo jun), and returned to his native province. With Xia Douyin's aid, he established a short-lived autonomous regime at Shashi. But when Shi's regime was crushed by the Beiyang-clique Hubei military governor Wang Zhanyuan, Xia rallied some 2,000 remnants of Shi's troops south of the Yangzi in Gong'an County. A great many of these, including Xia's old patron Zhang Sen, were Macheng natives, and not a few were Xia's own kin; they became, in effect, his personal army. Gradually this force made its way south to Changsha, where Xia put them at the service of the coalescing anti-Beiyang resistance. When generals of Hunan origin fell to bickering amongst themselves, he emerged as the most potent military force in Changsha.

In the late 1910s and early 1920s, the idea of a federalist system of provinces for the Chinese Republic, long cherished by some, gained growing popularity as a means to combat the heavyhanded dominance of the Beiyang militarists at Beijing. Hunan was at the forefront of this movement, initially under the sponsorship of the 1911 hero Tan Yankai. When Tan himself was deposed, in November 1920, the Provincial Assembly declared Hunan independent and eventually enacted a provincial constitution. Meanwhile, on July 21, 1921, a congress of more than 10,000 Hubei expatriates assembled in the Hunanese capital and determined to expel the outside militarists from their native province. A provincial government in exile was formed, and Xia Douyin was anointed commander of the so-named "Hubei Independence Army." The congress ordered him to lead an expedition north to liberate the "birthplace of the Republican Revolution." Initially his army had great success; by August 7, Xia had approached Wuhan and forced the detested Wang Zhanyuan to flee. But the Beiyang forces quickly recovered. On August 9, General Wu Peifu himself was placed in charge of the defense of Wuhan. He blew up the dikes at Mianyang, drowning a large portion of Xia Douyin's army just as it was crossing the Yangzi toward the provincial capital. What remained of his force gradually fell back to Changsha. The Hubei liberation movement, for the moment, had failed.[57]

Up to this point in his career, then, Xia Douyin appeared as a vigorous champion of provincial home rule, the republican principles of Sun Yat-sen, and resistance to military despotism. When the Beijing government in 1924 appointed Xiao Yaonan governor of Hubei, cynically declaring this appointment to be its answer to cries for Hubei self-rule (though Xiao was a Hubei native, he identified completely as a loyal subordinate of the Beiyang clique), Xia Douyin was unmoved. He remained at Changsha, rebuilding his strength in anticipation of the new revolution that was to come, from the south, in 1926. But Xia, while genuinely patriotic, was also fully in the mold of localist Macheng heroes of the past, men like Mei Zhihuan and Liu Junfu in the seventeenth century and Yu Yaxiang in the nineteenth. That is, despite his "modern" education and his "revolutionary" credentials, he remained totally out of sympathy with any breach of social discipline on the part of the underclass. He would have ample chance to put this violent animus on display in the decade to come.

Chaos

At least in the short term, the most significant legacies of the 1911 Revolution in Macheng County were a breakdown of the fragile social order that had obtained since the post-Taiping reconstruction, and descent into a chaotic war of all against all (*luan*). As we have seen throughout our story, the county was at all times subject to large-scale bandit predations. With the mushrooming number of firearms on the street following the midcentury rebellions, both the incidence and the ferocity of quasi-organized lawlessness rose as well.[58] But the breakdown of any semblance of central authority soon after the dynastic collapse—coupled with the transformation of much of China's lower elite into a militarized caste, through the replacement of the civil service examination curriculum by a military school education—raised the problem of routinized violent disorder to a level that, arguably, was unprecedented even in this perennially troubled locale. As the 1935 county gazetteer recorded in its section on military events, the impact of 1911 in this regard was felt most severely only a decade or so after the event:

> Although political and military unrest has plagued China from the very outset of the Republican era, its effect did not immediately extend to Macheng, and for a while the county remained relatively tranquil. Thus there is little to record here for these early years. There were only isolated groups of soldiers passing through from time to time. They would extort some money and then pass on without causing major disruption or harm to local people. . . . This changed dramatically, however, in 1925. Since that year, the entire county has been completely overrun with renegade troops [*kuibing*] and indigenous bandits [*tufei*].[59]

Contemporary observers were quick to note that these were paired phenomena. As intramilitarist struggles intensified, battalions of several thousand troops under a charismatic leader (like Xia Douyin) would routinely break off from their command structure and settle into a life of plundering local civilian populations. Frequently they would compete with indigenous bandits for their established mountain lairs (*chaoku*), dislodging the latter or stirring them into even more predatory behavior. Members of the two types of paramilitary forces, who in any case shared much in the way of personal background, floated back and forth between the two, or else the group as a whole would alter its identity and character between modes. Macheng's site on the northeastern Hubei border with Henan and Anhui—a historic interregional thoroughfare no longer of much use for commerce but still, unfortunately, heavily trafficked by military—was one of the most notorious areas of such activity throughout the nation.[60]

Beginning in 1925, the chronicle of events is a dreary one. Throughout that year, large-scale bandit gangs ravaged Macheng. Then, beginning after the new year of 1926, the festering conflict between the armies of Wu Peifu in Hubei and Zhang Zuolin in Henan began to throw off splinter groups of marauders to prey upon local societies. The first of these, led by General Lou Yunhao, occupied the Macheng County seat in January and refused to leave until it was paid a huge ransom, raised by subscription by Tao Xiang, president of the chamber of commerce.[61]

Then, in August, a notoriously undisciplined force under one of Zhang Zuolin's lieutenants, Yuan Ying, swept across the Dabie Shan into Macheng and again grabbed the county seat. Yuan systematically extorted hundreds of thousands of dollars out of the administration and the local economy; it was he, for example, who expropriated the assets of the fledgling Cotton Cloth Factory mentioned at the start of this chapter. Worse, he commissioned a number of longtime indigenous bandits as "militia commanders," dispatching them throughout the county to garner further tribute. It was these men who slaughtered the family of the venerable local-self-government leader Jiang Hualong when he refused to pay up. Yuan also dispatched a heavily armed bandit force to Dongshan's Muzidian, to extract "contributions" from that town's merchants. The bandits were met by a Dongshan militia group under Zheng Jiankui, who announced a guerrilla campaign of annihilation against the invaders. Macheng magistrate Liu Fang, justly anticipating a bloodbath, intervened to negotiate a solution: a payoff to Yuan Ying's troops and the incorporation of Zheng Jiankui's Dongshan militia into the county's (theoretically) integrated self-defense force (*ziweituan*). Yuan himself temporarily withdrew across the Dabie Shan into Henan's Shangcheng County in November, leaving his bandit clients to do as they would in Macheng and Huang'an.[62] They were still there, providing a local backdrop of chaotic collective violence, when the National Revolutionary Army and its agents of class-warfare mobilization arrived from the south the following month. The stage was set for massive carnage, and the ensuing events did not disappoint.

CHAPTER TEN

The Cauldron

BY THE LATTER YEARS of the 1920s, the county gazetteer observed, Macheng had become a bubbling cauldron (*dingfei*) of vicious hatreds and eruptive violence.[1] When the Nationalist Revolution inserted itself into this incendiary setting, offering its rhetoric of class warfare and its apocalyptic promises of revenge and redemption, the result was a bloodbath (*xuexi*)[2] of deeply disturbing proportions. As the American journalist Edgar Snow observed, with a mixture of political sympathy and humanistic horror, it was "a civil war with the intensity of a religious war."[3]

Economic Collapse

The county's agrarian economy—which in the late Ming had been rich enough to underwrite the accumulation of enormous family fortunes and the rise of a nationally prominent scholar-official elite, and which had effectively held its own throughout the Qing and early Republican eras—rapidly collapsed. The rural population had increased nearly 50 percent over the final quarter of the nineteenth century and the first quarter of the twentieth, while cultivable acreage had remained roughly stable. The crop mix had not appreciably changed. Nor was there any significant expansion of nonfarm employment: well into the late twentieth century, more than 95 percent of Macheng's population derived its livelihood primarily from agriculture.[4] Under these structural constraints, the specific problems of the late 1920s led to catastrophic consequences.

Local Communist and Nationalist accounts of the late 1920s and early 1930s paint remarkably similar pictures of economic crisis in Macheng. The year 1925 saw great drought in the summer, followed by near-total harvest failure in the fall in staple crops such as rice, wheat, peanuts, and cotton. Magistrate Li Ziqing restricted his intervention to prayers for rain. When outraged Macheng sojourners at Wuhan arranged for Li's dismissal, his successor asked for relief aid from the Provincial Assembly president, Macheng native son Qu Peilan. Unfortunately, this aid came in the form of paper currency, which quickly proved worthless. Attempts to replace it with copper cash stalled, and finally the already badly depleted county granaries were emptied for relief in kind. Although this got the county through the year, the next few harvests were also very poor; by the time some decent yields could be reported, such as those for wheat in the early 1930s, producers of this largely cash crop found that market demand had disappeared. First bandits and renegade militarists, and then the Nationalist and Communist revolutions, laid waste the land, expropriated harvests, and disrupted channels of marketing for rural produce. In the county's market towns, the shops of potential buyers, including many shops of considerable scale and longevity, shut their doors. The larger regional and extraregional marketing networks of the Huangbang guild fell apart suddenly and, for the most part, permanently. The linkage of these failures with Macheng's indigenous economic collapse was reciprocal: Huangbang merchants lost their sources of supply in the native county, while local agrarian producers lost their merchant buyers. Handicraft production of textiles and other items—the traditional supplement to agricultural incomes—rapidly dried up as foreign and domestic industrial competition, from which local producers had up to now been largely shielded, was first severely felt. By the late 1920s, after several successive years of harvest failure, large-scale rural flight became noticeable, and much formerly productive farmland was reported lying fallow.[5]

On the question of landlordism, the Communist and Nationalist reports, unsurprisingly, diverged. A 1934 Nationalist survey, despite the bleak picture it paints of Macheng's rural economy overall, suggests that land-tenure relations are not a serious contributor to the dismal economic outlook: 80 percent of Macheng farmers, it insists, are freeholding owner-cultivators (*zigeng nong*), and even a majority of the 20 percent of "tenants" own some portion of the land they till.[6] This view contrasts sharply with a 1929 Communist report, which, on the basis of its more variegated subcounty numbers, appears rather more convincing. In the foothills of the Dongshan, in east central Macheng, the report finds a remarkable lack of stratification, the great majority of the population being impoverished owner-cultivators; hired laborers were not an appreciable percentage of the population, since no one could afford to hire them. (Significantly, we are not given figures for the Dongshan highlands themselves, the areas surrounding Muzidian and Cassiawood River, since by 1929 the Communists had nearly no presence there.) In the highly stratified south—the environs of Songbu, Qiting, Zhongguanyi, and the county seat—more favorable agrarian conditions allowed greater land accumulation. There were nine households holding several thousands of *mou*, over 100 households with more than a 1,000 *mou*, and several hundred owning in the hundreds of *mou*. Apart from these substantial landlords, however, perhaps 50 percent of the population ("middle peasants") owned their farms and not infrequently leased a portion of this land to others. The remaining 50 percent were either tenants or laborers on the lands of the wealthier half of the population. But the biggest problem area was the north—the desiccated Dabie Shan townships of Chengmagang, Shunheji, and Huangtugang. While there were no really rich landlords here, and only 100 or so smaller ones, a full 75 percent of the population were tenants or hired laborers, most of these on lands of families only slightly better off than themselves. The latter sought to cling to their position of marginal superiority by extracting everything they could from their less fortunate neighbors, and rents ran as high as 60 percent of the crop.[7]

Beyond the property owned by individual landlords, of course, a large and growing portion of Macheng's arable land was held by corporations. As in the past, these included lineages (the West Village Cheng, for example, held thousands of *mou* as "sacrificial lands") and temples (the Buddhist Longtan temple of Huang'an held over 5000 *mou*, which it farmed by using its more than 100 indentured laborers) but also the proliferating number of new "public" entities like the Macheng Educational Association and the new "benevolent halls."[8]

Rents in twentieth-century Macheng were normally collected in kind, that is, in rice. Until the repeated poor harvests of the late 1920s, these were usually fixed rents, but after 1925 many landlords, to ensure a more reliable rental income, shifted to share rents. According to the 1929 Communist report, this added to the immiseration of many peasant households, which found it increasingly difficult to make it through the year on the consumption of their share of reduced harvests. In the south, rent conditions were far better than in the northern highlands, with rents averaging only about one-fifth of the crop. In the north, the nominal basic rent (*zhengke*) was one-half of the harvest, but in practice this was often expanded to two-thirds. In addition, there were numerous much-resented surcharges, or "bruising rents" (*zike* or *heike*), including supplementary assessments in wheat, in cotton, and in peanuts, as well as a noncontractual-labor service exaction (*renke*). The combined weight of these assessments was brutal, leading in growing numbers to loss of leasehold and to a turn to full rural proletarian status.[9]

Landlord-tenant relations in Macheng had always been acrimonious, as we have seen throughout our story, but they radically worsened with the economic collapse of the 1920s. Even Nationalist surveyors lamented the fact that loans of seed and draft animals by landlords to tenants, common elsewhere, were unheard of in Macheng, though usurious loans of food grain to tenants in extremis offered a routine supplement to landholders' incomes. At the first Hubei

Peasants' Conference, convened at Wuchang in March 1927 with representatives from Macheng and many other counties, there was repeated talk of serfdom and land slavery as being persistent in the province, and below we shall see clear intimations that servile tenancy as an institution survived in Macheng well into this era.[10] Tenants, compelled to address members of the landlord's family with such honorifics as "Gracious Master" (*kuoren laoye*) and the more colloquial "Mr. Riding Jacket" (*maguazi*), suffered ridicule in return, and they were obliged to perform extracontractual chores, such as bearing the master's sedan chair, and to present gifts and throw banquets for the lord to express gratitude for not being evicted. The local post-1949 "speak bitterness" literature is full of memories of petty cruelties on the part of masters; one Dabie Shan villager, for instance, recalled finding a dead fish at the side of a stream and trying to bring it home for his family's dinner, only to have his lord accuse him of stealing it and demand a large sum of cash to avoid criminal prosecution.[11]

Nationalist and Communist sources agree that inflation of commodity prices was a major social irritant. Whereas laborers' wages had risen seven to tenfold between the 1870s and the early 1930s, purchase prices of rice and other foodstuffs had risen much faster yet. Again, there was a significant wage differential between the core area in the southeast and the Dabie Shan highlands in the north—an ordinary farm laborer in the south was said to earn a higher annual wage (between 150 and 200 strings of cash) than a schoolteacher in the north—while commodity prices were nearly the same in both areas. Unsurprisingly, then, by the late 1920s localized small-scale grain riots were pandemic in the county, owing little, or so it is claimed, to the work of professional agitators.[12]

Finally, the clumsy acquisitiveness of the early Republican state, at all levels, was a major contributor to economic collapse and social tension. Local reporters noted the direct link between rapid price inflation and the succession of paper currencies issued by the government, currencies that depreciated even faster than food prices rose. Surtaxes on cultivated land and an infinitely expanding range of specialized fees had begun to proliferate in the late Qing, and their number and aggregate burden escalated greatly over the course of the 1920s: alcohol and tobacco taxes, animal-slaughter taxes, straw-sandals taxes, cooking-stove taxes, door-placard taxes, and so on. Commercial nuisance taxes were said to be one of the major reasons for the failure of small-town shops, the buyers whom rural commercial producers depended upon for their market. Even though the enhancement of public security forces, which were most often directed against the resistance movements of the underclass, was claimed as the justification for the new impositions, these taxes were often levied on that underclass itself. Nationalist sources in particular argue that, more than any other factor, it was unrestrained fiscal predation that led to the cauldronlike character of Macheng society in the late 1920s and early 1930s.[13] It was a revolutionary situation par excellence.

The Radical Generation

Lucien Bianco has argued that the Communist-led "peasant movement" of the late 1920s was in fact less a "class revolution" than a "generational revolution." "What is . . . more marked than the social origins of the activist peasants," Bianco observes, "is the generation gap between themselves and the others." The local leaders of the movement were most often "traitors to their class." They were sons (and, in a few instances, daughters) of "landlords" or "rich peasants," "intellectuals who returned to their villages to lead the revolution after having studied in the city." As for the movement's "foot-soldiers," it was "young villagers from every level [who] provided the revolution with its most enthusiastic and most numerous recruits."[14] Bianco's argument on the rural revolution's generational character is exquisitely borne out by the experience of Macheng, one of that revolution's most volatile and conspicuous sites.

A dictionary of revolutionary "martyrs" from Hubei Province provides capsule biographies of sixty-nine Macheng natives, among the very highest totals for any county in the province.[15] Within this group, two age cohorts are readily identifiable: about thirty-five were born in the years 1901–10, and another fourteen were born in the following decade. That is to say, most were in their teens or very early twenties at the height of the rural revolution in the county. Although native place within the county is not recorded for most of the Macheng "martyrs," nine of them are specifically listed as hailing from the Dabie Shan township of Chengmagang—"Horseback Ridge"—in the county's northwest. Roughly 40 percent are listed as having had education of some kind, sufficient to qualify them in Communist Party sociology as "revolutionary intellectuals" (*geming zhishifenzi*). But on the issue of education there is a marked difference between the two cohorts: those born during the late Qing almost invariably had schooling, while those born under the Republic typically did not. It was the youths of the earlier generation, educated by their parents (frequently at considerable financial sacrifice) in new-style schools of the early twentieth century, who became the first wave of the Communist Revolution in the eastern Hubei highlands.

The radicalization of Macheng's rural youth essentially began with one man: Dong Biwu (1886–1975), who would end his life as vice chairman of the People's Republic of China. Dong came from a literati family of the county seat of Huang'an, that portion of northwest Macheng that had been detached in the sixteenth century through the efforts of Li Zhi's chief antagonist, Geng Dingxiang. Biwu's early life was that of a modestly privileged young man of China's great transitional era. At the age of ten, he went to study with a tutor in Macheng's Songbu, site of the murder of the Swedish missionaries just three years earlier; his official biography claims that Songbu's residual atmosphere of antiforeignism strongly influenced his development. Nevertheless, after attaining a lower-level civil service examination degree at the age of fifteen, Dong went on to missionary school in Wuhan, where he pursued a fully Western curriculum, and then, in 1917, he graduated from law school in Japan. His political engagement proceeded apace. At Wuhan, in early 1911, he had joined the Revolutionary Alliance, and after the outbreak of the October Revolution he took a midlevel post in the new regime's financial department. With the perceived failure of the Republican Revolution over the mid- to late 1910s he affiliated with Sun Yat-sen's Revolutionary Party, but at Shanghai, in the wake of the 1919 May Fourth Movement, he converted to Marxism, eventually attending the founding meeting of the Chinese Communist Party as head of the Hubei provincial delegation. He returned to Wuhan as a labor organizer in the early 1920s, but with Wu Peifu's bloody suppression of the Jing-Han Railroad strike of 1923 he fled to Guangzhou, where he took a leading role in organizing the first Nationalist Party Conference in January 1924, forming the United Front between the Nationalist and Communist Parties, and planning the joint parties' Northern Expedition (or Nationalist Revolution).[16]

Throughout this time, Dong Biwu was also an educator as well as a charismatic evangelist of revolution among his adolescent students. In 1911, he taught in Macheng, at the county's Higher-Level Elementary School (established by Republican revolutionary martyr Qu Kaiyan), and in the early 1920s he founded the Awaken Huangzhou Middle School (Qihuang zhongxue) at Wuchang. In 1923, he returned for a term to the Higher-Level Elementary School, where he exercised a transforming influence upon a generation of Macheng youth and established a pipeline for these young men to move on to more sophisticated training in revolutionary theory at his Wuchang middle school. It was these radicalized youth who would prove the foundation of the "peasant" movement in late-1920s Macheng.[17]

The most senior of Dong's Macheng converts—a decade younger than Dong himself, but a decade older than most of Dong's other students—was Wang Youan (1896–1928). Wang hailed from a declining landlord family of Chengmagang township and was probably the single figure most responsible for forging the special link between that area and the rural class war of the 1920s and 1930s. Educated in local private schools and in the county's new Normal School, he moved on in 1918 to the Hubei First Normal School at Wuchang, where the events he observed quickly radicalized him. He became a key leader in the 1919

May Fourth demonstrations at Wuhan, and when, in 1922, Dong Biwu—now head of the Hubei branch of the newly founded Chinese Communist Party—returned to Wuhan from Shanghai, Wang was among his first recruits. After a year spent aiding Dong in labor organizing in the metropolis, he returned, likely at Dong's behest, to teach and recruit at Macheng's Higher-Level Elementary School. There he organized selected students into a Marxist-Leninist study group, mixing reading of *New Youth* and other New Culture periodicals with reading of the *Communist Manifesto* and local Marxist pamphlet literature. He mobilized student anti-imperialist demonstrations in the county seat and at Macheng's other major commercial centers, and sent his pupils back to Chengmagang and their other native townships to begin proselytizing class struggle among the increasingly impoverished rural population. In the spring of 1925, county authorities sought Wang's arrest, and he discreetly removed to Wuchang, where he taught and recruited at the Hubei Number Five Elementary School. He would, however, return.[18]

Among the dozens of Macheng students whom Dong Biwu and Wang Youan recruited to the cause through their schools, the most active were Baiguo township's Cai Jihuang (1905–27), Feng Shugong (1901–29) and Liu Xiangming (1904–28), Shunheji's Deng Tianwen (1905–27) and Liu Wenwei (1909–27), and Chengmagang's Ling Zhuzhong (1898–1931), Wang Hongxue (1899–1932), Xu Ziqing (1903–29), Wang Shusheng (1905–74), and Xu Qixu (1906–29). With the exception of Cai, who hailed from an important merchant-literati family, these young men were offspring of modestly prosperous agrarian households. As the list poignantly reveals, they were not destined for long lives: very few survived their twenties, and only one, Wang Shusheng (who in 1954 became China's deputy minister of defense) lived to witness the Japanese invasion and the eventual Communist victory of 1949.[19]

In 1923, when several pupils were expelled from the Italian Roman Catholic school in Macheng City, Wang Shusheng led his teenaged classmates from the Higher-Level Elementary School in a protest, trashing much of the mission's property. Here we see the antiforeignism for which Macheng had long been known beginning to evolve into a more ideologically driven anti-imperialism. The transformation was almost complete by the following year, when, in the wake of the announcement of the United Front at Guangzhou and the promulgation of the stirringly anti-imperialist *Guomindang Manifesto* (in the drafting of which Dong Biwu had a hand), the Higher-Level Elementary School students organized an Anti–Japanese Goods movement, seizing and burning foreign merchandise from stores in Macheng City and other local markets.[20]

In late 1924 and throughout 1925, many of the same young men, now away from home at Wuchang's Awaken Huangzhou Middle School, organized themselves into a Communist working group (*gongzuo zu*) to plan for action in their native county.[21] During the winter semester break of 1925–26, these students went home and began to implement their plans. This was a liminal moment in Macheng's radical mobilization, coming as it did in the wake of the disastrous harvest and the growing food crisis of late 1925. The students now reconstituted themselves as the Macheng Special Branch Committee of the Chinese Communist Party, within the broader United Front, and Wang Youan himself returned home from Wuchang to oversee their actions. They engaged in a frenetic propaganda campaign, publishing sporadic issues of journals with names like *Macheng qingnian* (Macheng Youth), *Gongzuo zhinan jin* (The Worker's Guide), *Xuanyan bao* (Manifesto), and *Zhandou bao* (Combat) and set up the Communist Youth League to recruit into the movement others of their age who were less educationally privileged than they were. They targeted especially the Dongshan townships, which, significantly, had until then produced few if any Communist converts. (Following the precedent of the late-Ming Forty-Eight Fort League, the Communist Youth League's span of organization was to encompass both slopes of the Dongshan, in Macheng and Luotian Counties, and for this purpose its headquarters was established at a historic hilltop fort on the county border.)[22] For these committed young rural "intellectuals," this must have been a time of heady excitement, but in fact it was still really only schoolboys' play. As they headed back to school at Wuhan in the spring of 1926, few probably had any sense of the magnitude of bloodshed that lay just ahead.

Politics Takes Command

When the armies of the Nationalist Revolution swept north to capture Wuhan in September 1926, the rules of the game in Macheng suddenly changed. Several of the county's native sons played key roles in that revolution's rapid triumph. Wang Caoru (1876–1926), from a wealthy Songbu family, had been an early student at the Baoding Military Academy and a participant in the 1911 Revolution. A professional soldier, he was recruited into the Communist Party in 1923, along with his commander, the flamboyant leftist general He Long. During the Northern Expedition's march northward through Hunan, Wang, allegedly betrayed by right-wing elements within the United Front itself, was ambushed and killed by Beiyang forces.[23] Wang's Baoding classmate Xia Douyin was also part of the Nationalist juggernaut. In Changsha in the early 1920s, as military leader of the Hubei government in exile, Xia had been approached by an emissary from Guangzhou—none other than his Huangzhou compatriot Dong Biwu—to lead an independent rising in the path of the planned Northern Expedition. In fact, he joined the Northern Expedition at Changsha and was one of the first of its generals to enter Wuhan, realizing his long-cherished dream of driving the Beiyang occupiers out of his native province. Appointed a member of Hubei Military Administration Committee, he briefly swept north to mop up Beiyang forces in Henan, but when the independent Sichuan militarist Yang Sen traversed the Yangzi gorges to challenge the Nationalists at Wuhan, Xia was dispatched upriver to confront the threat.[24]

The Nationalist regime that emerged at Wuhan in the last months of 1926 was overwhelmingly committed to a leftist social agenda, so much so that when the shadow national government relocated there from Guangzhou, in December, more conservative elements in the United Front alliance initially refused to take part in the move, proposing to set up an alternative "Nationalist" capital at Nanchang, Jiangxi. Ultimately a reconciliation was achieved, allowing Wuhan to be declared the unified Nationalist capital of China on January 1, 1927. An even more deeply leftist agenda fired the newly installed Nationalist administration in Macheng County itself. Within weeks of taking Wuhan, the regime dispatched a rather conservative party member from Huanggang County, Liu Fang, to serve as its initial county executive (*xianzhang*) in Macheng. But Liu found himself greatly outnumbered by other would-be political players, who not only were local natives but were also much more far-reaching in their definition of what the revolution was about. As the United Front armies had advanced toward central China, virtually all of the radical students produced by Macheng's Higher-Level Elementary School and Wuhan's Awaken Huangzhou Middle School had coupled their Communist affiliation with membership in the Nationalist Party, and when the new county government was formed, many of these young men—still patronized by the United Front luminary Dong Biwu—were rewarded with positions of real importance. Indeed, with so many of Dong's protégés in place in the county government's leadership, the socioeconomic restructuring of Macheng County would turn out to be, in effect, Dong's signature project. Cai Jihuang, twenty-one years old, was appointed the county's Nationalist Party Secretary and charged with local implementation of orders from Party Central. Wang Youan, Liu Xiangming, Xu Ziqing, and Wang Shusheng served as members of the Nationalist Party Committee at the county seat while at the same time establishing *Communist* Party offices in Chengmagang and their other native townships. The county-level Communist Party committee was set up shortly afterward, with its headquarters in the old Qing-era orphanage (*yuying tang*).

Grassroots mobilizing was carried out even more vigorously by the various "mass organizations" that the United Front national government authorized and sponsored at the local level: workers' associations (*gonghui*),[25] merchants' associations (*shanghui*), women's associations (*funūhui*), educational associations (*jiaoyuhui*), and, of most immediate impact, "peasant associations" (*nongmin xiehui*, or simply *nonghui*). Before we can get into the complex and dramatic story of the "peasant" movement in late 1926 and early 1927 Macheng, however, it is necessary to revisit the problem of ongoing militarization and the more general decline of public order against which the movement played itself out.

Total Militarization

Macheng's new United Front county administration had, first of all, to confront the same problem facing any governing authority, whatever its ideological agenda: securing the county from the predations of bandits and renegade troops. Indeed, with the defeat and disintegration of the Beiyang command structure in the Dabie Shan region, the problem of marauding, unaccountable military units, already out of hand in the mid-1920s, only worsened. The notoriously undisciplined Second Army forces of Yuan Ying reentered Macheng and Huang'an from Henan in late 1926, sporadically occupying both county seats and expropriating local public and private resources. In Macheng, Yuan's lieutenants despoiled the new Cotton Cloth Factory (the single institution constituting the local economy's "modern sector") and kidnapped the county chamber of commerce president, demanding a ransom of over 4,000 Mexican dollars from local salt-administration coffers for his release. Magistrate Liu Fang beseeched Wuhan for military aid, and Generalissimo Jiang Jieshi sent Battalion Commander Yan Zheng to help secure the area. Over the early months of 1927, Commander Yan and local militia forces, including some controlled by local "peasant associations" but most notably those under Dongshan local strongman Zheng Jiankui, drove Yuan's soldiers out of the county in a series of bloody battles.[26]

Zheng's militia was but one manifestation of a much broader militarization of Macheng society in the mid- to late 1920s. Armed paramilitary forces had been a prominent feature of the local scene for many centuries, as we have observed, but local sources insist that after the intensification of bandit and renegade troop activity, around 1925, the involvement of armed paramilitary forces reached levels unprecedented in local memory. The 1935 gazetteer records that, over the previous decade, "all able-bodied men from the entire county [had] been in a continual process of military training," at the various training grounds (*jiaochang*) carved out for this purpose in nearly every village and town. After 1925, these militia were linked into some twenty local confederations in the county, all heavily armed with automatic weapons (*kuaiqiang*) purchased from outside by collections of local elites.[27] As Lucien Bianco astutely notes, in Macheng and elsewhere these "self-defense corps" (*ziwei tuan* or *baowei tuan*), which in the very near future would fight to the death with Communist paramilitary forces, had not, in most instances, been created for this purpose; they were instead a response to the breakdown of public security in the Republican era and to the heightened predations of militarist forces claiming the mantle of the Republican state. Their goal first and foremost, Bianco reminds us, was the defense of rural *property* against all who would seize it, be that seizure via theft, extortionate taxation, or, ultimately, socialist redistribution.[28]

In the flush of "local self-government" (*difang zizhi*) enthusiasm that followed the 1911 Revolution, some twenty ward-level *baowei tuan* were authorized by the county government. Each would be led by a militia head (*tuanzong*) and comprise twenty or so militiamen (*tuanding*); expenses would be borne at the ward level, by some combination of surtaxes and subscriptions. In the absence of any real public security threat during the very early Republican era, however, for the most part this militia system, mandated from above, remained a dead letter.[29] When the real threat came, an essentially different, societally generated paramilitary system arose to confront it.

Despite repeated attempts by the county government to co-opt and integrate these new spontaneous militia units, both before and after the Nationalists' arrival in 1926, they remained essentially the private armies of landholding local elites and community "godfathers." Their most basic element lay in the kinship system, in the "descendants' armies" (*zidi bing*) commanded by strongmen known colloquially as "grandfather" (*die*), that most of the region's important lineages fielded for pursuit of their parochial interests.[30] The case of one of the earliest township-level self-defense forces shows well this process of negotiation among lineage, territorial community, and state. In July 1918 a bandit leader from Huang'an County crossed over into Macheng and besieged the walled commercial town of Zhongguanyi. Lin Dianhua, scion of the leading mercantile lineages of the town (whose history we traced in chapter 3), organized and financed the new Zhongguanyi Self-Defense Force (*Zhongguan baowei tuan*), which he commanded, to drive off the attackers. Over the course of the following decade, Lin's militia entrenched itself and assumed routine military control over the town and its environs. In 1925, the county administration promulgated a new, three-tier *baojia* public security system known as the *kuihuzhi* (ward and household system), into which paramilitary groups such as Lin Dianhua's were to be enfolded. In Zhongguanyi, however, and most likely throughout the county, the lower-level units of regimentation were explicitly fixed to units of kinship, and in fact bore the names of the families they represented. As it had ever been in Macheng, lineage domination was integral to the militarization of local society in the 1920s.[31]

It was the Zheng-dominated militia of northern Dongshan that became the most successful and expansive of these lineage-dominated groups. The Zheng were not a lineage of any distinguished pedigree: like their Muzidian neighbors the Xia, they had produced no upper-level civil or military degree holders over the Ming and Qing, but also like the Xia they had been local strongmen for many generations. Their new (or newly visible) militia was not, strictly speaking, a lineage army, since several of their nonkin neighbors were credited with a role in its founding, but it was primarily the creation of Zheng lineage elders Zheng Shancuo and Zheng Kangshi, the latter a man who had attained countywide prominence in 1918 through his directorship of the local education association. The militia's actual commander, as we have seen, was Zheng Jiankui (1895–1938). In April 1926, with renegade troops threatening the adjoining wards of Muzidian and Dongyizhou, the Zheng purchased a quantity of automatic weapons from Shangcheng County, across the Henan border, and mobilized a troop of some 2,000 men that they dubbed the Dongyizhou-Muzidian Militia Federation (Dong-Mu lianhe baowei tuan). In October, in the first of many government attempts to bureaucratize the Zheng army, it was renamed the Eighth Ward Militia Federation (Bakui liantuan), and then, under the new United Front regime, later that year, the Eighth Ward People's Self-Defense Army (Bakui renmin ziweijun).[32]

Under Zheng Jiankui's command, the militia had striking success on the battlefield. In mid-1926 it purged the area of a bloodthirsty bandit gang that had massacred the entire Xiong lineage of Zengshan and gone on to hold the town of Muzidian itself for ransom.[33] Then, as we have seen, it cooperated with United Front commander Yan Zheng to drive renegade general Yuan Ying and his *tufei* allies back across the border into Henan (according to local sources, by comparison to Yan Zheng's weak-kneed subordinates, Zheng Jiankui and his Dongshan stalwarts actually absorbed the greater part of the fighting in the Yuan Ying campaign). Zheng's army emerged from this campaign as the single most powerful military force in the area. In recognition of its critical de facto role in the county's overall defense, it was again rechristened in early 1927 the "*Macheng* People's Self-Defense Army," and in April of that year a portion of the force was permanently deployed to the county seat. Like other Dongshan militia leaders before him—Liu Junfu in the 1670s and Yu Yaxiang in the 1850s and 1860s—Zheng Jiankui had brought his demonstrably successful army down out of the peripheral eastern hills to assume military protection of Macheng as a whole. Zheng's own political stance, as yet unclear, would have a decisive effect on the outcome of the class war that lay just ahead on the local horizon.

Beyond renegade troops, bandits, and local militia, another element contributing to the violent mix of armed groups in Macheng County in the mid- to late 1920s was the organizations known generically as Red Spears (*hongqiang hui*). Contemporary observers and subsequent historians have much debated the essential character of these groups, and we do not need here to rehearse the details of these debates.[34] Briefly, the Red Spears were rural self-defense organizations in North China, practicing the traditional martial arts. They were dominated by landholders and had a very strong localist orientation, often attacking any outsiders to their village base. They resisted the encroachments of the Republican state, most especially its predatory land taxes and surtaxes but also other elements of "modernizing" change, such as Western-style schools. Red Spears chapters had a strong religious component, with belief in the capacity of members to generate, through devotional and other practices, impenetrability to weapons; one Red Spears motto in Macheng was "Since I have practiced *gongfu* for a hundred days, knives and spears cannot pierce me."[35] It is a matter of question, however, whether this religious orientation was so distinctive as to merit its being called a sect, or whether Red Spears beliefs and practices simply distilled those that were already common among the rural population as a whole.

Some scholars trace the origins of these groups to the White Lotus tradition; Suemitsu Takayoshi in 1932 specifically identified their origins in the Eight Trigrams sect, a White Lotus spinoff of the early nineteenth century.[36] Zhang Zhenzhi found an internal Red Spears history that claimed the group's origins in a dissident faction of the Taiping movement.[37] Others see the Red Spears' origins in the Nian; still others, in the local militia spawned to *combat* the Taiping and Nian. Many scholars, both those arguing for and those arguing against a White Lotus origin, detect a strong organizational influence left by the antiforeign Boxer movement of the turn of the twentieth century. All agree that there was a quantum increase in Red Spears activity at that time, and many find the first recorded use of the Red Spears name in village defense against Lao Yangren (Old Foreigner) and other unprecedentedly large and rapacious bandit gangs that terrorized the North China Plain in the mid- to late 1910s.[38] Nagano Akira pointed out in 1938—and the experience of Macheng definitely supports him—that the United Front's Northern Expedition of the 1920s itself further galvanized Red Spears formation and activity.[39]

Red Spears chapters were organized most basically on a village scale and were linked to one another through collective participation in a local marketing system. They were usually headquartered in a village temple or shrine, known for this purpose as a chapter hall (*huitang*) or incense hall (*xiangtang*). Financing came from initiation fees and often from an assessment on local landowners, which further suggests protection of property as a major organizational goal. Even the most localized chapters often featured a complex leadership structure, including a civil chapter headman (*huizhang*), a military commander (*tuanzhang* or *dashuai*), and a priestlike "head of studies" (*xuezhang*); the chapter itself was often simultaneously known as a "red study" society (*hongxue*). In most cases, each of these leaders was drawn from the ranks of the most substantial local landholders.

A written regulatory code for one Henan chapter, discovered by Suemitsu, offers perhaps our most revealing glance at such groups' orientation on the ground. Membership was restricted to property owners. The goals were stated as local defense against bandits (*tufei*), evil or anarchic troops (*ejun* or *luanjun*), and, explicitly, evil fiscal impositions (*eshui*). But a broad-ranging and highly conservative cultural agenda was also spelled out: requirements for strict observation of filial piety, both toward natural parents and toward teachers (*shizhang*)—that is, chapter leaders—and prohibitions against alcohol consumption and sexual promiscuity. Violent *chiarivari*-style recriminations were demanded against adulterers and other deviants from imposed behavioral norms.[40] The group thus promised the locality not only defense from external predators but also the imposition of uncompromising internal discipline in the face of threatening cultural change.

It was in Henan that the Red Spears movement took hold most deeply, contemporaries noted, most especially in the province's southwest but also in the counties of the southeast—Guangshan and Shangcheng—across the Dabie Shan from Macheng. This had always been a highly martial area, and its southern border with Hubei was routinely crossed by paramilitary forces; recall that in the 1850s, for example, the Macheng magistrate had invited in Shangcheng "braves" to help defend his county from the Taiping. Red Spear organization in southern Henan had proliferated in the late 1920s in response to banditry (a newspaper report from 1926 lauds a village Red Spear chapter that had invited menacing bandits to a banquet and beheaded forty-seven of them[41]) and undisciplined warlord strife. Throughout 1926, forces at least nominally loyal to Zhang Zuolin and to Wu Peifu had wrangled messily over this area, and the establishment of the United Front government at Wuhan in September actually made matters worse: armies of retreating Beiyang militarists, of the advancing Nationalists, and of the wild-card Nationalist Army (Guominjun) general Feng Yuxiang fought continually over the region though the end of that year and into the first half of 1927. Local Red Spear chapters sprang up and amalgamated, sometimes forging tactical alliances with various of these contenders for national power, but basically trying to protect their property and their home localities, using tactics that an English-language journalist recognized as "guerrilla warfare."[42] Many of these chapters actively supported the short-lived Henan independence movement of 1927 until that movement was bloodily crushed by Feng Yuxiang.[43] A mid-1927 report estimated the total number of Red Spear guerrillas in Henan at more than 600,000.[44]

These Red Spear units from the other side of the mountains would prove to be major players in Macheng's internal struggles of the late 1920s, but the county also spawned similar organizations of its own, on a somewhat lesser scale. In response to the escalating bandit disorders of 1925, a variety of spears associations (*qianghui*) began to appear throughout the county, and their number grew rapidly throughout the decade. There were more than a score of these, comprising thousands of members, in the central areas of Yanjiahe and Baiguo and in the southwestern river valley around Songbu. But the area of greatest Red Spears proliferation was in the north central Dabie Shan townships of Futianhe and Huangtugang (Yellow Ridge), adjacent to Henan. Communist documents report several dozen Red Spears chapters in Huangtugang as of mid-1927, with perhaps a few hundred members, but by 1929 the number of chapters had mushroomed to over 300, together enrolling "virtually the entire population."[45]

Macheng's indigenous spears associations seem to have differed somewhat from those across the provincial border in Henan. They were a later development overall and seem to have had a lower level of translocal organization. This is suggested, for example, in the far greater variety in their nomenclature: in addition to red spears, there were also white and black spears in the north, gold spears in the south, and organizations such as Songbu's Renyi hui (Benevolence and Propriety Association), which contemporaries saw as indistinguishable in function, but which did not have "spears" in their names at all.[46] Further, to the extent that the Henanese or Huaibei style of Red Spear chapter (the latter famously depicted by Elizabeth Perry) can be seen as mutual associations of small yeoman farmers banding together to defend their farms, the Macheng variants were nothing of the sort. They tended to be bands of bodyguards or goons organized in specific service to a local landholding strongman. In a typical case, a big boss (*da laoban*) of a northern village was said to have *compelled* his intimidated poorer neighbors into joining his Red Spear chapter, and to have imported a Henanese boxing master (*quanshi*)—less charitably referred to elsewhere as an itinerant thug (*liumang*)—to train and command them.[47] It is significant, I believe, that there are no reports at all of Macheng spears associations engaging in tax resistance or other antiestablishment activities of the sort common in Henan and beyond.

Despite this unpromising situation, the United Front and Communist Party activists made repeated attempts to turn Red Spears chapters to their cause. Following the advice of their Comintern advisors, Chinese Communist Party founders Li Dazhao and Chen Duxiu each wrote tracts in 1926 urging alliances with these groups, and a Party central committee meeting in Shanghai in July announced these "middle and poor peasants'" organizations as ripe for Party co-optation. As early as 1925, in advance of the Northern Expedition, on-the-ground efforts had been made to link up with Red Spears chapters in Henan.[48] In Macheng itself, consistently through the difficult years of the late 1920s, the local Party committee urged its agents to distinguish between those Red Spears chapters that were hopeless tools of the landlords and those that had latent revolutionary potential.[49] They even scored occasional success. In Cao Gate Village, a young Party member and martial arts adept named Wu Huanxian managed to form a Red Spears chapter of his own, linking it to those in neighboring villages through ties with his schoolmates there; Wu's organization was ultimately absorbed into the Red Army.[50] However, the overall record of Communist–Red Spears relations in Macheng was one of massive mutual carnage, as we shall see.

The Radicals Seize Power

The final element in the bloody mix of paramilitary organizations in 1920s Macheng was the explicitly revolutionary groups known as peasant associations (*nongmin xiehui,* usually abbreviated *nonghui*).[51] In the summer of 1925, advance agents of the Nationalist Party had set up a peasants department (*nongmin bu*) as part of its underground Party headquarters in Wuhan, followed in December by the Hubei Provincial Peasant Association. The same year, Guomindang agents set up a Macheng *nonghui* at the county seat, with a local literatus and Party member named Luo Qinglian as its initial *huizhang*.[52] Subsequent Communist sources, however, insist that this was a very traditional, top-down sort of institution, which, despite its impressive membership on paper, neither functionally nor organizationally bore any relationship to the genuinely radical organizations that began to spring up under similar names in the villages and market towns of the county the following year.

During the summer vacation of 1926, with the United Front armies sweeping up successfully from the south, many of Macheng's radical youths came home from their studies at Dong Biwu's Awaken Huangzhou Middle School at Wuhan to organize the rural populations in their respective townships. The year before, Dong himself had already paid a visit to the countryside around Songbu to conduct a survey of rural conditions and attitudes, preparatory to establishing grassroots *nonghui* dedicated to his own class-struggle agenda. In the summer and fall, Xu Ziqing, Wang Shusheng, and Wang Hongxue set up, with Dong's guidance, an underground peasant association at the Dongyue Temple in the town of Chengmagang, while Deng Tianwen, Cai Jihuang, and Liu Wenwei did the same in Shunheji. Two young activists of the Ye lineage announced the formation of the Zhongguanyi Peasant Association, commandeering the precincts of their lineage temple to serve as its meeting hall. Young activists of other townships followed suit. With the takeover of the area by United Front forces in October, these associations came out into the open. On Dong Biwu's orders, *nonghui* members were issued red, white, and blue Three Peoples Principles shoulder sashes proudly proclaiming their affiliation. The newly constituted Macheng Peasant Association was set up at the county seat in late 1926, with Cai Jihuang and Xu Ziqing as its directors, and a planning committee was formed to extend local organization into areas of the east and south where it had not previously taken hold. By April there were no fewer than 340 local branches, with a countywide total of 124,000 members.[53] It was largely a membership of male farmers who had at least some proprietorship of land, if only a leasehold: the county Communist Party committee broke down *nonghui* members in 1929 as nearly 40 percent owner-cultivators (10 percent of the total being "rich" and 20 percent "poor") and 60 percent tenants. Hired laborers made up less than 2 percent of the membership, and women only 1 percent.[54]

Much of the work in this era remained propaganda. Rural organizers introduced Party-approved slogans (*biaoyu*) among the illiterate rural population. Early and popular ones were "Down with corrupt officials and clerks" (*Dadao tanguan wuli*)—a sentiment that rural proprietors of any degree of wealth could share—and the more contentious and open-ended "Down with local bullies and evil gentry" (*Dadao tuhao lieshen*).[55] Local activists were aware of the limitations to this approach, as Macheng organizer He Yulin reported in 1929:

> I asked one tenant, "Are you a revolutionary?"
> He replied, "I am!"
> I then asked, "In what way are you a revolutionary?"
> He replied, "I kill local bullies and evil gentry."
> I asked, "And what then?" He could not answer. . . .
> Much more needs to be done in this area![56]

The "more" included a strenuous campaign to improve rural literacy so that Party directives, newspapers, and especially the leaflets (*chuandan*) that local activists printed in abundance could be read and understood. For this purpose, the Macheng and Huang'an organizers set up scores of "mass reading rooms," "mass-education schools," and "village night schools" over the winter of 1926–27 and were trumpeted as a national model in this activity by United Front authorities in Wuhan.[57]

Communist activists in Macheng, offspring of the local countryside as they were, were well positioned to make use of the area's popular culture in their efforts to win over their neighbors to the revolution. One medium they aggressively utilized was folk songs (*minge*). In a poorly educated population such as that of the Dabie Shan, as one local organizer said, "slogans work better than leaflets, but songs work best of all."[58] Particularly useful were the locally beloved "mountain songs" (*shange*) traditionally sung by shepherds, boatmen, and tea pickers, featuring call-and-response vocals accompanied by hand drums. During the first months of United Front rule, highland-born youths returned from Wuhan to write new, "progressive" lyrics to these familiar tunes. One, composed by Wang Youan in early 1928, went as follows:

> Waves of Marxist-Leninist thought refresh our minds.
> The warlords butcher our bodies and steal our grain.
> Workers and peasants of the world seize the reins of power.
> We the firstborn willingly sacrifice our lives in this cause.[59]

Activists also sought, with some success, to turn traditional local festivals to revolutionary ends, festivals that they themselves as children had of course enjoyed. Several activists used the forthcoming celebration of the New Year as an excuse to demand contributions of grain from local wealthy households, to allow the poor to celebrate in comfort. On the occasion of the Lantern Festival (the fifteenth of the first lunar month), one organizer staged a "civilized drama" (*wenming xi*) in his native Dabie Shan village, with actors portraying a "big-nosed foreigner," a warlord, and a landlord cavorting ludicrously in the main street and inviting public ridicule. To celebrate important revolutionary moments, new festivals were also invented almost as quickly as those moments occurred.[60]

The United Front party line dictated that local activism be directed against foreign "imperialists," and as the Wuhan regime's campaign for retrocession of the British concessions at Hankou and Jiujiang heated up, in early 1927, Macheng activists fanned out into the villages to remind farmers of the humiliation they had suffered at the hands of the British for eighty years. They were helped in this effort by the current dearth, and by the claim that it was due in part to the callous refusal of British imperialists to sell grain or make cash loans to the starving local people. On January 30, several of the peasant associations of central Macheng succeeded in staging a mass anti-British rally, said to be 10,000 strong, in front of the Catholic church at Baiguo.[61] Throughout the county, attacks on shopkeepers who were accused of hoarding food were frequently more virulent when it could be claimed that a merchant had also converted to a foreign faith.[62] Nevertheless, as time would show, and despite Macheng's proud and violent tradition of hostility to Christianity and other things foreign, the anti-imperialist cause among the rural populace was but a faint side current to what was clearly the revolution's main appeal: the opportunity to articulate and act upon long and very deep-seated hatreds toward the local masters (*laoye*).

It was these generations-old hatreds that, activists acknowledged, were their chief assets in the strikingly easy and rapid organization of peasant associations in Macheng.[63] In Chengmagang, Xu Qixu posted a threatening broadside on the gate of a neighbor's compound, bearing this poem:

> The poor all suffer miserably while you wealthy men live like kings.
> Why should some households be perennially poor and others perennially rich?

> You local bullies oppress impoverished people like us.
> You do no work, yet grab all the fine things for yourselves.
> The only way is for peasants to organize armed militia.
> Then, after a thousand years, even a barren tree may miraculously burst into bloom![64]

In Zhongguanyi and elsewhere, Peasant Association leaders convened "struggle sessions" against especially detested local magnates. They paraded these men through the streets—in scenes foreshadowing those of the Cultural Revolution—wearing dunce caps identifying them as "evil gentry" to be "smashed."[65] Wang Shusheng would later recall that this became something of a radical "vogue" in early 1927, the actions of young men infatuated with their newfound muscle. As Mao Zedong described it, based on his celebrated investigations in contemporaneous Hunan, "capping" was an act of rather great symbolic violence: local notables subjected to this treatment knew immediately that they would never again enjoy the respect of their neighbors.[66] But the orchestrated violence of the *nonghui* did not stop at the symbolic.

Over the winter and spring of 1926–27 the "peasant movement" in Macheng gradually shifted into a much more aggressive and violent mode. As Mao rather gleefully put it, "A revolution is not a dinner party." His famous report extolling agrarian violence in his native Xiang River valley was issued in March, to a highly mixed reception on the part of United Front higher-ups at Wuhan.[67] But Dong Biwu, the Huang'an and Macheng product currently serving as head of the National Government's "Peasants and Workers Bureau," was one of its most enthusiastic readers. Mao's pithy dictum would quickly prove all too applicable to Dong's native region.

In late December the Macheng county-level Peasant Association declared an immediate 25 percent reduction in rents and a maximum interest rate on loans of 20 percent, and throughout the next six months rent and debt-repayment resistance campaigns were very active throughout the county to enforce these. Local activists also hoped to initiate a campaign for land redistribution, but it proved, for the moment, less in consonance with actual demands by cultivators, and it never got off the ground. The peasant associations also directed their attacks against those bastions of elite domination in Macheng, the ancestral cult (denounced as a feudal superstition) and the lineage system, and against opium smoking and gambling. In a move rather deeply revealing of both United Front parties' prurient antipathy to Chinese popular culture, they also sought to shut down performances of "obscene" village operas (*yinxi*).[68]

The long legacy of virulent class antagonisms in the county clearly contributed to the uncommonly violent nature of these campaigns in Macheng. But, as recent scholars have come to see, the early peasant movement, in which Macheng played such a starring role, also tapped more general strains of violence

Smashing "local bullies and evil gentry." From *Fengyun bianhuan*.

inherent in village culture. As Susan Mann has observed, the land revolution in the countryside specifically empowered young men who had grown up with a construction of masculinity that was deeply violent in nature, and it further unleashed violence-prone cultural elements that had already been systematically cultivated in the martial arts tradition and institutionalized in local militia units.[69] Barend ter Haar argues, a bit more speculatively, that extreme violence against *tuhao lieshen* was legitimized by identification of such class enemies with the incarnate demons that popular religion presumed to lurk throughout the world.[70] I have not found evidence from 1920s Macheng of such explicit demonization, but I do not doubt that it was there. We have seen, after all, both that the "demonic paradigm" did deeply pervade Macheng popular culture and that Communist activists in the 1920s—local boys themselves—worked very energetically to infiltrate this culture and harness it to their violent revolutionary ends.

In the words of the Nanjing-era gazetteer, in the spring of 1927 "conditions throughout Macheng degenerated into chaos, as opportunistic thugs [that is, the *nonghui*] rampaged everywhere."[71] The hotheaded teenager Liu Wenwei organized the Peasants' Self-Defense Force in Shunheji and began armed intimidation of local landholders. On the Huang'an border, a female activist with the masculine nom de guerre Xia Guo'er (Son of China) led young indentured servants on temple lands to attack the landlords, accusing them of demonic behavior—"eating the people's flesh and drinking their blood."[72] Wu Huanxian organized a "struggle session" against the hated local magnate Fang Enkong, who was then executed by a crowd of villagers wielding fishing spears.[73] Other prominent members of the elite, such as Wu Huicun, Chen Yaoting, and Wang Zili, suffered similar fates.

While the Communist-led United Front activists sought somewhat successfully to direct the "peasant movement" through the vehicle of their *nonghui*, they did not have the arena of rural class warfare entirely to themselves. Just as Mao Zedong observed in Hunan, and as Lucien Bianco has recently emphasized, associations of enraged poor cultivators often took the initiative in class warfare, without the Party. A highly secretive jacquerie known as the Xiefu hui, or Terrorize the Wealthy Association, became active in Macheng and Huang'an in this era. Like its analogue the Red Spears, the Xiefu hui had sectarian content, and it devised a secret language to mask its activities. Unlike the Red Spears, however, it was exclusively an organ of the most immiserated: any farmer owning as much as a single *mou* of land was expressly forbidden to join. An abbreviated form of the society's name (*xiehui*, or terror association) was homonymous with an alternative abbreviation for the Communist-directed peasant associations (*xiehui*, or assistance associations), and the Xiefu hui clearly took advantage of this coincidence to carry out its tasks undetected. By all accounts, an uncompromising hatred of any person of wealth formed the society's basic agenda, and terrorist assassination was its preferred method of operation.[74]

Much of this rural violence was reported in the Chinese and Western press at Wuhan and established the county's growing national and international reputation as a radical hotbed. But the series of events that really put Macheng on the world's radar began in Chengmagang, during the terrible dearth of the winter of 1926–27, with what was essentially a family quarrel. The twenty-one-year-old Chengmagang native Wang Shusheng, as we have seen, had been a political firebrand since his student days at the county's Higher-Level Elementary School, and after the establishment of the United Front government at Wuhan he had been a very successful organizer of local peasant associations in his native township. He had something of a skeleton in his closet, however. Wang was the maternal nephew of one Ding Zhenyu, the most feared and detested landlord-strongman in all Chengmagang. Popularly known as the Tiger of the North, Ding was widely accused not only of mercilessly exploiting his tenants but also of routinely expropriating their women for his sexual pleasure. Wang Shusheng, clearly embarrassed by his kinship with Ding, resolved to cement his own revolutionary credentials by making his uncle an example of how an evil *tuhao* must be dealt with. As local hunger grew ever more acute in December, Wang rallied his followers in the peasant associations to loot Ding's well-stocked granaries. He then mounted a show trial for his uncle, in absentia, sentencing him to death for accumulated crimes against the people.[75]

But Ding Zhenyu was not the sort to take this lying down. He began to mobilize an alliance among his fellow Dabie Shan strongmen, drawing upon their collective paramilitary muscle and their links with local Red Spears chapters. Wang appealed to the United Front county administration, under magistrate Liu Fang, to take action against this "counterrevolutionary" activity, but the response was minimal. On December 20, Ding led simultaneous raids on peasant association headquarters in several of the township's market towns, seizing and executing their personnel. That very night, Wang Shusheng struck back. Leading a *nonghui* force some thousand men strong, he burst into Ding's fortified compound, engaged in fierce fighting with Ding's retainers, and placed Ding under arrest. A "struggle session" was organized, with tenants invited to denounce the captured "Tiger." Most vociferous among this group were several unmarried tenants who accused Ding and his goons of forcibly preventing them from marrying and setting up independent households (*chengbuliaojia*)—powerful evidence for the twentieth-century survival of agrarian servility in Macheng, at least in attenuated form. Over the following days and weeks, similar apprehensions and trials of "local bullies" were carried out by peasant association militias throughout Chengmagang and Shunheji townships.[76]

In Macheng City, the Nationalist magistrate Liu Fang grew alarmed at the apparent course the revolution was taking in his county. He turned for support to the two most potent sources of muscle he had at hand: Li Shunqing, president of the chamber of commerce, and Luo Youzhang, head of the county's highly conservative workers' association (*gonghui*), which had clashed repeatedly with leftist *nonghui* in the past. When Cai Jihuang, leader of the Macheng Peasant Association, announced that Ding Zhenyu and eighteen other *tuhao* prisoners were being brought to the county seat so that the magistrate could carry out their death sentences, Liu responded that these worthies must all be released instead, and he ordered all peasant associations in the county to disband immediately. Cai Jihuang, defying this order, withdrew from the city to Chengmagang, the heartland of the peasant associations' strength. The stalemate dragged on for more than a month as both sides braced themselves for a showdown.

Then, on February 2, the *nonghui* struck. In a scene reminiscent of those from the late Yuan, the late Ming, and the early Qing, an army of impoverished farmers from Macheng's peripheral highlands marched on and occupied the county seat. Several thousand strong, the peasant association militia of Chengmagang, with Cai Jihuang in command, forcibly arrested the "capitalist" Li Shunqing and the "scab" (*gongzei*) Luo Youzhang for crimes against the people and demanded that Magistrate Liu Fang sentence them to death. When Liu refused, Cai declared the magistrate stripped of his office. All power throughout Macheng, Cai proclaimed, now rested with the peasant associations.[77]

Meanwhile, events elsewhere also contributed to the ratcheting up of the level of violence in Macheng. A galvanizing incident came with the so-called "atrocity" (*can'an*) in southeast Hubei's Yangxin County, near the borders with Hunan and Jiangxi. There, on Chinese New Year's Day (February 27), the county magistrate and the head of the chamber of commerce—counterparts of Macheng's Liu Fang and Li Shunqing, who had perhaps learned from their example—took preemptive action of their own. They enlisted a group of a hundred or so Red Gang (Hongmen hui) members in a surprise attack on the county peasant association headquarters, doused the building with gasoline, and set it afire, incinerating nine *nonghui* leaders and United Front activists inside. A three-man committee, including Mao Zedong, was dispatched from Wuhan to investigate, and their investigation resulted in the issuance of new sets of provincewide regulations ordering the arrest, trial, and execution of local strongmen who might participate in such acts in the future. A provincial "Bring the Local Bullies to Justice Committee" (Shenpan tuhao lieshen weiyuanhui) was set up in Wuhan to oversee this task, with branch committees in eight Hubei counties, including Macheng.[78]

The following month, from March 4 to March 22, the first "congress" of the Hubei Provincial Peasant Association was held at Wuchang, sponsored and financially underwritten by the United Front national government. By this time, the provincial-level association claimed to represent in total some 800,000 cultivators in forty counties; the congress itself had nearly 200 participants, five of them, led by Liu Xiangmin, from Macheng.[79] The Hubei congress received extensive coverage in the leftist foreign-language press, which trumpeted its "historic" nature, comparable to the "enlightenment" of the medieval European peasantry and the resulting abolition of "serfdom." The conferees resolved that Nationalist county governments throughout the province would be thoroughly reorganized so as to make their leadership effectively coterminous with that of the respective county peasant associations. Those new governments would then dedicate themselves first and foremost to liquidating all public and corporate landholding in the county, and they would implement drastic tax and rent reductions on cultivators. What was most significant, district defense corps were to be purged of all "agents" of past "corrupt power holders." These new militias, though appointed by the county magistrate, would be composed almost exclusively of members of the peasant associations, and any alternative, "oppressive" paramilitary units were to be destroyed. Local elites would be stripped of all honorific titles and would be prohibited from gathering collectively to resist the dictates of the peasant associations.[80] This was, in effect, an unambiguous call for the seizure of local power, if necessary by violent means. It was also very close to the agenda that had already been accomplished, with apparent success, in Macheng.

The Macheng Atrocity

But organized elite resistance was strengthening in Macheng as well.[81] Over the course of the spring, Chengmagang's major landholders—led by Ding Zhenyu's son (and Wang Shusheng's cousin) Ding Yueping—sought to free their imprisoned fellow elites from the peasant associations' custody. In time-honored fashion, they sought help from across the mountainous provincial border, in Henan's Guangshan. There they recruited large numbers of Red Spears fighters to their cause, inviting them across the Dabie Shan into Macheng. At the same time, they impressed their own tenants and neighbors into additional Red Spears chapters, allegedly on pain of death. The society's membership thus grew very rapidly, not only in Macheng itself but also in adjacent Huang'an and Luotian Counties. With their newly expanded muscle, Ding Yueping and the Chengmagang elite led a series of increasingly aggressive assaults on local peasant association cells. Wang Shusheng and the other township *nonghui* leaders repeatedly asked for aid from the county administration, but Liu Fang's successor as Macheng magistrate, the Cantonese Fu Jiashu (the county had a dizzying series of nine different magistrates over the course of

1927 to 1928[82]) never complied; according to leftist sources, he had actually entered into a clandestine pact with the Chengmagang landholders in support of their suppression of the "peasant movement" in their township.

Finally, on April 3, Ding Yueping and his Red Spears led a simultaneous, well-planned attack on four ward-level peasant association and women's association headquarters in Chengmagang and the adjacent Huangtugang. They killed or wounded more than fifty individuals and abducted more than sixty others, many of whom they later executed. Then they destroyed the homes of major *nonghui* and Communist Party leaders in the area, making off, in many cases, with their female dependents.[83] Chengmagang *nonghui* head Wang Shusheng escaped to shelter in the county seat, where the county peasant association, under Cai Jihuang, still held the dominant power. Shortly thereafter, Luo Youzhang's rightist General Labor Association led a coordinated attack on the peasant association headquarters of the seventh ward, in the county's southwestern core, killing or wounding another fifty or so of its leaders. Cai Jihuang telegraphed Wuhan for military support, but for the moment none came.

Beginning on April 5, a force of several thousand Red Spears converged to besiege the Macheng county seat and root out the "Party bandits" (*dangfei*). The city was defended by a comparable number of armed peasant association members under Cai Jihuang and Wang Shusheng (the same force that had invaded and occupied the city some two months before). They were aided, we are told, by revolutionary urban laborers and shop clerks. At noon on the second day of the siege, several white-turbaned Red Spears, led by their martial arts teachers and convinced of their invulnerability to weaponry, launched assaults on several of the city gates, only to be repulsed, with horrific casualties, as the defenders poured pots of lime down on them from the city walls. Cai again sought reinforcements from the United Front provincial government at Wuhan, but when these arrived, in the form of a team of emergency guards (*jingbei dui*), they joined the besieging landlord force instead. So, too, did the city's own elite-led militia (*baowei tuan*). The entire scene eerily replicated that of the late Ming, with Macheng City occupied by an army of lower-class agrarian rebels and in turn besieged by a countermobilization of the rural elite.

Guo Zhiping, the newly arrived Macheng magistrate, who was a native of nearby Qishui County, prudently chose not to reveal his own sympathies in the war between the peasant associations and the rural elite. In this, of course, he reflected the increasingly conflicted attitude of his United Front superiors at Wuhan, as we shall see below. Rather than declare for a side, Guo opted to invite the single most powerful coercive force in all of Macheng—Zheng Jiankui and his Dongshan People's Self-Defense Army—to proceed to the county seat and prevent a bloodbath. Zheng agreed to do so, but, apparently by design, he dragged his feet in arriving, thus preserving, for the moment, his own perceived neutrality on the proper future course of the revolution.[84]

Wang Shusheng managed to slip out of the besieged city, bringing his personal report of the affair to Wuhan. There, the April attacks on Macheng *nonghui* headquarters were declared an "atrocity" (*can'an*), following the example of the Yangxin incidents of February, thereby claiming rhetorical legitimacy for the radicals' cause. (In a sense, of course, the Red Spears attacks were simply reprisals for the round of violence that the peasant associations in Chengmagang had themselves initiated.) The Macheng Atrocity Resolution Committee was dispatched to the scene by joint authority of the Central Peasant Bureau (under Dong Biwu), the Military Affairs Commission, the Provincial Nationalist Party Committee, and the Provincial Peasant Association. Delegates from each of these units were included in the investigation team, and upon their arrival in Macheng, they added Cai Jihuang (representing the Macheng County Peasant Association) and Xu Qixu (representing the Macheng Party Office) to their numbers. Given the constitution of the team, the *tuhao* leaders proved, unsurprisingly, to be totally unwilling to cooperate with their investigation, and on May 9 the Wuhan contingent returned to the capital.

No resolution of the standoff had been achieved, but the propaganda payoff for the radicals was huge. On May 12, the Nationalist government's most widely read Chinese-language organ, the *Minguo ribao,* carried as its lead story an account of how the entire national revolution had been endangered and the cause of justice frustrated by a group of "reactionary forces" in Macheng. Those "local bullies" in the county's northern section, the Dabie Shan townships of Chengmagang and Huangtugang, were identified as "especially vicious." The county's various local defense forces (*fangjun*) were condemned as unresponsive to properly constituted authority, though a prudent exception was made for Zheng Jiankui's People's Self-Defense Army of the Dongshan, which, the newspaper claimed (somewhat hopefully), stood in opposition to the "reactionary" elements. The account concluded by calling for a major military intervention by Wuhan in support of the beleaguered peasants of Macheng.[85]

What followed was an event of mythic significance, not only in the history of Macheng County but also in that of the overall revolution. Wang Shusheng had sought the intercession of Dong Biwu at Wuhan, and the latter had persuaded Mao Zedong to send a force of some three hundred Hubei and Hunan students at his Peasant Training Institute to proceed to Macheng and relieve the siege. The teenaged Macheng activist Liu Wenwei, who had been a student at Mao's institute since March, took command. On the evening of May 14, this group assembled at Wuchang's Yellow Crane Tower—the same site where Li Zhi had been attacked by Geng Dingxiang's supporters more than three centuries earlier—to shouts of "Crush the Macheng *tuhao*!" and "Power to the peasant associations!" Singing the "Internationale," the so-called "Student Army" then set out for Macheng. Although contemporary United Front sources indicate that the army was also dispatched with the blessing of the Guomindang Military Affairs Commission—formed the preceding March, and of which Jiang Jieshi (as well as Feng Yuxiang and Tan Yankai) was a member—Jiang had already by this time shown himself in violent opposition to the peasant movement and almost certainly did not concur. Indeed, a Maoist-era account of the incident claims that the Student Army also rallied to chants of "Down with Jiang Jieshi!" and "Defend Wuhan [from "right Guomindang" attack]!" Clearly, Macheng local politics and United Front national politics were by now very deeply intertwined.[86]

En route to Macheng, the Student Army engaged in several skirmishes with local Red and White Spears chapters. Arriving in the vicinity of the besieged city on May 17, they met with Zheng Jiankui, leader of the county's formidable People's Self-Defense Army. The surviving hagiographic accounts of the student army's victories do not record whether Zheng's forces actually joined them in the relief of the siege; given the ease with which the students defeated a numerically superior opponent, it seems likely that they did. What we *are* told is that the Red Spears and the landlord militia panicked at the arrival of this "spirit army" (*shenbing*) and immediately fled the scene. On May 18, the Student Army entered Macheng through the south gate, flying red banners proclaiming "Down with the *tuhao lieshen*!," "Down with feudalism!," and "Down with imperialism!," and (we are told, rather less convincingly) waving copies of Mao's *Report on an Investigation of the Peasant Movement in Hunan*.[87]

On the evening they entered the city, the Student Army and the county peasant association convened a compulsory mass meeting at the City God Temple to educate local inhabitants on the significance of what they had witnessed. The visitors then went to bed down in the precincts of the old civil service examination hall. Cai Jihuang, Wang Shusheng, and selected others organized themselves as the impromptu Committee to Prosecute Local Bullies and Evil Gentry and debated their course of action through the night. The next morning, following the dictates of the regulations established by the Provincial Peasant Association congress in March, a massive show trial was held for the various *tuhao* whom the radicals had held prisoner for months. Three of the convicted—Chamber of Commerce president Li Shunqing, "Tiger of the North" Ding Zhenyu, and one other—were condemned to death. They were dragged to an execution ground outside the city's west gate and decapitated, and their heads were marched around the city on poles as a lesson to others. Revolutionary violence in Macheng had reached a new level of terrorist display.[88]

Immediately after the executions, Cai Jihuang announced the start of a new "Northern Expedition" of his Student Army and the peasant association, intended to sweep clean or purge (*suqing*) all military power of the local bullies and sectarian bandits (*huifei*) from the Dabie Shan townships of Chengmagang and Huangtugang.[89] On May 20, the "Peasant Dare to Die Corps," led by Wang Shusheng, ambushed and assassinated Wang's cousin Ding Yueping at a banquet the latter was holding for Red Spears leaders from Henan, and then laid siege to the heavily fortified compound of Wang's executed uncle, "Tiger" Ding Zhenyu. A local Buddhist temple, which reformers of the previous generation had forcibly converted into a Western-style elementary school, was in turn appropriated by the Student Army as its Chengmagang barracks. Over several days, Wang's forces attacked one after another of the Red Spears' lairs and succeeded in killing a number of important martial arts teachers, including the much-feared "Six Demon King" Hu Youan. They linked up sequentially with other village *nonghui* militia, coordinated their activities with simultaneous offensives in Huang'an and other counties, and gradually amalgamated into a force of more than 20,000. (The number of combatants mushroomed so quickly that food supplies became a serious concern.) Local landholders who resisted them—in all, some 200 individuals—were seized, subjected to impromptu show trials, and put to death. The daily exploits of this revolutionary juggernaut were breathlessly cheered on by the Wuhan press, which nevertheless conceded that there were ghastly numbers of casualties on both sides.

A climax of sorts came on May 23 with the siege of what was reckoned to be the Red Spears' most daunting stronghold, the Fangjiawan fortress, protectively nestled in the Dabie Shan foothills and topped by numerous gun turrets. Under cover of a thunderstorm, the Student Army surrounded the fort overnight and pressed the attack the next morning, without success. Noting that the fortress contained a number of wooden cattle pens, however, a "dare to die" corps of the attackers managed to scale the walls and set these afire, incinerating many of the defenders and forcing the survivors to flee into the mountains. The following day, a mass rally to declare victory and promote the "glorious thought" of Mao Zedong was held in the market square of Chengmagang. On May 27, the student army returned to Macheng City and summoned the residents to a meeting of 10,000 persons. One speaker after another harangued the crowd on the momentous significance of this moment in the long term of Dabie Shan history, after which the students divided into eight teams to fan out and carry the message of liberation to all sectors of the county. The Macheng Atrocity Resolution Committee, in a story that ran as the lead in the Wuchang press, declared its avenging work successfully accomplished, and it disbanded.[90]

But Macheng's indigenous *nonghui* leadership was hardly satisfied that the job was done. A rather halfhearted "Eastern Expedition" was mounted in late May into the Red Spear–infested (but, until then, relatively pacific) Dongshan highlands, and then, a few days later, a more concerted thrust was launched across the Dabie Shan into Guangshan County, home to most of the mercenar-

Peasant Association headquarters, Chengmagang, northwestern Macheng. Photograph by the author.

ies in the Chengmagang elite's employ. Continuing the time-honored pattern of armed incursions back and forth across the provincial border, Macheng's *nonghui* militia and their supporters in the Student Army spent more than a week exterminating all resistance in contiguous southern Henan. When, on June 4, Mao's Student Army declared complete victory and began its withdrawal to Wuhan, there was some local grumbling that this declaration had come too soon. And, indeed, a series of Red Spear counterassaults over the following few days prompted provincial authorities to dispatch other United Front forces to Macheng to secure the gains that had been made. Red Spear forces had not in fact been defeated as decisively as had been hoped, and they continued sporadic terrorist attacks throughout the county and its neighbors throughout the summer.[91]

Still, this moment clearly represented a high tide of sorts in the fortunes of local leftists. Their principal targeted *tuhao* and *huifei* leaders had been killed. Macheng had gained for itself a growing international notoriety, as reporters from Japan and elsewhere overseas now routinely visited the county to observe the course of its glorious "peasant movement." As the Wuhan press reported in late May, "The conflict between reactionary forces and revolutionary forces in Macheng has escalated, over time, to a level unseen in any other county of Hubei."[92] But for local historians in the People's Republic, it was not this newfound celebrity that was the most significant legacy of the "atrocity" incident. Rather, it was that, in its wake, Communist Party and peasant association operatives in the county now came to organize themselves into a formalized military force, a countywide *nongmin ziweijun* (peasant self-defense army), supplemented by more sporadic *nongmin gansidui* (peasant suicide commandos), *chiweidui* (Red Guards), and even the occasional local unit styling itself (like Zou Pusheng's followers of the fourteenth century) the *hongjun* (Red Army).[93] The county had made the leap, as it so often had done in the past, into wholesale militarization. All inhibitions of civility and hegemony had effectively been removed, and Macheng slipped into yet another era of protracted total war.

CHAPTER ELEVEN

Immaturity

By the late spring and early summer of 1927, the cohort of young Communists in Macheng—Cai Jihuang, Wang Shusheng, Liu Wenwei, and others—seemed to have had their way in the county. With only modest outside support, they had successfully crushed their elite militia and Red Spears foes in most of western and northwestern Macheng and had even extended their string of battlefield victories beyond the county borders into (always troublesome) southern Henan. In this success, they enjoyed at least the passive acquiescence of the county's other major local armed presence, which dominated the eastern Macheng highlands: Zheng Jiankui's People's Self-Defense Army. Within the county seat, though they did not occupy the magistracy itself, they effectively called the shots in local administration, on the basis of their own intimidating numbers and the perceived support of the United Front national government, just half a day's travel down the Ju River in Wuhan. This "left Guomindang" government was headed by the venerable Republican revolutionary Wang Jingwei, but to all appearances it responded to the dictates of a collection of foreign Comintern advisors and domestic Communists, prominently including Huang'an's own native son Dong Biwu, teacher and patron of the Macheng communists. The government had consistently cheered on the ever-greater assertion of power in Macheng by its peasant associations, held this up as a national model, and actually sent military aid when called upon by the county's young radicals. But things were not as secure as they might have appeared: there were mounting challenges to the authority of Wuhan within the broader Nationalist revolutionary alliance, and the support of Wuhan itself would prove to be less than reliable. Macheng's "progressive" youths would shortly discover this—in most cases, at the cost of their lives.

The most formidable among Wuhan's opponents was of course the commander-in-chief of the still ongoing Northern Expedition, Generalissimo Jiang

Jieshi (Chiang Kai-shek). When most of the United Front parties had established themselves at Wuhan, in December of the previous year, Jiang had not accompanied them, choosing instead to establish a separate seat of power at the Jiangxi provincial capital of Nanchang. Though Jiang did not, for the moment, overtly challenge the legitimacy of Wuhan as the Nationalist government, over the first quarter of 1927 he continued to proclaim with growing stridency his dissatisfaction with Wuhan's radical leadership of the labor and peasant movements, and especially its domination by Comintern outsiders. As he pushed his Nationalist Revolutionary Army down the Yangzi, capturing by a combination of diplomacy and military force the major cities of Nanjing, Hangzhou, and Shanghai, he progressively distanced himself from Wuhan's control and treated disparate social elements in these conquered areas as he saw fit. In mid-March, in fact, he arrested and executed the major "mass movement" leaders in his base area of Jiangxi. Finally, on April 12, with the United Front of Communists, "left Guomindang," and Jiang's own "right Guomindang" still formally in place, he unleashed the dramatic wholesale purge in Shanghai and his other areas of control that over the next weeks would kill thousands of rural and urban leftists and become known as the White Terror.[1]

Xia Douyin Comes Home

Jiang's actions were watched closely by others under the sway of Wuhan, especially those who shared his discomfort with the class-warfare elements of the revolution. In Macheng itself, Jiang's increasingly visible efforts to put the brakes on mass movements and rally the forces of the "right Guomindang" are generally assumed to have inspired the violent reprisals against leftist organizers by local elite-led militias in early April, labeled by their opponents the Macheng Atrocity. Even more important, however, in the course of both local and national history, was the impact of Jiang's apostasy on the most powerful figure then in China of Macheng birth: the Dongshan general Xia Douyin.

Xia, it will be recalled, was a Hubei patriot of long pedigree who had taken a central role in the Northern Expedition's conquest of Wuhan. In recognition of this, he was made a member of the Nationalist regime's Hubei Provincial Political Affairs Commission. A nominal subordinate of Wuhan's supreme military commander Tang Shengzhi, Xia in late 1926 had been dispatched to western Hubei to secure the regime's flank from the threat posed by the Sichuan warlord Yang Sen. While there, Xia was commissioned to conduct mop-up or purge (*suqing*) operations against local bandits and remnant Beiyang forces, and he did so effectively enough to win repeated praise in Wuhan's official press.[2] But Xia's relations with United Front higher-ups were not uniformly smooth. For example, a major part of Wuhan's agenda in the wake of its conquest of central

China was rectification of its rather motley military command structure along with a campaign to "democratize" the army by achieving greater equality between officers and men (*guanbing pingdeng*). Xia Douyin's newly dubbed Independent 14th Battalion of the National Revolutionary Army was denounced by the reformers as especially feudal, with its commander exercising an unwonted proprietary attitude toward his troops—many of whom, of course, were his own kinsmen or Dongshan compatriots. Xia took these attacks badly, and the roots of his disaffection with the new regime grew apace.[3] Xia was naturally also distressed by the news he continued to hear of hair-raising attacks on fellow landholders in his native Macheng, and he hoped to put an end to this as well as to punish the Wuhan administration, which applauded such actions.[4]

Although the evidence is not fully clear, it seems that shortly after his April 12 coup, Jiang Jieshi at Shanghai sent a personal emissary to Xia in order to enlist him in an anti-Wuhan alliance. He did the same with respect to Xia's putative opponent on the far side of the Yangzi gorges, the Sichuan warlord Yang Sen, whom Jiang secretly designated commander of his own 20th Nationalist Army. Around May 10, in response to what some claim was a telegraphed go-ahead from Jiang, Xia mutinied and turned his army back toward Wuhan; his erstwhile foe Yang Sen slipped through the gorges and followed Xia's lead.[5] Given the growing prominence of Macheng émigrés in the Sichuan population since the fourteenth century, and their reputation as being among that population's most martial elements, it seems entirely possible that the army of Yang Sen itself, no less than that of Xia Douyin, was significantly composed of Macheng men who longed to rectify the situation in their still remembered and now nationally notorious native place.

In his march on Wuhan in mid- to late May, Xia carved a broad swath of bloodshed through western and southern Hubei. At the river town of Jiayu, he arrested the Guomindang Political Bureau head, Li Bogang, a man who had been among the most strident critics of the "feudal" style of Xia's army. In a dramatically staged crossing of the Yangzi at Jiayu's Huangshi Harbor on May 13, he proclaimed his intention to purge the Wuhan government of Communist and other leftist influences. To underscore his point, Xia released captive "local bullies" from the custody of the Jiayu Peasant Association, rallied the local elite militias, and seized and executed the peasant association's leaders. He did the same in each of the other counties that his army traversed.[6]

On May 18, the headline of Wuhan's leading English-language newspaper announced that the city had been thrown into a fever of excitement by reports of war. Xia Douyin's troops were encamped at Xianning County, a mere twenty miles from the capital, and skirmishes had been reported around the shores of Wuchang's East Lake. Xia's new ally Yang Sen was pressing eastward toward Wuhan from Shashi, in western Hubei, while some of Jiang Jieshi's forces were moving menacingly upstream from Nanjing. Remnant troops of the Beiyang warlord Wu Peifu still hovered along the capital's northern perimeters. Several of Wuhan's own commanders were suspected of sympathy for Xia's revolt. Refugees streamed into the city from all localities in Xia's path. The prospects for the United Front government, and for local mass movement leaders throughout the province who depended upon its patronage, looked increasingly desperate.[7]

An anti-Xia mass meeting was convened on May 19 at Wuhan by the regime's General Labor Union, joined by international delegates to a pan-Pacific trade union conference that the union had planned to convene the following day. The turncoat Macheng general was loudly denounced as a "running dog of Wu Peifu and Jiang Jieshi" and as "the representative of the *tuhao lieshen* class." The Provincial Peasant Bureau held its own emergency rally, warning local activists of a provincewide network of "local bullies," rightist militias, and Red Spears chapters that Xia and his sympathizers were effectively cobbling together as they rampaged their way through Hubei. Responding to such orchestrated public pressure, the nervous and internally fragmented Nationalist government dispatched the Communist general Ye Ting, along with a motley assortment of volunteer fighters, to intercept Xia Douyin; reinforcement forces loyal to Wuhan were summoned from Jiujiang and other Middle Yangzi cities. In a dramatic series of engagements over the next few days, Ye and his bedraggled supporters succeeded, rather startlingly, in pinning down Xia's forces at Xianning and decisively stalling his march on Wuhan.[8]

With his attempt at a national coup frustrated, Xia Douyin turned his energies to a two-month campaign of liquidation of all suspected leftists in rural areas to the capital's south, east, and north; as the Wuhan press colorfully put it, "Iron Hooves Trample Eastern Hubei."[9] In Xianning, Tongcheng, Chongyang, Tongshan, Puqi, Echeng, and Daye Counties, Xia successively linked up with local landlord militias and chapters of secret societies—including the Qingbang (Green Gang), which had already established its ties with Jiang Jieshi in the course of the Lower Yangzi White Terror—to topple leftist local administrations, shut down mass movement headquarters, and murder literally thousands of Communist, *nonghui*, and labor union leaders, often in the most grisly manner. In Tongshan, where the Atrocity Resolution Commission had been set up on the Macheng model to investigate and avenge attacks on local activist cells, Xia simply had the commission members rounded up and killed.[10] By early June, he had arrived in his home region of eastern Hubei, where he extended his bloody vendetta to the countryside in Huanggang, Huang'an, Luotian, and Huangmei; in the latter county, to cite but one example, he stumbled across a several-hundred-strong anti-Jiang Jieshi rally and massacred all in attendance.[11] Finally, in mid-July, Xia crossed over into Anhui, pausing to butcher leftists in the border counties of Susong and Taihu before proceeding downriver to join Jiang's rightist regime in Nanjing.[12]

Unsurprisingly, before departing Hubei, Xia Douyin took special pains to rectify conditions in his native Macheng. As Wang Shusheng described the county's White Terror in his oral history:

> Most of the officers [in Xia's army] were natives of the place and were familiar with conditions in the locality. In collusion with local landlords' militia forces, they sought out those connected with the peasant association and killed them off, sometimes whole families of them. Houses were burned, and the mountainside was combed region by region, village by village. Members of the Chinese Communist Party and the Communist Youth Corps, with relatively long years of membership, and major cadres of the peasant association were generally killed. Still larger numbers of innocent peasants were also killed.[13]

As Xia approached from the east, sweeping down from the Dongshan, panic-stricken leftist sympathizers from throughout Macheng fled to the peasant association–controlled county seat, where they begged Wuhan for military aid and prepared yet once again to withstand a siege. Meanwhile, urban elites plundered the accounts of the government post office to bring in additional mercenaries from Henan in support of their own cause. The situation in Macheng City for most of June was tense, uncertain, and frantic.[14]

But Xia Douyin proceeded toward the county seat only very slowly and, as it turned out, halfheartedly: he never in fact got there. Quite possibly he was deterred by the calamitous flooding of the Ju River in late June and early July, which, if it spared Macheng's southeastern core from military devastation, nevertheless killed hundreds outright and destroyed most of that year's crops.[15] Even without the floods, however, Xia's evident greater interest lay in avenging the miscarriage of the revolution in rural areas along his route, most especially in the Dongshan itself, and above all in the vicinity of his native Muzidian Town. Wuhan newspaper accounts of Xia's activities in this area are bloodcurdling. He torched farmhouses and merchant shops in the town and butchered hundreds of persons, many of them women and children. Village elites captured suspected local Communist sympathizers and presented them to Xia as tribute, to be gruesomely executed. In the southern Dongshan market of Huangshigang, one of Xia's officers attacked a rural schoolhouse, murdering the teacher and all twenty-three students inside. Similar massacres occurred throughout the county's eastern highlands.[16] By late July, Wuhan's *Minguo ribao* could report that throughout Macheng County the grassroots-level leadership (*xiaji ganbu*) of the agrarian revolution had been entirely wiped out.[17]

There is no question that Xia Douyin was viewed by many as a savior. In one friendly, near-contemporary account of his army's prolonged peregrinations through Hubei, it is recorded that he was jubilantly welcomed by "the people" (*minzhong*) in each county through which he passed.[18] While the credibility of this report depends critically upon how one chooses to delineate the category "people," there is no reason to disbelieve that Xia found some kind of welcoming audience everywhere he went. The landholding elite, pressed to the wall by the increased aggressiveness and violence of the peasant movement, naturally welcomed Xia's approach as key to their personal survival. But it is clear that he was also seen as the savior of civilization. The locally born, Western-trained social scientist Meng Guangpeng, in his preface to the 1935 Macheng County gazetteer—financed largely by Xia himself, to be sure, but also clearly reflecting a broad elite consensus in the county at this time—portrays the mass movement leadership as nothing but rapacious thieves and plunderers (*zeipi mijue*), purveying wild and socially dysfunctional theories akin to those of Li Zhi some four centuries earlier. Xia Douyin's contribution lay not merely in his restoration of social order in his native county but, more generally, in rectifying the minds of the people (*ren zhi xinsi*) in the direction of loyalty and sincerity (*zhongcheng*), hallmarks both of the civilized Chinese tradition and of Macheng's own local culture.[19]

Xia himself consistently presented his actions in the grandiose terms of Confucian paternalism. I am heartsick, he wrote, at the sores of affliction suffered by my native region, devastated as it has been by bandits, plagued by natural disasters, and perverted by heterodox and lewd (*xieyin*) ideas. The inherent vitality (*yuanqi*) of the people has been sapped, and it is my own awesome duty (*shuming*) to renew it.[20]

At the same time, the level of violence engaged in by Xia and his troops went well beyond even the norms of his violent day; it was horrific, ghoulish, and highly theatrical. Much of our knowledge of his violence comes, of course, from the reports of his enemies, but they are sufficiently convincing to have made even the deeply anti-Communist American scholar C. Martin Wilbur squeamish; with obvious embarrassment that a Guomindang general would act in such fashion, Wilbur termed Xia's style of butchery "pitiful."[21] In Huanggang, Xia was said to have used hot iron to sear the flesh of his captives, and in Luotian to have bound his victims to trees "and put them to death with one thousand cuts into which [he] rubbed sand and salt." He was fond of dousing suspected leftists with kerosene and setting them afire. (The Provincial Peasant Association, presented with this convenient excuse to target outlets of "imperialist" economic penetration, ordered its local operatives to torch all kerosene shops in their districts prior to Xia's arrival.) Xia's men, dreaded by local people as "snakes and scorpions" (*shexie*), reportedly tore infants from their mothers'

General Xia Douyin. From *Who's Who in China*, 4th edition, 1931.

breasts and dismembered them before their eyes. They collected buckets of ears of *nonghui* members to present to their commander.[22] In large measure, of course, such conduct was a reflection of the highly ideologized, even apocalyptic, tenor of the times. In part it was due to Xia's background as a student in Beiyang-dominated military academies and regiments. But very basically, it is clear, it grew out of the milieu in which Xia and most of his followers had been raised—the intrinsically violent local culture of Macheng and the Dongshan.

Gender War

Xia Douyin was particularly keen to torture and humiliate women. His troops routinely raped women in areas through which they passed, but this was an accustomed pattern in times of trouble throughout Chinese history, and the Macheng area had seen more than its share of it over the centuries. Xia's misogyny went very much further than this, and he exercised it in highly theatrical acts of antifemale terrorism. He was fond of grabbing women suspected of leftist sympathies, stripping off their clothes, and displaying them atop local opera stages to demonstrate their debauchery. And in one widely reported incident, in Macheng's neighboring Luotian County, he slit open the breasts of several naked women and pierced them with iron rods before parading them through the village streets.[23]

There was clearly an element of misogynist fantasy fulfillment in such behavior that ran deeply in Xia's own personality, and arguably in the local culture of which he was a product. But it was also a calculated tactical response to changes in the world that Xia and men like him observed with genuine horror. Late-imperial Chinese society was repressive in general of its female members, and in Macheng this repression seems almost to have reduced women to chattel status. Recall the eighteenth-century incident in which a reluctant bride was locked up for over a year in a false partition in a house (see chapter 1); neither in this story's survival in local folklore nor in its embellished retelling by Yuan Mei is the woman's imprisonment itself condemned as offensive to conventional morality. Recall as well the local population's violent response to what was perhaps Macheng's one recorded exercise of female agency, the decision of Mei Guozhen's daughter in the sixteenth century to accept Buddhist discipleship under Li Zhi and his monastic colleague Wunian. Extant lineage rules from late-imperial Macheng unanimously proclaim strict limits on female action, and this was emphasized all the more in their Republican-era revisions. A revised regulatory code of the Shi lineage, drawn up by a council of elders as late as 1946, offers a case in point. In the midst of ringing modernist rhetoric on the need to forge the nation (*guojia*) and on the critical role to be played in this project by the autonomous energies of the individual (*geren*)—for instance, through vigorous study of the natural sciences (*gezhong kexue*)—the code reiterates in stronger terms than ever before the demand for cloistering lineage females within the house, and it bewails the pernicious contemporary trend of women getting out into the larger society.[24] And Xia Douyin's Dongshan was yet more conservative in its attachment to older gender models than was the county as a whole: a Guomindang report of 1934, for example, notes that whereas in most parts of Macheng footbinding has become a thing of the past, in Dongshan it is still routine practice.[25]

But times were radically changing, at least in part because of political revolution. One aspect of this change was the ongoing contest over women (the society's surplus of males was due in part to the continuing practice of female infanticide) and over shifts in the marriage market. A legacy of the bondservant system pervasive in Macheng since the mid- to late-Ming periods was the inhibitions imposed by masters on the freedom of their tenants to marry and establish independent households, along with routine expropriation by the master of wives and daughters of their dependents. As we have seen, while the legal formalities of the bondservant system may have been gone by the 1920s, complaints about both kinds of gender-related practice on the part of landlords were still heard in Macheng in those years and were identified by rural males as one key stimulus for joining the peasant movement. From the Communist point of view, gender relations could be a double-edged sword. For instance, a 1929 report of the Macheng Party branch laments the obstacle posed to recruitment of some better-off dependents of estate-holding landlords. In the master's frequent absence, the report states, these rural overseers have complete run of his household, a privileged status that pointedly includes sexual relations with the master's womenfolk. What incentive do such men have to make revolution? Nevertheless, the report boasts, given the climate of extreme gender repression in Macheng, young activist males find their attractiveness to women, and their marital chances, significantly improved by their reputation for progressiveness in gender consciousness.[26] Conservatives were of course quick to accuse the same activists of exploiting their newfound muscle for sexual conquest: a common narrative was that leftist youth from formerly impoverished backgrounds blackmailed the widows of "rich peasants" to marry them, in order to safeguard their land from seizure and redistribution.[27] And throughout the Dabie Shan region, Red Spears chapters—which, as we have seen, took enforcement of conventional gender morality as one of their most basic mandates—spread hair-raising stories of young leftist females sharing men.[28]

There were indeed substantial grounds in the rhetoric of women themselves to establish at least the plausibility of this charge. It is really only in the era of the Nationalist Revolution that female voices begin to be heard at all in the local historical record, but then they are heard with great clarity and vigor. Indeed, if, as Lucien Bianco argues, the early, radical phase of the Nationalist Revolution is more accurately understood as a war between generations than as a war between classes, it was clearly also, to a not inconsiderable extent, a war between genders. From late 1926 through the middle of 1927, the revolution was very vocal about proclaiming as its mission a fundamental transformation of gender relations, and, as Christina Gilmartin points out, a person's stance on this issue became something of a litmus test of the genuineness of his or her basic commitment to revolutionary change in general.[29] It was also the issue that provoked the most deeply felt and violently expressed resistance.

Women themselves took the lead in the movement—notably urban women, but by no means exclusively so. In Hubei, provincewide membership in county women's associations (usually branches of local peasant associations) rose dramatically, from about 2,000 to 60,000 over the first half of 1927.[30] The movement's centerpiece in this era was the internationally reported First Hubei Provincial Women's Representative Conference, held in Hankou on March 8 (Women's Day) of 1927.[31] The meeting was accompanied by a mass rally and a parade of a reported several hundred thousand women in the city center. Alarmed conservative leaders were said to have hired prostitutes to march topless alongside the representatives, leading the press breathlessly to report that leftist Hubei women had held a "naked parade." The goings-on within the meeting itself, however, were no less dramatic. The conferees—led by the fiery orator Huang Mulan, and backed by Song Qingling, the prestigious widow of Sun Yat-sen, and by the wife of chief Comintern advisor Michael Borodin—resolved to push vigorously for greater work opportunities for women, at equal pay, and to lead a mass female-literacy campaign through the vehicle of supplementary-education schools (*buxi xuexiao*) for village women. They demanded an immediate end to footbinding. (Following up on this demand, the United Front government announced a deadline of May 16 for all women under thirty throughout its territories to have their feet unbound, and an impressive rate of compliance was achieved.[32]) The conferees denounced the venerable local charitable institution of *qingjie tang* (virtuous-widow halls), referring to them derisively as "cattle pens," and ordered their immediate transformation into women's industrial-training centers. But most provocative of all were the conference's resolutions on sexual and marital issues, and the accompanying waves of enthusiasm for shocking modes of sexual conduct.

The conference's resolutions could not have been more basic and far-reaching, identifying as their central target the entire corpus of cultural assumptions on personal propriety, interpersonal behavior, and family structure subsumed under the rubric of *lijiao* (ritual teachings). The conferees took direct aim, in other words, at what the vast majority of the Chinese elite held to be the very essence of civilization. These normative practices were, in the conference's graphic term, *chiren* (cannibalistic). There were resolutions to end specific abuses in the patrilineal family system: polygamy and concubinage, purchasing of brides (*maimai jiehun*), and minor marriage of *tongyangsi* (little daughters-in-law) brought into the groom's household effectively as servants. But demands quickly went much further, culminating in a resolution that local women's associations throughout the province aggressively push for *lihun jiehun juedui ziyou* (absolute freedom of divorce and marriage). A vogue of women demanding immediate divorce from their husbands, and choosing new mates, swept through Wuhan, and it was imitated to a more modest degree in the province's rural counties. Many women went even further, proclaiming contemptuously anti-male agendas such as *dushenzhuyi* (cellibatism) and a lesbian-tinged *funüzhuyi* (womanism).

Macheng, where a local women's association had been established the year before, sent its own representatives to the Hankou conference, and at least some women there were deeply influenced by its resolutions. Purchased and "little daughter-in-law" minor marriage were still routine practices in the county, and the local association took eradication of these practices as its principal aim, at least in the short term.[33] But the local impact of the movement seems to have come less from any institutionalized activities than from those of highly zealous individual women. Xiong Jiamou and Xiong Jiaxun, for example, were daughters of a lower-gentry village schoolteacher from the outskirts of Xia Douyin's hometown, Muzidian, and great-granddaughters of a Taiping-era *jinshi*. As their father gradually responded to the message of radicalization in the mid-1920s, they did as well, becoming leaders of the peasant association's women's auxiliary. They led active propaganda work throughout the Dongshan highlands, proclaiming messages such as "Women! Strike down the feudal marriage system!" For this, and for their unorthodox lifestyle—it was said, "In the Xiong family, the father is no proper father, and the daughters are no proper daughters!"—they were expelled from their lineage.[34] Luo Qijie came from an indigent Macheng family, which contracted her out at the age of nine as a "little daughter-in-law" in a family of neighboring Huang'an. When the groom's parents tried to bind her feet, she ripped off the bindings and ran away, joining the Communist Youth League and engaging in guerrilla warfare under the nom de guerre Baigan yimei (Sister Baigan). In defiant protest of the conventional marriage system, Luo returned to her native place and lived in open cohabitation with a leftist young man. Eventually she became a resistance leader and was executed by the Japanese in 1944.[35] And we have already met (see chapter 10) the young activist woman Xia Guo'er (nom de guerre "Son of China"), who led deadly "peasant self-defense corps" attacks on *tuhao* along the Macheng-Huang'an border throughout the late 1920s.[36]

As these examples suggest, the radicalization of women in the 1920s centrally included a violent aspect, a display of martial bravado. One manifestation was the revived cult of Mulan, the legendary Chinese women warrior; this was, for example, the chosen nom de guerre of the great Women's Day orator Huang Mulan. Another was the fashionable self-reference of activist women as (in English) "Amazons." During the first half of 1927, recruits from newly formed women's associations throughout central China were selected to attend Wuhan's Zhongyang junshi zhengzhi xuexiao (Central Military and Political Institute). These young women with unbound feet and short-clipped hair, dressed in gray uniforms with caps and riding boots, learned to march, ride horseback, and shoot rifles alongside their male classmates.

In mid-May, as Xia Douyin's army approached a panicked Wuhan, these students and a larger force of surrounding peasant women were mobilized into the *nüsheng dui* (Women's Brigade) and thrown into the field to help intercept Xia's march. From numerous memoir accounts—generated both at the time and later, under the solicitous patronage of the Women's Federation in the People's Republic—it is clear that the formation of this brigade was a galvanizing event in female consciousness and in the women's movement in central China. The Women's Brigade was largely organized by a twenty-four-year-old female Communist veteran of the Northern Expedition, Li Zheshi (Li Wenyi), then serving as director both of the Hubei Provincial Women's Association and of the Women's Department of the provincial government. At a rally for the Women's Brigade, prior to their departure, Li encouraged her troops: "If we don't succeed in slaughtering our foe, we cannot dare return to face the revolutionary masses." Shouting "Slay the enemy!," these 200-odd women warriors marched into battle, and they reportedly did in fact confront Xia's forces successfully at the town of Xiantao, contributing to his failure to reach his goal of Wuhan. One can only imagine how the specter of this troop of Amazons arrayed against him registered on the consciousness of the Dongshan general, already deeply embittered by the revolution's degenerate effects on gender relations and popular morality.[37]

There was probably no more visible or more incendiary marker of the radicalization of 1920s women than bobbed hair (*jianfa*). On October 11, 1926—the day after Chinese National Day, and a few weeks after United Front armies had captured Wuhan—a large crowd of women assembled outside the headquarters of the Hubei Women's Association and proclaimed their liberation from the old order by collectively shearing off their hair.[38] Long tresses, they argued, were nothing but "feudal tails," whereas bobbing gave one a "civilized head" (*wenming tou*). In United Front ideology, a woman's bobbing her hair went in tandem with her unbinding her feet; whereas the cutting of male queues had been the tonsorial symbol of the Republican Revolution, the cutting of women's long hair would be the emblem of the Nationalist. It signified not merely equality of the sexes but also a farewell to female vanity and a visible commitment to self-sacrifice in the national interest. In practical terms, United Front propagandists urged, the fifteen to thirty minutes a day that women had formerly spent arranging their long hair might now be applied to revolutionary pursuits.

As the revolution moved north through central Hunan in late 1926, it had vigorously proselytized hair bobbing among rural as well as urban women, and in the first few months of 1927, activists fanned out into the Hubei countryside to intensify the campaign in this province as well. But there was unanticipated female resistance along the way. Many Hunanese women, on rumors that

Female Communist guerrillas of the Dabie Shan, 1948, with bobbed hair. Bettman Archive.

the revolutionaries were going to seize them and forcibly cut their hair, fled to remote areas, and in Hubei many farm women threatened suicide should this happen to them, just as they would have done if threatened with other forms of sexual assault by conquering armies.[39] Consequently, the revolution's leadership felt obliged to go slow. During the mass rallies for Women's Day in March 1927, though virtually all the participants themselves sported short haircuts, the announced agenda included only a demand to end footbinding, not a parallel enforcement of hair bobbing. And as part of an overall slowdown of revolutionary activities in late spring, on June 21 the Hubei Peasant Association included in its "Resolution on the Question of Rural Women" an explicit prohibition on enforced haircutting by local activists.[40]

In Macheng, as probably elsewhere, the wearing of long hair by women was traditionally not only an aesthetic choice but also a sign of acceptance of the established marriage-and-family system: unmarried females tied their long hair into one or two pigtails (*bian*), whereas married women coiled theirs into a topknot (*wanji*).[41] Nevertheless, the county women's association, as early as its mid-1926 founding, had accorded equal emphasis to hair bobbing and the unbinding of feet in its campaign for liberationist change in women's bodies.

Activists like the Xiong sisters, Jiamou and Jiaxun, rallied farm wives even in backwoods Dongshan with slogans such as "Women! Cut your hair and unbind your feet [*jiantou fangjiao*]" as a demonstration of their opposition to "feudal" gender practices.[42]

In a way, in the Macheng area at least, revolutionary encouragement of female haircutting in the late 1920s was analogous to the 1645 Qing edict ordering male tonsure and adoption of the queue. In both instances, a seemingly trivial tonsorial innovation, largely incidental to the greater political cause, became a red flag igniting massive local resistance to the new regime. In both cases, it affected even persons who had initially made their peace with the conquerors, or who even, like Xia Douyin, had served in their vanguard. Both were seen by culturally conservative local males as fundamental affronts to cherished cultural values and challenges to the civilized social order. In Macheng, unsurprisingly, the first wave of male violence directed at hair bobbing came from the *chiarivari*-style defenders of traditional morality, the Red Spears. In their assault on leftist headquarters in Chengmagang and Huangtugang on April 3, 1927, Red Spear bands reportedly grabbed women they encountered who had bobbed hair, shackled them, and paraded them through the streets in shame.[43] In June, when Xia Douyin arrived as the avenging angel in his native county, he took the reprisals one step further, gruesomely torturing as well as debauching women with short haircuts.[44] But over the next few years, Xia gradually abandoned such theatrical violence in favor of a more direct and taciturn response: by 1930, he had given general orders to his troops that any woman discovered to have bobbed hair was to be shot and killed on the spot.[45]

Reeducating the Radical Generation

Over the course of April and May 1927, there was much debate within the United Front leadership at Wuhan about the seemingly unbridled vendettas of local peasant associations, in Macheng and elsewhere. Dong Biwu and Mao Zedong led the faction that argued for continued free license to local leaders to do as they saw fit, while others, including chief Comintern representative Michael Borodin, sought the imposition of a more moderate central control. On May 20, with the rightist armies of Xia Douyin and others virtually at the capital's gates, the Guomindang central committee met and issued a directive prohibiting local activists from unauthorized attacks on local elites. As reported by the *Hankow Herald*, the directive stated:

> Those landlords and [gentry] who oppose . . . and hinder the emancipation of the peasants are disclaimed by the Party. But evidence against them must first be found before they can be punished. If such evidence is established, they can then be taken to court for trial and punished according to law. [However,] those honest wealthy people who

are not opposed to the Revolution are under the protection of the Nationalist Government.[46]

This would be but the first in a series of central directives that would effectively pull the rug out from under the young local activists whom the same regime had been encouraging throughout the United Front territories, and nowhere more clearly than in Macheng.

The Wuhan regime—deeply divided internally, confused about the proper response to Jiang Jieshi's defection and bloody purges, threatened militarily on all sides, and uncertain about just which militarists to turn to for support—responded by essentially blaming the excesses of local activists for its plight. Between June 8 and June 10, the Hubei Provincial Peasant Association and the All-China Peasant Association held a series of emergency meetings and issued a series of directives and press releases announcing the immediate need to modify the course of the peasant movement in the province. These statements differed somewhat in their emphases, according to the political position of the speaker: some were more critical than others of what had gone on in the central China countryside, but they generally concurred in characterizing the failures of local peasant association leaders as those of "immaturity" (*youzhi*). It was said that the peasant movement had developed too rapidly, that it had outrun the ability of the center to exercise paternalist control, and that, in its youthful zeal, it had needlessly alienated individuals and groups in society who now, with Xia Douyin as their catalyst, had reacted crushingly against it. The countryside, it was said, was in a condition of anarchy. More stable and responsible local revolutionary administrations had to be set up, and economic productive capacity had to be safeguarded. It was necessary immediately to cease confiscations and redistribution of landlords' property without express direction from the center, and to seek closer cooperation among propertyless peasants, small landlords, merchants, and manufacturers. Most consistent among the injunctions issuing from these Wuhan meetings was that the families and properties of all revolutionary soldiers and officers—of men, that is, such as Xia Douyin and his followers—should be protected.[47]

Over the following weeks, further condemnations of local activist "immaturity" and orders to slow down the rural revolution issued steadily from the center. A resolution of the Hubei Provincial Peasant Association of June 21, for example, ordered an end to female activists' demands for "absolute freedom" of marriage and divorce. And in a summary report on revolutionary work in Hubei over the first half of the year, the Guomindang central committee affixed the blame for the numerous "peasant massacres" throughout the province squarely on the fact that "the orders of the Party and the Hubei Peasant Association were not carried out quickly and efficiently" by local activists.[48]

In late June, a disturbed Dong Biwu summoned a large number of these local activists—many of them, of course, his personal protégés—to Hankou for a conference of Hubei peasant association provincial and district representatives, its purpose being for him to hear their side of the story and formulate what would turn out to be the last effective defense of the rural strategy to date. He seems to have gotten an earful. At the close of the conference, on June 25, Dong issued a "manifesto" described by the *People's Tribune* under the headline "[Hubei] Peasants Deny Activities Immature."[49] The document paid dutiful respect to the idea of government leadership over local peasant associations but at the same time called for stepped-up attacks on local *tuhao* and an ongoing process of land redistribution under the supervision of local *nonghui*. Over the following week, however, a series of drafts and redrafts of the conference's final report were successively issued, each of which was more emphatic than its predecessor on the urgent need for "severe discipline" of local associations by the Party center. Village-level activists, it was announced, must be made to gain "a clearer and wider understanding of the general political situation, and of the policy and organization of the Party as a whole." A stricter hierarchy of peasant association levels and a clearer chain of command were established to serve these purposes.[50] On July 8, a leadership meeting of the Provincial Peasant Association was convened in order to provide a unified official interpretation of what had clearly been a lively and contentious conference of the rank-and-file two weeks before. Local branches were enjoined to support all the resolutions of the leadership and to follow the instructions of the Nationalist government for the identification and punishment of alleged class enemies. Somewhat poignantly, in light of the rightist terror going on in the Lower Yangzi and elsewhere (and in light of Comintern advisor Borodin's departure from Wuhan the very same day), the meeting concluded with the directive that Nationalist and Communist Party members should "closely cooperate" in managing the future course of the rural revolution.[51]

The gradual recognition, over the next week or two, of the impossibility of such cooperation, and the eventual collapse of the Wuhan government itself, only further undermined the activities (and indeed the survivability) of its dependent local activists. Between July 13 and July 16, Wang Jingwei gradually separated himself from the Communists in his government, and the Comintern pulled its advisors completely out of Wuhan. Between this time and Wang's own abandonment of Wuhan, on September 13, "counter-revolution . . . moved into the leftist capital," with the cities put under martial law. Dozens of labor movement activists were rounded up and shot.[52] The most articulate radical in the women's movement, Chen Dingyi, was executed in August, and her head was displayed atop Wuchang's main gate for three days.[53] As for the peasant movement, Guomindang officials announced that they were reclaiming leadership of it from the Communists, who had previously arrogated its leadership to themselves, and whose "puerile actions" had only brought disaster. "Party direction" and "strict revolutionary discipline," it was decreed, must be imposed on the local peasant associations in Hubei, which were to be reorganized accordingly. Implementation of a 25 percent rent reduction would be the most immediate task in the countryside, but no longer would any attacks on landlords or seizures of property be tolerated. As the *People's Tribune* reported in early August, "The Communists have been propagating a class war and a dictatorship of the peasantry and laborers. All these [sic] sugar-coated verbiage are used to deceive the public." In a major theoretical reformulation published on August 10 and titled "Correcting Several Varieties of Mistaken Thought," Wuhan leader Gu Mengyu posed the question "Does the Guomindang necessarily have a class base?" He answered his own question emphatically in the negative.[54]

Macheng County, a key site of such "puerile" actions on the part of the peasant movement when the center had loudly applauded them, now reclaimed the national spotlight as a model of *nonghui* reorganization. In the immediate wake of Wang Jingwei's break with the Communists, the Macheng Guomindang Party office issued a bulletin asserting for itself sole control of the local peasant movement, choosing, in so doing, to trumpet its own class-struggle credentials, by contrast with the "betrayal" of the peasants on the part of the "false" Guomindang regime of Jiang Jieshi.[55] Within days, however, the same office set up a "reorganized" education department in the county seat, its purpose being to "promote the revolution" by teaching "conformity to the Party line [*danghua*]." Teachers in all rural schools would need to be "screened" (*zhenbie*) and reeducated, to ensure conformity with the new agenda. A screening committee for village schoolteachers was established, and examinations on Party principles (*dangyi*) were administered to all incumbents and potential recruits. A sample question read: "Explain the importance of 'teaching conformity to the Party line' to the progress of the Nationalist Revolution."[56]

On the convenient (but largely false) argument that the lower-level leadership (*xiaji ganbu*) of Macheng's peasant movement had been completely wiped out by Xia Douyin's vendetta in his native county, the local Guomindang Party office convened the combined Party Affairs and Peasant Movement Training Institute at the county seat. Those who graduated on July 18 were treated to speeches by provincial Party officials who reminded them that closely adhering to Party guidelines was the only sure way to transform dark-age Macheng (*hei'an Macheng*) into a new glorious and enlightened Macheng (*guangming Macheng*). For what would effectively be the last time, attacks on genuinely counterrevolutionary "local bullies and evil gentry" were among the courses of action still condoned by Party higher-ups.[57]

But on June 23, *Minguo ribao* announced the formation of the Macheng

Army-Civilian Joint Welcoming Committee (*junmin lianhuanhui*) to receive troops of the Second Northern Expedition, which the Wang Jingwei regime had dispatched to Henan. The ostensible goal of this expedition was to pursue anti-imperialist goals in North China, now that Wang's rival Jiang Jieshi had demonstrated his complicity with foreign capitalists; clearly, however, sending such a force through Macheng and its neighboring counties was a timely means for Wuhan to enforce commitment to mass movement "reorganizational" efforts in these overly radicalized localities. The welcoming committee announced local class-inclusive solidarity in support of the new policies, and, despite the Wang regime's continued effort to portray itself as more representative of the masses than its rightist rivals, the committee pointedly avoided any mention of the county's recent violent experience of the rural revolution.[58]

What of Macheng's "progressive" youth, who so recently had found themselves in virtual control of the county administration? A week after Wang Jingwei's purge of the leftists, on July 15, the Communist Party central committee issued a declaration that it, not the Guomindang, was in charge of the rural revolution; Wang was accused of betrayal and of "hypocritically" giving tacit support to the brutal suppression of the peasant movement by Xia Douyin and his Red Spears allies.[59] But this was now of necessity an underground movement. In August, Dong Biwu himself—the most active advocate of the land revolution among the Wuhan leadership, and the personal patron of nearly all of Macheng's own young activists—was forced to hide out in Hankou's Japanese Concession and then to flee the city for Shanghai, Japan, and ultimately Moscow.[60] In Macheng, a violent and prolonged Party purge (*qingdang*) got under way in September, with a parallel "reorganization" of the county's Peasant Self-Defense Army.[61] Twenty-one-year-old *nonghui* leader Xu Qiyu escaped to join He Long's Communist army, en route to Jiangxi; there, at the beginning of August, he played a leading role in He's failed Nanchang Uprising.[62] Other young leftists, such as Wang Youan, Cai Jihuang, Wang Shusheng, and Liu Wenwei, abandoned the county seat for their native highland townships, Chengmagang and Shunheji, where they awaited the call to yet another round of rural revolution.

The Huang-Ma Uprising

That call came as the result of an emergency meeting of the Communist Party central committee, held at Hankou on August 7. The cause of the manifest disasters of the United Front policy was conveniently reduced to the "right opportunism" of Party chairman Chen Duxiu, who was replaced by a new leadership group headed by Qu Qiubai, and new strategies were laid out for local leadership in those areas of Hubei, Hunan, Jiangxi, and Guangdong where the Party felt it still had viable power. The meeting produced a stunningly radical call for direct seizure of political power in the localities, via a linked series of uprisings (*baodong*) envisioned as establishing, once and for all, "mass democracy" throughout the region. Local peasant associations were to reorganize themselves into hardened military units for this purpose, and all opposing local militias were to be "smashed." The property of all large and middle landlords, and all lineage and temple land, were to be seized and redistributed. The entire class of "local bullies and evil gentry" and "counterrevolutionary elements" was to be "liquidated" (*suqing*) at one stroke.[63] In essence, in response to the heinous violence of Xia Douyin and his allies, the newly autonomous Communist Party proposed a bloody vendetta of its own.

Guided by this "Spirit of August 7," the Hubei Provincial Communist Party held its own meeting a week later, calling for armed local uprisings throughout the province and the violent extermination (*baodong shajin*) of all class enemies. Six counties were specifically targeted for "autumn harvest uprisings" (*qiushou baodong*)—three of them were Macheng and its neighbors Huang'an and Luotian—to be conducted initially at the village level by newly militarized peasant armies. In mid-September, at the Chengmagang headquarters-in-exile of the Macheng Communist Party, this "Spirit of August 7" was in turn loudly proclaimed at a meeting and rally led by Cai Jihuang, Liu Wenwei, and Wang Shusheng, and the details were laid out for village-level uprisings to be conducted over the next few weeks. On September 26, by prearrangement, these young activists fanned out throughout the county, by boat and on horseback, mobilizing local sympathizers into action. The actions they orchestrated began the next day, under the unambiguous slogan "Kill the bullies and divide their land." Even the most sympathetic sources indicate that they were, across the board, savagely violent.[64]

Nowhere were they more so than in Chengmagang Township itself. Deep in the Dabie Shan mountain range, and only marginally productive in the best of times, this highly militarized area had been the scene of the most feverish peasant association activity since the outbreak of the Nationalist Revolution, and of the most brutal reprisals by Xia Douyin and his Red Spears allies. During the summer, Xia had conducted a scorched-earth counterinsurgency campaign in Chengmagang, forthrightly ordering his troops to kill all, raze all houses, and slaughter all livestock. When the "reorganized" Wuhan government suddenly—and shockingly (to local organizers)—ordered the cessation of all peasant association activities, the county government put the same Red Spears units in charge of enforcement of the new policies in Chengmagang. But when the government at the same time ordered the imposition of its promised 25 percent rent reduction, landholders in the northeast refused to comply and demanded autumn harvest rent payments as usual. (As Nationalist magistrate

Liu Gang complained, these Chengmagang "gentry" were a major obstacle to his anti-Communist campaigns in Macheng; by comparison to the elites of the county's urban core, they were old-style, narrowly self-interested, and impervious to appeals to the public good.[65]) This action seems to have been the final irritant that ignited a bloody wave of murders of landlords throughout the area, with the result that much of the township elite fled either to Wuhan or to the sanctuary offered by bandit gangs in the mountains.[66]

Between late September and early November, Chengmagang Township and the adjacent township of Qiliping, across the border in Huang'an, witnessed a ferociously bloody civil war between peasant association and Red Spears units, both of which linked up from below into ever-larger armed forces. By late October, it was estimated that *nonghui* militia members in Chengmagang itself numbered more than 20,000, with another 10,000 in Qiliping.[67] The Chengmagang forces were in possession of around eighty automatic weapons (*kuaiqiang*), but their more common armaments were swords and spears. These, we are told, were calculatedly produced to be somewhat longer than the short pikes favored by the Red Spears and allowed peasant association fighters to hack their enemies to death with some sense of impunity. This they did to more than a thousand Red Spears fighters in a few short encounters alone. As the Communist Party county committee reported at the time, their battle cry was a simple "Kill! Kill! Kill!" Village-level peasant associations competed over which of them could slaughter larger numbers of their foes.

But if the carnage along the Macheng-Huang'an border had by early November been largely "spontaneous," at least as perceived by Communist Party higher-ups, it presented them with an enticing opportunity to take the action a step further in a centrally directed way. Observing that the major Nationalist armies were embroiled in an internecine power struggle in central China, the Hubei Provincial Communist Party determined that the time was ripe for a major offensive.[68] A team of four veteran military officers was sent down by the Party to Chengmagang, where it established the Edong tewei (Eastern Hubei Special Committee) to plan the assault. Cai Jihuang was made a committee member, and Liu Wenwei, Wang Shusheng, and other local activists were dispatched throughout the border area to reorganize local peasant associations into more regimented commando units (*yiyong dui*) in preparation for the offensive.[69] The inspiration for the celebrated Huang-Ma Uprising, which would prove the last campaign for so many of Macheng's radical youth, came, in other words, from outside and above.

Most of Macheng's young Communists—in the midst of a rapidly deteriorating situation nationally, and, in their home county, facing an intensification of the White Terror at the hands of the Nationalists—threw themselves into a plan to cross over from Chengmagang into northern Huang'an, hook up with

Communist units there, and wrest political control of that county. Identified by crimson belts around their waist, they marched first on the walled Dabie Shan market town of Qiliping. On November 10, a commando unit armed with automatic weapons overran a small Nationalist gun emplacement outside the town. The commandos systematically torched the sprawling Longtan Temple—the largest corporate landholder in the area, but largely abandoned as the rebels approached—and occupied Qiliping itself. In town, they liquidated (*suqing*) all the "counterrevolutionaries" who had been bold enough to remain. Hearing of this, Nationalist Thirtieth Army forces charged with defending the Huang'an county seat prudently withdrew from their posts. On the night of November 13, some 20,000 Communist militia members marched south from Qiliping to Huang'an and entered the city at dawn with only token resistance; only one member of the attacking force died in the assault. For a while the insurgents braced for a counterattack, but, surprisingly, none came. That day they publicly executed Magistrate He Shouzhong and his chief of police, set fire to the county government offices, and arrested a few of the larger merchants but otherwise sought to keep the urban population calm.[70]

Over the next few days, the rebels busied themselves in setting up a revolutionary government in Huang'an—what Gregor Benton has called, in effect, the first "soviet" in central China.[71] The regime was conceived as more than simply countywide in scope; twenty-one of the Macheng Peasant Association leaders already present, for example, were designated delegates in the new government, and representatives from other eastern Hubei counties also participated. The leadership declared an eight-hour workday, set down regulations for continuing the land revolution, and reaffirmed its opposition to "imperialism." The disparate military units of the victors were reorganized into the Eastern Hubei Workers' and Peasants' Revolutionary Army, with Wang Shusheng made commander of its Second Regiment. On November 18, a 10,000-strong mass meeting was convened, at which a peasant government was formally declared, with a nine-member governing committee chaired by Cao Xuekai and including Macheng's Cai Jihuang. A succession of speakers affirmed the strategy of *baodong*—violent uprisings to seize local power—as appropriate in the current situation, thanked the Party central committee for its support, cautioned of the need to follow central directives (all governing-committee members were Party members as well), and pledged to continue the campaign of wholesale assassination of major local landholders. To underscore this point, several such individuals were ritually executed on the spot. Public killings of this sort were officially endorsed by the peasant government as an instrument of *shiwei* (intimidationist display).[72]

By late November, the new regime reckoned that it had consolidated its control of Huang'an City sufficiently to fulfill its larger goal of toppling the increasingly rightist Wuhan government. It launched a "southern expedition" for this purpose, linking up with local peasant associations along the way. Communist reports themselves concede that it was an exceptionally savage campaign. Red Spear units dominated much of the southern Huang'an countryside and usually fought to the death. The rebel forces forayed into neighboring Huanggang, where they plundered the estate of former Hubei military governor Xiao Yaonan. They held a mass rally in the southern Huang'an market town of Baliwan, where they celebrated their victories by publicly executing most of the town's elite and burning down their homes. A number of the more renowned landholders of the area were dragged back in chains to the county seat, where they were decapitated, and their heads were displayed atop the city gates.[73]

As Communist strategists had hoped, the audacious Huang-Ma offensive had taken the Guomindang authorities very much by surprise. What had not been predicted, however, was the speed and overwhelming force with which the Nationalist government, seemingly paralyzed by internal divisions, might respond. By late November, large numbers of Red Spears volunteers had been mobilized to enter Huang'an from the north, from across the Dabie Shan in Henan's Guangshan County. These were joined by regular troops dispatched northward from Wuhan and, in early December, by Nationalist troops sent in from the east, from Songbu City, the southwestern Macheng riverport that constituted the strongest base of anticommunist authority in that county. The fighting was exceptionally bloody, with very high casualties on both sides. Ultimately, on December 5, the Nationalists dislodged the peasant government—only twenty-one days after its creation—from Huang'an City. In the fever of the "southern expedition," the city had been left in the hands of only about seventy-five defenders (including a fifteen-man team of machine gunners from Macheng), and it was lost as easily as it had been gained. Within weeks, the Nationalists had driven the soviet's last personnel out of Huang'an County altogether. The Huang-Ma Uprising phase of local revolutionary history was over.[74]

A number of the peasant government leaders crossed into Huangpi County's Mulan Mountains and hid out successfully. Macheng's own Xu Ziqing escaped across the Dabie Shan into Shangcheng, continuing his organizational activities in Henan.[75] But most of the radicals were not so fortunate. Over the course of December and into the following spring, victorious Guomindang forces conducted a highly successful dragnet in Huang'an and Macheng Counties for participants in the November rising, a campaign characterized by local historians as a bloodbath (*xuexi*) and the absolute low point of revolutionary history in the region.[76] A very large portion of the remarkable cohort of Macheng County's "progressive" youth, so patiently recruited and trained by Dong Biwu and Wang Youan over the early 1920s, met violent ends in the immediate aftermath of the Huang-Ma adventure. Wang Youan himself returned to his native Chengmagang after the fall of Huang'an and continued leading a Peasant Self-Defense Army unit until the unit, betrayed by a spy, was ambushed by a rightist militia; dragged to Songbu, Wang was executed by the riverbank on February 17, 1928, while, it was reported, loudly singing the "Internationale." The Songbu-born revolutionary "intellectual" Cai Jihuang and the militant farmboy Liu Wenwei fell back to Shunheji, where they were betrayed by villagers to a rightist *mintuan* leader, and captured and executed on December 7, 1927; Cai was twenty-two; Liu, a mere twenty-one. Others of the same age who were tracked down and eliminated by *qingxiang tuan* ("clear the countryside" units) included Deng Tianwen, Wang Mianjin, Liu Xiangming, and Feng Shugong.[77]

The local Party committee reported on December 14 that the outcome of the Huang-Ma adventure triumphantly vindicated the center's strategy of *baodong*-style armed uprisings in the Dabie Shan, and the uprising is depicted today in local and Party histories as a great victory, due in large measure to behind-the-scenes direction by "central committee member Mao Zedong."[78] But Wang Shusheng, probably the most prominent of Macheng's "progressive" youth who survived the debacle, knew better. In his oral history, recorded by Zhang Guotao a few years later, Wang conceded, in hindsight, that the disastrous slaughter of partisans that followed was directly attributable to the disorganization, inexperience, and total lack of discipline demonstrated by the rebellion's leaders. Zhang Guotao himself added that it was only complete ignorance of conditions on the ground that had prompted the center (now discredited, to be sure) to order such suicidal folly in the first place. Zhang, curiously echoing the "reorganized" Wuhan government's allegations of immaturity on the part of peasant activists, concluded that the Huang-Ma Uprising and the events leading up to it had been from the outset "tantamount to indulging in child's play."[79]

CHAPTER TWELVE

Extermination Redux

REN YINGQI WAS one of those shadowy and thoroughly unpleasant individuals who seem so heavily to populate the history of Republican China. He hailed from Lushan County, in mountainous western Henan; his year of birth is unrecorded. Ren's biographer notes delicately that his background was in the greenwood (*lulin chushen*)—that is to say, he was a bandit. For whatever reason, very likely because he was fleeing from the law, he turned up in 1924 in Nationalist Canton, as commander of the Second Henanese Mixed Brigade. Two years later, he was back in Henan, serving as a division commander under Wu Peifu, only to defect again to the Nationalists on September 12, 1926, as his superior's position in central China crumbled at the approach of the United Front Northern Expedition. He was rewarded with a promotion to commanding general of the Twelfth Army of the National Revolutionary Army. In August of the following year, he entered Macheng.[1]

Xia Douyin had vacated the area in mid-July, after conducting rightist scorched-earth campaigns there for nearly two months. It may seem that Xia's and Ren's occupations of the county were of a piece. Both men were commanders of their own personal armies; both were at the time claiming to act as agents of the Nationalist government declared by Jiang Jieshi at Nanjing the preceding April; and both announced their overriding intent in Macheng to be that of conducting a thorough anti-leftist *qingdang* (Party purge). And yet the references to Ren Yingqi in the county gazetteer financed and directed by Xia Douyin some eight years later are uniformly scathing, no less so than those in the gazetteers produced under Communist rule in the People's Republic. There were very fundamental differences between the two Nationalist generals. Xia was a deeply chauvinistic Macheng native son, and Ren was an outsider. Ren's origins were in banditry, while Xia, though the product of an equally martial highland culture, had descended from many generations of bandit-suppressing local strongmen. And Xia's activities during his occupation, horrifically brutal as they were, were clearly and consistently ideologically driven. Ren Yingqi, by contrast, was manifestly an opportunist and used his ostensible mission of political rectification to go after any object of plunder that presented itself. Unsurprisingly, then, his most effective opponents in Macheng were none other than Xia Douyin's closest allies.

Sweeping into Macheng in August, Ren immediately deposed the incumbent magistrate and replaced him with one of his own Henanese henchmen. He quickly rounded up and slaughtered more than 600 peasant association activists and instituted a reign of terror in the villages. At the same time, however, he extorted, under threat of violence, huge sums of money from urban shopkeepers and from the *chengxiang shenfu* (gentry and wealthy of both town and countryside) and seized the assets of Macheng's few viable industrial enterprises, in most cases ending their operations forever.[2]

Ren Yingqi's troops were concentrated in the most developed, western portions of Macheng, the county seat and the Ju River Valley, but his sway extended over the entire county with the exception of its eastern highlands.[3] Resistance to Ren in that sector was led by the Dongshan strongman Zheng Jiankui, who, as we have seen, had been the county's most effective militia leader and local protector since the arrival of the National Revolutionary Army at Wuhan the year before. In hopes of crushing Zheng, Ren struck deals with a motley array of local bandit gangs in Luotian, Huanggang, and other "greenwood" havens throughout the broader Dongshan region. As a result of their intrusion and Zheng's stubborn defense of his turf, over the course of late 1927 and early 1928—the same period when the Huang-Ma Uprising was devastating northwestern Macheng—much of the county's eastern regions were effectively reduced to rubble.

An Interval of Home Rule

In late October of 1927, yet another military force swept into the county from the south, in the form of the Nineteenth National Revolutionary Army, Third Division, commanded by Zheng Zhong (1896–1950). A native of Macheng's north central Futianhe Township, in the heart of the Dabie Shan highlands (and thus apparently not related to Muzidian Township's Zheng Jiankui), Zheng Zhong had been a classmate of Xia Douyin at the Baoding Military Academy; over the course of the following decade, he would become Xia's right-hand man and the overwhelmingly dominant civil and military presence in Macheng County.[4] For the moment, he contented himself with occupying Baiguo Town—the "gateway to the Dongshan" (and, two and a half centuries earlier, Yu Chenglong's staging ground for his suppression of the Dongshan

Rebellion). From there he sought to drive Ren Yingqi, his fellow Nationalist, out of his native county. In January 1928, the merchants of the Macheng Local Origin Club at Wuhan subscribed funds to send additional mercenaries to aid the two Zhengs in this project, and in March the Nanjing government itself disavowed Ren and committed more of its troops to his defeat. In a major battle on March 19, Zheng Zhong succeeded in retaking the county seat, and in April he also retook Songbu and other Ju River market towns. Ren Yingqi hung on in the county until May and then slipped back across the Dabie Shan into Henan. With Ren gone and the Communists barely surviving after their Huang-Ma debacle, Zheng Zhong and Zheng Jiankui together exercised near-complete dominance of their native county. They took the occasion to install a native-born magistrate, Han Xuehai, and for a short time a nearly fully autonomous home rule prevailed in Macheng.

Zheng Jiankui, as we have seen, had up to this time presented a studied neutrality in the conflict between left and right. At the time of the Macheng Atrocity and its retaliatory aftermath, Zheng had even appeared to be something of an ally of Macheng's peasant association activists; though offering sanctuary to the occasional "local bully" or "evil gentry," he had pointedly refrained from armed intervention on either side. Most frequently, as in the campaign against Ren Yingqi, he acted the ideologically neutral protector of his native place from outside predators. He would have, it turned out, one more opportunity to play this role, in the winter of 1928–29. In December, a force of some 40,000 renegade troops under the Beiyang militarist known as Old Man Li[5] poured into northeast Macheng through the Pine Nut Pass, established their headquarters at Sheng Family Fort, and once again ransacked the surrounding Dongshan highlands. Zheng Jiankui mobilized his militia to set up a thirty-mile-long defense perimeter, headquartered at his hometown of Muzidian, and over the course of the winter he conducted a dogged and bloody campaign to drive out the intruders. He succeeded, killing Old Man Li himself, in late January.[6]

With the county's borders secured for the moment, Zheng Jiankui was free to turn his attention to crushing domestic insurgency—turn it to, in Communist historiography, "betraying the revolution." He allowed his Peasant Self-Defense Army to be incorporated into the Nanjing regime's military structure and turned it from defense of the mountain passes in the northeast to suppression of Communists in the northwest; Dongshan, in effect, leveled its armed power against Chengmagang. Ultimately, in March 1930, Zheng Jiankui would be placed by Nanjing in charge of the Luotian-Macheng-Shangcheng Tri-County Defense Command and, shortly afterward, of the Eyuwan Border Region Communist Extermination Command. By the time of his death from illness, in 1935, he held the command of the Guomindang Third Route Army.[7]

Cleansing the Countryside

Zheng Jiankui's rise from apolitical village-level militia leader to high-ranking Nationalist general was indicative of the broader process in Macheng, over the late 1920s and early 1930s, of local militia units gradually coalescing into larger countywide paramilitary forces, merging in function and sometimes in formal command structure into Nationalist armies and shifting their focus from defense of the locality from bandits and renegade troops to the overriding task of *qingxiang* (cleansing the countryside) and *suqing* (liquidating) Communist sympathizers.

In May 1928, newly appointed Macheng magistrate Ye Kaiyan, a native of the eastern Hubei county of Daye, established a system of twelve ward-level "clear the countryside" defense corps (*qingxiang baowei tuan*) oriented exclusively to Communist extermination.[8] Zheng Jiankui was made commander of the First Ward Corps and charged with patrolling the county seat and its immediate environs. In the city itself, a Clear the Countryside Committee (*qingxiang weiyuanhui*) was set up to coordinate countywide search-and-destroy operations. The system was to be financed by a per-*mou* surtax on the land tax, and a new commercial tax was to be levied on urban shops, replacing the ad hoc system of contributions and subscriptions that had largely financed local militia units up to this point. Nevertheless, Ye's new arrangement remained largely decentralized: assessments and collections of the tax remained the responsibility of the twelve ward-level militia commanders, and actual levies varied widely from ward to ward, giving rise to bickering and politicking at the township level over the subsequent years.

The following year, an effort to further standardize the *qingxiang* militia and its financing came at the hands of Ye's successor, the Japanese-educated Echeng County (Hubei) native Lu Bangbian. Lu not only established a formal county-level General Militia Department (*zongtuan bu*) and instituted a regime of routinized military exercises under a full-time director of training but also bureaucratized the countywide militia command structure under the leadership of a single commander-in-chief: himself. Thereafter, command of the county's overall militia apparatus—appropriately renamed, in 1931, the "Eradicate the Communists Militia" (*changong tuan*)—remained officially a collateral responsibility of the Macheng magistrate.

This arrangement could not have better suited the temperament of the man who succeeded to the magistracy in 1932 and remained in that post up until the Japanese occupation: Zheng Zhong, the locally born Nationalist general and client of Xia Douyin. Zheng devoted his full energies to the cause of killing Communists. He streamlined the county's twelve-ward structure to the nine wards that still exist today, and he expanded the ward-level militia headquarters into more multifunctional township administrative offices. He recruited a graduate of the Japanese-directed Beijing Police Academy named Hu Guanglu, a Mianyang (Hubei) native who had briefly preceded Zheng as Macheng magistrate in 1931, to stay in the county as commander of a more offensive complement to the county's militia apparatus, a system of nine ward-level *dadui* (brigades) and twenty-five subordinate *zhongdui* (companies); Zheng Jiankui served as Hu's second in command. There were also two *tewudui* (special-assignment brigades)—effectively a county secret police—one headquartered at the county seat and the other, under Zheng Jiankui's kinsman Zheng Maoqian, at Dongshan's Muzidian. By the mid-1930s, the county's full-time military force numbered 1,007 men, armed with over 900 rifles.

The new military apparatus proved extremely costly, especially since adjacent ward-level commanders often exerted simultaneous claims to tax the same local area.[9] In 1932, despite merchants' protests that the county's declining commercial economy could not support it, Zheng Zhong raised the shop tax 50 percent, to an aggregate total of more than $10,000 (*yuan*) per year. The next year he raised the land tax surtax an additional 20 percent, three-fifths of the assessment to be borne by the landlord and (ironically, given the purposes to which the revenues were put) two-fifths by the tenant. Once all conceivable locally generated sources of income had been exhausted, Zheng turned to the Macheng Local Origin Club at Hankou, which had on occasion in the past shown its willingness to contribute for defense of the home county. At the magistrate's request, guild members set up an internal subscription-raising mechanism (*xiejinhui*), eventually contributing several tens of thousands of dollars to the cause of anti-Communist "bandit extermination" in their native place.

One ward-level militia organization about which information survives is that for the Seventh Ward, centered on the market town of Zhongguanyi. The power behind this militia was Lin Renfu (1892–1950), an eighteenth-generation descendant of a Fujianese *jinshi* who had come to Macheng as a Ming official in the fourteenth century, and whose lineage had totally dominated the cloth, tea, and herbal-medicines trade of Zhongguanyi since that time. His father had been a *juren* of 1903, and Renfu was educated at the Hubei Number One Middle School in Wuhan. By far the wealthiest man in the area, Lin became president of the Zhongguanyi Chamber of Commerce in 1915 and, when the Seventh Ward militia commander was assassinated by Communists in 1929, assumed that post as well. As the county's militia system became more finely differentiated throughout the 1930s, Lin, through alliances with other local strongmen, progressively extended his control over a proliferating network of martial law subdistricts. He was extraordinarily effective at building up local arms caches, constructing defense works, and capturing and executing leftists—by one count, about 220 of these. Communist sources depict Lin as a sadistic torture master. Among his favored means of doing away with his foes were said to be cutting out their hearts, poisoning them slowly with hot pepper juice, boiling them in chestnut oil, and piercing them with hundreds of bamboo nails. Much to his satisfaction, he was popularly known as the King of Hell (Yanwang).[10]

In striking (and intended) resonance with the policies enacted so successfully in Macheng by Yu Chenglong during the San-fan Rebellion and by Hu Linyi during the Taiping wars, Nationalist officials linked the militarization of local society to a resurrected system of *baojia* household registration.[11] In mid-1932, Jiang Jieshi himself toured eastern Hubei in the process of setting up the Eyuwan Bandit-Extermination General Command (see below) and concluded his tour by proclaiming on August 1 a new code of *baojia* regulations for the Dabie Shan region; it was this model that Jiang would extend, in November 1934, to the entire territory under control of his Nanjing government, including most especially that in the environs of the Jiangxi Soviet.[12] The regulations specified that a *huzhang* (househead) be recognized for each stove-sharing familial unit, a *jia*-headman for each ten households, and a *bao*-headman for each ten *jia*. The latter two posts would be served in annual rotation by headmen of the subordinate units they encompassed. At all three levels, the headmen were assigned responsibility not only for members' good conduct but also for meeting the unit's tax, corvée, and military conscription requirements.

Ultimately, the *bao* leaders (*baozhang*) were responsible to the ward administration, but there was a key intermediary unit known as the *bao*-headmen's linked management office (*baozhang lianhe bangongchu*, shortened in popular usage to *lianbaochu*); between fifteen and twenty-five of these were envisioned per ward. The *lianbaochu* was headed by a director (*lianbao zhuren*), who exercised wide-ranging military, police, and judicial powers over his constituency, the last of these with the assistance of *lianbao*-level tribunals known as *tiaojie weiyuanhui* (mediation committees); as routine reports to higher-level military commands make clear, however, the *lianbaochu*'s central task was to exterminate local Communists.[13] The enormously powerful post of *lianbao* director was initially specified to be filled through election by the constituent *baozhang*. Nevertheless, evidence from Lin Renfu's Seventh Ward at Zhongguanyi suggests that, on the ground, many or most *lianbao* headships in Macheng were simply occupied by lineage branch heads, and *lianbaochu* offices were frequently merely reconfigured lineage temples.[14]

Nationalist authorities themselves became quickly aware that *lianbao* directors and *baozhang* in Macheng County had become what a 1934 survey team described as "hopelessly alienated" from their constituencies.[15] On the one hand, there was the growing, massive unpopularity of their duties. In addition to their role in collecting the increasingly onerous tax assessments and in making the proliferating and widely reviled corvée assignments for public works, probably the headmen's most detested function was in the area of military conscription. With the growing formal Nationalist military presence in the county, over 3,000 local residents were said to be pressed into service as military *yunmin* (bearers) *every day*, a task that the population universally sought to evade.[16] Then, in 1933, Nanjing promulgated a conscription law (*bingyi fa*) compelling all males between the ages of eighteen and forty-five to serve in the Nationalist Army and made *baozhang* and *lianbao* squarely responsible for meeting draft quotas; local resistance in Macheng prevented any effective implementation of this at all until 1937, and the county never really came close to meeting its annual quota of draftees until well into the anti-Japanese resistance era, in 1942.[17]

On the other hand, the quality of *baojia* personnel rapidly fell, as the most potentially effective indigenous elites either fled to Wuhan to avoid assassination by the Communists or sought to avoid headman service because of the damage it would cause their reputations. As Prasenjit Duara has demonstrated in detail for North China, the increasingly malodorous tasks of local leadership drove out local elites—who, bullies though they might have been, enjoyed at least some semblance of local cultural legitimacy and acted, at least in part, as brokers in the defense of local interests vis-à-vis outside predators—and replaced them with a class of rank opportunists.[18] The 1934 provincial survey team in effect acknowledged as much, complaining that most incumbents of even the relatively high-ranking *lianbao* post in Macheng were illiterate and unable to keep the most simple account books—a major liability in the eyes of a regime increasingly enamored of statistical intelligence about its population.[19] Intense dissatisfaction with incumbents' performance, in Macheng as in other areas of the Nationalist regime's domain, eventually led the regime to bureaucratize their selection. Each ward had its own training school for lower-level *baojia* functionaries, who, to judge by their uniformed ranks in a graduation photograph from the Fourth Ward school, were effectively local policemen.[20] By the mid-1930s, the eastern Hubei *baojia* regulations were amended to have higher-level *lianbao* headmen appointed directly by the province and undergo standardized instruction at the *xiangzheng renyuan xunliansuo* (Rural Administration Personnel Training Institute) in Wuhan.[21] The key element—co-optation of *existing* local strongmen, which had facilitated the success of Hu Linyi's mid-nineteenth-century *baojia* regimentation in Macheng, and still more that of Yu Chenglong in the late seventeenth century—thus eluded Nationalist authorities in the 1930s.

In one key respect, however, Nationalist *baojia* efforts in fact brought to a logical climax one cardinal element of both Yu's and Hu's programs of the Qing era: that of linking household registration, local militia mobilization, and cultural indoctrination. In Nationalist Macheng, under the guidance of Magistrate Zheng Zhong, this came to be known as "social militarization" (*shehui junshi*). In 1935, the county affixed a new militia command system (*zhuangding dui*) to its newly revivified *baojia* system. There were 1,128 *xiaodui* (teams) headed by *bao* headmen, under 265 *liandui* (linked teams) commanded by the *lianbao* directors, under nine *kuidui* (ward brigades) led by ward administrators, all under the *dadui* (battalion) commanded by Magistrate Zheng himself. Every able-bodied young man in the county was required to serve at least three months' duty, and at any given time there were about 60,000 men enrolled. Zheng also assumed the new post of Director of Social Military Training and Instruction (*shehui junshi xunlian jiaoguan*) for the county, and commanders at each level were charged with intensively indoctrinating their troops in patriotism and moral conduct.[22] To be sure, militia organization had been a prominent feature of Macheng society for centuries, and in times of stress, such as the Ming-Qing transition and the Taiping Rebellion, it had assumed a major role in shaping social organization more generally. But now, in the late 1930s, it had finally seized its seemingly destined place as the basic instrument of cultural production among the county's population.

The "New Life" in Macheng

"Social militarization" was a centerpiece of the larger Nationalist campaign to fundamentally refashion Macheng culture—and win the hearts and minds of the people in the war against Communism—under the general rubric of the New Life Movement (*xin shenghuo yundong*). As Steven Averill long ago argued, based on study of comparable highland areas in Jiangxi, as much as the New Life Movement may appear an anachronistic comic opera to Western observers, to its promoters on the ground it was deadly serious business.[23] Clearly, nowhere was it more serious than in Nationalist Macheng, which had been such a hotbed of agrarian radicalism and was even now witnessing a consolidation of soviet power in the Dabie Shan.

Over the early 1930s, the Nationalist Party in Macheng had imposed a series of organizational reforms and "ideological correctness" campaigns that clearly reflected the Party's Leninist roots. In October 1930, the provincial Party office sent down to the county the three-man Party Rectification Committee, which purged the existing authorities, with their suspected residual loyalties to Wang Jingwei's Wuhan regime, and set up in their place the new Provisional Party Committee. The local representative on the Party Rectification Committee was one Qu Fangcheng (1906–51), a twenty-four-year-old native of Zhangjiafan Ward in the southern Dongshan and a recent graduate of Wuhan's First Provincial National Learning Academy (Guoxueguan)—the font of right-wing

Guomindang ideological correctness in Hubei.[24] In January 1933 the Provisional Committee was again reorganized into the County Party Committee. Now Qu Fangcheng was granted the formal title of *ganshi* (director), a term favored by the Nationalists to denote a local organizational head with especially close ties and reporting responsibilities to the Party center. Over the next few years, Qu's jurisdiction as *ganshi* gradually expanded to Party leadership in the broader Dongshan-centered three-county region of Macheng, Luotian, and Yingshan. During the same period, Macheng's various mass organizations—its workers' association, its women's association, its teachers' association, its merchants' association, and above all its peasant associations—were also reorganized, some of them repeatedly, to bring their agendas and activities more closely in line with Nationalist Party goals. Their existing leadership structure, based on internally selected headmen (*huizhang*), was replaced by that of *ganshi*, Party members appointed by and responsive to Qu's local Guomindang apparatus. Macheng's cadre of Nationalist Party members, numbering 247 persons as of 1935, thus increasingly solidified its collective control over the county's society and politics.[25]

Adhering to Jiang Jieshi's dictum that suppression of Communism was a process 70 percent political and only 30 percent military, local Nationalist agents launched a multifront campaign of ideological warfare. Party head Qu Fangcheng assumed the collateral title of political commissar of elementary education in the eastern Hubei region. A new infrastructure of Party-run schools was implanted on the Macheng landscape. Local Party newspapers were founded, and a network of mass reading rooms was set up to ensure that as many local people as possible read (or heard read to them) the good word. Following the example of Communist activists just a few years earlier, Nationalist agents strove to assert hegemony over traditional festival celebrations, turning them to contemporary political ends, and to restructure the annual festival calendar to highlight "national days" and other politically inspired ritual performances. The Anti-Communist Propaganda Corps was set up in Macheng in 1931 to coordinate these new campaigns. The Rural Revival Work Training School was also set up, relying both on appeals to personal moral example (*geren daode*) and to newfangled social-science methodologies (statistical analysis, use of pie charts, and so on) to teach its several hundred trainees how to regenerate the countryside and hence exterminate the Communists.[26] Eventually all of this activity was subsumed under the blanket control of the New Life Movement Promotion Association, established locally in March 1934, with Zheng Zhong (county magistrate and militia commander) and Qu Fangcheng (Party head) as its co-directors.

In Macheng, at least, the New Life Movement grew less out of optimism at the bright future Nationalist rule might offer than out of a deep recognition on the part of Guomindang authorities of the desperate current situation. The 1934 Hubei Province county-by-county survey already cited, undertaken in tandem with the formation of the New Life agenda, yielded an extraordinarily bleak picture of contemporary Macheng's economy, society, and culture—a picture every bit as bleak as one their Communist foes might have painted, but with a radically different set of solutions. It begins with a narrative of the county's proud history of passionate heroism (*kangkai*) and fearsome rectitude (*jijie*). Under Mei Zhihuan in the late Ming, and under Yu Yaxiang in the Taiping era, local braves (*xiangyong*) from Macheng had not only rallied to loyalist causes at home but also spilled forth from county borders to quell fanatical rebel movements in the wider region. As recently as 1928 (the unstated reference is to Xia Douyin) they had done the same, doing their ancestors proud. Now, however, this local animating spirit (*tuqi*) had become exhausted. The heirs to Macheng's proud tradition of local leadership had turned pessimistic and negative (*xiaoji*), no longer daring to shoulder responsibility (*bugan fuze*). Both the material condition of the county (*jianshe*) and the enterprising spirit of its population (*shiye*) had fallen into decadence (*luohou*). The great elite lineages of Macheng (*haoshen dazu*), their backs broken by decades of predatory exactions, no longer took to heart the public interest (*bugong*). Ordinary people (*xiaomin*) could not make ends meet. Under these conditions, the self-sacrificing spirit of transcendent local identity (*difang xinyang*) had been lost, replaced by a disastrously divisive rural-urban gap (*chengxiang zhenyu zhi jian*) and an antisocial individualism (*gerenzhuyi*) on the part of the young. The cure for Macheng's manifest cultural despair, in the New Life view, could come only from the top: the gentry class (*shishen jieji*), aggressively led by a cadre of inspired local officials, had to recapture the virtue (*daode*) it had so abundantly displayed in the county's past.[27]

The éminence grise behind the Macheng report in this 1934 provincial survey was none other than the county's most eminent native son, Xia Douyin himself, who in 1933 had become "chairman" of Hubei Province and, the following year, had left that post to assume command of the larger anti-Communist extermination force in the Middle Yangzi provinces (see below). Xia's presence was even more pervasive in the recompiled Macheng County gazetteer of 1935, which Xia, along with his client, Magistrate Zheng Zhong, largely financed.[28] If the 1934 survey offered a critique and an agenda of required New Life remedies, the gazetteer of the following year was more a celebration of what had already been achieved in such a short time. This achievement is certified by a preface contributed by no less an authority than Meng Guangpeng—the very man who had compiled the Hubei provincial survey the year before.[29]

The 1935 gazetteer is a remarkable document. It is a wealth of information and as such has been a major source for this book. But it is also a monument to the Nationalist Party's single moment of triumph in Macheng County, and to its vision of what a progressive and enlightened, albeit peripheral, county ought to look like. The chief editor was Yu Jinfang (1861–1938), a septuagenarian native of Baiguo popularly known as Affectionate Old Grandpa (*chunhui laoren*). Yu had been one of the county's last and proudest civil service examination successes, receiving his *jinshi* in 1894 and the honor of posting to the Hanlin Academy. As an expert in financial administration, he had served the Qing on the board of revenue, as county magistrate in Guangzhou and Guizhou, and as provincial treasurer of Yunnan. In the wake of the 1911 Revolution, while a member of the Hubei Provincial Assembly, he had been called to Beijing by Yuan Shikai to aid in the process of Qing abdication. Subsequently he had returned to his native county, where he served in a variety of senior managerial posts in the county hospital, local schools, and the office of entrepreneurial development. He had published both an elementary medical textbook and a collection of poetry.[30]

The gazetteer as a whole, but most especially the prefaces by Yu Jinfang, Meng Guangpeng, and magistrate Zheng Zhong, spells out an agenda for instructing and civilizing (*jiaohua*) the Macheng population that both relies on a particular reading of local history and exhibits a striking resonance with the moral dictates of those figures in that history whom the Nationalist intellectuals find most to their taste. Meng, the Henanese, begins by noting the obvious strategic centrality of Macheng at times of national crisis. Hu Linyi saw this, Meng says, and constructed forts and mobilized militias to defend this critical locality. But Hu also understood the deeper necessity for *jiaohua* as a strategy of defense. Macheng people, fortunately, are by nature upright, according to Meng, who invites the reader to recall, for instance, how they tossed out Li Zhi when he espoused his heterodox theories in the county. But some time later the influence of Li's pernicious teachings inspired a host of *jianmin* (traitorous people) who defamed the Sage and the Way, and these people then had to be subdued. Again in the Northern Expedition, a glorious victory for civilization was threatened by the heterodox thieves and plunderers who sprang up in Macheng in the expedition's wake. Thank heaven, Meng says, that honorable gentlemen such as Xia Douyin and Zheng Zhong once again arrived to vanquish the deviants. The moral, for Meng Guangpeng, is clear: there will always be rebellion (*bian*) and disorder (*luan*), especially in this vulnerable locality, but there is also a constant way to deal with it: tighter ideological control. That is, Meng says, solicitous attention must be paid to rectifying popular mentality (*renxin*) and customs (*fengsu*). Above all, Meng recommends stress on the Four Cardinal Virtues (*siwei*): ritual propriety (*li*), upright conduct (*yi*), humility (*lian*), and shame (*chi*).[31] As for Magistrate Zheng, he notes that his basic purpose in convening the county's venerable scholars to recompile the gazetteer is to illuminate the virtues of loyalty and righteousness (*zhongyi*), filiality and partisanship (*xiaoyou*), and fidelity and self-sacrifice (*jielie*). It is the duty of these elites, Zheng says, to promote civilization (*xuanhua*) and instruct and supervise (*jiaodu*) their social inferiors.[32] The venerable Yu Jinfang, in turn, offers his own sage advice on how such moral values should be promoted. The necessary first step, he writes, is to enforce strict and respectful adherence (*zunshi*) to the Confucian family rituals (*sili*)—the underpinning, that is, of lineage control. Historically in the county, Yu observes, every time deviant Daoist or Buddhist practices crept into these performances (the clear unstated reference is to Li Zhi) social breakdown followed shortly thereafter. And the most important aspect of ritual correctness, he says, is that the manner of the ritual performance should conform to the celebrant's social station (*shisu geru qifen*); the very essence of ritual correctness is deference.[33] All in all, the 1935 gazetteer, produced in the immediate wake of local class revolution by a group of men with Western-style educations but a New Life social agenda, displays a remarkable continuity with the discourse of hierarchy enunciated by the county's most conservative culture heroes of the past.[34]

Guerrilla War and the Emergence of Eyuwan

The hopeful agenda laid out by New Life campaigners, heartfelt though it might have been, seems terribly out of touch with the reality of life on the ground in Macheng and the Dabie Shan during the Nationalist decade. In no place in China, it would seem, was civil war more pervasive, continuous, and devastating than in this strategic highland region. After the debacle of the Huang-Ma Uprising of late 1927 and the highly effective Nationalist White Terror that followed, Macheng's underground Communist leadership launched what they termed a guerrilla war (*youji zhanzheng*), a war that never really ended until 1949 but that was at its most pitched in the years around 1930. Over the winter of 1928–29, the Communists concentrated on assassinations of ward-level functionaries (their biggest kill being Huang'an County public security bureau chief Cao the Butcher).[35] Then, in March, the Nationalist military situation in the eastern Hubei region suddenly deteriorated as war broke out between Jiang Jieshi and the Guangxi clique at the same time as a maverick Nationalist officer named Xia Fengshi began an insurrection in Macheng itself. Granted this opportunity, a newly formed Red Army (*hongjun*) division in southern Henan forayed across the mountains and, linking up with village-level Red Guards units (*chiweidui*) on the Macheng side, over the summer fought to consolidate control of a forty-mile swath of borderland stretching west from the Pine Nut Pass. They targeted (murderously) the dozen or so largest landholding lineages of the area and began the process of land redistribution. A report of Macheng magistrate Liu Gang from June of that year expresses frustration at just how successful this Communist strategy of selected terrorist assassinations was in demonstrating their power to the local populace, and at how easily the assassins could disappear like rabbits into their holes after their work was done.[36] In August, however, Xia Douyin was placed in personal command of the Nationalist Thirteenth Division at Macheng City, and over the fall he won back much of the territory that the Red Army had gained, in the process exterminating several thousand Communist sympathizers. Thousands of other local residents were massacred during this campaign—a rather minor and inconclusive one, as it turned out—and over 6,000 farmhouses were razed.[37]

The year 1929 was also marked by two significant, related events in Communist history, the ascendancy of the "Li Lisan line" and the formation of local soviets. Both had major impacts on Macheng County. In the spring, Moscow appointed the Hunanese labor organizer Li Lisan (1899–1967) chair of the Chinese Communist Party, and Li remained in that post until his purge in September of the following year. Locally in Macheng, as nationally, Li's line was associated with adventurous seizures of power and expansionist military campaigns. In the summer of 1929, Li's overriding goal was to capture Wuhan and other major central China cities such as Jiujiang, Changsha, and Nanchang. Occupying the county seats of Macheng and Huang'an was seen as a step toward this end, and rural organization in those counties was accordingly subordinated to this larger purpose. That is, the countryside received little of the Party's available financial and military resources (which were diverted to urban organization) while at the same time land confiscations and attacks on village elites were stepped up, largely in order to extract food supplies from the already strained rural economy to underwrite projected risings in the cities. One result in Macheng was growing rural disaffection with the Communist cause.[38]

The chief implementer of the Li Lisan line in Macheng was an ambitious Chengmagang farm boy named Wang Hongxue. Wang (1899–1932) came from a ruined landlord family and was among the first generation of revolutionary youth in Macheng to have been recruited from the county's schools by Wang Youan. He joined the Party in 1927 and led a team of arsonists (*huogongdui*) during the terrorist campaigns in his native area the next year; he then played a minor role in November's Huang-Ma Uprising, emerging as one of its few survivors. At this point, he began his real rise to prominence. In March 1929, with local rural leadership decimated by the Huang-Ma debacle, Wang formed a new peasant committee (*nongmin weiyuanhui*) in his native township; membership was limited to those who could provide two guarantors, and able-bodied members were also expected to serve in the committee's military arm, a "Red Guards" unit. Wang's organization was unusually radical in its attacks on landholders and in its confiscation of property. With Li Lisan's formal installation as Party chairman in June, Wang was tapped to expand his peasant committee to all of Macheng, and three months later he was also handed the post of county Party secretary.[39]

The parallel developments in Communist strategy during this era were the gradual turn from guerrilla to positional warfare, and the attempt to govern territory (in large part for fiscal extraction to fund adventures elsewhere) through the instrument of "Soviets." Macheng and its environs saw several of these, of varying scales. Though most were in peripheral areas of the northern highlands, there were also some in the urban core. Taking advantage of Guomindang infighting in the spring of 1929, for example, local Communists boldly set up the "Zhongguanyi-Songbu Border Area Working Committee" (*Zhong-Song bianqu gongzuo weiyuanhui*) in the county's most commercialized, and most securely Nationalist-controlled, southwestern quadrant. The following year, a Party professional was sent down to organize a fiscal-administrative structure for the area, and the Zhongguanyi-Songbu Border Area Working Committee was renamed the "Zhong-Song Border Area Soviet." A statue of Lenin was proudly erected at the soviet's headquarters in the market town of Xiyang. Its commando teams (*youjidui*) undertook terrorist assassinations in Songbu, while its Red Guard units launched an intensified wave of land seizures and "struggle sessions" against the area's suburban landholders, the wealthiest in all Macheng. The Zhong-Song Soviet survived until September 1932, when it was betrayed by one of its leaders and its headquarters was overcome by the dreaded secret police of the King of Hell, Lin Renfu. The remaining leaders fled to the county's northern highlands, only to be captured and executed almost immediately.[40]

Much larger, more enduring, and critically important in the broader history of the Chinese civil war was what became known as the "Eyuwan Soviet," in the Dabie Shan. Eyuwan occupied a several-hundred-square-mile swath of hardscrabble hillside in northern Macheng and Huang'an Counties, with adjacent portions of Henan's Shangcheng and Guangshan and Anhui's Jinzhai. At its height, the soviet governed a population of some 3.5 million—over 1 million more than its famous counterpart to the south in Jiangxi.[41]

The site of Eyuwan had been known for centuries as a refuge of bandits and splinter groups of rebels,[42] and there was more than a touch of the greenwood in both the cultural style and the patterns of association of early Communist leaders in these mountains. They relied on the goodwill of preexisting bandit gangs in the area in order to survive, struck ad hoc alliances with some of them, and, in the view of many, behaved much like social bandits themselves—sweeping into a locality, knocking off a few class enemies, and expropriating their stocks of food for their own livelihood.[43] One of the most venerable and adaptable of Party activists in the area, Chengmagang's Wang Shusheng, recounted in his oral history that he found himself at one point in 1929 running for his life through the greenwood among a group of eighteen men, half of whom were Party comrades and the other half traditional bandits. One night, the bandits decided that the Communists—inviting, as they did, intensified government pursuit—were no longer useful allies. They demanded all of the group's arms and food supplies in exchange for allowing the others to live, and they disappeared into the woods.[44]

The organizational history of what became known as the Eyuwan Soviet was chaotic, dictated by local and factional identities, by repeated efforts at centralizing reorganization (*gaizao*), and above all by conditions on the battlefield. Greatly simplified, a special committee to control Red areas in Chengmagang was renamed a soviet by Wang Shusheng in March 1929. It collapsed in September but was succeeded by, variously, the Macheng County Soviet Government under Wang Hongxue, the Edong (Eastern Hubei) Special Committee, the Eyu (Hubei-Henan) Border Special Committee, the Eyuwan (Hubei-Henan-Anhui) Border Region Government, and finally, under orders from Li Lisan's Party central, the Eyuwan Soviet in March 1930. Although Wang Shusheng, Wang Hongxue, and other local activists retained some authority within this expanded entity; beginning with the 1930 reorganization the larger share of power within its complex leadership structure rapidly shifted into the hands of outsiders. Its most powerful figure was the Shanxi-born Fourth Red Army commander Xu Xiangqian (1901–90), a Whampoa Military Academy graduate and hero of the Northern Expedition, who had converted to the Communist cause at Wuhan in 1927.[45] A key subordinate was Xu Haidong, a former pottery worker from Huangpi whom Edgar Snow immortalized as the most strongly class-conscious man he ever met, imbued with a deep and unshakable hatred of all persons of wealth. The following May, with the arrival of new leadership from the Party central committee in Shanghai, the Soviet was reorganized yet again. Its capital was established at the market town of Xinji, in Guangshan (Henan), and Macheng—the regional movement's acknowledged birthplace—was relegated to the status of a subdistrict headquarters.[46]

Encircle and Exterminate

In March 1930, to counter this growing Communist territorial claim, Jiang Jieshi's Nationalist government reposted its most trusted local native, General Xia Douyin, from Anhui to Wuhan as Hubei provincial public security chief. According to Xia's (hostile) biographer, his long tenure in that post was marked not only by his accustomed brutality but also by an increasingly wanton personal corruption. He amassed a huge fortune, largely by skimming the profits of Wuhan's interregional opium trade, and used the proceeds to acquire luxurious townhouses in both Wuchang and Hankou, a 1,000-acre estate on the shores of suburban East Lake, and an expansive portfolio of properties in his native Macheng. He frequented the Wuhan brothels, taking several of the most famous prostitutes as his concubines and enriching these women's families as well. Much of his effort, it is claimed, went to subverting and discrediting his superior, Hubei governor He Chengjun. The great Yangzi flood of the summer of 1931 gave Xia his chance: he successfully fixed the blame for the flood's disastrous consequences on He, got the governor removed, and inherited, informally at first, his rival's power.[47]

Whatever the level of Xia's personal venality, however, there is no doubt about his genuine commitment to liberating his native place from Communist influence, regardless of the cost in lives. Immediately upon his return to Hubei, he deployed a sizable contingent of Nationalist regulars to his home township in the Dongshan, Muzidian, and over the course of 1930–31 he repeatedly called in reinforcement battalions from other provinces. Meanwhile, his local ally Zheng Jiankui gradually pieced together a militia alliance spanning both slopes of the Dongshan (Macheng and Luotian) and the Dabie Shan (Macheng and Shangcheng), an alliance strikingly reminiscent, in its multicounty scope and its mission of counterinsurgency, of the Forty-Eight Fort League constructed three centuries earlier by Mei Zhihuan. Zheng's intensive recruitment drive over the summer allowed him the manpower to reorganize his militia alliance into more than forty brigades, including a crack "dare to die" commando unit (*gansidui*).

Just as Communist strategy had turned from a shifting guerrilla warfare to the defense of relatively fixed soviet bases, Nationalist strategy evolved from a more generalized war of exterminating by sweeping clean (*qingjiao*) to a positional one of exterminating by encirclement (*weijiao*). With the necessary forces now in place, the First Encirclement Campaign was launched against the newly declared Eyuwan Soviet in December 1930, with Xia Douyin personally in command. The Second Encirclement Campaign followed in the spring of 1931, and the Third Campaign took place that summer. Despite high military and civilian casualties, as well as scorched-earth destruction of great swaths of farmland, none of these campaigns remotely achieved their objectives.[48]

In fact, the fighting in Macheng and its environs over this period, while steadily escalating in ferocity and casualty rates, appears less like any organized campaign than an intensification of the anomic violence that had characterized the immediate past. In Chengmagang and the adjacent townships of northwest Macheng, along the borders with Huang'an and Guangshan Counties, the Communists continued to receive much popular support. In the winters of both 1930–31 and 1931–32, their forces—now usually designated one or another unit of the new Red Army—enjoyed waves of battlefield success in this area, and by the spring of 1932 they were pushing south toward the Ju River Valley, forcing the Nationalists to reinforce the threatened urban centers of Songbu and Qiting. In September 1931, a passing Communist army briefly and half-heartedly besieged the county seat itself. But the bloodiest fighting in these years took place in the county's northeast, around the strategic three-province border of Hubei, Henan, and Anhui. The Pine Nut and Long Ridge Passes were the great prizes to be controlled here, and both changed hands repeatedly between 1930 and 1932. Not only was this area the key to the defense of the Eyuwan Soviet, whose nerve center was now just north of the passes, it also incorporated, on the south side, the northern Dongshan, the home turf of both Xia Douyin and Zheng Jiankui. Zheng's expanding militia organization bore the brunt of the fighting on the government side, while Xia, from Wuhan, continually sent waves of reinforcement troops into the area to secure his native place. It seems clear that the Communists specifically sought out targets they knew to lie close to Xia's heart. In July 1930, while besieging the northern Dongshan's central market town of Muzidian, they briefly occupied and razed Cassiawood River (Mujihe), the satellite market that was Xia's ancestral home, and the following January they ambushed and, over the course of a horrifically bloody three-day firefight, wiped out Xia's personal regiment nearly to a man.[49]

The mountain fortresses—*shanbao* and *shanzhai*—that centuries of violence had bequeathed to Macheng and its surrounding counties, and that had played so central a role in the great conflicts of the past, found renewed significance in the Nationalist-Communist civil war. As the United Front forces first assumed control of the county in 1927 and then degenerated into bloody struggles among themselves, local elites scurried to reconstruct their venerable strongholds. In some cases, they did this so well that they were able to sustain virtually autonomous fiefdoms for years, with populations numbering into the thousands. Many of these renovated forts were enormous, defended by dozens of high-tech artillery emplacements and fielding substantial militias of their own; they maintained an overt peace with the dominant Nationalist regime but successfully defied its dictates as they wished. Some of the fortress lords explicitly identified themselves with the gentry heroes of the Taiping era (one dubbed himself "the new Zeng Guofan"), maintaining a local elite- and lineage-based stability in the juncture between barbaric rebels, on the one side, and a militarily and ideologically unreliable state, on the other. Wang Shusheng in his oral history cited with grudging admiration the case of one Dabie Shan fortress lord known as Gu the Dog (Gu Gouzi), who instituted model reformist social policies within his personal domain while continually resisting the hegemony of both the Chinese Communist Party and the Nationalists.[50]

With dramatically new weaponry, forts were less impregnable than they had been in the past, but they remained prizes of war fought over by all sides, the

Red Army included. The Tengjiabao on the eastern border with Luotian county, the Yangsizhai on the northwest border with Henan, and the Shuizhai in the southwest core outside Zhongguanyi, were all sites of protracted engagements. Wang Shusheng proudly renamed one Taiping-era Chengmagang stronghold the "Victory Attained Fort" (Desheng zhai) after capturing it, and he even returned to the site after the Communist triumph in 1949 to write a very bad poem commemorating its capture. More commonly, however, the Communists tore forts down as quickly as they captured them, just as the Qing forces had done with these bothersome strongholds of elite-led localism in the 1640s.[51]

Nationalist armies, likewise no friends of local elite autonomy, often did the same. But Xia Douyin, the Nationalist official of Dongshan local elite stock, knew the historic value of forts in counterinsurgency warfare. Macheng's great military heroes of the late Ming, Mei Guozhen and Mei Zhihuan, had both emphasized this in the conduct of their field campaigns in defense of the dynasty and of the native place. Explicitly following the example of Hu Linyi's anti-Taiping campaigns (in which his own forebears had so valiantly fought), Xia Douyin constructed *diaobao* (blockhouses), 484 of them in the two years 1933–34 alone. These were built most densely not in Dongshan, where the old-style fortresses were concentrated, but rather in the northwestern Dabie Shan townships of Chengmagang and Shunjihe, where the greatest Communist menace lay. It seems unlikely that these *diaobao* were the same sorts of feudal estates as the *shanzhai*, with communal and production functions accompanying the military ones, but they were routinely manned by large armed forces. Like the *shanzhai*, the blockhouses were individually named, and each had an identified builder/proprietor—sometimes a military unit, but often enough a member of the local elite (some named "Xia," but also some "Mei" and other venerable Macheng surnames).[52] As a direct successor to the *qingye* scorched-earth strategies of the late-imperial era, the *qingjiao* extermination campaigns of the early 1930s combined fort building with an attempt to starve out the insurgents.

Liquidation

The ultimate success of this policy was aided immeasurably by events within the Eyuwan Soviet itself. On April 9, 1931, Zhang Guotao (1897–1979) arrived in Eyuwan, sent by Party headquarters in Shanghai to establish a Central Branch Bureau (*zhongyang fenju*) in the soviet and accomplish its unification (*yiyuanhua*) with the Party center. Zhang, though hailing from a wealthy landlord-merchant family of Pingxiang County, Jiangxi, had accrued by this time an impressive revolutionary résumé. He had been a sympathetic youthful observer of the 1906 Ping-Liu-Li Uprising and of the 1911 Revolution in his home county. He had studied at Beijing University, where he participated in the May Fourth demonstrations of 1919, and was recruited to Marxism by Chen Duxiu and Li Dazhao. He had accompanied Chen and Li to the founding meeting of the Chinese Communist Party in Shanghai in 1921. After a sojourn in Moscow, where he took active part in the 1922 Congress of the Toilers of the Far East, he returned to China to work as a labor organizer. Zhang's Moscow ties enabled his rapid rise in influence when, in 1931, Li Lisan was dismissed as Chinese Communist Party chairman and replaced by the "returned student" Wang Ming. Though not himself one of Wang's cohort of "twenty-eight Bolsheviks" (two of the twenty-eight, Shen Zemin and Chen Changhao, accompanied Zhang to Eyuwan), Zhang came to the Dabie Shan as the new Party leadership's chosen agent to reverse the "errors" of the Li Lisan line and simultaneously to bring Communist activities in the region under much stricter central control. His effort to do so took the form of a genocidal Party purge that, among other things, cost the lives of most remaining Communists of indigenous Macheng origin who had managed to survive Xia Douyin's White Terror.[53]

Zhang Guotao's status as a "traitor" to the Communist Party—after his relationship with Mao Zedong fell apart during the Long March, he was expelled in 1938 and subsequently emerged as a Nationalist central committee member—has inclined Party historians to assign him all blame for the brutality of the Eyuwan purges.[54] Yet he certainly did not invent them. For example, Xu Qixu, a well-to-do youth recruited by Wang Youan at the county Higher-Level Elementary School, and Xu Ziqing, an impoverished cooking-oil peddler, had both been pioneer activists in Chengmagang's peasant movement. Following the debacle of the Huang-Ma Uprising, both young men crossed the Dabie Shan into southern Shangcheng County, where Xu Ziqing carved out a base area to administer in the name of the Party. In March 1929, his base was incorporated into the Eyuwan Special District, and Ziqing was appointed district Party secretary. Xu Qixu became one of Eyuwan's military commanders and orchestrated a rural uprising in the mountains that spring. However, both young men soon found themselves beset by "political problems" (*zhengzhi wenti*). A work team sent down from the Party central committee in May "reorganized" the special district, expelling some 40 percent of its 500 cadres. Team leader Chen Guling took exception to the Xus' incorporation of "local bullies" into the base area's leadership and to their overly lenient handling of traitorous elements (*panbian fenzi*); he ordered the executions of the twenty-six-year-old Xu Ziqing in July and of the twenty-three-year-old Xu Qixu in August.[55]

Farther afield, but probably a more direct precedent for Zhang Guotao's bloodletting, was the Futian incident of 1930. Toward the end of that year, Mao Zedong in the Jiangxi Soviet arrested several thousand of his opponents on grounds that they belonged to an "AB tuan" (anti-Bolshevik league). On December 8, a battalion political commissar rebelled, set the prisoners free, and arrested some 100 of Mao's supporters in turn. Others also rebelled, setting up rival soviets of their own. The rebellion failed, however, and in the end Mao and his allies executed several thousand of the dissidents.[56] Zhang Guotao's own relationship with Mao was always rather testy, from the time they were both at Beijing University in the late 1910s until their feud led to Zhang's own purge in 1938. Relations between Zhang's Eyuwan Soviet and Mao's Jiangxi Soviet were likewise highly competitive; an effort in late 1931 to unite the two bases administratively into a single Chinese soviet republic, with Zhang as Mao's subordinate, never achieved any effective reality.[57] Yet Zhang closely watched what Mao was doing in Jiangxi, and Mao's dramatic attack on his opponents there emboldened Zhang to enforce his own will in Eyuwan, at any cost to longtime Communist partisans. In reporting his purges to the Party central committee, Zhang in effect dared his superiors to condemn his mass murders while tolerating those of Mao: "We have been inspired by the lessons of Futian to root out [our enemies] here."[58]

Zhang Guotao's purge of counterrevolutionary elements (*suqing fangeming*, or simply *sufan*) in Eyuwan was initially directed against officers in the Fourth Red Army headquarters at Baiqueyuan (White Sparrow Garden), Shangcheng. These commanders, the flamboyant general Xu Jishen most prominent among them, resented taking orders from Zhang and his young "returned student" colleagues. For his part, Zhang decried the "warlord-bandit" behavior of Xu Jishen and his army and its easy way with appropriating food and abducting and raping women from the populations they encountered. According to Zhang, officers and men chafed at restrictions imposed on their behavior and grumbled that life was much better in the various White Armies that they periodically engaged. In the summer of 1931, Zhang claimed that this disgruntlement had prompted a large number of lower-level commanders to form a local anti-Bolshevik league—akin to the one Mao had exposed in Jiangxi—in sympathy with Wang Jingwei's "Reorganizationist Faction" (*gaizu pai*) and other third-party political movements. Zhang Guotao's report of the situation to the Party central committee notes the discovery of countless spies of every political persuasion throughout the Red Army; Zhang, clearly eager to turn up any possible excuse for eliminating opponents and consolidating his own control, nevertheless sounds genuinely paranoid about his safety.

On top of this, Zhang had disagreed with his commanders over military strategy almost from his first arrival in Eyuwan. In late spring of 1931, in the lull between the Nationalists' Second and Third Encirclement Campaigns, the military people sought to seize the chance for a "southern expedition" of their own, striking out from their southern Henan base into Huangzhou and Qizhou Prefectures of eastern Hubei. They argued that moving into this more productive agricultural area would both relieve food shortages in the soviet and divide

Nationalist forces in Wuhan from those farther down the Yangzi. Zhang Guotao was more cautious, dismissing the commanders' plans as smacking of the "left adventurous" Li Lisan line. In summer, Zhang reluctantly agreed to expand operations more modestly into contiguous portions of Anhui Province, the counties of Liu'an and Yingshan. But when the commanders took these areas, they defied Zhang's orders and pushed further south through the passes into Hubei's Dongshan, taking the Luotian county seat on August 8. Emboldened by the ease of their success, the officers bridled at Zhang's restraints, and on September 13, at the market town of Mabu in Anhui's Liu'an County, they publicly resolved to disregard further orders from the Eyuwan secretariat. But Zhang Guotao, it turned out, held the stronger hand. Accompanied by loyalist troops, he proceeded to Mabu and arrested the mutineers. Over the next two months he tried and executed hundreds, perhaps thousands, of Fourth Red Army personnel, including General Xu Jishen.[59]

The military housecleaning was only the tip of the iceberg of the *sufan* campaign in Eyuwan. The more fundamental targets of the campaign would in fact prove to be county-level Party leaders and the modestly prosperous farmers who had up to then made their peace with Eyuwan Soviet hegemony. And no counties within the Eyuwan jurisdiction came under Zhang's censure more heavily than did Macheng and Huang'an, where, Zhang insisted, the number of *yiyi fenzi* (deviant elements) was perhaps as high as 20,000.[60] Ironically, Zhang added, this was a legacy of the fact that these counties had been the region's very first and most enthusiastic participants in the peasant movement of the mid- to late 1920s. As a result, revolutionary leadership there had fallen to the earliest local converts to the Communist cause, "rural intellectuals" of landlord or rich peasant background, most of whom, in the heyday of the United Front, had actually accepted membership in the Guomindang. Then, when the United Front gave way to the White Terror, the survivors among this group had adopted a terrorist, guerrilla-warfare campaign dismissed by Zhang as *tufei xingwei* (bandit behavior); not a few local Party members, Zhang said, had in fact been *zhenzheng tufei* (true bandits) themselves. For these reasons, Zhang Guotao and his "returned student" allies deeply distrusted the indigenous leadership of Macheng and Huang'an, and immediately upon their arrival they began to effect that leadership's "remoulding" (*gaizao*); this was not yet exactly a purge (*suqing*), but very quickly it would become one.[61]

The major instruments of Zhang Guotao's purification drive were the public security bureaus (*baoweiju*) that he set up in each county shortly after his arrival. Because of the deep suspicion Zhang held for Macheng, the public security bureau of that county, at Kexing Bridge in Shunheji Ward, received his special attention and was particularly aggressive in rooting out spies. It was headed by a Shunheji native named Chen Wenfu, offspring of a family that produced several Communist martyrs, but who himself would become one of the most vilified characters in the county's revolutionary history. Commanding a corps of some 100 secret police, Chen apprehended and "insanely butchered" (*fengkuangde dusha*) in all an estimated 1,175 alleged reorganizationists, Li Lisan remnants, and anti-Bolshevik leaguers, including thirty-two county-level cadres, eighty-four ward-level cadres, 189 *xiang*-level cadres, and sixty-eight village-level cadres. In a field outside Chen's headquarters, human remains piled up like a mountain—remembered today as White Bone Mound—to be devoured by neighborhood dogs. In one midnight raid at the market town of Xiyang, according to popular lore, Chen sent two special deputies ahead to mark the houses of all residents *not* suspected of being reorganizationists, but the two fell asleep before accomplishing their mission, and 114 innocent persons were inadvertently massacred by Chen's thugs.[62]

Over the course of the summer and fall of 1931, Zhang Guotao issued a series of proclamations and convened several mass meetings in which he identified the targets of the *sufan* campaign, in ever-widening terms. Finally, in November, he announced the results of his investigation of the Fourth Red Army—it contained within it, he reported, some 10,000 to 20,000 counterrevolutionaries—and he explicitly expanded his purge of the military into a cleanup of local Party administrations and peasant associations. The Eyuwan central branch sent a directive to all county-level cadres, ordering them to step up the purge. The result was a near-hysterical witch-hunt, a frenzied effort by local cadres to save their own hides by coming up with expanding lists of counterrevolutionaries among their colleagues. Over the winter, according to the Party historian Sheng Renxue, virtually every local Party member or Communist activist throughout the Eyuwan Soviet area who hailed from a landlord, rich peasant, or intellectual background was liquidated (*qingxi*).[63]

The carnage spilled well beyond Party ranks. One of the major charges leveled by Zhang Guotao against the purged Eyuwan leaders was that they had paid insufficient attention to class struggle. Indeed, he noted the irony that whereas implementers of the Li Lisan line had been castigated as leftist adventurists for their overconfident efforts at territorial expansion, in fact this leftism disguised a more basic rightist error: their territorial adventures were possible only because they had systematically neglected the land revolution.[64] In meetings of the First Representative Congress of the Eyuwan Soviet on June 28 and July 1, from which rich peasants and intellectuals as well as landlords were excluded, Zhang laid out his plan to greatly intensify land confiscations, this time with rich peasants as the principal target. At a follow-up meeting on October 1, he ordered the complete and equal redistribution of all land under the Eyuwan Soviet's control. In some local communities, however, including several in Chen Wenfu's Shunheji Ward, the revolution went even further: seized land was not redistributed at all but instead was collectivized under experimental units known as "economic communes" (*jingji gongshe*).[65]

This was by no means a bloodless revolution. Zhang complained upon his arrival that, though earlier Eyuwan leaders had always told the Party central committee that they were dutifully killing landlords and rich peasants, the leaders had been doing nothing of the sort.[66] Zhang set out to rectify this situation, vowing on June 28 to eradicate (*xiaomie*) the region's landlord and rich peasant classes once and for all.[67] The man whom Zhang appointed in July as chairman of the Eyuwan Soviet, Guangshan County's Gao Jingting, was well suited to carrying out this task; having seen, as a young man, his father, his wife, and his infant son murdered by rich peasants, Gao was possessed by a fierce class hatred that prompted him to massacres that even his fellow Communists felt to be inhumanly cruel.[68] In Macheng and Huang'an Counties, by Zhang Guotao's own account, the conduct of the land revolution in 1931 was especially violent.[69]

By the end of the year, resistance against Zhang Guotao's brutal leadership was rising throughout the Eyuwan Soviet area. In January 1932, when public security bureau agents arrived at the Huang'an market town of Xianju to make an arrest, they were met with a demonstration by a crowd estimated at 50,000, shouting "Down with the butcher Zhang!" Zhang declared their actions a "counterrevolutionary riot" and arrested some 600 of the protesters, most of whom he ordered shot.[70] Throughout much of 1932, amidst renewed leadership conflicts over strategy and a deteriorating military situation, Zhang launched a second round of purges and executions, most notably in Macheng itself. In May, the county's Party committee was systematically decimated. Its secretary, the former Red Guard organizer and Li Lisan protégé Wang Hongxue, was arrested by Chen Wenfu, public security chief, and hauled off to Henan for execution. So, too, were longtime *nonghui* leader Ling Zhuzhong and Communist Youth League secretary Chen Zefeng; another veteran cadre, Liao Songkun, escaped execution only when General Xu Xiangqian personally vouched for his impeccably poor class origins and his battlefield heroism.[71] Wang Shusheng, who had been recruited in the early 1920s by Dong Biwu, was away on maneuvers and thus was virtually the sole survivor among the cadre of Macheng's "progressive" youth. He escaped the purge, but—in an action with intriguing hints of a misogynist witch-hunt—his sister, along with Fourth Army commander Xu Xiangqian's wife, was denounced as a "reorganizationist" and shot.[72] By September, however, the momentum of the bloodbath was winding down, and accounts were being settled. Chen Wenfu himself, Macheng's dreaded public security chief, fell afoul of Zhang Guotao and was arrested and executed. By the end of the year, Chen's bureau as a whole had been shut down by Party authorities, and his secret police had been disbanded.[73]

The Eyuwan *sufan* campaign of 1931–32 remains a matter of contention, ambiguity, and Party secrecy. (For example, the Hubei Provincial Archives contains a promising documentary file on the affair, but it remains "not open" to scholars.[74]) Estimates of the total number of the campaign's victims vary widely, from Zhang Guotao's own untenably low figure of 600 to Gregor Benton's guess of upwards of 10,000; official Communist sources usually place the number at 2,500.[75] What this meant was the near-final extinction of the Party's base of indigenous supporters in the Dabie Shan region.[76] It seems clear that this was at least a semideliberate strategy. The highly cultivated Zhang Guotao, even afforded the distance of his 1960s Hong Kong retirement, was brutally dismissive of the peasant mentality of the Dabie Shan partisans, expressing great frustration at the effort it took to get these bumpkins to understand even the most straightforward directives from the Party central committee. He chafed as well at the petty localisms that divided these local activists, noting most especially the resentment of natives of Huang'an and Macheng at the intrusion of comrades from outside.[77]

Shanxi-born Fourth Army commander Xu Xiangqian, no friend of Zhang Guotao, essentially shared Zhang's exasperation at the deeply localist orientation of Macheng and Huang'an. As Xu wrote in his memoirs:

> The revolutionary ardor of the peasant masses of Huang-Ma is very high, but they view the Communist Party as *their very own thing*. . . . If the Party holds a secret meeting to discuss strategy, they angrily exclaim, "How can you hold a meeting and exclude us?" It takes a great deal of effort to make them understand. Slogans such as "Kill the local bullies and evil gentry" resonate deeply with these people, but what a soviet is, very few of them comprehend.[78]

But Zhang Guotao's condescension toward the Dabie Shan "peasants" largely masks the real conflict, which was with the proprietary attitude of the indigenous rural elite. As we have seen, the flourishing Communist movement that Zhang Guotao encountered in the region, and most especially Macheng within that region, was largely the creation of a cadre of rural intellectuals with deep local roots. There was a *class* problem with these people, from the point of view of the Party central committee, but it was even more profoundly a problem of *localism*. Not unlike the generations of Macheng-bred scholar-officials of late-imperial times, "progressive" youth like Wang Hongxue cherished a devotion to wider moral causes, but also an even more profound sense of a mission to make things right in their own native place. They clearly saw themselves in part—as Mei Zhihuan, Yu Yaxiang, and even Xia Douyin had done before them—as *local* saviors and patrons. Indeed, even today, in local history and collective memory of the Communist movement in Macheng, that movement is seen as an essentially homegrown affair: it was an effort to rescue the *locality* from its precarious condition in the Republican era.[79] From the point of view of a bureaucratic Party hierarchy imposed from outside, and perhaps especially for a functionary as personally insecure as Zhang Guotao, this sort of romantic heroism (*yingxiong langman*)—so characteristic of the Dabie Shan—was intolerable, and Zhang was determined to root it out.[80] In this sense, the Eyuwan purges in Macheng were simply one more bloody instance of conflict between local leaders and a larger, centralizing regime, a conflict that had plagued the area for centuries.

Macheng Abandoned

Zhang Guotao's *sufan* purges coincided with a dramatic turn for the worse in the Eyuwan Soviet's military position, which would shortly bring about the soviet's demise. The loss of personnel and morale brought by the purges themselves was one important factor, but there were others. Conditions in the soviet areas were terrible. Food shortfalls became ever more severe; by the latter half of 1931, vegetables had almost disappeared from the residents' meager diet. Clumsy experiments in collective agriculture crippled production, and the soviet's heavyhanded imposition of controls on distribution of food and other staples, already in desperately short supply, severely alienated local people. The "four vermin" (flies, mosquitoes, bedbugs, and lice) afflicted the region, and disease (malaria, dysentery, skin diseases) became rampant. There was virtually no medical aid. Over the winter of 1931–32, the Soviet was struck by a devastating epidemic, in which two-thirds of the population fell ill. This was most critical in the Hubei sector: in Huang'an county alone, some 10,000 persons were said to have died. Zhang Guotao, not implausibly, linked this catastrophe to the accelerating witch-hunts of the *sufan* purge, which shifted into its most hysterical phase at precisely the moment the epidemic reached its height.[81]

An ill-considered southern offensive into Hubei also played a major part in the Eyuwan Soviet's collapsing security. This campaign revived the wrangling between the soviet's political and military leadership. Fourth Army commander Xu Xiangqian opposed the offensive from the start, noting the rapid new buildup of Nationalist troops in the area, while Zhang Guotao, who just months before had cashiered and executed much of his officer corps on grounds of adventurist territorial expansionism, now demanded just such expansion. He made his case primarily on the basis of the need to capture food supplies for relief of the soviet's starving population, but his biographer claims that Zhang, unique among Eyuwan leaders in seeing the struggle as basically anti-imperialist in nature, had as his real goal to strike a blow at the foreign presence in Wuhan. In any case, in the summer of 1932 the Eyuwan Red Army, in time-honored Chinese rebel tradition, sent the bulk of its military force south over the Dabie Shan to plunder and besiege Macheng, Huang'an, and Luotian.

At the beginning of the year, Communist forces had already captured and razed Macheng's ancient capital, Qiting, and they continued to enjoy some presence in the Ju River Valley in the county's southeast. In early July, the Eyuwan Soviet launched a sudden coordinated attack on many of the county's secondary cities and towns. The Eyuwan forces were remarkably successful, managing to take Zhongguanyi, Baiguo, Futianhe, Huangtugang, and several lesser market towns. But they could not hold these, losing most of them to Nationalist forces within a few days, and then alternately taking and losing them throughout the remainder of the month. At the same time, following in the footsteps of many others who had swooped in from the county's peripheries over the centuries, they launched a protracted siege of the Macheng county seat. On July 31, Zhang Guotao, facing continually reinforced Nationalist defenders, ordered a concentration of his forces in an effort to take the city once and for all. He got distracted, however, when, on August 7, his Fourth Army managed to capture the county seat of adjacent Huang'an; three days later, Zhang ordered a halt to the siege of Macheng and a diversion of these troops to reinforce Huang'an. This action did no good: on August 15, Huang'an was retaken by the Nationalists. The Eyuwan Soviet's southern offensive was over, and its surviving troops, badly weakened, straggled back over the mountains into Henan. The campaign's most significant legacy was the near-total destruction of the 1932 harvest in the most agriculturally productive portion of the Dabie Shan, at a moment when the region as a whole could least afford this loss.[82]

At around the same time, the Nationalists began to approach Eyuwan with a new level of seriousness. In May, Jiang Jieshi personally toured the area and established the new Eyuwan Bandit Extermination General Command (*Eyuwan sansheng jiaofei zongsiling bu*), naming himself its head. He posted one of his closest Party allies, Yang Yongtai, to Wuhan as head of the Military Affairs Commission and administrative coordinator of the paired campaigns against the Eyuwan Soviet.[83] It was newly appointed Hubei governor Xia Douyin, however, who, as the most senior and politically reliable native of the area, was assigned by Jiang direct military command of that summer's Fourth Encirclement and Extermination Campaign. Launched at the same time as Zhang Guotao's own ill-conceived Macheng offensive, this campaign decisively turned the tide of the war.[84]

The Fourth Encirclement differed dramatically from the first three in that it was a radical scorched-earth campaign, euphemistically termed the *sanguang* (three emptyings). In so-called bandit areas, all able-bodied men were killed, all buildings were burned, and all crops were either seized or destroyed. Nationalist "killer squads" massacred every man, woman, and child in suspect villages, and village wells were poisoned to prevent rehabitation. Japanese newspapers reported that 100,000 persons were either murdered or deliberately starved to death in Huang'an County alone, and the death toll throughout the Eyuwan Soviet areas was at least twice that. The grisly strategy worked. A government offensive into the heartland of the Eyuwan Soviet in southeast Henan and adjacent Anhui captured the soviet's headquarters at Xinji on September 9, and Mabu, Yingshan, and Shangcheng fell quickly thereafter. By late fall, nearly 80 percent of the territory that had once been held by the Eyuwan Soviet was securely in Nationalist hands. In October, Zhang Guotao and what was left of his soviet administration fled the region for Sichuan, accompanied by the great bulk of the Fourth Red Army under Xu Xiangqian and the last surviving Communist leader of Macheng birth, Wang Shusheng. A rump force, dubbed the Twenty-Fifth Red Army, under Xu Haidong, was left behind. With the Fourth Army's departure, the Nationalists declared the new, Fifth Extermination campaign, and over the winter of 1932–33 the slaughter of civilians throughout the Dabie Shan intensified even further, with what Edgar Snow described as "singular savagery."[85]

But Xu Haidong, the Huangpi potter and implacable foe of any person of wealth, proved surprisingly resilient. Over the first half of 1933, he not only held out but even recovered some of the former soviet territories. Frustrated Nationalist authorities responded by raiding Xu's home village and "exterminating" sixty-three of his relatives, including women and infants.[86] As the fighting dragged on inconclusively, Jiang Jieshi grew ever angrier at the seeming ineffectiveness of Xia Douyin. In the summer, he visited Wuhan and stripped Xia of his governorship, publicly ridiculing him for having so long demanded, "Hubei for the Hubeinese" and then, once actually granted control of the province, proving inept to govern it.[87] Fighting in Macheng County continued, bloodily but inconclusively, until, over the winter of 1933–34, Nationalist forces began to enjoy a series of dramatic victories. In November 1934, even the redoubtable Xu Haidong was forced to abandon the area, joining up with Mao and Zhu De on the Long March to Yan'an. The few remaining Communist partisans in the Dabie Shan retreated to hide out in the "deep mountains" (*shenshan milin*). Nationalist forces quickly and efficiently completed their *qingjiao* (extermination).[88]

The Nationalist moment of triumph in Macheng did not, of course, endure for long. The dreams of a "New Life" in the county, wistfully portrayed in Xia Douyin and Zheng Zhong's 1935 county gazetteer, went up in smoke with the Japanese invasion of 1938. On October 26 of that year, after days of heavy air bombardment, Japanese troops occupied Macheng City and all of the county's major urban centers. Xia and Zheng fled west, to join the Nationalist exile regime in Sichuan. Over the next dozen years, such Nationalist and Communist luminaries as Jiang Jieshi, Li Zongren, Guo Morou, Li Xiannian, and Deng Xiaoping would each spend time in the county in the course of the resistance and civil wars.[89] But the centuries-old pattern of locally generated leadership, conflict, and violence was now a thing of the past—and here, appropriately, is where our saga ends.

The decade of the late 1920s and early 1930s was a horrifically brutal time for Macheng, though not uniquely so in the county's violent history. International journalists found in the county material for their most gruesome accounts of savagery and barbarism in the Chinese Revolution. Edgar Snow, most famously, described the carnage in Macheng as "a civil war with the intensity of a religious war," and, in an unconscious echo of the Red Turban Rebellion of the fourteenth century (of which he was surely unaware) invoked the term "Manichaean" to characterize the totalizing class hatreds that turned the campaigns around Eyuwan into crusades of fratricidal annihilation.[90] Local collective memory also records particular horrors, such as Communist guerrillas' murder of some 3,000 members of elite households along the Chengmagang-Guangshan border in the summer of 1929, and the massacre of all in attendance at a landlord's funeral in August 1935.[91] Given the eventual triumph of the Communists and their ability largely to control local history, Nationalist atrocities in and around the county became even more the stuff of legend. These included the Wanzishan Massacre of January 1933, in which tens of thousands of the inhabitants of a Red-controlled area were said to have been liquidated, among them 300 patients incinerated within a makeshift hospital. Local accounts tell of entire lineages of known Communists systematically eliminated, regardless of sex and age, and of persons, feeling spongy ground underfoot, digging up mass graves—in one case, 3,500 persons who in a single night had been buried alive.[92]

But deliberate slaughter was hardly the sole cause of mass death in Macheng in these years. Famine and immiseration were already severe in the county itself even while it was being inundated with famine refugees from Henan and Anhui.[93] Many of these years, and most notably 1931 and 1934, were marked by near-total drought, and serious earthquakes repeatedly struck the Dabie Shan hills. While epidemics racked the highlands, cholera killed thousands in the county's urban core.[94] The most concise index of the horrors that Macheng experienced in these years was demographic collapse: a population drop of nearly 20 percent between 1923 and 1941. In Chengmagang and Shunheji, the two townships most severely visited by civil war, the loss was more startling yet: a population decline from 180,000 to fewer than 50,000 in the eight years between 1926 and 1934.[95]

With the establishment of the People's Republic in 1950, the Nationalist magistrate Zheng Zhong, the "King of Hell" ward leader Lin Renfu, and many other county officials of the Nanjing decade were hunted down throughout China and hauled back to Macheng. There they either died in prison, like Zheng, or, like Lin, were executed by "people's courts." General Xia Douyin was more fortunate. He managed to get appointed to the Communist government's Commission to Restore Order (*zhian weiyuanhui*) and then prudently withdrew to Hong Kong, where he died peacefully the following year.[96] There is no actual evidence for such a meeting, but it is fascinating to imagine Xia and his fellow Hong Kong exile Zhang Guotao—both now retired from the heat of events—sitting down in the Colony over a cup of tea and quietly reminiscing about the thousands of persons each had murdered in Macheng.

Conclusion

IN A POIGNANT recent book, David Der-wei Wang has explored the morbid fixation of twentieth-century Chinese literary culture with decapitation, starvation, cannibalism, and other aspects of the violence that had become such a banal component of the national experience. Since historians both then and now, Wang argues, have seemed insensitive to the "seemingly endless brutality" in the enormous casualty figures they have toted up, novelists and essayists were left the task of recording "the moral and psychological aftermath of China's violence and pain." To some extent, this awareness of the centrality of violence formed a "counter-discourse" within the classical canon itself, but it assumed much greater prominence with the work of Li Zhi in the late sixteenth century, and then with literary accounts of the Ming-Qing transition, as wanton human slaughter became ever more routine. In the mid-twentieth century, spurred especially by the genocidal fallout from the Nationalist Revolution, repulsion and horror at "the monster that is history" became the dominant literary theme.[1] The people of Macheng County, as we have seen, were in the forefront throughout this long and tortuous historical experience, simultaneously the monster's agents and its victims.

Between the expulsion of the Mongols in the mid-fourteenth century and the invasion of the Japanese in the mid-twentieth, Macheng experienced two eras of notable prosperity. The first, in the mid- to late-Ming, featured the development of an export agriculture, parlayed into a surprising degree of scholar-official success and empire-wide cultural prominence; the second, peaking in the mid-Qing, was based on the profits of its merchant diaspora but was accompanied by the county's gradual retreat into political and cultural marginality. The two eras were marked by different structures of power within Macheng. The former period was dominated by wealthy and highly cultured estate-holding gentry of the central and southwestern core, organized into large and intermarried lineages; in the latter era, these literati magnates, while they retained their estates, were overshadowed by a succession of more modestly educated strongmen—beginning with Liu Junfu, in the 1670s, and continuing through Yu Yaxiang, Zheng Jiankui, and Xia Douyin—who spilled down from the Dongshan to exercise military overlordship in the county as a whole. Both eras were routinely punctuated by bloodshed, and both concluded with moments of truly appalling carnage, in the 1630s–50s and the 1920s–30s. With a single exception—the White Lotus rebellion of 1796–1805—the county found itself near the center of every episode of empirewide violent disorder—of *luan*—during these seven centuries. Several of these episodes, in fact, it had helped precipitate. This was no coincidence.

What is there about Macheng—this particular, seemingly nondescript locality—that gave rise to such a disturbing record of savage violence? Where does a monster like Xia Douyin, the Guomindang scourge of god, or like Lin Renfu, the dreaded King of Hell ward boss, come from? If Macheng was relatively extreme in this regard—this seems the case, though on the basis of this single local study we cannot say *how* extreme—why was this so?

It was evidently not just physical ecology, which the county shared with many other Chinese localities. The Dabie Shan, unlike similar mountainous areas within the broader Middle Yangzi macroregion, was not a late-settled region of intense land reclamation and immigration. In the Han River highlands to the west, for example, these processes gave rise in the mid-Qing to peculiarly exploitative land-tenure relations and, with dramatic ecological decay in the generation or two after settlement, eruptive social tensions; one result was the massive White Lotus rebellion of the late eighteenth century. The Dabie Shan, by contrast, was one of the longest-settled regions of the Chinese empire; over the late-imperial and Republican eras, its population grew steadily but evenly, by no means out of step with that of the country as a whole. Nor were confrontations with non-Han "aborigines" a social irritant, as was the case throughout the Qing in the highlands of the Middle Yangzi's southwest. Indeed, though Macheng continued to receive modest waves of immigrants from various parts of China (most notably Jiangxi) during the Ming and the Qing, I have found no evidence that ethnic animosities played any role at all in the generation of local social conflict. And whereas still other Middle Yangzi highland areas, such as Hunan's Ping-Liu-Li, had taken part in the mining boom of the mid-Qing and thus come to host large numbers of familyless, violence-prone male miners, Macheng did not; it had, to be sure, its share of small-scale mines, but its economy has always been overwhelmingly agrarian.[2]

The most suggestive regional comparison for Macheng, in fact, is probably not a mountainous area at all but rather the nearby Huaibei floodplain of eastern Henan and northern Anhui and Jiangsu, studied by Elizabeth Perry.[3] Perry's Huaibei was also a highly militarized, fort-dominated site of chronic collective violence and, like Macheng, was terrorized by the Nian in the 1860s and the Red Spears in the 1920s and 1930s. Both regions were strategic crossroads (*bingchong*) targeted by aspirants to national power throughout imperial and Republican history. But here, too, the differences are at least as striking as the similarities. A distinctive feature of Huaibei was its "ecological fragility," notably its susceptibility to flooding, which Perry sees as the major contributor to both the region's endemic violence (a basic "strategy of survival") and its lack of severe and enduring social stratification (the result of persistent downward mobility pressures and of a relatively undeveloped market system). By contrast, Macheng's agrarian ecology was not especially "fragile." Natural disasters and failed harvests were routine, to be sure, but seem to have been no more frequent or severe than in most other parts of China. And Macheng's fertile mountain valleys did in fact allow rather successful commercialization of agriculture, accumulation of wealth, concentration of landholding, and social stratification. This was likely one reason why it differed so greatly from Perry's Huaibei in its fervent receptivity to Communist revolutionary appeals.

At the same time, like Huaibei, Macheng throughout most of its history was a locality of little national significance—a small place (*xiao difang*)—and its inhabitants knew it.[4] Their home district was not Nanjing or Beijing, nor was it Suzhou or Shanghai, or even Wuchang or Hankou. For one anomalous moment, lasting from the late fifteenth to the early seventeenth centuries, the county did succeed in promoting itself onto the empire's cultural map, but very quickly afterward it lapsed again into the obscurity and marginality to which it had always been accustomed. This sense of geographic inferiority—what may be called a small-place consciousness (*xiao difang yizhi*)—underlay, I believe, the aggressive sense of local pride that Macheng people consistently demonstrated, their fierce urge to regional autonomy, and the bloody conflicts with centralizing forces that punctuated the county's history. Late-imperial commentators repeatedly remarked on the exaggerated localist sentiment (*bangfeng*) that imbued Macheng, and on the pride as well as the distress that its people felt at being left on their own as an "orphaned locality" (*gucheng*) in times of trouble.[5] Central-local tensions erupted most dramatically in the autonomous claims of the late-Yuan Tianwan regime, in the resistance movements of the Forty-Eight Fort League and the Dongshan rebels in the Ming-Qing transition, and in the struggle with Party Central in the 1930s that precipitated the Eyuwan purges. But these tensions were present under the surface the whole time. Macheng people had *attitude*.

Patterns of dominance and resistance *within* Macheng were locally distinctive. Personal servitude in agriculture, accompanied by elite control over the creation of households and reproduction on the part of the rural workforce, was both more ubiquitous at its late-Ming peak and survived longer (in attenuated form, even into the twentieth century) in Macheng than in most other Chinese localities. While forts existed in other parts of China, their centrality in shaping both local society and local culture in Macheng had few parallels elsewhere—they lay at the very core of the county's identity. The real compulsions of the decimal-group household regimentation system (*baojia*) and the intensity of local militarization (*tuanlian*) were unusually great here, and both had a persistent impact on local social relations. The use of these instruments by armed local elites to assert great coercive power over their neighbors, usurping in the process at least some of the prerogatives of the central state, took place earlier and more thoroughly in Macheng than elsewhere; whereas, as Philip Kuhn has demonstrated, for most parts of central China this was a function of the Qing's nineteenth-century *decline*, here it dated no later than the dynasty's *consolidation* of authority in the 1670s (see chapter 7). When state power did forcefully reassert itself under the Nationalists, it refashioned *baojia* and *tuanlian* into a totalizing cult, in the "social militarization" of the New Life era. Throughout this process, the consistent loser was Macheng's rural underclass, and it responded by mobilizing for armed resistance in a succession of ways, the Communist-led rural revolution being merely the most recent.

The structure of local collective violence conformed to complex, historically generated patterns. Class tensions were strong and persistent but manifested themselves most violently when facilitated by the incursion of wider conflicts (the late-Yuan, late-Ming, San-fan, and Taiping rebellions; the Nationalist and Communist Revolutions). Yet these tensions were consistently cross-cut by this small locality's urge to resist outside centralizing forces, an urge affecting both commoner and elite. Intraelite feuding was also chronic. Conflicts between city and countryside, and between the economic core in the southwest and the mountainous peripheries (Dongshan, Chengmagang), were familiar aspects of the local conflict repertoire. The siege of the county seat by rural paramilitary forces (both elite- and subaltern-led), and flight into the highlands when things got tough, were well-practiced, culturally sanctioned routines.

These routines were but one part of a broader culture of violence in the county. The strongman fortmaster (*baozhang*) as a cultural type was a dominant feature of local consciousness, along with the "greenwood" (*lulin*) ethos of the *Water Margin*–style outlaw subculture—a peculiarly muscular variant of the Confucian tradition.[6] As we have seen, Macheng had (not coincidentally) played a central role in the textual history of the *Water Margin* itself, that quintessential literary repository of the *haohan* (tough guy) tradition. As W. J. F. Jenner notes, perhaps the most terrifying thing about this tradition is its portrayal of the most gruesome and irrational violence as "simple childish fun."[7] Violence in Macheng was many things, but not least among these things was *play*.

The martial arts were unusually developed in Macheng, especially a particular local variety of *quanshu*, institutionalized in scores of boxing academies. Boxing associations (*quanhui*) proliferated, mutating when called upon into the various more politicized *hui* that we have seen as such central actors in the county's violent history, from the Liren hui (Village Benevolent Association) of the seventeenth century to the Hongqiang hui (Red Spears), the Xiefu hui (Terrorize the Wealthy Association), and the Nongmin xiehui (Peasant Associations) of the twentieth. Most of Macheng's countless local militia leaders and military degree–holders over the late-imperial era were products of these boxing schools, and it was an easy transition for persons brought up in this tradition to move into twentieth-century military schools—schools such as the Baoding Academy (alma mater of Xia Douyin, Zheng Zhong, and much of the county's Nationalist leadership) and its counterpart, Mao Zedong's Wuhan Peasant Training Institute (spawning ground of many of Macheng's early Communist leaders).[8]

But the local culture of violence, in which not only natives but local state agents participated, went well beyond the robustly martial to feature a terrorist aspect as well—violence for purposes of theatrical display. Grisly dismemberment of heads, ears, hearts, and breasts was an accustomed part of this culture, as was the practice of systematic annihilation of an enemy's kin. The discourse encountered in local writings, both official and unofficial, is heavy with the titillating language of piled-up corpses, rivers of blood, bloodbaths, and the rich symbolism of the color red.[9] Even under the People's Republic, popular historiography has reveled in this language, from Cai Ji'ou's 1958 *Ezhou xueshi* (The bloody history of Hubei) to Guo Mu's 1997 *Diexue Dabieshan* (The blood-drenched Dabie Shan) and countless local revolutionary memoirs. For local people, by the middle of the twentieth century the deceptively innocuous term *qing* (pure, clean, cleansed) must have assumed an all-too-familiar aura of terror, through its patterned usage in such euphemisms for genocide as *qingye*, *qingxiang*, *qingjiao*, *qingxian*, and *suqing*.

This culture of violence was systematically reproduced through the instruments of history and collective memory. Tragic/heroic episodes of the past were kept very much alive, reshaped, and contested through the processes of official historiography, notably in the seven county gazetteers produced between 1535 and 1993. Therein could be found, continually reprinted, poems on martial virtues by such famous native sons as Mei Guozhen and Wang Shusheng, stirring accounts of past battles, practical blueprints for militia organization, and elaborate martyrologies of fallen heroes. Shifting treatments of heroes and villains from the county's past—local natives such as Zou Pusheng, Mei Zhihuan, Tang Zhi, Zhou Wenjiang, Bao Shirong, Qu Kaiyan, Xia Douyin, and Liu Wenwei, and outsiders like Zhang Xianzhong, Li Zhi, Yu Chenglong, Hu Linyi, and Zhang Guotao—served as touchstones for articulating the political stance of the regime in power at the time of each gazetteer's compilation. Alongside this was a more popular historiographic tradition, growing initially out of the Wansong and other private academies. Among its most striking products is the meticulously researched yet stirringly romanticized account of the Forty-Eight Fort League by Wang Baoxin. Wang's 1908 book is a vivid testament to how the past (the loyalist/localist rebellion of the seventeenth century) could be used as inspiration for contemporary (anti-Manchu) revolution, and ultimately for the savage class warfare preached by Wang's friend and partisan Dong Biwu.[10]

Still more encompassing repositories of collective memory, such as folktales, recounted, often with irony and humor, vicious incidents of the past like lineage vendettas and bandit attacks as well as the bloody deeds of such rebels as Zhang Xianzhong.[11] Local folk songs celebrated past battles and were rewritten in turn to serve the needs of current combatants.[12] The distinctive Macheng local opera tradition also embodied an ethos of violence and resistance, so much so that its chief purveyor, the Tianfutai troupe, was forcibly disbanded by the Japanese a century after its 1837 founding.[13] Physical monuments to past violence dotted the terrain: graves, steles, forts, relics of old battles, and temples to bandit-suppressing warrior gods. Local residents could readily recount the heroic campaigns, stretching back to the Warring States era, associated with each of the county's famous Five Passes. Most tellingly, the mountain grotto sacred to the county's patron deity, the Daoist immortal Ma Gu, visibly recalled that fourth-century maiden's defiant release of local conscript labor on the battlement that gave the county its name, hence ever after providing the archetype of resistance to outside commandism.

The combined weight of such influences seems to have given rise to a local culture that was persistently and systemically violent. In our early chapter on the late-Yuan rebellions in Macheng, we noted Edgar Snow's characterization of this set of cultural attitudes as "Manichaean."[14] By this Snow meant an absolute and uncompromising hatred of one's enemies that would sanction, across the spectrum of political ideology, the most grisly and inhuman actions against them. It was a mind-set, as the 1882 county gazetteer put it with some pride, "bent on total extermination" (*shazei zhiguo zhi si*).[15] This, it would appear, was a mentality that Macheng people had patiently learned over many centuries.

REFERENCE MATTER

Abbreviations

The following abbreviations are used in the Appendix, the Notes, and the Selected Bibliography.

DMB	L. Carrington Goodrich and Chaoying Fang, eds. *Dictionary of Ming Biography, 1368–1644*. New York: Columbia University Press, 1976.
ECCP	Arthur Hummel, ed. *Eminent Chinese of the Ch'ing Period, 1644–1912*. Washington D.C.: U.S. Government Printing Office, 1943–44.
HBTZ	*Hubei tongzhi* (Consolidated gazetteer of Hubei Province), Republican era, n.d.
HGO	Hubei Gazetteer Office
HPA	Hubei Provincial Archives
HPL	Hubei Provincial Library
MCA	Macheng County Archives
MCXDMZ	Macheng County Place Name Leadership Group, comp., *Hubei sheng Macheng xian diming zhi* (Gazetteer of place names in Macheng County, Hubei Province). Macheng, 1984.
MCXJZ	*Macheng xian jianzhi* (Brief Gazetteer of Macheng County). Macheng: Macheng County People's Government, 1981.
MCXZQB	Yu Jinfang, ed. *Macheng xianzhi, qianbian* (Gazetteer of Macheng County, part 1), orig. 1935. Taibei: Chengwen, 1975.
MCXZXB	Yu Jinfang, ed. *Macheng xianzhi, xubian* (Gazetteer of Macheng County, part 2), orig. 1935. Taibei: Chengwen, 1975.
MQA	Number One Historical Archives, Beijing (Ming-Qing Archives).
MQDA	Institute of History and Philology, comp. *(Xiancun Qingdai Neige dagu yuancang) Ming Qing dang'an* (Ming and Qing archives from the surviving holdings of the Qing Grand Secretariat). Taibei: Academia Sinica, 1986.

MSLLZ — *Ming shilu leizuan: Hubei shiliao juan* (Veritable records of the Ming, topically selected: materials on Hubei history). Wuhan: Wuhan chubanshe, 1991.

NMZZ — History Department, Chinese People's University, and First Historical Archives, comp. *Qingdai nongmin zhanzheng shi ziliao xuanbian* (Collected materials on the history of peasant wars in the Qing dynasty). Beijing: Chinese People's University Press, 1984.

SKQS — *Wenyuange siku quanshu dianzibian* (Electronic edition of the *Siku quanshu* [of 1783]). Hong Kong: Chinese University of Hong Kong Press, 1999.

1670 XZ — Qu Zhenqi, ed. *Macheng xianzhi* (Gazetteer of Macheng County), orig. 1670. Macheng: Gazetteer Office, 1999.

1795 XZ — Jiang Tingming, ed. *Macheng xianzhi* (Gazetteer of Macheng County), orig. 1795. Macheng: Gazetteer Office, 1999.

1882 XZ — Guo Qinghua, ed. *Macheng xianzhi* (Gazetteer of Macheng County), orig. 1882. Macheng: Gazetteer Office, 1999.

1993 XZ — Yan Yizhou, ed. *Macheng xianzhi* (Gazetteer of Macheng County). Beijing: Hongqi chubanshe, 1993.

Official population figures for Macheng County, 1391–1984

Year	Total population	Males	Females	Households
1391	105,112			15,609
1512	145,095			
1556	148,240			19,380
1619	116,234			10,605
1694	110,387			
1715				10,781
1756				10,920
1795	283,888			
1876	368,312			
1912	462,371			111,494
1923	579,585	327,236	252,349	119,914
1941	467,835			
1949	584,509			
1964	718,975	373,698	345,177	
1984	977,467			201,989

Sources: *MCXZQB* 3:1–3; *1993 XZ*, 71, 75 (for sex ratios); *MCXZXB* 3:1 (for 1923); *MCXZXB* 9:3 (for 1912); *MCXDMZ*, 1 (for 1984).

Notes

Sources not included in the Selected Bibliography are cited in full here, when complete citation data are available. Sources included in the Selected Bibliography are cited here in shortened form: surname of the author, editor, or compiler (and given name, if needed for clarity); page number(s), if relevant; and additional information (for example, title or year of publication) that may be necessary to identify and distinguish sources. A key to the abbreviations used in the notes begins on page 329.

Introduction

1. *1993 XZ*, 13.
2. Hofheinz, 73–74. Others have noticed this as well. A more recent study terms Macheng "the very core area of the Communist Revolution" in central China, and CCP historians themselves speak routinely of "the truly glorious revolutionary tradition" of this distinctive locality; see Wou, 123–29. See also Liu Manrong, 77.
3. Three classic works in this tradition are Sorel, Benjamin, and Arendt.
4. I draw here upon Coser (a work based largely on the ideas of the early-twentieth-century German sociologist Georg Simmel), as well as on Marx, on Fox, and on Riches.
5. A pioneering study is that by Davis. I have found especially useful the work of Nirenberg.
6. Nirenberg, 131.
7. Riches, 11–12.
8. Harrell, 1, 8.
9. All these examples are drawn from Morohashi.
10. See Mann, "The Male Bond in Chinese History and Culture."
11. See Louie.
12. See Lewis.
13. ter Haar, "Rethinking 'Violence' in Chinese Culture." David Robinson has likewise cautioned against overestimating the shift from martial to civil values among the elite, often dated to the Tang-Song transition; see Robinson, 171.
14. Boretz, 97. Boretz's study is among several recent ones arguing in this way: see

also Ho; Antony, "Banditry and the Culture of Violence in Late Imperial South China" (I am grateful to Professor Antony for permission to cite his paper, and for enlightening conversations on this topic).

15. Robinson, 167.

16. See Chen Pingyuan. For a classic study, see also Ruhlmann.

17. Ssu-ma; see also J. J. Y. Liu.

18. Jenner. See also the discussion of the ambivalent but usually admiring application of the term *haojie* (outstandingly able person, especially in the use of force) in Robinson, 21.

19. The following paragraphs are based on ter Haar, "China's Inner Demons," and on ter Haar, *Ritual and Mythology of the Chinese Triads*, chap. 6. Though arguing to different effect, von Glahn similarly stresses the ubiquitous presence of demons in Chinese popular consciousness.

20. See Wolf. Robert Hymes, among others, criticizes Wolf's taxonomy for its oversimplification, without, as I see it, dismissing its general veracity; see Hymes, *Way and Byway*, 3–5.

21. As ter Haar, "China's Inner Demons," concedes, the demonic world of popular religion "precisely opposed" the ordered world of the literati All-under-Heaven, the latter stressing as it did harmonic integration instead of violent conflict. This does not mean, however, that most Chinese literati did not share in this system of popular belief. A better way of conceiving this relationship, it seems to me, is to see the literati as having proposed a more orderly cosmological system precisely as a way to keep at bay the forces of demonic disorder, which they fully understood as being out there but deemed too dangerous to formally acknowledge.

22. See ter Haar, *Ritual and Mythology of the Chinese Triads*, chap. 6. See also Antony, "Demons, Gangsters, and Secret Societies in Early Modern China."

23. See ter Haar, *Ritual and Mythology of the Chinese Triads*, 236–62.

24. Blight, 397.

25. Halbwachs (French original published posthumously, 1950). See also Nora; Confino; Spiegel.

26. Nora, 7–9.

27. For a particularly nice example of this, see Zhongguanyi Township Gazetteer Compilation Office, ed. The series *Macheng wenshi ziliao*, seven volumes to date, contains much more along these lines as well.

28. *1993 XZ*, 485.

29. Wang Baoxin; see also "Nongmin qiyi lingxiu Bao Shirong."

30. My reference, of course, is to Stone's celebrated apologia for narrative history.

31. Jelavich, 84.

32. Perdue, "The Qing Empire in Eurasian Time and Space," 60. Perdue echoes Charles Tilly's description of the task of social history as investigating the links "between very large structural changes . . . and the changing experiences of ordinary people"; see Tilly, 11. For a manifesto of microhistorical method, see Levi. For analyses of the movement's goals, see Muir; see also Iggers, chap. 9.

33. An agenda of *Annal*ist history is laid out in Braudel. There are two applications of the *longue durée* method to China which I much admire: Schoppa, and Dardess, *A Ming Society*.

34. Wang Shizhen, "Wanyai Huang gong muzhi ming"; *MCXZQB*, 5:2, 8:4, 8:26.

35. The classic example is the identification of "great agrarian cycles" by Le Roy Ladurie.

36. See Will.

37. See Skinner, especially 16–28, 219–20.

Chapter 1

1. For example, the Five Passes were sites of watershed defenses of the Southern Song against the Jin, in 1222, and against the Yuan, in 1246; see *1670 XZ*, *juan* 2.

2. See Yi. According to the Kangxi-era county gazetteer, Macheng is a short 240 *li* northeast of the Hubei provincial capital of Wuchang but 2,540 *li* overland (nearly twice that distance by water) southwest of Beijing; see *1670 XZ*, *juan* 1.

3. Wang Baoxin, 1:6. Wang exaggerated just a bit: the average elevation of Macheng is 500 meters above sea level, but mountain villages throughout the county can be found at elevations of 1,300 meters and higher; see *MCXDMZ*, 1.

4. In the wake of the New Culture Movement vogue of popular dialectology, twentieth-century Macheng gazetteers delight in offering long glossaries of local vernacular terms and nonstandard pronunciations (*fangyan*); see, for example, *MCXZXB*, 1:10–13; *1993 XZ*, 544–68. The popular characterization of the county as having the shape of a horse's hoof appears in *1993 XZ*, 25.

5. There was another spurt of growth in the first several decades of the People's Republic. Of course, neither this nor the earlier eighteenth-century one contradicts our expectations, based on Chinese population history more generally.

6. That the late-Ming demographic collapse began as early as the mid-sixteenth century, as these figures suggest, is not what one would be led to suspect from the literature on China's so-named seventeenth-century crisis. The Macheng figures are skewed, however, by the fact that a portion of the county was administratively severed in 1563 for inclusion in the newly created county of Huang'an. The true demographic collapse in both counties more likely took place only in the 1620s.

7. There was almost certainly a third period of sharp demographic decline, not accurately represented by these figures: that of the mid-nineteenth-century rebellions. The *1993 XZ*, 71, lists a population for 1859 (the eve of the Taiping invasion) of 283,888. If credible, this figure would suggest uninterrupted growth through the 1860s and 1870s to a total of 368,312 in 1876. However, as revealed by *MCXZQB*, 3:2–3, originally published in 1935, this figure for 1859 actually represents the population in 1795 and evidently was simply copied over in 1859 from an earlier source. My strong suspicion is that the actual population in 1859 was quite a bit higher than this, and that the 1876 figure represents not new growth so much as a recovery to levels that had been attained by the eve of the Taiping and Nian campaigns and then lost during those years.

8. *1993 XZ*, 71, 75.

9. See Watson.

10. Buck, 25.

11. That is, 742,466 out of a total 1,044,967 *mou*; see *MCXZQB*, 3:3–12.

12. For but one example, see the Yongzheng emperor's edict of 1731, in *Shizong Xianhuanagdi zhupi yuzhi* (Vermilion edicts of the Yongzheng emperor).

13. See, for example, the 1858 stele erected by Magistrate Yi Guanghui outside the county seat (text reprinted in *MCXZQB*, 15:19–20). The same sentiments were echoed in the early twentieth century by Wang Baoxin, 1:6, and, in the People's Republic, in *MCXJZ*, 40–41.

14. Liu Xian; Wang Shizhen, "Macheng Mu hou junfu gongxu," in *SKQS*; Wou, personal communication.

15. Wang Baoxin, 1:6.

16. Xiong Ji, preface to *MCXJZ*; this work is now lost, but the preface is reprinted in the gazetteers of both 1882 and 1993. Biographical entries for most of the individuals mentioned in Xiong's text can be found in *Zhongguo renming da zidian*. For examples of similar rehearsals of the county's military history, see Meng Guangpeng, preface to *MCXZQB*; see also *1993 XZ*, 340. On the Western Zhou battlements, see *1993 XZ*, 526–27.

17. The earliest written source for this legend may be that by the celebrated late-Ming literatus Wang Shizhen (1526–90), who, as we shall see, had many connections within the scholar-official world of Macheng County; see Wang Shizhen, *(Youxiang) Liexian quanzhuan*, 308–9. Note, however, that there are many other stories, from different eras and localities, that merge into that of the female deity Ma Gu, popularly worshipped today throughout Chinese society; for a survey, see Zong and Liu, 719–24.

18. See, for example, Mei Guolou, "Ma Gu Dong shi," and Li Wei, "Ma Gu Xian Dong fu," both in *1882 XZ*, *juan* 3; *MCXZQB*, 123–24; *1993 XZ*, 485; *Zhongguo renming da zidian*, 215, 1128.

19. For example "Jinyu huangmin" (Admonitions to famine refugees), orig. 1674, in Yu Chenglong, 2:61–62; *1882 XZ*, 39:5; *MCXZQB*, 15:6–7; *MCXZXB*, 2:4–5.

20. *HBTZ*, *juan* 73.

21. As recounted to Zhang Guotao; see Chang, 220.

22. This structure was inherited by the Qing and remained in place until the heady "local self-government" (*difang zizhi*) movement of the early twentieth century prompted a frenetic series of drawing and redrawing of subcounty units, which coalesced by 1927 into the nine wards (*qu*) that survived through much of the People's Republic. See *MCXZQB*, 1:35; *MCXZXB*, 1:2, 9:1–11.

23. *MCXZQB*, 1:35, 3:2–3.

24. *1882 XZ*, *juan* 10; *MCXJZ* 40–41; *MCXDMZ*, 473–76; *Macheng xianwei baogao*, 5.237; personal observation, May 2004.

25. The following paragraphs draw on *1670 XZ*, *juan* 2; *MCXZQB*, 1:41–42; *1993 XZ*, 63–64, 412–15; and *MCXDMZ*, 31–34, 39–40.

26. Baiguo today is much larger still than it was in the period examined in this book, having nearly doubled in size as merchants from other commercial centers relocated there under the Japanese occupation. See *1993 XZ*, 414; *MCXDMZ*, 39–40.

27. "Shihuo zhi" (Essay on political economy), in *1882 XZ*, *juan* 10.

28. *1882 XZ*, *juan* 10; *MCXDMZ*, 157–60; *1993 XZ*, 92–93, 414–15; personal observation, May 2004.

29. *1993 XZ*, 483–84.

30. This is clearly depicted in the topographic map "Shanshui quantu," in *1882 XZ*. See also *1670 XZ*, *juan* 1; *MCXDMZ*, 1.

31. This paragraph draws on *1882 XZ*, 25:4–11; *1993 XZ*, 415; and *MCXDMZ*, 605–10, 829–33.

32. See, for example, *MCXZXB*, 5:24.

33. Wang Baoxin, 2:12. Wang hailed from the eastern slopes of the Dongshan, in Luotian County.

34. For one relatively early example, see the 1653 memorial of Huguang governor Ji Riyi, in *NMZZ*, 1*xia*.252–53.

35. Cited from the now lost 1535 county gazetteer, in *1670 XZ*, *juan* 3. Variants of this quatrain appear in later gazetteers through the twentieth century, though with the more pejorative terms occasionally softened.

36. "Yuanyou yao" (Minstrel song), reproduced in *MCXZQB*, 1:45.

37. Zhou Weiqu, "Dongshan Jiyong xu" (Preface to a collection of commemorative chants on the Dongshan), orig. 1674, reproduced in *1795 XZ*, *wenzheng* 2, and in *MCXZQB*, 14:21. We will elaborate on the context of this remark in chap. 7.

38. See, for example, *Macheng xianwei baogao*, 234–35.

39. Liu Tingju, "Qian yihou xinjian xiancheng xu" (Commemorative essay on Magistrate Qian's reconstruction of the city wall), in *MCXZQB*, 2:1. See also *MCXZXB*, 2:4–5.

40. Hu Linyi, "Macheng xian pingchen ge jushen chouban juanyu qingxing bi" (Endorsement on a petition of the Macheng magistrate regarding gentry-managed logistics bureaus), in Hu Linyi, 2:1012. On this general phenomenon in imperial history, see Franke.

41. See, for example, memorials of Huguang viceroy Luo Xiujin, SZ 7/8, and of Hubei censor Nie Jie, SZ 9/6, in *MQDA*, A12–6, A14–161. See also Yu Chenglong, 1:55–56. On the conventional notion of *neiying*, or fifth-columnism, see Wakeman, "Localism and Loyalism during the Ch'ing Conquest of Kiangnan," 59–60.

42. Meng Guangpeng, preface to *MCXZQB*.

43. Wang Shizhen, *Yanzhou sibu gao, xugao*, in *SKQS*, 90:24.

44. For samples of these reports, see Wu Jingdao, memorial of SZ 6/7/3, *MQDA*, A10–100; *1882 XZ*, 37:7–9; *Huangzhou fuzhi* (1884 ed.), *juan* 10; *MCXZQB*, 5:20; *MCXZXB*, 5:24–26, 5:48–49.

45. Robinson, 100, *passim.* A key contention of Robinson's work, again supported by Macheng sources, is that widespread banditry in North China was not new to the era of Ming decline but was chronic even during the dynasty's most effective years.

46. Chen Tingjing, *Wuting wenbian*, 41:5–6.

47. *1993 XZ*, 356.

48. On this incident, see *MCXZXB*, 5:23–25, 10:1, 11:11. For representative reports of other bandit activities, see various entries for Zhengde 6 and 7 in *MSLLZ*, 620–24; Hubei governor Hui Jixun, memorial of GX 18/7/28, *Gongzhong dang Guangxu chao zouzhe*, 7:293–95; *1882 XZ*, 37:7–9; *MCXZQB*, 2:2, 5:20; *Huang'an gongzuo baogao: guanyu "Huang-Ma baodong" de jingguo*, 11–14; *Minguo ribao* (Republican Daily News, Hankow), Jan. 18, 1927, and Feb. 6, 1927; *People's Tribune* (Hankow), June 10, 1927.

49. Mei Guozhen, "Yu mou liangchu" (To an unnamed grain intendant), in *1670 XZ*, *juan* 10.

50. For the twentieth century, there is a large literature on who became bandits, and on their relationship to other "forces of disorder." See, among other works, Zhang Zhenzhi; Nagano, especially 237–38, which offers details on full-time bandits in 1930s Dabie Shan; Dai; Cai Shaoqing, *Minguo shiqi de tufei*. At a later point, this study will consider Elizabeth Perry's contributions to the debate.

51. See, for example, *MQDA*, A10–100; "Xuan wei Chen Huihui yu" (Proclamation announcing the pacification of Chen Huihui), in Yu Chenglong, 1:64–65. David Robinson also notes the ease with which late-imperial official sources labeled disparate social forces as bandits, and the problem this creates for the historian; see Robinson, 25, 67.

52. Chang, 215; Billingsley, 34–35. Bandits within their ranks, both real and imagined, were also a major target of purges by local Communist leaders in the 1930s, as we shall see.

53. In monthly reports submitted to provincial authorities during the Nanjing era, Macheng officials reported the names of captured Communist guerrillas and local bandits, recognizing that these were two distinct categories but recording them together; see "Macheng zhengfu banli hongjun tufei anjian yuebao biao" (Monthly summaries of case reports on captured Communists and local bandits), 1929–1934, HPA.

54. For example, Zhang Qun, *Hubei xianzheng gaikuang*, 508–9; *MCXZXB*, 5:48–49.

55. *MCXZQB*, 2:13, 2:18, 7:5.

56. Ibid., 15:33.

57. *Huangzhou fuzhi shiyi*, *juan* 6. For background on the rather illustrious Liu family, see *MCXZQB*, 8:3–4, 8:9, 9:27. One suspects that this unflattering story may have had its origins with other local Macheng lineages that harbored some resentment against the Liu.

58. Taniguchi, "Yu Seiryū no hōkō hō ni tsuite," 73. According to Nicola di Cosmo, *niaoqiang* were originally of Portuguese design, Japanese modifications of which had been introduced into China during the mid-sixteenth century by pirates along the southeast coast. Their dissemination to the Dabie Shan highlands did not take long and was no doubt affected by the many local men who had served in military posts on the coastal frontier; see di Cosmo, 132–33.

59. Wang Baoxin, 3:5. David Robinson, who is keen to emphasize the ubiquitous presence of swords, cudgels, bows, and other weapons throughout rural China during the Ming, nevertheless sees access to firearms as largely a state monopoly in this era. Macheng, again, looks to have been ahead of the curve; see Robinson, 91–96, 133.

60. *MCXZXB* 5:22–23; *Huang'an gongzuo baogao: guanyu "Huang-Ma baodong" de jingguo*, 11–14.

61. Yu Chenglong, 2:13.

62. *1993 XZ*, 514; *MCXZQB*, *juan* 8.

63. Huangfu, in *SKQS*, 49:2–3.

64. *Ming shi*, in *SKQS*, 302:18.

65. Li Xian, "Zhongyi dafu Haungzhou zhifu zhishi Teng jun mubiao," in Li Xian, *Gurang ji*, in *SKQS*, 16:14–15.

66. The Mei-Geng dispute will be treated in chap. 4. For another feud involving the Mei, see Mei Guozhen, "Yu Liu yihou shu" (Letter to Magistrate Liu), in *1670 XZ*, *juan* 10.

67. *Ming shilu*, entry for Chongzhen 1, in *MSLLZ*, 1009.

68. For the local folklore version, see *1993 XZ*, 485–86.

69. Yuan Mei, "Shu Macheng yu" (The legal case at Macheng), in Wang Yingzhi, 2:162–64. I thank my colleague Tobie Meyer-Fong for bringing the Yuan Mei version of this story to my attention.

70. See Liu Jianye.

71. According to Liu Jianye's highly fanciful elaboration, the problem stemmed from Ms. Yang's immodesty: when the aspiring scholar Tu invited literati acquaintances to his house, his beautiful wife routinely burst into their midst to exchange jokes with the men, to Tu's mortification.

72. The 1935 county gazetteer shows that Chen Ding became Macheng magistrate in 1735, and it credits that *nengli* (capable official) with resolution of this famous case, thus establishing some basis for it in historical fact; see *MCXZQB*, 6:19, 7:12. It seems likely to me that Chen, perhaps in retirement, may have been Yuan Mei's principal source for his story.

73. See Bianco.

74. Wang Shizhen, "Macheng Mu hou junfu gongxu," in *SKQS*, 59:26. Wang draws an allusion from the *Shi ji* in order to compare social behavior in Macheng to that among particular species of mountain goats observing an extreme hierarchical pecking order.

75. See, for example, *1670 XZ*, *juan* 10; *1882 XZ* 37:7; Cai Ji'ou, 30–31; He Yulin, 34.

76. *MCXZQB*, 7:15; *1993 XZ*, 560. On the routinization of late-imperial grain riots and local official quasi-tolerance, see Wong.

77. *Ming shi*, in *SKQS*, 166:14.

78. Mei Guolou, "Caoyun jiezhe ji" (Record of grain-tribute commutation), in *MCXZQB*, 3:9. The Mei lineage—major property holders in Macheng's south central plain, and in immediate shipping range of the county seat—would clearly have been among those most aggrieved by the original commutation scheme.

79. *MCXZQB*, 7:13.

80. He Yulin, 34.

81. Wang Baoxin, 2:13–15.

82. *Chinese Recorder* 23 (June 1892); *Chinese Recorder* 47 (Feb. 1916); Cai Ji'ou, 27; *1993 XZ*, 11–12, 514, 536. I am grateful to the Swedish historian Marie-Christine Skuncke for providing me additional information on this incident. On the Duanwu festival as a more general flash point for attacks on nonlocals in central China, see, for example, Perdue, "Insiders and Outsiders."

83. *Ming shilu*, entry for Jiajing 3/1, in *MSLLZ*, 629; *1670 XZ*, *juan* 3; *MCXZQB*, 5:13; *1993 XZ*, 12.

84. *1882 XZ*, 37:8.

85. Meng Guangpeng, preface to *MCXZQB*; *MCXZQB*, 2:1.

86. Mei Zhihuan, "Yu Huangzhou sili Zhou Zhitian" (To Huangzhou magistrate Zhou Zhitian), in Mei Zhihuan, 3:25; *Fengyun bianhuan*, 43–47.

Chapter 2

1. Ye Ziqi, 41. Ye's capsule biography can be found in *Zhongguo renming da zidian*, 1300.
2. Meng Siming, 170–206; Schurmann, 22–32; Yang Na, 120.
3. See Johnson.
4. *1670 XZ*, 6:1.
5. Hu Wokun, in *SKQS*, 5:27; Ouyang Xiu, in *SKQS*, 25:1.
6. See Hartwell; see also Hymes, *Statesmen and Gentlemen*.

7. Su Shi, in *SKQS*, 11:20; *1670 XZ, juan* 9; *1882 XZ*, 4:13–15; *MCXZQB*, 15:20–22. On Chen Zao and his relationship with Su, see *Zhongguo renming da zidian*, 1097.

8. Zhang's campaign against heterodox beliefs may not have had a lasting impact, but the temple he founded certainly did. Over the centuries, it accrued a variety of other deities beyond Fuzhu shen, and through the twentieth century it was popularly regarded as one of the most efficacious (*ling*) sites of divine invocation in the entire region; see *MCXZQB*, 2:11–13. On the persistent late-imperial literati crusades against *yinsi*, see Schneewind.

9. Su Shi, in *SKQS*, 11:20.

10. *1882 XZ*, 2:27, 9:1–9; *MCXZQB*, 4:29–35; Wang and Lei, 243.

11. *1670 XZ*, 6:1; *MCXZQB*, 8a:1; *MCXJZ*, 21. On the 1315 Yuan restoration of the civil service examination, see Endicott-West, 97.

12. *1670 XZ*, 5:1–2; *Huang'an xianzhi* (1697), 1:2. On Yuan local government in general, see Endicott-West, *passim*.

13. Wang Baoxin, 1:6.

14. Smith, 89–94. See also Schurmann, 6.

15. Endicott-West, 105–19.

16. See Meng Siming.

17. *MCXZQB*, 10:62. The Zou lineage was headquartered in the portion of northwest Macheng that was detached in the late sixteenth century to form part of the new Huang'an County; for the prominence of the Zou in this new jurisdiction, see *Huang'an xianzhi* (1697), *juan* 3.

18. Liu Shen, "Qin shi yitian jibei" (Stele recording the charitable estate of the Qin family), in *MCXZXB*, 14:14–15.

19. *MCXZQB*, 8:26–27.

20. According to Schurmann, 22–32, such large concentrations of land in private, often mercantile, hands was typical in the former Southern Song domains under the Mongols.

21. Wu Han, 26; Yang Na, 109–10; Schurmann, 31–32; Mote, 37–41.

22. Quan Heng, 19–21; Wang and Lei, 437–39; Dreyer, 18–19.

23. Wang and Lei, 446–47.

24. *1882 XZ*, 37:6; *MCXZQB*, 15:2.

25. Basic sources on Zou's rebellion include *Yuan shi* (1976 ed.), 2.892–93 (pagination corresponds to *juan* 42 in *SKQS*); *Ming shi* (1974 ed.), 7.3687–89 (pagination corresponds to *Ming shi, juan* 123, in *SKQS*); and Xu Qianxue, in *SKQS*, 174:8. A capsule biography appears in *1993 XZ*, 560.

26. On Huaqiao, see *1795 XZ*, 3:4. Zou is identified as a native of that place by Wang Baoxin, 1:6.

27. *1993 XZ*, 9; Yang Na, 109–10.

28. Ye Ziqi, 43; *1670 XZ, juan* 3; Wu Han, 21–27; Wang and Lei, 444; Yang Na, 109–10.

29. Ye Ziqi, 51; Wang Baoxin, 1:6–7; Romeyn Taylor, "Hsu Shou-hui," in *DMB*, 600–602.

30. Quan, 21; Ye Ziqi, 44; Wang and Lei, 440–41; John W. Dardess, "Han Lin-er," in *DMB*, 485–88.

31. Dreyer, 15.

32. The basic sources on the founding of Tianwan are Ye Ziqi, 51; *Yuan shi, juan*

42, in *SKQS*; *1670 XZ*, *juan* 3; *Huangzhou fuzhi* (1884), 10*xia*:17; *Hubei tongzhi*, 1777–78; and Wang Baoxin, 1:6–7. Wang mentions the existence (in 1907) of the *Tianwan guozhi* (Gazetteer of the Tianwan realm), but I have found no independent confirmation of its survival. For modern treatments, see also Wang and Lei, 445–51; Yang Na, 109–10; Qu Shulin.

33. Yang Na, 120.

34. Quan Heng, 23; *HBTZ*, 1778; Wang and Lei, 446–47.

35. *HBTZ*, 1779; Wang Baoxin, 1:7; Chen Shisong, ed., 5.19–27; Entenmann, 160–65; John W. Dardess, "Ming Yu-chen," in *DMB*, 1069–73.

36. Quan Heng, 28–29; Ye Ziqi, 44; Wang Baoxin, 1:7; Wang and Lei, 451–52; Romeyn Taylor, "Hsu Shou-hui," in *DMB*, 600–602; Dreyer, 21. On Toghto's dismissal, see Dardess, "Shun-ti and the End of Yüan Rule in China," 578–81.

37. Ye Ziqi, 51.

38. *Yuan shi*, *juan* 45, in *SKQS*; Ye Ziqi, 52; *HBTZ*, 1778; Wang and Lei, 454–58; Yang Na, 125.

39. Macheng County Place Name Leadership Group, comp., 1105.

40. *Yuan shi*, *juan* 445, in *SKQS*; *Ming shi*, *juan* 123, in *SKQS*; Ye Ziqi, 53–54; Wang Baoxin, 1:7; Wang and Lei, 467–69.

41. *Yuan shi*, *juan* 195, cited in Wang and Lei, 449.

42. Cited in Yang Na, 120. The parallel with the treatment of "counterrevolutionaries" in the Great Proletarian Cultural Revolution is hard to ignore.

43. Meng Siming, 210–12, *passim*.

44. See, for example, Yang Na; Qu Shusen; Wang and Lei.

45. Mote, 39.

46. Tang, 20:40; Ye Ziqi, 3:14.

47. Yang Na, 120; Qu Shulin, 104; Wang and Lei, 450.

48. Cited in Yang Na, 120.

49. Wang Shizhen, "Wanyai Huang gong muzhi ming" (Tomb inscription for Mr. Huang of Wanyai), in Wang Shizhen, *Yanzhou sibu gao, xugao*, in *SKQS*, 95:20–29.

50. "Lu shi jiazhen zhuan" (Biography of the martyr Ms. Lu), in Tang, 20:40–41.

51. See especially Qu Shulin, 104–6.

52. Biography of Wei Zhongli, *Yuan shi*, *juan* 195, cited in Wang and Lei, 450.

53. Ye Ziqi, 51–52.

54. Qu Shulin, 104–5; Yang Na, 109.

55. Thompson, 49 (emphasis in original).

56. *MCXZQB*, 4:1.

57. Yang Na, 122–24; Qu Shulin, 105; Wang and Lei, 444.

58. *MSLLZ*, 606–7.

59. Ye Ziqi, 61.

60. See ter Haar, "China's Inner Demons," 37.

61. Yang Na, "Tianwan Dahan hongjin jun shi shulun," 121.

62. Wu Han, 21–27.

63. Lieu, 260–61.

64. Yang Na, 121.

65. Shek, 97–101, 108.

66. Snow, 295.

67. For Song Lian (1310–81), Yuan-era *jinshi* and compiler of the *Yuan shi* under the Ming, see his *Song Wenxian gong quan ji* (Complete works of Song Lian) (Taibei: Zhonghua shuju, 1965). A substantial portion of this work is devoted to accounts of how Tianwan armies "killed the great families and plundered their estates" (*shalie jushi*). For Tang, Quan, and Ye Ziqi, see citations above.

68. *MCXZQB*, 15:27.

69. *Ming shi*, entry for Zhizheng 25/8, extracted in *MSLLZ*, 606.

70. *1993 XZ*, 9.

71. Chen Shisong, ed., 5:171.

72. Hu Zhaoxi, 70.

73. Entenmann, 165–66.

74. The total in Hechuan was 40 percent, in Guang'an it was 54 percent, and in other Sichuan counties it was also strikingly high; see Hu Zhaoxi, 69, 74–78.

75. Entenmann, 173–74.

76. Wang Gang, 83–84. On the history of the "Great Xia" state, see Chen Shisong, ed., 19–27; see also Wang and Lei, 467–69.

77. *MCXZQB*, 10:65–68. The fact that biographies of Yang and other successful émigrés were to be found in gazetteers of Macheng itself suggests the strength of continuing native-place and diaspora ties.

Chapter 3

1. Mao Fengshao, "Macheng zhi lue xu" (preface to the 1535 Macheng County gazetteer), in *1993 XZ*, 607.

2. The county population grew from 104,180 to 145,095 in the 100 years between 1412 and 1512, and it rose to 148,240 in 1556; see *1670 XZ*, 3:1.

3. The chronology of *zaiyi* (catastrophic and unusual events) in the 1935 county gazetteer leaves a record of only very sporadic failed harvests between the founding of the Ming and the late sixteenth century, in contrast to frequent such reports for the immediately prior and subsequent periods; see *MCXZQB*, 15:2–4.

4. Ibid., 8:26–27.

5. See Iwami.

6. Satō Fumitoshi, 169.

7. *1670 XZ*, 3:5–10; see also *Huangzhou fuzhi* (1884), 3:67. Given the persistent disorder of the late sixteenth and early seventeenth centuries, I believe it is a safe assumption that these products were not newly introduced in that era, and that the 1535 gazetteer, had it survived, would have reflected a nearly similar catalogue of products. Most of the items in this impressive 1670 list, I believe, were new to the early and mid-Ming.

8. *MCXJZ*, 40–41.

9. *Li shi xiafen zongpu*; *MCXZQB*, 8:26–27.

10. *MCXZQB*, 1:42; Zhang Jianmin, 438.

11. *1670 XZ*, 3:4–5.

12. *MCXZQB*, 4:35.

13. Li Wenzhi, "Lun Qingdai qianqi de tudi zhanyou guanxi."

14. See Yasuno. See also Masaaki for a somewhat restructured English-language version of work on which Yasuno drew, and which originally appeared in *Shigaku zasshi*

(1957–58). The labor-relations aspects of the Ming land concentration—most notably the rise of servility—will be discussed in chap. 5.

15. For example, one student of Frederick Mote—who, as we saw in the last chapter, is quite skeptical of class-analysis historiography in general—concludes from his own highly cautious analysis that the widespread land concentration of the mid-Ming is undeniable, despite its susceptibility to politicized overstatement; see Heijdra, especially 277–78.

16. The clearest evidence of this comes from *Xicun Cheng shi zongpu*. Unfortunately, the most unequivocal descriptions of this process in this genealogy (see, for example, 2:7–19) describe events of the early and mid-Qing rather than the Ming. The origins of the lineage's power locally, both as merchants and landlords, lay in the fourteenth and fifteenth centuries, however, and it seems fair to assume that a similar application of commercial profits to land acquisition characterized that earlier era as well.

17. The best local evidence comes from the case of Magistrate Mu Wei, discussed below. The broader prevalence of land concentration via commendation in the late Ming has been explored by many scholars (see, for example, Li Wenzhi, "Lun Qingdai qianqi de tudi zhanyou guanxi"), and their work is nicely summarized in Elvin, chap. 15.

18. *1882 XZ*, 9:1–9.

19. See Wang Libo. The site of this temple in the 1920s fell in the jurisdiction of Huang'an County, but through most of the Ming it lay in Macheng.

20. We saw in chap. 2 two late-Yuan examples of formation of a charitable estate by the Qin; for a substantial Ming example, see *Xicun Cheng shi zongpu*, *juan* 2.

21. Wou, 122, 410.

22. *1993 XZ*, 81–82.

23. Zhang Qun.

24. Wang Shusheng, cited in Chang, 221; *1993 XZ*, 232–33.

25. "Zhoushi zupu xu" (preface to the Zhou lineage genealogy), in Geng, 11:32–34.

26. Personal visit, May 2004.

27. *MCXZQB*, 8:26–27. On the naming of streets in the newly built county seat, see *1670 XZ*, *juan* 2.

28. Zhongguanyi Township Gazetteer Compilation Office, ed., 2–3. Zhang Qun, 2.511, likewise stresses that collective dwelling by kinship is the local norm.

29. Cited and discussed in Han Hengyu, 98. Timothy Brook has written very perceptively on similar phenomena in the Ming-era Lower Yangzi region; see Brook, "Funerary Ritual and the Building of Lineages in Late Imperial China," and Brook, "Family Continuity and Cultural Hegemony."

30. *MCXZXB*, 1:9.

31. Perdue, "Insiders and Outsiders," 170, 173; Rowe, "Success Stories"; Beattie, 26–27; Dennerline, "Marriage, Adoption, and Charity in the Development of Lineages in Wu-hsi from Sung to Ch'ing," 177, 181–82; Brook, "Family Continuity and Cultural Hegemony." As for Jiangxi itself, John W. Dardess's detailed study of Taihe County, in the Gan River Valley, notes that a few subsequently prominent lineages were creations of the Yuan-Ming transition but that the majority established themselves in earlier eras of dynastic transition; see Dardess, *A Ming Society*, 112–13. Dardess adds that by the late fourteenth century Taihe was already largely "full," and that consequently "it became an

exporter of population rather than an importer." Obviously, the evidence from other central China localities supports this view.

32. See *Li shi xiafen zongpu*, especially the 1805 preface by the "expectant magistrate" Li Yuda, 1:5–7.

33. Li Xunmu, preface, orig. 1805, in *Li shi xiafen zongpu*, 1:9–10; Li Xunmu, "Fenxiu congpu shuyao" (Criteria for dividing the revised genealogy into three branches), orig. 1800, in *Li shi xiafen zongpu*, 1:26–27.

34. Liu Ruxi, preface, in *Li shi xiafen zongpu*, 1:3–4.

35. See *Shi shi zongpu*, especially the 1924 preface by Shi Dianhao, *juan* 2.

36. *Shi shi zongpu, juan* 4.

37. See *Xicun Cheng shi zongpu*, especially Cheng Yinnan, comp., "Chengshi shouxing yuanliu kao" (An investigation of the origins and evolution of the Cheng surname), in ibid. One must wonder, of course, whether the link to one of the indisputably great mercantile lineages of Huizhou was not an after-the-fact invention, based upon the happy coincidence of a common surname.

38. *Xicun Cheng shi zongpu*, 2:23.

39. Beyond the evidence of the genealogy itself, see *MCXZQB, juan* 8, *passim*.

40. Self-described as a fellow villager (*tongli*) of the Cheng, Yu Jinfang was enlisted to write the preface to the lineage's 1919 genealogy. On Cheng Yinnan, see *MCXZXB*, 8:1, 13:1.

41. I have consulted two identically titled versions of the Macheng Lin genealogy, the *Lin shi zongpu* of 1873 and that of 1947.

42. An interesting history of this temple, on an island in the Ju River, and its endowment property is reprinted as "Dahezhou shand xinkai di ji" (Record of the land newly reclaimed on Dahe Island), in ibid. (1947 ed.).

43. See *Chen shi zongpu*; *Xiong shi zongpu*; *Zhou shi congpu*; *Liuxiu Cai shi zongpu*; *Wucheng Zeng shi congpu*. The Zhou claimed ultimate descent from the Duke of Zhou (d. 1094 BCE) via the Hunanese neo-Confucian Zhou Dunyi (1017–1073 CE); the Zeng claimed descent from Confucius' disciple Zengzi (505–436 BCE).

44. The Shi and the Lin, in fact, each provide two separate sets of rules compiled at different points in time. This circumstance allows some reflection on shifts in lineage strategies in response to changing environments, an issue to which we shall return in chap. 10. The rules appear in *Shi shi zongpu*, 3:8–15, 3:15–22; in *Xicun Cheng shi zongpu*, 1:12–21; in *Lin shi zongpu* (1873 ed.), 1:22–25, 1:29–33; and in *Chen shi zongpu, juan* 1.

45. *Shi shi zongpu*, 1:22.

46. See especially ibid., 3:17, 3:20.

47. Ibid., 3:14. We will return to the makeup of this underclass in chap. 5.

48. *Xicun Cheng shi zongpu*, 1:17–18.

49. The rules here closely echo Confucianized exhortations on "doing well by doing good" in the contemporary genre of merchant guides; see Lufrano.

50. *Xicun Cheng shi zongpu*, 2:18–19.

51. *1670 XZ, juan* 10.

52. On the Zou's prominence in Huang'an, see *Huang'an xianzhi* (1697), 9:3.

53. *MCXZQB*, 9:26–27.

54. Liu Bian, "Chongxiu ruxue ji" (Commemorative essay on the reconstruction of the Confucian school-temple) (ca. 1535), in *1882 XZ*, 8:3.

55. Mao Fengshao, "Macheng zhi lue xu" (Preface to the 1535 Macheng County gazetteer), in *1993 XZ*, 607.

56. Guo Qinghua, "Xuanju zhi" (Preface to lists of examination degree winners), in *1882 XZ*, 14:1.

57. Macheng's experience here was certainly very striking, but it was not unique. A similarly successful process of systematic promotion of native sons into upper official ranks is described by Dardess for Jiangxi's Taihe County in the same mid-Ming era, and by Beattie for Anhui's Huizhou Prefecture in the early and mid-Qing; see Dardess, *A Ming Society*; see also Beattie. The late-nineteenth-century experience in this regard of Hunan's Xiang River Valley is widely known.

58. *1882 XZ*, 8:1–9; *MCXZQB*,4:6–26.

59. *1882 XZ*, 9:9–11; *MCXZQB*, 4:35; *1993 XZ*, 470.

60. *MCXZQB*, 2:20–21.

61. Lists of these degree winners by name appear in *1795 XZ*, *juan* 12, and *MCXZQB*, *juan* 8.

62. Brook, "Family Continuity and Cultural Hegemony," 29–30.

63. Zhang Jianmin, 614–16.

64. *Huangzhou fuzhi* (1500 ed.), 9:45–47. For more on Li's career, see below.

65. Time-series and comparative data drawn from Zhang Jianmin, 614–16.

66. This document, known as the "Macheng Ming kemu zongbian," was apparently compiled in manuscript during the Ming itself but was not included in published county gazetteers prior to the 1882 Macheng County gazetteer; see *1882 XZ*, 14:33–34. It was reprinted again in the 1935 Macheng County gazetteer; see *MCXZQB*, 8a:26–27.

67. *MCXZQB*, 9:27, 9:29–30, 9:43.

68. *1882 XZ*, 8:9–10, 14:1; *MCXZQB*, 4:23–25, 8b:26–34, *juan* 9, *passim*; *MCXJZ*, 22.

69. *MCXZQB*, 2:37–40.

70. *1882 XZ*, 40:14–15; *MCXZQB*, 15:25. The very fact that this quasi-humorous anecdote (*yishi*) was repeatedly included in county gazetteers suggests that it was the source of a rather smirky local pride and was also considered illustrative of how successful native sons ought to behave toward *tongxiang* junior scholars.

71. *Huang'an xianzhi* (1697 ed.), 9:3; *MCXZQB*, 9:25–26, 15:22.

72. *Ming shilu*, entry for Chenghua 6/5 (1470), in *MSLLZ*, 1345; *Ming shi*, in *SKQS*, 189:1–3; *1882 XZ*, 32:18; *MCXZQB* 9:1–4, 9:28; *MCXJZ*, 22. For his bold youthful memorial impeaching the powerful grand secretary Liu Jiyin, Li Wenxiang also won mention in a canonical history of Confucian orthodoxy; see Huang Zongxi, in *SKQS*, 9:11.

73. *MCXZQB*, 8:4, 9:27, 9:29. Liu Xun's biography is in *Zhongguo renming da zidian*, 1462.

74. Liu Tianhe, *Wenshui ji*, in *SKQS*. Liu's official correspondence from his long tenure as Shaan-Gan governor general was collected in his memoirs; see Liu Tianhe, *Dufu zouyi*, in *SKQS*.

75. *Ming shilu*, entry for Jiajing 24/12, in *MSLLZ*, 1353–54; *Ming shi*, in *SKQS*, 200:19–21; *1882 XZ*, 8:9–10, 32:5; *MCXZQB*, 9:4–6, 9:32–33; *Zhongguo renming da zidian*, 1434, 1447; Liu Hong, "*Yipeng xue, Jinping mei, Macheng*." We will return to Liu Chengxi and Liu Tong below.

76. *Zhoushi jiacheng* (The rise of the Zhou family), unseen by this author but cited in *MCXZQB*, 9:7–8. It must be pointed out that, given the presence of several prominent

lineages in Macheng bearing the Zhou surname, and given the unavailability of genealogies for any of these, my breakdown of Zhou scholar-officials by lineage is somewhat tentative. Most especially, I believe (but cannot be certain) that the lineage including Zhou Hongzu discussed here is that of the Xindian Zhou, and that the lineage including Hongzu's near-contemporary Zhou Sijing (discussed below) is a different one, very likely that of the Juedanshan Zhou. My chief evidence in this regard is negative: despite many textual references to familial relations among the Zhou, none exists to link the two large groups of Zhou men bearing, respectively, the "Hong" generational character and the "Si" generational character.

77. *MCXZQB*, 9:28–29, 9:45–46.

78. *1882 XZ*, 18:12–13, 18:6–28; *MCXZQB*, 8b:34, 9:7–8, 14:25; *MCXJZ*, 23–24. Hongzu merited a biography; see *Ming shi*, in *SKQS*, 215:5–7. All three of these Zhou luminaries have entries in *Zhongguo renming da zidian*, 526.

Chapter 4

1. Liu Hong, "*Yipeng xue, Jinping mei, Macheng*."

2. Yuan Hongdao, *Xiaobi tang ji*, ed. Li Changgeng (1608); Zhou Qun, 40–43; Chaves, 23. For a concise account of Yuan's poetic innovations, see Nienhauser, ed., 955–56.

3. Tu Lien-che, "Chiao Hung," in *ECCP*, 145–46. Celebrated for having been awarded first place in the palace examination of 1589, Jiao had been a student of Macheng's Geng Dingxiang, on whom more below.

4. *MCXZQB*, 1:29–30, 2:27; *MCXJZ*, 37–39.

5. Yuan Zhongdao, "Longhu" and other poems, in Pan Zenghong, 3:1, 3:13, *passim*; *1882 XZ*, *juan* 3.

6. *MCXZQB*, 15:11–12.

7. *MCXJZ*, 24–25; Ray Huang, 154–55.

8. See *Mei shi zupu*, a modern edition in a Mei tradition of genealogy writing claiming to date from the late sixteenth century. See also Qian, "Mei Changgong zhuan," 1.

9. *Mei shi zupu*, 19:1; *MCXZQB*, 9:30. As one outcome of the factional conflicts of the Hongzhi era, Mei Ji was cashiered from his post, but, family sources claim, he remained a hero in Huizhou for his championing of local interests.

10. Qian, *Muzhai chuji*, 3.1628. I thank Wang Fan-sen for bringing this source to my attention.

11. *MCXZQB*, 9:33, 9:36, 14:1–4; *1993 XZ*, 488; *Zhongguo renming da zidian*, 1004.

12. The Mei intermarried strategically within Macheng, most densely with the county's indisputably most powerful lineage, that of Grand Secretary Liu Tianhe. Mei Guozhen himself married two wives from the Liu lineage and betrothed three of his daughters to Liu sons (local historian Li Min, personal communication). The local prominence of the Mei survived even into the Maoist era: in the 1960s, the head of the Macheng Women's Bureau was a Mei daughter; see Mei Jiwen.

13. *Mei shi zupu*, 19:8; Jiang, 27. Dozens of Mei's poems are printed in *1670 XZ*, *juan* 9 and *juan* 10, with several of these repeatedly reprinted in subsequent gazetteers. His collected memorials (*Mei Kesheng zoushu*) and his various accounts of rebel pacification campaigns in the northwest (*Zheng Pei zouyi* and *Xizheng ji*) were all published in the early seventeenth century.

14. Mei Guozhen, letters to Li Zhi, reprinted in Pan, 4:1–2.

15. *Ming shi* (1974 ed.), 5976–79. For an outline of Mei's ideas on fortification, see Mei Guozhen, "Jiabao bianbao shu." On the Pubei Rebellion and Mei's decisive role in quashing it, see Swope.

16. *Ming shilu*, entry for Wanli 33/8, in *MSLLZ*, 1356–57; *MCXZQB*, 8b:34. The details of Mei Guozhen's official career are recorded at some length in *MCXZQB*, 9:9–16 and are summarized in *1993 XZ*, 488, in *MCXJZ*, 24, and in *Zhongguo renming da zidian*, 1004.

17. Mei Guozhen, "Yuqi liangshu" (Letter to the provincial grain commissioner), orig. ca. 1590, in *1670 XZ*, *juan* 10.

18. Mei Guozhen, "Song yihou Liu Yibai ruqin xu" (Letter of presentation to the throne of Magistrate Liu Wenqi), orig. 1601, in *1670 XZ*, *juan* 9.

19. Mei Guolou, "Caoyun jiezhe ji" (Record of grain tribute commutation), orig. ca. 1595, in *MCXZQB*, 3:9.

20. Wang Shizhen, "Macheng Mu Hou junfu gongxu," in *SKQS*, 59:26–28.

21. Ibid.

22. Wang Shizhen, "Wanyai Huang gong muzhi ming" (Tomb inscription for Mr. Huang of Wanyai), in Wang Shizhen, *Yanzhou sibu gao, xugao*, in *SKQS*, 95:20–29.

23. *1670 XZ*, *juan* 7. See also Mao Fengshao, "Macheng zhi lue xu" (Preface to the 1535 Macheng County gazetteer), in *1993 XZ*, 607; *MCXZQB*, 8:13.

24. Huang Juan, "Mu hou yisi xu" (Commemorative essay in honor of Magistrate Mu), in *1670 XZ*, *juan* 9. Huang's essay portraying the heroic efforts of Mu Wei became an entrenched component of local elite lore, reprinted in subsequent county gazetteers down through the early twentieth century; see *MCXZQB*, 7:4–5.

25. *1882 XZ*, 14:32.

26. Wang Shizhen, "Macheng Mu Hou junfu gongxu," in *SKQS*.

27. Mei Guozhen, "He Mu hou yingjiang xu" (On Magistrate Mu's commendation), in *MCXZQB*, 7:5.

28. *1882 XZ*, 18:13–14; *MCXZQB*, 8b:34, 9:8–9; Julia Ching, "Keng Ting-hsiang," in *DMB*, 718–20.

29. *MCXZQB*, 9:9; *Zhongguo renming da zidian*, 836–37. I follow Jin Jiang in romanizing Dinglii ("lii," principle) with a double vowel, in order to differentiate him from his brother Dingli ("li," strength).

30. Geng Dingxiang, "Ti Jingye xiansheng yulu" (A proposal endorsing the writings of Lu Nan [Lu Jingye]), in Geng, 16:8–10.

31. Geng Dingxiang, "Ti Huang'an xiangyue" (A proposal to institute the community compact system in Huang'an county), in Geng, 16:7–8. For models of how *xiangyue* was actually implemented in other localities during this period, see McDermott, "Emperor, Elites, and Commoners," 299–351; see also Hauf. On *tongmin* as a rallying cry for reform, see Handlin.

32. Geng Dingxiang, "He Wang Hou Shao'ai xinzheng jiangli xu" (A proposal that Magistrate Wang receive imperial commendation for his innovative policies), in *MCXZQB*, 7:6–7.

33. The following paragraphs draw primarily upon *Huang'an xianzhi* (1697 ed.), 1:2–12. See also *1993 XZ*, 10.

34. *Huang'an xianzhi* (1697 ed.), *juan* 9, *passim*.

35. Ibid., 9:4, 10a:14.

36. *Juedanshan Zhou shi zongpu* (n.d.). I thank local historian Li Min for making available to me her photocopy of this genealogy, the original of which is held in the Hong'an County Archives.

37. Hai Rui's testimonial, "Zeng Zhou Liutang rujin," was, unsurprisingly, reprinted in successive Macheng gazetteers; see, for example, *1882 XZ*, 33:5–6. It is also the proud subject of a recent article by a Macheng local archivist and historian; see Liu Hong, "Hai Rui jingzhong de qingquan," 46.

38. No fewer than five letters to Zhou Sijing are included in Zhang Juzheng's collected correspondence; see Ray Huang, 258. Biographical entries on the Zhou brothers appear in *MCXZQB*, 9:32, 9:47, and in *Zhongguo renming da zidian*, 533.

39. *MCXZQB*, 5:11–12.

40. Twenty-one letters from Geng to Zhou, most on this subject, are reprinted in Geng, 3:35–63. This collection also includes a preface that Geng contributed to the Zhou lineage's published genealogy; see ibid., 11:32–34.

41. Standard treatments of Li's life and career include Shimada, chap. 3; Rong; Zhu Qianzhi; and K. C. Hsiao, "Li Chih," in *DMB*, 807–18.

42. *MCXZQB*, 9:8–9, 10:63–64. For a detailed analysis of the Confucian-Buddhist syncretism of this period, and of Li Zhi's pivotal position in this, see Araki. For its social impact, see Brook, *Praying for Power*. For general discussions of the Taizhou school and this intellectual circle, see Shimada, chap. 2; de Bary, 145–248; Dimberg; and Peterson, 708–88.

43. Rong, 45–47.

44. *Huang'an xianzhi* (1697 ed.), 12:15–16.

45. Li Zhi, "He Xinyin lun" (On He Xinyin), in Li Zhi, *Fenshu*, 88–90; Li Zhi, "Yu Jiao Yiyuan taishi" (Letter to Jiao Hong), in Li Zhi, *Xu fenshu*, 27–29; Rong, 53–55. For the ambiguous circumstances of He Xinyin's death, see Dimberg, 50–54, and Peterson, 734–35.

46. Li Zhi, "Ta Zhou Youshan" (Reply to Zhou Sijing), in Li Zhi, *Xu fenshu*, 1:25; Yuan Zhongdao, "Longhu" (Dragon Lake), in Pan, *Li Wenling waiji*, 3:1. For analysis of this pattern of patronage, see Brook, *Praying for Power.*

47. Zhou Qun, 40–43; Rong, 72–73; *MCXZQB*, 10:63–64. The multistranded links among Li Zhi, Jiao Hong, and Yuan Hongdao during this period are nicely treated in Chow, 134–38; Chow emphasizes in particular that Li's "deceptively reclusive life" in Macheng was in fact "but one point in the intricate and well-connected" network of commercialized literary production in the late Ming. The Dragon Lake Group is a source of intense local pride in Macheng today. It is immortalized in such local history collections as Ling and Li, eds., which brings together several hundred poems, letters, and essays by members of the circle, and in local accounts the group is extolled for its "progressive" thought, especially in contrast to that of the wider region; see, for example, Zhou Rucheng. Dragon Lake itself no longer exists, apart from some scattered marshy pools, having been reclaimed as farmland by local residents.

48. "Saying Goodbye to the Monk Wu-nien," trans. Jonathan Chaves, in Chaves, 48–49. Mei Zhihuan's collected works contain no fewer than twenty-four letters to Wunian as well as an epitaph and an inscription for the monk's portrait; see Mei Zhihuan, 4:5–17, 6:39, 7:29–31.

49. Li Zhi, "Yu Zhou Youshan" (To Zhou Sijing), in Li Zhi, *Xu fenshu*, 11; see also

Jiang. On the complex relationships among Li Zhi, the Yuan brothers, Jiao Hong, and Wunian, see also Chow, chap. 3.

50. Yuan Zhongdao, "Li Wenling zhuan," in *SKQS*, 541:9–11.

51. Several of Li's Macheng poems, one of which expressly extols liquor and conviviality ("Hoisting the Winecup with Liu Yuancheng in Mid-Autumn at Dragon Lake"), were collected in *1670 XZ, juan* 10.

52. Liu Hong, "Sixiangjia yu guaiseng: Li Zhi."

53. Li Zhi, "Da Zhou Erlu," in Li Zhi, *Fenshu*, 259; see also Jiang.

54. "On Hearing That a Girl of the Ts'ui Family Has Become a Disciple of the Buddhist Master Wu-nien—Playfully Offered to the Master," trans. Jonathan Chaves, in Chaves, 77–78.

55. On Mei Danran's subsequent role as a patron of Buddhist temples in Macheng, see *MCXZQB*, 2:15. For examinations of her relationship to Li, see Shi Shi, "Mei Danran dui Li Zhi you aiqing ma?" and Shi Shi, "Ye tan Li Zhi yu Mei Danran."

56. Ray Huang, 208; Zhu Qianzhi, 7.

57. Key statements of Li's position may be found in Li Zhi, "Da Geng Sikou" (Reply to Minister Geng) and "You yu Jiao Ruohou" (Again to Jiao Hong), in Li Shi, *Fenshu*, 29–39, 48–50. See also Zhu Qianzhi, 6–9; Rong, 61–63.

58. Geng Dingxiang, letter to Zhou Sijiu, in Geng, 3:54–57.

59. Ibid., 3:59–61. For a discussion of how the notions of *mingjiao* and *fenbie* figured more generally in the late-Ming orthodox Confucian defense of the hierarchical social order and in the attack on Buddhist syncretic influences, see Araki, 213–14, 218.

60. For an explication of Li's logic on this point, see de Bary.

61. Geng Dingxiang, letter to Zhou Sijiu, in Geng, 3:61–63.

62. Liu Tong, "Li Zhuowu muji" (Tomb inscription for Li Zhi), in *1670 XZ, juan* 10; Pan, 4:21–23; Rong, 64–65.

63. See Rong, 68–70; Zhu Qianzhi, 8. See also Jiang.

64. Liu Hong, "Sixiangjia yu guaiseng: Li Zhi," 36.

65. Mei Guozhen, preface to Li Zhi, *Cangshu*, 3. Geng Dingli's preface argues that the Way can be understood only through consideration of the diversity of human opinions, including those of "the good Mr. Li," not through any artificially imposed consensus; see Geng Dingli, preface to Li Zhi, *Cangshu*, 5. On this period of Li's life, see Rong, 74–89.

66. Irwin, 75. Irwin argues that Li's contributions to the novel include better development of characters, a straightening out of aspects of the plot, and provision of geographic coherence for the action. As Kai-wing Chow notes, however, scholars "are not in accord regarding the degree and level of Li's contribution" to the novel as we know it today; see Chow, 135.

67. Irwin, 75–86; Li Min, "Longhu ju shi Yang Dingjian"; Wang Ling.

68. Jenner, 8, 19.

69. Rong, 103–4.

70. Among many sources on this incident—none of them very satisfactory—one of the more detailed is that by a local Macheng archivist; see Liu Hong, "Sixiangjia yu guaiseng: Li Zhi." On Ma Jinglun, see *Zhongguo renming da zidian*, 869.

71. Ma Jinglun, "Yu Li Linye Dujian zhuanshang Xiao Sikou" (To Councillor Li Linye, for upward transmission to Judge Xiao), in Pan, 4:24–27.

72. Ma Jinglun, "Yu dongdao shu" (Letter to the authorities), in Pan, 4:18–21.

73. Ma Jinglun, "Yu dangdao shu" ([Second] letter to the authorities), in Pan, 4:21–23. Ma's accusations are also treated in Rong, 105, and in Jiang, *passim*.

74. Two surviving letters from Mei to Li on these matters are reprinted in Pan, 4:1–2.

75. Mei Zhihuan, "Gongjian Li zhangzhe" (Eulogy for Master Li), in Mei Zhihuan, 7:17–19.

76. See Jiang.

77. Ray Huang, 217.

78. Mei Zhihuan, 18.

79. Rong, 81.

80. Mei Guozhen, "Yu Liu yihou shu" (Letter to Magistrate Liu), in *1670 XZ, juan* 10.

81. Mei Guozhen, "Song yihou Liu Yibai ruqin xu" (Letter of presentation to the throne of Magistrate Liu Wenqi), in *MCXZQB*, 7:7–8.

82. See, for example, Rong, 58–59; Zhu Qianzhi, 6, 21–22.

83. See Shimada, especially 178–79, 235–36, 253; de Bary, especially 188, 199; Ray Huang, 195. Peterson, 751, *passim*, chooses the less controversial term "relativism" in preference to "individualism" but agrees that Li represents the culmination of the late-Ming quest for a protoliberal "moral autonomy." In post-Mao Chinese scholarship, it should be noted, the interpretation of Li as a champion of "individualism" and other liberal values has also found increasing favor; see, for example, Ling and Li, eds., *passim.*

84. Ray Huang, 197.

85. Liu Tong, "Li Zhuowu muji" (Tomb inscription for Li Zhi), in *1670 XZ, juan* 10. The biographical notice appears, among other places, in *1670 XZ, juan* 8, and in *MCXZQB*, 10:63–64.

86. Meng Guangpeng, prefaces to parts 1 and 2 of the 1935 Macheng County gazetteer; see *MCXZQB*, *MCXZXB*.

87. Li Zhi, "Li Zhi zai Diaoyutai jiangxue"; Liu Hong, "Sixiangjia yu guaiseng: Li Zhi," 11, 36–37; *MCXJZ*, 25.

88. Gu Yanwu, *Yuan chaoben Rizhi lu*, 540. I thank Wang Fan-sen for bringing this source to my attention.

89. See Jiang. On the Donglin critique of Li in general, see Hucker, "The Tung-lin Movement of the Late Ming Period," 144–45.

90. Mei Zhihuan's enactment of the heroic ideal will be treated in chap. 5, and that of Liu Tong in chap. 6.

Chapter 5

1. Mei Guozhen, "Song yihou Liu Yibai ruqin xu" (Letter of presentation to the throne of Magistrate Liu Wenqi), in *MCXZQB*, 7:7–8.

2. Wu Weiye, 10:10.

3. *MCXZQB*, 9:26 (citing Zou Laixue, fifteenth century), and *1670 XZ, juan* 7 (biography of Huang Juan, early sixteenth century).

4. Wu Weiye (1609–72), from Taicang County, Jiangsu, was a founding member of the Restoration Society (Fushe) and its most celebrated early success, having passed the

metropolitan examination of 1631 in first place. He served the Ming as a junior councillor (*shao canshi*), but resigned after falling out with Ma Shiying (on whom more below, in chap. 6). See *ECCP*, 882–83; *Zhongguo renming da zidian*, 319–20; Chow, 234. On Wu's literary response to the Ming collapse, see Wai-yee Li, "History and Memory in Wu Weiye's Poetry," in Idema, Li, and Widmer, 99–148.

5. The term *dianpu* was the analytical crux of the great work on Song-dynasty agrarian servility by Sudō Yoshiyuki, *Chūgoku tochi seido shi kenkyū* (Studies in the history of Chinese land-tenure systems) (Tokyo: University of Tokyo Press, 1954). For a candid attempt to sort out just what degree of personal servility the term actually implied, see Elvin, chaps. 6, 15.

6. *1670 XZ*, *juan* 3.

7. Wu Weiye, 10:10.

8. The noted mid-nineteenth-century Buddhist monk Yaochan, for instance, came from a servile farm family in Dongshan; see *1882 XZ*, 25:10–11.

9. The literature is large and growing. The pioneering work was probably that done in the 1930s by Xie; see Xie Guozhen, "Mingji nubian kao," 257–89. Subsequent work by Chinese scholars includes Fu Yiling, "Ming-Qing zhi ji de 'nubian' he diannong jiefang yundong" (Bondservant rebellions and tenants' liberation movements in the Ming-Qing transition), in Fu Yiling, *Ming Qing nongcun shehui jingji* (Rural society and economy in the Ming and Qing) (Beijing: Sanlian shudian, 1961), and Fu Yiling, "Mingmo nanfang de 'dianbian,' 'nubian.'" See also Han Hengyu; Wei, Wu, and Lu; Ye Xian'en; and Jing. In Japanese, see Oyama; see also Yasuno. Among recent Western-language studies, see Mixius; see also Heijdra.

10. Ye Xian'en, 232.

11. Fu Yiling, "Ming-Qing zhi ji de 'nubian' he diannong jiefang yundong." Similarly forceful arguments for the historical uniqueness of Ming-Qing agrarian servitude are also advanced in Xie Guozhen, "Mingji nubian kao," and in Han Hengyu.

12. Biography of Huang Juan in *1670 XZ*, *juan* 7.

13. Heijdra, 275–77.

14. Ye Xian'en, especially 298–302.

15. See Jin. Jin's report has been utilized by several scholars; see especially Satō Fumitoshi, which uses Jin's work most extensively.

16. Huang Juan, "Mu hou yisi xu," *1670 XZ*, *juan* 9. For general discussions of the relationship between commendation of land and of persons, see Oyama, 130–35; Han Hengyu, 97; and Li Wenzhi, "Lun Qingdai qianqi de tudi zhanyou guanxi," 77.

17. Heijdra, 275–77.

18. See Wei, Wu, and Lu.

19. For a general history of legislation on the question of personal commendation, see Jing, 149–51.

20. Among many studies of the Yongzheng "emancipations," see Terada; Pei Huang, *Autocracy at Work: A Study of the Yung-Cheng Period, 1723–1735* (Bloomington: Indiana University Press, 1974); and Feng Erkang, *Yongzheng zhuan* (Biography of the Yongzheng emperor) (Beijing: Renmin chubanshe, 1985), 377–86.

21. Biographies of Mei drawn upon in the following paragraphs include those in *Mei shi zupu*, 19:14–16; *Ming shi*, *juan* 248, in *SKQS*; *MCXZQB*, 9:18–22; Wang Baoxin, 3:2–6; and *Zhongguo renming da zidian*, 1004. Especially rich in personal detail are two

biographical prefaces to Mei's writings; see Wan, "Xingzhuang"; Qian, "Mei Changgong zhuan."

22. See, for example, Mei Zhihuan, "Qi Liu tongren" (To Comrade Liu), in Mei Zhihuan, 3:20–24, discussed further below.

23. Mei Zhihuan, 4:5–17, 6: 39, 7:29–31.

24. Mei Zhihuan, "Cong junxing, er" (On military campaigns, no. 2), in *1882 XZ*, 35:24.

25. Wang Baoxin, 3:4.

26. Mei merited an entry in a collective biography of Donglin partisans; see Chen Ding, in *SKQS*, 20:12–17.

27. Li Changgeng, preface to Feng, *Chunqiu hengku.*

28. An alternate name for the *Spring and Autumn Annals.*

29. Mei Zhihuan, preface to Feng, *Linjing zhiyue.*

30. See Elman, *Classicism, Politics, and Kinship*, 152–53.

31. See Wang Ling.

32. For the routine late-Ming use of such "paratextual" devices as lists of contributing readers (*canyue*) to generate sales of books, see Chow, 119–20. As Chow shows (125–26), Feng Menglong was an accomplished hand at supplementing his income through such practices. Chow also provides (223–29) an interesting discussion of the politicization during this period of literary societies (*wenshe*) such as that formed by Mei Zhihuan and Feng Menglong in Macheng.

33. Dardess, *Blood and History in China*, 109.

34. See the *canyue* in Feng, *Linjing zhiyue.*

35. Mei Zhihuan, preface to Feng, *Linjing zhiyue.* For Feng's Donglin ties and his frustrated political career, see *DMB*, 450–53.

36. Dardess, *Blood and History*, chap. 1; *ECCP*, 1.176–77.

37. Dardess, *Blood and History*, chap. 3.

38. See McDermott, "Friendship and Its Friends in the Late Ming," 1.67–96; see also Kutcher.

39. Qian, "Mei Changgong zhuan," 9; Wang Baoxin, 3:2–4.

40. Qian, "Mei Changgong zhuan" (dated Chongzhen 17/2/6). On Qian's career see *ECCP*, 1.148–50; Wakeman, *The Great Enterprise, passim*; Ko, 203–5, 274–78; Kang-I Sun Chang, "Qian Qianyi and His Place in History," in Idema, Li, and Widmer, 199–218.

41. Qian, *Muzhai chuji*, 3.1628.

42. Li's biography in the *Ming shi*, in *SKQS*, 256:9–13, records that he died of old age during the Ming-Qing transition. See also Wang Baoxin, 3:5. 3:11; *MCXZQB*, 9:22–25; *MCXJZ*, 24; *Zhongguo renming da zidian*, 403.

43. On Macheng in particular, see Satō Fumitoshi, 181–83; on central China more generally, see Fu Yiling, *Ming-Qing fengjian tudi suoyouzhi lungang*, 125, *passim.*

44. *MCXZQB*, 10:18.

45. *MCXZQB*, 7:7.

46. Wu Weiye, 10:10.

47. *1670 XZ*, *juan* 3; *1882 XZ*, 13:10, 37:10; *MCXZQB*, 5:13; *1993 XZ*, 10; Satō Fumitoshi, 173–74.

48. For the spread into neighboring Luotian, see, for instance, Volkmar.

49. Fu Yiling, "Mingmo nanfang de 'dianbian' 'nubian'," 64; Fu Yiling, *Ming-Qing fengjian tudi suoyouzhi lungang*, 125.

50. Mei Zhihuan, "Yu Tang futai" (To Governor Tang), in *1670 XZ*, *juan* 10.

51. Taniguchi, "Minmatsu Shinsho no hōsai ni tsuite," 2–3. As ter Haar points out, late-imperial bandits often assumed the posture of exorcists in the ongoing war of humans against demons, taking such names as The King Who Weeds and Levels and The Exterminator King (Shajin wang); see ter Haar, "China's Inner Demons," 35.

52. Mei Zhihuan, "Yu Hong zhitai" (To Governor-General Hong) and "Yu You Kundou xiangguo" (To Grand Secretary Yao Kundou), in Mei Zhihuan, 3:17–18, 3:28–29 (respectively).

53. These campaigns are described in excruciating detail in *1670 XZ*, *juan* 3; *1882 XZ*, 37:10–13; *MCXZQB*, 5:13–14, 7:19–20; *Huang'an xianzhi* (1869 ed.), 10:1–2; and *Huangzhou fuzhi* (1884 ed.), 10*xia*:18–20. A biography of Magistrate Liu Xingyao appears in *MCXZQB*, 7:8–9, and a biography of of Governor Song Yihao appears in *Zhongguo renming da zidian*, 346.

54. Wang Baoxin, 3:5.

55. Wu Weiye, 5:10.

56. Mei Zhihuan, 3:20–24.

57. Wan, "Xingzhuang," 15.

58. Ibid., 16.

59. Qian, "Mei Changgong zhuan," 7.

60. Mei Zhihuan, "Cong junxing, yi" (On military campaigns, number one), in *1882 XZ*, 35:24.

61. Mei Zhihuan, "Yu Zhuozhou Feng xiangguo" (To Grand Secretary Feng), in Mei Zhihuan, 3:30–31. The infamous Feng Quan (1595–1672) had cooperated with the eunuch Wei Zhongxian in his persecution of the Donglin party. He was dismissed in 1628 upon the fall of Wei and then resurfaced as a so-called twice-serving minister under the conquering Qing. See *Zhongguo renming da zidian*, 1226, and *ECCP*, 240–41.

62. Mei Zhihuan, *juan* 3, *passim*; *1670 XZ*, *juan* 10.

63. Mei Zhihuan, "Yu Huangzhou sili Zhou Zhitian" (To Huangzhou Prefect Zhou Zhitian), in Mei Zhihuan, 3:25–26.

64. Wan, "Xingzhuang," 13.

65. Mei Zhhuan, "Qi Liu tongren," in Mei Zhihuan, 3:20–24.

66. Wan, "Xingzhuang," 16; Qian, "Mei Changgong zhuan," 7–8.

67. Wang Baoxin, 3:5.

68. *1882 XZ*, 4:6; *MCXZQB*, 2:13, 2:18.

69. Mei Zhihuan, "Qi Liu tongren," in Mei Zhihuan, 3:23–24.

70. Mei Zhihuan, "Yu Huangzhou sili Zhou Zhitian," in Mei Zhihuan, 3:25.

71. The following paragraphs are drawn above all from Wan, "Xingzhuang," and from Wang Baoxin, 3:5.

72. Mei Zhihuan, 3:20–29.

73. A good study of this phenomenon is Franke.

74. See Perry, especially 88–94.

75. *Yuan shi*, in *SKQS*, 59:20.

76. Mei Guozhen, "Jiabao bianbao shu," 452:13–14; Zou Hexin, "Shizishan ji" (History of Shizishan), in *MCXZQB*, 1:12; Wang Baoxin, 1:6–7; *1993 XZ*, 526–30.

77. Lu Xiangsheng, "Lizhai bingcun qingye shefu zengbing choouxiang shu" (Memorial on setting up forts, village alliances, and scorched-earth policies, and on requesting more troops and rations), in Lu Xiangsheng, 2:19–22; Takeo, especially 147–52; Kuhn,

Rebellion and Its Enemies in Late Imperial China, 41–42. Lu's biography appears in Chen Ding, in *SKQS*, 5:14; it also appears in *Zhongguo renming da zidian*, 1594–95.

78. Lu Xiangsheng, "Gongbao fangwei xiejiao shu" (Further report on regional defense and joint rebel-extermination campaigns) and "Tongbing ru Yu shu" (Memorial on leading troops across the Henan border), in Lu Xiangsheng, 3:12–17.

79. Lu Xiangsheng, "Lizhai bingcun qikuan" (Seven regulations for setting up forts and village alliances), in Lu Xiangsheng, 2:38–41.

80. *1882 XZ*, *juan* 3; *MCXZQB*, 1:12, 5:2–10; *Huangzhou fuzhi* (1884 ed.), 10:16–19; Macheng County Place Name Leadership Group, comp., 157–60; Wang Baoxin, 1:9–10.

81. *1882 XZ*, 40:7; *MCXZQB*, 2:13; Wang Baoxin, 2:13.

82. Macheng County Place Name Leadership Group, comp., 1096, 1102.

83. Wang Baoxin, 3:22.

84. Mei Zhihuan, "Yu Zhuozhou Feng xiangguo," in Mei Zhihuan, 3:30–32.

85. Both Song and Shi would soon be martyred in the Ming cause: Song committed suicide after a 1643 defeat by Li Zicheng in the Han River highlands, and Shi died in the disastrous defense that he orchestrated against Qing forces at Yangzhou in 1645. See Wang Baoxin, 4:1–2; *Zhongguo renming da zidian*, 174, 346.

86. Wang Baoxin, 1:7–10; Taniguchi, "Minmatsu Shinsho no hōsai ni tsuite," 2–3; Zhu Xizu, ed., 26–27.

87. I have not been able to locate Wu Dezhi's complete text, but it is cited at length in Zhu Xizu.

88. See, for example Strand; see also Goodman.

89. Wang Baoxin, 1:8.

90. Wang's repeated invocation of the word *qun* (herd), the term for "sovereign political community" favored by his contemporary Liang Qichao, cannot be coincidental; see Hao.

91. Wang Baoxin, 1:6. On Wang's life and work, I am guided by a personal conversation with the eminent Wuhan University historian (and Huang'an native) Feng Tianyu. See also Zhu Xizu, 26. It is intriguing that Wang's 1914 book has been republished three times in Taiwan—in 1966, 1971, and 1972—but never in the People's Republic.

Chapter 6

1. Wan, "Xingzhuang," 17.

2. The genealogy of one Macheng lineage in the MCA, *Zhou shi zupu*, claims that several thousand of its members alone perished in the carnage of the dynastic transition.

3. Board of War, memorial of Chongzhen 13/9/23, in Zheng and Sun, eds., 278–88; Board of War, memorial of Chongzhen 14/12/19, in Institute of History and Philology, comp., *Ming-Qing shiliao* 7:648; *Ming shi*, in *SKQS*, 260:21, 263:2; *1670 XZ*, *juan* 3; *MCXZQB*, 5:14; *1993 XZ*, 10; Wang Baoxin, 1:12–16.

4. Wang Baoxin, 1:14–15.

5. Board of War, memorial of Chongzhen 16/4/21, in Zheng and Sun, eds., 400–402.

6. See "Nongmin qiyi lingxiu Bao Shirong."

7. The basic sources on Tang Zhi's rebellion are Ji, 376–78; Peng, 128–29; Dai and Wu, 16:3–11; Wu Weiye, 10:10–14; *1670 XZ*, *juan* 3; *Huangzhou fuzhi* (1884), 10*xia*:20; *Hubei tongzhi*, 1790; *MCXZQB*, 5:14–15; and Institute of Qing History, Chinese People's

University, comp., 512. Useful secondary treatments include Wang Baoxin, 1:18–22; Satō Fumitoshi, 175–76; Zhang Jianming, 206–10; Fu Yiling, *Ming Qing nongcun shehui jingji*, 101–2; and Li Wenzhi, *Wan Ming minbian*, 86.

8. *1993 XZ*, 348; Wou, 106. For an attempt to chart the elusive history of the *hui* organizational form, see Ownby.

9. The genesis of these associations on the Li lineage estates has prompted some chroniclers to mistakenly write the "Li" of "Liren hui" with the character for the surname Li instead of the character for "village" (the result translatable as "Association of Li People"), or even to read "Liren hui" as a personal name, "Li Renhui"; see Ji, 378 and, apparently following him, Parsons, 150.

10. See, for example, the various revisions of the Shi lineage rules, *Shi shi zongpu*, 3:8–22. On the ideology of fraternal associations in more recent eras of Chinese history, see Alitto; see also Esherick, *The Origins of the Boxer Uprising*.

11. Wu Weiye, 10:10; *Ming shi*, in *SKQS*, 294:4.

12. Satō Fumitoshi, 184.

13. On Zhou Wenjiang, see Wang Baoxin, 1:18, and *1993 XZ*, 560. Not nearly enough is known about Zhou Wenjiang and his motivations. Although this cannot be determined with certainty, he was likely from one of Macheng's historically eminent Zhou lineages: *wen* was a common generational character among Macheng men of the Zhou surname who passed the civil service examinations in this era; see *MCXZQB*,8:28. Mixius, 32, observes that Zhou Wenjiang's participation suggests the possibility of broader lower-gentry sympathy to the bondservant rebellion, but it is also possible that he was acting simply as an opportunistic individual. His subsequent behavior certainly demonstrates an adept ability to shift his cause.

14. *1993 XZ*, 485; *MCXJZ*, 7.

15. Ji, 378; Qian, "Mei Changgong zhuan," 10.

16. Gu Yingtai, 4.1327. On this work and its author, see *ECCP*, 426–27. See also Peng, 128; Wang Baoxin, 1:16.

17. Ji, 376–77; Wang Baoxin, 3:20.

18. *MCXZQB*, 9:49.

19. Gu Yingtai, 4.1327; Wang Baoxin, 1:18; *MCXZQB*, 8*xia*:13.

20. Dai and Wu, 16:11.

21. Wang Baoxin, 1:20–21.

22. *ECCP*, 761–62; Struve, 23–24, 53–54.

23. *ECCP*, 558; Dennerline, *The Chia-ting Loyalists*, 59–62; Struve, 18–22.

24. *Hubei tongzhi*, 1790; Wang Baoxin, 3:9–10.

25. See Hu Zhaoxi.

26. See, for example, ibid., 66–68, 87–89. See also Chen Shisong, ed., 5.178; Entenmann, 160–70.

27. Wang Baoxin, 1:22.

28. Ibid., 1:11–12.

29. Ibid., 1:22–23; *1993 XZ*, 489.

30. Wakeman, "Romantics, Stoics, and Martyrs in Seventeenth-Century China."

31. Lienche Tu Fang, "Liu Tong," in *DMB*, 968–70.

32. See Liu and Yu. Lienche Tu Fang, "Liu Tong," in *DMB*, calls this work a masterpiece of Chinese literature.

33. Liu Tong, "Zhaishe ci" (Ode to the village community), in *1993 XZ*, 488–89.

Other poems by Liu appear in all surviving Macheng gazetteers, beginning with that of 1670. On Liu's life and politics, see *MCXZQB*, 9:72; *MCXJZ*, 25.

34. This and the following paragraph are based on biographies of Cao Yinchang and Zhou Sun in Wang Baoxin, 3:13–15; *MCXZQB*, 9:68–69; and *1993 XZ*, 488–89. See also Taniguchi, "Minmatsu Shinsho no hōsai ni tsuite," 12.

35. Wakeman, "Localism and Loyalism during the Ch'ing Conquest of Kiangnan," 47.

36. *Huangzhou fuzhi shiyi*, 1:17; Wang Baoxin, 1:2–3, 1:23; Taniguchi, "Minmatsu Shinsho no hōsai ni tsuite," 8–9; Struve, 17–19, 32–34, 53–54. A biography of Jin Shenghuan appears in *ECCP*, 166–67.

37. Wakeman, "Localism and Loyalism during the Ch'ing Conquest of Kiangnan," 43.

38. Wang Baoxin, 1:27.

39. *1670 XZ*, *juan* 2; *MCXZQB*, 6:13; Wakeman, "Localism and Loyalism during the Ch'ing Conquest of Kiangnan," 55–63.

40. Jiang Yuxu, memorial of Shunzhi 2/11, in *NMZZ*, 1*xia*.240–41. Jiang—a veteran Ming counterinsurgency specialist, *jinshi* of 1631, and protégé of Lu Xiangsheng himself—had gone over the Qing cause and continued to ply his specialty. See Lu Xiangsheng, "Baopu tuigong Jiang Yuxu shu" (Memorial recommending magistrate Jiang Yuxu for promotion), in Lu Xiangsheng, 1:29–30.

41. Zhang Jianming, 210–13.

42. Wang Baoxin, 1:7–8.

43. Ibid., 3:10–13.

44. Ibid., 1:1–5. On Prince Tang (Zhu Yunjian), see Struve, 77–84, and *ECCP*, 196–98.

45. Wang Baoxin, 2:1–3.

46. He Mingluan, memorial of Shunzhi 2/12, in *NMZZ*, 1*xia*.241–43; "Xu Yong chuan" (Biography of Xu Yong), in *Erchen chuan* (Biographies of twice-serving officials), *juan* 1, reprinted in Xie Guozhen, *Qingqu nongmin qiyi ziliao jilu*, 201; *Zhongguo renming da zidian*, 784.

47. On these strategic options, see Hucker, "Hu Tusng-hsien's Campaign Against Hsü Hai," 274; see also Wills. For their use in the Qing campaigns against loyalist holdouts in the Lower Yangzi, see Wakeman, "Localism and Loyalism during the Ch'ing Conquest of Kiangnan," 65.

48. Lu used this idiom repeatedly throughout his Dabie Shan campaigns. Writing from Macheng itself in late 1635, for example, he differentiated his desired strategy of *hejjiao dagu* (massive extermination at one blow) from *fenjiao xiaogu* (piecemeal extermination); see Lu Xiangsheng, "Qing chi gelu yuanbing shu" (Request to coordinate the armies of the various routes), in Lu Xiangsheng, 3:26–27.

49. He Mingluan, memorial of Shunzhi 2/12/20, in *NMZZ*, 1*xia*.241–43; *Huangzhou fuzhi shiyi*, 1:17; Wang Baoxin, 1:24; Xie Guozhen, *Qingqu nongmin qiyi ziliao jilu*, 201–3; Taniguchi, "Minmatsu Shinsho no hōsai ni tsuite," 10–11; Zhang Jianming, 210–12.

50. He Mingluan, memorial of Shunzhi 3/6/21, in Institute of History and Philology, comp., *(Xiancun Qingdai Neige dagu yuancang) Ming Qing dang'an*, A4–131 (title shortened hereafter to *Ming Qing dang'an*); Wang Baoxin, 1:24; *Huangzhou fuzhi shiyi*, 1:18; *MCXZQB*, 9:37; *1993 XZ*, 560.

51. Luo Xiujin, memorial of Shunzhi 3/7/14, in Institute of History and Philology, comp., *Ming Qing dang'an*, A4–189.

52. Luo Xiujin, memorial of Shunzhi 3/12/7, reprinted in Xie Guozhen, *Qingqu nongmin qiyi ziliao jilu*, 203–4.

53. Wang Baoxin, 1:1, 1:23. On the Yongli emperor (Zhu Youlang), see *ECCP*, 193–95; see also Struve, 99–105, 176–78.

54. Luo Xiujin, memorial of Shunzhi 7/8, in Institute of History and Philology, comp., *Ming Qing dang'an*, A12–6.

55. He Yongshng, memorial of Shunzhi 5/intercalary 4, in Xie Guozhen, *Qingqu nongmin qiyi ziliao jilu*, 205; Zhang Jianming, 212–13.

56. *1670 XZ*, *juan* 3; *Huangzhou fuzhi* (1884), 10*xia*:21.

57. Wu Jingdao, memorial of Shunzhi 6/7/3, in Institute of History and Philology, comp., *Ming Qing dang'an*, A10–100; Luo Xiujin, memorial of Shunzhi 7/8, in Institute of History and Philology, comp., *Ming Qing dang'an*, A12–15.

58. Wang Baoxin, 1:25–26, 3:10–15.

59. Chi Riyi, memorial of Shunzhi 6/11/7, in Xie Guozhen, *Qingqu nongmin qiyi ziliao jilu*, 205; Board of War memorials of Shunzhi 7/9 and Shunzhi 7/11, in Institute of History and Philology, comp., *Ming Qing dang'an*, A12–25, A12–68; *1993 XZ*, 488; Taniguchi, "Minmatsu Shinsho no hōsai ni tsuite," 12. On Hong Chengchou, the former colleague of Lu Xiangsheng in the campaigns against the late Ming rebels, see Lu Xiangsheng, 3:15–17; *Zhongguo renming da zidian*, 670; and Dennerline, *The Chia-ting Loyalists*, 49–50.

60. During these years, Hong Chengchou was an object of widespread ridicule and vilification on the part of his fellow former Ming officials, whom he sought to persuade to capitulate to the Qing as he himself had done; see Dennerline, *The Chia-ting Loyalists*, 299.

61. Wang Baoxin, 1:25–26, 3:14–15.

62. *MCXZQB*, 9:69.

63. Memorial of Hubei censor Nie Jie, Shunzhi 9/6, in Institute of History and Philology, comp., *Ming Qing dang'an*, A14–161; *1993 XZ*, 10.

64. *1670 XZ*, *juan* 3; *1882 XZ*, 38:2; *Huangzhou fuzhi* (1884), 10*xia*:21.

65. Hong Chengchou, memorial of Shunzhi 13/1/23, in Institute of History and Philology, comp., *Ming Qing dang'an*, A25–92.

66. See, for example, Zheng Siwei, memorial of Shunzhi 8/4/18, in Institute of History and Philology, comp., *Ming Qing dang'an*, A12–167. On the persistent peacekeeping problems posed by Macheng immigrants to Sichuan, see Hu Zhaoxi, 89.

67. Cited in Taniguchi, "Minmatsu Shinsho no hōsai ni tsuite," 2.

68. Wang Baoxin, 1:1.

69. Xie Guozhen, *Qingqu nongmin qiyi ziliao jilu*, 207–8.

70. Taniguchi, "Minmatsu Shinsho no hōsai ni tsuite," 13. See also Satō Fumitoshi, 185–86.

71. Xie Guozhen, *Qingqu nongmin qiyi ziliao jilu*, 201; Taniguchi, "Minmatsu Shinsho no hōsai ni tsuite," 11. On the dangers inherent in such anachronism, see Wakeman, "Localism and Loyalism during the Ch'ing Conquest of Kiangnan," 85.

72. Wakeman, "Localism and Loyalism during the Ch'ing Conquest of Kiangnan," 73, *passim*.

73. See, for example, Li Wenzhi, "Lun Qingdai qianqi de tudi zhanyou guanxi," 78.

74. Jing, 87–89.

75. Satō Fumitoshi, 177.

76. The most basic source on the 1651 bondservant rebellion is the one found in *1670 XZ*, *juan* 3. Another extended treatment appears in an essay titled "Macheng jianu zhi bian" (Rebellion of family servants in Macheng), in *Hubei tongzhi*, *juan* 69, reprinted in Institute of Qing History, Chinese People's University, comp., 512; it serves as the source for discussions of the event in Fu Yiling, *Ming Qing nongcun shehui jingj*, 103, and in Mixius, 32. A more in-depth scholarly treatment appears in Satō Fumitoshi, 177–78. Significantly, while the *1670 XZ* account is reprinted in most subsequent Macheng County gazetteers (see, for example, *1882 XZ*, 38:1–2), a seemingly deliberate case of "social amnesia" led to the incident's complete omission from part 1 of the rightist-produced Macheng County gazetteer of 1935; see *MCXZQB*.

77. Zou Xing's biography appears in *MCXZQB*, 9:37. We will return to his life and career more fully in the following chapter.

78. On the Yongzheng-era *tanding rudi* reforms, see Guo Songyi, "Lun 'tanding rudi,'" *Qingshi luncong* 3 (1982), 1–62.

79. *Huang'an xianzhi* (Tongzhi ed.), 10:2, cited in Institute of Qing History, Chinese People's University, comp., 512; Wei, Wu, and Lu, 140.

80. Jin, 273.

81. Satō Fumitoshi, 185–86. For a slightly different but analogous case of this alliance in the Ming-Qing transition, see Dennerline, "Fiscal Reform and Local Control."

82. Satō Fumitoshi, 187. One manifestation of this concern was that greater attention was paid to prohibiting runaway bondservants from enlisting in Qing military forces.

83. The key edict of 1727 was codified in the *Da Qing huidian shili* (Guangxu ed.), *juan* 810, and is cited extensively in Wei, Wu, and Lu, 109. See also Jing, 236–51; Terada, 124–41.

84. See Ye Xian'en.

85. *1882 XZ*, 25:10–11.

86. Cited in Institute of Qing History, Chinese People's University, comp., 400.

87. *People's Tribune* (Hankow), March 22, 1927.

88. *Shi shi zongpu*, 3:9–10.

Chapter 7

1. *MCXZQB*, 8*xia*:1–12.

2. *MCXZQB*, 9:37, 9:51–53.

3. *MCXZQB*, 8*xia*:3–5, 8*xia*:32, 9:37.

4. Wang Baoxin, 2:1–3.

5. Liu Fengyuan, 229–39, 280–95.

6. *Huang'an xianzhi* (1869 ed.), 10:2.

7. The most detailed secondary accounts are Taniguchi, "Yu Seiryū no hōkō hō ni tsuite," 69–70, *passim*, and the semipopular Wang Youdong, chap. 5.

8. Yu Chenglong, *juan* 1.

9. Chen Tingjing, "Yu gong benchuan." The portion relevant to the 1674 Dongshan Rebellion is found in Chen Tingjing, *Wuting wenbian*, 41:7–14, reprinted with only slight alterations in *1882 XZ*, 38:3–11. Chen Tingjing was a Shanxi native, *jinshi* of 1658, and a career metropolitan official. He rose to the rank of grand secretary after 1703 and is perhaps best known as one of the principal editors of the *Kangxi zidian* (Kangxi dictionary). See his biography by Tu Lien-che in *ECCP*, 101.

10. Zhou Weiju, "Dongshan ji yongxu" (Ballad of the Dongshan), in *1795 XZ*, *wenzheng* 2. The editor of the Guangxu-era county gazetteer, Guo Qinghua, similarly dismisses the Dongshan rebels as *beini* (turncoats); see *1882 XZ*, preface to *juan* 37.

11. See Wang Baoxin.

12. *1882 XZ*, 40:32–33. While this passage sheds new and surprising light on the background of the Wu Sangui Rebellion, it arguably says even more about Han anxieties regarding the voodoo magic encountered as part of early modern imperial expansion and contact with the aboriginal other.

13. The specific pairing of the "precious sword" and the "letter from Heaven" in messianic movements has a long tradition in this region. In the next chapter, we will see its recurrence in eastern Hubei in the eighteenth century. As late as 1982, a messianic leader in Xinshao County, Hunan, announced himself as bearing the same two emblems of authority. See Anagnost; ter Haar, "China's Inner Demons," 41. The letter is typically written in invisible ink. On the more general meaning of demon-slaying swords in anti-Qing movements, see ter Haar, *Ritual and Mythology of the Chinese Triads*, 286, 320, 334–36.

14. Yu Chenglong, 1:72–75; Wang Baoxin, 2:4; *MCXZQB*, 6:15.

15. Yu Chenglong, 1:52; Wang Baoxin, 2:4.

16. *MCXZQB*, 9:37.

17. "Dongshan tuzei" (The Dongshan Rebellion), in *Hubei tongzhi*, 1791–93.

18. Beyond Yu's own writings and his detailed biography by Chen Tingjing, see *MCXZQB*, 7:10; *ECCP*, 937–38; *Zhongguo renming da zidian*, 15; and Stuart and Rawski, 109.

19. Yu Chenglong, 1:49–50; Chen Tingjing, *Wuting wenbian*, 41:7–8.

20. "Chu fu Dongshan qianpian" (Broadside calling for the pacification of Dongshan) and "Quan fanjian guinong yu" (Proclamation ordering cultivators to return to your farms), in Yu Chenglong, 1:50–52.

21. "Anwei gebao yu" (Proclamation of reassurance to the various townships), in Yu Chenglong, 1:52–53.

22. It is probably not accidental that Yu's use of the phrase *guanji minbian* echoes the language used by the genuine self-proclaimed rebel Liu Qingli, to justify his own actions.

23. Yu's antipathy to Zou Xing, which is definitely not shared by Zou's biographers in Macheng County gazetteers (where Zou is presented as the repeated savior of the county and the virtuous father of a grand secretary, no less), is never fully explained. Did Yu suspect Zou of having orchestrated the slandering of the Xu Family Fort elites as rebels? Did he believe Zou complicit in the clerical tax racket that Yu saw as underlying the whole mess (see below)? Both?

24. "Shen Zhang futai shifang wugu xiang" (Report to Governor Zhang requesting dismissal of charges against the innocent), in Yu Chenglong, 1:54–55.

25. "Bao Dongshan jiufu xiang" (Report on my pacification mission to Dongshan), in Yu Chenglong, 1:55–56.

26. See, for example, Zhou Weiju, "Dongshan ji yongxu" (Ballad of the Dongshan), in *1795 XZ*, *wenzheng* 2. *Huangzhou fuzhi* (1884), 10*xia*:22; Wang Baoxin, 2:5–6.

27. Chen Tingjing, "Yu gong benchuan," in *1882 XZ*, 38:3–7. For explication of this classic recognition scene, see Henry, especially 10. As Henry notes, such scenes figured repeatedly in the fictional writings of Feng Menglong, who had sojourned in Macheng half a century earlier and contributed significantly to the county's literati culture.

28. Stripped of all imperial rhetoric, Yu's matter-of-fact characterization of the Three Feudatories Rebellion as a "north-south war" seems jarring in such a dedicated agent of the Qing.

29. Yu Chenglong, 1:55–65; Wang Youdong, chap. 5.

30. Wang Baoxin, 2:5–6.

31. "Zhaofu shijun xiang" (Report of bringing to a close the matter of pacification), in Yu Chenglong, 1:72–75.

32. For the remainder of 1674, Yu shuttled back and forth between Wuchang, Huangzhou City, and various areas of the field in Macheng.

33. *1882 XZ*, 38:6–7. There is little evidence that this cadastral survey project bore much fruit, or indeed that it was at all central to Yu's agenda for social control in Macheng.

34. "Jinzhi xiazha jiufu shimin yu" (Proclamation prohibiting extortion of repacified gentry and commoners), in Yu Chenglong, 1:66–67.

35. Hsiao, 26–28.

36. On this statecraft genealogy, see Rowe, *Saving the World*, 388–92.

37. Hsiao, 43–48; Taniguchi, "Yu Seiryū no hōkō hō ni tsuite," 63–67.

38. Taniguchi, "Yu Seiryū no hōkō hō ni tsuite," 62.

39. Hsiao, 46 (emphasis in original).

40. "Sanlihe jiazhang" (The headman of Three Mile River), in *1993 XZ*, 485.

41. Yu Chenglong, 2:50.

42. The classic text is Gu Yanwu, "Junxian lun," 1:6–9. On the broader scapegoating of *yamen* clerks by Qing officials and local elites, see Ch'u and, with more sophistication, Reed. Major studies of the *fengjian* critique of predatory bureaucratism include Lien-sheng Yang; Min; and especially Kuhn, "Local Self-Government under the Republic."

43. Yu Chenglong, 2:48–50.

44. Ibid., 1:70.

45. In later incarnations of the *baojia* system in Macheng—and, as we shall see, there were very many baroque elaborations of Yu's scheme in the centuries to follow—this functionary is usually referred to instead as a *paizhang* (*pai*-unit headman), a term that suggests a bureaucratization of the post, a turn away from the kinship-based nature of the system that was so central for Yu Chenglong.

46. Yu also prescribed a number of additional posts with titles like *zongbao* (*bao* coordinator) and *yuanzhu* (master of the battlements), but it is, frankly, difficult to discover exactly how they fit into his three-tiered hierarchy; see Yu Chenglong, 1:67–68.

47. Hsiao, 68, *passim*. Hsiao also argues that this impossible agenda was one of the reasons why the system quickly degenerated into an on-paper-only reality.

48. This is pointed out in Taniguchi, "Yu Seiryū no hōkō hō ni tsuite."

49. "Shang Zhang futai shanhou shiyi bin" (Petition to Governor Zhang regarding reconstruction matters), in Yu Chenglong, 1:76–78.

50. Ibid., 1:78.

51. Wang Baoxin, 2:5–6.

52. Yu Chenglong, 1:65–66.

53. "Qingli baojia yu" (Directive to clear up the *baojia* system), in Yu Chenglong, 1:66–67.

54. "Shenxuan xiangyue yu" (Directive to select with care community compact leaders), in Yu Chenglong, 2:44–48.

55. "Jinyu huangmin" (Directive of prohibition for famine refugees), in Yu Chenglong, 2:61–62.

56. Yu Chenglong, 1:75–76, 2:50–52; *1882 XZ*, 38:6–7; Taniguchi, "Yu Seiryū hōkō hō ni tsuite," 73–74.

57. See Kuhn, *Rebellion and Its Enemies in Late Imperial China.*

58. Ibid.

59. The following paragraphs are drawn in part from Hubei governor Zhang Chaozhen, memorial of KX 13/12, in *Da Qing Shengzu Rendi shilu* (Veritable records of the Kangxi reign), 51:1–2; Yu Chenglong, *juan 3*, *passim*; *1882 XZ*, 38:6–7, 38:12–14; and *Hubei tongzhi*, 1791–93.

60. Wang Baoxin, 2:10.

61. Again, the higher stipends were for the musketeers.

62. The full list of local elites for whom Yu requested official honors is found in Yu Chenglong, 3:42–46, and in *1882 XZ*, 38:14.

63. *1882 XZ*, 38:13; Wang Baoxin, 2:11; Yu Chenglong, 2:50–52.

64. "Nongmin qiyi lingxiu Bao Shirong," 40.

65. Yu Chenglong, 2:50–52.

66. "Xiaoyu He Shirong zuzhong pai" (Declaration to the membership of He Shirong's lineage), in ibid., 3:21–22; "Nongmin qiyi lingxiu Bao Shirong."

67. Yu Chenglong, 3:38–39.

68. Ibid., 3:47–48.

69. "Xugong xiangwen" (Detailed report on those deserving of official honors), in ibid., 3:44–46.

70. Yu Chenglong, *juan* 2, *passim.*

71. *Huangzhou fuzhi* (1884), 10*xia*:22; *HBTZ*, 1792; Wang Baoxin, 2:5–6; Taniguchi, "Yu Seiryū no hōkō hō ni tsuite," 69.

72. Yu Chenglong, 1:64–65.

73. "Shenbao Dongshan fushi yijun xiang" (Announcement that the Dongshan incident has been concluded), in Yu Chenglong, 1:63.

74. Yu Chenglong, 1:67–68, 1:70–72; Taniguchi, "Yu Seiryū no hōkō hō ni tsuite," 75.

75. Yu Chenglong, 3:1–2, 3:2–3; Satō Fumitoshi, 178, 186–87.

76. At one point, Yu describes Zou as a *taopu*, which may be read simply as an epithet, "thieving villain," or, more literally, as "bandit-bondservant"; see Yu Chenglong, 1:64.

77. Taniguchi, "Yu Seiryū no hōkō hō ni tsuite," 74.

78. Yu Chenglong, 3:3–4.

79. Chen Tingjing, "Yu gong benchuan," in *1882 XZ*, 7:10–12.

80. Yu Chenglong, 3:1–2; Wang Baoxin, 2:8; *Hubei tongzhi*, 1792.

81. Yu Chenglong, 3:1–4.

82. Memorial of Zhang Chaozhen, KX 13/9, in *Da Qing Shengzu Rendi shilu* (Veritable records of the Kangxi reign), 49:15–16; Yu Chenglong, 3:5–12.

83. See, for example, the variety of small-scale bondservant uprisings in Huangzhou Prefecture catalogued in the 1688 memorial of Jiang Fan, in Institute of Qing History, Chinese People's University, comp., 513–14.

84. "Guifeng yi ping / Longtan yi qing / ji geng ji zhong / wanshi yong ning." The text of this poem was continually reprinted over the years in local sources (*1882 XZ*, 5:16; *HBTZ*, 1793; *MCXZQB*, 14:26; "Nongmin qiyi lingxiu Bao Shirong," 40) as well as in Yu's own collected works; see Yu Chenglong, 3:51.

85. *1795 XZ*, *wenzheng* 2; *1882 XZ*, 38:7, 38:12–14; *MCXZQB*, 14:21.

86. Wang Baoxin, 2:12.

87. *MCXZQB*, 15:27–28.

88. *MCXZQB*, 7:10.

89. These oral tales were transcribed and published in two vernacular story collections by the early-twentieth-century popular writer Chu Renxun (1874–1928), and they continue to be widely read in China today; see Chu, "Yu gong'an."

90. *Yidai lianli Yu Chenglong* (Yu Chenglong, an incorruptible official for all time), CCTV series, 2000–2001.

91. "Nongmin qiyi lingxiu Bao Shirong"; *1993 XZ*, 10.

92. See, for example, *1795 XZ*, *wenzheng* 2.

93. Wang Baoxin, 2:12.

Chapter 8

1. *1882 XZ*, *juan* 10; *MCXZXB*, 3:28; Li Hua, 57; Zhang Jianmin, 438–39.

2. *Xiakou xianzhi*, 5:27; Cai Yiqing, "Xianhua Hankou" (Leisurely chats about Hankou), *Xinsheng yuekan* 6:1–2 (ca. 1934), 78.

3. See, for example, *Shi shi zongpu*, *juan* 7 *passim*; *Lin shi zongpu* (1947), *juan* 2 *passim*; and *Xicun Cheng shi zongpu*, *juan* 2 *passim.*

4. *Xicun Cheng shi zongpu*, 3:23.

5. *MCXZQB*, 9:61, 10:29–35.

6. *1795 XZ*, 3:12–14.

7. *MCXZQB*, 1:42; Macheng County Place Name Leadership Group, comp., 31–34.

8. *1993 XZ*, 169–71; *MCXJZ*, 40–41.

9. *1882 XZ*, 8:9–10; *MCXZQB*, 4:23–25, *juan* 8 *passim*; Zhang Jianmin, 614–19.

10. Brook, "Family Continuity and Cultural Hegemony," 30. From Ming to Qing, Yin County's total *jinshi* production declined from 293 to 131.

11. *1882 XZ*, 9:9–11; *MCXZQB*, 4:35–36. For this trend empirewide, see the various contributions to Elman and Woodside, eds.

12. *MCXZQB*, 9:78.

13. The dichotomy of Han learning and Song learning in the Qing context has been worked out in detail in a large number of studies by Benjamin Elman; see, for example, Elman, *From Philosophy to Philology*. The relationship of Song learning to statecraft,

and its specific embodiment in mid-Qing central China, is analyzed in Rowe, *Saving the World*, especially chap. 4.

14. The following paragraphs draw on *1882 XZ*, 18:60–61, 32:4, 34:83–100; *MCXZQB*, 9:38–40, 9:61, 9:79–81; and *MCXJZ*, 26.

15. The Jiang-Han shuyuan was a venerable institution that served in the nineteenth century as the semiofficial center of higher learning for Hubei Province as a whole. It was condemned as old-fashioned and was abolished in the 1880s by Zhang Zhidong, who replaced it with his own Jingxin shuyuan, featuring a partially Western curriculum. See Ayers, 21.

16. This lengthy text, "Jie ninü wen," is reproduced in *1882 XZ*, 34:83–89.

17. See McMahon.

18. Mann, *Precious Records*. For my own take on the relationship of stability and development during this era, see Rowe, "Social Stability and Social Change."

19. See *zhiyu* (supplement) to *1882 XZ*; *MCXZQB*, 2:2–36, 3:13–19, 15:41–42; *MCXZXB*, 3:4–5.

20. See, for example, the extensive register of Cheng lineage property in *Xicun Cheng shi zongpu*, *juan* 2.

21. Ibid., 2:18–19.

22. *MCXZQB*, 1:24–25.

23. Liang Gongzhen, *Beidongyuan bilu* (Jottings from the Northeast Garden), 4:3, extracted in Institute of Qing History, Chinese People's University, comp., 400. On the Yongzheng "emancipations," see, for example, Terada; Wei, Wu, and Lu, 169–82; Jing, 236–51. For a synopsis of the large literature on this subject see Rowe, "Social Stability and Social Change."

24. *1993 XZ*, 340.

25. Wang Fengrong, "Qiting juncheng Wang gong kanluan bei" (Stele recording Qiting subprefect Wang's handling of the disorder), reproduced in *MCXZQB*, 14:26–27. On this rebellion more broadly, see Shaanxi circuit censor Jiang Fan, memorial of KX 27, in Institute of Qing History, Chinese People's University, comp., 513–14.

26. My account of Ma Chaozhu's rebellion is summarized from ter Haar, *Ritual and Mythology of the Chinese Triads*, 236–62.

27. See Suzuki; Jones and Kuhn, 107–62.

28. Qin Cheng'en, memorial of QL 59/10/8, in MQA. I am grateful to Blaine Gaustad for providing me with a copy of this document.

29. *1882 XZ*, 40:32–33.

30. Indeed, of the 556 local document files on *nongmin yundong lei: bimi shehui* (peasant rebellions: secret societies, catalogue nos. 367.4–367.83) into which the palace memorials (*zhupi zouzhe*) held in Beijing's Number One Historical Archives are organized (covering the Yongzheng through Guangxu reigns, and including materials on the White Lotus Rebellion), there is not a single file related to Macheng County. As the evidence of this study clearly suggests, that fact cannot be due either to a lack of profound social tensions in the county or to any lack of sectarian beliefs generally; it must reflect instead the awesome disciplinary power of the Qing local elite.

31. *Huang'an xianzhi* (1869 ed.), 10:3; *Huangzhou fuzhi* (1884 ed.), 10*xia*:24; *1882 XZ*, 38:10–11; *MCXZQB*, 2:11–13 and 5:16.

32. *1882 XZ*, 39:1–2; *Huangzhou fuzhi* (1884), 10*xia*:24–25; *MCXZQB*, 5:21–22. For the

classic analysis of *mintuan* or *tuanlian* mobilization in the Taiping era, see Kuhn, *Rebellion and Its Enemies in Late Imperial China*, especially 196–200, dealing with militia mobilization in Macheng's neighboring Huanggang County.

33. JenYu-wen, 176, places this Taiping force at 20,000–30,000, but this estimate seems unlikely and is not supported by local sources.

34. Yao Guozhen and Han Baochang were evidently the sorts of officials whom the court assigned to county-level service in Hubei when it became clear that the area would be in the direct path of the rebels. Both were very likely bannermen (Yao hailed from Fengtian, and Han from Beijing), neither held an examination degree of any sort, and both had risen through the lowest orders of the bureaucracy on the basis of demonstrated military competence. See their biographies in *MCXZQB*, 7:20–21.

35. This number includes the 342 for whom both name and year of death are recorded, plus a percentage of the more than 400 whose names are given but whose dates of death are listed as unknown; see *MCXZQB*, 10:44–55.

36. *MCXZQB*, 9:61–62, 9:82.

37. *1882 XZ*, 6:13; *MCXZQB*, 5:16–17, 10:27–28; *MCXZXB*, 11:9–10; *1993 XZ*, 347.

38. In addition to being mentioned in the sources cited above, these events are chronicled in a special essay titled "Macheng tuanlian shimo" (The full story of the Macheng militia), in the Republican-era *Hubei Provincial Gazetteer*; see *HBTZ*, *juan* 74, 1882–83.

39. Hu Linyi, "Fu shunying binqing tianzhao yongding pi" (Endorsement on an assistant battalion commander's request to recruit more braves), in Hu Linyi, 2.989–90. A biographical entry on Hu Linyi by Ssu-yu Teng appears in *ECCP*, 333–35. His military innovations are analyzed in Kuhn, *Rebellion and Its Enemies in Late Imperial China.* For discussions of Hu's civil administrative reforms in Hubei, see William T. Rowe, *Hankow: Commerce and Society in a Chinese City, 1776–1889*, and Rowe, "Hu Lin-i's Reform of the Grain Tribute System in Hupeh, 1855–58."

40. See *1993 XZ*, 11. See also *Huangzhou fuzhi* (1884), 10*xia*:29–31; *1882 XZ*, 39:5; *MCXZQB*, 5:18.

41. *Huangzhou fuzhi* (1884), 10*xia*:30.

42. Guanwen and Hu Linyi memorials of XF 8/1/15, XF 8/1/20, and XF 8/2/13, in MQA; Hu Linyi, memorial of XF 8/3/26, in Hu Linyi, 1.441–43; *Huangzhou fuzhi* (1884), 10*xia*:31–32. A biography of Magistrate Wang Dunren appears in *MCXZQB*, 7:15–16.

43. Guanwen and Hu Linyi memorial of XF 8/3/26, in MQA; *MCXZQB*, 5:18; *1993 XZ*, 347; Jen Yu-wen, 328.

44. Guanwen and Hu Linyi, memorial of XZ 8/4/23, MQA.

45. For the gory details, see Guanwen and Hu Linyi, memorials of XF 8/4/14, XF 8/5/11, and XF 8/5/18, in MQA; Yinggui memorial of XF 8/5/16, in MQA; Li Mengqun memorial of XF 8/5/19, in MQA.

46. Guanwen and Hu Linyi memorial of XZ 8/6/4, in MQA; Guanwen memorials of 8/7/14 and 8/8/20, in MQA.

47. *1882 XZ*, 5:22–24; *MCXZQB*, 15:19–20.

48. *MCXZQB*, 7:21, 10:37–38, 10:44–55.

49. *1882 XZ*, 6:4–15.

50. "Shihuo zhi" (Essay on political economy), in *1882 XZ*, *juan* 10.

51. *1882 XZ*, 6:3–4; *Hubei tongzhi*, 1882–83.

52. Hu Linyi, "Macheng xian binfu xiujian diaolou pi" (Endorsement on petition of the Macheng magistrate to construct blockhouses), in Hu Linyi, 2.1027.

53. Hu Linyi, "Zha Huangzhou fu yu binbao diaoka zhangcheng" (Posted regulations on blockhouses and guardposts in Huangzhou Prefecture), in Hu Linyi, 2.987.

54. Hu Linyi, "Macheng xian binchen difang qingxing pi" (Endorsement on report on local conditions by the Macheng magistrate), in Hu Linyi, 2.1008–9.

55. For the relationship between mid-Qing demographic and economic change in the highlands and the outbreak of the White Lotus Rebellion, see Suzuki; see also Rawski.

56. See Hibino, 141–47; Kuhn, *Rebellion and Its Enemies in Late Imperial China*, 45–50; biographies of Mingliang and Lebao, *ECCP*, 579–80, 444–46 (respectively).

57. Yan Ruyi, "Sansheng shannei bianfang lun" (Essays on frontier defense in the mountains of the three-province borderland), especially no. 4, *Baozhai* (Forts), and no. 5, *Tuanlian* (Militia), in *Huangchao jingshi wenbian*, 82:12–17. On Yan's career and influence, see work in progress by McMahon.

58. Zheng Qinghua, introductory essay to "great military events" section, in *1882 XZ*, *juan* 37.

59. For example, Zhang Supu, a Huangbang sojourner in Chongqing who returned to his native township to help feed his starving neighbors, and the merchant Liu Huanzhang, who financed and oversaw relief dispensaries in Songbu; see *MCXZQB*, 10:29–32.

60. Hu Linyi, "Macheng xian binchen gejushen chouban juanlun qingxing pi" (Endorsement on report of the Macheng magistrate regarding gentry management of subscription drives), in Hu Linyi, 2.1012.

61. *MCXZQB*, 5:22–26, 7:16, 10:27; *HBTZ*, 1883.

62. Kuhn, *Rebellion and Its Enemies in Late Imperial China*, 179; Perry, chap. 4. Perry also provides a copious bibliography of Chinese- and Japanese-language studies of the Nian.

63. *HBTZ*, 1861.

64. Cited in Luo, *Xiangjun bingzhi*, 37.

65. *Huangzhou fuzhi* (1884), 10*xia*:32–33; *MCXZQB*, 5:18–19. For a biographic entry on Cheng Daxi, see *MCXZQB*, 7:18.

66. *MCXZQB*, 9:62.

67. *HBTZ*, 1883.

68. *MCXZQB*, 5:22.

69. See, for example, the biography of the merchant Cheng Zhiyi in *Xicun Cheng shi zongpu*, 2:30–32, and that of the Qing general Xiang Baifu in *MCXZQB*, 7:18.

70. *Huangzhou fuzhi* (1884), *10xia*:34–36; *HBTZ*, 1864; Jen Yu-wen, 473–74.

71. Guanwen memorials of TZ 3/6/8, TZ3/6/23, TZ 3/7/4, TZ 3/7/20, TZ 3/7/26, TZ 3/8/1, and TZ 3/8/6, in MQA; Zhang Zhiwan and Mao Changxi memorials of TZ 3/7/28 and TZ 3/8/13, in MQA; Zeng Guofan memorial of TZ 3/7, in MQA.

72. Guanwen memorial of TZ 5/11/21, in MQA; Bayang'a memorial of TZ6/1/15, in MQA; *Huangzhou fuzhi* (1884), 10*xia*:36–37.

73. Zheng Qinghua, introductory essay to "major events" section, in *1882 XZ*, between *juan* 36 and *juan* 37.

74. The individual's name was Yu Mouchuan, and the account records that Mou-

chuan's son, Yu Yashi, bore both the same surname and generational character (Ya) as Yu Yaxiang; see biography of Yu Cheng in *1993 XZ*, 561.

75. *MCXZQB*, 9:82; *Hubei tongzhi*, 1883.

76. *1993 XZ*, 11. On the Gelaohui and its relationship to the Xiang army, see Cai Shaoqing, *Zhongguo bimi shehui*, 48–78, and Cai Shaoqing, "On the Origins of the Gelaohui."

77. *MCXZQB*, 5:22.

78. *1993 XZ*, 560.

79. *MCXZQB*, 10:28.

80. Huangbang merchants such as Cheng Zhiyi, who contributed 1,000 taels silver to the reconstruction project for Macheng's examination hall, also financed the rebuilding of his lineage temple and, in addition, the city wall of his place of sojourn, Taiping County in Sichuan; see *Xicun Cheng shi zongpu*, 2:32.

81. *1882 XZ*, 39:13; *MCXZQB*, 2:20–21, 3:16–19.

82. *1882 XZ*, 39:13; *MCXZQB*, 4:27–29, 10:27.

83. *MCXZQB*, 4:32, 9:63, 9:79–82.

84. *1882 XZ*, 5:22–24, 39:14–21, *juan* 26 to 31 *passim.* For a study of eulogies, commemorations, and ruins in the wake of another, similarly apocalyptic conflict, see Blight.

85. *1882 XZ*, 39:14–21. Guo's career in Macheng is recorded in *MCXZQB*, 6:31–32.

86. See especially Meng Guangpeng, preface to *MCXZQB.*

Chapter 9

1. *MCXZXB*, 10:3–5.

2. Su Yunfeng, 329–456.

3. *MCXZXB*, 3:39.

4. For example, *Lin shi zongpu* (1947), *juan* 2.

5. Macheng was not listed among the province's major cotton producers in the survey "Agricultural Production in Hupeh during 1934." On the dual economy in cotton, see Feuerwerker.

6. *1993 XZ*, 413.

7. See Chen Bozhuang; see also Zhang Ruide.

8. Su Yunfeng, 447. Macheng's first telegraph links to the outside came only in the 1920s, first at Songbu, in 1921, and three years later at the county seat.

9. *MCXZXB*, 7:5; Su Yungfeng, 409–10. A Songbu chamber of commerce followed in 1916, as did similar organs in other Macheng townships, but only in the 1930s.

10. *Chinese Recorder*, 47 (Feb. 1916), 132; *1993 XZ*, 11. For a discussion of Yu Dongchen's movement, see Wyman.

11. *MCXZXB*, 15:4–5; *1993 XZ*, 536.

12. *1993 XZ*, 12.

13. *MCXZXB*, 2:2–4.

14. *1993 XZ*, 413.

15. *MCXZQB*, 9:40–42. On the Jingxin Academy, see Liu Ping, 244–46.

16. *MCXZQB*, 9:63.

17. Ibid., 4:41–42, 8*xia*:12, 10:32; *1993 XZ*, 12.

18. Li Min, "Kaopeng youlai"; *MCXZQB*, 4:36–41; *MCXZXB*, 4:10–14; *1993 XZ*, 11–12, 470, 531, 579–80; *MCXJZ*, 41–42.

19. See Xiang Yunlong.

20. Zheng Zhong, preface to *MCXZQB*.

21. *MCXZXB*, 4:1–10. This was as well an era of vigorous private reconstruction of many lineage temples in the county, also with the end of providing moral "instruction" to their constituencies.

22. Ibid., 2:18–19. On these types of institutions in Yangzi Valley localities, see Rankin; see also Rowe, *Hankow*.

23. *MCXZQB*, 5:26; *MCXZXB*, 5:21–23, 5:57.

24. Esherick, *Reform and Revolution in China.*

25. Macheng County Grain Bureau, 1. Unfortunately, the details of this overhaul and its background are not recorded in this source.

26. Cai Ji'ou, 30–31.

27. *MCXZXB*, 3:4–5.

28. Ibid., 9:1–11.

29. Ibid., 11:11–12.

30. *MCXZQB*, 10:34.

31. See Wang Baoxin. The preface is dated Guangxu 34/3 and signed at Xuannan Ward, Beijing.

32. The following paragraphs are based on Yu Peihong; *MCXZXB*, 11:4; *1993 XZ*, 561; and *MCXJZ*, 26.

33. Tu and Dai, eds.; 356; *MCXZXB*, 11:11; *MCXJZ*, 27.

34. Fairly detailed biographies of Qu Kaiyan appear in *MCXZXB*, 11:10–11, and *1993 XZ*, 579.

35. *MCXZQB*, 8*xia*:25–26.

36. Cai Ji'ou, 1.

37. Xie Shiqin, 492.

38. Cai Ji'ou, 28–29. For English-language accounts of the failed rebellion of Tang Caichang's Independence Army, see Joseph W. Esherick, *Reform and Revolution in China*, 28–33, and Bays, 78–91.

39. Zhang and Lin, 3:88–92; Esherick, *Reform and Revolution in China*, 194.

40. *MCXZXB*, 11:11; Cai Ji'ou, 111–12; Xie Shiqin, 493; Esherick, *Reform and Revolution in China*, 198.

41. Qu Peilan (1877–1928) was an alumnus of the Jingxin Academy and the Liang-Hu Academy, a "returned student" from Japan, and dean of the Shinan Teacher's College at Wuhan; see *MCXZXB*, 11:5.

42. Zhou Longxiang (1878–1912) was a *shengyuan* and an old classmate of Qu Kaiyan at the Liang-Hu Academy, where he participated in Qu's anti-Manchu study group in the early 1890s. After a tour of study in Japan, he assumed the Liang-Hu's headmastership. Upon the outbreak of the Wuchang Rebellion, he attached himself immediately to the revolutionary government, largely managing the new regime's foreign relations. He is said to have had a great deal of influence over Li Yuanhong in the Republic's first year, especially in dealing with the administration of Hubei Province. See *1993 XZ*, 579–80.

43. *MCXZQB*, 5:20–21.

44. Ibid., 9:63.

45. *MCXZXB*, 2:2.

46. Zhang Sen (1887–1928) studied the Confucian curriculum in his youth but, like many of his Dongshan compatriots, was more deeply attracted to the *Sunzi* and other classics of military strategy. A graduate of Macheng's new Higher-Level Elementary School, he became a leader of student protests while at Baoding and, later, a Hubei Army and Guomindang military officer. See *MCXZXB*, 11:2–3.

47. *MCXZXB*, 4:14–17; Zheng Hengwu, "Xia Douyin de yisheng," 77–88. I thank Steven MacKinnon for bringing the latter source to my attention.

48. Alitto, 225 (emphasis added).

49. *MCXZXB*, 8:1, 11:5.

50. Ibid., 11:9.

51. *MCXZQB*, *juan* 8.

52. Ibid., 10:17–18, 10:24, 10:26, 10:30.

53. See Meskill.

54. *MCXZQB*, 9:61–62; *MCXZXB*, 11:9–10.

55. Luo Ergang, "Qingji bingwei jiangyou de qiyuan."

56. Wang Zhongxing; *Who's Who in China*, 4th ed., 145–46; *Who's Who in China*, 6th ed., 82; Zheng Hengwu, "Xia Douyin de yisheng," 77–78; *MCXZQB*, 4:42; *1993 XZ*, 572–73; Tian and Huang, 230.

57. Zheng Hengwu, "Xia Douyin de yisheng," 78–79; Tian and Huang, 71; Li Chien-nung, 401–8.

58. For example, memorial of Hubei governor Wei Jixun, Guangxu 18/7/28, *Guanzhong dang Guangxu chao zouzhe*, 7:293–95.

59. *MCXZXB*, 5:23.

60. See especially Nagano, 237–38, *passim*. See also He Xiya; Billingsley, 34–35, *passim*; Cai Shaoqing.

61. *Hankow Herald*, Jan. 8 1926; *Hubei xianzheng gaikuang*, 508–9; *MCXZXB*, 5:48, 11:8–9.

62. *MCXZXB*, 5:24, 10:4, 11:12.

Chapter 10

1. *MCXZXB*, 3:41.

2. The term and variants of it recur routinely in popular historiography of this period of Macheng history; see, for example, Guo Mu.

3. Snow, 298.

4. *MCXDMZ*, 1; *1993 XZ*, 71.

5. Macheng magistrate Liu Gang, report to Hubei provincial governor Fang, June 12, 1929, HPA; *Macheng xianwei baogao*, 234–35; *Hubei xianzheng gaikuang*, 508–12; He Yulin, 34; *MCXZXB*, 3:28, 15:9.

6. *Hubei xianzheng gaikuang*, 510.

7. *Macheng xianwei baogao*, 238–39; Li Min, "Hong tudi shang de huaguo"; Wou, 104–6.

8. *Xicun Cheng shi zongpu*, *juan* 2; Wang Libo; *MCXZXB*, 4:4–10.

9. *Macheng xianwei baogao*, 239; *Hubei xianzheng gaikuang*, 510. Note that the Na-

tionalist survey explicitly (and almost certainly inaccurately) denies the existence of rent surcharges in Macheng.

10. *People's Tribune* (Hankow), March 22, 1927.

11. *Huang'an wei guanyu 'Huang-Ma baoyun' jingguo qingxing gei zhongyang de baogao* (Report of the Huang'an County Committee on the Progress of the Huang'an Uprising), Dec. 14, 1927, HPA; Xinxian County Party School, 8.22.

12. He Yulin, 34; *MCXZXB*, 1:8; *Macheng xianwei baogao*, 238. This last point strongly reinforces the arguments of Bianco.

13. The newly assessed *juan* (fees) are catalogued in *MCXZXB*, 3:39–42, and *Macheng xianwei baogao*, 235.

14. Bianco, 43–44.

15. Tu and Dai, eds.

16. Klein and Clark, 874–80. Dong's official biography is *Dong Biwu nianpu* (Chronological biography of Dong Biwu); see Dong Biwu Nianpu Working Group, comp., especially 7, 10 (for Dong's Songbu experience).

17. *1993 XZ*, 223, 490; *MCXJZ*, 9; Li Min, "Kaopeng youlai"; Dong Biwu Nianpu Working Group, comp., 29, 44–53; Wou, 116.

18. Tu and Dai, eds., 20–21; *1993 XZ*, 223, 564.

19. Capsule biographies of several of these young men appear in Tu and Dai, eds., 26, 96, 439–40, 445–46, 469, 571–72, 574–75. For Wang Shusheng's official biography, see Wang Shusheng Biography Working Group, comp.

20. *1993 XZ*, 12, 562–63, 573.

21. *1993 XZ*, 223.

22. *1993 XZ*, 233, 520.

23. "Beifa jiangling Wang Caoru"; *1993 XZ*, 562.

24. *Hankow Herald*, May 18, 1927; *MCXZXB*, 11:3; Tian and Huang, 93, 230.

25. The first "red" Workers' Association was set up by Cai Jihuang in his native town of Baiguo in January 1927; see *Macheng gonghui zhi*, 2.

26. *Minguo ribao* (Republican Daily News, Hankow), Jan. 6, 1927, Jan. 18, 1927, Jan. 20, 1927, Jan. 28, 1927, and Feb. 8, 1927; *People's Tribune* (Hankow), June 10, 1927; *MCXZXB*, 5:24–25, 10:3–5.

27. *MCXZXB*, 5:23; *1993 XZ*, 340.

28. Bianco, 4–5, 10.

29. *MCXZXB*, 5:49–51.

30. *Huang'an gongzuo baogao: guanyu "Huang-Ma baodong" de jingguo*, 3–4.

31. *Fengyun bianhuan*, 1; *MCXZXB*, 11:7. Note that the character *kui* in *kuihuzhi* is Matthews no. 1599, normally pronounced *qu*, but Macheng sources are emphatic that locally, in reference to the 1925 system, it was read *kui*.

32. *1993 XZ*, 340, 568–69; *MCXZXB*, 4:1.

33. *MCXZXB*, 5:23–24. It seems suggestive, at least, that the leader of Macheng's bandit-extermination struggle in the early years of the People's Republic (discussed in chap. 1) was also surnamed Zheng.

34. Accounts consulted here include Xiang Yunlong, 35–41; Zhang Zhenzhi, chap. 2; Suemitsu, 113–44; Nagano; and Perry, 197–224, *passim*. In addition to groups explicitly calling themselves Red Spears, there were parallel groups with names such as White

Spears (*baiqiang*) and Black Spears (*heiqiang*); for an attempt to distinguish among these, see Dai, 132–36. In the Macheng area, all behaved similarly.

35. "Gong dao bairi, dao qiang buru." Another went: "With body toughened like metal, and belly imbibing cosmic energy (*lianqi*), I can resist knives and deflect lances, and bullets cannot penetrate my body"; see *1993 XZ*, 537.

36. Suemitsu, 116–17. On the Eight Trigrams sect, see Naquin.

37. Zhang Zhenzhi, 131.

38. On this, see also Kuhn, *Rebellion and Its Enemies in Late Imperial China*, 34.

39. Nagano, 326–29.

40. Suemitsu, 115–31.

41. *Hankow Herald*, June 23, 1926.

42. Ibid., Feb. 26 1927. See also the *Herald* editions of Jan. 8, 1926, May 26, 1926, and Aug. 7, 1927. A sense of the military chaos in this area during the months before and after the arrival of the Nationalists can be gained from Sheridan, chap. 9.

43. Zhang Zhenzhi, 145.

44. Xiang Yunlong, 37.

45. *Huang'an xianwei guanyu "Huang-Ma baodong" jingguo xingqing gei zhongyuan de baogao* (a revised and edited version of this document has been published as *Huang'an gongzuo baogao: guanyu "Huang-Ma baodong" de jingguo*, 3.1–15); *Macheng xianwei baogao*, 244–45.

46. *Macheng xianwei baogao*, 245; *MCXZXB*, 5:25; *1993 XZ*, 537.

47. *MCXJZ*, 14.

48. Dai, 217–18; Perry, 213–16.

49. *Macheng xianwei baogao*, 247; He Yulin, 31.

50. Wou, 117–18.

51. Throughout this study, I have avoided translating *nong* or *nongmin* as "peasants" because of the ideological and/or orientalist nature of that patronizing English word. In most instances, "farmers" or "cultivators" is a more accurate and value-free rendering of the Chinese. In the case of *nongmin xiehui*, however, the ideological content of the term was deliberately intended by the organizations' founders, and indeed *nongmin* itself was a direct translation of the Marxist category "peasant"; "peasant associations" thus seems the most appropriate translation.

52. *MCXZXB*, 7:4–5; *1993 XZ*, 233; Tian and Huang, 192–93.

53. *Fengyun bianhuan*, 4, 8–9; *1993 XZ*, 12, 232, 562–64; *MCZXZ*, 10.

54. *Macheng xianwei baogao*, 240.

55. *Fengyun bianhuan*, 8; *1993 XZ*, 230. On the rather fuzzy referent of the term "local bullies and evil gentry," see Alitto, 239–42, and Kuhn, "Local Self-Government under the Republic."

56. He Yulin, 43.

57. *Minguo ribao* (Republican Daily News, Hankow), Jan. 28 1927; *MCXZXB*, 7:2–4.

58. *Macheng xianwei baogao*, 247.

59. *1993 XZ*, 493. In 1981, the Macheng Cultural Office published a collection of 255 of these progressive folk songs, a collection I have not seen. The Communist practice of appropriating Macheng's vibrant folk song traditon for political purposes continued throughout the Maoist era; see, for example, "Hubei Macheng nongmin geyao."

60. Xinxian County Party School, 8.25; *MCXZXB*, 7:2–4.

61. *Minguo ribao* (Republican Daily News, Hankow), Feb. 9, 1927, and March 7, 1927.
62. *Fengyun bianhuan*, 9.
63. *Minguo ribao* (Republican Daily News, Hankow), Feb. 8, 1927.
64. Tu and Dai, eds., 445.
65. *Fengyun bianhuan*, 8–9; Chang, 213.
66. Mao Tse-tung, "Report on an Investigation of the Peasant Movement in Hunan (March 1927)."
67. Mao, "Report," 28 (where the "dinner party" comment appears). For a discussion of the report's reception in Wuhan, see Schram, 94–103.
68. *Minguo ribao* (Republican Daily News, Hankow), March 7, 1927; *Macheng xianwei baogao*, 239; Chang, 213–14; He Yulin, 34; *1993 XZ*, 233.
69. Mann, "The Male Bond in Chinese History and Culture." Mann bases this argument largely on evidence from Friedman, Pickowicz, and Selden.
70. ter Haar, "China's Inner Demons," 28–29.
71. *MCXZXB*, 15:9.
72. See Wang Libo.
73. See Xinxian County Party School.
74. *Huang'an xianwei guanyu "Huang-Ma baodong" jingguo xingqing gei zhongyuan de baogao; Huang'an gongzuo baogao: guanyu "Huang-Ma baodong" de jingguo*, 4.
75. *MCXJZ*, 10–11; *1993 XZ*, 574.
76. *Minguo ribao* (Republican Daily News, Hankow), May 16, 1927; *1993 XZ*, 230; *MCXJZ*, 10–11; Tu and Dai, eds., 574.
77. *Macheng gonghui zhi*, 1; Tu and Dai, eds., 571–72; *1993 XZ*, 563–64.
78. Tian and Huang, 195–96.
79. *Hankow Herald*, March 4, 1927; *1993 XZ*, 232; Tian and Huang, 194.
80. *People's Tribune* (Hankow), March 22 and 24, 1927. The author of these articles may have been the American communist Earl Browder.
81. The most important source of the following paragraphs is a long and detailed article in *Minguo ribao* (Republican Daily News, Hankow), May 16, 1927. See also *MCXJZ*, 12–14.
82. *MCXZXB*, 6:2.
83. *Minguo ribao* (Republican Daily News, Hankow), Apr. 5 1927. The entire report of the attack in this Wuhan newspaper is printed in bold, enlarged typeface.
84. *MCXZXB*, 5:25.
85. *Minguo ribao* (Republican Daily News, Hankow), May 12, 1927. See also *MCXZXB*, 5:25; *1993 XZ*, 12, 223.
86. *Minguo ribao* (Republican Daily News, Hankow), May 22 and May 27, 1927; *1993 XZ*, 562; Liu Manrong, 78.
87. *Minguo ribao*, May 22 and May 27, 1927. Briefer and more matter-of-fact accounts of the relief of the siege appear in *MCXZXB*, 5:25, *1993 XZ*, 12, and *MCXJZ*, 12–14.
88. *1993 XZ*, 230, 564; Liu Manrong, 79.
89. The following paragraphs are based on *Minguo ribao* (Republican Daily News, Hankow), May 21, 1927, May 22, 1927, May 26, 1927, May 27, 1927, May 28, 1927, May 30, 1927, May 31, 1927, June 2, 1927, and June 6, 1927. See also *1993 XZ*, 348, 531; Liu Manrong, 80; Guo Mu, chap. 3.

90. *Minguo ribao* (Republican Daily News, Hankow), May 28, 1927; *1993 XZ*, 348; *MCXJZ*, 14.

91. *Minguo ribao* (Republican Daily News, Hankow), June 4, 1927, June 7, 1927, June 9, 1927, and June 11, 1927.

92. *Minguo ribao* (Republican Daily News, Hankow), May 22, 1927.

93. *1993 XZ*, 341–42; *MCXJZ*, 39–40.

Chapter 11

1. Standard treatments of this protracted rupture between Jiang Jieshi and the United Front left can be found in Isaacs, 143–44, 175–85; see also Wilbur, 78–112.

2. *Minguo ribao* (Republican Daily News, Hankow), Jan. 11, 1927, and Jan. 16. 1927.

3. Zheng Hengwu, "Xia Douyin de yisheng," 80–81.

4. *Minguo ribao* (Republican Daily News, Hankow), June 25, 1927.

5. General accounts of Xia's mutiny appear in Zheng Hengwu, "Pingding Xia Douyin, Yang Sen panluan"; Pi and Ouyang, 522–24; Tian and Huang, 203, 231–32; Wilbur, 126–28. On the likely orchestration of Xia's actions by Jiang Jieshi, see *People's Tribune* (Hankow), June 21, 1927; *MCXZXB*, 11:3; Zheng Hengwu, "Xia Douyin de yisheng," 81.

6. *Hankow Herald*, May 18, 1927; *Minguo ribao* (Republican Daily News, Hankow), June 11, 1927; *MCXZXB*, 11:3; Zheng Hengwu, "Xia Douyin de yisheng," 83; Zheng Hengwu, "Pingding Xia Douyin, Yang Sen panluan." For personal memoirs of Xia's march by purported eyewitnesses, see the works by Shi Heng, Han Ling, and Lan Wenwei; I thank Steven Mackinnon for bringing these three sources to my attention.

7. *Hankow Herald*, May 18, 1927, and May 19, 1927; Wilbur, 126.

8. *Hankow Herald*, May 21, 1927; *People's Tribune* (Hankow), May 20 and 22, 1927; *Minguo ribao* (Republican Daily News, Hankow), June 1, 1927, and June 12, 1927; Wu Zhongya.

9. *Minguo ribao* (Republican Daily News, Hankow), June 14, 1927.

10. Ibid., May 23, 1927, May 24, 1927, May 25, 1927, June 1, 1927, and June 14, 1927; *People's Tribune* (Hankow), May 24 and June 21, 1927; Zheng Hengwu, "Xia Douyin de yisheng," 82–83; Zheng Hengwu, "Pingding Xia Douyin, Yang Sen panluan," 186–89.

11. *Minguo ribao* (Republican Daily News, Hankow), June 4, 1927, June 14, 1927, June 27, 1927, June 30, 1927, July 2, 1927, and July 18, 1927; *People's Tribune* (Hankow), July 21, 1927.

12. *Minguo ribao* (Republican Daily News, Hankow), July 18, 1927; Pi and Ouyang, 524.

13. Wang, oral history, in Chang, 214.

14. *Minguo ribao* (Republican Daily News, Hankow), June 19, 1927, June 24, 1927, June 27, 1927, and June 28, 1927.

15. *Minguo ribao* (Republican Daily News, Hankow), July 18, 1927.

16. *Hankow Herald*, June 26, 1927; *Minguo ribao* (Republican Daily News, Hankow), June 22, 1927, June 25, 1927, and July 5, 1927.

17. *Minguo ribao* (Republican Daily News, Hankow), July 28, 1927.

18. *MCXZXB*, 11:3.

19. Meng Guangpeng, preface to *MCXZQB*.

20. Xia, handwritten "introduction" to Xia, ed.

21. Wilbur, 128.

22. For phrases cited in this passage, see Isaacs, 227. See also *Minguo ribao* (Republican Daily News, Hankow), June 12–13, 1927, and June 22, 1927; Xie Bingying.

23. *Minguo ribao* (Republican Daily News, Hankow), June 12–13, 1927, and June 22, 1927; Isaacs, 227.

24. "Xinzeng jiashun yin" (Extracts from newly-amended lineage rules), in *Shi shi zongpu*, 3:15–22.

25. Zhang Qun, 517.

26. *Macheng xianwei baogao*, 237, 242.

27. Wou, 127. In a directive of early summer, the United Front regime itself acknowledged and prohibited such compulsory marriages; see *People's Tribune* (Hankow), July 6, 1927.

28. Gilmartin, 196.

29. Ibid., 180.

30. Wang Zheng, 345.

31. The chief sources for the following paragraphs on the Women's Representative Conference are announcements and resolutions from the conference itself in addition to journalistic accounts of it in *Minguo ribao* (Republican Daily News, Hankow) and *Hubei funü* (Journal of the Hubei Women's Association); these are collected and reprinted in All-China Women's Federation, Research Department on the History of the Women's Movement, comp., 741–45, 760–67, 779–80. See also Wang Zheng, 296–302.

32. Gilmartin, 187.

33. *1993 XZ*, 233.

34. See "Xiong Miannan funü."

35. Tu and Dai, eds., 334.

36. Wang Libo, file GM2–118–2.

37. *Minguo ribao* (Republican Daily News, Hankow), May 22, 1927; See Xie Bingying; see also Gilmartin, 188–91. Among the prolific memoir accounts, see Li Wenyi, 12–14; Hu Langui, 86–98; Lü Ruzhen, 154–58; Fu Hao.

38. Gilmartin, 182.

39. *Hankow Herald*, Jan. 15 1927; Gilmartin, 192–93.

40. "Hubei sheng nongxie dahui: Duiyu nongcun funü wenti jueyi an," in All-China Women's Federation, Research Department on Women's Movement History, comp., 708.

41. *1993 XZ*, 540.

42. "Xiong Miannan funü," 8; *1993 XZ*, 233.

43. *Minguo ribao* (Republican Daily News, Hankow), May 16, 1927.

44. Ibid., June 22, 1927.

45. Snow, 300–304.

46. *Hankow Herald*, May 22, 1927. For a discussion of the debates at Wuhan, see Wilbur, 117–24.

47. *People's Tribune* (Hankow), June 9 and 11, 1927; *Minguo ribao* (Republican Daily News, Hankow), June 12–13, 1927. The principal spokesmen for Wuhan on this issue were Ren Xu, head of the All-China Peasant Association, and Cai Yishen, a member of the central committee. Ren clearly enunciated more critical and moderationist policies than Cai. On the confused leadership situation at this time in Wuhan, see Isaacs, 252–71.

48. *People's Tribune* (Hankow), June 25, 1927; All-China Women's Federation, Research Department on Women's Movement History, comp., 708.

49. *People's Tribune* (Hankow), June 26, 1927.

50. Ibid., June 29, 1927, July 1, 1927, July 2, 1927, July 6, 1927, and July 12, 1927. These reports also contain detailed (and sometimes conflicting) instructions on land reform, village militia organization, and other matters that need not detain us here.

51. *People's Tribune* (Hankow), July 13, 1927.

52. Wilbur, 144–45, 158.

53. Gilmartin, 181.

54. *Minguo ribao* (Republican Daily News, Hankow), Aug. 10, 1927; *People's Tribune* (Hankow), Aug. 3, 1927, Aug. 5, 1927, and Aug. 11, 1927; *Hankow Herald*, Aug. 9 1927.

55. *Minguo ribao*, July 19, 1927.

56. *Minguo ribao*, July 23, 1927.

57. *Minguo ribao*, July 28, 1927.

58. *Minguo ribao*, July 23, 1927.

59. "Zhongyang duiyu Wuhan fandong shiju zhi tonggao" (Party central committee declaration on the current reactionary political situation in Wuhan), July 24, 1927, in Central United Front Department and Central Party Archives, comp., 7–9.

60. Klein and Clark, 876–77.

61. *1993 XZ*, 223, 341.

62. *Hankow Herald*, Aug. 9, 1927; *MCXJZ*, 30–31.

63. "Zhongguo Gongchandang de zhengzhi renwu yu celue de jue'an" (Resolutions on the political mission and strategies of the Chinese Communist Party), Aug. 21, 1927, in Central United Front Department and Central Party Archives, comp., 32–43; Tian and Huang, 334–35; Isaacs, 279–80; Wilbur, 150–51.

64. *MCXJZ*, 15–16; Tian and Huang, 336–37.

65. Macheng magistrate Liu Gang, report to Hubei provincial governor Fang, June 12, 1929, HPA.

66. This and the following paragraphs rely heavily on *Huang'an xianwei guanyu "Huang-Ma baodong" jingguo xingqing gei zhongyuan de baogao*, file GM2-117.

67. Tian and Huang, 340.

68. On the details of this Nationalist power struggle see Wilbur, 158–59.

69. *1993 XZ*, 564; *MCXJZ*, 17.

70. *Huang'an gongzuo baogao: guanyu "Huang-Ma baodong" de jingguo*; *Huang'an xianwei guanyu "Huang-Ma baodong" jingguo xingqing gei zhongyuan de baogao*; Wang Libo; *1993 XZ*, 348–49.

71. Benton, 310.

72. *Huang'an gongzuo baogao: guanyu "Huang-Ma baodong" de jingguo*, 8–9.

73. Ibid., 10.

74. *Huang'an xianwei guanyu "Huang-Ma baodong" jingguo xingqing gei zhongyuan de baogao*; *Huang'an gongzuo baogao: guanyu "Huang-Ma baodong" de jingguo*, 11–14; Tian and Huang, 341.

75. *1993 XZ*, 566; *MCXJZ*, 18.

76. *1993 XZ*, 230.

77. Tu and Dai, eds., 21, 96, 572; *1993 XZ*, 13, 564–65.

78. See especially Huang-Ma Uprising Compilation Group, ed.; enlivened by stir-

ring illustrations, folk songs, and imagined dialogue, this colloquial work climaxes with "Twenty-One Days of Glory" and devotes only a few pages to the rebellion's disastrous outcome. Only a bit more muted is the work by Guo Mu.

79. *Huang'an gongzuo baogao: guanyu "Huang-Ma baodong" de jingguo*, 15; Chang, 214.

Chapter 12

1. Ren's easy way with loyalties later showed itself in his abandoning Jiang Jieshi's Nationalists for Feng Yuxiang in the North China campaigns of the early 1930s. His luck ran out in 1934, when he was captured and executed by Nationalist authorities in Tianjin; see Zhang Xianwen et.al., comp., *Zhonghua minguo shi da cidian* (Historical dictionary of Republican China) (Nanjing: Jiangsu guji chubanshe, 2001), 699–700; Jordan, 280.

2. *Macheng xianwei baogao*, 233, 243; *Huang'an gongzuo baogao: guanyu "Huang-Ma baodong" de jingguo*, 15; *MCXZXB*, 10:5; *1993 XZ*, 13.

3. The following paragraphs are based largely on *MCXZXB*, 5:25–26.

4. *1993 XZ*, 590–91; *MCXZXB*, 8:2–5.

5. Li Jianbang, popularly known as Old Man Li (Li Laomo), after a stock character in the *zaju* opera tradition.

6. *MCXZXB*, 5:26–27; *1993 XZ*, 349.

7. *1993 XZ*, 569.

8. The following paragraphs are based largely on *MCXZXB*, 3:40–41, 5:49–53, and on *1993 XZ*, 340–41, *bianhuan*, 2–4. Note that private anti-Communist militia units continued to exist alongside those that the Guomindang County administration more or less successfully brought under its control. For example, Macheng's local Roman Catholic community, headed by a resident Italian priest known as Li Daochun—a man with increasingly obvious sympathies with the Fascist government in his native country—operated its own Blessed Virgin Anti-Communist Army (*Fangong Shengmu jun*) throughout the 1930s. Father Li remained in Macheng as a collaborator under the Japanese occupation and was finally expelled by the new Communist regime in 1951. See *1993 XZ*, 537.

9. Wou, 111, 407.

10. *Lin shi zongpu* (1947), *juan* 2; *Fengyun bianhuan*, 2–3, 43–47; *1993 XZ*, 572. The establishment of the Lin lineage in Macheng is treated in chap. 3, above. Lin, self-styled King of Hell, sought sanctuary with a lineage branch in Chengdu when Macheng was taken by the Communists in 1949 but was extradited home and executed by the People's Government the following year.

11. The following paragraphs follow Zheng Hengwu, "Eyuwan sansheng 'jiaozong' shishi baojia lianzuo fa."

12. On the Nationalist use of *baojia* in the encirclement of the Jiangxi Soviet, and in "reconstruction" of the area after the soviet's collapse, see Averill.

13. See, for example, the series of reports from Macheng's Fourth Ward in 1936, held in the HPA under the title "Siqu zhuan Macheng chengyi lianbao bangongchu banshi" (Reports of activities of the Fourth Ward Baojia Linked Management Office, forwarded by Macheng County).

14. *Fengyun bianhuan*, 3.

15. *Hubei xianzheng gaikuang*, 2.507–8.

16. *Hubei xianzheng gaikuang*, 2.514.

17. *1993 XZ*, 345.

18. See Duara.

19. *Hubei xianzheng gaikuang*, 2.507.

20. *Macheng disichu baojia xunlianban tongxue lu* (Graduation program for Fourth Ward Baojia Training School), 1937, MCA.

21. Zheng Hengwu, "Eyuwan sansheng 'jiaozong' shishi baojia lianzuo fa," 234. On the general phenomenon of this bureaucratization, see Kuhn, "Local Self-Government under the Republic."

22. Macheng magistrate Zheng Zhong, "Zhengli baojia suqing lingfei fang'an" (Proposal for reorganizing *baojia* and mopping up remnant bandits), Feb. 15, 1934, HPA; *1993 XZ*, 341; Zheng Hengwu, "Eyuwan sansheng 'jiaozong' shishi baojia lianzuo fa," 235–36.

23. See Averill, who was of course arguing against Mary Clabaugh Wright's contemptuous dismissal of the New Life; see also Wright, introduction.

24. *1993 XZ*, 591.

25. *MCXZXB*, 7:1–5; *1993 XZ*, 233. It is noteworthy that the Guomindang-appointed director of Macheng's merchant association was one Mei Yuqi—very likely a descendant of Mei Guozhen and Mei Zhihuan, who had been so central to the county's society and politics in the late Ming.

26. Eyuwan Border Area Bandit-Extermination Command, Huang-Ma Branch.

27. *Hubei xianzheng gaikuang*, 2.517–18.

28. With a contribution of 1,000 Mexican dollars, Xia was by far the largest contributor to the gazetteer project; Magistrate Zheng ranked second, at 300 dollars. See "Juanhu xingming," in *MCXZXB*.

29. Meng Guangpeng, a native of Shangqiu, Henan, was a statistician and a respected Guomindang expert on local governance. In 1933, he was appointed director of Hubei Province's Office of Popular Administration (*minzheng ting*), in which capacity he supervised the compilation not only of the massive six-volume *Hubei xianzheng gaikuang* in 1934, but also of the provincial cadastral survey the following year (see Meng Guangpeng).

30. *1993 XZ*, 577.

31. *MCXZXB*; Meng Guangpeng, preface to *MCXZQB*. There is a similar emphasis on adherence to the *siwei* in several of Macheng's lineage regulatory codes, especially in their Republican-era revisions; see, for example, *Shi shi zongpu*, 3:8–21.

32. See Zheng Zhong, preface to *MCXZXB*.

33. *MCXZXB*, 1:43–44.

34. Perhaps unsurprisingly, the echoes are most striking of all with Geng Dingxiang's passionate espousal (contra Li Zhi) of moral and social distinction (*fenbie*) and purification of popular mores (*zunsu weifeng*) as correctives to social disorder. But there are also strong resonances with the rhetoric of Mei Guozhen, Mei Zhihuan, Yu Chenglong, and Hu Linyi as well as with local lineage regulatory codes of all eras.

35. *Macheng xianwei baogao*, 240–41; Tu and Dai, eds., 445–46.

36. Macheng magistrate Liu Gang, report to Hubei provincial governor Fang, June 12, 1929, HPA.

37. *Macheng xianwei baogao*, 233; *MCXZXB*, 5:27; *1993 XZ*, 349; Xinxian County Party School, 8.27; Chang, 218; Wou, 122, 410.
38. *1993 XZ*, 230–34; McColl, 51–52.
39. *1993 XZ*, 234, 566; Tu and Dai, eds., 26.
40. *Fengyun bianhuan*, 4–20.
41. Benton, 304; *MCXJZ*, 18.
42. For but one example of this area's chronic role as hiding ground for rebels—in this case, a Taiping offshoot (*fengu*)—see Zhang Zhiwan and Mao Changxi, memorial of TZ 3/8/13, in MQA.
43. Billingsley, 256–58.
44. Chang, 215.
45. For an account of Xu's Eyuwan experience, see Xu Xiangqian.
46. *Macheng xianwei baogao*, 242; *1993 XZ*, 13, 224; Snow, 295; Klein and Clark, 348–50; McColl, 46–47. Xu Xiangqian eventually rose to become, by the 1970s, a member of the central committee and marshal of the People's Republic of China.
47. Zheng Hengwu, "Xia Douyin de yisheng," 84–88.
48. For routine reports of Communists captured and killed between 1929 and 1934, see *Macheng xian zhengfu banli Hongjun tufei anjian yuebao biao* and *Chaocheng yuanlai gongfei mingdan*. For general assessments of the campaigns' success, see *MCXZXB*, 5:29–34; Pi and Ouyang, 546; McColl, 53.
49. *MCXZXB*, 5:35–40; *1993 XZ*, 13; McColl, 57.
50. Chang, 224–25; *MCXZXB*, 5:7.
51. *Fengyun bianhuan*, 33–35; *MCXZXB* 5:29–30; *1993 XZ*, 230, 348, 490; *MCXJZ* 14–15; Tu and Dai, eds., 574–75.
52. *MCXZXB*; Meng Guangpeng, preface to *MCXZQB*; Meng Guangpeng, *MCXZQB*, 5:1–21; *1993 XZ*, 345–46.
53. The best study of the Eyuwan purge is Chen Yongfa. See also Sheng, 30; Benton, 307, 313–14. For Zhang Guotao's early life, see Klein and Clark, 38–43.
54. For example Guo Mu, 425–26. See also Chen Yongfa, who adopts a moderate position: the purges would probably have taken place even without Zhang, but Zhang certainly made them more bloody than they would otherwise have been.
55. Both men were shortly afterward rehabilitated and declared martyrs; see *1993 XZ*, 224, 565–66; Tu and Dai, eds., 439–40, 445–46.
56. Guillermaz, 216–17.
57. Klein and Clark, 40.
58. Zhang Guotao, "Suqu fazhan jingguo ji sufan shengli de yuanyin: Zhang Guotao gei Zhongyang de baogao," 295.
59. Ibid., 290–95. See also Chang, 241; Sheng, 30–35; Guillermaz, 217.
60. Chen Yongfa, part 1, 25.
61. Zhang Guotao, "Suqu fazhan jingguo ji sufan shengli de yuanyin: Zhang Guotao gei Zhongyang de baogao," 288–90.
62. Li and Chen; *Fengyun bianhuan*, 19–20; *1993 XZ*, 329, 567, 569; Zhang Guotao, "Suqu fazhan jingguo ji sufan shengli de yuanyin: Zhang Guotao gei Zhongyang de baogao," 294. Chen Yongfa, part 2, offers a detailed reconstruction of the mechanism of the purge.
63. Sheng, 36–37.

64. Zhang Guotao, "Suqu fazhan jingguo ji sufan shengli de yuanyin: Zhang Guotao gei Zhongyang de baogao," 289; Chang, 242.

65. *1993 XZ*, 417.

66. Zhang Guotao, "Suqu fazhan jingguo ji sufan shengli de yuanyin: Zhang Guotao gei Zhongyang de baogao," 290.

67. Sheng, 32.

68. Benton, 308–9, 317. Gao was eventually executed as a "mountain toppist" in 1939 by New Fourth Army commander Ye Ting.

69. Zhang Guotao, "Suqu fazhan jingguo ji sufan shengli de yuanyin: Zhang Guotao gei Zhongyang de baogao," 293–94.

70. Chen Yongfa, part 1, 26; Sheng, 39.

71. Tu and Dai, eds., 26, 299, 469, 575; *1993 XZ*, 566.

72. Xu Xiangqian, 162–63.

73. *1993 XZ*, 329.

74. The file is listed in the archive's catalogue as "Eyuwan bianji shishengwei disizi kuangda huiyi yu muqian xingshi ji dang de zhongxin renwu, dang de zuzhi wenti, fangeming pai bije douzheng sufan wenti de jueyi" (Resolutions of the Fourth Eyuwan Border Area Plenum on the current problems of Party center responsibility, Party organization, and the struggle against and purge of counterrevolutionaries). HPA, file GM, 2–1–66.

75. Chang, 276; Benton, 307; Xu Xiangqian, 152–63; Guo Mu, 425; *MCXJZ*, 18.

76. Chen Yongfa, part 3, 127; Benton, 307; Xiaorong Han, "Patterns of Central-Local Relations in Soviet China, 1927–1935."

77. Chang, 240–41, 253, 274.

78. Xu Xiangqian, 73 (emphasis added).

79. See, for example, "Weiye chui ceshi, fengfan liu guxiang" (While accomplishing great things of historical importance, his heart was always in his native place), testimonial statement prepared by the Macheng County Party Committee on the 100th anniversary of Wang Shusheng's birth (unpublished draft).

80. Chen Yongfa, part 2, 68–69; Benton, 311. For broader geographic perspectives on this tension, see Bianco, 26–28; see also Xiaorong Han, "Localism in Chinese Politics Before and After 1949."

81. Zhang Guotao, "Suqu fazhan jingguo ji sufan shengli de yuanyin: Zhang Guotao gei Zhongyang de baogao," 294; Chang, 263–64; *1993 XZ*, 417–18.

82. *MCXZXB*, 5:35–41, 7:6; *1993 XZ*, 223, 231; Sheng, 41–42.

83. The Cantonese Yang Yongtai (1880–1936) was a veteran of the 1911 and 1913 Revolutions and a former Guangdong governor. He was consistently right of center within the Nationalist political spectrum and was a staunch ally of Jiang Jieshi in the interparty conflicts of the 1930s. Shortly after his appointment as Hubei governor in 1936, he was assassinated by a factional opponent. See Boorman and Howard, 4.17–19.

84. Zheng Hengwu, "Xia Douyin de yisheng," 85; Zheng Hengwu, "Eyuwan sansheng 'jiaozong' shishi baojia lianzuo fa," 234–36; Sheng, 40.

85. *1993 XZ*, 231; Snow, 300–304; Benton, 315–18; Sheng, 43; Klein and Clark, 38–43, 346–48, 931–33.

86. Benton, 317.

87. Xia remained in his post as director of the Provincial Public Security Bureau,

reportedly incensed at his personal geomancer for having predicted he would hold the governorship for nine years rather than the nine months he was actually in office; see Zheng Hengwu, "Xia Douyin de yisheng," 86–87.

88. *1993 XZ*, 224, 230–31.

89. *1993 XZ*, 14.

90. Snow, 295–304.

91. *MCXZXB*, 5:27–29; Benton, 309.

92. For representative examples, see Li and Chen; *Fengyun bianhuan*, 22–24; Xinxian County Party School, 8.28; *1993 XZ*, 13, 231.

93. "Edong yimin banfa" (Regulations for dealing with refugees in eastern Hubei), filed with twelve related documents, May–July 1935, HPA.

94. *MCXZXB*, 3:14–18, 7:6; *1993 XZ*, 13.

95. Li and Chen, 31.

96. Zhang Hengwu, "Xia Douyin de yisheng," 88; *Fengyun bianhuan*, 47; *1993 XZ*, 572–73, 591.

Conclusion

1. See David Der-wei Wang, especially 2, 4–6, 79.

2. A "backyard steel furnace" was set up in Macheng during the Great Leap Forward and promoted as something of a national model but was closed as a failure after merely four years of operation. See Wagner, 52–56; *1993 XZ*, 186.

3. See Perry.

4. This paragraph draws upon observations by Gang Zhao, based on his reading of an early draft of this book.

5. For but one example, see Magistrate Guo Qinghua's introductory essay to the "major events" section, *1882 XZ*, between *juan* 36 and 37.

6. On the strongman (or "man of force") as a cultural type, see Meskill; see also Robinson, 20, *passim*. On the *lulin* ethos, see Alitto, especially 229–31.

7. See Jenner, 12.

8. *1993 XZ*, 514–15; *Minguo ribao* (Republican Daily News, Hankow), June 12–13, 1927.

9. Macheng's splinter county Huang'an (literally, Yellow Peace) has even been renamed, in the Communist era, "Hong'an" (Red Peace).

10. Wang Baoxin (c. 1860–1944) was a Luotian native, an expert on local gazetteers, and, later, a professor at both Wuhan University and Beijing University (information provided by Wuhan University historian Feng Tianyu, a Huang'an native and a family friend of both the Wangs and the Dongs).

11. See, for example, *Huangzhou fuzhi shiyi*, *juan* 6, HPL; *1993 XZ*, 485–86.

12. For a relatively recent selection, recast so as to emphasize the goals of the Great Leap Forward, see "Hubei Macheng nongmin geyao."

13. See Miu.

14. See Snow, 295.

15. *1882 XZ*, 39:15.

Selected Bibliography

"Agricultural Production in Hupeh during 1934." *Chinese Economic Journal and Bulletin* 17.2 (1935), 164–75.

Alitto, Guy S. "Rural Elites in Transition: China's Cultural Crisis and the Problem of Legitimacy." *Select Papers from the Center for Far Eastern Studies* 3 (1978–79), 218–77.

All-China Women's Federation, Research Department on Women's Movement History, comp. *Zhongguo funü yundong lishi ziliao* (Historical materials on the Chinese women's movement). Beijing: Renmin chubanshe, 1986.

All-China Women's Federation and Whampoa Military Academy Alumni Association, comp. *Da geming hongliu de nübing* (Female soldiers in the Nationalist Revolution). Beijing: Zhongguo funü chubanshe, 1991.

Anagnost, Ann. "The Beginning and End of an Emperor: A Counterrepresentation of the State." *Modern China* 11.2 (Apr. 1985), 147–76.

Antony, Robert J. "Banditry and the Culture of Violence in Late Imperial South China." Paper presented at the annual meeting of the Association for Asian Studies, San Diego, Calif., March 6, 2004.

———. "Demons, Gangsters, and Secret Societies in Early Modern China." *East Asian History* 27 (June 2004), 71–98.

Araki, Kengo. "Minmatsu ni okeru Ju Butsu chowarron no seikaku" (The nature of Confucian-Buddhist syncretism in the late Ming). *Nihon Chūgoku gakkai hō* 18 (1966), 210–24.

Arendt, Hannah. *On Violence.* San Diego, Calif.: Harcourt Brace Jovanovich, 1970.

Averill, Steven. "The New Life in Action: The Nationalist Government in South Jiangxi, 1934–37." *China Quarterly* 88 (Dec. 1981), 594–628.

Ayers, William. *Chang Chih-tung and Educational Reform in China.* Cambridge, Mass.: Harvard University Press, 1971.

Baiguo qu gaikuang (General information about Baiguo). Baiguo: Baiguo Township Office, 1986. HGO.

Bays, Daniel H. *China Enters the Twentieth Century: Chang Chih-tung and the Issues of a New Age, 1895–1909.* Ann Arbor: University of Michigan Press, 1978.

Beattie, Hilary. *Land and Lineage in China: A Study of T'ung-ch'eng County, Anhwei, in the Ming and Ch'ing Dynasties.* Cambridge: Cambridge University Press, 1979.

"Beifa jiangling Wang Caoru" (The Northern Expedition general Wang Caoru). *Macheng wenshi ziliao* 1 (1987), 6–7.

Benjamin, Walter. "Critique of Violence," orig. 1921. In Walter Benjamin, *Reflections: Essays, Aphorisms, Autobiographical Writings*, ed. Peter Demetz. New York: Schocken Books, 1978.

Benton, Gregor. *Mountain Fires: The Red Army's Three-Year War in South China, 1934–1938*. Berkeley: University of California Press, 1992.

Bianco, Lucien. *Peasants without the Party: Grass-Roots Movements in Twentieth-Century China*. Armonk, N.Y.: M. E. Sharpe, 2001.

Billingsley, Phil. *Bandits in Republican China*. Stanford, Calif.: Stanford University Press, 1988.

Blight, David W. *Race and Reunion: The Civil War in American Memory*. Cambridge, Mass.: Harvard University Press, 2001.

Boorman, Howard L., and Richard C. Howard. *Biographical Dictionary of Republican China*. New York: Columbia University Press, 1967–1979.

Boretz, Avron A. "Martial Gods and Magic Swords: Identity, Myth, and Violence in Chinese Popular Religion." *Journal of Popular Culture* 29.1 (1995), 93–109.

Braudel, Fernand. "History and the Social Sciences: The *Longue Durée*." In Fernand Braudel, *On History*, trans. Sarah Matthews. Chicago: University of Chicago Press, 1980.

Brook, Timothy. "Family Continuity and Cultural Hegemony: The Gentry of Ningbo, 1368–1911." In Joseph W. Esherick and Mary Backus Rankin, eds., *Chinese Local Elites and Patterns of Dominance*. Berkeley: University of California Press, 1990.

———. "Funerary Ritual and the Building of Lineages in Late Imperial China." *Harvard Journal of Asiatic Studies* 49.2 (Dec. 1989), 465–99.

———. *Praying for Power: Buddhism and the Formation of Gentry Society in Late Ming China*. Cambridge, Mass.: Council on East Asian Studies, 1993.

Buck, John Lossing. *Land Utilization in China: Statistics*. Nanjing: Nanking University Press, 1937.

Cai Ji'ou. *Ezhou xueshi* (The bloody history of Hubei). Shanghai: Longmen lianhe shuju, 1958.

Cai Shaoqing. *Minguo shiqi de tufei* (Local bandits in the Republican era). Beijing: Renmin chubanshe, 1993.

———. "On the Origins of the Gelaohui." *Modern China* 10.4 (Oct. 1984), 481–508.

———. *Zhongguo bimi shehui* (Secret societies in China). Hangzhou: Zhejiang renmin chubanshe, 1989.

Cai Yiqing. "Xianhua Hankou" (Leisurely chats about Hankou). *Xinsheng yuekan* 6.1–2 (ca. 1930), n.p.

Central United Front Department and Central Party Archives, comp. *Zhonggong zhongyang tudi geming qianqi tongyi zhanxian wenjian xuanbian* (Selected Chinese Communist Party central committee documents on the land revolution during the First United Front). Beijing: Dang'an chubanshe, 1990.

Chang, Hao. *Liang Ch'i-ch'ao and Intellectual Transition in China, 1980–1907*. Cambridge, Mass.: Harvard University Press, 1971.

Chang Kuo-t'ao (Zhang Guotao). *The Rise of the Chinese Communist Party, 1928–1938: The Autobiography of Chang Kuo-t'ao*. Lawrence: University Press of Kansas, 1972.

Chaocheng yuanji gongfei mingdan (Submitted lists of Communists captured in Macheng), May 16, 1930. HPA.
Chaves, Jonathan. *Pilgrim of the Clouds: Poems and Essays from Ming China*. New York: Weatherhill, 1978.
Chen Bozhuang. *Ping-Han yanxian nongcun jingji diaocha* (An examination of the rural economy along the Beijing-Hankou Railroad). Shanghai: Jiaotong daxue yanjiusuo, 1936.
Chen Ding. *Donglin liezhuan* (Biographies of Donglin partisans), orig. 1711. *SKQS*.
Chen Pingyuan. *Qiangu wenren xiake meng: wuxia xiaoshuou leixing yanjiu* (The millennia-old dream of the literati: A study of the genre of knight-errant story). Beijing: Renmin wenxue chubanshe, 1992.
Chen shi zongpu (Genealogy of the Chen lineage), 1937. MCA.
Chen Shisong, ed. *Sichuan tongshi* (General history of Sichuan). Chengdu: Sichuan University Press, 1993.
Chen Tingjing. "Yu gong benchuan" (Draft biography of Yu Chenglong). In Chen Tingjing, *Wuting wenbian* (Selected works of Chen Tingjing), orig. 1708. Taibei: Commercial Press, 1972; reprinted, with slight modifications, in *1882 XZ*.
Chen Yongfa. "Zhengzhi kongzhi he qunzhong dongyuan: Eyuwan sufan" (Political control and mass mobilization: The Eyuwan purge), part 1. *Dalu zazhi* 86.1 (1993), 20–38.
———. "Zhengzhi kongzhi he qunzhong dongyuan: Eyuwan sufan" (Political control and mass mobilization: The Eyuwan purge), part 2. *Dalu zazhi* 86.2 (1993), 67–78.
———. "Zhengzhi kongzhi he qunzhong dongyuan: Eyuwan sufan" (Political control and mass mobilization: The Eyuwan purge), part 3. *Dalu zazhi* 86.3 (1993), 120–29.
Chen Zilong. *Huang Ming jingshi wenbian* (Compendium of statecraft writings from the Ming dynasty), orig. 1640. Taibei: Guolian chubanshe, 1964.
Chow, Kai-wing. *Publishing, Culture, and Power in Early Modern China*. Stanford, Calif.: Stanford University Press, 2004.
Chu Renxun. "Yu gong'an" (Legal cases of Mr. Yu). In Chu Renxun, *Qingdai chaoben gong'an xiaoshuo* (Storybook of Qing legal cases). Tianjin: Baihua wenyi, 1996.
Ch'u, Tung-ts'u. *Local Government in China under the Ch'ing*. Cambridge, Mass.: Harvard University Press, 1962.
Confino, Alon. "Collective Memory and Cultural History: Problems of Method." *American Historical Review*, Dec. 1997, 1386–1403.
Coser, Lewis A. "Some Social Functions of Violence." *Annals of the American Academy of Political and Social Sciences* 364 (March 1964), 8–18.
Da Qing lichao shilu (Veritable records of successive reigns of the Qing dynasty). Taibei: Hualian chubanshe, 1964.
Dai Li and Wu Shu. *Huailing liukou shizhong lu* (Complete account of the rampaging rebels in Huailing), orig. 1673. Taibei: Zhengzhong shuju, 1985.
Dai Xuanzhi. *Hongqiang hui, 1916–1949* (The Red Spears, 1916–1949). Taibei: Shihuo chubanshe, 1973.
Dardess, John W. *Blood and History in China: The Donglin Faction and its Repression, 1620–1627*. Honolulu: University of Hawai'i Press, 2002.
———. *A Ming Society: T'ai-ho County, Kiangsi, Fourteenth to Seventeenth Centuries*. Berkeley: University of California Press, 1996.

———. "Shun-ti and the End of Yüan Rule in China." In Denis Twitchett and John K. Fairbank, eds., *Cambridge History of China,* vol. 6: *Alien Regimes and Border States, 907–1368.* Cambridge: Cambridge University Press, 1994.

Davis, Natalie Zemon. "The Rites of Violence." In Natalie Zemon Davis, *Society and Culture in Early Modern France.* Stanford, Calif.: Stanford University Press, 1965.

de Bary, William Theodore. "Individualism and Humanitarianism in Late Ming Thought." In William Theodore de Bary, ed., *Self and Society in Ming Thought.* New York: Columbia University Press, 1970.

Dennerline, Jerry. *The Chia-ting Loyalists: Confucian Leadership and Social Change in Seventeenth-Century China.* New Haven, Conn.: Yale University Press, 1981.

———. "Fiscal Reform and Local Control: The Gentry-Bureaucratic Alliance Survives the Conquest." In Frederic Wakeman, Jr., and Carolyn Grant, eds., *Conflict and Control in Late Imperial China.* Berkeley: University of California Press, 1975.

———. "Marriage, Adoption, and Charity in the Development of Lineages in Wu-hsi from Sung to Ch'ing." In Patricia Buckley Ebrey and James L. Watson, eds., *Kinship Organization in Late Imperial China, 1000–1940.* Berkeley: University of California Press, 1986.

di Cosmo, Nicola. "Did Guns Matter? Firearms in the Qing Formation." In Lynn A. Struve, ed., *The Qing Formation in World-Historical Time.* Cambridge, Mass.: Harvard University Asia Center, 2004.

Dimberg, Ronald G. *The Sage and Society: The Life and Thought of Ho Hsin-yin.* Honolulu: University of Hawai'i Press, 1974.

Dong Biwu Nianpu Working Group, comp. *Dong Biwu nianpu* (Chronological biography of Dong Biwu). Beijing: Zhongyang wenxian chubanshe, 1991.

Dreyer, Edward L. *Early Ming China: A Political History, 1353–1435.* Stanford, Calif.: Stanford University Press, 1982.

Duara, Prasenjit. *Culture, Power, and the State: Rural North China, 1900–1942.* Stanford, Calif.: Stanford University Press, 1988.

Edong yimin banfa (Procedures for dealing with famine refugees in eastern Hubei). 1935. HPA.

Edong yimin shiwu zuzhi zhangcheng (Regulations for the Eastern Hubei Famine Refugee Management Office). 1935. HPA.

Elman, Benjamin. *Classicism, Politics, and Kinship: The Ch'ang-chou School of New Text Neo-Confucianism in Late Imperial China.* Berkeley: University of California Press, 1990.

———. *From Philosophy to Philology: Intellectual and Social Aspects of Change in Late Imperial China.* Cambridge, Mass.: Council on East Asian Studies, 1984.

———, and Alexander Woodside, eds. *Education and Society in Late Imperial China.* Berkeley: University of California Press, 1994.

Elvin, Mark. *The Pattern of the Chinese Past.* Stanford, Calif.: Stanford University Press, 1973.

Endicott-West, Elizabeth. *Mongolian Rule in China: Local Administration in the Yuan Dynasty.* Cambridge, Mass.: Council on East Asian Studies, 1989.

Entenmann, Robert Eric. "Migration and Settlement in Sichuan, 1644–1796." Ph.D. diss., Harvard University, 1982.

Esherick, Joseph W. *The Origins of the Boxer Uprising.* Berkeley: University of California Press, 1987.

———. *Reform and Revolution in China: The 1911 Revolution in Hunan and Hubei.* Berkeley: University of California Press, 1976.

Eyuwan Border Area Bandit-Extermination Command, Huang-Ma Branch. *Xingfu nongcun gongzuo renyuan shunlianban biye dianli* (Graduation program for graduating class of Rural Revival Work Training School), 1935. MCA.

Feng Menglong. *Chunqiu hengku* (An expansive treasury on the *Spring and Autumn Annals*), orig. 1625. Shanghai: Shanghai guji chubanshe, 1993.

———. *Linjing zhiyue* (Monthly companion to the Unicorn Classic). In Feng Menglong, *Feng Menglong quanji* (Complete works of Feng Menglong), orig. 1620. Shanghai: Shanghai guji chubanshe, 1993.

Fengyun bianhuan nianernian, 1927–1949 (Twenty-two years of unpredictable change). Songbu: Zhongguanyi Township Gazetteer Compilation Office, 1986.

Feuerwerker, Albert. "Handicraft and Manufactured Cotton Cloth in China, 1871–1910." *Journal of Economic History* 30 (June 1970), 338–78.

Fox, Robin. "The Violent Imagination." In Peter Marshall and Anne Campbell, eds., *Aggression and Violence.* Oxford: Basil Blackwell, 1982.

Franke, Herbert. "Siege and Defense of Towns in Medieval China." In Frank A. Kierman, Jr., and John K. Fairbank, eds., *Chinese Ways in Warfare.* Cambridge, Mass.: Harvard University Press, 1974.

Friedman, Edward, Paul Pickowicz, and Mark Selden. *Chinese Village, Socialist State.* New Haven, Conn.: Yale University Press, 1991.

Fu Hao. "Zai tao Xia Douyin panluan de rizi li" (A day-by-day account of Xia Douyin's mutiny). *Wuhan wenshi ziliao* 15 (1984), 64–73.

Fu Yiling. *Ming-Qing fengjian tudi suoyouzhi lungang* (An outline of the feudal landownership regime of the Ming and Qing). Shanghai: Shanghai renmin chubanshe, 1992.

———. *Ming Qing nongcun shehui jingji* (Rural society and economy in the Ming and Qing). Beijing: Sanlian shudian, 1961.

———. "Ming-Qing zhi ji de 'nubian' he diannong jiefang yundong" (Bondservant rebellions and tenants' liberation movements in the Ming-Qing transition), in Fu Yiling, *Ming Qing nongcun shehui jingji* (Rural society and economy in the Ming and Qing). Beijing: Sanlian shudian, 1961.

———. "Mingmo nanfang de 'dianbian,' 'nubian'" (Tenant and bondservant uprisings in late-Ming south China). *Lishi yanjiu*, May 1975, 61–67.

Geng Dingxiang. *Geng Tiantai xiansheng wenji* (Writings of Mr.Geng Dingxiang), orig. 1590. Taibei: Wenhai, 1970.

Gilmartin, Christina Kelley. *Engendering the Chinese Revolution: Radical Women, Communist Politics, and Mass Movements in the 1920s.* Berkeley: University of California Press, 1995.

Gongzhong dang Guangxu chao zouzhe (Palace memorials from the Guangxu reign), in *Gongzhong dang lichao zouzhe* (Palace memorials from successive reigns of the Qing dynasty). Taibei: National Palace Museum, 1973–75.

Goodman, Bryna. *Native Place, City, and Nation: Regional Networks and Identities in Shanghai, 1853–1937.* Berkeley: University of California Press, 1995.

Goodrich, L. Carrington, and Chaoying Fang. *Dictionary of Ming Biography, 1368–1644.* New York: Columbia University Press, 1976.

Gu Yanwu, "Junxian lun" (On the prefectural system). In Gu Yanwu, *Tinglin shiwen ji* (Poetry and prose of Gu Yanwu). Shanghai: Commercial Press, 1929.

———. *Yuan chaoben Rizhi lu* (Original draft edition of the *Rizhi lu*). Tainan: Weiyi shuye zhongxin, 1975.

Gu Yingtai. *Mingshi jishi benmo* (Complete history of the Ming), orig. 1658. Shanghai: Commercial Press, 1934.

Guillermaz, Jacques. *A History of the Chinese Communist Party, 1921–1949*. New York: Random House, 1972.

Guo Mu. *Diexue Dabieshan: Huang-Ma baodong jishi* (The blood-drenched Dabie Shan: The story of the Huang-Ma Uprising). Beijing: Jiefang jun wenyi chubanshe, 1997.

Halbwachs, Maurice. *The Collective Memory*, trans. Francis J. Ditter, Jr., and Vida Yazdi Ditter. New York: Harper and Row, 1980.

Han Hengyu. "Luelun Qingdai qianqi de dianpu zhi" (The bondservant system in the early Qing). *Qingshi luncong* 2 (1980), 88–110.

Han Ling. "Taofa Xia Douyin, Yang Sen panluan qin liji" (A personal recollection of the campaign against Xia and Yang). *Wuhan wenshi ziliao* 15 (1984), 60–63.

Han, Xiaorong. "Localism in Chinese Politics Before and After 1949: The Case of Feng Baiju." *Chinese Historical Review* 11.1 (Spring 2004), 23–56.

———. "Patterns of Central-Local Relations in Soviet China, 1927–1935," paper presented at the annual meeting of the Association for Asian Studies, San Diego, California, March 4–7, 2004.

Handlin, Joanna. *Action in Late Ming Thought: The Reorientation of Lü Kun and Other Scholar-Officials*. Berkeley: University of California Press, 1983.

Harrell, Stevan. "Introduction" to Jonathan N. Lipman and Steven Harrell, eds., *Violence in China: Essays in Culture and Counterculture*. Albany: State University of New York Press, 1990.

Hartwell, Robert M. "Demographic, Political, and Social Transformations of China, 750–1550." *Harvard Journal of Asiatic Studies* 42.2 (Dec. 1982), 365–442.

Hauf, Kandice. "The Community Covenant in Sixteenth-Century Ji'an Prefecture, Jiangxi." *Late Imperial China* 17.2 (Dec. 1996), 1–50.

He Changling, ed. *Huangchao jingshi wenbian* (Compendium of statecraft writings from the present dynasty), orig. 1826. Taibei: Guofeng chubanshe, 1963.

He Xiya. *Zhongguo taofai wenti zhi yanjiu* (A study of the bandit problem in China). Shanghai: n.d., 1925

He Yulin. "Zhonggong Edongbei tewei He Yulin gei Zhongyang de baogao: Huang-Ma dichu zhengzhi, jingji, junshi, ji dangde gongzuo qingkuang" (Report to the Center by Northeast Hubei Committee member He Yulin on the political, economic, military, and Party situation in Huang'an and Macheng), orig. May 7, 1929. In *Eyuwan geming genjudi* (The Eyuwan revolutionary base area). Zhengzhou: Henan renmin chubanshe, 1989, 3.24–49.

Heijdra, Martinus Johannes. "The Socio-economic Development of Ming Rural China (1368–1644): An Interpretation." Ph.D. diss., Princeton University, 1994.

Henry, Eric. "The Motif of Recognition in Early China." *Harvard Journal of Asiatic Studies* 47.1 (1987), 5–30.

Hibino Takeo. "Goson boei to kempeki shoya" (Rural defense and the policy of *jianbi qingye*). *Tōhō gakuhō* 22 (1953), 141–55.

History Department, Chinese People's University, and First Historical Archives, comp. *Qingdai nongmin zhanzheng shi ziliao xuanbian* (Collected materials on the history of peasant wars in the Qing dynasty). Beijing: Chinese People's University Press, 1984.

Ho, Virgil Kit-yiu. "Butchering Fish and Executing Criminals: Public Executions and the Meanings of Violence in Late Imperial and Modern China." In Göran Aijmer and Jon Abbink, eds., *Meanings of Violence: A Cross-Cultural Perspective*. Oxford: Berg, 2000.

Hofheinz, Roy, Jr. "The Ecology of Chinese Communist Success: Rural Influence Patterns, 1923–45." In A. Doak Barnett, ed., *Chinese Communist Politics in Action*. Seattle: University of Washington Press, 1969.

Hsiao, Kung-chuan. *Rural China: Imperial Control in the Nineteenth Century*. Seattle: University of Washington Press, 1960.

Hu Langui. "Nüsheng dui canjia pingban zhantou ceji" (A record of frontline action in the Women's Brigade campaign). In All-China Women's Federation and Whampoa Military Academy Alumni Association, comp., *Da geming hongliu de nübing* (Female soldiers in the Nationalist Revolution). Beijing: Zhongguo funü chubanshe, 1991.

Hu Linyi. *Hu Linyi ji* (Works of Hu Linyi). Changsha: Yuelu shushe, 1995.

Hu Wokun. *Qiantong* (Compendium on money), orig. Song period. *SKQS*.

Hu Zhaoxi. *"Zhang Xianzhong du Shu" kaobian (lianzhe Huguang dian Sichuan)* (An investigation of "Zhang Xianzhong butchers Sichuan," with an analysis of the repopulation of Sichuan from Huguang). Chengdu: Sichuan renmin chubanshe, 1980.

Huang, Ray. *1587, A Year of No Significance: The Ming Dynasty in Decline*. New Haven, Conn.: Yale University Press, 1981.

Huang Zongxi. *Ming ru xue'an* (Biographies of Ming Confucians), orig. 1676. *SKQS*.

Huang'an gongzuo baogao: guanyu "Huang-Ma baodong" de jingguo (Report on work in Huang'an: regarding the Huang-Ma Uprising), orig. Dec. 14, 1927. In *Eyuwan geming genjudi* (The Eyuwan revolutionary base area). Zhengzhou: Henan renmin chubanshe, 1989, 3.1–15.

Huang'an xianwei baogao (Report of the Huang'an County Committee), orig. 1929. In Central Archives, comp., *Eyuwan suqu geming lishi wenjain huiji* (Collected documents on the revolutionary history of the Eyuwan Soviet). Beijing: Central Archives, 1985, 5.204–14.

Huang'an xianwei guanyu "Huang-Ma baodong" jingguo xingqing gei zhongyuan de baogao (Report of Huang'an County Committee on the "Huang-Ma Uprising"), Dec. 14, 1927. HPA.

Huang'an xianzhi (Gazetteer of Huang'an County), ed. Liu Chengju, orig. 1697. Beijing: Zhonghua quanguuo tushuguan wenxian shuwei fuzhi zongxin, 1999.

Huang'an xianzhi (Gazetteer of Huang'an County), 1869. HPA.

Huangfu Fang. *Huangfu sixun ji* (Collected works of Huangfu Fang), orig. 1550. *SKQS*.

Huang-Ma Uprising Compilation Group, ed. *Huang-Ma qiyi* (The Huang-Ma Uprising). Huanggang: Hubei renmin chubanshe, 1978.

Huangzhou fuzhi (Gazetteer of Huangzhou Prefecture), orig. 1500. Shanghai: Guji shudian, 1965.

Huangzhou fuzhi (Gazetteer of Huangzhou Prefecture), orig. 1884, ed. Ying Qihou. Taibei: Chengwen, 1976.

Huangzhou fuzhi shiyi (Gazetteer of Huangzhou Prefecture, lacunae), orig. 1909, ed. Liu Jinrong. HPL.

"Hubei Macheng nongmin geyao" (Peasant folk songs from Macheng, Hubei). *Shikan* 3 (March 1958), 5–6.

Hubei tongzhi (Consolidated gazetteer of Hubei Province), Republican era, n.d.

Hubei xianzheng gaikuang (General survey of county administration in Hubei). Comp. by Zhang Qun. Wuhan, 1934. HPL.

Hucker, Charles O. "Hu Tsung-hsien's Campaign Against Hsü Hai, 1556." In Frank A. Kierman, Jr., and John K. Fairbank, eds., *Chinese Ways in Warfare*. Cambridge, Mass.: Harvard University Press, 1974.

———. "The Tung-lin Movement of the Late Ming Period." In John K. Fairbank, ed., *Chinese Thought and Institutions*. Chicago: University of Chicago Press, 1957.

Huguang tongzhi (Consolidated gazetteer of Huguang), orig. 1733. *SKQS*.

Hummel, Arthur, ed. *Eminent Chinese of the Ch'ing Period, 1644–1912*. Washington D.C.: U.S. Government Printing Office, 1943–44.

Hymes, Robert P. *Statesmen and Gentlemen: The Elite of Fu-chou, Chiang-hsi, in Northern and Southern Sung*. Cambridge: Cambridge University Press, 1986.

———. *Way and Byway: Taoism, Local Religion, and Models of Divinity in Sung and Modern China*. Berkeley: University of California Press, 2002.

Idema, Wilt L., Wai-yee Li, and Ellen Widmer, eds., *Trauma and Transcendence in Early Qing Literature*. Cambridge, Mass.: Harvard University Asia Center, 2006.

Iggers, Georg G. *Historiography in the Twentieth Century: From Scientific Objectivity to the Postmodern Challenge*. Hanover, N.H.: Wesleyan University Press/University Press of New England, 1997.

Institute of History, Chinese Academy of Social Sciences, comp. *Ming-Qing shiliao* (Sources on Ming and Qing history). Beijing: Zhonghua shuju, 1987.

Institute of History and Philology, Academia Sinica, comp. *(Xiancun Qingdai Neige dagu yuancang) Ming Qing dang'an* (Ming and Qing archives from the surviving holdings of the Qing Grand Secretariat). Taibei: Academia Sinica, 1986.

Institute of Qing History, Chinese People's University, comp. *Kang-Yong-Qian shiqi chengxiang renmin fankang douzheng ziliao* (Materials on urban and rural resistance struggles in the Kangxi, Yongzheng, and Qianlong reigns). Beijing: Zhonghua shuju, 1979.

Irwin, Richard Gregg. *The Evolution of a Chinese Novel: Shui-hu-chuan*. Cambridge, Mass.: Harvard University Press, 1953.

Isaacs, Harold R. *The Tragedy of the Chinese Revolution*. Stanford, Calif.: Stanford University Press, 1961.

Iwami Hiroshi. "Kōkan juku, tenka soku" (When Huguang has a good harvest, the empire has enough to eat). *Tōyōshi kenkyū* 20.4 (1962), 175.

Jelavich, Peter. "Method? What Method? Confessions of a Failed Structuralist." *New German Critique* 65 (Spring–Summer 1995), 75–86.

Jen, Yu-wen. *The Taiping Revolutionary Movement*. New Haven, Conn.: Yale University Press, 1973.

Jenner, W. J. F. "Tough Guys, Mateship, and Honour: Another Chinese Tradition." *East Asian History* 12 (1996), 1–33.

Ji Liuqi. *Mingji beilue* (North China campaigns of the late Ming), orig. early Qing. Beijing: Zhonghua shuju, 1984.

Jiang, Jin. "Heresy and Persecution in Late Ming Society: Reinterpreting the Case of Li Zhi." *Late Imperial China* 22.2 (Dec. 2001), 1–34.

Jin Changzhen. "Qingyan zhupu" (Request to tighten the legislation on bondservants). In Li Yu, comp., *Zizhi xinshu* (New administrative handbook), orig. 1663; reprinted in Li Yu, *Li Yu quanshu* (Complete works of Li Yu). Hangzhou: Zhejiang guji chubanshe, 1991, 16.271–73.

Jing Junjian. *Qingdai shehui de jianmin dengji* (Debased status in Qing society). Hangzhou: Zhejiang renmin chubanshe, 1993.

Johnson, David G. *The Medieval Chinese Oligarchy.* Boulder, Colo.: Westview Press, 1977.

Jones, Susan Mann, and Philip A. Kuhn. "Dynastic Decline and the Roots of Rebellion." In John K. Fairbank, ed., *Cambridge History of China*, vol. 10: *Late Ch'ing, 1800–1911, Part 1.* Cambridge: Cambridge University Press, 1978.

Jordan, Donald A. *The Northern Expedition: China's National Revolution of 1926–1928.* Honolulu: University of Hawai'i Press, 1976.

Juedan shan Zhou shi zupu (Genealogy of the Zhou lineage of Juedan shan), n.d. Huang'an County Archives.

Klein, Donald W., and Anne B. Clark. *Biographic Dictionary of Chinese Communism, 1921–1965.* Cambridge, Mass.: Harvard University Press, 1971.

Ko, Dorothy. *Teachers of the Inner Chambers: Women and Culture in Seventeenth-Century China.* Stanford, Calif.: Stanford University Press, 1994.

Kuhn, Philip A. "Local Self-Government under the Republic: Problems of Control, Autonomy, and Mobilization." In Frederic Wakeman, Jr., and Carolyn Grant, eds., *Conflict and Control in Late Imperial China.* Berkeley: University of California Press, 1975.

———. *Rebellion and Its Enemies in Late Imperial China: Militarization and Social Structure, 1796–1864.* 2d ed. Cambridge Mass.: Harvard University Press, 1980.

Kutcher, Norman. "The Fifth Relationship: Dangerous Friendships in the Confucian Context." *American Historical Review* 105.5 (Dec. 2000), 1615–1629.

Lamley, Harry J. "*Hsieh-tou*: The Pathology of Violence in Southeastern China." *Ch'ing-shih wen-t'i* 3.7 (Nov. 1977), 1–39.

Lan Wenwei. "Wo shi zen yang cedong Xia Douyin panluan de" (How I plotted the strategy for Xia Douyin's mutiny). *Wuhan wenshi ziliao* 15 (1984), 74–76.

Le Roy Ladurie, Emmanuel. *The Peasants of Languedoc.* Urbana: University of Illinois Press, 1976.

Levi, Giovanni. "On Microhistory." In Peter Burke, ed., *New Perspectives on Historical Writing.* University Park: Pennsylvania State University Press, 2001.

Lewis, Mark Edward. *Sanctioned Violence in Early China.* Albany: State University of New York Press, 1990.

Li Chengbin and Chen Yi. "Youqing luxian zaocheng de peiju: jianji Kexing qiao can'an" (A tragedy of the left-deviation line: The atrocity at Kexing Bridge). *Macheng wenshi ziliao* 1 (1987), 29–31.

Li Chien-nung. *The Political History of China, 1840–1928.* Stanford, Calif.: Stanford University Press, 1956.

Li Hua. "Qingdai Hubei nongcun jingji zuowu de zhongzhen he difang shangren de huoyue" (Rural products and merchant activity in Qing Hubei). *Zhongguo shehui jingji shi yanjiu*, Feb. 1987, 50–60.

Li Min. "Hong tudi shang de huaguo: Macheng geming jianjie" (The blossoming of a Red Area: A brief introduction to the revolution in Macheng). Unpublished paper.

———. "Kaopeng youlai" (Origins of the examination hall). *Macheng wenshi ziliao* 7 (2003), 164–68.

———. "Longhu jushi Yang Dingjian" (Yang Dingjian, a literatus who lived at Dragon Lake). In Ling Lichao and Li Min, eds., *Li Zhi qiren* (Li Zhi the man). Macheng: Macheng Gazetteer Office, 2002.

Li shi xiafen zongpu (Genealogy of the third branch of the Li lineage). Songbu: Tongsentang, 1947.

Li Wenyi. "Funü geming de pengyang" (Whipping up the women's revolution). In All-China Women's Federation and Whampoa Military Academy Alumni Association, comp., *Da geming hongliu de nübing* (Female soldiers in the Nationalist Revolution). Beijing: Zhongguo funü chubanshe, 1991.

Li Wenzhi, "Lun Qingdai qianqi de tudi zhanyou guanxi" (On land-tenure relations in the early Qing). *Lishi yanjiu*, May 1963, 75–108.

———. *Wan Ming minbian* (Popular uprisings in the late Ming). Shanghai: Shanghai shudian, 1989.

Li Xian. *Gurang ji* (Collected works of Li Xian), orig. ca. 1460. *SKQS*.

Li Zhi. *Fenshu* (Burn this book!). Beijing: Zhonghua shuju, 1959.

———. *Cangshu* (Hide this book!). Beijing: Zhonghua shuju, 1959.

———. *Xu Fenshu* (Burn this book, continued). Zhonghua shuju, 1975.

"Li Zhi zai Diaoyutai jiangxue" (Li Zhi's lectures at the Diaoyutai pavilion). *Macheng wenshi ziliao* 1 (1987), 37–38.

Lieu, Samuel N. C. *Manichaeism in the Later Roman Empire and Medieval China: A Historical Survey*. Manchester: Manchester University Press, 1985.

Lin shi zongpu (Genealogy of the Lin lineage), 1873.

Lin shi zongpu (Genealogy of the Lin lineage), 1947.

Ling Lichao and Li Min, eds. *Li Zhi yu Longhu* (Li Zhi and Dragon Lake). Macheng: Hubei yinxiang yishu shubanshe, 2002.

Liu Fengyun. *Qingdai sanfan yanjiu* (A study of the Qing Three Feudatories). Beijing: Renmin daxue chubanshe, 1994.

Liu Gang. Untitled report of Macheng magistrate Liu Gang to Hubei Provincial Government, June 12, 1929. HPA.

Liu Hong. "Hai Rui jingzhong de qingguan" (An honest official esteemed by Hai Rui). *Hubei dang'an*, March 2001, 46.

———. "Sixiangjia yu guaiseng: Li Zhi" (Li Zhi: philosopher and ascetic). *Hubei dang'an*, Nov. 2000, 36–37.

———. "*Yipeng xue, Jinping mei, Macheng*" (The novels *Yipeng xue, Jingping mei,* and Macheng). *Hubei dang'an*, Sept. 2000, 36–37.

Liu, James J. Y. *The Chinese Knight-Errant*. London: Routledge and Kegan Paul, 1967.

Liu Jianye. "Yongzheng Macheng shaqi an" (A case of wife-murder in Yongzheng-era Macheng). *Falü yu shenghuo*, Dec. 1995, 31–41; Jan. 1996, 42–45; Feb. 1996, 44–47.

Liu Manrong. "Xuesheng jun Macheng jiaofei" (The student army exterminates bandits in Macheng). *Wuhan daxue xuebao* 25.3 (May 1978), 77–80.

Liu Ping. *Zhang Zhidong zhuan* (Biography of Zhang Zhidong). Lanzhou: Lanzhou daxue chubanshe, 2000.

Liu Tianhe. *Dufu zouyi* (Memoirs of Shaanxi governor-general Liu), orig. ca. 1540. *SKQS*.

———. *Wenshui ji* (On river conservancy), orig. ca. 1540. *SKQS*.

Liu Tong and Yu Yizheng. *Dijing jingwu lue* (Guide to the Imperial Capital), orig. 1635. Taibei: Guangwen, 1969.

Liu Xian. "Qin shi yitian jibi" (Stele recording the charitable estate of the Qin family). *MCXZXB*, 14:14–15.

Liuxiu Cai shi zongpu (Genealogy of the Cai lineage). 6th ed. Macheng County Museum, 2003.

Louie, Kam. *Theorising Chinese Masculinity: Society and Gender in China*. Cambridge: Cambridge University Press, 2002.

Lü Ruzhen. "Ji Wuhan fenxiao nüsheng dui" (A record of the Wuhan campus' Women's Brigade). In All-China Women's Federation and Whampoa Military Academy Alumni Association, comp., *Da geming hongliu de nübing* (Female soldiers in the Nationalist Revolution). Beijing: Zhongguo funü chubanshe, 1991.

Lu Xiangsheng. *Lu Zhongsu gong ji* (Works of Lu Xiangsheng), 1875.

Lufrano, Richard. *Honorable Merchants: Commerce and Self-Cultivation in Late Imperial China*. Honolulu: University of Hawai'i Press, 1997.

Luo Ergang. "Qingji bingwei jiangyou de qiyuan" (The late-Qing origin of personal armies). *Zhongguo shehui jingji shi yanjiu* 5.2 (1937), 235–50.

———. *Xiangjun bingzhi* (Military history of the Xiang Army). Beijing: Zhonghua shuju, 1984.

Macheng County Grain Bureau, comp. *Macheng xian liangshi zhi* (Gazetteer of grain and tax matters in Macheng County). Macheng, 1989.

Macheng County Place Name Leadership Group, comp. *Hubei sheng Macheng xian diming zhi* (Gazetteer of place names in Macheng County, Hubei Province). Macheng, 1984.

Macheng disiqu baojia shunlianban tongxue lu (Class list for Macheng Fourth Ward *Baojia* Training School), 1937. MCA.

Macheng gonghui zhi (Gazetteer of the Macheng Workers' Association). Macheng: Macheng General Workers' Association, 1990. HGO.

Macheng shi renwu zhi (Gazetteer of Macheng persons). Macheng: Macheng Gazetteer Office, 1987. HGO.

Macheng xian gaikuang (General information about Macheng County). Macheng: Macheng Gazetteer Office, 1984. HGO.

Macheng xian jianzhi (Brief gazetteer of Macheng County). Macheng: Macheng County People's Government, 1981.

Macheng xian liangshi zhi, 1840–1985 (History of tax and provisioning in Macheng, 1840–1985). Macheng: Macheng Provisioning Bureau, 1989. HGO.

Macheng xian zhengfu banli Hongjun tufei anjian yuebao biao (Monthly reports of Red Army soldiers and local bandits captured in Macheng), 1929–1934. 24 items. HPA.

Macheng xianwei baogao (Report of the Macheng County Committee), orig. May 26, 1929. In Central Archives, comp., *Eyuwan suqu geming lishi wenjain huiji* (Collected documents on the revolutionary history of the Eyuwan Soviet). Beijing: Central Archives, 1985, 5.233–48.

Macheng xianzhi (Gazetteer of Macheng County), ed. Qu Zhenqi, orig. 1670. Macheng: Macheng Gazetteer Office, 1999.

Macheng xianzhi (Gazetteer of Macheng County), ed. Jiang Tingming, orig. 1795. Macheng: Macheng Gazetteer Office, 1999.

Macheng xianzhi (Gazetteer of Macheng County), orig. 1882, ed. Guo Qinghua. Macheng: Macheng Gazetteer Office, 1999.

Macheng xianzhi (Gazetteer of Macheng County), ed. Yan Yizhou. Beijing: Hongqi chubanshe, 1993.

Macheng xianzhi, qianbian (Gazetteer of Macheng County, part 1), orig. 1935, ed. Yu Jinfang. Taibei: Chengwen, 1975.

Macheng xianzhi, xubian (Gazetteer of Macheng County, part 2), orig. 1935, ed. Yu Jinfang. Taibei: Chengwen, 1975.

Mann, Susan. "The Male Bond in Chinese History and Culture." *American Historical Review* 105.5 (Dec. 2000), 1600–1614.

———. *Precious Records: Women in China's Long Eighteenth Century*. Stanford, Calif.: Stanford University Press, 1997.

Mao Tse-tung (Zedong). "Report on an Investigation of the Peasant Movement in Hunan (March 1927)." In Mao Tse-tung (Zedong), *Selected Works of Mao Tse-tung*. Beijing: Foreign Languages Press, 1967.

Marx, Emmanuel. *The Social Context of Violent Behaviour: A Social Anthropological Study in an Israeli Immigrant Town*. London: Routledge and Kegan Paul, 1976.

McColl, Robert W. "The Oyüwan Soviet Area, 1927–1932." *Journal of Asian Studies* 27.1 (Nov. 1967), 41–60.

McDermott, Joseph P. "Emperor, Elites, and Commoners: The Community Pact Ritual in the Late Ming." In Joseph P. McDermott, ed., *State and Court Ritual in China*. Cambridge: Cambridge University Press, 1999.

———. "Friendship and Its Friends in the Late Ming." In Institute of Modern History, comp., *Family Process and Political Process in Modern Chinese History*. Taipei: Academia Sinica, 1992.

McMahon, Daniel. "The Yuelu Academy and Hunan's Nineteenth-Century Turn toward Statecraft." *Late Imperial China* 26.1 (June 2005), 72–109.

Mei Guozhen. "Jiabao bianbao shu" (Memorial on enhancing and linking battlements on the frontier), orig. 16th–17th c. In Xu Fouyuan, ed., *Huang Ming jingshi wenbian* (Collected writings on statecraft from the Ming dynasty). Taibei: Guolian, 1964.

Mei Jifa. "Nongmin Mei Qinsheng koutou shi" (The peasant-poet Mei Qinsheng). *Macheng wenshi ziliao* 1 (1987), 74–80.

Mei Jiwen. "Yao wo bugeming, chufei taiyang zong xibian chulai!" (If I'm not revolutionary, let the sun rise in the west!), *Zhongguo funü*, Feb. 1964, 18–20.

Mei shi zupu (Genealogy of the Mei lineage), ca. 1990. Macheng County Museum.

Mei Zhihuan. *Mei Zhongcheng yigao* (Draft writings of Mei Zhihuan), orig. ca. 1640. Beijing: Beijing chubanshe, 2000.

Meng Guangpeng. *Hubei tudi celiang huibian* (Statistical survey of Hubei farmland). Wuchang: Hubei sheng zhengfu minzheng ting, 1935.

Meng Siming. *Yuandai shehui jieji zhidu* (The class system in Yuan society). Beiping: Harvard-Yenching Institute, 1938.

Meskill, Johanna M. *A Chinese Pioneer Family: The Lins of Wu-feng, Taiwan, 1729–1895*. Princeton, N.J.: Princeton University Press, 1979.

Min, Tu-ki. "The Theory of Political Feudalism in the Ch'ing Period." In Tu-ki Min, *Na-*

tional Polity and Local Power: The Transformation of Late Imperial China, ed. Philip A. Kuhn and Timothy Brook. Cambridge, Mass.: Council on East Asian Studies, 1989.

Ming shi (Ming dynastic history). Beijing: Zhonghua shuju, 1974.

Ming shilu leizuan: Hubei shiliao juan (Veritable records of the Ming, topically selected: Materials on Hubei history). Wuhan: Wuhan chubanshe, 1991.

Miu Jinghao. "Tianfutai xiban de jianli ji qi fazhan" (The founding and development of the Tianfutai theatrical troupe). *Macheng wenshi ziliao* 1 (1987), 71–74.

Mixius, W. Andreas. *"Nu-pien" und die "Nu-p'u" von Kiangnan: Aufstände Abhängiger und Unfreier in Südchina, 1644/45*. Hamburg: Gesellschaft für Natur und Völkerkunde Ostasiens, 1980.

Morohashi Tetsuji. *Dai Kan-Wa jiten* (Great Chinese-Japanese dictionary). Tokyo: Taishūtan shoten, 1966–68.

Mote, Frederick W. "The Rise of the Ming Dynasty, 1330–1367." In Frederick W. Mote and Denis Twitchett, eds., *The Cambridge History of China*, vol. 7: *The Ming Dynasty, 1368–1644, Part 1*. Cambridge: Cambridge University Press, 1988.

Muir, Edward. "Introduction: Observing Trifles." In Edward Muir and Guido Ruggiero, eds., *Microhistory and the Lost Peoples of Europe: Essays from 'Quaderni Storici'*. Baltimore, Md.: Johns Hopkins University Press, 1991.

Nagano Akira. *Shina hei, tohi, kōsōkai* (Soldiers, bandits, and Red Spears in China). Tokyo: Sakaue shoen, 1938.

Naquin, Susan. *Millenarian Rebellion in China: The Eight Trigrams Uprising of 1813*. New Haven, Conn.: Yale University Press, 1976.

Nienhauser, William, Jr., ed. *The Indiana Companion to Traditional Chinese Literature*. Bloomington: Indiana University Press, 1986.

Nirenberg, David. *Communities of Violence: Persecution of Minorities in the Middle Ages*. Princeton, N.J.: Princeton University Press, 1996.

"Nongmin qiyi lingxiu Bao Shirong" (The peasant rebel leader Bao Shirong). *Macheng wenshi ziliao* 1 (1987), 39–40.

Nora, Pierre. "Between Memory and History: *Les lieux de Mémoire*." *Representations* 26 (Spring 1989), 7–24.

Ouyang Xiu. *Wenzhong ji* (Works of Ouyang Xiu), orig. Song period. *SKQS*.

Ownby, David. *Brotherhoods and Secret Societies in Early and Mid-Qing China: The Formation of a Tradition*. Stanford, Calif.: Stanford University Press, 1996.

Oyama Masaaki. "Large Landownership in the Jiangnan Delta Region during the Late Ming–Early Qing Period." In Linda Grove and Christian Daniels, eds., *State and Society in China: Japanese Perspectives on Ming-Qing Social and Economic History*. Tokyo: University of Tokyo Press, 1984.

Pan Zenghong. *Li Wenling waiji* (Additional materials regarding Li Zhi), orig. ca. 1599. Taibei: Weiwen tushu chubanshe, 1977.

Parsons, James B. *Peasant Rebellions of the Late Ming Dynasty*. Tucson, Ariz.: Association for Asian Studies, 1970.

Peng Sunyi. *Pingkou zhi* (A record of pacification of the rebels), orig. ca. 1650. Shanghai: Guji chubanshe, 1984.

Perdue, Peter C. "Insiders and Outsiders: The Xiangtan Riot of 1819 and Collective Action in Hunan." *Modern China* 12.2 (Apr. 1986), 166–201.

———. "The Qing Empire in Eurasian Time and Space: Lessons from the Galdan Campaign." In Lynn A. Struve, ed., *The Qing Formation in World-Historical Time*. Cambridge, Mass.: Harvard University Asia Center, 2004.

Perry, Elizabeth J. *Rebels and Revolutionaries in North China, 1845–1945*. Stanford, Calif.: Stanford University Press, 1980.

Peterson, Willard. "Confucian Learning in Late Ming Thought." In Denis Twitchett and Frederick W. Mote, eds., *The Cambridge History of China*, vol. 8: *The Ming Dynasty, 1368–1644, Part 2*. Cambridge: Cambridge University Press, 1998.

Pi Mingxiu and Ouyang Zhiliang. *Wuhan shigao* (Draft history of Wuhan). Beijing: Zhongguo wenshi chubanshe, 1992.

Qian Qianyi. "Mei Changgong zhuan" (Biography of Mei Zhihuan). In Mei Zhihuan, *Mei Zhongcheng yigao* (Draft writings of Mei Zhihuan), orig. ca. 1640. Beijing: Beijing chubanshe, 2000.

———. *Muzhai chuji* (First collection of works by Qian Qianyi). Taibei: Wenhai chubanshe, 1986.

Qu Shulin. "Yuanmo hongjinjun de zhengquan jianshe" (The Red Turban Army's establishment of an administrative regime in the late Yuan). *Yuanshi luncong* 1 (1982), 91–108.

Quan Heng. *Gengshen waishi* (Unofficial history of the late Yuan), orig. ca. 1380. Taibei: Yiwen yinshuguan, 1966.

———. *Muzhai chuji* (First collection from the Shepherd's Studio). Taibei: Wenhai, 1986.

Rankin, Mary Backus. *Elite Activism and Political Transformation in China*. Stanford, Calif.: Stanford University Press, 1986.

Rawski, Evelyn S. "Agricultural Development in the Han River Highlands." *Ch'ing-shih wen-t'i* 3.4 (1975), 63–81.

Reed, Bradley W. *Talons and Teeth: County Clerks and Runners in the Qing Dynasty*. Stanford, Calif.: Stanford University Press, 2000.

Riches, David. "The Phenomenon of Violence." In David Riches, ed., *The Anthropology of Violence*. Oxford: Basil Blackwell, 1986.

Robinson, David. *Bandits, Eunuchs, and the Son of Heaven: Rebellion and the Economy of Violence in Mid-Ming China*. Honolulu: University of Hawai'i Press, 2001.

Rong Zhaozu. *Li Zhi nianpu* (Chronological biography of Li Zhi). Beijing: Sanlian shudian, 1957.

Rowe, William T. *Hankow: Commerce and Society in a Chinese City, 1776–1889*. Stanford, Calif.: Stanford University Press, 1984.

———. *Hankow: Conflict and Community in a Chinese City, 1796–1895*. Stanford, Calif.: Stanford University Press, 1989.

———. "Hu Lin-i's Reform of the Grain Tribute System in Hupeh, 1855–58." *Ch'ing-shih wen-t'i* 4.10 (Dec. 1983), 33–86.

———. *Saving the World: Chen Hongmou and Elite Consciousness in Eighteenth-Century China*. Stanford, Calif.: Stanford University Press, 2001.

———. "Social Stability and Social Change." In Willard J. Peterson, ed., *Cambridge History of China*, vol 9: *The Ch'ing Empire to 1800*. Cambridge: Cambridge University Press, 2002.

———. "Success Stories." In Joseph W. Esherick and Mary Backus Rankin, eds., *Chinese Local Elites and Patterns of Dominance.* Berkeley: University of California Press, 1990.

Ruhlmann, Robert. "Traditional Heroes in Chinese Popular Fiction." In Arthur F. Wright, ed., *The Confucian Persuasion*. Stanford, Calif.: Stanford University Press, 1960.

Satō Fumitoshi. "Kōsan ken, Majō ken dohen kō" (A study of bondservant rebellions in Guangshan and Macheng Counties). In *Min Shin shi ronsō* (Studies in Ming-Qing history). Tokyo: Ryōgen shoten, 1977.

Schneewind, Sarah. "Competing Institutions: Community Schools and 'Improper Shrines' in Sixteenth-Century China." *Late Imperial China* 20.1 (June 1999), 85–106.

Schoppa, R. Keith. *Xiang Lake: Nine Centuries of Chinese Life*. New Haven, Conn.: Yale University Press, 1989.

Schram, Stuart. *Mao Tse-tung*. Rev. ed. Harmondsworth: Penguin, 1967.

Schurmann, Herbert Franz. *Economic Structure of the Yüan Dynasty*. Cambridge, Mass.: Harvard University Press, 1956.

Shek, Richard. "Ethics and Polity: The Heterodoxy of Buddhism, Maitreyism, and the Early White Lotus." In Kwang-Ching Liu and Richard Shek, eds., *Heterodoxy in Late Imperial China*. Honolulu: University of Hawai'i Press, 2004.

Sheng Renxue. *Zhang Guotao nianpu ji yanlun* (Biography and discussion of Zhang Guotao). Beijing: Liberation Army Press, 1985.

Sheridan, James E. *Chinese Warlord: The Career of Feng Yü-hsiang*. Stanford, Calif.: Stanford University Press, 1966.

Shi Heng. "Pingding Xia Douyin, Yang Sen panluan de jingguo" (My experience in quelling the Xia-Yang mutiny). *Wuhan wenshi ziliao* 15 (1984), 51–59.

Shi Shi. "Mei Danran dui Li Zhi you aiqing ma?" (Was Mei Danran in love with Li Zhi?) In Ling Lichao and Li Min, eds., *Li Zhi qiren* (Li Zhi the man). Macheng: Macheng Gazetteer Office, 2002.

———. "Ye tan Li Zhi yu Mei Danran" (Further discussion of Li Zhi and Mei Danran). In Ling Lichao and Li Min, eds., *Li Zhi qiren* (Li Zhi the man). Macheng: Macheng Gazetteer Office, 2002.

Shi shi zongpu (Genealogy of the Shi lineage). Songbu: Zongbotang, 1946.

Shimada Kenji. *Chūgoku ni okeru kindai shii no zasetsu* (The frustration of modern thought in China). Tokyo: Chikuma shohō, 1949.

Shizong Xianhuangdi zhupi yuzhi (Vermilion edicts of the Yongzheng emperor). *SKQS*.

Siqu zhuan Macheng chengyi lianbao bangongchu banshi tongce (General regulations of the *lianbao* office of Macheng Fourth Ward), March 11, 1934. HPA.

Skinner, G. William, ed. *The City in Late Imperial China*. Stanford, Calif.: Stanford University Press, 1977.

Smith, Paul Jakov. "Impressions of the Song-Yuan-Ming Transition: Evidence from *Biji* Memoirs." In Paul Jakov Smith and Richard von Glahn, eds., *The Song-Yuan-Ming Transition in Chinese History*. Cambridge, Mass.: Harvard University Asia Center, 2003.

Snow, Edgar. *Red Star over China*, orig. 1938. New York: Grove Press, 1973.

Sorel, Georges. *Reflections on Violence*, orig. 1908. Cambridge: Cambridge University Press, 1999.

Spiegel, Gabrielle M. "Memory and History: Liturgical Time and Historical Time." *History and Theory* 41.2 (May 2002), 149–62.

Ssu-ma Ch'ien. *Records of the Historian: Chapters from the* Shih Chi *of Ssu-ma Ch'ien*, trans. Burton Watson. New York: Columbia University Press, 1969.

Stone, Lawrence. "The Revival of Narrative: Reflections on a New Old History." *Past and Present* 85 (Nov. 1979), 3–24.

Strand, David. "Community, Society, and History in Sun Yat-sen's *Sanmin zhuyi*." In Theodore Huters, R. Bin Wong, and Pauline Yu, eds., *Culture and State in Chinese History: Conventions, Accomodations, and Critiques*. Stanford, Calif.: Stanford University Press, 1997.

Struve, Lynn A. *The Southern Ming, 1644–1662*. New Haven, Conn.: Yale University Press, 1984.

Stuart, Jan, and Evelyn S. Rawski. *Worshiping the Ancestors: Chinese Commemorative Portraits*. Washington, D.C.: Freer and Sackler Galleries, 2001.

Su Shi (Dongpo). *Dongpo quanji* (Complete works of Su Dongpo), orig. Song period. *SKQS*.

Su Yunfeng. *Zhongguo xiandaihua de quyu yanjiu: Hubei sheng, 1860–1916* (A regional study of Chinese modernization: Hubei Province, 1860–1916). Taibei: Institute of Modern History, 1981.

Suemitsu Takayoshi. *Shina no himitsu kessha to jizen kessha* (Secret societies and philanthropic societies in China). Dairen, 1932.

Suzuki Chūsei. *Shinchō chūki shi kenkyū* (A study of the mid-Qing period). Toyohashi: Aichi Daigaku Kokusai mondai kenkyūjo, 1952.

Swope, Kenneth M. "All Men Are Not Brothers: Ethnic Identity and Dynastic Loyalty in the Ningxia Mutiny of 1592." *Late Imperial China* 24.1 (June 2003), 79–130.

Tang Guifang. *Tang shi san xiansheng ji* (Works of three gentlemen of the Tang lineage), orig. ca. 1380. Beijing: Shumu wenxian chubanshe, 1987.

Taniguchi Kikuo. "Minmatsu Shinsho no hōsai ni tsuite" (Forts in the late Ming and early Qing). *Tōkai shigaku* 9 (1973), 1–15.

———. "Yu Seiryū no hōkō hō ni tsuite" (Yu Chenglong's *baojia* system). *Tōyōshi kenkyū* 34.3 (1975), 62–80.

ter Haar, Barend J. "China's Inner Demons: The Political Impact of the Demonological Paradigm." In Woei Lien Chong, ed., *China's Great Proletarian Cultural Revolution: Master Narratives and Post-Mao Counternarratives*. Lanham, Md.: Rowman and Littlefield, 2002.

———. "Rethinking 'Violence' in Chinese Culture." In Göran Aijmer and Jon Abbink, eds., *Meanings of Violence: A Cross-Cultural Perspective*. Oxford: Berg, 2000.

———. *Ritual and Mythology of the Chinese Triads: Creating an Identity*. Leiden: Brill, 1998.

Terada Takanobu. "Yōseitei no semmin kaihōrei ni tsuite" (On the Yongzheng emperor's emancipation of debased peoples). *Tōyōshi kenkyū* 18.3 (1959), 124–41.

Thompson, E. P. *The Making of the English Working Class*. New York: Vintage, 1966.

Tian Ziyu and Huang Huawen. *Hubei tongshi: Minguo juan* (General history of Hubei: Republican era). Wuhan: Huazhong shifan daxue chubanshe, 1999.

Tilly, Charles. "Retrieving European Lives." In Olivier Zunz, ed., *Reliving the Past: The Worlds of Social History*. Chapel Hill: University of North Carolina Press, 1985.

Tu Yunheng and Dai Qinhe, eds. *Hubei yinglie cidian* (Dictionary of Hubei martyrs). Wuhan: Hubei renmin chubanshe, 1997.

Volkmar, Barbara. "The Physician and the Plagiarists: The Fate of the Legacy of Wan Quan." *The East Asia Library Journal* 9.1 (Spring 2000), 32–34.

von Glahn, Richard. *The Sinister Way: The Divine and the Demonic in Chinese Religious Culture.* Berkeley: University of California Press, 2004.

Wagner, Donald B. *Dabieshan: Traditional Chinese Iron-Production Techniques Practiced in Southern Henan in the Twentieth Century.* London: Curzon Press, 1985.

Wakeman, Frederic, Jr. *The Great Enterprise: The Manchu Reconstruction of Imperial Order in China.* Berkeley: University of California Press, 1985.

———. "Localism and Loyalism during the Ch'ing Conquest of Kiangnan: The Tragedy of Chiang-yin." In Frederic Wakeman, Jr., and Caroline Grant, eds., *Conflict and Control in Late Imperial China.* Berkeley: University of California Press, 1975.

———. "Romantics, Stoics, and Martyrs in Seventeenth-Century China." *Journal of Asian Studies* 43.4 (1984), 631–66.

Wan Yanqi. "Xingzhuang" (Biographical sketch). In Mei Zhihuan, *Mei Zhongcheng yigao* (Draft writings of Mei Zhihuan), orig. ca. 1640. Beijing: Beijing chubanshe, 2000.

Wang Baoxin. *Qi Huang sishiba zhai jishi* (Record of the Forty-Eight Forts of Qi-Huang), orig. 1908. Taibei: Wenhai, 1971.

Wang, David Der-wei. *The Monster That Is History: History, Violence, and Fictional Writing in Twentieth-Century China.* Berkeley: University of California Press, 2004.

Wang Duanming and Lei Jiahong. *Hubei tongshi: Song Yuan juan* (General history of Hubei: Song and Yuan). Wuhan: Huazhong shifan daxue chubanshe, 1999.

Wang Gang. "'Hubei dian Sichuan' wenti tanlun" (Preliminary discussion of the problem of "Hubei fills up Sichuan"). *Shehui kexue yanjiu,* March 1979, 82–90.

Wang Libo. "Huang-Ma qiyi qianhou de bianduan huiyi" (Recollections of the Huang Ma Uprising), Feb. 1950. HPA.

Wang Ling. "Feng Menglong Macheng zhi xing" (Feng Menglong's sojourn in Macheng). *Fujian luntan,* Apr. 1988, 45–47.

Wang Shizhen. "Macheng Mu Hou junfu gongxu" (Magistrate Mu Wei's tax-equalization reforms in Macheng). In Wang Shizhen, *Yanzhou sibu gao* (Draft writings on various subjects), orig. 1577. *SKQS.*

———. *Yanzhou sibu gao* (Draft writings on various subjects), orig. 1577. *SKQS.*

———. *Yanzhou sibu gao, xugao* (Draft writings on various subjects, 2d collection), orig. ca. 1630. *SKQS.*

———. *(Youxiang) Liexian quanzhuan* ([Illustrated] lives of the Daoist immortals), orig. ca. 1600. Taibei: Xuesheng shuju, 1989.

Wang Shusheng Biography Working Group, comp. *Wang Shusheng zhuan* (Biography of Wang Shusheng). Beijing: Dangdai Zhongguo chubanshe, 2004.

Wang Yingzhi, ed. *Yuan Mei chuanji* (Complete works of Yuan Mei). Suzhou: Jiangsu guji chubanshe, n.d.

Wang Youdong. *Tianxia diyi lianli: Yu Chenglong* (The empire's most incorrupt official: Yu Chenglong). Taiyuan: Shanxi renmin chubanshe, 2000.

Wang Zheng. *Women in the Chinese Enlightenment: Oral and Textual Histories.* Berkeley: University of California Press, 1999.

Wang Zhongxing. "Wo suo zhidao de Xia Douyin" (The Xia Douyin that I knew). *Macheng wenshi ziliao* 1 (1987), 50–54.

Watson, James L. "Self-Defense Corps, Violence, and the Bachelor Subculture in South China." In James L. Watson and Rubie S. Watson, *Village Life in Hong Kong: Politics, Gender, and Ritual in the New Territories.* Hong Kong: Chinese University of Hong Kong, 2004.

Wei Qingyuan, Wu Qiyan, and Lu Su. *Qingdai nupi zhidu* (The bondservant system under the Qing). Beijing: Renmin daxue chubanshe, 1982.

Who's Who in China. 4th ed. Shanghai: China Weekly Review, 1931.

Who's Who in China. 6th ed. Shanghai: China Weekly Review, 1950.

Wilbur, C. Martin. *The Nationalist Revolution in China, 1923–1928.* Cambridge: Cambridge University Press, 1983.

Will, Pierre-Etienne. "Un Cycle Hydraulique en Chine: La Province du Hubei du XVIe au XIXe Siècle." *Bulletin de l'Ecole Française d'Extrême Orient* 68 (1980), 262–87.

Wills, John E., Jr. "Contingent Connections: Fujian, the Empire, and the Early Modern World." In Lynn A. Struve, ed., *The Qing Formation in World-Historical Time.* Cambridge, Mass.: Harvard University Asia Center, 2004.

Wolf, Arthur P. "Gods, Ghosts, and Ancestors." In Arthur P. Wolf, ed., *Religion and Ritual in Chinese Society.* Stanford, Calif.: Stanford University Press, 1974.

Wong, R. Bin. "Food Riots in the Qing Dynasty." *Journal of Asian Studies* 41.4 (August 1982), 767–88.

Wou, Odoric Y. K. *Mobilizing the Masses: Building Revolution in Henan.* Stanford, Calif.: Stanford University Press, 1994.

Wright, Mary Clabaugh. *The Last Stand of Chinese Conservatism: The T'ung-Chih Restoration, 1862–1874.* Stanford, Calif.: Stanford University Press, 1957.

Wu Han. *Zhu Yuanzhang dazhuan* (Biography of Zhu Yuanzhang). Beijing: Yuanliu chubanshe, 1991.

Wu Weiye. *Suikou jilue* (Brief record of rebel pacification), orig. early Qing. Taibei: Guangwen shuju, 1968.

Wu Zhongya. "Tao ping Yang-Xia panluan de zhanchang shikuang" (The true story of the Yang-Xia mutiny). *Wuhan wenshi ziliao* 14 (1983), 91–95.

Wucheng Zeng shi zongpu (Genealogy of the Wucheng Zeng lineage), 1936. In possession of the family.

Wyman, Judith. "The Ambiguities of Chinese Antiforeignism: Chongqing, 1870–1900." *Late Imperial China* 18.2 (Dec. 1999), 86–122.

Xia Douyin, ed. *Hubei difang zhangzhi zhengli huiyi* (Meeting on the rectification of Hubei local administration), Sept. 1, 1932. HPA.

Xiakou xianzhi (Gazetteer of Xiakou County), 1920.

Xiang Yunlong. "Hongqiang hui de qiyuan ji qi shanhou" (The origins and repacification of the Red Spears). *Dongfang zazhi* 24.21 (1927), 35–41.

Xicun Cheng shi zongpu (Genealogy of the Cheng lineage of West Village), 1919.

Xie Bingying. "Letters of a Chinese Amazon," trans. Lin Yutang. In Lin Yutang, ed., *Letters of a Chinese Amazon and War-Time Essays.* Shanghai: Commercial Press, 1930, 3–47.

Xie Guozhen. "Mingji nubian kao" (Bondservant rebellions in the late Ming). In Xie Guozhen, *Ming Qing zhijian danshe yundong kao* (Factional movements in the Ming-Qing transition). Taibei: Taiwaan Commercial Press, 1967, 257–89.

———, ed. *Qingqu nongmin qiyi ziliao jilu* (Selected materials on peasant rebellions of the early Qing). Shanghai: Xin zhishi chubanshe, 1956.

Xie Shiqin. *Shu gong suibi* (Random jottings of Mr. Shu). In Documents Office, Institute of Modern History, Chinese Academy of Social Sciences, comp., *Xinhai geming ziliao* (Materials on the 1911 Revolution). Beijing: Zhonghua shuju, 1961.

Xinxian County Party School. "Shanxiang nuhuo" (Fires of rage in a mountain township). *Shixue yuekan*, Aug. 1965, 22–32.

"Xiong Miannan funü" (Xiong Miannan and his daughter). *Macheng wenshi ziliao* 1 (1987), 7–8.

Xiong shi zongpu (Genealogy of the Xiong lineage), ca. 1942. MCA.

Xu Qianxue. *Zizhi tongjian houbian* (Sequel to the Mirror for Governance), orig. 1690. *SKQS*.

Xu Xiangqian. *Lishi de huigu* (Historical reminiscences). Beijing: Liberation Army Press, 1987.

Yang Guo'an. "Shehui dongdang yu Qingdai Hubei xiangcun zhong de zhaibao" (Social upheaval and rural forts in Qing Hubei). *Ming Qing shi*, Feb. 2002, 45–49.

Yang, Lien-sheng. "Ming Local Administration: Feudalism and Centralism in the Chinese Tradition." In Charles O. Hucker, ed., *Chinese Government in Ming Times: Seven Studies*. New York: Columbia University Press, 1969.

Yang Na. "Tianwan Dahan hongjin jun shi shulun" (History of the Red Turban armies of the Tianwan and Great Han regimes). *Yuanshi luncong* 1 (1982), 109–36.

Yanjiahe qu gaikuang (General information about Yanjiahe). Yanjiahe: Yanjiahe Township Office, n.d. HGO.

Yasuno Shōzō. "Meimatsu Shinsho Yūsokō chū ryūiki no dai tochi shoyū ni kansuru ikkosatsu" (Large landownership in the Middle Yangzi region in the late Ming and early Qing). *Tōyōshi kenkyū* 20.4 (1962), 61–88.

Ye Xian'en. *Ming Qing Huizhou nongcun shehui yu dianpu zhi* (Rural society and the bondservant system in Ming Qing Huizhou). Hefei: Anhui renmin chubanshe, 1983.

Ye Ziqi. *Caomuzi* (Notes from prison), orig. 1378. Beijing: Zhonghua shuju, 1959.

Yi Guanghui. "Baigu ta beiji" (Stele of the White Bones Pagoda). *MCXZQB*, 15:19.

"Yu Cheng shengping jianjie" (A critical introduction to the life of Yu Cheng). *Macheng wenshi ziliao* 1 (1987), 35–37.

Yu Chenglong. *Yu qingduangong zhengshu* (Official correspondence of Yu Chenglong), orig. 1683. Taibei: Wenhai, 1976.

Yu Peihong. "Yu Cheng geming shilue" (Brief account of Yu Cheng's revolutionary activities). *Macheng wenshi ziliao* 3 (1990), 37–66.

Yuan Mei. *Yuan Mei quanji* (Complete works of Yuan Mei). Nanjing: Jiangsu guji chubanshe, 1993.

Yuan shi (Yuan dynastic history). Beijing: Zhonghua shuju, 1976.

Yuan Zhongdao. "Li Wenling zhuan" (Biography of Li Zhi). In He Fuzheng, comp., *Wenchang bianti huixuan* (Literary compositions selected and arranged by type), 541:9–22. *SKQS*.

Zhang Guotao. "Suqu fazhan jingguo ji sufan shengli de yuanyin: Zhang Guotao gei Zhongyang de baogao" (Report of Zhang Guotao to the Party Center on the origins, progress, and reasons for victory of the purge in the Soviet Area), orig. Nov. 25, 1931. In Sheng Renxue, *Zhang Guotao nianpu ji yanlun* (Biography and discussion of Zhang Guotao). Beijing: Liberation Army Press, 1985.

Zhang Jianmin. *Hubei tongshi: Ming Qing juan* (General history of Hubei: Ming and Qing). Wuhan: Huazhong shifan daxue chubanshe, 1999.

Zhang Kaiyuan and Lin Zengping. *Xinhai geming* (The 1911 Revolution). Beijing: Renmin chubanshe, 1981.

Zhang Ruide. *Ping-Han tielu yu Huabei de jingji fazhan, 1905–1937* (The Beijing-Hankou Railroad and economic development in north China, 1905–1937). Taibei: Institute of Modern History, 1987.

Zhang shi sanxiu jiapu (Genealogy of the Zhang lineage), orig. 1876. 3d ed. Wuhan Municipal Library.

Zhang Yunfei. "Mei Guozhen de aimin sixiang" (Mei Guozhen's populist thought). *Macheng wenshi ziliao* 7 (2003), 176–83.

Zhang Zhenzhi. *Geming yu zongjiao* (Religion and revolution). Shanghai: Minzhi shuju, 1929.

Zheng Hengwu. "Eyuwan sansheng 'jiaozong' shishi baojia lianzuo fa" (Regulations enacting *baojia* organization issued by the Eyuwan "Extermination Command"). *Wuhan wenshi ziliao* 41–42 (1990), 234–36.

———. "Pingding Xia Douyin, Yang Sen panluan" (Suppressing Xia Douyin and Yang Sen's rebellion). *Wuhan wenshi ziliao* 41–42 (1990), 184–89.

———. "Xia Douyin de yisheng" (The life of Xia Douyin). *Wuhan wenshi ziliao* 15 (1984), 77–88.

Zheng Tianting and Sun Yue, eds. *Mingmo nongmin qiyi shiliao* (Historical materials on late Ming peasant rebellions). Shanghai: Zhonghua shuju, 1954.

Zheng Zhong. *Zhengli baojia suqing lingfei fang'an* (Program for reorganizing *baojia* and mopping up remnant bandits), Feb. 15 and 17, 1934. 2 items. HPA.

Zhongguo renming da zidian (Chinese biographical dictionary). Shanghai: Commercial Press, 1980.

Zhou Qun. *Yuan Hongdao pingzhuan* (Critical biography of Yuan Hongdao). Nanjing: Nanjing University Press, 1999.

Zhou Rucheng. "Qiantan Li Zhi sixiang zai Macheng de fayu huanjing" (The development of Li Zhi's thought in the Macheng context). In Ling Lichao and Li Min, eds., *Li Zhi qiren* (Li Zhi the man). Macheng: Macheng Gazetteer Office, 2002.

Zhou shi zongpu (Genealogy of the Zhou lineage), 1992. MCA.

Zhu Qianzhi. *Li Zhi: Shiliu shiji Zhongguo fanfengjian sixiang de xianquzhe* (Li Zhi: A sixteenth-century pioneer of antifeudal Chinese thought). Wuhan: Hubei renmin chubanshe, 1957.

Zhu Xizu. "Jiaobu *Qi-Huang sishiba zhai jishi* ba" (Colophon to the *Qi-Huang sishiba zhai jishi*). In Zhu Xizu, ed., *Mingji shiliao tiba* (Colophons to sources on late Ming history). Beijing: Zhonghua shuju, 1961.

Zhupi zouzhe: Nongmin yundong lei. Beijing: China Number One National Archives, file nos. 5, 36, 43, 97, 98, 121, 122, 167, 265.

Zong Li and Liu Qun. *Zhongguo minjian zhushen* (Chinese popular deities). Shijiazhuang: Hebei renmin chubanshe, 1986.

Selected Glossary

anfen 安分
Baigu ta 白骨塔
Baiguo 白果
Baijiao cheng 拜教城
Bailian jiao 白蓮教
Baiqueyuan 白雀園
baiyi 百一
Baiyun zhai 白雲寨
Bakui renmin ziweituan 八區人民自衛團
bangfeng 邦風
bao (violent) 暴
bao (fort) 堡
Bao Peng 鮑鵬
Bao Shirong 鮑世榮
baodong 暴動
baodong shajin 暴動殺盡
baojia 保甲
baokang 暴抗
baoqi 暴起
baojian 寶劍
baowei ju 保衛局
baowei tuan 保衛團
baozhang (baojia leader) 保長
baozhang (fort master) 堡長
bian 辮
biaoyu 標語
bingchong 兵衝
binggong zhengfa 秉公正法
bingyi fa 兵役法
buxi xuexiao 補習學校
Cai Jihuang 蔡濟璜
Can'an 慘案
Cangshu 藏書
cangtou shizhu 蒼頭弑主
canyue 參閱
Cao Yinchang 曹胤昌
Caojiahe 曹家河
chachang 茶場
changjue 猖獗
Changling guan 長嶺關
changing tuan 剗共團
changping cang 常平倉
Changshun zhou 常順州
chaoku 巢窟
Chen Huihui 陳恢恢
Chen Tingjing 陳廷敬
Chen Wenfu 陳文富
Chen Youliang 陳友諒
Chen Yucheng 陳玉成
Chen Zao 陳慥
Cheng Chaoer 程朝二
Cheng Daji 成大吉
Cheng Xuehan 程學瀚
chengbuliaojia 成不了家
Chengmagang 乘馬崗
chengnei shishen 城內士紳
chengshen 城紳
Chibi 赤壁
chifei 赤匪
chihuo 赤禍
chiren 吃人
chiweidui 赤衛隊
chizi nongbing 赤子弄兵

choujia 仇家
chouren 讐人
Chujun 楚軍
Chunqiu 春秋
Chunqiu hengku 春秋衡庫
chushi 出世
Cihua si 慈化寺
congshi 從始
congtian tanding 從田攤丁
cuifu yipin 摧富益貧
cunshu 村塾
Dabie shan 大別山
dahu 大戶
daluhuachi 達魯花赤
Dan Yanyang 單言揚
danghua 黨化
dangyi 黨義
daosu weifeng 導俗維風
Daoyi 道一
Daxiong dong 大雄洞
Deng Tianwen 鄧天文
Desheng zhai 得勝寨
diaobao 碉堡
diaolou 碉樓
Diaoyutai 釣漁台
dianpu 佃僕
die 爹
difang zizhi 地方自治
difangzhuyi 地方主意
Ding Yueping 丁岳平
Ding Zhengsong 丁正松
Ding Zhenyu 丁枕魚
dingfei 鼎沸
Dinghui si 定惠寺
Dizhu gong 帝主宮
Dong Biwu 董必武
Donglin 東林
Dongshan 東山
Dongyue shen 東岳神
dushenzhuyi 獨身主意
Edong tewei 鄂東特委
Enyi ju 恩義局
Eyuwan 鄂豫皖
fan 畈
Fang Jihua 方繼華
fangpu 放僕
feihuan 匪患
fenbie 分別
Feng Menglong 馮夢龍
fengjian 封建
Feng Tingxiang 馮廷
fengzeng 封贈
Fenshu 焚書
fupin xiang'an 富貧相安
funü hui 婦女會
funüzhuyi 婦女主意
Fushe 復社
Futianhe 福田河
Fuzhu shen 富主神
gaizao 改造
ganshi 幹事
Gaodeng xiaoxue 高等小學
gege shajin 箇箇殺盡
Gelaohui 哥老會
Geng Dingli 耿定力
Geng Dinglii 耿定理
Geng Dingxiang 耿定向
Geng Yingqu 耿應衢
Gong Xiazi 龔瞎子
Gong Jinghan 龔景瀚
gongfei 共匪
gonghui 工會
gonglun 公論
gongzuo zu 工作組
Gu Yanwu 顧炎武
Guangshan 光山
guanji minbian 官激民變
guantian 官田
guanxiang 關廂
Guanwen 官文
Guanxue 關學
gucheng 孤城
guibing 鬼兵
Guifeng shan 龜峯山
guimen 閨門
guinong 歸農
guiyue 規約
Guo Qinghua 郭慶華
Guoxueguan 國學館
Hai Rui 海瑞
han 悍
Han Liner 韓林兒
Han Shantong 韓山童
Hankou minguo ribao 漢口民國日報

Hanren 漢人
haohan 好漢
haojie 豪傑
haoshen dazu 豪紳大族
He Lingluo 何零落
He Shirong 何士榮
He Xinyin 何心隱
heng 横
hengcai 恒財
Hong Chengchou 洪承疇
Hong Louxian 洪樓先
Hongjin 紅巾
Hongjun 紅軍
Hongmen hui 紅門會
Hongqiang hui 紅槍會
Hu Anguo 胡安國
Hu Linyi 胡林翼
Huaibei 淮北
Huang Jinlong 黄金龍
Huang Juan 黄卷
Huang Mulan 黄木蘭
Huang Wumeng 黄武孟
Huang-Ma 黄麻
Huang'an 黄安
Huangbang 黄幫
Huangbo zhai 黄栢寨
Huanggang 黄岡
Huangtugang 黄土崗
Huangzhou 黄州
Hubei jingguo jun 湖北靖國軍
hui 會
Huiche shuyuan 迴車書院
huifei 會匪
huiguan 會館
huijia shunan 毀家紓難
huitang 會堂
Huiyun an 慧雲菴
Husheng bao 護生堡
huzhang 戶長
jia daoxue 叚道學
jiagui 家規
jiahe 假合
jianbi qingye 堅壁清野
jianfa 剪髮
Jiang Hualong 江化龍
Jianghan shuyuan 江漢書院
jiangxue 講學
jiantou fangjiao 剪頭放脚
jianxi 奸細
jiao 勦
Jiao Hong 焦竑
jiaofei 教匪
jiaofu 勦撫
jiaohua 教化
jiaoren 教人
jiaoxun zidi 教訓子弟
jiaoyang 教養
jiaoyu hui 教育會
Jiaoyu ju 教育局
jiaozhu 勦主
jiashu 家塾
jiazhang 甲長
jicai 積財
Jiezi shu 戒子書
Jin Changzhen 金長真
jingbei dui 警備隊
jingcha 警察
jinjian zhiluan 禁奸止亂
jingshi 經世
Jingxin shuyuan 經心書院
jinzhan 盡斬
Jiuguo tuan 救國團
jiuhu yizhu 救護儀註
jiukuang 酒狂
Ju shui 舉水
Juedan shan 蕨淡山
juji shanzhong yishibuzu
聚集山中衣食不足
junliang 均糧
kaiken 開墾
kamen 卡門
kansha 砍殺
Kongmiao 孔廟
kuaiqiang 快槍
kuang 狂
kuangfu changluan 狂夫倡亂
kuanghan 狂悍
kui 區
kuibing 潰兵
kuihu zhi 區戶制
kuoren laoye 闊人老爺
Lao Huihui 老回回
Laoye 老爺
lerang 樂壤

li 戾
Li Changgeng 李長庚
Li Gongmao 李公茂
Li Keming 李克明
Li Keshen 李克慎
Li Laomo 李老末
Li Lisan 李立三
Li Peixiang 李培祥
Li Shengqi 李省七
Li Shunqing 李舜卿
Li Tianbao 李添保
Li Wenxiang 李文祥
Li Youshi 李有實
Li Zhao 李釗
Li Zheshi 李哲時
Li Zhengfang 李正芳
Li Zhi 李贄
Li Zicheng 李自成
lianbao 聯保
lianbaochu 聯保處
liancun fa 聯村法
Lianghu shuyuan 兩湖書院
liangmin 良民
liangzhi 良知
lie 烈
lieshen 劣紳
lihun jiehun juedui ziyou 離婚結婚絕對自由
lijiao 禮教
Lin Dianhua 林殿華
Lin Gusong 林古松
Lin Mian 林棉
Lin Renfu 林仁敷
Linjing zhiyue 麟經指月
liren 里仁
Liren hui 里仁會
Liu Fang 劉芳
Liu Gang 劉剛
Liu Jintang 劉金堂
Liu Junfu 劉君孚
Liu Qingli 劉青黎
Liu Qiao 劉僑
Liu Congzheng 劉從政
Liu Mingmeng 劉名夢
Liu Tianhe 劉天和
Liu Tong 劉侗
Liu Wenwei 劉文蔚
liumang 流氓
lixue 理學
liyi zhi ren 力役之人
Longhu 龍湖
Longtan 龍潭
Lu Jinxi 陸晉錫
Lu Xiangsheng 盧象昇
luan 亂
lulin 綠林
Luo Hongsheng 羅鴻升
Luo Qijie 羅七姐
Luo Xiujin 羅繡錦
Luotian 羅田
Ma Gu 麻姑
Ma Gu xiandong 麻姑仙洞
Ma Jinglun 馬經綸
Ma Qiu 麻秋
Ma Shiying 馬士英
Mabu 麻埠
Macheng 麻城
maguazi 馬褂子
maishen 賣身
mancheng liuxue 滿城流血
Manmo jiao 滿摩教
Mao Fengshao 毛鳳韶
Mei Danran 梅澹然
Mei Guolou 梅國樓
Mei Guosen 梅國森
Mei Guozhen 梅國楨
Mei Heng 梅亨
Mei Ji 梅吉
Mei Tian 梅鈿
Mei Zhihuan 梅之煥
Mei Zhiyuan 梅之熉
Mei Zeng 梅增
meng 猛
Meng Guangpeng 孟廣澎
Mi-le 彌勒
Mi-tuo 彌陀
miaohe 妙合
mincai 民財
minfei 民肥
Ming Chengzu 明承祖
Ming Yuzhen 明玉珍
minge 民歌
Mingjiao (Doctrine of Light) 明教
mingjiao (Confucian orthodoxy) 名教

mingli 名禮
Mingwang 明王
mingxian 名賢
Mingzhu 明主
minqing 民情
minsheng 民生
mintian 民田
mintuan 民團
Mu Wei 穆煒
Mulan 木蘭
Muxihe 木樨河
Muzidian 木子店
nangeng nüye 男耕女饁
nanren 南人
neiying 內應
Ni Wenjun 倪文俊
Nian 捻
niaoqiang 鳥槍
nonghui 農會
nongmin gansidui 農民敢死隊
nongmin xiehui 農民協會
nongmin qiyi 農民起義
nubian 奴變
nuli 奴隸
nupu 奴僕
nupu xiaren 奴僕下人
panpu 叛僕
paoluo 炮烙
Peng Yingyu 彭瑩玉
Peng Zungu 彭遵古
piaohan 慓悍
pingjia 平價
Pinnong ju 貧農局
pocan burenyan 破慘不忍言
pujitang 普濟堂
Qi-Huang sishiba zhai 蘄黃四十八寨
Qian Qianyi 錢謙益
qianghui 槍會
Qihuang zhongxue 啟黃中學
qijia 起家
Qiligang 七里崗
Qiliping 七里坪
Qin Chaoqing 秦朝卿
Qingbang 青幫
qingdang 清黨
qingjiao 清勦
qingjie tang 清節堂
qingxi 清洗
qingxiang tuan 清鄉團
qingyao bofu 輕傜薄賦
qingye 清野
Qishui 蘄水
Qiting 岐亭
qiushou baodong 秋收暴動
Qizhou 蘄州
Qu Fangcheng 屈方誠
Qu Kaiyan 屈開埏
Qu Peilan 屈佩蘭
Qu Zhenqi 屈振奇
quanshi 拳師
quanshu 拳術
Quanxue suo 勸學所
quzhang 區長
Ren Yingqi 任應岐
renke 人課
renqing 人情
renshi 人市
Renyi hui 仁義會
Rizhi hui 日知會
Rizhi lu 日知錄
Runing 汝寧
rushan 入山
Saichepuhua 賽徹普化
sanguang 三光
santai bajing 三臺八景
shandou 善鬬
Shangcheng 商城
shange 山歌
shanghui 商會
shanhou ju 善後局
shanzhai 山寨
shanzhu 山主
shantang 善堂
shanyu 山愚
shazei zhiguo zhi si 殺賊致果之思
shecang 社倉
shehui junshi 社會軍事
Shen Huilin 沈會霖
Shengren tang 聖人堂
shengsi qiechi 生死切齒
Shenzhuang 沈庄
Shi Kefa 史可法
Shi Xianfu 施賢輔
Shi Xingchuan 石星川

Shicheng wang 石城王
Shicheng zhai 石城寨
shifei 是非
shihuan zhi jia 仕宦之家
shimin sixiang 市民思想
shipu 世僕
shiwei 施威
shixue 實學
Shiyang 陽
Shizi shanzhai 什子山寨
shizu 始祖
Shubao 舒保
Shuihu zhuan 水滸傳
Shunheji 順河集
shupu 贖僕
sichan 祀產
sili 四禮
siqi 思齊
siwei bade 四維八德
Song Lian 宋濂
Song Yilin 宋一麟
Song Yihe 宋一鶴
Songbu 宋埠
Songzi guan 松子關
Su Dongpo 蘇東坡
sufan 肅反
suqing 肅清
suqing fangeming 肅清反革命
Taichang 泰昌
Taiping xiang 太平鄉
tanding rudi 攤丁入地
Tang Caichang 唐才常
Tang Guifang 唐桂芳
Tang Zhi 湯志
tanya yaofen 彈壓妖氛
taopu 逃僕
Teng Song 滕松
tewu dui 特務隊
Tian Hui 田蕙
Tianfutai 天福泰
Tianjiazhai 田家寨
tianshu 天書
Tianwan 天完
tiaojie weiyuanhui 調解委員會
Tingchuan xiang 亭川鄉
Toghto 脫脫
Tongmeng hui 同盟會
tongpu 僮僕
touxian 投獻
tuanding 團丁
tuanlian 團練
tuanzong 團總
tufei 土匪
tuhao 土豪
tujin 屠盡
tuqi 土氣
Wang Baoxin 王葆心
Wang Caoru 王操如
Wang Ding 王爋
Wang Gen 王艮
Wang Guangshu 王光樹
Wang Hongxue 王宏學
Wang Jingwei 汪精衛
Wang Ming 王明
Wang Shizhen 王世貞
Wang Shusheng 王樹聲
Wang Youan 王幼安
Wanghua shan 望花山
wanji 挽髻
Wanren yaigao 萬人崖高
Wansong shuyuan 萬松書院
weifa 圍法
weifang ying 衛防營
weijiao 圍勦
Wen Zhenmeng 文震孟
Wenmiao 文廟
wenming tou 文明頭
wenming xi 文明戲
wenshe 文社
Wu Lin 吳林
Wu Sangui 吳三桂
Wu Weiye 吳偉業
Wu Zhaotai 吳兆泰
wujia kegui 無家可歸
wulai 無賴
wulun 五倫
Wumu yuewang 武穆岳王
Wunian 無念
wushu 武術
wuye jianmin 無業奸民
wuye kewu 無業可務
wuyong 武勇
Xia Ding'an 夏鼎安
Xia Douyin 夏斗寅

Xia Shipeng 夏士鵬
Xia Wu 夏梧
Xia Zhongkun 夏仲昆
xiang 鄉
xiangbing 鄉兵
Xiangjun 湘軍
xiangshen 鄉紳
xiangtang 香堂
xiangxian si 鄉賢祀
xiangyong 鄉勇
xiangyue 鄉約
xiangzheng renyuan xunliansuo 鄉政人員訓練所
Xianju xiang 仙居鄉
xianyin 縣尹
xiangyin yizhu 鄉飲儀註
xiaochun 小蠢
Xiaogan xiang 孝感鄉
xiaomie 消滅
xiaqi 俠氣
Xicun 西邨
xidi 洗地
Xiefu hui 脇富會
Xieshuo 邪說
Xin shenghuo yundong 新生活運動
Xindian 新店
Xingzhong hui 興中會
Xinji 新集
xiong 兇
Xiong Ji 熊吉
Xiong Jiamou 熊家模
Xiong Jiaxun 熊家訓
xiongni wangming zhi tu 兇逆亡命之徒
xizi hui 惜字會
Xu Ding 徐鼎
Xu Haidong 徐海東
Xu Jishen 許繼慎
Xu Qixu 徐其虛
Xu Xiangqian 徐向前
Xu Shouhui 徐壽輝
Xu Yong 徐勇
Xu Ziqing 徐子清
xuegong 學宮
xuehui 學會
xuetang 學堂
xuexi 血洗
Xujiabao 徐家堡
Yan Boyu 閻伯璵
Yan Ruyi 嚴如熤
Yang Dingjian 楊定見
Yang Lian 楊連
Yang Pei 楊霈
Yang Sen 楊森
Yanjiahe 閻家河
Yantianhe 鹽田河
Yanwang 閻王
yanyi 嚴邑
Yao Guozhen 姚國振
yaoren 妖人
Ye Kaiyan 葉開演
Ye Ziqi 葉子奇
Yi Daosan 易道三
Yi Guanghui 易光蕙
yimin 遺民
yimin zhimin 以民治民
yinchun yizhu 迎春儀註
yinde 陰德
yingxiong 英雄
yingxiong langman 英雄浪漫
yinshi fujia 殷實富家
yinshi liangshan 殷實良善
yinxi 淫戲
yishi hui 議事會
yitian 義田
yixue 義學
yiyi fenzi 異議分子
yiyong dui 毅勇隊
yiyuanhua 一元化
Yongli 永曆
yongmian 擁面
youji zhanzheng 游擊戰爭
youjidui 游擊隊
youzhi 幼稚
Yu Cheng 余誠
Yu Chenglong 于成龍
Yu Jinfang 余晉芳
Yu Linxie 余林燮
Yu Poquan 余潑泉
Yu Yaxiang 余雅祥
Yu Yingyun 余應雲
Yuan Hongdao 袁宏道
Yuan Mei 袁枚
Yuan Xian 袁銑
Yuan Ying 袁英

Yuan Zhongdao 袁中道
Yuan Zongdao 袁宗道
yuanqi 元氣
Yuanzhou 遠州
yueshu 約束
Yuewang miao 岳王廟
Yujun 豫軍
yushou haodou zhi lei 遊手好鬬之類
Yushou ju 與守局
yuzhai 寨
zanghuo 臧獲
Zeng Guofan 曾國藩
Zengjiawan 曾家彎
zhai 寨or砦
zhaini 寨逆
Zhan Zhaozhu 詹兆朱
Zhan Zhonglian 詹鍾廉
Zhang Chaozhen 張朝珍
Zhang Guotao 張國燾
Zhang Sen 張森
Zhang Xianzhong 張獻忠
Zhang Xingqi 張行七
Zhang Xiyun 張錫雲
Zhangjiafan 張家畈
zhangtian 丈田
zhanguo 斬馘
Zhao Yufeng 趙玉峯
zhaofu 招撫
zhen daoxue 真道學
zhenbie 甄別
Zheng Jiaju 鄭家駒
Zheng Jiankui 鄭漸逵
Zheng Kangshi 鄭康時
Zheng Zhong 鄭重
Zhengke 正課
zhengsu 正肅
zhengzhi wenti 政治問題
zhenji 真幾
zhian weiyuanhui 治安委員會
Zhidao hui 直道會
Zhifoyuan 芝佛院
Zhixue hui 恉學會
zhongbao 中飽
Zhongguanyi 中館驛
zhongyang fenju 中央分局
Zhongyi ju 忠義局
Zhou Ailiu 周愛六
Zhou Hongmo 周宏謨
Zhou Hongyue 周宏鑰
Zhou Hongzu 周宏祖
Zhou Jian 周鑑
Zhou Longxiang 周龍驤
Zhou Meigong 周美公
Zhou Sijing 周思敬
Zhou Sijiu 周思久
Zhou Sun 周損
Zhou Tiezhao 周鐵爪
Zhou Weiju 周維秬
Zhou Weizhen 周維楨
Zhou Wenjiang 周文江
Zhu Jue 朱玨
zhuangding dui 壯丁隊
zhumeng 主盟
Zhushan zhai 朱山寨
zhuangtian 莊田
zhuangyuan 莊園
zhulian jiuzu 株連九族
zidi bing 子弟兵
zike 紫課
Zili hui 自立會
zimai 自賣
ziran zhi zhenji 自然之真幾
Ziwei hou miao 紫微侯廟
ziwei tuan 自衛團
zizhi qu 自治區
zongbao 總保
zongju 總局
zongtuan bu 總團部
Zou Han 鄒瀚
Zou Junsheng 鄒君升
Zou Laixue 鄒來學
Zou Pusheng 鄒普勝
Zou Qianba 鄒遷八
Zou Shicong 鄒士璁
Zou Xing 鄒惺
zupu 族譜
Zuo Liangyu 左良玉
Zuo zhuan 左傳

Index